# MASSACRES [illegible]



Most cultural and legal codes agree [illegible] ns, whether in peacetime or war, is prohibited. This is the norm of [illegible] ity, widely considered to be a fundamental moral and legal principle. Yet despite this fact, the deliberate killing of large numbers of civilians remains a persistent feature of global political life. What is more, the perpetrators have often avoided criticism and punishment. Examining dozens of episodes of mass killing perpetrated by states since the French Revolution late eighteenth century, this book attempts to explain this paradox. It studies the role that civilian immunity has played in shaping the behaviour of perpetrators and how international society has responded to mass killing. The book argues that although the world has made impressive progress in legislating against the intentional killing of civilians and in constructing institutions to give meaning to that prohibition, the norm's history in practice suggests that the ascendancy of civilian immunity is both more recent and more fragile than might otherwise be thought. In practice, decisions to violate a norm are shaped by factors relating to the norm and the situation at hand, so too is the manner in which international society and individual states respond to norm violations. Responses to norm violations are not simply matters of normative obligation or calculations of self-interest but are instead guided by a combination of these logics as well as perceptions about the situation at hand, existing relations with the actors involved, and power relations between actors holding different accounts of the situation. Thus, whilst civilian immunity has for the time being prevailed over 'anti-civilian ideologies' which seek to justify mass killing, it remains challenged by these ideologies and its implementation shaped by individual circumstances. As a result, whilst it has become much more difficult for states to get away with mass murder, it is still not entirely impossible for them to do so.

# Massacres and Morality

*Mass Atrocities in an Age of Civilian Immunity*

ALEX J. BELLAMY

OXFORD
UNIVERSITY PRESS

OXFORD
UNIVERSITY PRESS

Great Clarendon Street, Oxford, OX2 6DP,
United Kingdom

Oxford University Press is a department of the University of Oxford.
It furthers the University's objective of excellence in research, scholarship,
and education by publishing worldwide. Oxford is a registered trade mark of
Oxford University Press in the UK and in certain other countries



First Edition published in 2012
First published in paperback 2014



Published in the United States of America by Oxford University Press
198 Madison Avenue, New York, NY 10016, United States of America

British Library Cataloguing in Publication Data
Data available

Library of Congress Cataloging in Publication Data
Data available

ISBN 978–0–19–928842–7 (Hbk.)
ISBN 978–0–19–871476–7 (Pbk.)

*For Isaac*

# *Contents*

# *Acknowledgements*

This book was nearly six years in the writing and during that time changed its character almost completely. For that reason alone, my most sincere thanks are owed to Dominic Byatt at Oxford University Press for showing forbearance above and beyond the call of duty, sticking with the project (and me), and for providing wise counsel at critical points along the way. Thanks are also owed to others at OUP, including Carla Hodge, Kim Allen, and Subramaniam Vengatakrishnan, who helped make the finished product much better than the draft manuscript I gave them.

In the early stages, research for this book benefitted from a University of Queensland Research Excellence Award which gave me relief from teaching. I was able to complete the book thanks to the support of Griffith University.

Research was ably assisted by my research assistants, Regan Neal and Kimberley Nackers who ensured that I always had plenty of reading.

As ever, my friend and colleague Paul D. Williams offered constructive criticisms, guidance, and excellent advice on all aspects of the book. I have written this before, but I will say it again: I admire your scholarship and treasure your friendship. Other colleagues also provided guidance along the way, most notably Richard Devetak and Jason Sharman.

Finally, my deepest debt is owed to my beloved Sara—wife, wonderful mother to our son, friend, wise counsellor, critic of sloppy draft chapters, and constant source of support and inspiration. Nothing would be possible without her.

This book is dedicated to my son, Isaac, in the hope that his life will be lived untouched by the horrors recounted in these pages and that his generation can do a better job than mine of protecting the innocent from the scourge of mass atrocities.

# Introduction

The intentional killing of civilians, whether in peacetime or war, is morally prohibited. Most of the world's major ethical traditions and legal codes forbid the deliberate killing of people who are neither members of the armed forces nor guilty of some crime punishable by death.[1] This is the norm of civilian immunity, widely regarded as a fundamental prescriptive norm and moral principle. Yet despite the fact that most peoples agree that killing civilians is wrong, such killing remains a persistent feature of global political life.[2] To make matters worse, those that commit these grave wrongs are as likely to succeed in their plans as they are to be punished for their misdeeds.[3]

Taking the apparent disjuncture between a shared moral norm prohibiting the intentional killing of civilians and a history of recurrent violations of that norm, this book examines the struggle for civilian immunity over the past two centuries. It studies the role that civilian immunity has played in shaping the behaviour of perpetrators and how international society has responded to serious violations. It argues that although international society has made impressive progress in legislating against the intentional killing of civilians and in constructing institutions to give meaning to that prohibition, the norm's history in practice suggests that the ascendancy of civilian immunity is both more recent and more fragile than might otherwise be thought.

[1] For instance, compare the various chapters in Vesselin Popovski, Gregory M. Reichberg, and Nicholas Turner (eds), *World Religions and Norms of War* (Tokyo: United Nations University Press, 2009).

[2] See Paul Huth and Benjamin Valentino, 'Mass Killing of Civilians in Time of War, 1945–2000', in J. Joseph Hewitt, Jonathan Wilkenfeld, and Ted Robert Gurr, *Peace and Conflict 2008* (Boulder: Paradigm, 2008); and Ekaterina Stepanova, 'Trends in Armed Conflicts: One-Sided Violence Against Civilians', in *SIPRI Yearbook 2009: Armaments, Disarmament and International Security* (Oxford: Oxford University Press, 2009).

[3] See Alex De Waal and B. Conley-Zilkic, 'Reflections on How Genocidal Killings are Brought to an End', *Social Science Research Council*, 22 December 2006; and Alex J. Bellamy, 'Military Intervention' in Donald Bloxham and Dirk Moses (eds), *The Oxford Handbook of Genocide Studies* (Oxford: Oxford University Press, 2009).

It is not only rogue states or shadowy terrorists that intentionally kill civilians.[4] In the little over two hundred years covered by this book, all of the world's major powers have intentionally killed civilians at some point.[5] Indeed, each of the current permanent five members of the UN Security Council has a history that includes the intentional killing of civilians. The USA did so in its wars against indigenous Americans, in its colonial war in the Philippines, in the Second World War, Korea, and Indochina; the Soviet Union in its many massive domestic purges, in Poland, and elsewhere in occupied Europe during and immediately after the Second World War, and in Afghanistan; the UK in the Boer War and other colonial enterprises and in the Second World War; France during its own revolution, in the Peninsular War, in response to domestic uprisings in the nineteenth century, and in Algeria and elsewhere in its empire in the following century; and communist China in repeated purges and ill-fated schemes of social transformation. It is a sad fact that despite the enormous attention paid to preventing mass atrocities and holding the perpetrators to account in the past few years, new cases of mass killing remain as likely to end with outright victory for the perpetrators as with their defeat and punishment. Of the many ways in which episodes of mass atrocities might be ended, intervention or punishment by foreign powers is still among the least likely.[6]

Thanks largely to its persistence and apparent ubiquity, contemporary mass killing is often explained without reference to the norm of civilian immunity. Mass killing has been portrayed as, variously, a rational tool employed to accomplish radical social transformations or eliminate perceived enemies, a useful strategy for defeating certain types of insurgencies, a means by which governments unable to prevail over their enemies with conventional military means might succeed, and (in the case of non-state actors) a product of the conditions in which groups originate.[7] Where the norm of civilian immunity is found to encourage actors to wage war more discriminately, it is said to do so in tandem with other developments such as technological progress which

[4] A point emphasized by Alexander B. Downes, *Targeting Civilians in War* (Ithaca: Cornell University Press, 2008).

[5] Of course, mass killing itself has a much longer history and in the course of that history it is not unusual to see the epoch's great powers at the forefront of bloodletting. See Ben Kiernan, *Blood and Soil: A World History of Genocide and Extermination from Sparta to Darfur* (New Haven: Yale University Press, 2007); and Mark Levene and Penny Roberts (eds), *The Massacre in History* (New York: Berghahn Books, 1999).

[6] De Waal and Conley-Zilkic, 'Reflections on How Genocidal Killings are Brought to an End' and Bellamy, 'Military Intervention'.

[7] Respectively, Benjamin Valentino, *Final Solutions: Mass Killing and Genocide in the 20th Century* (Ithaca: Cornell University Press, 2004), esp. ch. 3 and 4; Benjamin Valentino, Paul Huth, and Dylan Balch-Lindsay, 'Draining the Sea: Mass Killing and Guerrilla Warfare', *International Organization*, 58, 2004, pp. 375–407; Downes, *Targeting Civilians*; and Jeremy M. Weinstein, *Inside Rebellion: The Politics of Insurgent Violence* (Cambridge: Cambridge University Press, 2007).

permits some wealthy states to fight wars both effectively and discriminately.[8] The general implication here, though, is that civilian immunity is too weak to inhibit behaviour.

But amidst all the violence, there is evidence of civilian immunity at work. Most obviously, although it has not propelled bystanders to act in its defence in every case, the norm has helped motivate international society to construct a web of rules and institutions aimed at preventing mass killing, protecting the victims, and punishing the perpetrators. Seven developments are especially worth noting in this regard. First, international human rights and humanitarian law has gradually outlawed arbitrary killing in almost all of its forms. Second, the establishment of an International Criminal Court (ICC) in 2002 with international jurisdiction to prosecute individuals for the deliberate killing of civilians. Third, the expansion of global humanitarian action to include the protection of civilians from mass violence.[9] Fourth, the adoption of resolutions by the UN Security Council advancing a broad civilian protection agenda that encourages compliance with International Humanitarian Law and reiterates the Council's commitment to enforcing the law when it deems necessary.[10] Fifth, the establishment of international peace operations specifically charged with protecting civilians.[11] Sixth, the development of regional initiatives in Europe, Africa, and Latin America aimed at preventing harm to civilians and protecting potential victims of mass violence. Seventh, the international commitment to the Responsibility to Protect (RtoP) principle in 2005 and its reaffirmation by the UN Security Council in 2006 (Resolution 1674) and 2009 (Resolution 1894) and the UN General Assembly in 2009.[12]

There is also evidence to suggest that civilian immunity is a factor that weighs on potential perpetrators.[13] Mass atrocities are not normally an actor's

[8] Ward Thomas, *The Ethics of Destruction: Norms and Force in International Relations* (Ithaca: Cornell University Press, 2001).

[9] For instance, see Oxfam International, *Beyond the Headlines: An Agenda for Action to Protect Civilians in Neglected Conflicts* (Oxford: Oxfam GB for Oxfam International, 2003) and International Committee of the Red Cross (ICRC), *Enhancing Protection for Civilians in Armed Conflict and Other Situations of Violence* (Geneva: ICRC, September 2008).

[10] For an overview, see Security Council Report, *Protection of Civilians* (Cross-Cutting Report No. 2, 14 October 2008).

[11] For a comprehensive examination, see Siobhan Wills, *Protecting Civilians: The Obligations of Peacekeepers* (Oxford: Oxford University Press, 2009); and Victoria K. Holt and Tobias C. Berkman, *The Impossible Mandate? Military Preparedness, The Responsibility to Protect and Modern Peace Operations* (Washington, DC: The Henry L. Stimson Center, 2006).

[12] For more details, see Alex J. Bellamy, *Responsibility to Protect: The Global Effort to End Mass Atrocities* (Cambridge: Polity, 2009); Gareth Evans, *The Responsibility to Protect: Ending Mass Atrocity Crimes Once and for All* (Washington DC: The Brookings Institution, 2008); and Ban Ki-moon, *Implementing the Responsibility: Report of the Secretary-General*, A/63/677, 12 January 2009.

[13] This is in line with Jeffrey Legro's argument that norms are one of several factors that influence behaviour. See Jeffrey W. Legro, 'Which Norms Matter? Revisiting the "Failure" of Internationalism', *International Organization*, 51 (1), 1997, p. 32.

first course of action. Indeed, more often than not, groups choose not to resort to deliberately killing civilians even when they stand to gain and have the means to do so.[14] Massacring civilians is usually entered into reluctantly and only after alternative strategies have been contemplated and found wanting. Massacres are inhibited by a combination of fears about the potential for retribution against ones own population, a mutual interest—common to all forms of social life—in maintaining rules governing conflict in order to limit damage to the underlying social order, the potential for third party intervention or punishment, and ideologies or moral codes that prohibit the intentional killing of civilians.[15] Other than fears of retribution, which is an entirely self-regarding concern only operable when there is an unusually high degree of parity between the perpetrators and the victims, the other inhibitors of massacres are grounded in civilian immunity—the level of rule-utility attached to it, its capacity to generate punishment, and its ability to inhibit behaviour through internalization.

We might also be tempted to see civilian immunity at work in the decline of the overall incidence of massacres in the past few decades.[16] But the reality is decidedly mixed and unclear. Even if we could establish an overall decline in the intentional killing of civilians, there may be many potential reasons for it other than the workings of civilian immunity. Alternative explanations for a reduction of civilian killing might include the decline of interstate war, a lessening of great power interference in civil wars, a reduction of ideological conflict, the population size of countries over which wars are fought, the technologies used in war, the increased interconnectedness of national economies, and growing recognition that killing civilians may be counter-productive as a counter-insurgency strategy.[17] These concerns notwithstanding, it is useful to understand the overall picture of the current context—as messy

[14] The tendency to use atrocities as a last resort is widely recognized by the literature. See Downes, *Targeting Civilians*; Valentino, *Final Solutions*; Stathis N. Kalyvas, *The Logic of Violence in Civil War* (Cambridge: Cambridge University Press, 2006); and Daniel Chirot and Clark McCauley, *Why Not Kill Them All? The Logic and Prevention of Political Mass Murder* (Princeton: Princeton University Press, 2006).

[15] Fears of intervention and retribution are identified by Downes, *Targeting Civilians* and Valentino, *Final Solutions*. It was most evident as an inhibitor in the early days of the Second World War. See Jeffrey W. Legro, *Cooperation Under Fire: The Conduct of the Air War in the Second World War* (New York: St. Martin's Press, 1992). The others are identified by Chirot and McCauley, *Why Not Kill Them All?*, pp. 95–6.

[16] A view presented by Evans, *Responsibility to Protect*, p. 14,

[17] See Human Security Research Group, *Human Security Report, 2009/10: The Causes of Peace and the Shrinking Costs of War* (Oxford: Oxford University Press, 2011); Erik Melander, Magnus Oberg, and Jonathan Hall, 'Are "New Wars" More Atrocious? Battle Severity, Civilians Killed and Forced Migration Before and After the End of the Cold War', *European Journal of International Relations*, 15 (3) 2009, p. 508; and Alex J. Bellamy and Paul D. Williams, 'On the Limits of Moral Hazard: Rebellion, Intervention and the Responsibility to Protect', *European Journal of International Relations*, 18 (3), 2012.

and complicated as it is. The following analysis draws on a dataset of 103 episodes since 1945 where at least 5,000 civilians in any given year were intentionally killed.

Based on this dataset, Figure I.1 shows the number of new episodes of mass killing in any given year for each year between 1945 and 2008. The annual number of new episodes fluctuates between six and zero with little in the way of an obvious trend. The trendline indicates a slight upwards trend in the incidence of new cases from the 1940s until the late 1970s/early 1980s, followed by a gradual decline that accelerated in the first decade of the twenty-first century. We should be cautious about this result, however, because the trendline obscures some significant peaks in the late 1990s and is heavily influenced by the absence of new episodes in the period between 2006 and 2008.

An alternative way of analysing the same data is to consider the overall number of ongoing episodes in any given year (Figure I.2).

Figure I.2 shows that the number of episodes in any given year increased steadily from the late 1940s to the 1980s and then declined thereafter. There were slight increases at the beginning and end of the 1990s, but these were not

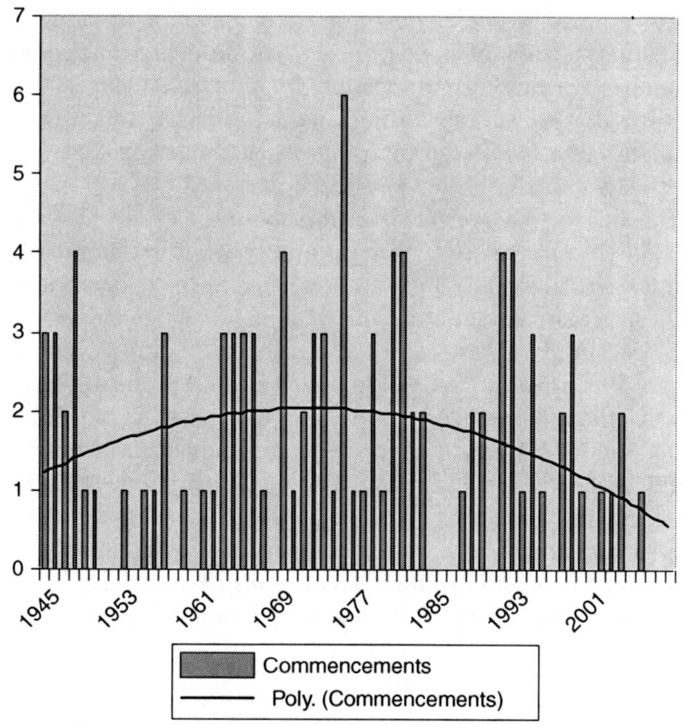


**Fig. I.1** Commencements of mass atrocities per year: 1945–2008

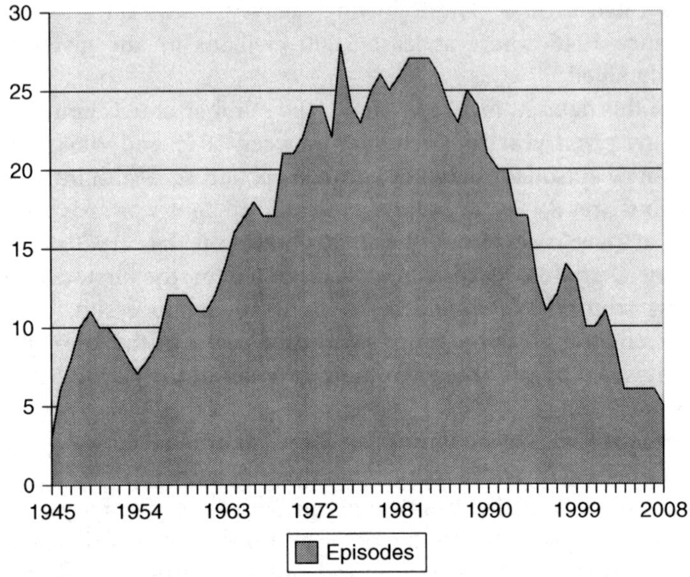


**Fig. I.2** Number of episodes each year: 1945–2008

sufficient to reverse the overall downwards trend. Comparing Figures I.1 and I.2 suggests that the bulk of any decline in the overall incidence of episodes of mass atrocities was caused by the ending of protracted episodes. We might infer from this that only a small proportion of the decline can be accounted for by the tendency of actors to refrain from selecting mass atrocities as a strategy in the first place.

This brings us to an associated question about the extent of killing once an episode erupts. We might see civilian immunity at work inhibiting the scale of mass killing. There are a number of challenges which make it difficult to identify the aggregate amount of civilian killing in any given year. In particular, there are almost always wide discrepancies in the estimated casualty figures even in relatively small and localized cases. For instance, estimates of how many civilians were killed during the 1993 massacres in Burundi range from 50,000 to 250,000.[18] Adding further complexity is the fact that the rate of killing tends to be uneven and data are not sufficiently precise to record this. The best we can do, therefore, is a rough approximation based on the available casualty estimates and the date ranges provided. Selecting the median casualty estimate for each case and assuming an even distribution of killing over time, Figure I.3 shows an estimate of the aggregate level of mass atrocities for each

[18] This is partly a product of the hazards of estimation in situations where hard evidence is very limited but is also caused by differences over whether to count both direct and indirect deaths. See Sara E. Davies, *Global Politics of Health* (Cambridge: Polity, 2010), ch. 7.

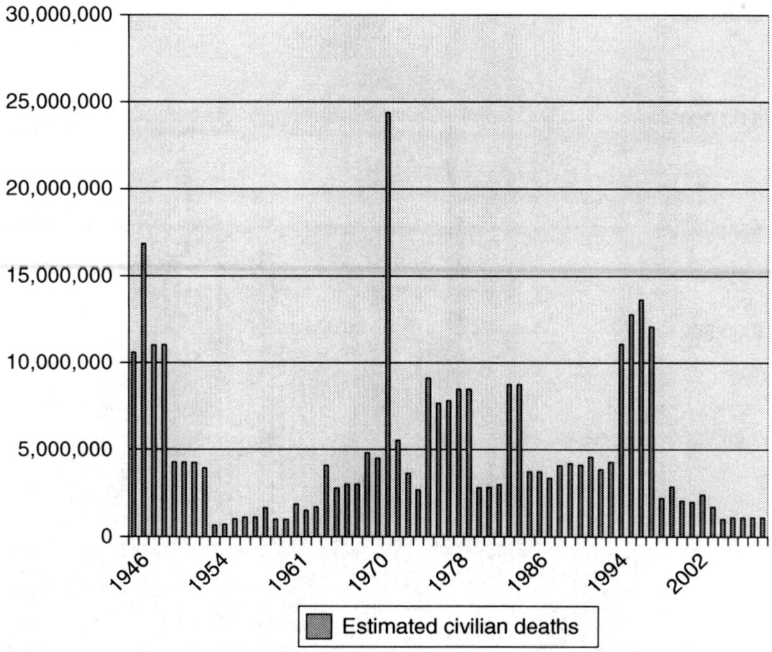


**Fig. I.3** Estimated number of killings each year: 1945–2008

year since 1945. Because the scale of killing in individual episodes varies from a few thousand to several million, there is wide variation across individual years. Figure I.3 highlights four notable peaks of mass killing caused by a handful of extremely severe cases: the Chinese civil war, Indian partition, East Pakistan, the Indochina wars, the regime induced famines in Ethiopia and North Korea, and the Rwandan genocide.

From this we can discern a slight trend whereby the estimated average rate of killing gradually increased from the mid-1950s to the mid-1990s and declined thereafter. But the trend is not altogether clear and is less pronounced than the trends relating to the commencement of episodes and the aggregate number of episodes in a given year. But if we exclude the outlying cases of massive mass killing, however, the trend becomes clearer (Figure I.4).

Because the downwards trend in the scale of killing is not as pronounced as the trends in commencements or aggregate number of episodes, it is not clear from these figures whether the reduced number of killings is primarily a product of fewer episodes (i.e. actors choosing to not use mass atrocities) or reduced average lethality (i.e. actors being restrained from killing higher numbers of civilians once they embark on a campaign of mass atrocities). To shed light on this question, Figure I.5 sets out the average number of killings per episode in a given year, excluding the outlying cases. It shows that

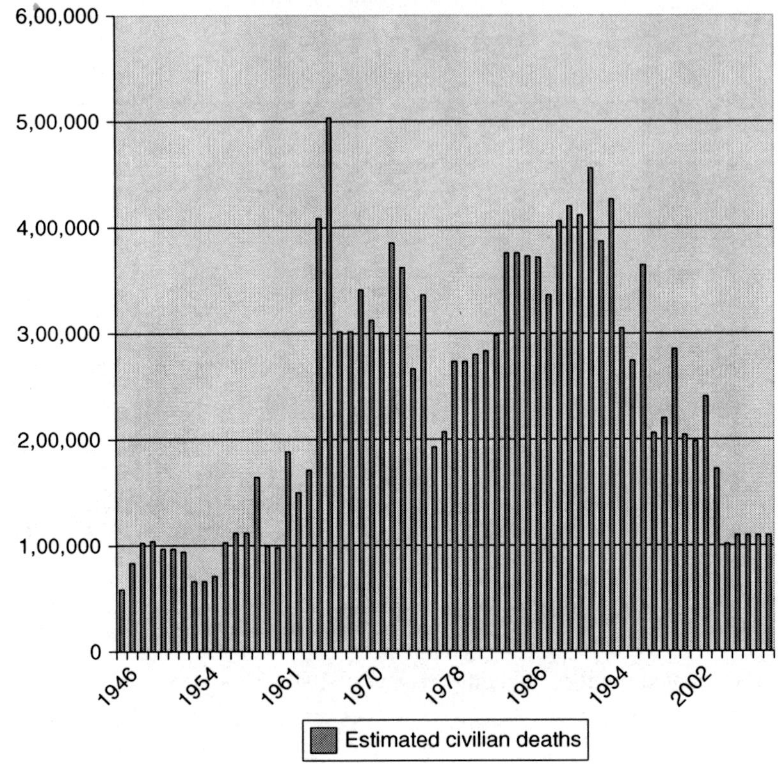


**Fig. I.4** Estimated number of killings each year excluding outlying cases: 1945–2008

there has been no downward trend in the average lethality of episodes. To the contrary, with the exception of the 'mega cases', the trend across the whole period is upwards with the average annual level of killing per episode plateauing in the twenty-first century at a level somewhat higher than its previous plateau between the mid-1960s and mid-1970s (around 18,000 per year, compared to around 16,000 per year).

Given the aforementioned problems with the data, we should not read too much into these figures. With due caution, we can posit four general insights. First, the past two decades have seen a decline in the overall number of civilians deliberately killed in any given year. Second, this is related to a reduction of the aggregate number of on-going episodes. Third, there has been a slight downturn in the average number of new episodes each year. Fourth, excluding a handful of 'mega cases' the average lethality of individual episodes has increased over the past forty years. Even excluding the 1994 Rwandan genocide, average lethality reached a peak in the 1990s and declined slightly thereafter but has settled in the early twenty-first century at a level significantly higher than that of the 1950s and 1960s. In the end, then,

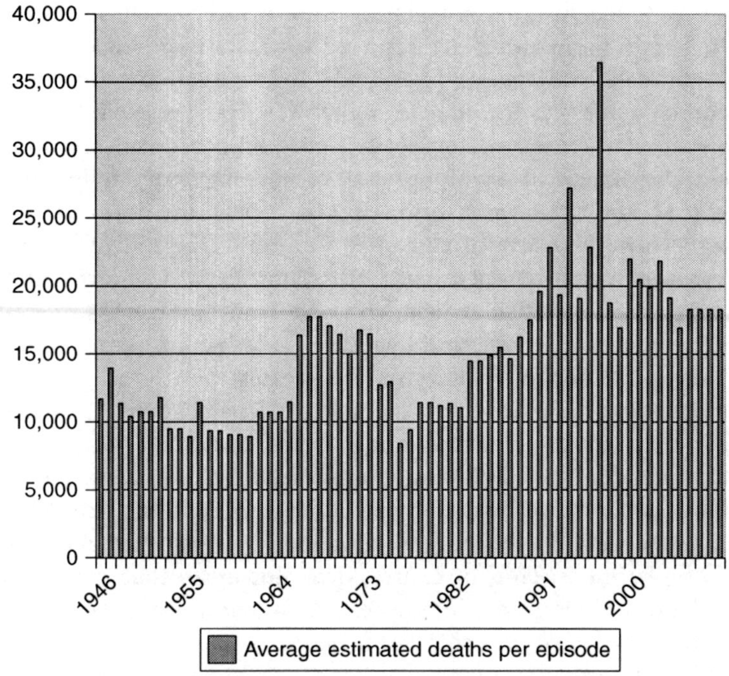


**Fig. I.5** Average number of deaths per episode, excluding outlying cases

numbers provide a mixed and uncertain picture about the impact of civilian immunity on the practice of mass killing. To make sense of this we need to know more about the role of civilian immunity in individual cases and how that role has changed over time. How do political leaders exempt themselves from shared norms and justify norm violating behaviour? How and why is there such marked variation in the determination of international society and individual states to defend the norm against violations? How and why have the politics surrounding these two issues changed over time? Addressing these questions is the purpose of this book.

## MASSACRES AND MORALITY

Actors sometimes violate norms because they calculate that doing so might serve their interest. But humans—both individually and as social actors—need a rationale to justify their behaviour.[19] Vaughn Shannon argues that political

[19] But cf. Alexander B. Downes, 'Review of Hugo Slim, *Innocent Civilians . . .*', *Journal of Strategic Studies*, 33 (1) 2010, p. 169.

leaders have to feel justified in violating a norm such as civilian immunity in order to satisfy their own personal need for a positive self-image (and to close cognitive dissonance) and to 'sell' their violation to domestic and international audiences in order to maintain social approval.[20] Actors who cannot exempt themselves from compliance with a norm are unlikely to violate it. The capacity to exempt oneself from being bound to follow a norm is influenced, according to Shannon, by two things: the norm itself and the situation. Norms that are difficult to interpret authoritatively, limited by parameters or which compete with other norms to define the normative characteristics of a particular behaviour are easier to exempt oneself from than determinate, universal, and hegemonic (i.e. admitting no competitors in its issue-area) norms.[21] Likewise, the greater the degree of uncertainty about a situation, the more actors are able to plausibly deny or excuse norm violations or portray their behaviour as being consistent with other, more important, norms. Thus, as Shannon argues, 'violation is motivated by self-interest but is permitted by the nature of the norm and the situation, which condition one's ability to define a situation in a way that allows socially accepted violation'.[22] This, of course, does not mean that the society as a whole will not still disapprove of the behaviour, but it does indicate that *there are situations in which an actor can believe that it is behaving in a socially acceptable way whilst violating norms, and can persuade others to share that belief.*[23]

Just as decisions to violate a norm are shaped by things relating to the norm and the situation, so too is the manner in which international society and individual states respond to norm violations. Responses to norm violations are not simply matters of normative obligation (logics of appropriateness) or calculations of self-interest (logics of consequences) as some constructivists and realists would respectively have it, but are instead guided by both these logics as well as perceptions about the nature of the situation at hand, pre-existing social relations with the actors involved, and power relations between actors holding different accounts of the situation.[24]

Taking these theoretical insights as my starting point, in this book I argue that between the late-eighteenth and mid-twentieth centuries, civilian

[20] Vaughn P. Shannon, 'Norms Are What States Make of Them: The Political Psychology of Norm Violation', *International Studies Quarterly*, 44, 2000, p. 300.

[21] This is an adaptation of Shannon, 'Norms Are What States Make Them', p. 300. Shannon does not himself include other norms.

[22] Shannon, 'Norms Are What States Make of Them', p. 300.

[23] Shannon, 'Norms Are What States Makes of Them', p. 304.

[24] This builds on the thinking set out by Richard K. Hermann and Vaughn P. Shannon, 'Defending International Norms: The Role of Obligation, Material Interest and Perception in Decision-Making', *International Organization*, 55 (3) 2001, pp. 621–54. Hermann and Shannon identify three main factors: (1) material interest; (2) felt normative commitment; (3) perception.

immunity coexisted with two competing 'anti-civilian' ideologies.[25] These ideologies, which I have labelled *necessity* and *selective extermination*, provided a rationale for the intentional killing of civilians and grounds for justifying such killing in certain situations and to some audiences at least. For a variety of reasons, largely associated with the rise of liberal doctrines of humanitarianism, human rights, and self-determination, the transformation of broadcasting technologies, and the ebb and flow of great power politics, these ideologies became less widely accepted as justifications for killing civilians. Nonetheless, many political leaders continued to believe that killing civilians could serve a useful purpose in certain situations. Violence against civilians was sometimes seen as being part and parcel of strategic air campaigning, low-level guerrilla warfare, counter-insurgency operations, campaigns to radically transform societies, and occasionally as being necessary for maintaining order. Some perpetrators agonized over the morality of their choices. More often, though, they agonized only over how to justify their behaviour to their own and international societies in order to maintain support and avoid punishment. This was a serious consideration, especially after the Second World War as international society moved incrementally to translate a weak norm based on a shared ethical principle into an embedded norm replete with legal rules and institutions empowered to enforce those rules.

With the norm-based route to self-exemption from civilian immunity effectively closed by the demise of anti-civilian ideologies, the key to getting away with mass atrocities came to rest largely with presenting the situation in certain ways. Perpetrators of mass killing employed a variety of strategies designed to create and leverage uncertainty, enabling them to claim that their behaviour was consistent with the norm of civilian immunity when in reality it was anything but.[26] They got away with it so often because even in a context where there was agreement about shared norms, judgements about legitimacy and the consequences that flow from being seen to be acting illegitimately are not framed exclusively by the consistency of behaviour with shared norms or by the quality of justificatory arguments. Instead, legitimacy judgements and the consequences that flow from them are mediated by contextual factors

[25] Hugo Slim, *Killing Civilians: Method, Madness and Morality in War* (New York: Columbia University Press, 2008), pp. 121–79. The phrase refers to political doctrines or ideas which hold that certain groups of civilians do not enjoy the protection of civilian immunity and provide reasons or justifications. On the role of ideology in mass milling more generally, see Jacques Semelin, *Purify and Destroy: The Political Uses of Massacre and Genocide* (New York: Columbia University Press, 2007); and Eric D. Weitz, *A Century of Genocide: Utopias of Race and Nation* (Princeton, NJ: Princeton University Press, 2003).

[26] The idea of leveraging uncertainty is drawn from Colin H. Krahl, 'In the Crossfire or the Crosshairs? Norms, Civilian Casualties, and US Conduct in Iraq', *International Security*, 32 (1) 2007, pp. 7–46.

which influence whose stories are likely to be believed, the manner in which events are interpreted, the importance attached to particular norms and their violation, and the extent to which actors will take it upon themselves to expend resources defending norms and punishing violators.[27] The most salient factors differ from case to case, but particularly important to the story of civilian immunity are the extent to which information clearly pointed to the intentional and widespread killing of civilians (shaping perceptions), prior judgements based on existing social relations about the relative legitimacy of the actors involved (including judgements about sovereignty claims), the presence (or absence) of interests that counterbalanced concerns about norm violations, and the relative power of actors that supported either of the parties involved. Even in the post-Cold War period—when changes in the underlying context made it undeniably harder to plausibly exempt oneself from civilian immunity—perpetrators were occasionally able to avoid international criticism. Most notable in this regard were Russia's wars in Chechnya and the Rwandan Patriotic Front's (RPF) massacres in Rwanda and Zaire. Both entailed massive and systematic violations of civilian immunity yet neither attracted much criticism, let alone punishment.

These cases were exceptions to the general rule, but they help demonstrate that the struggle for civilian immunity is far from won. They point to the persistence of situational forces that might enable leaders to justify mass killing and inhibit efforts to defend the norm. The rise to prominence of Al Qaeda and its ideology of selective extermination grounded in radical Islamism and a US-led War on Terror which, whilst remaining formally faithful to civilian immunity, partially resurrected the ideology of necessity, show that the norm itself continues to confront significant challenges and may be weakened by practice in ways that would make it easier for future perpetrators to exempt themselves from compliance. The struggle for civilian immunity will therefore persist for the foreseeable future; a struggle between the norm itself, various competing ideas and ideologies, and strategic rationality whose outcome in specific situations is heavily influenced by contextual factors.

To understand the role that norms play in shaping behaviour and to chart how they change over time, it is important to see them within the social context in which they operate—in this case, cases where civilians are intentionally killed.[28] After briefly clarifying the meaning and scope of civilian immunity and the politics of legitimacy in Chapter 1, the book offers a history of civilian immunity in practice. My focus is principally on the manner in

[27] Hermann and Shannon, 'Defending International Norms'.

[28] The theory underpinning this method is discussed in more detail in Alexander Wendt, 'The Agent-Structure Problem in International Relations Theory', *International Organization*, 41 (3) 1987, esp. p. 365; and Martha Finnemore and Kathryn Sikkink, 'International Norm Dynamics and Political Change', *International Organization*, 52 (4) 1998, p. 890.

which perpetrators attempted to justify their use of violence against civilians, the reception those arguments received and the factors that affected that reception, though where appropriate I also examine the perpetrators' own dialogue and debates about targeting civilians. Because the role of civilian immunity is heavily influenced by the social context and human agency, it is difficult to identify general patterns by looking at a handful of cases in detail. Therefore, the study examines a relatively large number of cases involving various types of mass killing in order to better understand the interplay of norms, actors, and contexts and identify patterns and changes. The thinking behind this approach is set out in more detail in the following chapter.

The book takes the French Revolution as its starting point, because this event marked the beginning of the period in which international society began to seriously consider codifying shared moral principles about civilian immunity into international legal rules.[29] What follows is loosely organized into two sections. The first section spans the period from the French Revolution to the end of the Second World War in which civilian immunity evolved from being a moral principle into a shared, convention-dependent, ethical norm. For much of this period, the norm competed with two anti-civilian ideologies (necessity and selective extermination) that provided grounds for legitimizing the intentional killing of civilians in certain situations and among certain parts of international society. Thanks largely to the second of these ideologies, selective extermination, the norm of civilian immunity was generally understood to apply only to relations between 'civilized'/European countries and was not widely thought to extend to colonized peoples.

The second section covers the period from the end of the Cold War to the 'war on terror' at the beginning of the twenty-first century, during which time the norm of civilian immunity grew gradually stronger and became a customary principle of international law, embedded in several different legal regimes. Although civilian immunity had largely prevailed over necessity in the early twentieth century, selective extermination continued to find support inside the communist world. Outside the communist bloc, perpetrators generally preferred to leverage uncertainty in order to claim that their behaviour was not inconsistent with civilian immunity. During the Cold War especially, the politics of civilian immunity were heavily conditioned by contextual factors, mainly those connected to the strategic interests of the superpowers. Towards the end of the Cold War, improvements in global communications made it more difficult for perpetrators to avoid responsibility for mass atrocities,

[29] At least one macro-history of genocide starts from a similar starting point on the grounds that the rise of the West, modernity and the nation-state are the key structures underlying genocide and that genocides can be explained as much by reference to great power politics as other factors. See Mark Levene, *Genocide in the Age of the Nation-State*, Vol. I: *The Meaning of Genocide* (London: I. B. Tauris, 2005); and Mark Levene, *Genocide in the Age of the Nation-State*, Vol. II: *The Rise of the West and the Coming of Genocide* (London: I. B. Tauris, 2005).

whilst the end of the Cold War itself removed many of the strategic interests that had earlier inhibited the condemnation and punishment of norm violators. Together, this made it more difficult—but not impossible—for actors to 'get away' with violating the norm of civilian immunity. But this is not a teleological account and challenges to the norm persist. The September 11 terrorist attacks on New York and Washington, DC brought to prominence a new ideology of selective extermination, influenced by radical Islamism. In responding to this new challenge, the USA courted necessity as an excuse for violating the spirit—and some would say the letter—of civilian immunity. Had either radical Islam's appeal to selective extermination or the USA's appeal to necessity been sustained and legitimated, either could have seriously damaged the norm of civilian immunity—and may prove to yet.

The book's principal argument is that the ascendancy of civilian immunity is both relatively recent and fragile, and that its application in particular settings is heavily influenced by context. Although it is has become progressively more difficult to get away with mass atrocities, certain contexts continue to make that a very real possibility for some. What is more, challenges to the norm's pre-eminence are recurrent. To those who share my conviction that civilian immunity is an important principle that moderates humanity's tendency towards grave inhumanity, this book sounds a wake up call. The battle for civilian immunity is perpetual and should be waged everywhere that the norm is challenged. There is simply no room for complacency.

Before proceeding it is necessary to clarify a few points of terminology. This book is about grave violations of the norm of civilian immunity—that is, the deliberate killing of civilians. For my purposes, that includes the indiscriminate killing of civilians where civilian targets and areas are attacked but without specific intent to kill civilians. I use the terms 'massacre', 'mass killing', and 'atrocities' interchangeably throughout the book to refer to the intentional killing of multiple civilians or a campaign of civilian killing. Sometimes I refer to campaigns or strategies of 'terror' to denote the systematic use of violence against civilians. I refer to 'genocide' only where the killing is committed with the intent to destroy a definable group in whole or in part and other legal terms such as 'crimes against humanity', 'war crimes', and 'ethnic cleansing' only in the specific way intended by international law—recognizing that violations of civilian immunity may be violations of different laws in different contexts. When I refer to 'terrorism' I mean the use of relatively low-level violence against civilians by non-state actors. Where this is targeted violence against individual civilians, I use 'assassination'. Civilian immunity is understood here to be an ethical norm—a groundnorm—upon which legal rules are based. This is discussed in greater detail in the following chapter. Where I refer to 'non-combatant immunity', I am referring to the specific legal prohibition on targeting 'non-combatants'. Finally, there is some overlap between the anti-civilian ideology of necessity and the principle of 'military necessity'.

Especially in relation to counter-insurgency warfare, 'military necessity' sometimes permitted the killing of civilians as a reprisal for guerrilla attacks on regular forces. By the early twentieth century, however, the principle of 'military necessity' rarely permitted the deliberate slaying of civilians, though such slaying was often justified by reference to broader principles of necessity.[30]

[30] This trend can be traced to the promulgation of General Orders No. 100 by the US government in 1863 (better known as the Lieber code). Here, necessity was defined as 'those measures which are indispensable for securing the ends of the war, and which are lawful according to the modern law and usages of war'. This nodded in the direction of a concept of necessity that included civilian immunity but the Code itself gave considerable discretion to commanders on this issue. See Richard Shelly Hartigan, *Lieber's Code and the Law of War* (Chicago: Precedent, 1983), p. 48; and Ernest Nys, 'Francis Lieber—His Life and Work: Part II', *American Journal of International Law*, 5 (2) 1911, p. 383.

# 1

## Civilian Immunity and the Politics of Legitimacy

This chapter examines two conceptual issues that underpin most of what follows. The first part clarifies what I understand to be the norm of civilian immunity and how that norm relates to rules relating to the killing of civilians in wartime, peacetime, and in genocide, each of which are governed by their own international legal regimes (International Humanitarian Law, International Human Rights Law, and the Genocide Convention, respectively). The second part examines how norms inhibit behaviour and frame the responses of third parties.

### CIVILIAN IMMUNITY

Civilian immunity overlaps with—but is distinct from—a number of different international legal rules.[1] The norm is a moral belief, shared by most of the world's major ethical traditions and embedded in different parts of international law, that it is wrong to intentionally kill people who are neither members of the armed forces nor criminals legitimately convicted of crimes that carry the death penalty.[2] Under the rubric of the doctrine of double-effect,

[1] This is not unique to civilian immunity. Many laws are derived from ethical norms but remain distinct from them. See Sarah Percy, *Mercenaries: The History of a Norm in International Relations* (Oxford: Oxford University Press, 2007), pp. 18–19.

[2] There is an extensive literature on this. See, among others, Paul Christopher, *The Ethics of War and Peace: An Introduction to Legal and Moral Issues* (Englewood Cliffs, NJ: Prentice Hall, 1994), pp. 9–10; Sun Tzu, *The Art of War* trans. Samuel Griffith (Oxford: Oxford University Press, 1963), pp. 76–8; James Turner Johnson, *Morality and Contemporary Warfare* (New Haven: Yale University Press, 1999), pp. 168–86; Richard Shelly Hartigan, *The Forgotten Victim: A History of the Civilian in War* (Chicago: Precedent Publishing, 1982); James Turner Johnson, *Ideology, Reason and the Limitation of War: Religious and Secular Concepts 1200–1740* (Princeton: Princeton University Press, 1975); James Turner Johnson, *Just War Tradition and the Restraint of War: A Moral and Historical Enquiry* (Princeton: Princeton University Press,

the norm does permit the *unintended* killing of civilians in war so long as: (1) the object of the attack has a military purpose; (2) the expected civilian casualties are proportionate to the expected military utility; (3) civilian casualties are not the means by which the military objective will be achieved; and (4) combatants take steps to minimize the risk of civilian casualties as far as possible.[3]

Although stated in different ways, the principle of civilian immunity can be found as a long-standing rule in several ethical traditions (e.g. Christian just war, Islamic traditions, and Hindu traditions) and a number of others contain elements of civilian immunity (the Hebrew Bible, ancient Chinese philosophy). It is worth noting, though, that some major ethical traditions—notably Japan's warrior ethos (*bushi*) and the imperial Chinese tradition—contained little, if any, protection for civilians.[4] Moreover, some contemporary Western philosophers have also raised a number of arguments against civilian immunity. Among others, they include the utilitarian view that it should be permissible to kill civilians if the overall good exceeds the overall harm; the argument that civilians who benefit from injustice and oppression may be justly killed; Michael Walzer's doctrine of supreme emergency which permits the killing of civilians in times of dire necessity; and the realist injunction that ethics have no part to play in war.[5] But ethical traditions

1981); Torkel Brekke (ed.), *The Ethics of War in Asian Civilizations: A Comparative Perspective* (London: Routledge, 2006); Nick Allen, 'Just War in the *Mahabharata*', in Richard Sorabji and David Rodin (eds), *The Ethics of War: Shared Problems in Different Traditions* (Aldershot: Ashgate, 2006), p. 139; Davood Feirahi, 'Norms of War in Shia Islam', in Vesselin Popovski, Gregory M. Reichberg, and Nicholas Turner (eds), *World Religions and Norms of War* (Tokyo: United Nations University Press, 2009), pp. 273–4; Richard Bonney, *Jihad: From Qur'an to bin Laden* (Basingstoke: Palgrave, 2004).

3 Michael Walzer, *Just and Unjust Wars: A Moral Argument with Historical Illustrations* (New York: Basic Books, 1977), p. 156; and Colm McKeogh, *Innocent Civilians: The Morality of Killing in War* (Basingstoke: Palgrave, 2002), pp. 64–5.

4 Karl Friday, 'Might Makes Right: Just War and Just Warfare in Early Medieval Japan', in Brekke *Ethics of War in Asian Civilizations*, p. 175; and Mark E. Lewis, 'The Just War in Early China', in Brekke, *Ethics of War in Asian Civilizations*, p. 185.

5 See Robert E. Goodin, *Utilitarianism as Public Philosophy* (Cambridge: Cambridge University Press, 1995), pp. 3–28 and 265–88; George I. Mavrodes, 'Conventions and the Morality of War', in C. Beitz, M. Cohen, T. Scanlon, and A. J. Simmons (eds), *International Ethics: A Philosophy and Public Affairs Reader* (Princeton: Princeton University Press, 1990), p. 81; Saul Smilansky, 'Terrorism, Justification and Illusion', *Ethics*, 114 (4), 2004, p. 791; Kai Nielsen, 'Violence and Terrorism: Its Uses and Abuses' in Burton M. Leiser (ed.), *Values in Conflict* (New York: Macmillan, 1981), pp. 435–49; Burleigh Taylor Wilkins, *Terrorism and Collective Responsibility* (London: Routledge, 1992); Frantz Fanon, *The Wretched of the Earth* (London: Grove Press, 1965), pp. 34–7; Seumas Miller, 'Civilian Immunity, Forcing the Choice, and Collective Responsibility', in Igor Primoratz (ed.), *Civilian Immunity in War* (Oxford: Oxford University Press, 2007), pp. 113–35; Jeff McMahan, 'The Ethics of Killing in War', *Ethics*, 114, 2003, pp. 693–733; Walzer, *Just and Unjust Wars*, pp. 251–5. For a critical evaluation of these approaches, see Igor Primoratz, 'Civilian Immunity in War: Its Grounds, Scope and Weight', in Igor Primoratz (ed.), *Civilian Immunity in War* (Oxford: Oxford University Press, 2007).

with nothing to say about civilian immunity are a distinct minority and were not widely held in the modern age and public debates about the ethics of killing civilians have not been perceptibly influenced by the lively and creative arguments of philosophers who believe that we might sometimes justly kill the unarmed. Neither has precluded the emergence of international consensus about establishing civilian immunity in international law.

Potential confusion about the scope of the norm of civilian immunity arises because international law governing the protection of civilians from arbitrary violence distinguishes between different settings and crimes. It is useful, therefore, to think of civilian immunity as a 'groundnorm' upon which various international legal regimes are built.[6] The most fundamental difference between the legal rules and ethical norm is the distinction that some laws make between wartime rules and peacetime rules. However, one of the gravest forms of violation—genocide—enjoys its own legal regime that makes no distinction about the context in which that crime is committed.

Civilian immunity is most closely associated with International Humanitarian Law (IHL) sometimes known as the 'laws of war'. By the end of the twentieth century, civilian immunity had come to be considered a customary principle of international law—legally binding on all states regardless of whether they had acceded to specific treaties.[7] Rules governing war are as old as war itself, but the period between the 1860s and the outbreak of the First World War was something of a 'golden era' for international treaty-making on the subject.[8] The 1864 Geneva Convention gave formal recognition to the International Committee of the Red Cross (ICRC) and its mission to protect people from the ravages of war and established the principle of legal protection for those playing no part in armed hostilities (in this case wounded soldiers). But it did not apply to civilians and only enjoyed declaratory status, drawing sharp criticism from Florence Nightingale among others.[9] The 1868 St Petersburg Declaration was the first to impose legally binding obligations on belligerents. It nodded towards civilian immunity in its preamble by stating that

[6] Drawing on Hans Kelsen, as a groundnorm civilian immunity might be thought of as providing the basis and rationale for a variety of laws and regimes aimed at protecting civilians from arbitrary violence in different contexts. Different legal try to give meaning to civilian immunity in different settings. For Kelsen's theory, see Hans Kelsen, *General Theory of Law and State* (Cambridge, MA: Harvard University Press, 1949). I refer to the goundnorm as 'civilian immunity' and legal rules embedded in IHL as 'non-combatant immunity'.

[7] Theodor Meron, 'The Geneva Conventions as Customary Law', *American Journal of International Law*, 81 (2) 1987, pp. 348–70; and Michael Byers, *War Law: International Law and Armed Conflict* (London: Atlantic Books, 2005), p. 116.

[8] See James Brown Scott, 'The Codification of International Law', *American Journal of International Law*, 18 (2) 1924, pp. 260–80.

[9] Caroline Moorhead, *Dunant's Dream: War, Switzerland and the History of the Red Cross* (New York: Carroll and Graf Publishers, 1998), p. 47.

the only legitimate object of war was the enemy's military.[10] In 1899, the first Hague conference reaffirmed and expanded the scope of the St Petersburg Declaration and prohibited the use asphyxiating or deleterious gases and the use of dum-dum bullets. A second and more inclusive Hague conference was convened in 1907, producing the Convention on the Laws and Customs of War on Land. This moved more decisively towards codifying civilian immunity, forbidding the bombardment of undefended towns and villages (Article 25), requiring that military commanders give due warning before commencing a bombardment (Article 26), and demanding that 'in sieges and bombardments all necessary steps must be taken to spare, as far as possible, buildings dedicated to religion, art, science or charitable purposes, historic monuments, hospitals and places where the sick and wounded are collected, provided they are not being used at the time for military purposes' (Article 27).[11] Protected groups included the ill, wounded, prisoners of war, the inhabitants of undefended places, those in defended places who departed when given an opportunity to do so, and all inhabitants once hostilities ceased (except spies and insurgents). The 1923 Hague rules governing aerial warfare forbade the use of aerial bombardment to terrorize the enemy's civilian population.

The conscience-shocking Holocaust created additional momentum for the rapid advancement of civilian immunity as a principle of the laws of war in the late 1940s—described by Stephen Neff as a 'humanitarian revolution' which marked a shift in 'the very nature and purpose of the rules governing the prosecution of armed conflict'.[12] During the Second World War, the ICRC had drafted articles for a new convention aimed at protecting the victims of war. A meeting of experts was convened in Stockholm in 1947, which produced a draft convention that was then put to states at a 1949 conference in Geneva.[13] Although there was broad agreement on the general principles, especially on the need to strengthen protection for civilians and prisoners of war, there was much less agreement on how to achieve these goals.[14] In the end, common Article 3 prohibited 'violence to life and person' against any person 'taking no active part in the hostilities'. The Geneva Conventions

[10] Preamble of the 1868 St Declaration. For a discussion, see Hilaire McCoubrey, *International Humanitarian Law: Modern Developments in the Limitation of Warfare* (Dartmouth: Ashgate, 1998), p. 19; and Ingrid Detter De Lupis, *The Law of War* (Cambridge: Cambridge University Press, 1987), p. 135.

[11] Sceptics point out that the Conventions did not specifically refer to non-combatants and note that the use of terms like 'undefended towns' gave attackers considerable latitude. George H. Aldrich, 'The Laws of War on Land', *American Journal of International Law*, 94 (1) 2000, p. 50. Contrast with James Turner Johnson, 'Maintaining the Protection of Non-Combatants', *Journal of Peace Research*, 37 (4) 2000, p. 431.

[12] Stephen C. Neff, *War and the Law of Nations: A General History* (Cambridge: Cambridge University Press, 2005), p. 340.

[13] Geoffrey Best, *War and Law Since 1945* (Oxford: Clarendon Press, 1994), pp. 80–4.

[14] Best, *War and Law Since 1945*, pp. 111–20.

granted more protection to civilians in international wars than in civil wars, but Article 3 (which applied to both) nevertheless marked a breakthrough, establishing non-combatant immunity as an international legal principle.

Within a decade or so of their enactment, it had become clear to many that there were significant gaps in the Conventions. Not least, there was no prohibition of indiscriminate bombardment, no proportionality clause, and the rule of non-combatant immunity was relatively vague.[15] Added to this were calls for the protections afforded to civilians in international wars to be extended to civilians in internal conflicts. Between 1974 and 1977, states returned to Geneva to negotiate additions to the Conventions. The first Additional Protocol significantly extended the legal protection afforded to civilians. Stating the legal principle of non-combatant immunity more clearly than previous treaties, it demanded that:

> The civilian population as such, as well as individual civilians, shall not be the object of attack. Acts or threats of violence the primary purpose of which is to spread terror among the civilian population are prohibited (Article 51 (2)).

The protocol also insisted that attacks should be strictly limited to military objectives, defining these as 'those objects which by their nature, location, purpose or use make an effective contribution to military action and whose total or partial destruction, capture or neutralization, in the circumstances ruling at the time, offers a definite military advantage'.[16] In other words, combatants were forbidden from attacking civilians or their property, though so-called 'dual use' facilities remained lawful targets.[17] Soldiers were also obliged to evaluate the proportionality of their attacks, with Article 51 (5) outlawing attacks on military objects which 'may be expected to cause' excessive civilian casualties. The Protocol also forbade the indirect targeting of civilians through attacks calculated to destroy vital civilian infrastructure or cause starvation. In short, though it did not grant internal wars the same legal status as international wars nor provide non-state belligerents with the rights enjoyed by their state-sanctioned counterparts, the first Geneva Protocol established a comprehensive and universal principle of discrimination based on the 'groundnorm' of civilian immunity.[18] This principle holds that it is as bad to kill civilians in indiscriminate fire as it is to target them directly and that no meaningful distinction should be made between the two. Thus, bombing a

[15] Best, *War and Law Since 1945*, pp. 106–7; and Judith Gail Gardam, 'Proportionality and Force in International Law', *American Journal of International Law*, 87 (3) 1993, pp. 391–413.

[16] Article 52 of the 1977 Geneva Protocol I.

[17] A provision that has since been questioned by writers who suggest that dual-use facilities that perform vital civilian functions should be immune from attack. See Henry Shue and David Wippman, 'Limiting Attacks on Dual-Use Facilities Performing Indispensable Civilian Functions', *Cornell International Law Journal*, 35, 2002, pp. 559–79.

[18] Neff, *War and the Law of Nations*, p. 368.

city centre violates civilian immunity even if there is no specific intent to kill civilians. This provided the catalyst for subsequent conventions banning weapons considered inherently indiscriminate.[19] For example, the 1980 Convention on Conventional Weapons and subsequent amendments banned weapons such as booby traps, lasers, and weapons that injure by creating fire and heat, on the grounds of their inherently indiscriminate nature.[20] The cases for the 2000 Convention prohibiting the manufacture, sale, and use of landmines and the 2008 Convention banning cluster munitions were also articulated on these grounds, with some considerable success.[21] Beginning in the mid-nineteenth century, therefore, international society has gradually legislated on the norm of civilian immunity in wartime, though it was not until 1977 that the targeting of civilians and the indiscriminate use of force in both internal and international wars were prohibited.

However, around one-third of all the major episodes of violence against civilians were committed outside a context of war.[22] These too represent violations of civilian immunity and are prohibited by international human rights law.[23] The basic right to life was put forth in the 1948 Universal Declaration of Human Rights. Article 3 of the Declaration stated that 'everyone has the right to life . . . ' and subsequent articles forbade torture and inhuman treatment (Article 4) and arbitrary arrest and detention (Article 9). This right to life was reiterated in the UN's Convention of Civil and Political Rights (1994), which declared that 'every human being has the inherent right to life. This right shall be protected by law. No one shall be arbitrarily deprived of his life' (Article 6 (1)). This Convention also prohibited torture (Article 7) and arbitrary detention, Article 9 (1) declaring that '[E]veryone has the right to liberty and security of person. No one shall be subjected to arbitrary arrest or detention. No one shall be deprived of his liberty except on such grounds and in accordance with such procedure as are established by law'. Different elements of these rights were given their own international treaties. Torture, for instance, was expressly prohibited by an extensive range of human rights conventions, including a specific UN convention on torture and a variety of regional treaties.

[19] Louise Doswald-Beck, 'The Civilian in the Crossfire', *Journal of Peace Research*, 24 (3) 1987, p. 253.

[20] See David Kaye and Steven A. Solomon, 'The Second Conference of the 1980 Convention on Certain Conventional Weapons', *American Journal of International Law*, 96 (4) 2002, pp. 922–36.

[21] See Richard Price, 'Reversing the Gunsights: Transnational Civil Society Targets Land Mines', *International Organization*, 52, 1998, pp. 613–44.

[22] Alex J. Bellamy, 'Mass Atrocities and Armed Conflict: Links, Distinctions and Implications for the Responsibility to Protect', *Stanley Foundation Policy Analysis Brief*, January 2011.

[23] Geoffrey Best argues that there is an important connection between the laws of war and human rights law. See Best, *War and Law Since 1945*, pp. 70–2. For an overview, see Bertrand G. Ramcharan, (ed.), *The Right to Life in International Law* (The Hague: Martinus Nijhoff, 1985).

It is also widely considered a 'crime against humanity'.[24] All this led the ICRC to conclude that 'no possible loophole is left; there can be no excuse, no attenuating circumstances' in which torture may be permitted.[25]

To add a further layer of confusion, one particularly extreme type of anti-civilian behaviour, genocide, has its own legal regime. Only a year after prominent lawyer and activist Raphael Lemkin first coined the term, the UN General Assembly unanimously agreed an international convention outlawing genocide.[26] The 1948 *Convention on the Prevention and Punishment of the Crime of Genocide* is generally considered to be customary international law.[27] Article 1 of the Convention prohibits the crime of genocide and establishes the duty of states to prevent it and punish the perpetrators.[28] In 2008, the International Court of Justice (ICJ) ruled that the Article 1 obligation to prevent genocide requires that states 'employ all means which are reasonably available to them'.[29] Article 2 defined genocide as the commission of a number of acts (including killing members of a group) 'committed with intent to destroy, in whole or in part, a national, ethnical, racial or religious group as such'. This definition was subsequently adopted by the International Criminal Tribunals for former Yugoslavia and Rwanda (ICTY and ICTR respectively) and the Rome Statute of the International Criminal Court (ICC) (Article 6). Although criticized for being too restrictive, because it applies only to the destruction of national, ethnic, racial, and religious groups (and not, for example, socio-economic groups such as the *kulaks* in the Soviet Union), it is generally accepted as definitive.[30]

These different strands of law were brought together by international society in 2005, when the UN General Assembly made its unanimous commitment to the Resposibility to Protect (RtoP) principle. RtoP holds that all states have a duty to protect their populations from grave breaches of civilian

[24] Philip Setunga and Nick Cheeseman (eds), *Torture: A Crime against Humanity* (Hong Kong: Asian Human Rights Commission, 2001). Almost all of the world's states are party to one or more conventions forbidding torture. Nigel S. Rodley, *The Treatment of Prisoners Under International Law* (Oxford: Clarendon Press, 1987), p. 45.

[25] Jean Pictet (ed.), *The Geneva Conventions of 12 August 1949—Commentary: III Geneva Convention Relative to the Treatment of Prisoners of War* (Geneva: ICRC, 1960), p. 39.

[26] William A. Schabas, *Genocide in International Law* (Cambridge: Cambridge University Press, 2000), p. 14; and Samantha Power, *A Problem from Hell: America and the Age of Genocide* (New York: Basic Books, 2002), esp. pp. 42–72.

[27] See Caroline Fournet, *The Crime of Destruction and the Law of Genocide: Their Impact on Collective Memory* (Aldershot: Ashgate, 2007), p. 99; and Jan Wouters and Sten Verhoeven, 2005. 'The Prohibition of Genocide as a Norm of *Ius Cogens* and Its Implications for the Enforcement of the Law of Genocide', *International Criminal Law Review* 5(3), 2005, p. 405.

[28] Schabas, *Genocide in International Law,* p. 2; and Fournet, *Crime of Destruction*, p. 37.

[29] See Mark Gibney, 'Genocide and State Responsibility', *Human Rights Law Review* 7(4), 2007, p. 772; and Marko Milanovic, 'State Responsibility for Genocide: A Follow-Up', *European Journal of International Law* 18(4) 2007, p. 686.

[30] On the criticism, see Martin Shaw, *What is Genocide?* (Cambridge: Polity, 2006). For a discussion, see Wouters and Verhoeven, 'The Prohibition of Genocide', p. 403.

immunity (genocide, war crimes, ethnic cleansing, and crimes against humanity) and that this duty applies irrespective of the context.

As understood here, therefore, the norm of civilian immunity underpins various legal regimes which prohibit the intentional killing of civilians in different contexts. The norm is related to, but distinct from, the legal rules it informs. Each of these legal rules has a different status—for instance IHL is commonly regarded as customary law, whereas the customary status of the Convention on Civil and Political Rights is disputed—and different mechanisms for ensuring or encouraging compliance.[31] Except for the crime of genocide, international law distinguishes between wartime rules and peacetime rules, whereas the underlying ethical norm makes no such distinction. That grave breaches of civilian immunity may be committed in wartime and peacetime was recognized formally by international society in its unanimous commitment to RtoP in 2005.

Having identified what I mean by the norm of civilian immunity and how it relates to various legal rules, it is important at this point to clarify the norm's nature and quality. In other words, what sort of norm is it and in what basic ways has the norm itself (rather than the way in which it is used) changed? Because this book is principally concerned with how the norm of civilian immunity has functioned in practice and how this has changed over time, in subsequent chapters I do not examine the more general extent of international support for the norm or its domestic internalization except where this relates directly to individual cases. In his landmark book, *Ethics of Destruction*, Ward Thomas helpfully distinguished between moral principles and ethical norms and identified two types of ethical norm. According to Thomas, a moral principle is a 'proposition or tenet that expresses an abstract judgment about right or wrong'. These tend to be quite abstract (e.g. 'it is wrong to kill without justification') and hold true for the bearer even if held by only one person or by small groups.[32] By contrast, ethical norms, whilst based upon moral principles, imply a degree of intersubjective agreement. In other words, the moral principle is *shared*. Often, the process of negotiating an ethical norm makes it more specific than the abstract moral principle. For example, the injunction 'it is wrong to kill without justification' might become 'it is wrong to intentionally kill civilians (with the double-effect caveat duly noted)'. Whilst a moral principle might influence the personal choices of those that adhere to it, because they are intersubjective ethical norms are likely to influence social behaviour more generally. When talking about civilian immunity in different

[31] For a comprehensive account, see Jacob Blaustein Institute for the Advancement of Human Rights, *Compilation of Risk Factors and Legal Norms for the Prevention of Genocide* (New York: Jacob Blaustein Intstitute, 2011).

[32] Thomas, *Ethics of Destruction*, pp. 27–8.

historical periods, therefore, we need to know whether we are talking about a moral principle or an ethical norm.

We also need to be aware that not all norms carry equal weight. Thomas helpfully distinguishes two types of norm based on their capacity to influence behaviour. The first, and weakest, are 'convention-dependent' norms. As their name suggests, convention-dependent norms 'rely heavily on precedence and patterns of reciprocal adherence'.[33] In other words, actors comply with the norm only insofar as that compliance is reciprocated. Once a norm is violated by one party, the obligation on the others to comply is relieved or relaxed. The second type of norm, according to Thomas, is an *internalized* norm. Thomas argues that once a norm becomes internalized, 'it is not simply one among a number of considerations that must be factored into the calculus of foreign policy decision-making. It instead becomes one of the foundational assumptions upon which that calculus is premised'.[34] The more deeply internalized a norm becomes, the more it becomes taken for granted, naturalized, and habitually practised. Such norms are insulated from normal processes of decision-making.[35] Where the use of force is concerned, most norms—even powerful ones such as the prohibition on the use of nuclear weapons—cannot be said to be entirely internalized because norm violation remains an option that decision-makers are prepared to contemplate in some situations.[36] We might, therefore, helpfully add an additional type of norm between 'convention-dependent' and 'internalized' norms. I will label this type, *embedded* norms. Embedded norms enjoy high levels of intersubjective agreement and group members are expected to comply irrespective of patterns of reciprocity. Whilst recognizing that a norm is embedded in international social relations, individual actors may nonetheless consider violating the norm in order to achieve cherished goals and occasionally follow through with norm-violating behaviour. All other things being equal, the violation of embedded norms can be expected to provoke criticism and punitive action from other members of the society in which the norm is embedded. This significantly increases the transaction costs associated with norm-violating behaviour—a point discussed in more detail below. In general, a norm that

[33] Thomas, *Ethics of Destruction*, p. 34.

[34] Thomas, *Ethics of Destruction*, p. 38.

[35] For an example of this 'taken for granted' quality in a different context (diplomatic practice), see Janice A. Thompson, 'Norms in International Relations: A Conceptual Analysis', *International Journal of Group Tensions*, 23 (1), 1993, p. 73.

[36] See Michael Walzer's discussion of supreme emergencies: Walzer, *Just and Unjust Wars*. On the status of the nuclear taboo, see Richard Price and Nina Tannenwald, 'Norms and Deterrence: The Nuclear and Chemical Weapons Taboos', in Peter J. Katzenstein (ed.), *The Culture of National Security: Norms, Identities and World Politics* (New York: Columbia University Press, 1996).

is embedded is more likely to guide behaviour than a convention-dependent norm, even though the norm is not internalized by the actor in question.

This brings us Thomas' analysis of the changing status of the norm of civilian immunity over time. Thomas argues that, in relation to aerial bombing, the first part of the twentieth century saw civilian immunity evolve from a moral principle into a convention-dependent norm which rapidly unravelled at the beginning of the Second World War. In the post-war era, the norm was gradually internalized (I would say embedded) in some places, resulting in the progressive reduction of civilian casualties caused by aerial bombardment. Thomas argues that this transformation can be explained by reference to four factors.[37] First, there was increased moral outrage about terror bombing. The Second World War's atrocities provoked unprecedented levels of moral outrage. This was exacerbated by the second factor, the revolution in broadcasting technology which created the potential for almost instant images of civilian suffering to be transmitted into living rooms around the world. Third, Thomas argues that the threat of mutual nuclear destruction and the Korean War experience created the impression that terror bombing was ineffective.[38] Finally, advances in military technology—especially in relation to targeting—made some Western states capable of distinguishing between soldiers and civilians to a much higher degree than before. According to Thomas, this created a mutually supportive relationship between the Western way of high-technology war and the norm of civilian immunity, through which the West legitimized its own use of force whilst denying legitimacy to those unable to fight in the same way.[39]

From this, we can distinguish four types of ethical belief: moral principle, convention-dependent norm, embedded norm, and internalized norm. Thomas also provides us with a basis for making general claims about the status of civilian immunity in different historical periods. The periodization I offer here is only a general rule of thumb because whilst the strength of norms undoubtedly affects their role in shaping behaviours and perceptions, it is impossible to be precise about their strength and function in the abstract because their effects are closely related to, and dependent upon, the social context.[40] With those caveats in mind, we can identity two stages of progression in the norm of civilian immunity. In the first stage, the 'long nineteenth century' spanning the period 1789–1945, civilian immunity began to be translated from a widely held moral principle common to different ethical

[37] Thomas, *Ethics of Destruction*, pp. 170–1.

[38] In my view, this claim is less compelling than the others, for reasons that should be made clear in subsequent chapters.

[39] See Christopher Coker, *Humane Warfare* (London: Routledge, 2001); and Martin Shaw, *The New Western Way of War: Transfer War and its Crisis in Iraq* (Cambridge: Polity, 2005).

[40] On the importance of contingency and the limits of generalization, see J. Samuel Barkin, *Realist Constructivism* (Cambridge: Cambridge University Press, 2010), pp. 147–52.

traditions into a convention-dependent norm. The norm was weak and limited by its coexistence with the two anti-civilian ideologies mentioned earlier and the fact that it applied only to part of the world. The shocks of the Second World War saw civilian immunity rapidly become an embedded norm, indicated by its incorporation into international law, and become internalized in some places. Even at the beginning of the twenty-first century, however, civilian immunity was more embedded than internalized, as the final two chapters of this book will demonstrate.

## THE POLITICS OF LEGITIMACY

How should a shared norm like civilian immunity influence behaviour? How might norm violators exempt themselves? What factors influence the willingness of international society to defend its norms? Many constructivists hold that shared norms, typically understood as intersubjectively agreed 'standards of appropriate behaviour for actors with a given identity', serve as 'meaningful constraints' on behaviour.[41] This is because, whether as a result of coercion, self-interest, psychological need, or socialization and the norm's own legitimacy, it is widely accepted that actors prefer to be seen to be acting legitimately by complying with shared norms and will be inhibited from acting in ways that cannot be plausibly justified to others.[42] Social actors require a positive self-image. When cognitive dissonance—a discrepancy between behaviour and beliefs—is created by the public adoption of prohibited behaviours such as killing civilians, actors are much more likely to articulate beliefs, values, and attitudes that justify the behaviour than they are to modify their behaviour.[43] This need is amplified for political actors as they require not only a positive self-image, but also the approval of domestic and foreign constituencies.[44]

It is also commonly thought that violations of shared norms are likely to generate collective punishment. For instance, in their classic study of norms, Martha Finnemore and Kathryn Sikkink argue that those who violate shared

[41] Martha Finnemore and Kathryn Sikkink, 'International Norm Dynamics and Political Change', *International Organization*, 52 (4), 1998, p. 891; Thomas, *Ethics of Destruction*, p. 181; and Friedreich V. Kratochwil and John Gerard Ruggie, 'International Organization: The State of the Art of the Art of the State', *International Organization*, 40, 1986, p. 765.

[42] Ian Hurd, 'Legitimacy and Authority in International Politics', *International Organization*, 53 (2), 1999, pp. 379–408; and Alexander Wendt, *Social Theory of International Politics* (Cambridge: Cambridge University Press, 1999).

[43] Philip Zimbardo, *The Lucifer Effect: How Good People Turn Evil* (London: Rider, 2007), pp. 219–20.

[44] Vaughn P. Shannon, 'Norms Are What States Make of Them: The Political Psychology of Norm Violation', *International Studies Quarterly*, 44, 2000, p. 300.

norms are likely to be punished with 'ridicule' and 'diplomatic and economic pressure'.[45] We might add force and coercion to the list of potential punishments.[46] Given that civilian immunity is a widely shared ethical norm that has become embedded as a customary rule of international law, we should expect it to inhibit mass atrocities and dictate that violators receive 'ridicule', 'diplomatic and economic pressure', or other forms of punishment. Yet, as I noted in the introduction, mass killing remains a recurrent feature of world politics and the criticism and punishment of violators remains inconsistent at best. Among the various possible explanations are Gary Goertz's claim that states are likely to impose sanctions only when their interests are harmed by norm-violating behaviour and Janice Bially Mattern's suggestion that even in these circumstances shared identities might limit the scope for sanctions.[47] Whilst Goertz's expectation is somewhat confounded by examples of sanctioning behaviour absent obvious self-interest (such as the US effort to capture the Somali warlord Muhammed Farah Aideed in 1993), the argument developed here builds on both insights by suggesting that perceptions, pre-existing relationships with actors involved in violent episode, interests, and power influence the extent to which bad behaviour is tolerated and criticism of norm violations backed up with punishment.

All this implies that civilian immunity sometimes fails to inhibit behaviour because perpetrators might calculate that the risk of potential punishment is outweighed by the utility of mass killing. This, in turn, suggests that they believe they can secure *sufficient legitimacy* and avoid punishment.

Legitimacy can be attached to behaviours and actors. Both are relevant for this study and it is the relationship between the two that is especially important. Behaviour is legitimate if it is seen to correspond with agreed standards of behaviour (norms) and actors are legitimate in particular realms if they correspond to agreed criteria. For example, recognition of statehood is commonly linked to an entity having control (even if only nominally) over a particular territory, the capacity to enter into international treaties, and domestic authority related to self-determination.[48] One of the central claims that I will advance in this book is that perpetrators are likely to get away with mass atrocities if they succeed in preventing the illegitimacy of their behaviour ('behaviour-legitimacy') from being translated into illegitimacy as actors

[45] Finnemore and Sikkink, 'International Norm Dynamics', pp. 902–4.

[46] Finnemore and Sikkink overlook coercion and force as compliance generating mechanisms. See Shannon, 'Norms Are What States Make of Them', p. 297.

[47] Gary Goertz, *International Norms and Decision-Making: A Punctuated Equilibrium Model* (Lanham: Rowman & Littlefield, 2003), p. 236; and Janice Bially Mattern, *Ordering International Politics: Identity, Crisis and Representational Force* (New York: Taylor and Francis, 2005).

[48] For a definitive account, see James Crawford, *The Creation of States in International Law*, second edition (Oxford: Oxford University Press, 2006).

('actor-legitimacy') among important audiences. This is what I label *sufficient legitimacy.*

When attempting to legitimize behaviour that violates a norm, actors use a variety of strategies to explain and justify their actions. These arguments are attempts to provide a self-exemption to the norm and justify the behaviour to others. This might include an assertion that a particular norm ought to be applied to the situation at hand and that the behaviour in question is consistent with that norm.[49] Behaviour is considered legitimate to the extent that these claims are validated by other group members.[50] As a rule of thumb, the greater the extent of the validation, the more legitimate a behaviour may be deemed to be. The social quality of legitimacy, however, means that behaviour is seldom wholly legitimate or illegitimate and that it is generally more accurate to speak in terms of degrees of legitimacy. To achieve *sufficient* legitimacy though, norm-violating behaviour need not be validated by external actors. Instead, sufficient legitimacy requires only that external actors *excuse* the behaviour (i.e. say that it is wrong but understandable in the circumstances) or *tolerate* it (i.e. say that it is wrong but that either the alternatives or the prospective punishments would be worse). In some cases, perpetrators might believe they have sufficient legitimacy even when they are condemned by others, for instance when verbal attacks are not translated into crippling punishments. We might organize these different responses along a continuum (Table 1.1).

Different audiences determine the material consequences that flow from differing degrees of legitimacy. Actors will rarely be in complete agreement about the legitimacy of a particular behaviour. Therefore, exactly *who* makes these judgements matters very much in terms of determining the effects of legitimacy judgements.[51] The relative power and influence of those who defend or criticize perpetrators—both domestically and internationally—is a critically important influence on the role played by civilian immunity in individual cases. It also shapes perpetrator behaviour, especially if they try to shield themselves from punishment by associating with a great power or group of states. In those contexts, justificatory strategies might be skewed exclusively to winning the support or tolerance of only a handful of external actors. This was most notable during the Cold War, when the patronage of one of the superpowers was generally sufficient to prevent the punishment of behaviour judged to be illegitimate by a majority of states.

[49] Neta C. Crawford, *Argument and Change in World Politics: Ethics, Decolonization and Humanitarian Intervention* (Cambridge: Cambridge University Press, 2002), p. 24

[50] Thomas Franck, *Recourse to Force: State Action Against Threats and Armed Attacks* (Cambridge: Cambridge University Press, 2002), p. 185; and Ian Clark, 'Legitimacy in a Global Order', *Review of International Studies*, 29:S1, 2003, p. 80.

[51] Coleman conceptualizes this in terms of different 'audiences'. Katharina P. Coleman, *International Organisations and Peace Enforcement* (Cambridge: Cambridge University Press, 2007), pp. 24–5.

**Table 1.1.** Degrees of legitimacy

| Legitimacy judgements | Likely Response | Generic description |
|---|---|---|
| *Behaviour:* legitimate<br>*Actor:* legitimate<br>*Overall:* legitimacy | Validate | External actors accept perpetrator's justifications. |
| *Behaviour:* weak illegitimate<br>*Actor:* legitimate<br>*Overall:* sufficient legitimacy | Excuse | External actors express concern about the perpetrator's behaviour but on balance suggest that it is excused by the context. |
| *Behaviour:* illegitimate<br>*Actor:* legitimate<br>*Overall:* sufficient legitimacy | Tolerate | External actors are critical of the behaviour but do not offer vocal condemnation or consider serious punishment. |
| *Behaviour:* illegitimate<br>*Actor:* borderline legitimate/illegitimate<br>*Overall:* borderline sufficient legitimacy | Condemn | External actors are critical of the behaviour, condemn the perpetrators, and may impose minor diplomatic sanctions. |
| *Behaviour:* illegitimate<br>*Actor:* illegitimate<br>*Overall:* illegitimate | Punish | External actors condemn the behaviour and the perpetrators and impose punishments. |

Even allowing for the complexity introduced by sufficient legitimacy and divergent audiences, the basic claim that norms inhibit behaviour that cannot be plausibly justified draws an obvious criticism. This criticism holds that because self-exemptions are obviously self-serving and social norms must be interpreted and applied in specific contexts norms cannot guide behaviour because, as Wittgenstein put it, '[w]hatever I do is compatible with some interpretation of the rule'.[52] According to this perspective, shared norms cannot inhibit behaviour because actors are entirely free to select which norms to apply in what circumstances. But although actors are free to employ arguments strategically and the veracity of the arguments used does not determine the extent to which they succeed in securing sufficient legitimacy, there are limits on what can be plausibly argued. Addressing his own conundrum, Wittgenstein maintained that the premise that actors are free to apply rules however they see fit cannot be sustained because norms are not decontextualized guides to how we must act, but are constituted and governed by the societies they inhabit and constitute. Actors are therefore not entirely free to select whatever argument they like because interpretations of a norm are monitored by the community as a whole.[53] Moreover, the purpose of making justificatory arguments in the first place is

[52] Ludwig Wittgenstein, *Philosophical Investigations*, trans. G. E. M. Anscombe (New York: Macmillan, 1953), p. 198.

[53] Wittgenstein, *Philosophical Investigations,* pp. 151 and 185.

to *persuade* oneself and, more importantly, others about the legitimacy of a course of action.[54] Implausible arguments—those that apply norms in ways that are obviously contrary to shared understandings or that defy shared understanding about the situation at hand—are unlikely to be persuasive. Therefore, there is a limited range of arguments that an actor can use to justify behaviour. Whilst we might expect contestation about the appropriate interpretations of norms and events, arguments are not infinitely malleable. As Quentin Skinner famously argued, actors 'cannot hope to stretch the application of the existing principles indefinitely, correspondingly, [the actor] can only hope to legitimate a restricted range of actions'.[55] If norms were infinitely malleable, political leaders would never be believed and normative arguments would serve no purpose.[56] What is important, however, is the *degree* of plausibility required and the extent to which it is the plausibility of the argument that determines the legitimation of norm-violating behaviour and the consequences which flow from that.

Norms cannot by themselves prevent actors from choosing a course of action.[57] When behaviour is prohibited by a norm, actors might calculate that the expected utility of norm violation is sufficiently high and the perceived interests at stake sufficiently important to compensate for the anticipated criticism and punishment. But even powerful actors are limited in the costs they can tolerate. The question, therefore, becomes one of securing *sufficient legitimacy*. Given that norm-violating behaviour is unlikely to be welcomed, the principal task of a strategy for justifying such behaviour is to minimize its perceived illegitimacy and ensure that it is not translated into a perception that the perpetrating actor itself is illegitimate. This is important because legitimate actors, even those that occasionally act in illegitimate ways, are less likely to be punished than illegitimate actors. What actors hope for when they violate well-established norms is that they can minimize and tolerate the immediate costs and prevent the erosion of their legitimacy as an actor. The next section examines strategies that actors might use to achieve this.

## Justifying Non-Compliant Behaviour

The capacity for actors to exempt themselves from norms is shaped by the norm and the situation. The capacity of various justificatory strategies to offer a plausible justification for norm-violating behaviour is therefore influenced

[54] Martha Finnemore, *National Interests in International Society* (Ithaca: Cornell University Press, 1996), p. 141.

[55] Quentin Skinner, 'Analysis of Political Thought and Action', in James Tully (ed.), *Meaning and Context: Quentin Skinner and His Critics* (Cambridge: Polity, 1988), p. 117.

[56] E. H. Carr, *The Twenty Years' Crisis 1919–1939* (London: Macmillan, 1946), p. 92.

[57] Kratochwil and Ruggie, 'International Organization', p. 767.

by the determinacy of the norm in question, parameters placed upon the norm's applicability and the existence of other norms that might be invoked to support overriding the norm in question. In relation to determinacy, the more precisely a norm indicates the behaviour it expects in a given situation, the stronger its compliance-pull because actors cannot use ambiguities in the norm itself to mask behaviour that contradicts its purpose.[58] Indeterminacy is produced by a combination of uncertainty among group members about what is expected, disagreements about what ought to be expected, and a shared interest in preserving flexibility for the future.[59] At its core, civilian immunity is a highly determinate norm because its demand is unambiguous. In practice, however, judging compliance is complicated by the fact that the norm prohibits only the *intentional* killing of civilians and intent is a property largely internal to the perpetrator. The same point holds in relation to the norm's parameters. On the one hand, there appears to be a universal injunction against the intentional killing of civilians. On the other, however, the norm is embedded in different legal regimes applying to war, peacetime, and genocide and the types of legal remedies available in each regime are different. In addition, civilian immunity co-existed with two brands of anti-civilian ideology that provided rationales for mass atrocities. Although the norm of civilian immunity eventually reached a point of ascendancy over these ideologies, such that they became ineffective as sources of legitimacy for mass killing, the values and beliefs that underpinned them remained evident in the arguments presented by perpetrators, suggesting that they continued to hold some purchase. Therefore, whilst on the whole civilian immunity appears to be quite a strong norm when measured in terms of its determinacy, universality and hegemony, we do not have to look far to see gaps and uncertainties that present opportunities for perpetrators to exempt themselves. Nonetheless, compared to other norms, civilian immunity presents something of a hard case to would-be perpetrators because of the basic clarity of what it requires.

The first potential justificatory strategy for violators of this norm is to contest the norm's substance and/or authoritativeness and propose new ones in its place. This is a potentially risky option because when used to justify concurrent behaviour that violates the old norm it logically requires an admission of guilt. Success requires intersubjective agreement about the superiority of the new norm in a context in which the prevailing standards of behaviour are defined by the old norm.[60] As a result, this option is usually

[58] Thomas Franck, *The Power of Legitimacy Among Nations* (New York, Oxford University Press, 1990), p. 52; Friedreich V. Kratochwil, 'Contract and Regimes: Do Issue Specificity and Variations of Formality Matter?', in Volker Rittberger (ed.), *Regime Theory and International Relations* (Oxford: Clarendon Press, 1993), pp. 84–93; and Martin Hollis and Steve Smith, *Explaining and Understanding International Relations* (Oxford: Clarendon Press, 1990), p. 184.

[59] Franck, *Power of Legitimacy*, pp. 52–4.

[60] Finnemore and Sikkink, 'International Norm Dynamics', p. 897.

open only to the most powerful actors and even they will find it difficult to legitimize new norms unless there is a groundswell of dissatisfaction with the old. Because it is relatively unambiguous and based on a deeply held moral consensus, since its emergence as an ethical norm there have been few concerted attempts to replace or significantly revise civilian immunity. The closest we came to a serious attempt to rewrite the rules was the US Attorney-General's argument that in the wake of the 11 September 2001 terrorist attacks, the Geneva Conventions were obsolete. As I show in Chapter 8, this suggestion won very little international support.

A second potential strategy is to plead mitigation by arguing that the situation made it too difficult for the actor to comply with the norm and that others should recognize that they could not reasonably expect compliance in such circumstances.[61] Borrowing Thomas Franck's 'jurying' metaphor, actors might admit to violating the norm but argue that the exceptional circumstances should serve as mitigation.[62] As with the first strategy, this is a risky approach because it requires an admission of guilt and reasonable expectations that the group is prepared to accept exceptions to the general rule.

The third strategy—commonly used before the 'humanitarian revolution' of the post-Second World War period—is to appeal to other norms. Martha Finnemore argues that 'determining which rules and norms apply in different situations involves sophisticated reasoning processes' and this strategy aims to take advantage of this uncertainty.[63] Norms are inconsistent, sometimes contradictory and do not share ethical content. New norms are often grafted onto old ones and there is no pre-given hierarchy of norms. Where hierarchies emerge, it is usually over time through processes of contestation and legitimation. As Finnemore pointed out:

> [t]o understand how norms work, we need to understand the complexity, contradictions and indeterminacy of the larger normative system in which political action takes place. Any policy decision of consequence is taken within a dense web of normative claims that often conflict with one another.... After all, if the prescriptions of norms and values were always clear or if they never conflicted with one another, we would not have to make any decisions; we would just follow the prescriptions.[64]

Actors might therefore justify violating one norm by arguing that their behaviour is consistent with other, more relevant or important, norms. Breaches of a particular norm might be regarded as acceptable if they are

[61] Kratochwil and Ruggie, 'International Organization', p. 765.

[62] Martha Finnemore, 'Paradoxes in Humanitarian Intervention' in Richard Price (ed.), *Moral Limit and Possibility in World Politics* (Cambridge: Cambridge University Press, 2008), pp. 150–1.

[63] Finnemore, *National Interests*, p. 29.

[64] Finnemore, 'Paradoxes', p. 198.

justified by reference to higher-order principles especially if those principles would be violated by compliance with the norm.[65] This was precisely the function played by the anti-civilian ideologies described earlier. *Necessity* was prefaced on a shared understanding among governments that killing civilians was sometimes the only way to defeat insurgents, generally thought to be illegimate by states.[66] Necessity permitted legitimate governments to justify killing civilians in order to punish guerrilla movements but also limited the scope of killing that could be plausibly justified to that which was necessary to achieve the purpose. The second anti-civilian ideology, *selective extermination*, worked differently. It was prefaced on a mindset which held that the protection of civilian immunity applied only to particular groups. Certain characteristics were ascribed to other groups in order to place them outside the bounds of human society or, to use Helen Fein's terminology, 'outside the universe of [moral] obligation'.[67] Thus, European and settler states agreed that 'barbarians' or 'uncivilized' peoples in the colonised world were not protected because they did not behave in a civilized fashion, were not wholly rational and could not be tamed or civilized without a degree of violence. Because it divides the world into insiders and outsiders, however, *selective extermination* can only operate as a plausible justification *within* the groups that espouse it and its capacity to secure sufficient legitimacy for mass atrocities is therefore directly linked to the size and material power of the 'in group' as well as to the extent to which group members accept the ideology. Thus, arguments that employed this logic to justify the mass killing of natives by colonial states and settlers were plausible only within colonizer societies. They succeeded for so long in part because they persuaded key constituencies within those societies and in part because the colonizers were numerous and powerful. Twentieth-century fascist and communist variants fared less well largely because there was less support for them among the world's most powerful states and societies. These ideologies were seldom wholly effective in persuading communities to support the commission of mass atrocities. 'In-group' members sometimes rejected the ideology or doubted the necessity of mass killing. To shore-up support, therefore, perpetrators sometimes augmented selective extermination arguments with other strategies such as denial or the use of euphemisms.

[65] Harald Muller, 'The Internalization of Principles, Norms and Rules by Governments: The Case of Security Regimes', in Volker Rittberger (ed.), *Regime Theory and International Relations* (Oxford: Clarendon Press, 1993), pp. 277–313.

[66] For a detailed account, see Karma Nabulsi, *Traditions of War: Occupation, Resistance and the Law* (Oxford: Oxford University Press, 1999).

[67] Helen Fein, *Genocide: A Sociological Perspective* (London: Sage, 1993), p. 50; and Helen Fein, 'Revolutionary and Anti-Revolutionary Genocides: A Comparison of States Murders in Democratic Kampuchea, 1975 to 1979, and in Indonesia, 1965 to 1966', *Comparative Studies in Society and History*, 35 (4) 1993, p. 815. Also see Leo Kuper, *Genocide: Its Political Uses in the Twentieth Century* (New Haven: Yale University Press, 1981), p. 41.

The fourth potential strategy is to deny violating the norm. This strategy has become central to the politics of mass atrocities since the post-Second World War 'humanitarian revolution' brought civilian immunity into the ascendancy. The use of denial provides counter-factual validity to the norm of civilian immunity because reluctance to openly justify mass killing behaviour demonstrates a degree of deference to the norm and fear that open violation is likely to draw criticism and punishment. Actors making this argument may be required to go to considerable lengths to cover-up evidence of atrocities and make it appear *as if* they were complying with the norm. Actors may simply deny that they are deliberately targeting civilians. Given conditions that make it difficult to distinguish soldiers from civilians (as in urban war or counter-insurgency), that make external scrutiny difficult, or a context where the interests of powerful external actors are served by turning a blind eye, actors may argue that they are not *intentionally* killing civilians or may deny that civilians are being killed at all. Sometimes, actors modify their behaviour in order to reduce the *appearance* of norm violation. This may include (but is not limited to) prosecuting a handful of low-ranking perpetrators to sustain the argument that atrocities which attract publicity were perpetrated by 'rogue elements' and not as a matter of policy, limiting the commission of atrocities to regions less likely to attract international media attention, and offering humanitarian assistance to the survivors. Other strategies include challenging the facts of the case by denying massacres or claiming that the victims were not civilians, arguing that civilian deaths were not intentional, arguing that other groups were responsible for civilian deaths, and blaming the victims for supporting insurgents or acting as 'human shields'. Although the role of norms is always contingent on social context, the success or failure of this particular justificatory strategy hinges almost entirely on the situation.

There are therefore at least four ways in which actors might attempt to secure sufficient legitimacy for norm-violating behaviour. The likelihood of success, I argued earlier, was largely dependent on the context. The following section briefly examines some of the key contextual factors that influence the extent to which external actors will validate, excuse, tolerate, criticize, or punish norm-violating behaviour.

## Contextual Factors

What constitutes a breach of a norm, and the consequences that flow from this judgement, 'is not simply an "objective description" of a fact but an intersubjective appraisal'.[68] As such, the extent to which external actors

[68] Kratochwil and Ruggie, 'International Organization', p. 774.

validate, excuse, or tolerate norm-violating behaviour is influenced by more than just the plausibility of the justification measured against the known facts of the case. The capacity of perpetrators to justify their norm-violating behaviour and the response to that behaviour is heavily influenced by the situation.[69] This view is in line with claims that persuasive argumentation is more likely in less politicized and more insulated settings than in highly political settings where contextual intervening variables exert greater effect.[70] Drawing on extant theories of communicative action and legitimacy, this section identifies five important contextual factors that might influence the process of legitimation, shaping the capacity of perpetrators to justify their behaviour and the willingness of external actors to defend the norm. It should be stressed, though, that this does not exhaust the range of potential factors and both the specific factors themselves and as well as the roles they play will differ from case to case.

The first relates to perceptions. How external actors perceive a situation influences how they respond.[71] All other things being equal, external actors are much more likely to punish clearly apparent atrocities committed by obvious perpetrators than they are to punish the perpetrators of atrocities where uncertainty remains as to the nature of the situation. Precisely how external actors make sense of a situation is influenced to some extent by all of the contextual factors and is also plagued by problems of incomplete information and misperception, but perceptions are most immediately shaped by the explanations proffered by the perpetrators, their relation to the *reported facts* of the case at the time, and the nature of the relationship between the two sets of actors.[72] Evaluating the extent to which the perpetrator's action corresponds with shared norms and the plausibility of its justificatory arguments, third parties have recourse only to the known facts at the time and are influenced by dominant interpretations of those facts. Given that states face strategic uncertainty about future preferences and interests, they tend to be risk averse and are unlikely to adopt strong positions when faced with incomplete, inconsistent, or uncertain information unless such a position corresponds closely with existing preferences, interests, and future

[69] On the importance of context for persuasive argumentation see Nicole Deitelhoff, 'The Discursive Process of Legalization: Charting Islands of Persuasion in the ICC Case', *International Organization*, 63, 2009.

[70] See, for example, Abram Chayes and Antonia Handler Chayes, *The New Sovereignty: Compliance with International Regulatory Agreements* (Cambridge, MA: Harvard University Press, 1995); Jeffrey Checkel, 'Why Comply? Social Learning and European Identity Change', *International Organization*, 55 (3), 2001; and Alistair Iain Johnston, *Social States: China in International Institutions* (Princeton, NJ: Princeton University Press, 2007).

[71] Hermann and Shannon, 'Defending International Norms', p. 650.

[72] On perceptions in world politics generally, see Robert Jervis, *Perception and Misperception in International Politics* (Princeton, NJ: Princeton University Press, 1976).

expectations.[73] As such, we can expect that incomplete information and unclear interpretation, aided by factors such as geographical remoteness, contexts of war or generalized chaos, and tight government restrictions and censorship of the media, will grant perpetrators more latitude in the selection of plausible justificatory arguments and increase the likelihood of its explanations being accepted by others. Conversely, extensive reporting and the dissemination of accurate information reduces the range of plausible justifications that are available to perpetrators and increases the likelihood of external actors perceiving the situation as one characterized by norm violations—identifying a credibility gap between the perpetrator's rhetoric and reported behaviour that increases the risk of criticism and punishment.[74] Extensive coverage of clear mass atrocities can also force governments to formally respond to a situation and can restrict the range of legitimate positions that bystanders might adopt. By contrast, when atrocities are not clearly reported, external actors can avoid having to adopt positions and might find it easier to tolerate or excuse norm-violating behaviour that does not challenge their interests.

The second contextual factor relates to the pre-existing social relations between parties to an episode of mass killing and external actors. In most cases, external actors have relations with one or more of the parties and have already formed judgements about their legitimacy relative to other relevant actors. This matters because when external actors make judgements about the legitimacy of a behaviour and the consequences that flow from this, who is presenting an argument or interpretation may sometimes matter more than what is being argued.[75] Because identities are 'inherently relational', judgements about the legitimacy of an actor are never made in isolation of the social context.[76] They are therefore relative. Actors and behaviours are judged to have more or less legitimacy than others and these judgements inform assessments about the legitimacy of the behaviour or actor relative to other relevant behaviours and actors. Actors that are thought legitimate, or whose purposes are considered legitimate, are likely to get away with norm-violating behaviour to a greater extent than actors whose legitimacy is already in doubt. As Hermann and Shannon put it, '[t]here is a tendency to defend norms more

[73] See Joseph M. Grieco, 'Anarchy and the Limits of Cooperation: A Realist Critique of the Newest Liberal Internationalism', *International Organization*, 42 (3), 1988, pp. 485–507; and Oran Young, *International Cooperation: Building Regimes for Natural Resources and the Environment* (Ithaca: Cornell University Press, 1989).

[74] See Gary J. Bass, *Freedom's Battle: The Origins of Humanitarian Intervention* (New York: Alfred A. Knopf, 2008), pp. 25–38.

[75] Checkel, 'Why Comply? Social Learning and European Identity Change', *International Organization*, 55 (3).

[76] Alexander Wendt, 'Anarchy is What States Make of It: The Social Construction of Power Politics', *International Organization*, 46, 1992, p. 397.

actively when violated by foes than when they are violated by friends'.[77] Relative legitimacy achieves this effect in two primary ways. Third parties that consider an actor and its purposes to be more legitimate than other relevant actors are predisposed towards accepting that actor's justifications. They are therefore more likely to validate justifications for norm-violating behaviour, and may do so even if those justifications are not particularly plausible.[78] In contrast, third parties that consider an actor, or its purposes, less legitimate than other relevant actors are likely to reject even relatively plausible justificatory arguments. The likelihood of a particular actor validating, excusing, or tolerating the justifications of another is therefore shaped by the pre-existing relationship between those actors.

Alternatively, actors might make different judgements about the legitimacy of the act and that of the perpetrator, influencing the extent to which perceived illegitimacy generates punishment. They might condemn the commission of mass atrocities but nevertheless refuse to punish the perpetrators or withdraw material and political support because although they find the specific behaviour objectionable, overall they believe that the perpetrator is more legitimate than other relevant actors. Who might be considered a relevant actor for comparative purposes changes from context to context and is decided by the external actors themselves. External actors may doubt the perpetrator's legitimacy relative to all other members of the group as a whole (e.g. international society), but still rate it more highly than that of other actors thought relevant to the context. It is this ranking of actors thought relevant to the case that is important when external actors form judgements about legitimacy and the consequences that flow from it. An additional consideration here is sovereignty. Mutual recognition of sovereignty, the basic rules of international society (especially non-interference), and a shared interest in maintaining order, means that governments might enjoy more legitimacy when killing their own populations than when targeting foreign populations.[79]

A third potential contextual factor relates to the interests and policy priorities of external actors. In other words, the importance attached to the case at hand and to defending the norm of civilian immunity relative to other policy concerns which might dictate validating, tolerating, or excusing norm violations or refraining from punishing those violations. Such interests are not pre-given and are constituted by factors such as identity, social norms, political preferences, social relations, and judgements about the expected relative utility of different courses of action. It is not only important to know whether or not

[77] Hermann and Shannon, 'Defending International Norms', p. 651.

[78] See Richard K. Hermann and Vaughn P. Shannon, 'Enacting International Norms: American Elite Thinking About Interests and Obligation'. Paper presented at the 1999 Annual APSA Conference, Atlanta, GA.

[79] For a powerful defence of this conception of international society, see Robert Jackson, *The Global Covenant: Human Conduct in a World of States* (Oxford: Oxford University Press, 2000).

an actor believes that a course of action violates a particular norm, we also need to know how much the actor cares about that judgement relative to other things it cares about and to what extent it is prepared to sacrifice other concerns in order to defend the norm. Actors may criticize violations but regard them as less important than other concerns, reducing the likelihood that the illegitimacy of an action will undermine the legitimacy of the perpetrator or that illegitimacy will produce punishment. The factors which shape interests and the level of priority afforded to defending civilian immunity include social relations between the two entities, the strategic importance of the actors involved, the episode's geographic location, the relationship between the perpetrator or victims and great powers, the degree of domestic agitation in favour of or against the perpetrators, and the expected utility associated with different courses of action.

A fourth contextual factor relates to the relative power of the groups of actors that choose to validate, excuse, tolerate, criticize, or punish the norm violation. As defined by Michael Barnett and Raymond Duvall, power has four aspects—two of which are directly relevant here. 'Compulsory power' relates to an actor's capacity to shape the 'circumstances and/or actions' of another through the employment of material, symbolic, or normative resources, whereas 'institutional power' refers to the ability of actors to achieve these effects through institutions which mediate relations between the actor and its target.[80] The balance of power is an important consideration because perpetrators are primarily concerned about securing *sufficient* legitimacy, not necessarily absolute levels of international legitimacy. The relative compulsory and institutional power of the actors who support or reject justificatory arguments (or some position in between the two) determines the number of actors who need to be persuaded. For instance, a communist state during the Cold War need have only persuaded the Soviet bloc—a relatively small subsection of international society—of its case to secure sufficient legitimacy and avoid punishment because the Soviet Union and it allies had more than sufficient power to shield the perpetrator from punishment. The same applied for rightist dictatorships in Latin America vis-à-vis the USA. In view of this, it might be anticipated that perpetrators develop expectations about the degree of legitimacy that is sufficient to avoid punishment. These expectations may be as, if not more, consequential than the availability of plausible justifications in determining whether or not they decide to commit mass atrocities.

The fifth is the perpetrator's own material and institutional power. The basic idea here is that powerful states are much more likely to avoid punishment than weak states, simply because their power increases the costs

[80] Michael Barnett and Raymond Duvall, 'Power in Global Governance', in Michael Barnett and Raymond Duvall (eds), *Power in Global Governance* (Cambridge: Cambridge University Press, 2005), pp. 3 and 13–17.

associated with punishment. For this reason, realists have tended to argue that legitimation is simply a product of the degree of compulsory power held by the perpetrators. According to this perspective, norms might cloak the exercise of power in moral language but they cannot constrain powerful actors.[81] Moreover, power imbalances are likely to inhibit criticism of the strong by the weak.

Together, these—and other—contextual factors influence the interpretation and persuasiveness of a perpetrator's justificatory arguments, shaping legitimacy judgements and determining whether illegitimacy will be translated into punishment. Contextual factors can magnify or nullify judgements about the legitimacy of mass atrocities and the consequences that flow from those judgements. Indeed, in many of the cases explored in the following chapters, contextual factors proved more important in determining responses to mass killing than either the justifications proffered by perpetrators or the extent to which the norm was embedded.

## CONCLUSION

This chapter has clarified what I mean by the norm of civilian immunity and how the norm has changed over time. I argued that civilian immunity is best understood as a 'groundnorm'—a shared ethical norm prohibiting the deliberate killing of civilians that finds different forms of legal expression. Drawing on the work of Ward Thomas, I suggested that during the 'long nineteenth century' (1789–1945), civilian immunity was gradually translated from a widely held moral principle embedded in different ethical traditions into a 'convention-dependent' norm. During this period, the norm was weak and limited by its coexistence with the two anti-civilian ideologies described in the introduction. The shocks of the Second World War created intense political impetus that propelled civilian immunity to the status of an embedded norm, indicated by its incorporation into international law, though the extent of its internalization remained patchy.

In the second part of the chapter, I argued that political actors generally prefer to gain social approval for their behaviour and tend to seek legitimacy by appealing to shared norms. This should mean that norms inhibit behaviour that cannot be plausibly justified. But as I noted in the introduction, both norms themselves and the social situations in which they operate provide actors with opportunities to claim self-exemptions. Only where opportunities for self-exemptions are closed is the norm likely to inhibit actors who would otherwise choose to violate it for whatever reason. The manner in which third

[81] Carr, *Twenty Years' Crisis*, p. 111.

parties respond to norm violations are also varied because they are mediated by contextual factors and dependent on other judgements. These factors influence whose stories are likely to be believed, the manner in which events are interpreted, the importance attached to particular norms and their violation relative to other concerns, and the extent to which actors will take it upon themselves to expend resources defending norms and punishing violators. It is often shifts in the social context rather than changes to the norm itself that alter the capacity of civilian immunity to inhibit behaviour and prompt states to act in its defence.

The rest of the book shows how the norm's uses and effects have changed over time by examining the way that perpetrators have tried to secure sufficient legitimacy for themselves, the responses of domestic and international societies, the factors that shaped those responses, and the consequences.

# 2

# State Terror in the Long Nineteenth Century

This chapter examines mass atrocities committed by states from the French Revolution to the 1930s. There was no formal international legal prohibition on the killing of civilians, but during this period the widely held moral principle of civilian immunity was gradually translated into a shared ethical norm. Despite the absence of legal rules prohibiting the killing of civilians, governments were generally not thought to be entitled to kill civilians without special justification though the European and colonial worlds were governed by quite different standards.[1] For much of this period, state-based mass atrocities could be legitimized by reference to the two anti-civilian ideologies described in the Introduction, with the choice of ideology being shaped by the context. Within Europe, governments justified the violent suppression of protestors and the killing of civilians in counter-insurgencies by reference to necessity. Necessity served as both an enabler and a constraint on mass atrocities in that it permitted their use whilst limiting the circumstances in which they might be legitimately employed and the scale of permissible killing. The capacity of necessity-based arguments to secure sufficient legitimacy for mass killing was shaped, principally, by two considerations: the legitimacy of the perpetrating regime relative to those they attacked, measured in terms of its domestic and international standing; and perceived compliance with the limits imposed by necessity. The moral principle of civilian immunity played an indirect role by influencing the amount and type of killing that could be justified by reference to necessity, growing in relative importance as the period unfolded.

In contrast, European colonialists referred to variants of the ideology of 'selective extermination' to justify mass atrocities against non-Europeans in the colonized world. This was supported at the beginning of the period by a widely (but not unanimously) held consensus among Europeans that 'uncivilized' (i.e. colonized) peoples were not protected by European moral conventions. If the exclusion of non-European peoples from moral protections excused mass

[1] See Edward Keene, *Beyond the Anarchical Society: Grotius, Colonialism and Order in World Politics* (Cambridge: Cambridge University Press, 2002), p. 7.

killing, racist doctrines espousing a colonial 'civilizing mission' sometimes made a virtue of it, creating a permissive normative environment that enabled colonial powers and settler communities to employ, and normally get away with, mass atrocities.[2] Of course, liberals sometimes employed this same doctrine for the opposite purpose—to enjoin restraint by demanding that colonizers protect the welfare of the colonized. This fact notwithstanding, inasmuch as it provided a rationale for excluding groups from moral protection against mass killing and valorized some forms of killing, this justificatory framework provided the structural foundations for the value systems that underpinned the totalitarian ideologies of selective extermination in the twentieth century.[3]

In cases where governments failed to persuade others sufficiently of the legitimacy of using mass atrocities, they received criticism and were occasionally subjected to punishment. The level of plausible justification required to avoid criticism or punishment was lower if the victims were associated with insurgency-style warfare and much lower again if they were non-Europeans. Although states were occasionally criticized for terrorizing these groups, they were seldom subjected to punishment.

The French Revolution—which is where this chapter begins—marked the beginning of a profound transformation of international society away from an order founded on absolute monarchs and empires towards a society of sovereign states constituted, nominally at least, by the will of their people.[4] This transformation had a profound impact on the politics of mass atrocities and opened the door for activists like Henri Dunant to demand the translation of civilian immunity from moral principle into a shared ethical norm (see Chapter 1)—a precursor to its adoption as a legal rule. During this period, two interrelated movements connected to the rise of liberalism—popular sovereignty and humanitarianism—challenged the normative order, impacting upon the legitimization of mass atrocities.[5]

The bases of government legitimacy began to change as authority claims based on the supposed 'divine rights' of monarchs were challenged by the

[2] For a detailed account of the 'standard of civilisation' as an international norm, see Geret Gong, *The Standard of 'Civilization' in International Society* (Oxford: Clarendon Press, 1984). The relationship between racism and the civilizing mission is exemplified by John Stuart Mill's essay 'Civilization' in *Collected Works*, Vol. 18: *Essays on Politics and Society* (London: Routledge, 1977), pp. 119–47.

[3] The idea that colonial attitudes were the precursor to twentieth-century totalitarianism can be found in Hannah Arendt, *The Origins of Totalitarianism* (New York: Schocken, 1951).

[4] See Brad R. Roth, *Governmental Illegitimacy in International Law* (Oxford: Oxford University Press, 2000), especially chs 2 and 3.

[5] See Mlada Bukovansky, *Legitimacy and Power Politics: The American and French Revolutions in International Political Culture* (Princeton, NJ: Princeton University Press, 2002); and Christian Reus-Smit, *The Moral Purpose of the State* (Princeton, NJ: Princeton University Press, 1999). It is important to note that in this period 'humanitarianism' was thought to extend only to Europeans and was not universal in scope.

increasingly popular idea that political authority derived from the will of the people.[6] The doctrine of popular sovereignty made it theoretically possible for non-state actors to justify political violence against civilians by claiming authority derived from the will of the people, giving rise to various uprisings and insurgencies that often provided the context for mass atrocities. Occasionally, however, when a government failed to suppress an armed rebellion effectively and resorted to what others saw as disproportionate or unnecessary mass atrocities, doubt was cast on its right to rule that particular territory, altering the balance of relative legitimacy between the state and its opponents. Sometimes, when these judgements aligned with the strategic interests of key external powers, foreign powers took punitive action against the state that perpetrated mass atrocities. In two cases (Greece (1821) and Cuba (1898)), the government's loss of legitimacy provided a catalyst for foreign intervention. In a third (Armenia (1915)) it helped forge an, albeit temporary, consensus around internationally sanctioned secession. Colonial possessions were judged according to a different standard but even here there is a (single) case of a European ruler losing international recognition partly because of the excessive use of mass atrocities (Leopold's Congo).

Judgements about the legitimacy of the actors involved also influenced the degree of violence governments could get away with. Increasingly conditioned by the idea of popular sovereignty, judgements about a government's entitlement to rule a particular territory framed assessments about the degree of violence that could be justified by necessity. A government whose claim to authority confronted well-supported claims for national self-determination found itself subject to greater opprobrium for slighter or equal uses of mass killing than governments whose authority claims were less challenged. Moreover, whereas at the beginning of the period governments had a generally recognized right to use reprisals against civilians in occupied territories irrespective of the legitimacy of their claim to the land they occupied, by the First World War even limited reprisals drew sharp criticism in cases where their right to govern was in doubt. By the early twentieth century, there were even suggestions that non-state actors had a *right* to resist military occupation in these circumstances, something that would have been unthinkable a century earlier.

The other relevant aspect of liberalism's rise was the emergence of humanitarianism and the gradual transformation of civilian immunity from moral

[6] See, *inter alia*, Bukovansky, *Legitimacy and Power Politics*, pp. 1–10; Theda Skocpol, *States and Social Revolutions* (Cambridge: Cambridge University Press, 1979); Charles Tilly, *Coercion, Capital and European States AD 990–1990* (Oxford: Basil Blackwell, 1990); Andreas Osiander, *The States System of Europe, 1640–1990* (Oxford: Clarendon Press, 1994); Paul W. Schroeder, *The Transformation of European Politics, 1763–1848* (Oxford: Clarendon Press, 1994); and Franco Venturi, *The End of the Old Regime in Europe, 1768–1789*, 2 vols, trans. R. Burr Litchfield (Princeton, NJ: Princeton University Press, 1989).

principle to shared norm. The 1899 and 1907 Hague Conventions, discussed in Chapter 1, formalized the idea that 'military necessity' could not be used as a justification for breaking the laws of war—though the laws still permitted reprisals against civilians during insurgencies. Through the so-called Martens principle, the Conventions also insisted that civilians remained 'under the protection' of 'the laws of humanity, and the requirements of public conscience'.[7] Even this, however, did not entirely preclude the use of necessity as a justification for mass atrocities by states, because the Hague system permitted lawful reprisals and applied only between mutually recognized belligerents.[8] Nevertheless, as the century progressed, liberal humanitarianism had three effects on the principle of necessity as a justification for mass atrocities. First, the threshold at which governments began to incur criticism for using mass atrocities was lowered. In other words, by the end of the period 'necessity' arguments could be used to justify less violence against civilians than was the case at the beginning of the period. Second, the degree of international criticism and likelihood of punitive action increased, though calculations about interests remained dominant in influencing third party decisions to punish perpetrators. Third, the victim's status became an increasingly important consideration. Where victim groups were judged to have legitimate grounds for self-determination, the use of force against their civilians was typically judged more harshly than in other cases. Despite these changes, however, without a legal ban on the killing of civilians, necessity could still provide a plausible justification for mass atrocities in some circumstances. Necessity came to be understood as both justification and constraint, a logic set out most clearly in 1863 in President Lincoln's *General Orders No. 100*, otherwise known as the 'Lieber Code'.[9] As the century progressed, the constraints outweighed but did not entirely replace the enablers.

This chapter proceeds in four parts. The first focuses on the 'Great Terror' of the French Revolution. The second considers the use of mass killing to suppress domestic uprisings, focusing on the Greek insurrection in 1821, the 1848 uprisings in Paris and Vienna, the suppression of the Paris Commune in 1871, and the Armenian genocide in 1915. The third section examines the use of atrocities as reprisals to suppress wartime insurgencies. This section focuses

[7] Article 22 of the 1907 Hague Convention (IV) Respecting the Laws and Customs of War on Land. See Theodor Meron, 'The Martens Clause, Principles of Humanity, and Dictates of Public Conscience', *American Journal of International Law*, 94 (1), 2000. According to Paul Weidenbaum, the Hague Convention rendered obsolete the view that necessity could be used to justify illegal measures. Thus, 'military necessity . . . cannot overrule the laws of warfare'. Paul Weidenbaum, 'Necessity in International Law', *Transactions of the Grotius Society*, 24, 1938, p. 129.

[8] Weidenbaum, 'Necessity in International Law', p. 130.

[9] Judith Gardam, *Necessity, Proportionality and the Use of Force by States* (Cambridge: Cambridge University Press, 2004), pp. 4–8.

on the Napoleonic peninsular war, the Franco-Prussian War, Cuba, the Boer War, and German reprisals in Belgium at the beginning of the First World War. The final part focuses on colonial terror and the ideology of selective extermination. Recognizing that European powers frequently used atrocities in the colonial world, it focuses on their use to 'pacify' and settle lands (focusing on the US 'conquest' of the West), to extract financial profits (Leopold's Congo 'Free State'), and to suppress resistance (focusing on the Herero genocide).

## THE FRENCH REVOLUTIONARY TERROR (1793–1794)

The 'Great Terror' of the French Revolution (1793–94) is often portrayed as the quintessential expression of state terror and sometimes even as its etymological genesis.[10] For some, the Jacobin Terror was an inevitable consequence of the 1789 revolution.[11] For others, it was a contingent response to the threat of counter-revolution manifested by the Vendéan and Federalist revolts, the royal family's flight to Varennes and military interventions by Prussia and Britain.[12] There is equally little agreement on precisely how many people were killed, but most estimates place the figure somewhere between 15,000 and 20,000, excluding the destruction of the Vendée.[13] The vast majority of these victims died not on the infamous guillotine in Paris but in the government-led reprisals that followed armed rebellions in Lyon, Marseilles, Bordeaux, Nantes, and Toulon. The brutal repression that followed the 1793 uprising in Vendée is estimated to have accounted for around 130,000 lives.[14]

[10] For instance, Jerzy Waciorski, *Le Terrorisme Politique* (Paris: A. Pedone, 1939), p. 98. For a discussion, see George Armstrong Kelly, 'Conceptual Sources of Terror', *Eighteenth Century Studies*, 14 (1) 1980, pp. 20–1. According to Andrew Sinclair, a history of terror could be dated 'Before and After Robespierre': Andrew Sinclair, *An Anatomy of Terror: A History of Terrorism* (London: Pan Books, 2004), p. 74.

[11] François Furet, *Interpreting the French Revolution* (Cambridge: Cambridge University Press, 1981); and Simon Schama, *Citizens: A Chronicle of the French Revolution* (New York: Alfred A. Knopf, 1989).

[12] For instance, Arno J. Mayer, *The Furies: Violence and Terror in the French and Russian Revolutions* (Princeton: Princeton University Press, 2002); and Timothy Tackett, 'Conspiracy Obsession in a Time of Revolution: French Elites and the Origins of the Terror, 1789–1792', *American Historical Review*, 105 (3) 2000, pp. 691–713.

[13] See Donald Greer, *The Incidence of the Terror During the French Revolution: A Statistical Interpretation* (Gloucester, Mass: Peter Smith, 1966), pp. 25–6; and Beatrice F. Hyslop, 'Historical Publications since 1939 on the French Revolution', *Journal of Military History* 20 (3) 1948, pp. 245–6.

[14] See Mark Levene, *Genocide in the Age of the Nation-State*, Vol. II: *The Rise of the West and the Coming of Genocide* (London: I. B. Tauris, 2005), p. 110.

It is commonly argued that the defining feature of the Terror was the use of indiscriminate violence to spread fear and thereby restore order in the fracturing republic.[15] On closer inspection, however, the deliberate creation of fear through indiscriminate killing played a relatively minor role, with the Terror geared more to the punishment of individuals and groups thought guilty of anti-revolutionary behaviour.[16] This was hardly surprising given that one of the Jacobins' principal philosophical inspirations, Montesquieu, had argued that terror understood as the creation of fear was the governing principle of despotism.[17] Instead, the revolutionary government argued that executions were necessary to punish criminals and maintain order. Where whole groups were targeted, as in the Vendée, the government employed collective responsibility arguments, claiming that the whole region had supported the rebellion and was therefore guilty of treason.[18]

The Terror was formally legislated as a means of punishing those guilty of plotting against the state. When it passed the enabling legislation in 1792, the National Convention decreed that those who sought to restore monarchy, undermine the sovereignty of the people, or destroy the unity of France would be guilty of treason and punished by death.[19] In the face of foreign invasion and mob violence, Danton called for 'judicial measures to punish counterrevolutionaries', proposing 'a new-fledged tribunal speaking the law'. Leading Jacobins, Robespierre and Marat, endorsed Danton's plea, demanding measures that would 'put in fear the counterrevolutionaries and save the people from the temptation of joining in wild murder'.[20] Robespierre envisioned the Terror as a judicially sanctioned instrument of state policy.[21] With important exceptions, such as the reprisals referred to earlier and the political executions of the Hébertists and Dantonists at the Terror's climax, the majority of its victims were targeted on a nominally individual basis. There is a broad

[15] E.g. Bronislaw Baczko, 'The Terror before the Terror? Conditions of Possibility, Logic of Realization', in Keith Michael Baker (ed.), *The French Revolution and the Creation of Modern Political Culture*, Vol. IV: *The Terror* (Oxford: Pergamon Press, 1994), p. 32; also see, Hoffmann, *Inside Terrorism* (New York: Columbia University Press, 2006), pp. 16–17; C. Townshend, *Terrorism: A Very Short Introduction* (Oxford: Oxford University Press, 2002), ch. 3.

[16] To be sure, the Terror was punctuated by indiscriminate massacres, notably the Vendée, suppression, the September 1793 prison massacre, the 1794 killing of political opponents guilty of no crimes against the state, and the slaughter of those only guilty by loose association at worst. See David A. Bell, 'Violence, Terror and War: A Comment on Arno Mayer's *The Furies*', *French Historical Studies*, 24 (4) 2001, p. 562; François Furet, 'A Commentary', *French Historical Studies*, 16 (4) 1990, p. 797; Schama, *Citizens*, pp. 632, 636.

[17] Baron de Montesquieu, *Spirit of the Laws*, ed. Ann M. Cohler, Basia Collier Miller, and Harold Samuel Stone (Cambridge: Cambridge University Press, [1748] 1989).

[18] Levene, *Genocide*, pp. 104–5.

[19] National Convention decrees of 4 December 1792 and 16 December 1792.

[20] Both cited by Mayer, *The Furies*, pp. 190–1.

[21] Mayer, *The Furies*, pp. 101–3. This view was challenged by revolutionary radical, Marat, who viewed the Terror as a bottom-up expression of popular vengeance.

consensus that with the exception of the Vendée, between 1792 and 1794 approximately 90 per cent of all the Terror's victims were judicially sanctioned executions involving individuals accused of insurrection, collusion, or plotting against the republic.[22] Of course, the quasi-judicial process instituted by the Jacobins was deeply flawed, but not all of those who were denounced were imprisoned and only around half of those accused of crimes warranting execution were in fact executed.[23]

Where revolutionary radicals advocated measures beyond the law, they did so by reference to the principle of necessity. One of the most notorious, Saint-Just, who was responsible—among other things—for a massacre in Lyon, defended his actions by insisting that 'one must rule by the sword those who cannot be ruled by justice'.[24] After the arrest of the Girondin deputies, Saint-Just argued that the government was 'compelled to sacrifice the freedom of a few to the salvation of all. . . . Nothing resembles virtue so much as a great crime'.[25] In contrast to Robespierre, Saint-Just argued that it was legitimate to extend the Terror beyond the law but even he insisted that Terror be limited to what was necessary to defeat the republic's enemies.[26]

The Terror was conceived as the judicially sanctioned killing of people believed guilty of crimes against the people and state. Many revolutionaries seemed to be aware that mass killing contradicted the liberties set out in the Declaration of the Rights of Man and the Citizen but they insisted that exceptional measures were legitimate if necessary for the defence of the republic.[27] Not even radicals like Marat, Couthon, and Saint-Just defended killing those not implicated in crimes against the state to establish a general state of fear.[28] According to Saint-Just and Couthon, the Terror's principal

[22] Greer, *The Incidence of Terror*, p. 81; Mona Ozouf, 'Jacobins: Fortune et Infortune d'un mot', in *L'école de la France: Essais sur la Révolution, l'utopia et l'enseignment* (Paris: Editions Sociale, 1984), p. 242; and Tackett, 'Conspiracy Obsession', p. 692. Elsewhere, Tackett argues that although most instances of repression targeted specific individuals, this was sometimes simply because they were members of a particular social or political group. Timothy Tackett, 'The Flight to Varennes and the Coming of the Terror', *Historical Reflections/Reflexions Historiques*, 29 (3) 2003, p. 485.

[23] Greer, *The Incidence of Terror* and David Garrioch, 'Revolutionary Violence and Terror in the Paris Sections', in Robert Aldrich and Martyn Lyons (eds), *The Sphinx in the Tuileries* (Sydney: University of Sydney, 1999), pp. 67–76.

[24] Saint-Just cited by Marc Bouloiseau, *The Jacobin Republic 1792–1794,* trans. Jonathan Mandelbaum (Cambridge: Cambridge University Press, 1987), p. 94.

[25] Cited by Peter Gay, 'Rhetoric and Politics in the French Revolution', *American Historical Review*, 66 (3) 1961, p. 671.

[26] Kelly, 'Conceptual Sources of the Terror', p. 18.

[27] Norman Hampson, *Prelude to Terror: The Constituent Assembly and the Failure of Consensus, 1789–1791* (Oxford: Basil Blackwell, 1988), pp. 165–6.

[28] Though their justifications for executing Danton, Desmoulins, and other former leaders were far from plausible. Saint-Just accused them of plotting against the republic by spreading fears about food shortages and therefore encouraging counter-revolution. See Bouloiseau, *The Jacobin Republic*, p. 117.

purpose was to 'destroy' or 'annihilate' the republic's enemies, not to frighten them into submission.[29] This is not to say that fear played *no* role in the Terror's justification or function.[30] But to the extent that the Terror instilled fear in the republic's enemies, this was a by-product of measures primarily aimed at punishing those believed guilty of plotting against the republic.

The principal criticism of the Terror levelled by French émigré aristocrats, the Catholic Church and France's continental neighbours focused not on the killing itself but on the republic's right to rule. In July 1791, Leopold II of Austria summoned monarchs to discuss measures to 'secure the liberty and honour of the Most Christian King and his family and to set bounds on the dangerous extremism of the French Revolution'.[31] In the Pillnitz declaration that followed, Austria and Prussia agreed to restore 'the foundations of monarchical government' in France.[32] Their objectives were more clearly spelled out in the Brunswick manifesto, which accused the revolution of overthrowing 'legitimate government' and committing 'daily outrages' against the royal family. Austro-Prussian intervention would halt attacks on 'Church and Throne' but had 'no intention of interfering in the internal affairs of France' beyond restoring the monarchy and punishing the 'rebels'. The kings warned that if Louis were harmed they would wreak 'an exemplary and ever-memorable vengeance' on Paris.[33] After the execution of King Louis, the European monarchs invaded France hoping to punish those they thought guilty of 'regicide' and restore the Bourbon monarchy. The sentiment was shared by French Royalists even before Louis' execution. In 1792, Montmorin, a former royalist minister wrote, to the Comte de la Marche, with the approval of the Queen, suggesting that 'I think we will have to strike the Parisians with Terror'.[34] This is one of many examples of supporters of the *Ancien Regime* speaking approvingly of terror. The monarchs issued the Brunswick manifesto demanding the 'severe and exemplary punishment of all crimes' and recommending that retribution run to '44,000 executions or one in each commune'.[35] The key point here is that it was not the Terror itself that exercised European governments. Austria and Prussia were moved by what they saw as the illegitimacy of republican government, not by the Terror per se. The Catholic Church endorsed both the idea that the revolutionary government was illegitimate and that mass killing would be needed to punish

[29] Greer, *The Incidence of Terror*, p. 19.

[30] In 1793, for instance, the Paris sections called upon the Convention to 'bring fear into the hearts of our enemies'. Cited by Bronislaw Baczko, 'The Terror Before the Terror?', p. 31

[31] Cited in Mayer, *The Furies*, p. 549.

[32] John Hall Stewart, *A Documentary Survey of the French Revolution* (New York: Macmillan, 1951), pp. 223–4.

[33] The text of the Brunswick manifesto is reproduced in Stewart, *A Documentary Survey*, pp. 307–11.

[34] Cited by Albert Mathiez, *Révolution Française*, Vol. III (Paris: Biblioteque Mediations, 1985), p. 90.

[35] Cited by Mayer, *The Furies*, p. 187.

wrongdoers. Pope Pius VI insisted that 'the innocent blood of Louis XVI would rise to heaven . . . and provoke a divine fury', reminding the French that 'God, the just avenger of crimes, had often inflicted terrifying punishments for altogether lesser transgressions'.[36]

Britain's position was somewhat different. The primary British concern was the question of whether the French republic would behave as a legitimate international actor. Indeed, it welcomed the 1789 revolution.[37] Britain was also reluctant to intervene to restore the monarchy and refused to endorse Bourbon restoration throughout the 1790s.[38] Prime Minister Pitt was primarily concerned about the French republic's ability to honour its international obligations. The fulfilment of treaty obligations, Pitt believed, required that a government have the support of its people. As neither the Bourbons nor the revolutionary government enjoyed such support, France could not in his view fulfil its international responsibilities. This, in turn, jeopardized British security, warranting the use of limited force against France.[39] Charles James Fox, leader of the opposition, shared these views and condemned both the revolutionaries and the monarchists for committing atrocities.[40] In January 1794, the British government stated that 'the Revolution of 31 May established an entirely new form of government in France more atrocious than any of the former systems and *more incompatible with the Safety of other Countries*'.[41] Later that year, the Pitt government listed the 'Levee on masse, Requisition, Prehension, Armed People, Use of Capital of Country' as the French republic's crimes and in 1799, some five years after the 'Great Terror', Pitt commented that 'we ought never to think of peace with a revolutionary Jacobin government' irrespective of whether or not it engaged in terror.[42] Britain's position was perhaps most clearly summarized in 1795 by George Canning, the future foreign secretary, who insisted that:

> It is not the form of Government there [in France], but its power & will to afford and maintain Security to other Countries, that we consider as indispensable, that about Monarchy, or Republicanism, or Revolutionary Committees, or this or that set of men or set of principles, we have no care or consideration—further than as they go to promise or to make improbable, the secure maintenance of Peace, if on other grounds peace should be desirable.[43]

[36] Cited by Mayer, *The Furies*, p. 188.

[37] Hampson, *Prelude to Terror* and Alfred Cobban, 'An Age of Revolutionary Wars: An Historical Parallel', *The Review of Politics*, 13 (2) 1951, pp. 131–41.

[38] Jennifer Mori, 'The British Government and the Bourbon Restoration: The Occupation of Toulon, 1793', *The Historical Journal*, 40 (3) 1997, pp. 706 and 713.

[39] Mori, 'The British Government', p. 704.

[40] Lord John Russell (ed.), *Memorials and Correspondence of Charles James Fox*, Vol. III (London: Richard Bentley, 1835), pp. 39–40.

[41] Emphasis added, cited by Mori, 'The British Government', p. 716.

[42] Mori, 'The British Government', p. 716.

[43] George Canning, 26 January 1795, cited by Mori, 'The British Government', p. 717.

In other words, Britain was less interested in the conduct of the French government than it was in the preservation of European order.

Others were more explicit in their condemnation of the Terror but also addressed the perceived illegitimacy of the Jacobin government. Edmund Burke's critique began well before the Terror when, in response to the 1789 revolution, he insisted that the people of France had thrown off 'law and morals' along with their monarch, potentially undermining the entire basis of European civilization.[44] Two years before the Terror, Burke insisted that 'those who have made the exhibition of the fourteenth of July are capable of every evil. They do not commit crimes for their designs; but they form designs that they may commit crimes. It is not their necessity, but their nature that impels them'.[45] During the Terror, he insisted that 'these philosophers are fanatics . . . they are carried with such an headlong rage towards every desperate trial that they would sacrifice the whole human race to the slightest of their experiments'.[46] For Burke, the Terror was the inevitable consequence of the overthrow of monarchy. The illegitimacy of the violence, however, was intimately connected to the revolutionary government's illegitimacy.

Ironically, one group that shared Burke's view were the Thermidorians ultimately responsible for the overthrow of the Terror. Jacobins themselves, the Thermidorians turned against the Terror after it was used to remove Robespierre's political opponents, arguing that a legitimate tool for dealing with genuine enemies of the republic had been subverted in a manner inimical to liberty. The Jacobin society at L'Aigle declared the Terror antithetical to liberty stating that 'the system of terror only suits slaves'.[47] What became known as 'Robespierrism' was labelled a threat to the revolution.[48]

In summary, the perpetrators of the Terror claimed that they held the authority to enforce the law and that their victims were guilty of crimes against the state. The republican government did not claim a right to use Terror indiscriminately to maintain order by spreading fear. Instead, it maintained that the emergency it confronted made exceptional measures necessary to

[44] Letter to William Windham, 27 September 1789, in Michael A. Mosher, 'The Skeptic's Burke: Reflections on the Revolution in France, 1790–1990', *Political Theory*, 19 (3) 1991, p. 402. Also, Edmund Burke, *Reflections on the Revolution in France*, ed. Conor Cruise O'Brien (London: Penguin, 1987 [1790]), p. 173.

[45] Edmund Burke, 'Thoughts on French Affairs' (1791), reproduced in Louis Bredvold and Ralph G. Ross (eds), *The Philosophy of Edmund Burke* (Ann Arbor: The University of Michigan Press, 1960), p. 246.

[46] Letter to a Noble Lord (1796), reproduced in Bredvold and Ross, *Philosophy of Edmund Burke* (Ann Arbor: The University of Michigan Press, 1960), p. 234.

[47] Michael L. Kennedy, 'The "Last Stand" of the Jacobins Clubs', *French Historical Studies*, 16 (2), 1989, p. 338.

[48] See Michael L. Kennedy, *The Jacobin Club of Marseille* (Ithaca: Cornell University Press, 1994), pp. 136–7.

protect the republic. The general right of a government to adopt such measures was tacitly recognized by both domestic critics and foreign governments alike. For most foreign governments, it was the revolutionary government's right to rule and not its mass killing that lay at the heart of the problem. Indeed, the émigrés, Austrians, and Prussians advocated their own atrocities as retribution for regicide. Other critics, such as Edmund Burke, did not disentangle the legitimacy of the regime from that of the Terror.

Albeit with significant contextual variation, this pattern was repeated throughout the nineteenth century. When responding to domestic uprisings with violence against civilians, political leaders tended to insist either that they were only targeting those guilty of crimes against the state or that they were conducting legitimate reprisals in response to crimes committed by rebels. On many occasions, those justifications were endorsed by other states on the grounds that legitimate governments were entitled to take the necessary steps to maintain order but, as I mentioned earlier, the degree of toleration declined as the century progressed. Such violence was more likely to be criticized when doubts were raised about the regime's right to rule or where violence extended beyond the execution of those implicated in plots against legitimate governments. Where these two factors combined, governments were more likely to censure or punish their peers for committing atrocities.

## DOMESTIC REPRESSION

During the nineteenth and early twentieth centuries, European states resorted to violence on more than 300 occasions in response to domestic insurrections.[49] Often, this involved the intentional killing of civilians—those not engaged in armed conflict or found guilty of a particular crime punishable by death. The Ottoman Empire used mass atrocities in its efforts to quell uprisings in Serbia (1807 and 1817) and Greece (1821–30), and committed genocide against the Armenians (1915). Austria, Prussia, France, and Russia all used more limited atrocities to quash liberal uprisings in 1848, and the French army killed approximately 20,000 civilians and surrendered insurgents in the immediate aftermath of the fall of the Paris commune in 1871. International reactions to these atrocities were primarily determined by judgements about the legitimacy of the perpetrator and the extent to which the killing was judged necessary. Where a government's authority was widely recognized and its use of atrocities believed necessary, mass killing was generally tolerated or excused, and sometimes validated. But in cases where atrocities were

[49] For a list, see Sandra Halpern, *War and Social Change in Modern Europe: The Great Transformation Revisited* (Cambridge: Cambridge University Press, 2004), pp. 312–444.

employed by regimes whose right to rule the territory concerned was in doubt or where violence was judged unnecessary or excessive, foreign actors were sometimes prepared to criticize the perpetrators and occassionally impose punishments. With the rise of humanitarianism described earlier and in Chapter 1, the amount of civilian killing that attracted criticism was generally lower towards the end of the period than it was at the beginning.

## Greek War of Independence (1821–1827)

The response of European governments to the Greek war of independence demonstrates that even in cases where a government's right to rule was acknowledged, that government did not enjoy an inexhaustible right to employ mass atrocities. This case shows that although necessity could be called upon to justify mass atrocities, the principle also imposed constraints by delegitimizing killing perceived as being unnecessary. Additionally, this case demonstrates that even in the early nineteenth century, governments could fail to secure sufficient legitimacy for mass atrocities and that when they do so other members of international society might punish them—in this case with military intervention.[50] This outcome was made possible by a combination of Ottoman actions and important contextual factors including public support for Greek nationalism and the convergence of great power interests.

In 1821, the Greek population in Morea rebelled against Ottoman rule, unleashing a wave of violence against soldiers and civilians alike.[51] When the town of Tripolista fell to the Greeks, the rebels slayed 8,000 Turkish soldiers and civilians.[52] The Ottoman authorities and Turkish communities responded with a wave of reprisals. Turkish mobs attacked Greek civilians in Smyrna and the government hanged the Orthodox Patriarch in Constantinople.[53] The rebellion soon turned into a protracted insurgency with both sides using reprisals against civilians. In 1822, Ottoman forces massacred around 20,000 civilians on the island of Chios and carried thousands more into slavery. The crisis escalated in 1824 when the Ottoman leader in Egypt, Ibrahim Pasha, intervened in support of the Turks. The Egyptians launched a campaign of mass killing and slave-taking. At Kasas, they killed 500 civilians and took 2,000 into slavery and at Psara, 8,000 Greeks were slaughtered or dragged into

[50] Gary J. Bass, *Freedom's Battle: The Origins of Humanitarian Intervention* (New York: Alfred Knopf, 2008), pp. 45–152.

[51] The rebellion itself was described as a 'war of extermination' against Turks in Morea, see J. A. R. Marriott, *The Eastern Question: A Study in European Diplomacy* (Oxford: Blackwell, 1940), p. 205.

[52] Douglas Dakin, *The Struggle for Greek Independence 1821–1833* (London: B. T. Batsford, 1973), p. 67.

[53] M. S. Anderson, *The Eastern Question 1774–1923* (London: Macmillan, 1966), p. 54.

slavery.[54] Rumours abounded that Ibrahim planned to kill or enslave the entire Greek population of Morea and repopulate the region with North Africans.[55]

The Ottoman government argued that these measures were legitimate reprisals against the rebels and rejected foreign interference. Throughout the crisis, it refused to see the Greek rebels as anything other than outlaws and insisted that it did not have to justify its actions to international society because a legitimate ruler was entitled to use whatever means it deemed necessary to suppress insurrection.[56] At the outset, Western European governments tended to support the Turkish position for a mixture of strategic and normative reasons. Britain and Austria feared that Turkish weakness would be exploited by Russia. Their foreign ministers, Castlereagh and Metternich, agreed that the 1815 Vienna settlement gave Turkey the right to govern Greece.[57] International sympathy for the Greeks was further tempered by discomfort about Greek atrocities. For largely strategic reasons, the Russian government was much more sympathetic to the Greek cause but unwilling to act unilaterally.[58]

By 1827, the British and French positions had markedly changed for at least three reasons. First, the litany of massacres described above brought public opinion firmly behind the Greeks, making a pro-Turkish policy politically unfeasible.[59] Second, the protracted conflict created a problem with piracy in the Aegean Sea that was damaging international trade. This cast doubt on the Ottomans' ability to fulfil their treaty obligations. Third, Britain and France were concerned that Russia might use the war and public sympathy for the Greeks as a pretext for unilateral intervention.[60] Wanting to see the conflict speedily resolved, the two powers endorsed a plan to coerce the Turks into accepting an autonomous Greek state that would be a tributary to the Ottoman Empire. Together with Russia, they despatched a naval fleet to blockade Egyptian forces—though with orders to not use force except in self-defence. The London Treaty (6 July 1827) explained the grounds for intervention as

[54] Dakin, *Greek Struggle for Independence*, p. 122.

[55] C. W. Crawley, *The Question of Greek Independence: A Study of British Policy in the Near East, 1821–1833* (Cambridge: Cambridge University Press, 1930), p. 77; and Dakin, *Greek Struggle for Independence*, p. 229.

[56] Anderson, *The Eastern Question*, p. 67.

[57] According to the Vienna settlement, not only were states not entitled to violate the territorial integrity of other fully sovereign states, no state 'had an unrestricted right to revolutionise itself'. Martin Wight, 'International Legitimacy', *International Relations*, 4 (1) 1972, p. 3. For a discussion, see Ian Clark, *Legitimacy in International Society* (Oxford: Oxford University Press, 2005), pp. 91–6.

[58] Anderson, *The Eastern Question*, p. 61.

[59] See C. W. Crawley, *Question of Greek Independence: A Study of British Policy in the Near East, 1821–1833* (Cambridge: Cambridge University Press, 1930), p. 77.

[60] Simon Chesterman, *Just War or Just Peace? Humanitarian Intervention and International Law* (Oxford: Oxford University Press, 2001), p. 31.

being to prevent 'all the disorders of anarchy', end the endemic piracy in the region, and put a 'stop to the effusion of blood' and 'evils of every kind'.[61] An exchange of fire between the fleets at Navarino escalated into a full-scale naval engagement that resulted in the destruction of the Ottoman fleet. Among his explanations for the engagement, the allied fleet commander pointed to reported Turkish atrocities in the area.[62] Without their fleet, the Ottomans were forced to accept Greek autonomy.

Although it was widely recognized that sovereigns had a right to use violence against rebellious subjects, even civilians, this case suggests that they did not have an inexhaustible right to commit mass atrocities. As early as 1827, this right was conditioned by necessity, which both justified *and limited* the legitimate killing of civilians within Europe. The Chios massacre and rumours about Ibrahim's plans for repopulating Morea were viewed with alarm by European publics. This made it more difficult for governments predisposed to supporting the Ottomans to justify their position. Moreover, the Ottoman argument that it did not need to provide special justifications for its actions was not widely accepted.[63] Having already damaged perceptions of the Ottoman's right to rule Greece, the combination of these normative concerns with strategic imperatives pushed the European powers towards humanitarian intervention.

## Paris and Vienna Uprisings (1848)

In 1848, European governments confronted a series of uprisings. In France, Prussia, and the Habsburg Empire, a mixture of nationalists, liberals, and socialists attempted—with some initial success—to overthrow monarchical governments in the name of popular sovereignty.[64] The French monarchy was deposed and Metternich's rule in Austria came to an end; but by year's end, order had been restored and the rebels suppressed. In both France and Austria, the governments of early 1848 were deposed almost without a fight but the final restoration of order was accompanied by atrocities. Although Habsburgs atrocities were more limited than French atrocities, they received

[61] Preamble of the London Treaty, reproduced in John Westlake, *International Law*, 2nd edn (Cambridge: Cambridge University Press, 1910), p. 319, n. 3.

[62] C. M. Woodhouse, *The Battle of Navarino* (London: Hodder and Stoughton, 1965), p. 37; and Dakin, *Greek Struggle for Independence*, pp. 229–30.

[63] The Ottomans experienced a similar fate in Lebanon in 1860. See Ellery C. Stowell, *Intervention in International Law* (Washington, DC: John Byrne and Co., 1921), p. 66; Chesterman, *Just War or Just Peace?*, pp. 32–3; and Bass, *Freedom's Battle*, pp. 100–51.

[64] Helmut Pogge von Strandmann, '1848–1849: A European Revolution?', in R. J. W. Evans and Helmut Pogge von Strandmann (eds), *The Revolutions in Europe, 1848–1849* (Oxford: Oxford University Press, 2000), pp. 1–3.

more criticism thanks to perceptions that it was a less legitimate regime deriving from sympathy for Hungarian and Italian claims to self-determination. This contrast demonstrates the role played by judgements about the relative legitimacy of the actors involved in shaping responses to mass atrocities.

In the French case, a new republican government was able to quickly assert its authority and then use that authority to successfully defend the use of violence against civilians.[65] In June 1848, Parisian radicals who had fared badly in national elections took to the streets to protest the closure of 'national workshops'.[66] Approximately 15,000 workers took to the streets (some suggested 50,000), erecting barricades and seizing parts of eastern Paris. A state of siege was declared and National Guards summoned from the provinces. Once the city had been retaken, government forces sought out protestors, summarily executing 2,000–3,000 and arresting 12,500. Of those, 4,500 were later deported to Algeria.[67]

Members of the new government justified the killing on the grounds of necessity. According to one of the Constituent Assembly's most prominent members, Alexis de Tocqueville, the National Guard was 'eager to defend society against the threat of anarchic doctrines and to put an end to the intolerable dictation of the chronically insurgent Parisian workers'.[68] Later, he wrote that 'the measures they caused to be taken were indispensable for the safety of the country'.[69] This view was widely supported. Even Karl Marx, perhaps the French government's loudest critic, held the insurgents partly responsible for the bloodshed. He lamented that their refusal to contemplate concessions and the 'nonsense' idea that a single class could rule 'has led in Paris to a bloody outcome'.[70] Marx also denounced the 'June days' as 'bourgeois terrorism'.[71] Liberals and conservatives across Europe welcomed the suppression of the rebels who had, they claimed, threatened to destroy the institutions of religion and family. Britain viewed the republican government as an inevitable consequence of the French monarchy's misrule but when the

[65] See Geoffrey Bruun, *Revolution and Reaction: 1848–1852* (New York: Van Nostrand, 1958), p. 27; Jean Sigmann, *1848—The Romantic and Democratic Revolutions in Europe* (London: Allen and Unwin, 1973), p. 210; and Peter N. Steans, *1848: The Revolutionary Tide in Europe* (New York: W. W. Norton, 1974), p. 78.

[66] Sigmann, *1848*, p. 227.

[67] Geoffrey Ellis, 'The Revolution of 1848–1849 in France', in Evans and von Strandmann, pp. 32–3; and Sigmann, *1848*, p. 41.

[68] Cited by Stearns, *1848*, pp. 89–90.

[69] Alexis de Tocqueville, *The Recollections of Alexis de Tocqueville*, J. P. Mayer (ed.), trans. A. D. de Mattos (New York: Harvill, 1949), pp. 172–3.

[70] Karl Marx, speech to the Democratic Club of Cologne, 4 August 1848. Cited by Sperber, *The European Revolutions: 1848–1851* (Cambridge: Cambridge University Press, 1994), p. 200.

[71] Karl Marx, 'Class Struggles in France', in Eugene Kamenka (ed.), *The Portable Karl Marx* (Hardmondsworth: Penguin, 1983), pp. 283, 285.

Paris mob seized control of part of the capital, Viscount Palmerston, the British Foreign Secretary, wrote that 'power has passed into the hands of a mob ignorant of the principles of government, of morality and of justice'.[72] Later, he too welcomed the revolt's suppression.[73]

Austria's experience in 1848 provides an instructive comparison to the French experience. In February, demonstrators in Vienna forced Metternich's resignation and the army's withdrawal from Vienna.[74] Hungarian nationalists led by Kossuth invaded Austria with the intention of assisting the Viennese rebels. Kossuth's army was defeated outside Vienna and withdrew to Hungary where it was annihilated by a Russian intervention. In late October, after offering an armistice that was rejected by the rebels, the Habsburg army bombarded Vienna before storming it. In the days that followed, between 2,000 and 4,300 people were killed, including 1,300–1,500 Habsburg soldiers.[75] As in Paris, Habsburg soldiers committed summary executions once the fighting was over. Approximately 1,500 people were killed in these executions and between 2,400 and 10,000 arrested.[76] Special military tribunals were created to try those arrested and twenty-five suspected leaders were executed.

As with the French, the Habsburg government justified its actions by reference to necessity. Emperor Franz Ferdinand explained, 'we see ourselves compelled, according to our royal duty, for the maintenance of the security and the law, to take the following measures and to command their enforcement . . . until the disturbed peace and order in the country shall be restored'.[77] This claim was accepted by some foreign governments, though doubts about the legitimacy of Vienna's rule over Hungary gave rise to international criticism of the Habsburgs' repression of the rebels.

Whereas Russia openly supported the Habsburgs and intervened against the Hungarians, the French government offered rhetorical support to the rebels though it refrained from providing material support for fear of undermining its own claim to be a stable and legitimate government. Britain's position was ambivalent. On the one hand, the British government was concerned about the maintenance of the 1815 European order but on the other hand it criticized the Habsburg regime. At the peak of the crisis in

[72] Letter to King Leopold I of Belgium, 15 June 1848. Reproduced in Evelyn Ashley, *The Life of Henry John Temple, Viscount Palmerston*, Vol. 1 (London: R. Bentley and Son, 1876), p. 96. On Britain's attitude more generally, see Leslie Mitchell, 'Britain's Reaction to the Revolution', in Evans and Strandmann, *The Revolutions in Europe*, p. 85.

[73] Sperber, *The European Revolutions*, p. 200.

[74] Steans, *1848*, p. 96; Denis Mack Smith, 'The Revolutions of 1848–1849', in Evans and Standmann (eds), *The Revolution in Europe*, p. 63; Sperber, *The European Revolutions*, p. 215.

[75] Cf. J. A. S. Granville, *Europe Reshaped 1848–1878* (London: Harvester Press, 1976), p. 126; and Steans, *1848*, p. 121.

[76] Cf. Steans, *1848*, p. 121; and Granville, *Europe Reshaped*, p. 124.

[77] Phineas Camp Headley, *Life of Louis Kossuth: Governor of Hungary* (London: Darby and Miller, 1852), pp. 123–4.

Vienna, Palmerston wrote that 'as to poor Austria, every person who attaches value to the maintenance of a balance of power in Europe must lament her present helpless condition'.[78] After the restoration of Habsburg rule, however, Britain provided refuge to Kossuth and refused to extradite Hungarian immigrants wanted for prosecution by the Austrians.[79] Palmerston's view was clearly expressed in 1849 when he wrote that 'the Austrians are really the greatest brutes that ever called themselves by the undeserved name of civilised men'.[80] The US government was similarly exercised by what it saw as the brutal treatment of the Hungarians. It despatched a diplomatic mission to Vienna to demand an end to the oppression of Hungary.[81] The Habsburg government was also roundly criticized for executing Robert Blum, a commissioner from the Frankfurt National Assembly who had joined the Viennese rebels. Blum's execution became something of a *cause célèbre* among European liberals.[82] What is significant here for our purposes is the fact that although the Habsburg crackdown was less bloody and more restrained than the French, the government in Vienna was criticized more sharply than its counterpart in Paris. This was mainly because its right to govern other European peoples—and thus its right to use force against them—was doubted in some circles, whilst the legitimacy of the French national state was not.

## Fall of the Paris Commune (1871)

The brief reign of terror that accompanied the collapse of the Paris Commune in 1871 bucked the trend of relative restraint displayed in 1848 and serves as a prologue to the effects of the injection of totalitarian ideology into the justification of atrocities. This case is also interesting because whilst the French government's legitimacy was generally recognized, its recourse to mass killing was widely criticized as unnecessary, suggesting that even legitimate governments did not enjoy an unlimited right to kill their own civilians and that the amount of anti-civilian violence that could be justified by reference to necessity was diminishing.

After the collapse of the French army in the Franco-Prussian war, the Parisian public overthrew the government and established the Paris

[78] Letter to King Leopold I, 15 June 1848.

[79] R. J. W. Evans, '1848–1849 in the Habsburg Monarchy', in Evans and von Strandmann (eds), *The Revolutions in Europe*, p. 200.

[80] Letter of 9 September 1849 to Ponsonby, the British Minister in Vienna. Reproduced in Ashley, *The Life of Henry John Temple*, Vol. 1, p. 139.

[81] See Arthur J. May, 'Contemporary American Opinion of the Mid-Century Revolutions in Central Europe', doctoral dissertation, University of Pennsylvania, Philadelphia, 1927, p. 54.

[82] See Axel Körner, 'The European Dimension in the Ideas of 1848', in Axel Körner (ed.), *1848: A European Revolution? International Ideas and National Memories* (London: Palgrave, 2000), p. 5.

Commune, which was immediately besieged by Prussia.[83] When government forces retook Paris in late May 1871, they summarily executed 20,000–25,000 civilians and prisoners. The majority were communard prisoners, executed without trial. The remainder were simply shot where they stood.[84]

On the eve of the commune's fall, Adolphe Thiers—head of the French government—justified what was to come by insisting that 'the cause of justice, order, humanity, civilisation has triumphed. . . . Expiation will be complete. It will take place in the name of the law, by the law and within the law'.[85] Government supporters believed that they had been presented with a rare opportunity to finally eradicate what Thiers reportedly labelled 'the vile multitude'.[86] As Paris fell, *Le Figaro* editorialized that 'never has such an opportunity presented itself for curing Paris of the moral gangrene that has been consuming it for the past twenty years. Parisians must submit to the laws of war, however terrible they may be. Today, clemency equals lunacy'.[87] Some government supporters went further, arguing that the communards and their allies were not civilized humans. A Catholic missionary described them as savages whilst a government-sponsored commission of inquiry found that France had been threatened by a 'barbarian invasion'.[88] Despite demands for a wholesale 'cleansing' of revolutionaries, Thiers himself later wrote that he gave 'strictest instructions that the rage of the soldiers was to be contained' and military commanders were instructed to avoid 'unnecessary violence'.[89] In practice, government forces did not exercise restraint and the government did little to enforce its orders.[90] Prisoners were arbitrarily killed as were civilians thought sympathetic to the commune.[91]

[83] See Alistair Horne, *The Fall of Paris: The Siege and the Commune 1870–1871* (London: Macmillan, 1965), p. 37; and John Plamenatz, *The Revolutionary Movement in France 1815–1871* (London: Longmans, 1952), pp. 141–3.

[84] The commune also used terror. Most infamously, under its 'Law of Hostages' the commune seized clerics and merchants whose sympathies might be expected to lie with the government and threatened to execute them as reprisals for the killing of communard prisoners. As the commune fell, the Archbishop and fifty other hostages were taken out of prison and shot. See Roger L. Williams, *The French Revolution of 1870–1871* (London: Weidenfeld and Nicolson, 1969), pp. 137–45.

[85] Cited by Horne, *The Fall of Paris*, p. 377.

[86] According to a commission of inquiry created by the government to investigate the commune. See Roger Price, 'Conservative Reactions to Social Disorder: The Paris Commune of 1871', *Journal of European Studies*, 1, 1971, p. 351.

[87] Cited by Horne, *The Fall of Paris*, p. 414.

[88] Roger Price, 'Conservative Reactions to Social Disorder: The Paris Commune of 1871', *Journal of European Studies*, 1, p. 345.

[89] Williams, *The French Revolution*, p. 150.

[90] 'During the fighting we can do nothing', Thiers wrote of the terror, 'and it would be useless to wish to interfere'. Cited in Robert Tombs, *The War Against Paris 1871* (Cambridge: Cambridge University Press, 1981), p. 185.

[91] Horne, *The Fall of Paris*, pp. 403–4.

As reports of the killings spread, the French government was criticized, particularly in Britain. The *London Standard*, which had earlier vilified the commune lamented 'the wholesale executions of men, women and children' which 'must disturb the conscience of those who suffered them to take place'.[92] *The Times* was also highly critical of the commune but condemned Thiers, proclaiming: 'The laws of war! They are mild and Christian compared with the inhuman laws of revenge under which the Versailles troops have been shooting, bayoneting, ripping up prisoners, women and children'. Two days later, it stated: 'the French are filling up the darkest page in the book of their own or the world's history . . . the Versailles troops seem inclined to outdo the communists in their sheer lavishness of human blood' and, later, 'human nature shrinks in horror from the deeds that have been done in Paris . . . the wholesale executions . . . sicken the soul'.[93] For its part, whilst recognizing the Thiers government, the British government expressed disquiet at the killing. Indeed, fear of British intervention encouraged the French government to end the killings and deliver relatively lenient penalties to surviving prisoners. Of the 40,000 prisoners who survived, only twenty-six were executed.[94] Although Prussian forces assisted in defeating the commune, both Bismarck and the Kaiser expressed shock at the bloody repression.[95] By week's end, Parisian opinion had also turned against the crackdown.[96]

## The Armenian Genocide (1915)

During the nineteenth century, the Ottoman Empire employed atrocities on several occasions to repress internal rebellions. In addition to the massacres in Greece (mentioned above) and Serbia in 1875 (which elicited almost no foreign criticism), an 1876 revolt in Bulgaria was suppressed by massacres, giving Russia a pretext for war in 1877.[97] In 1894–96, Turkish authorities responded to an uprising sparked by a tax dispute by massacring between 80,000 and 120,000 Armenians.[98] For this they were sharply criticized by

[92] *London Standard*, 10 June 1871. Cited by Royden Harrison, *The English Defence of the Commune 1871* (London: Merlin Press, 1971), p. 96.

[93] *The Times*, 29 and 31 May, and 1 June 1871, cited by Horne, *The Fall of Paris*, p. 417.

[94] Horne, *The Fall of Paris*, p. 418.

[95] See Otto Pflanze, *Bismarck and the Development of Germany*, Vol. 11: *The Period of Consolidation, 1871–1880* (Princeton, NJ: Princeton University Press, 1990), p. 296; and Allan Mitchell, *Bismarck and the French Nation 1848–1890* (New York: Pegasus, 1971), pp. 73–80.

[96] The Parisian middle-class initially welcomed the arrival of government troops and suppression of the commune, Tombs, *War Against Paris*, p. 185.

[97] Peter Balakian, *The Burning Tigris: The Armenian Genocide and America's Response* (New York: Perennial, 2004), p. 160.

[98] See Richard G. Hovannisian, 'The Historical Dimension of the Armenian Question, 1878–1923', in Richard G. Hovannisian (ed.), *The Armenian Genocide in Perspective* (New Brunswick:

Britain, France, and the USA. The British Ambassador described the killings as 'shocking atrocities' noting that Armenians were treated like 'wild beasts'. British Prime Minister William Gladstone famously referred to the Ottoman Sultan as 'the great assassin' and the Salisbury government which came to power in 1895 contemplated unilateral action in the Dardenalles.[99] The French Ambassador was also critical, pointing to 'organised massacres' permitted by the government. The German government privately expressed disquiet at the killings but publicly argued that the Ottoman government was entitled to act in this fashion.[100] But these massacres were just a precursor to the 1915 genocide.

The roots of the Armenian genocide lay in a combination of Turkish nationalism and its goal of transforming the ailing empire into a modern national state dominated by Turks, an ideology of Turkish superiority, the mass killing and displacement of Turks from the Balkans during the struggles in Greece, Serbia, and Bulgaria and an associated doctrine of Turkish superiority, fears about the possible dismembering of Anatolia, and an apparent alliance between Armenians and Russians. Turkish fears grew following Turkey's catastrophic defeat at Sarikamis and the allied landings at Gallipoli.[101] In early 1915, the first reports emerged of the disarming and killing of Armenians in the Ottoman armies, many of whom had only recently been forcibly recruited into labour battalions. On 24 April 1915, a few days after the Gallipoli landings, over 2,000 Armenian leaders in Constantinople were arrested and deported. Only a handful survived.[102] On 27 May, the government instructed all Anatolian Armenians to present themselves for deportation to the Mesopotamian desert for the duration of the First World War. Many deportees were taken straight to their deaths, drowned in the Black Sea. Others were set upon as they travelled. Women were systematically raped before being killed. Many were sold into servitude. Children were massacred or carried off. For the few that made it to Mesopotamia, all that awaited them

Transaction Publishers, 1998), pp. 22–4; and Vahakn H. Dadrian, 'The Signal Facts Surrounding the Armenian Genocide and the Turkish Denial Syndrome', *Journal of Genocide Research*, 5 (2) 2003, p. 27.

[99] See Robert Melson, *Revolution and Genocide: On the Origins of the Armenian Genocide and the Holocaust* (Chicago: University of Chicago Press, 1992), pp. 61–2; Vahakn N. Dadrian, *Warrant for Genocide: Key Elements of the Turko-Armenian Conflict* (New Brunswick: Transaction Publishers, 2004), pp. 86–7; Balakian, *The Burning Tigris*, p. 233; Donald Bloxham, *The Great Game of Genocide: Imperialism, Nationalism and the Destruction of the Ottoman Armenians* (Oxford: Oxford University Press, 2005), pp. 53–4.

[100] Dadrian, *Warrant for Genocide*, p. 89.

[101] See Michael Mann, *The Dark Side of Democracy: Explaining Ethnic Cleansing* (Cambridge: Cambridge University Press, 2005), pp. 111–39; and Taner Akçam, *A Shameful Act: The Armenian Genocide and the Question of Turkish Responsibility* (New York: Metropolitan Books, 2006), pp. 47–103.

[102] Bloxham, *Great Game of Genocide*, p. 78.

was death. Desert camps were left without food or water and disease was rife.[103] There is little agreement about how many Armenians were killed in the genocide but most historians put the toll at between 800,000 and 1.2 million people.[104]

Today, the Turkish government and its allies deny that the mass killing of Armenians was intended as a matter of state policy, a line of argument first adopted by the Kemalist government in 1920.[105] But at the time of the genocide and immediately afterwards the Turkish government acknowledged the massacres and offered some justifications.[106] Indeed, some leading figures spoke openly about their intent to annihilate the Armenians. For instance, Interior Minister Talât Pasha told the German Consul General in Istanbul: 'what we are talking about . . . is the elimination of Armenians'; elsewhere he said 'the intention of the deportation [of Armenians] is annihilation'.[107] This left foreign diplomats based in Turkey with little doubt about the government's plans. Indeed, several German diplomats posted in different cities across Anatolia reported the same basic point: that the government had embarked on a policy of annihilating the Armenians.[108] Why, though, was it necessary to deport and/or kill *all* Armenians? Taner Akçam argues that the Young Turks were animated by a belief in the Turks as a 'ruling-nation' and a desire to establish a modern national state governed by Turks. Within this schema, Turkish nationalists would permit non-Muslims to remain in Turkey only if they accepted Turkish domination. Those who resisted would have to be removed or annihilated. This doctrine of selective extermination, Akçam shows, was developed in the late nineteenth century and crystallized in response to the Ottoman defeat in the 1912–13 Balkan Wars, which caused the displacement of some 800,000 Muslims. The Young Turks were concerned that their schemes would provoke foreign intervention and delayed acting

[103] There are many first hand accounts of the deportations and killings. They include, Henry H. Riggs, *Days of Tragedy in Armenia: Personal Experiences in Harpoot 1915–1917*; (Ann Arbor, Gomidas Institute, 1997); and Arnold J. Toynbee (ed.), *The Treatment of the Armenians in the Ottoman Empire* (London: Hodder and Stoughton, 1916).

[104] See Balakian, *Burning Tigris*, p. 179; Christopher J. Walker, 'World War I and the Armenian Genocide', in Richard G. Hoannisian (ed.), *The Armenian People From Ancient to Modern Times*: Vol. II, *From Dominion to Statehood: The Fifteenth to the Twentieth Century* (New York: St. Martin's Press), pp. 271–2; Melson, *Revolution and Genocide*, pp. 146–7; and Richard G. Hovannisian, 'Introduction', in Richard G. Hovannisian (ed.), *Remembrance and Denial: The Case of the Armenian Genocide* (Detroit: Wayne State University Press, 1999), p. 15.

[105] Vigen Guroian, 'Collective Responsibility and Excuse Making: The Case of the Turkish Genocide of the Armenians', in Hovannisian (ed.), *The Armenian Genocide in Perspective*, p. 137; and see Balakian, *Burning Tigris*, p. 328.

[106] Including to the US Ambassador; see Henry Morgenthau, *Ambassador Morgenthau's Story* (New York: Doubleday, 1918), p. 26.

[107] Cited by Akçam, *Shameful Act*, pp. 156 and 168.

[108] Akçam, *Shameful Act*, e.g. pp. 121, 156, and 175. Austria's Ambassador Pallavinci made the same observation, p. 122.

until the First World War provided them with the cover they needed.[109] But, other than in unguarded comments to foreign diplomats, this is not how the Turkish nationalists justified their actions to the outside world. Fearing that its campaign of deportation and mass killing would attract foreign intervention, the Turkish government was careful to lay out a case that it thought would appeal to international society, especially its main ally Germany, and the USA which had not declared war on Turkey. The nationalists did not argue that the killing was necessary to establish a modern national state but instead pointed to the necessity of self-defence against a rebellious people in league with a foreign enemy (Russia). The necessity case was set out most clearly in a government document published in French in 1916, responding to charges that it was slaughtering the Armenians:

> The primary necessity to assure internal order and external security of the country has made indispensable the removal of Armenians from places where their presence was considered to be dangerous.... During the application of these measures, regrettable acts of violence have sometimes been committed, but however regrettable these acts might have been, they were inevitable because of the profound indignation of the Moslem population.[110]

To sustain this argument, the Young Turks insisted that the Armenians posed a dire threat.[111] Throughout 1914 and early 1915, they presented evidence of Armenian plans to revolt against the government and join the Russians.[112] Unchecked, they argued, this Russo-Armenian alliance endangered the survival of the Turkish state. Mass deportations were therefore legitimate because, in dire emergencies, necessity overrides other legal considerations. According to this narrative, the killings and other deaths were unintended by-products of humane policies.[113] These arguments were augmented by claims that the Turks were not, in fact, killing large numbers of Armenian civilians. It was often claimed that bands of Armenians were themselves engaged in the mass killing of Turkish Muslims.[114]

According to this account, the deportations were necessary to remove treasonous Armenians living near the contested border with Russia and the killings were either necessary to enforse the deportations, unintended by-products, or legitimate responses to attacks by Armenian bandits. Here, the

[109] Akçam, *Shameful Act*, on concerns about foreign intervention p. 104; on the First World War as cover, pp. 107, 155, and *passim*.

[110] Reproduced and trans. in Joseph Guttman, 'The Beginnings of Genocide', *Turkish Armenocide*, Documentary Series No. 2 (Philadelphia: Armenian Historical Research Association, 1965), p. 11.

[111] Balakian, *Burning Tigris*, p. 181.

[112] See Guroian, 'Collective Responsibility', p. 141.

[113] Dadrian, *Warrant for Genocide*, inside cover and Talaat Pasha, 'Posthumous Memoirs of Talaat Pasha', *Current History*, 15, November 1921, pp. 294–5.

[114] 'Posthumous Memoirs of Talaat Pasha', p. 294.

Turks resorted to a key element of the necessity argument as it applies to counter-insurgency (see below): the impossibility of distinguishing combatants from civilians. In a 1916 interview with the German newspaper *Berliner Tageblatt*, Talât Pasha explained that 'we have been reproached for making no distinction between the innocent Armenians and the guilty; but that was utterly impossible in view of the fact that those who were innocent today might be guilty tomorrow'.[115] According to this view, Armenian insurgents should be blamed for all civilian deaths.

To secure domestic support, the secular nationalists advanced religious arguments, proclaiming a holy war against Armenians. The Sultan proclaimed the First World War a *jihad*, calling upon Muslims everywhere to 'massacre' Christians living in Muslim lands.[116] Though most amongst their leadership were atheists, the Young Turks were more than happy to use religious injunctions to encourage Muslims to implement government policy. Shortly before the formal proclamation of *jihad*, the Young Turk leadership declared that 'our religious sentiments direct us to free the Muslim world from the domination of the infidels . . . we fight for our nation, our religion and our national ideal'.[117] The proclamation of *jihad* encouraged Turks to participate in the Armenian genocide on the grounds that it was a religious duty.[118]

The genocide was strongly condemned by governments and publics in Europe and North America.[119] Not even Turkey's German ally was willing to publicly defend the genocide and the German consul in Istanbul interceded with the government on several occasions to protect Catholic and Protestant Armenians. Most foreign governments and publics judged that Turkey had seriously overstepped the limit of what could be justified by reference to necessity. Such was the level of criticism that Turkey's right to govern Armenia—previously uncontested—was seriously challenged. Barring a resurgence of American isolationism in the wake of the First World War and profound disagreements amongst the allies over how best to govern post-war Turkey, that right would have been rescinded and Armenia transferred to an international protectorate. That strategic concerns, self-interest, and disagreements overtook moral outrage after 1920 does not diminish the fact that the genocide was widely considered at the time to be a grave crime.

The Turkish community itself was not uniformly supportive of the genocide. In Van, Trebizond, and Urfa, the authorities saw fit to pass decrees

[115] Quoted in Henry Morgenthau, *Secrets of the Bosphorus* (London: Hutchinson, 1918), p. 221.

[116] Text reproduced in Andre N. Mandelstam, *Le sort de l'Empire ottoman* (Lausanne: Payot, 1917), pp. 45–6.

[117] Declaration of 11 November 1914, cited in Yves Ternon, *The Armenians: History of a Genocide*, 2nd edn, trans. Rouben C. Cholakian (Ann Arbor: Caravan Books, 1990), p. 161.

[118] Krikoris Balakian, *Hai Koghkotan* (Beirut: Plenetta Printing, 1977), pp. 227–8.

[119] Akçam, *Shameful Act*, p. 213.

prohibiting Muslims from sheltering Armenians, on penalty of death, suggesting that the practice was widespread.[120] Some local governors, such as Tashin Bey, refused to implement the deportation order. Bey was removed from his post; other uncooperative functionaries were killed.[121] Between September and December 1915, a lone Turkish Senator, Ahmed Riza, publicly raised concerns about the deportations and massacres, describing them as 'inimical to the principles of law and justice'.[122] Immediately after the war, the new Turkish government expressed its own repudiation of the genocide by prosecuting several prominent Young Turk leaders. Among other things, the Young Turks were charged by Turkish courts with the 'massacre and liquidation of the Armenian people'.[123]

Governments and publics in the USA, Britain, and France condemned the massacres and many voices called for the perpetrators to be punished and for Turkey to lose its right to rule the Armenians. On 24 May 1915, Britain, France, and Russia declared that 'in view of these new crimes of Turkey against humanity and civilization the Allied governments announce publicly . . . that they will hold personally responsible . . . all members of the Ottoman government and those of their agents who are implicated in such massacres'.[124] This statement, issued on the insistence of the Russian Foreign Minister Sazanov, was the first to refer to 'crimes against humanity'—Britain and France worrying that the reference to 'crimes against Christianity and civilisation' in the Russian draft would offend Muslims in their empires.[125] Britain listed the punishment of the Turks as one of its central war objectives, writing to President Wilson in December 1916 that it aimed to achieve 'the liberation of nations living under the bloody injustice of the Turks'.[126] France also identified 'the liberation of peoples who now lie beneath the murderous tyranny of the Turks' as one of its 'supreme goals of the war'.[127]

US Ambassador to Turkey, Henry Morgenthau, condemned the killing, whilst prominent commentators such as former President Theodore Roosevelt called for tough action against the Turks. Morgenthau worked hard to alleviate the plight of the Armenians. His memoirs recount several occasions where he approached the Young Turk leadership requesting relief for the Armenians and an end to the killing. He left the Turkish government in no doubt as to the

[120] Walker, 'World War I', p. 267.

[121] Akçam, *Shameful Act*, p. 166.

[122] See Vahakn N. Dadrian, 'A Review of the Main Features of the Genocide', *Journal of Political and Military Sociology*, 22 (1) 1994, pp. 8, 9, n. 47, and p. 25.

[123] Taner Akçam, *From Empire to Republic: Turkish Nationalism and the Armenian Genocide* (London: Zed Books, 2004), p. 166. Also see Ternon, *The Armenians*, p. 211.

[124] *Foreign Relations of the United States*, 1915 Supp. 981 (1928); US National Archives, Record Group 59, 867.4016/67 (28 May).

[125] Akçam, *A Shameful Act*, p. 214.

[126] Akçam, *A Shameful Act*, p. 214.

[127] Akçam, *A Shameful Act*, p. 214.

American position on the genocide.[128] In domestic political circles the principal agitator for intervention on behalf of the Armenians was former president Theodore Roosevelt. Roosevelt described the genocide as 'the greatest crime of the war' and condemned what he saw as the pacifist sentiments that held sway over President Woodrow Wilson, whom he described as an 'abject coward' and 'the worst president since [James] Buchanan'.[129] Indeed, Roosevelt—who had taken America to war with Spain at least in part because of its ill-treatment of the Cubans (see below)—argued that the massacres provided strong grounds for war with Turkey: 'We are guilty of a peculiarly odious form of hypocrisy when we profess friendship for Armenia and the downtrodden races of Turkey, but don't go to war with Turkey'.[130] Several American-based intellectuals and newspaper editors expressed similar views. Bertrand Russell, teaching at Harvard in 1914, wrote that the Turks 'displayed a supremacy in cruelty and barbarism by torturing and degrading the Christians under their rule'.[131] Ezra Pound argued that 'tyranny in the modern world is most visible in . . . the Armenian massacres'.[132] In 1915 alone, the *New York Times* published 145 articles on the genocide, more than half of which were placed in the first three pages of the newspaper.[133] *The Times* used phrases like 'systematic race extermination' to describe what would later be labelled genocide.[134]

Woodrow Wilson was sympathetic to these arguments and after the war tried to persuade Congress to accept a League of Nations mandate for Armenia. In December 1915, Wilson wrote that 'the situation with regard to the Armenians is indeed nothing less than appalling'.[135] But US foreign policy during the genocide was constrained by two considerations, prompting the policy of non-interference so sharply criticized by Roosevelt. First, the Wilson administration was committed to a policy of non-interference in Turkish affairs.[136] Second, some American missionaries in Turkey worried that tough measures would provoke Turkish reprisals against them.[137] After the war, Wilson was unclear about how the principle of self-determination set out in his fourteen points should apply and he ultimately adopted a contradictory stance that gave succour to the Turkish nationalists. Point twelve called for the

[128] See, for example, Morgenthau, *Secrets of the Bosphorous*, pp. 220–1.

[129] Balakian, *Burning Tigris*, pp. 293–4.

[130] In Balakian, *Burning Tigris*, pp. 307–8.

[131] Bertrand Russell, *Pacifism and Revolution 1916–1918* (ed. Richard Pempel) (London: Routledge, 1995), p. 89.

[132] Timothy Materer (ed.), *The Selected Letters of Ezra Pound to John Quinn, 1915–1924* (Durham, NC: Duke University Press, 1991), p. 221.

[133] Marjorie Housepian Dobkin, 'What Genocide? What Holocaust? News from Turkey, 1915–1923: A Case Study', in Hovannisian (ed.), *The Armenian Genocide*, p. 98.

[134] Balakian, *Burning Tigris*, p. 282.

[135] Cited by Balakian, *The Burning Tigris*, p. 304.

[136] Bloxham, *The Great Game*, p. 186.

[137] Balakian, *Burning Tigris*, pp. 305–6.

freeing of races from Turkish misrule and oppression, which was judged to imply at least autonomy for Armenia. But the same point also called for the preservation of a Turkish state covering areas where Turks were in the majority—providing a basis for the denial of Armenian autonomy or independence.[138] Wilson battled with isolationists in the Senate over a proposed League of Nations mandate for Armenia.[139] The President argued that as a great power, the USA had a responsibility to help build a better future for the decimated Armenian population and that without international protection, the Armenians would remain at the mercy of the Turks.[140] He was opposed by Henry Cabot Lodge, a Republican isolationist and Chair of the Senate Foreign Relations Committee. Though not demurring from American condemnation of the genocide, Lodge argued that there were limits to America's international responsibilities.[141]

There were similar reactions in Britain, France, Italy, and Russia to the genocide and Turkey's justifications were widely rejected. Both sides of British politics condemned the Turks, though the liberals were especially animated by what they saw as Britain's historic responsibility for the fate of the Armenians because, in the 1880s, Britain had blocked Russian moves to take control of Armenian populated areas. Liberal Prime Minister Lloyd George described the Turks as 'a cancer on humanity, a wound that has worked its way into the flesh of the earth that it has misruled'.[142] He declared that 'when the peace conditions are announced the Turks will see what heavy punishment will be meted out to them for their madness, their blindness and their crimes. . . . The punishment will be such it will satisfy even their greatest enemies'. Although it was not altogether clear what form the 'punishment' would take, Lloyd George was adamant that Britain would not repeat its past mistakes: 'what would become of Mesopotamia should be left to the Paris congress. Yet there is something that should not be allowed to happen again. The Turks bloody dictatorship [over the Armenians] will not be restored'.[143] *The Times* and *Guardian* voiced their support, publishing an identical article in late 1916 which argued that 'one thing remains to be said about Armenia: the whole people of this country was massacred and cleansed in the worst atrocity the world has ever seen since the birth of Jesus Christ. That country should never

[138] Akçam, *A Shameful Act*, p. 227.

[139] Britain, France, and Italy were all reluctant to assume responsibility for the new republic. See David Lloyd George, *Memoirs of the Peace Conference* (New Haven: Yale University Press, 1939), p. 810.

[140] Balakian, *Burning Tigris*, p. 302.

[141] Balakian, *Burning Tigris*, p. 362. The Senate voted 52–23 against the mandate and almost all the territory set aside for a new Armenian state in Anatolia was reoccupied by the Turks between 1920 and 1922 amid fresh massacres.

[142] Cited by Akçam, *From Empire to Republic*, p. 72.

[143] Akçam, *A Shameful Act*, p. 216.

again and in no conditions be left in the hands of Turkey'.[144] Winston Churchill described the killings as a 'general massacre', noting that 'the clearance of the race from Asia Minor was about as complete as such an act, on a scale so great, could well be . . . there is no reasonable doubt that the crime was planned and executed for political reasons'.[145] These sentiments were widely shared by intellectuals and commentators. Lord Bryce and Arnold Toynbee compiled what remains as one of the most definitive and damning accounts of the genocide.[146] At war's end there was a broad consensus that Turkey should be punished but, as in the USA, strategic considerations were ultimately privileged and Turkey's perpetrators let off the hook.[147] But although Britain continued to call for the prosecution of those responsible for the killings, it became more hesitant in the wake of the Bolshevik revolution to punish Turkey more thoroughly, fearing that this would open the door to the Soviets.[148]

French Foreign Minister, Aristide Briand, insisted that 'France will not forget the terrible trials of the Armenians'.[149] As the genocide progressed, the French military conducted limited interventions to assist Armenians. In August and September 1915, the French Third Naval Squadron rescued around 4,000 Armenian survivors from near Antioch.[150] The Italian government also condemned the genocide, Prime Minister Vittorio Orlando declaring, 'say to the Armenian people that I make their cause my cause'.[151] Russian attitudes were shaped by a mixture of sympathy for the Armenians and a well-established strategic interest in extending Russian influence in the Black Sea region. Both pre- and post-revolution governments in Russia condemned the genocide, the Tsarist regime initiating the joint declaration condemning Turkey's 'crimes against humanity'.[152]

The one prominent exception to this pattern of public condemnation was Turkey's ally, Germany. Not only did Germany not publicly condemn the

144 Cited by Akçam, *A Shameful Act*, p. 235.

145 Winston Churchill, *The World Crisis*, Vol. 5: *The Aftermath* (London: Butterworth, 1929), p. 405.

146 Published as Arnold Toynbee (ed.), *The Treatment of Armenians in the Ottoman Empire*. It was accompanied in the same year by a confidential publication entitled, *Key to Names of Persons and Places Withheld from Publication in the Original Edition of 'The Treatment of Armenians . . .': Documents Presented to Viscount Grey of Fallodan by Viscount Bryce*, Miscellaneous no. 31, 1916.

147 On calls for punitive action, see E. L. Woodward and Rohan Butler (eds), *Documents on British Foreign Policy, 1919–1939*, Vol. 4: (London: HMSO, 1952), p. 661. On the privileging of strategic concerns immediately after the war, see Bloxham, *The Great Game*, p. 138.

148 Akçam, *A Shameful Act*, p. 225.

149 Quoted in *Le Temps*, 7 November 1918, p. 6.

150 Bloxham, *The Great Game*, p. 138.

151 Cited by Hovannisian, 'The Historical Dimensions of the Armenian Question, 1878–1923', in Hovannisian (ed.), *The Armenian Genocide*, p. 31.

152 Bloxham, *The Great Game*, pp. 136–7.

genocide, there were also suggestions that some German officials collaborated with the killing. Other officials and missionaries, like Johannes Lepsius, interceded on the Armenians' behalf and tried to raise the issue with Berlin.[153] In defence of its position, the German government argued that military necessity gave priority to the Turkish alliance.[154] Speaking on the government's behalf, on 29 September 1915, von Jagow told the *Reichstag* that: 'Much as we deplore the fate of the Armenians from the point of view of pure humanity, our sons and brothers are nearer to us than the Armenians. They are spilling their blood in terrible battles and they depend for their security upon Turkey's support. The Turks are rendering us a valuable service by protecting the flank of our military position. You, gentlemen, will agree with me that we could not break off our alliance on account of the Armenian question'. But although it was prepared to tolerate the genocide, Germany did not endorse it and neither did it go out of its way to excuse it.[155]

After the war, the victors agreed to the basic idea of removing Armenians from Turkish rule but differed on how to achieve it. The UK called for an American mandate, which the USA rejected; Wilson suggested that France occupy Anatolia until political arrangements could be established, but France and Italy disagreed about the terms of occupation and France grew increasingly reluctant to make a large military commitment. The punishment of individuals was actively pursued by the British but opposed by the French on the grounds that it created animosity. There were also legal problems owing to the fact that the laws of war did not actually prohibit the mistreatment of a government's own population. The new Turkish government tried to obviate the need for an international tribunal by launching its own trials. They succeeded in taking the momentum away from the British. Finally, the West's preoccupation with Germany, the rise of Bolshevism, and the competition for favour with the post-war Kemalist regime in Turkey, made punishment of Turkey much less of a priority for the great powers.[156] In the end, the Turkish trials collapsed and those Armenians that had not been deported from Anatolia remained under Turkish rule.

[153] Akçam, *A Shameful Act*, p. 214; and Leo Kuper, *Genocide: Its Political Uses in the Twentieth Century* (New Haven: Yale University Press, 1981), p. 107.

[154] Cited by J. Ellis Barker, 'Germany, Turkey and the Armenian Massacres', *Quarterly Review*, no. 233, January–April 1920, p. 385.

[155] Harry Stuermer, 'Germany and the Armenian Atrocities', *Current History*, November 1917, Morgenthau, *Secrets of the Bosphorous*, pp. 246–7; and Vahakn N. Dadrian, 'Documentation of the Armenian Genocide in German and Austrian Sources', in Israel Charny (ed.), *The Widening Circle of Genocide: A Critical Bibliographic Review*, Vol. 3 (New Brunswick: Transaction, 1994), p. 100.

[156] On the competition for favour, see Helen Fein, *Genocide: A Sociological Perspective* (London: Sage, 1993).

## Summary

The use of atrocities to quell domestic uprisings (both real and imagined) was commonly justified as being necessary for the preservation of order. Governments argued that they were entitled to take extraordinary measures to maintain order, even if this meant intentionally killing sometimes large numbers of civilians. In some cases, the use of atrocities *was* limited and constrained by necessity. In such cases, European society tended to tolerate atrocities and accept that states were entitled to sometimes kill civilians. But in at least three cases (the Greek insurrection, Paris commune, and Armenian genocide), atrocities were less constrained and international responses were characterized by sharp condemnation and sometimes punitive action. This suggested that a government's right to kill its own people was not unlimited. In two of these three cases, serious doubt was expressed about the perpetrators' right to rule the victimized people.[157] That condemnation of the Armenian genocide was so widespread points to the fact that popular sovereignty and humanitarianism were helping to reshape attitudes towards mass atrocities, giving necessity somewhat less purchase as a potential source of legitimacy. In this case, Turkey's claim to be doing only that which was necessary for security was widely rejected. After war's end, various political concerns ultimately protected Turkey from international punishment, demonstrating that the consequences that flow from illegitimate behaviour are heavily conditioned by political context.

## REPRISALS AND COUNTER-INSURGENCY

In the early nineteenth century, military law prohibited 'unnecessary' violence against civilians.[158] But in the face of an emerging 'republican' doctrine of war which called entire nations to arms, it was just as widely accepted that regular armies were entitled to kill civilians in reprisal for guerrilla attacks and to summarily execute captured insurgents as murderers.[159] Established states

[157] Martha Finnemore argues that this was part of an emerging right of intervention when Christians were harassed by non-Christian rulers. See Martha Finnemore, *The Purpose of Intervention: Changing Beliefs About the Use of Force* (Ithaca: Cornell University Press, 2003).

[158] Lance Janda, 'Shutting the Gates of Mercy: The American Origins of Total War, 1860–1880', *The Journal of Military History*, 59 (1) 1995, p. 10.

[159] Although hardly new, insurgency warfare became a strategy of choice for nationalist movements by which states defeated in open battle or non-state actors could continue to wage war on the more powerful. For an overview of the issues, see H. Nickerson, 'Mass War Begins' in G. B. Turner (ed.), *A History of Military Affairs* (New York: Harcourt Brace, 1952), p. 32; C. Hesse, 'Silences and the History of Representations of War', *The Journal of Military History*, 57 (5) 1993, pp. 143–4; and Nabulsi, *Traditions of War: Occupation, Resistance and the Law* (Oxford: Oxford University Press, 1999), pp. 177–240.

considered this new form of 'people's war' to be a dangerous development because it repudiated long-standing conventions about who was entitled to wage war, how war might be fought, and when a war might be deemed to have ended. As a French military jurist explained in 1902, 'our goal... is to humanise war, by which we mean that it must be regularised'. Insurgencies constituted 'a certain atrocity... the most terrible aggravation of war'.[160] This view had earlier been forcefully presented by General von Moltke, commander of Prussian forces in the Franco-Prussian War whose army confronted French irregulars—the notorious *francs-tireurs* (see below). It is worth quoting von Moltke at length:

> The [French] government still tries... to rouse the unfortunate population of the provinces to a new resistance, to put down which will entail the destruction of whole towns. Then, too, nagging of the francs-tireurs has to be paid for by bloody reprisals, and the character of the war becomes more vindictive. It is bad enough that armies sometimes have to butcher one another; there is no necessity for setting whole nations against each other—that is not progress, but rather a return to barbarism. How little can even the *levee en masse* of a nation, even so brave a one as this, do against a never so small but well-trained division of troops! Our liberals, who preach the arming of the people, should see its success in this campaign.[161]

In the USA, the 1863 Lieber Code moderated the approach by calling for the humane treatment of civilians whilst subjecting guerrillas to martial law. In practice, during the US Civil War, Generals Sheridan and Sherman granted no quarter to irregulars and in the face of the *francs-tireurs* insurgency in France, Sheridan advised Otto von Bismarck to burn villages in order to terrorize the population into submission—a piece of advice rejected by Prussian commander von Moltke.[162] At the Brussels conference on the limitation of war in 1874, the Russian delegation proposed a ban on volunteer forces that were not subject to sovereign command and insisted that the civilian population in occupied territories 'act in conformity with the laws and usages of war, so as to prevent the struggle becoming cruel and barbarous'.[163] Given that guerrillas seemed to challenge the conventions of war themselves, extraordinary measures—such as reprisal killings—came to be seen as acceptable ways of meeting the threat.

The most prominent justifications for the use of atrocities as a reprisal for insurgency were claims of military necessity supported by the argument that guerrillas were unlawful and immoral. Proponents argued that in such

[160] A. Brenet, *La France et l'Allemagne devant le droit international pendant les operations militaries de la guerre de 1870–1871* (Paris: A. Rousseau, 1902), p. 26.

[161] Cited by John Horne and Alan Kramer, *German Atrocities, 1914: A History of Denial* (New Haven: Yale University Press, 2001), p. 142.

[162] Ian F. W. Beckett, *Modern Insurgencies and Counter-Insurgencies: Guerrillas and their Opponents since 1750* (London: Routledge, 2001), p. 31.

[163] James Lorimer, *The Institutes of the Law of Nations: A Treatise on the Jural Relations of Separate Political Communities*, Vol. 2 (Clark, NJ: Lawbooks Exchange, 2005 [1876]), p. 356.

campaigns 'where a whole population engages in warfare, the distinction between combatant and non-combatant disappears'.[164] It was in relation to reprisals, though, that the rise of humanitarianism had its most noticeable impact during this period. Whereas early in the nineteenth century the right to use reprisals was widely understood, by the early twentieth century many politicians, lawyers, and public commentators in Europe and North America maintained that not even clear necessity could justify reprisals against civilians, a view rejected by German politicians, soldiers, and intellectuals—for which Germany was heavily criticized. As noted earlier (and in Chapter 1), this transformation was formalized by the prohibition of, among other things, the deliberate killing of non-combatants in reprisals, by the 1899 Hague Conventions, though the provisions were limited in scope. Article 50 of the 1899 Convention prohibited the mistreatment of the civilian population in occupied territories, except for that for which it could be 'regarded as jointly or severally responsible', permitting broad latitude to the occupiers.[165]

## The Peninsular War (1808–1814)

The term *guerrilla* (one who fights in a small war) has its origins in the Spanish insurgency against Napoleon between 1808 and 1814. After the effective collapse of the Spanish army in the face of the French invasion, various guerrilla groups launched insurgencies against French forces. The French responded by refusing quarter, summarily executing captured insurgents, and employing reprisals against the civilian population. In campaigns in Aragon and Navarre (1808–09), French forces killed any individual, including priests, found in possession of weapons, utterly destroyed any town or village that offered resistance, plundered cattle, and assumed that anyone absent from their home was a guerrilla and should be treated accordingly.[166] After the fall of Tarragona to the French in 1811, some 15,000 residents—guerrillas and civilians alike—were massacred as a reprisal for the death of French troops and as a warning to others.[167] The French justified their strategy by arguing that the insurgents had placed themselves and the civilian population beyond legal and moral protection, that they and their supporters were bandits not soldiers, and that guerrilla tactics made it

[164] Dunbar Rowland, *Andrew Jackson's Campaign Against the British* (New York: Ayer co., 1926), p. 159.

[165] Lassa Oppenheim, *International Law* (London: Longman, 1912), pp. 175–6.

[166] Don W. Alexander, *Rod of Iron: French Counterinsurgency Policy in Aragon During the Peninsular War* (Washington, Delaware: Scholarly Resources Inc., 1985), pp. 24–7; and John Lawrence Tone, *The Fatal Knot: The Guerrilla War in Navarre and the Defeat of Napoleon in Spain* (Chapel Hill: University of North Carolina Press, 1994), p. 86.

[167] Martyn Lyons, *Napoleon Bonaparte and the Legacy of the French Revolution* (New York: St. Martin's Press, 1994), p. 223.

impossible to distinguish soldiers from civilians, making every Spaniard a potential guerrilla and therefore a legitimate target.[168]

Despite being at war with France, Britain generally accepted these justifications. William Napier, a British government observer in Spain, insisted that 'all armies have the incontestable right to defend themselves when they are engaged in hostilities. An insurrection of armed peasants is military anarchy' and in such circumstances 'men cannot be restricted in the customs of regular war'. Thus, 'despite the apparent injustice', the French had every right to refuse quarter and burn villages, because these acts rested on 'the principle of necessity'.[169] Indeed, the British themselves expressed revulsion at atrocities committed by Spanish irregulars. As Sir Thomas Graham put it in 1810, 'we never can have such allies again, bad as their conduct often has been and much as we have daily reason to complain of it'.[170] Wellington himself hardly ever mentioned the guerrillas in his despatches and on one of the rare occasions where he did, wrote that the war's barbarism was largely 'occasioned by the irregularities of the soldiers, and their cruelties authorised and encouraged by their chiefs'.[171] After initial shock at French reprisals, British commentators on the peninsular war observed that 'the cruelty complained of was only the infliction of legitimate punishment for such conduct [on the part of the guerrillas]'.[172] The British viewed the 'cruel insurgents' as 'almost useless in any serious operation'.[173] Indeed, Napier noted that Spain's 'undisciplined bands' were as big a threat to the country as the enemy.[174] What this demonstrates for our purposes is that at the beginning of the nineteenth century, governments enjoyed a broadly recognized right to kill civilians as reprisals against guerrilla warfare.

## Prussia and the francs-tireurs (1870–1871)

Prussia's campaign against the *francs-tireurs*—groups of French civilians who launched insurgency attacks against occupying Prussian forces in

[168] Nablusi, *Traditions of War*, p. 31; and Alexander, *Rod of Iron*, pp. 26–7.

[169] In Nablusi, *Traditions of War*, p. 30.

[170] Graham to Bunbury, 12 July 1810, in Charles Esdaile, 'War and Politics in Spain, 1808–14', *The Historical Journal*, 31 (2) 1988, p. 317.

[171] Wellington, General Order, 9 July 1813, in Antony Brett-James (ed.), *Wellington at War 1794–1815: A Selection of His Wartime Letters* (London: Macmillan and Co., 1961), p. 271. On the absence of references in Wellington's despatches, see Walter Laqueur, *Guerrilla: A Historical and Critical Study* (London: Weidenfeld and Nicolson, 1977), p. 39.

[172] *Napier's Peninsular War*, Vol. II, p. 451, reported in 'On the Limits of Irregular Warfare', *The Times*, 22 October 1870, p. 22.

[173] Wellington cited by Gunther Rothenberg, 'Age of Napoleon' in Michael Howard, George J. Andreopoulos, and Mark R. Shulman (eds), *The Laws of War: Constraints on Warfare in the Western World* (New Haven: Yale University Press, 1994), p. 96.

[174] Laqueur, *Guerrilla*, p. 39.

1870–71—marked an important turning point for the legitimacy of reprisals. French insurgents were refused quarter and summarily executed as criminals. Civilians were killed to deter insurgent activities, used as human shields, and executed as reprisals for the killing of Prussian troops.[175] Although Prussia presented a coherent defence of its actions and many observers were deeply sympathetic to its *casus belli*, it was widely criticized nevertheless. Indeed, Prussia's use of atrocities helped turn international opinion against its role in the Franco-Prussian War.

The Prussian case rested on its claim that necessity was a legal principle that granted occupying powers a right to use reprisals when confronting illegal insurrections by irregular soldiers. Prussian military thinking distinguished between *Kriegsmanier* (custom of war) and *Kriegraison* (reason of war) whereby the former was binding in ordinary circumstances but was overridden by the latter in times of necessity.[176] Indeed, the Prussians argued that it was a soldier's *duty* to maintain or restore public order by setting aside the customs of war when faced with insurgents.[177] Thus, Crown Prince Friedreich noted in his diary that reprisals were 'ghastly, but necessary to prevent worse misfortune'.[178]

The use of atrocities was criticized in a Europe not unsympathetic to Prussia's case for war. British public and government opinion sided firmly with Prussia at the beginning of the war, believing that France had provoked conflict on the feeblest pretext. Prussia also found some initial support for its counter-insurgency. According to one correspondent in *The Times*, 'The Germans . . . have no alternative but to put down by every means in their power those disguised combatants, and the responsibility for these and all other consequences of the employment of soldiers without uniforms rests with the French'.[179] Similar views were expressed in the American media, where blame was apportioned equally to both sides.[180] Over time, however, British opinion changed, largely as a result of the humanitarian effects of the siege of

[175] See Michael Howard, *The Franco-Prussian War: The German Invasion of France, 1870–1871* (London: Rupert Hart-Davis, 1961), p. 251; Thomas Rockrämer, 'Daily Life at the Front and the Concept of Total War', in Stig Förster and Jorg Nagler (eds), *On the Road to Total War: The American Civil War and the German Wars of Unification 1861–1871* (Cambridge: Cambridge University Press), p. 508. Individual towns were sometimes forced to pay compensation for 'criminal' attacks on Prussian forces. Geoffrey Wawro, *The Franco-Prussian War: The German Conquest of France in 1870–1871* (Cambridge: Cambridge University Press, 2003), p. 238; Mark R. Stoneman, 'The Bavarian Army and French Civilians in the War of 1870–1871: A Cultural Interpretation', *War in History*, 8 (3) 2001, p. 273; Manfred Messerschmidt, 'The Prussian Army From Reform to War', in Förster and Nagler (eds), *On the Road to Total War*, p. 277.

[176] J. Stone, *Legal Controls of International Conflict: A Treatise on the Dynamics of Disputes and War-Law* (London: Stevens, 1959), p. 352.

[177] Nablusi, *Traditions of War*, p. 31.

[178] H. O. Meisner (ed.), *Kaiser Friedreich III: Das Kriegstagbuch von 1870/1871* (Berlin: Mittler, 1926), p. 78; and Wawro, *The Franco-Prussian War*.

[179] 'On the Just Limits of Irregular Warfare', *The Times*, 22 October 1870, p. 7.

[180] 'The Stories of Prussian Cruelties', *New York Times*, 1 November 1870, p. 4.

Paris and Prussian reprisals against civilians. Indeed, the commander of the forces besieging the city, Von Moltke, was reluctant to bombard Paris partly because he feared that moral outrage in Britain might compel the government there to adopt a pro-French position.[181] This view demonstrated a good understanding of British attitudes. Writing in *The Times*, Edward Hamley described Prussia's war conduct as 'horrible'. The requisition of civilian goods by the army was 'nothing but a system of organised plunder' and their method of combating the *francs-tireurs* best described as a 'system of terrorism'.[182] Prussia's war conduct was even criticized by Prussian Crown Prince, Frederick III, who described von Moltke's strategy as a 'war of extermination' and complained about the summary execution of French civilians on the slenderest of pretexts.[183]

## Cuba (1898) and the Boer War (1900–1902)

Reaction to Spanish reprisals against Cuban non-combatants in 1898 and British tactics against Boer insurgents and civilians from 1900 provide further evidence of the reduction of necessity as a plausible justification for reprisals against civilians. In the Cuban case, the use of reprisals by Spain against Cuban civilians prompted consternation in the USA, creating an impetus for military intervention that reached a crescendo after the sinking of the *USS Maine.*[184] In the Boer case, Britain presented a legal defence of reprisals that failed to stem the tide of criticism from domestic liberals.

After trying, and failing, with alternative counter-insurgency strategies, in 1896 Spain reacted to a nationalist insurgency in Cuba with a strategy characterized by *reconcentration.* The result was 'one of the most terrible catastrophes in the history of the Americas'.[185] Civilians in sensitive areas were ordered to remove themselves to camps near military headquarters and were not permitted to travel without permission. Military commanders were authorized to take summary action against suspected insurgents and people suspected of aiding insurgents were made subject to martial law.[186] Conditions in the camps were atrocious, with food and water shortages, disease, and a draconian punitive system. By 1898, half a million people had been uprooted from their homes and around 100,000 Cuban civilians had died as a result of *reconcentration*, though some extravagant American reports put

[181] Howard, *Franco-Prussian War*, p. 256.

[182] *The Times*, 22 February 1871.

[183] See Howard, *Franco-Prussian War*, pp. 378–8, n. 6.

[184] Wrongly attributed to Spanish action at the time. It is now commonly thought that the sinking was caused by an explosion in an arms store on the ship.

[185] John Lawrence Tone, *War and Genocide in Cuba, 1895–1898* (Chapel Hill: University of North Carolina Press, 2006), p. 193.

[186] David F. Trask, *The War with Spain in 1898* (New York: Macmillan, 1981), p. 8.

that figure at 400,000.[187] General Weyler, the commander of Spanish forces in Cuba, justified the strategy as a lawful response to guerrilla warfare, noting after the event (in 1906) that both the British (in the Boer War, below) and Americans (in the Philippines, 1899–1902) had used identical tactics. Weyler also pointed to decrees issued by Union commanders during the US Civil War demanding the evacuation of civilians from Confederate areas as a precedent for his policy.[188]

Among European governments there was considerable sympathy for the Spanish position. The Kaiser insisted that Spain was entitled to use whatever measures it thought necessary to suppress the rebellion, a view endorsed by the French, Austrian, and Russian governments.[189] Indeed, American Naval officer and scholar, French Ensor Chadwick has commented that *reconcentration* was unexceptional and conformed with the rules of war as they were understood at the time.[190] In 1902, when the US government reconsidered Weyler's strategy in light of its own experiences in the Philippines, it concluded that the Spanish had not violated accepted military practice.[191] But these were minority elite opinions and none of the European governments that sympathized with Spain's position were prepared to take a stand against the USA. Politicians and the popular press in the US vigorously condemned *reconcentration* and cited it as a *casus belli* for war with Spain.

The American media published accounts of Spanish atrocities and generally (with a few exceptions) sided with the 'Cuban patriots'.[192] For example, on 17 May 1896, *New York World* wrote of 'blood on the roadsides, blood in the fields, blood on the doorsteps . . .' and Joseph Pullitzer's *World* warned that 'a new Armenia lies within eighty miles of the American coast'.[193] Theodore Roosevelt argued the case for war with Spain, as did conservative Senator Redfield Proctor (Vermont). Proctor described Weyler's strategy as 'barbarity' and argued that misgovernment and mistreatment meted out to Cuba constituted grounds for war.[194] The sinking of the *USS Maine* in Havana harbour,

[187] See Ernest R. May, *Imperial Democracy: The Emergence of America as a Great Power* (New York: Harcourt, Brace and World, 1961), p. 127; and Phillip S. Foner, *The Spanish-Cuban-American War and the Birth of American Imperialism, 1895–1902*, Vol. 1. (New York: Monthly Review Press, 1972), p. 77.

[188] Valeriano Weyler y Nicolau, *Mi mando en Cuba: historia militar politica de la última guerra separatista*, Vol. 1 (Madrid: Felipe, 1906), p. 25. The strategy was also used in the Caucuses by Russia in the 1840s and had echoes in the US policy of housing its indigenous peoples on reservations. See Beckett, *Modern Insurgencies*, p. 36.

[189] See Trask, *War with Spain*, pp. 45–6.

[190] Tone, *War and Genocide*, p. 195.

[191] Tone, *War and Genocide*, p. 195.

[192] See, for instance, *The Cuban Crisis as Reflected in the New York Press (1895–1898)* (New York: Octagon Books, 1965), pp. 94, 201–2, and 233–4.

[193] Both cited by Tone, *War and Genocide*, p. 218.

[194] The *Wall Street Journal* reported that Proctor's speech converted many to the cause of war with Spain. See David Traxel, *1898: The Birth of the American Century* (New York: Alfred Knopf, 1998), pp. 116–17.

described as 'dirty [Spanish] treachery' by the US media, strengthened the war-party's case.[195] When President McKinley requested Congressional authority to intervene in Cuba, he listed ending the bloodshed in Cuba, protecting US citizens, precluding further damage to trade and property, and removing a menace to peace as his reasons.[196] Thus, Spanish mistreatment of Cuban civilians played a prominent role in prompting US intervention.

After early successes, Boer rebels in British South Africa were gradually defeated in the field and from late 1900 resorted to guerrilla tactics.[197] This presented the British forces with major problems. As Winston Churchill explained:

> [t]he roving enemy wore no uniforms... they mingled with the population, lodged and were succoured in farmhouses... and sprang into being, now here, now there, to make some formidable and bloody attack upon an unwary column or isolated post. To cope with all this the British military authorities found it necessary to clear whole districts of their inhabitants and gather the population into concentration camps.[198]

The British burnt farms (over 30,000) and removed civilians to concentration camps. At its peak, over 116,000 Boers were housed in concentration camps and between June 1901 and May 1902 around 18,150 died of disease, most of them women and children.[199] The British argued that it was legitimate to treat Boer insurgents as criminals rather than soldiers and that, once caught, they should be executed. Unlike Cuba, though, civilians were rarely executed without trial and the British provided medical assistance to civilians and rebels alike.[200]

Britain offered two arguments to justify its strategy. First and most important, it argued that because the Boers were engaged in an insurgency, the normal rules of war gave way to considerations of military necessity. The British government argued that 'it became a military necessity to destroy all the resources of the Boers in the field' including buildings, food, and cattle.[201] As the insurgents were using Boer farms as bases, farmers were providing rebels with provisions, and the rebels were hiding amongst civilians, it was

[195] See Richard Gott, *Cuba: A New History*, p. 99.

[196] President McKinley, Message to Congress, 11 April 1898. See May, *Imperial Democracy*, p. 157; and Trask, *War with Spain*, p. 52.

[197] See Denis Judd and Keith Sturridge, *The Boer War* (London: John Murray, 2003), p. 187.

[198] Winston Churchill, *My Early Life 1874–1904* (London: Scribner, 1966), p. 369.

[199] For a balanced account, see A. C. Martin, *The Concentration Camps 1900–1902: Facts, Figures and Fables* (Cape Town: Howard Timmins, 1957), p. 6.

[200] See Byron Farwell, *The Great Anglo-Boer War* (New York: Harper and Row, 1976), pp. 334–5 and 349. On at least one occasion in 1901, however, Kitchener proposed the complete removal of the Boers from southern Africa as punishment. Bill Nasson, *The South African War 1899–1902* (London: Arnold, 1999), p. 210.

[201] S. B. Spies, *Methods of Barbarism? Roberts and Kitchener and Civilians in the Boer Republics January 1900–May 1902* (Cape Town: Human & Rousseau, 1977), p. 19.

impossible to engage the insurgents directly. Attacking farms was seen as the only effective way of prosecuting the war.[202] Second, the government argued that because the Boers were not signatories to the Hague Convention's rules on land warfare and were not conducting regular military operations, the rules of war did not apply. In this context, reprisals against Boers were not unlawful. Although this argument won some support (from the German government, for instance) it was rejected by many liberals on the grounds that emerging international humanitarian law (and especially the 'Martens principle') applied irrespective of whether the Boers had signed the Hague treaty and that the laws of war did not reflect the moral standards expected by liberal society.[203] In other words, British behaviour might be legal, but it was not legitimate.

The German government validated the British strategy. Germany's official account of the Boer War insisted that after mid 1901, 'those [Boers] still in the field were often no longer recognisable externally as combatants'.[204] By contrast, British liberals were scathing in their condemnation. The leader of the Liberal opposition party, Sir Henry Campbell-Bannerman asked 'when is a war not a war? When it is carried on by methods of barbarism in South Africa'.[205] Likewise, future British Prime Minister, Lloyd George, condemned the 'scorched earth' policy.[206] Emily Hobhouse established the Women's South Africa Conciliation Committee to lobby government to improve conditions in the camps and expose the appalling conditions there, causing immense embarrassment to the British government.[207]

## German Reprisals in Belgium (1914)

The liberal argument against reprisals evident in the Cuban and Boer cases became a principled consensus amongst the First World War allied powers in the wake of German reprisals against Belgian civilians. Although there is little evidence of concerted Belgian resistance to German occupation, the diaries of German soldiers show that they believed themselves to be subject to a new *francs-tireurs* insurgency.[208] In response, the German army summarily

202 Martin, *The Concentration Camps*, p. 5.

203 A. Pearce Higgins, *The Hague Peace Conferences and Other International Conferences Concerning the Laws and Usages of War: Texts of Conventions with Commentaries* (Cambridge: Cambridge University Press, 1909), p. 211; and Spies, *Methods of Barbarism*, pp. 11–19.

204 Cited by David James, *Lord Roberts* (London: Hollis and Carter, 1954), p. 358.

205 Cited by Judd and Sturridge, *The Boer War*, p. 194.

206 See David Nash, 'The Boer War and its Humanitarian Critics', *History Today*, 49 (6), 1999, p. 43.

207 Martin, *The Concentration Camps*, pp. 22–3; and Nash, 'The Boer War', p. 49.

208 John Horne and Alan Kramer, 'War Between Soldiers and Civilians, 1914–1915', in Roger Chickering and Stig Förster (eds), *Great War, Total War: Combat and Mobilization on the Western Front, 1914–1918* (Cambridge: Cambridge University Press, 2000), p. 163; and Horne and Kramer, *German Atrocities*, e.g. pp. 96–7.

executed civilians suspected of assisting the rebels, massacred hundreds of civilians as punishment for attacks on German troops, took hostages, used human shields, and burnt property, including the university library at Louvain.[209] In total, approximately 5,000–6,000 Belgian civilians were killed in German reprisals.[210]

The German government justified its actions by applying a modified version of the justifications offered by the British in the Boer War. Rather than arguing, as the British had done, that the laws of war did not apply to insurgents, Germany argued that the rebels violated the law and behaved contrary to the morality of war. Thus, unlawful insurgency activity was rightly met with 'just punishment' by German troops.[211] The moral responsibility for reprisals, they argued, should lie with the Belgian government, which had initiated and supported an unlawful rebellion.[212] These justifications drew on ideas that had become deeply ingrained in German military thinking. In 1878, Prussian strategist Julius von Hartmann had written that 'where the People's War breaks out, terrorism becomes a principle of military necessity'.[213] The German *War Book* published in 1902, confirmed this view. It insisted that only soldiers wearing proper insignia were entitled to belligerent status; anyone else engaging in combat was to be regarded as a criminal and treated accordingly.[214] These ideas also found their way into military training. Officers were taught to expect civilian resistance and that such resistance was unlawful. They were taught that aspects of the Hague Conventions that might lend protection to insurgents (such as Article 2) 'did not comply with the German viewpoint, since it opened the door to *franc-tireur* war'.[215]

These arguments cut very little ice with international society, as the German army itself recognized.[216] The British response was summed up by the lawyer

[209] Documented in Horne and Kramer, *German Atrocities*, pp. 8–40; and contemporaneously by Arnold J. Toynbee, *The German Terror in Belgium* (London: Hodder and Stoughton, 1917) and a commission of inquiry chaired by Lord Bryce.

[210] Horne and Kramer, 'War Between Soldiers', pp. 156–7. The Germans were not alone in employing reprisals during the First World War. Hungarian forces operating in Serbia killed approximately 2,000 Serb civilians 'under circumstances of the most revolting cruelty'. R. W. Seton-Watson and George M. Trevelyan, press release, February 1915 in R. W. Seton-Watson, *R. W. Seton-Watson and the Yugoslavs: Correspondence, 1906–1941*, Vol. 1 (London: British Academy, 1976), p. 197.

[211] Also see Horne and Kramer, 'German "Atrocities"', p. 10.

[212] Barbara W. Tuchman, *August 1914* (London: Constable, 1962), pp. 309 and 312; and J. H. Morgan, *A Dishonoured Army: German Atrocities in France* (London: Spottiswoode, 1916), pp. 23–4.

[213] Cited in Horne and Kramer, *German Atrocities*, p. 143.

[214] Nicolleta F. Gullace, 'Sexual Violence and Family Honor: British Propaganda and International Law during the First World War', *American Historical Review*, 102 (3), p. 741.

[215] See Horne and Kramer, *German Atrocities*, pp. 149–50.

[216] Tuchman, *August 1914*, p. 314.

Coleman Phillipson. Phillipson argued that 'the Germans resorted to proceedings which are not only inadmissible from the humanitarian standpoint, but are directly prohibited by the Hague regulations'.[217] Lord Bryce commented in a letter to an American correspondent that 'surely the main principle of all warfare by land and sea is that the lives of noncombatants must not be taken.... The Germans, however, seem to have no respect for innocent life whatever. They murdered thousands of non-combatants in Belgium without remorse on the allegation that here and there somebody, being a civilian, had shot at their troops'.[218] Similar arguments were presented in the media: *The Times* described the burning of Louvain as 'a ruthless holocaust'.[219] This rejection of the claim that necessity justified reprisals against civilians was supported by Allied arguments focusing on German crimes against women and children. In particular, the Belgian government argued that German 'atrocities are beyond counting' and that 'the civilian population is massacred, the inhabitants are killed, women and children are brutalised in the most odious fashion'.[220] Rejecting the claim of military necessity was also fundamental to British appeals for American intervention. According to Lord Bryce, the case for American intervention centred not on Belgian neutrality, the balance of power or Germany's territorial ambitions, but on the massacre of Belgian civilians.[221] Although American officials and media reports expressed some scepticism about the more sensational reports, outrage at the atrocities helped turn public opinion against Germany. Indeed, *The New York Tribune* insisted that the sexual abuse of Belgian women was a crime worse than the killing of Americans aboard the *Lusitania*.[222]

## Summary

During the nineteenth and early twentieth centuries, the doctrine of reprisals against civilians as a response to guerrilla warfare was transformed from a basic legal principle to a practice widely seen as illegitimate. Although governments continued to argue about its legality and the applicability of the Hague Conventions to irregular war, from the 1860s onwards liberals in North

[217] Coleman Phillipson, *International Law and the Great War* (London: T. Fisher Unwin, 1915), p. 149.

[218] Cited by Gullace, 'Sexual Violence, p. 733.

[219] 'The Crime of Louvain', *The Times*, 3 September 1914, p. 4.

[220] Both cited in Horne and Kramer, *German Atrocities*, p. 177.

[221] Bryce to Eliot, 1 July 1915, in Gullace, 'Sexual Violence', p. 738.

[222] On American attitudes to the reports and the way that atrocity stories helped change public opinion, see Trevor Wilson, *The Myriad Faces of War: Britain and the Great War 1914–1918* (Oxford: Polity Press, 1986), p. 190; and Kevin J. O'Keefe, *A Thousand Deadlines: The New York City Press and American Neutrality, 1914–17* (The Hague: Martinus Nijhoff, 1972), pp. 26–33.

America and Britain criticized the killing of civilians, even in cases where much of the killing was indirect or unintended (as in the Boer War). In two cases (Cuba and the First World War), liberal reactions against reprisals contributed support for intervention against the perpetrators while in two other cases (Franco-Prussian War and the Boer War), reprisals turned domestic and/or international opinion against those who employed them. But the laws of war did not catch up with these liberal sensibilities until after the Second World War. The Nuremberg tribunal limited the scope of reprisals by finding that collective punishment was only lawful if the victims were demonstrably integrated within an organization guilty of some unlawful act and the 1949 Geneva Conventions prohibited the collective punishment and intimidation of non-combatants in occupied territories and 'reprisals against protected persons'.[223]

## COLONIAL TERROR AND SELECTIVE EXTERMINATION

Between 1789 and the Second World War, Western states waged almost perpetual war outside Europe, much of it against civilian populations. Fifty-eight full-scale wars were waged outside Europe between 1807 and 1912 and force was used to suppress uprisings on many more occasions.[224] In addition to the cases described below, atrocities was used by the British to suppress opponents in southern Rhodesia, Uganda, and India;[225] by Australian settlers to clear the land of indigenous peoples;[226] by the Italians in Abyssinia (1935–39) where some 250,000 Ethiopians were killed many in summary mass killings and gas attacks;[227] by the Dutch in Java;[228] by the USA in the Philippines

[223] Convention IV, articles 33 and 34. See Geoffrey Best, *War and Law Since 1945* (Oxford: Clarendon Press, 1994), pp. 192–5 and 311–18.

[224] Halpern, *War and Social Change*, pp. 6–7.

[225] See Sir Henry Colville, *The Land of Nile Springs: Being Chiefly an Account of How We Fought Kabarega* (London: Edward Arnold, 1895); Robert Pickering Ashe, *Chronicles of Uganda*, 2nd edn (London: Frank Cass, 1971); John Beattie, *Bunyoro: An African Kingdom* (New York: Holt, Rinehart and Winston, 1960).

[226] Ben Kiernan, *Blood and Soil: A World History of Genocide and Extermination from Sparta to Darfur* (Yale: Yale University Press, 2007), pp. 249–309.

[227] The Italian colonial minister imagined an 'Ethiopia without Ethiopians'. Enzo Traverso, *Origins of Nazi Violence*, trans. Janet Lloyd (New York: New Press, 1996), p. 61. Graziani, the Italian viceroy in Ethiopia, adopted a policy of mass executions and deliberately gassed non-combatants in order to terrorize the population into submission. Also see Angelo Del Boca, *The Ethiopian War 1935–1941* (Chicago: University of Chicago Press, 1965), p. 214; and John Gooch, 'Re-Conquest and Suppression: Fascist Italy's Pacification of Libya and Ethiopia, 1922–39', *Journal of Strategic Studies*, 28 (6) 2005, pp. 1006 and 1022.

[228] Michael Adas, *Prophets of Rebellion: Millenarian Protest Movements Against the European Colonial Order* (Chapel Hill: University of North Carolina Press, 1979), pp. 174–80.

(1899–1902) at the cost of some 200,000 lives;[229] and in German East Africa (Tanzania) as well as South West Africa.[230] In their colonial territories, the great powers were much less inhibited in their use of mass atrocities than they were in Europe. They justified their killing by reference to an ideology of selective extermination that was structurally similar to that used to justify the totalitarian mass killing of the twentieth century (see Chapter 3).

Colonial ideologies of selective extermination rested on two claims—the first excused mass killing, whilst the second made a virtue of it. First, it was commonly maintained that moral and legal protections applied only to 'civilized' peoples. For instance, in 1923, Reeves argued that 'international law is not applicable to uncivilised peoples and could have no influence upon them. It is merely a body of rules and customs that have grown up among nations more or less similar for use among themselves'.[231] Likewise, Colonel Fuller of the British army argued that 'against peoples possessing a low civilisation, war must be more brutal in type' a position endorsed by the 1914 British manual of military law which held that 'the rules of international law apply only to warfare between civilised nations . . . they do not apply in wars with uncivilised states and tribes where their place is taken by the discretion of the commander'.[232] Some leading British thinkers continued to make this argument even into the Second World War. In 1942, the British refused to countenance the prosecution of Italians for crimes committed in Abyssinia on the grounds that it considered that country 'outside the confines of European statesmanship'.[233] This attitude was also expressed during an American Senate Committee exploring US conduct in the Philippines (in 1900). Asked whether American conduct exceeded the bounds of 'civilised warfare', General Robert Hughes replied simply that 'these people [Filipinos] are not civilized'.[234] Likewise, an American newspaper correspondent in Manila wrote in 1900 that colonial forces 'do not regard the shooting of

[229] Stuart Creighton Miller, *'Benevolent Assimilation': The American Conquest of the Philippines, 1899–1903* (New Haven: Yale University Press, 1982).

[230] Thomas Pakenham, *The Scramble for Africa, 1876–1912* (London: Weidenfeld and Nicolson, 1997), p. 620. In 1899, the German authorities near Kilimanjaro killed 2,000 Africans who refused to pay a 'hut tax'. Hans Wagener, *Falsche Propheten: Gouverneur von Liebert und seine Presse* (Charlottenburg: 1900).

[231] Cited in Elbridge Colby, 'How to Fight Savage Tribes', *American Journal of International Law*, 21 (2) 1927, pp. 279–80.

[232] Fuller, *'The Reformation of War'*, p. 191. Also see British War Office, *British Manual of Military Law*, 1914, p. 235, para. 7.

[233] This wording comes from a 1942 Foreign Office Memorandum, cited in Richard Pankhurst, 'Italian Fascist War Crimes in Ethiopia: A History of Their Discussion, from the League of Nations to the United Nations', *Northeast African Studies*, 6 (1–2) 1999, pp. 89 and 93.

[234] Cited by Helmut Walser Smith, 'The Logic of Colonial Violence: Germany in Southwest Africa (1904–1907); the United States in the Philippines (1899–1902)', in Hartmann Lehmann and Hermann Wellenreuther (eds), *German and American Nationalism: A Comparative Perspective* (Oxford: Berg, 1999), p. 225.

Filipinos just as they would the shooting of white troops . . . the soldiers feel they are fighting with savages'.[235]

Excluding colonized peoples from the moral and legal protections that inhered between 'civilized' peoples could excuse their mass killing. The second basic component of the colonial ideology of selective extermination—the colonists' 'civilising mission'—sometimes helped make a virtue of it. A significant amount of colonial violence was framed by what David Maybury-Lewis described as 'metanarratives of modernity' and in particular the idea of progress.[236] The annihilation of indigenous Tasmanians, for instance, was partly justified as an attempt to 'bring them to civilisation'.[237] This line of thinking was underwritten by popular philosophers of government and law at the time. For example, John Locke's influential theory of government provided grounds for justifying colonial expansion by maintaining that only those who cultivated the land were entitled to own it—separating out the rights owing to 'civilized' peoples and 'uncivilized', though in applying it specifically to the North American case Locke wrongly assumed that indigenous Americans did not cultivate the land.[238] Noted international lawyer Emmerich de Vattel shared Locke's view that colonization of uncultivated lands was entirely lawful because cultivation was a sign of civilization. Uncivilized peoples had no such rights to government, property, and security. The potentially genocidal logic of this line of thinking was not lost on the Swiss lawyer. He accepted that 'nations are justified in uniting together as a body with the object of punishing, and even exterminating, such savage peoples'.[239] Of course, as I noted in the Introduction, the 'civilizing mission' was also sometimes employed by those opposing the abuse of colonized peoples and calling for restraint. Most notably, British liberals referred to this principle in their denunciation of Leopold's excesses in the Congo (see below).

This ideology helped permit and sometimes valourize the mass killing of non-Europeans even for some of those noted for their commitment to humanistic values and criticism of atrocities in the European world. Most obvious as an example of how the different moral worlds produced radically

[235] H. L. Wells, *The Watchman* (Boston), 27 July 1900, cited in Richard E. Welch Jr., 'American Atrocities in the Philippines: The Indictment and the Response', *Pacific Historical Review*, XLIII (2), 1974, p. 241.

[236] David Maybury-Lewis, 'Genocide Against Indigenous People', in Alexander Laban Hinton (ed.), *Annihilating Difference: The Anthropology of Genocide* (Berkeley: University of California Press, 2002), p. 45.

[237] Maybury-Lewis, 'Genocide', p. 45.

[238] John Locke, *Second Treatise of Government* (New York: Pearson Education, 1952 [1690]). In fact, some indigenous groups, including the Cherokee, did cultivate land. See Kiernan, *Blood and Soil*, p. 329.

[239] Emmerich de Vattel, *The Law of Nations or the Principles of Natural Law Applied to the Conduct and to the Affairs of Nations and of Sovereigns*, trans. C. G. Fenwick (Washington, DC: Carnegie Institution, 1916 [1758]), p. 246.

different understandings about the legitimacy of mass killing is the position of Theodore Roosevelt. We noted earlier that Roosevelt was a strident critic of Spanish atrocities in Cuba and of the Armenian genocide, arguing in relation to both that the USA ought to intervene to punish the perpetrators. Matters were very different, however, when it came to the killing of indigenous American civilians. Roosevelt described the massacre of 105 indigenous men and women and 28 men by forces under the command of a former Methodist minister, Colonel Chivington, at Sand Creek in 1864, as 'as righteous and beneficial a deed as ever took place on the frontier'.[240] Thanks to this ideology of selective extermination, killing indigenous and colonized peoples was seen in some quarters as morally and legally blameless because these peoples were not as endowed with human faculties and rights as Europeans. Sometimes it was portrayed as necessary for human progress. For those committed to new anthropological sciences and Social Darwinism, the extinction of indigenous and colonized peoples was a natural inevitability—a product, simply, of their biological inferiority and not of European malfeasance.

Colonial atrocities occasionally elicited criticism, principally (but not exclusively) from liberals and socialists who rejected the idea that ordinary morality did not apply in the colonial world and held that the 'civilizing mission' established a duty to care for colonized peoples.[241] Governments were generally reluctant to criticize each other in all but the most extreme cases, principally because of the broad consensus around the two claims set out above and concerns about the legitimacy of their own conduct. In the remainder of this section I consider three illustrative cases of colonial terror employed to acquire and clear land for settlement (in the American west), secure economic gain (Leopold's Congo), and repress a rebellion (the annihilation of the Herero).

## Settlement and Pacification in America (*c.* 1830–1875)

Mass atrocities characterized relations between Europeans and indigenous Americans from the first settlement of Europeans in 1607. Taken together, the various campaigns of mass killing, forced displacement, biological killing, enslavement, and deliberate starvation constitute history's longest, and one of its most 'successful', periods of genocide. Whereas the indigenous population of North America stood at around seven to ten million in 1600, only 237,000

[240] Cited in Paul R. Bartrop, 'Punitive Expeditions and Massacres' in A. Dirk Moses (ed.), *Genocide and Settler Society: Frontier Violence and Stolen Indigenous Children in Australian History* (New York: Berghahn Books, 2004), p. 209.

[241] For an example from Winston Churchill, see Shula Marks, 'Class, Ideology and the Bhambatha Rebellion' in Donald Crummey (ed.), *Banditry, Rebellion and Social Protest in Africa* (London: James Currey, 1986), p. 352.

remained in the 1890s.[242] Mass atrocities directly accounted for only a small fraction of this massive population decline, but they helped establish the context that enabled disease, hunger, and depredation to exert a massive toll.[243] Indigenous peoples in Australia shared a similar fate, with their population declining from around 750,000 in 1788 when the first colonists arrived to 31,000 by 1911.[244] Although it may not have directly accounted for the demographic decline of indigenous America, genocidal mass killing was certainly responsible for the virtual extinction of more than one indigenous nation. The fate of north California's Yuki people stands out only because of the rapidity of their demise. The fall of Mexican California and ensuing gold rush in 1847 produced a massive influx of settlers and prospectors looking to make their fortunes and future lives on Yuki land. With state sanction, Yuki men were systematically killed; women and children were seized as slaves; their land was seized and communities displaced. Of an original 20,000 Yuki, only 3,500 remained in 1854, and only 168 in 1880.[245]

After gaining independence from Britain, the USA pursued a relentless campaign of westward expansion and several states attempted to resolve their 'Indian problem' by expelling or exterminating indigenous populations. Whilst genocide was never proclaimed as a matter of state policy, during the War of Independence itself many of America's political leaders, military commanders, and agrarian settlers openly declared their genocidal intent. For instance, North Carolina's delegation to the US Continental Congress proclaimed that 'the duties of a Christian' included action against the Cherokee race 'to extinguish the very race of them and scarce to leave enough of their existence to be a vestige in proof that the Cherokee nation once was'.[246] Thomas Jefferson expressed a similar intent towards the Cherokee, writing '[n]othing will reduce these wretches so soon as pushing war into the heart of their country. But I would not stop there. I would never cease pursuing them while one of them remained on this side of Mississippi'.[247] In January 1780, Jefferson ordered the extermination of four groups of indigenous Americans (Shawnees, Mingos, Munsies, and Wyandots) before thinking better of it and instructing his military commander to decide for himself whether to exterminate or expel them.[248] After independence, America's western expansion proceeded apace and genocidal sentiments were put into practice. Most

[242] Ward Churchill, *A Little Matter of Genocide: Holocaust and Denial in the Americas from 1492 to the Present* (San Francisco, CA: City Light Books, 1997), p. 97.

[243] See Russell Thornton, *American Indian Holocaust and Survival: A Population History since 1492* (Norman, OK: University of Oklahoma Press, 1987).

[244] Adam Jones, *Genocide: A Comprehensive Introduction* (London: Routledge, 2006), p. 78.

[245] Jones, *Genocide*, p. 75.

[246] Cited by Kiernan, *Blood and Soil*, p. 318.

[247] Cited by Kiernan, *Blood and Soil*, p. 319.

[248] Kiernan, *Blood and Soil*, p. 323.

notable in this regard were the genocides in Texas and California and the clearing of the Great Plains.

Immediately after the US Civil War, the American government used atrocities to enforce a policy expelling Indigenous Americans to reservations where they would be 'civilized' by 'Indian agents'. Atrocities were used to coral people into reservations, punish those that fled and as retribution for violence against white settlers. The army took on the role of defending white land claims and providing settlers with security even if that meant exterminating Indigenous Americans. As Sherman exclaimed, 'we must act with vindictive earnestness against the Sioux, even to their extermination, men, women and children'.[249] After a series of skirmishes in the mid-west around Fort Laramie in 1867, Sherman presented Indigenous Americans with an ultimatum: accept white rule and assimilate, or face annihilation.[250] Later that year, Sherman handed command of the army to Sheridan, who conducted 619 operations against the mainly civilian native population, completing the conquest of the west.[251] In 1873, Sheridan commanded: 'let it be a campaign of annihilation, obliteration, and complete destruction'.[252] Sheridan's strategy involved annihilating his enemy principally by attacking their food supplies during winter when alternative sources were hard to come by. US forces destroyed foodstuffs and forced Indigenous Americans either to surrender or retreat through the snow, where most died of starvation or disease.[253] Two years later, Sheridan defended the destruction of Texan buffalo herds on the grounds that it obliterated both the Native American economy and their way of life.[254]

The massacres and forced displacement were typically justified by reference to necessity, the fact that the rules of civilized conduct did not apply to Indigenous Americans, and to the settlers' great civilizing mission. In relation to the first, it was commonly argued that the slaughter of women, children, and unarmed men was blameless because moral principles such as civilian immunity applied only to 'civilized' peoples. It was not possible to wage effective war on Indigenous Americans in any other way, the argument

[249] Cited in Lloyd Lewis, *Sherman: Fighting Prophet* (New York: Harcourt, Brace and Co., 1958), p. 597. These were not, of course the first genocidal campaigns against native American tribes. For a list of earlier campaigns, see Jeremy Black, *Introduction to Global Military History: 1775 to the Present* (London: Routledge, 2005), p. 75; and for a more detailed account of the pattern of genocidal war, see Kiernan. *Blood and Soil*, pp. 213–48.

[250] Lewis, *Sherman*, p. 598.

[251] Paul Andrews Hutton, *Phil Sheridan and His Army* (Lincoln: University of Nebraska Press, 1985), p. 345.

[252] Cited by Clarence D. Clendenen, *Blood on the Border: The United States Army and the Mexican Irregulars* (New York, Macmillan, 1969), p. 66.

[253] Russell F. Weigley, *The American Way of War: A History of United States Military Strategy and Policy* (New York: Macmillan, 1973), pp. 159–60.

[254] Hutton, *Phil Sheridan*, p. 246.

followed, because they used only 'treacherous tactics', placing themselves beyond the pale of civilization.[255] Atrocities were sometimes explained away as the only way of prevailing upon native peoples and, indeed, sometimes as the most 'humane' way of doing so. As Elbridge Colby put it in the *American Journal of International Law* in 1927, 'to a fanatical savage, a bomb dropped out of the sky on the sacred temple of his omnipotent God is a sign and a symbol that that God has withdrawn his favour. A shell smashing into a putative inaccessible village stronghold is an indication of the relentless energy and superior skill of the well-equipped civilized foe. . . . If a few "non-combatants"—if there be any such in native folk of this character—are killed, the loss of life is probably far less than might have been sustained in more prolonged operations of a more polite character'.[256] Although much of the violence was caused by the clearing of indigenous peoples from their lands by settlers, it was commonly portrayed as a defensive action to protect settlers and their property rights.[257]

In addition to being excused on account of the victims' putative lack of civilization, atrocities and other depredations were sometimes justified on the grounds that they helped protect civilization itself. Frank Baum, author of *The Wizard of Oz*, put it this way: 'our only safety depends on the total extirmination [sic] of the Indians. Having wronged them for centuries we had better, in order to protect our civilization, follow it up by one more wrong and wipe these untamed and untenable creatures from the face of the earth'.[258] All this helped create a permissive normative context for mass atrocities.

Although individual massacres were criticized both at home and abroad, there was little systematic criticism and nor was there much in the way of punishment. Most of those who led and fought in the genocidal campaigns were honoured with land and bounty payments and the few that were scolded or prosecuted for massacring Indians received only the lightest of sentences. Where there was criticism, it came principally from liberals in America and Britain.[259] For instance, one massacre in 1865 was described as 'brutal and inhuman . . . a dastardly outrage upon humanity and a lasting disgrace to our boasted civilization' by the *Atlanta Constitution*.[260] Overseas, whilst the

[255] See General Nelson A. Miles, *Serving the Republic* (New York: Harper and Brothers, 1911), pp. 113–14.

[256] Colby, 'How to Fight Savage Tribes', p. 287.

[257] Edward Keene, *Beyond the Anarchical Society: Grotius, Colonialism and Order in World Politics* (Cambridge: Cambridge University Press), p. 71; and Hutton, *Phil Sheridan*, p. 185.

[258] One of many to make such arguments was Frank Baum. Writing in the *Aberdeen Saturday Pioneer*, he wrote, 'He wrote much the same thing on several occasions'. See Susan Forsyth, *Representing the Massacre of American Indians at Wounded Knee, 1890–2000* (Lewiston, NY: Edwin Mellen, 2003), pp 30, 35–6, 39.

[259] Black, *Global Military History*, p. 76.

[260] Cited in Frederick E. Hoxie, *A Final Promise: The Campaign to Assimilate the Indians, 1880–1920* (Cambridge: Cambridge University Press, 1984), p. 2.

British government remained largely silent, two of London's newspapers offered radically different assessments of American conduct. Reporting an uprising by the Sioux in 1891, the *Illustrated London News* referred to the indigenous Americans as 'savage insurgents'. In sharp contrast, *The Times* noted that the uprising was a consequence of 'injudicious and inconsiderate' management on the part of the government.[261] This was about as stern as international criticism of the USA got. Its claim to sovereignty was uncontested by the European powers and its argument that atrocities were a necessary part of warring with 'savages' was generally accepted by governments and societies engaged in their own colonial experiments.

## Exploitation in Congo (1880–1907)

Between 1880 and 1907, King Leopold of Belgium presided over a system of terror and atrocity in his personal empire in the Congo.[262] During this period, the Congo's population was halved from around twenty million to ten million as a result of mass killing, forced labour, mass displacement, and disease.[263] Congolese men were required to work for the regime to satisfy an annual rubber quota. Those that refused to do so were killed.[264] Women and children were taken from villages as officially sanctioned hostages to force the men to work.[265] Sometimes this was done individually; on other occasions entire populations were seized. Others were forced to transport rubber by foot over vast distances. Congolese were whipped, tortured, and shot for offences that included looking at Europeans in an 'inappropriate' fashion.[266] It order to keep account of ammunition provided to Congolese soldiers loyal to the government, hands and ears were cut from victims and presented to the regional governors as evidence that it had been used efficiently.[267] Such brutality increased rubber production significantly, earning huge profits for Leopold and his investors.

[261] Cited in Forsythe, *Representing the Massacre*, pp. 41–2.

[262] Captured in literature by Joseph Conrad, *The Heart of Darkness and Other Tales* (Oxford: Oxford University Press, 1998). Between 1892 and 1910, Leopold's 'Congo Free State' was a unique form of government, see Samuel H. Nelson, *Colonialism in the Congo Basin 1880–1940* (Athens, OH: Ohio University Press, 1994), p. 84.

[263] Victoria Brittain, 'Colonialism and the Predatory State in the Congo', *New Left Review*, 236, July/August 1999, p. 133.

[264] Roger Anstey, *King Leopold's Legacy: The Congo Under Belgian Rule 1908–1960* (Oxford: Oxford University Press, 1966), p. 7.

[265] Nelson, *Colonialism in the Congo Basin*, p. 94.

[266] See Adam Hochschild, *King Leopold's Ghost* (Boston: Houghton Mifflin, 1998), pp. 225–32.

[267] Martin Ewans, *European Atrocity, African Catastrophe: Leopold II, the Congo Free State and its Aftermath* (London: Routledge Curzon, 2002), p. 164.

Leopold generally denied accusations that his government committed atrocities.[268] On closer scrutiny, however, government by atrocity was justified by reference to the putative 'inhumanity' of the Congolese, the necessity of violence for maintaining order, and the requirements of the civilizing mission. Indeed, the 'civilizing mission' lay at the heart of Leopold's claim to sovereignty over the Congo. The 'Free State', he argued, would bring 'civilisation and trade' to the region.[269] This allowed violence against the civilian population to be portrayed as not only necessary to protect whites but also as being in the best interests of its victims. Standing in the way of the civilizing mission, Leopold and his allies argued, was the incivility and savagery of the Congolese. They were considered lazy and little better than animals, and were generally treated as such.[270] European officials told stockholders that it was necessary 'to encourage' African production though a 'prolonged educative' relationship with Europeans.[271] Leopold himself put it more bluntly, 'in dealing with a race composed of cannibals for thousands of years it is necessary to use methods that will best shake their idleness and make them realise the sanctity of work'.[272] Such ideas were endorsed by *The Times* in London, which agreed that 'a system of compulsion closely akin to slavery would be necessary before the natives of the Congo Free State could be trained to regular voluntary labour'.[273]

The Congo Free State was more heavily and widely criticized than other cases of colonial atrocities because its violence was overt, prolonged, obviously devastating, attached directly to financial gain, and contrary to the principles of free trade. Opposition began in the liberal middle class in Britain and America. In Britain, the campaign was led by E. D. Morel whose *West African Mail* described the Congo as 'legalised infamy . . . accompanied by unimaginable barbarities and responsible for a vast destruction of human life'.[274] Morel was supported by Mary Kingsley, whose travel books repudiated Leopold's claim that the lands were vacant when first colonized, and the writer Arthur Conan Doyle in establishing the Congo Reform Association.[275] In 1903, *Pall Mall* editorialized that 'the cruel slavery in the Congo Slave State—for it ought to be so called—is a standing disgrace to Christian civilisation'.[276] The

268 'King Leopold Denies Charges Against Him', *New York Times*, 11 December 1906.

269 William Bain, *Between Anarchy and Society: Trusteeship and the Obligations of Power* (Oxford: Oxford University Press, 2003), p. 68.

270 Hochschild, *King Leopold's Ghost*, p. 121.

271 Nelson, *Colonialism in the Congo Basin*, p. 83.

272 In Hochschild, *King Leopold's Ghost*, p. 118.

273 In Ewans, *European Atrocity*, p. 177.

274 In Hochschild, *King Leopold's Ghost*, p. 186.

275 Hochschild, *King Leopold's Ghost*, p. 188; and Robert Weisbord, 'The King, the Cardinal and the Pope: Leopold II's Genocide in the Congo and the Vatican', *Journal of Genocide Research*, 5 (1) 2003, p. 37.

276 *Pall Mall*, 20 August 1903.

*Liverpool Mercury* described the Congo as 'hell on earth' and the *Westminster Gazette* published cartoons condemning Leopold's regime.[277] In the USA, Mark Twain published a pamphlet with photos of Leopold's African victims and described the Congo as 'the ghastliest episode in all human history'.[278] Protestant churches rallied opposition to the Congo regime while a Baptist clergyman charged Leopold with 'a crime without an equal in all of history'.[279] Sweden was also a centre of opposition, as missionaries in the Congo sent home reports detailing systematic terror.[280] The regime was also criticized by Belgian socialists and an eminent Belgian professor of law, Felicien Cattier, who labelled it as little more than a financial enterprise, denouncing its agents for betraying Christian and civilized values.[281]

Criticism and punishment from European governments was much slower to emerge in part because of great power politics but also because of concerns about the precedent criticizing Leopold would create for the continent's other colonial powers. When it did come, criticism focused on Leopold's failure to fulfil the 'civilizing mission' established by the 1885 Treaty of Berlin which also recognized Leopold's sovereignty. Almost entirely concerned with free trade, the treaty also committed colonial rulers to 'watch over the preservation of the native tribes, and to care for the improvement of the conditions of their moral and material well-being' (Article 5).[282] The question of atrocities in the Congo was first raised in the British House of Commons in April 1897. Sir Charles Dilke moved that the government consider international action through the parties to the 1885 Berlin Treaty to secure 'equitable treatment of the natives' in the Congo Free State. Later that year, Lord Salisbury, the British Foreign Secretary, described Leopold's regime as 'horrible' and the Foreign Office despatched a commission of enquiry.[283] The ensuing report found that 'the root of the evil lies in the fact that the government of the Congo is above all a commercial trust . . . their first duty is to show a profit . . . the treatment of the natives is . . . intentionally bad'. It concluded that 'the great decrease in population . . . were to be attributed above all else to the continued effort made during many years to compel the natives to work India-rubber . . . there had

[277] Weisbord, 'The King', pp. 37–8.

[278] J. Smith (ed.), *Mark Twain on the Damned Human Race* (New York: Hill and Wang, 1994), p. 193.

[279] In Weisbord, 'The King', p. 38.

[280] Hochschild, *King Leopold's Ghost*, pp. 125–8.

[281] Felicien Cattier, *Etude sur la Situation de l'Etat Indépendent du Congo* (Brussels: Kessinger Publications, 2009 [1906]).

[282] See W. M. Roger Louis, 'The Berlin Congo Conference', in Prosser Gifford and W. M. Roger Louis (eds), *France and Britain in Africa: Imperial Rivalry and Colonial Rule* (New Haven: Yale University Press, 1971), pp. 180–6; and Arthur Berriedale Keith, *The Belgian Congo and the Berlin Act* (Oxford: Clarendon Press, 1919), pp. 58–63.

[283] In S. J. S. Cookey, 'Great Britain and the Congo Question, 1892–1913' (unpublished PhD thesis, University of London, 1964), p. 60.

been much loss of life, accompanied by a somewhat general mutilation of the dead, as proof that the soldiers had done their duty'.[284]

Britain floated the idea of reconvening the Berlin conference to examine the Congo situation but this was rejected by France, which operated a very similar system to Leopold's in French Congo.[285] Political agitation continued nonetheless. In 1904, British MPs called for trade sanctions, the despatching of gunboats and cooperation with the US to reform the Free State. But the British government continued to prefer inaction on the grounds that there was no consensus about reconvening the Berlin conference. However, European opinion was gradually changing. Towards century's end, Germany began to criticize the Free State and relations between Belgium and the USA and UK worsened as a result of the war of words on Congo. This eventually prompted Belgium to assume sovereignty over the Free State in 1908, a move subsequently recognized by the great powers.[286]

## The Herero Genocide (1904–1907)

Like Leopold's Congo, the government of German Southwest Africa was informed by a racist worldview that varied between portraying Africans as 'noble savages' and depicting them as sub-human and animal-like.[287] For example, in 1907 Paul Rohrbach, the colony's economic adviser, wrote that from the 'point of view of the economy' the local natives were 'useless, provid[ing] no justification for the preservation of this race'.[288] When the Herero rebelled, the Germans initially responded with a conventional military campaign. Governor Leutwein rejected annihilation on the grounds that it would be too difficult to achieve and counter-productive, given the colony's reliance on Herero labour.[289] Having secured a difficult but not decisive victory at Oviumbo, Leutwein ordered a strategic pause and retreat. This was mistakenly interpreted by the German General Staff as a defeat and Leutwein was replaced in June 1904 with General von Trotha who was instructed to use 'all necessary means' to crush the rebellion.[290] Upon arrival, Trotha explained to Leutwein

[284] Cited by Ewans, *European Atrocity* pp. 193 and 196.

[285] Ewans, *European Atrocity*, p. 183.

[286] Tony Ward, 'State Crime in the Heart of Darkness', *British Journal of Criminology*, 45 (4) 2005, p. 437.

[287] For a detailed account of German depictions, see Dan Stone, 'White Men with Low Moral Standards? German Anthropology and the Herero Genocide', in A. Dirk Moses and Dan Stone (eds), *Colonialism and Genocide* (London: Routledge, 2008), esp. pp. 181–91.

[288] Quoted by Israel Goldblatt, *History of Southwest Africa* (Cape Town: JUTA, 1971), p. 147.

[289] Horst Drechsler, *'Let Us Die Fighting': The Struggle of the Herero and Nama Against German Imperialism (1884–1915)* (London: Zed Books, 1980), p. 148.

[290] Isabel V. Hull, 'Military Culture and the Production of "Final Solutions" in the Colonies: The Example of Wilhelminian Germany', in Robert Gellately and Ben Kiernan (eds), *The Specter*

that he intended to interpret his mandate to the full: 'the Emperor only said that he expected me to crush the rebellion by fair means or foul . . . it was and remains my policy to apply this force by unmitigated terrorism and even cruelty. I shall destroy the rebellious tribes by shedding rivers of blood and money'.[291] Trotha doggedly pursued a decisive battle but having failed to achieve this at the battle of Waterberg, German forces pursued combatants and civilians alike into the desert, cutting off access to water and any means of escape. German forces pursued and harried the fleeing civilians, shooting on sight those they encountered.[292] On 2 October, Trotha issued what has been aptly described as a genocidal order: 'The Herero people will have to leave the country. Otherwise, I shall force them to do so by means of guns . . . Every Herero, whether found armed or unarmed . . . will be shot'.[293] Where there had been approximately 80,000 Herero in 1884, only 15,130 survived in 1911.[294]

The annihilation of the Herero was justified by reference to the logic of selective extermination used by other colonists. As did other perpetrators of mass killing in the colonial world, Trotha argued that wars in Africa could not be waged in conformity with the rules governing civilized warfare.[295] In similar vein, referring to the Herero during a 1904 debate in the *Reichstag*, Ludwig zu Reventlow supported this general line and told his colleagues: 'do not apply too much humanity to bloodthirsty beasts in the form of humans'.[296] This logic permitted the exclusion of the Herero from the moral protections usual in civilized war. As Trotha reportedly commented on his arrival in South West Africa, 'no war may be conducted humanely against nonhumans'.[297] As was the case in America, some Germans maintained that civilization itself depended on the defence of white peoples in Africa even to the point of exterminating the indigenous population. Rohrbach opined that 'to secure the peaceful white settlement against the bad, culturally inept and predatory native tribe, it is possible that its actual eradication may become

*of Genocide: Mass Murder in Historical Perspective* (Cambridge: Cambridge University Press, 2003), p. 146.

[291] In Dreschler, *'Let us Die Fighting'*, p. 154.

[292] The mortality rate was approximately 70 per cent. See Benjamin Madley, 'From Africa to Auschwitz: How German South West Africa Incubated Ideas and Methods Adopted and Developed by the Nazis in Eastern Europe', *European History Quarterly*, 35 (3) 2005, p. 450.

[293] Cited by Dreschler, *'Let us Die Fighting'*, pp. 156–7. On its genocidal qualities, see Rachel Anderson, 'Redressing Colonial Genocide Under International Law: The Hereros' Cause of Action Against Germany', *California Law Review*, 93 (4) 2005, p. 1161.

[294] Horst Drechsler, *'Let Us Die Fighting'*, p. 164.

[295] See Jurgen Zimmerer, 'The Birth of the *Ostland* out of the Spirit of Colonialism: A Postcolonial Perspective on the Nazi Policy of Conquest and Extermination', *Patterns of Prejudice*, 39 (2), p. 209.

[296] In Madley, 'From Africa to Auschwitz', p. 440.

[297] Cited by Hull, 'Military Culture', p. 154.

necessary'.[298] Likewise, the German Colonial Society maintained that: 'anyone familiar with the life of the African and other less civilised non-white peoples knows that Europeans can assert themselves only by maintaining the supremacy of their race at all costs'.[299] This translated into a widely held view that the Germans should not negotiate with the Herero but should instead punish them for having the temerity to challenge white rule. The Kaiser forbade negotiations without his prior consent and the liberal newspaper, *Berliner Zeitung*, called for the 'punishment' of the Herero but qualified this a few weeks later in response to alleged German atrocities by noting that while 'a certain strictness is necessary, this must not degenerate into brutality'.[300]

When it became known in Germany, the extermination policy was widely criticized. Chancellor Bernhard von Bülow lobbied to have it rescinded and replaced by an order instructing German troops to take prisoners. Some of the criticism, it must be stressed, was driven by concerns that extermination would prove counter-productive by depleting local labour. For example, whilst excusing the extermination of 'useless' races, Rohrbach—an economist—criticized it as 'wasteful'.[301] Likewise, the German army's Chief of Staff, General von Schlieffen accepted Trotha's assessment that Germany confronted a 'race war [that] can be concluded only by the destruction or complete servitude or one of the parties' but believed that Trotha lacked the necessary resources to prosecute it successfully.[302]

But there were others such as Chancellor Bülow who objected to the extermination order chiefly on moral grounds. After learning of it, Bülow wrote to the Kaiser requesting that the order be superseded by one instructing German forces to accept prisoners. Describing his position as a 'matter of conscience', Bülow argued that the shooting of all the men and expulsion of all the women and children were 'contrary to the principles of Christianity and humanity'. A 'complete and systematic annihilation of the Herero', the Chancellor maintained, 'would exceed all the demands of justice'. Bülow also pointed to Schlieffen's argument about the military problems associated with this policy, endorsed the view that extermination would prove disastrous to the colony's economy, and argued that it would 'demolish Germany's reputation among the civilised nations and feed foreign agitation against us'.[303] August Bebel, leader of the Social Democratic Party shared this sense of moral outrage and condemned the 'barbarous treatment of the Hereros'.[304]

[298] In Madley, 'From Africa to Auschwitz', p. 441.
[299] Cited by Madley, 'From Africa to Auschwitz', p. 440.
[300] Cited by Hull, 'Military Culture', p. 150.
[301] Isabel V. Hull, *Absolute Destruction: Military Culture and the Practices of War in Imperial Germany* (Ithaca, NY: Cornell University Press, 2005), p. 50.
[302] Hull, *Absolute Destruction*, p. 64.
[303] Hull, *Absolute Destruction*, p. 64.
[304] Cited by Drechsler, *'Let us Die Fighting'*, p. 151.

The liberal media in Germany also criticized the policy. M. J. Bonn, for instance, ridiculed von Trotha's racist justification for genocide.[305] Intense lobbying by Bülow persuaded the Kaiser to overrule the extermination order, instruct German forces to take prisoners, and eventually to recall Trotha. But prisoners were taken to concentration camps, where malnourishment and disease caused death rates significantly higher than those experienced by Boer civilians in British camps, completing the destruction of the Herero.[306]

Outside Germany, the genocide attracted relatively little attention. Perhaps, as Mahmood Mamdani suggests, 'the genocide of the Herero was simply an extreme instance of the general tendencies of colonialism. The history of European colonies is rife with massacres and forced marches, conscript labour and expulsions. Colonial powers often stopped at nothing to subdue their restive populations; "annihilation" was always an option'.[307] Some liberals in Britain criticized the killing as a breach of the 1885 Berlin Treaty. But the British government did little to intervene, though its administration in South Africa permitted two hundred Herero who had escaped to British controlled Walvis Bay to remain in British ruled territory, even shipping them to Cape Town.[308] But the British colony also profited from the war by supplying German troops.[309] Moreover, several British officials expressed sympathy with the Germans. Lord Milner, the British High Commissioner in South Africa, told a German representative that he 'considered the rebellion in the German Protectorate a threat to the peace of the whole of South Africa' and that the British government would assist the Germans in whatever way they could. Milner's successor, Lord Selbourne, said much the same, noting that German success would assist the British colony. Furthermore, the British premier of the Cape Colony, Starr Jameson, indicated that his sympathies lay with the Germans.[310] There was certainly no suggestion at the time that Germany should be punished.

## Summary

The justifications offered for mass atrocities committed by settlers and colonial powers in the non-European world clearly demonstrate the role played by an ideology of selective extermination in helping perpetrators to secure sufficient legitimacy. In the eyes of most European governments, the 'standard of

[305] M. J. Bonn, 'Die wissenschaftliche Begründung der Trothaschen Eingeborenenpolitik', *Franfurter Zeitung*, 14 September 1909.
[306] Isabel V. Hull, 'Military Culture', p. 159.
[307] Mahmood Mamdani, 'A Brief History of Genocide', *Transition*, 10 (3) 2001, p. 32.
[308] Dreschler, *'Let us Die Fighting'*, p. 167.
[309] Dreschler, *'Let us Die Fighting'*, p. 218.
[310] All from Dreschler, *'Let us Die Fighting'*, p. 219.

civilization' separated peoples into two normative orders—one governed by moral rules that inhibited mass atrocities to some extent, the other governed by a much more permissive moral framework that selectively placed non-Europeans beyond protection and justified mass atrocities against them. The colonial doctrine of selective extermination made mass killing appear to be a blameless enterprise and the civilizing mission made a virtue of it. This enabled colonial perpetrators of mass killing to justify and sometimes legitimize behaviour that would have been considered utterly intolerable in the 'civilized' world.

That said, the limits of selective extermination were also in evidence, most notably in the case of the Congo where liberal states eventually exerted diplomatic pressure to remedy the worst of the excesses and in German opposition to the Herero genocide. In both these cases, selective extermination proved incapable of persuading some individuals and groups who drew on alternative moral traditions. This suggests that whilst it may provide an effective framework for persuading oneself and other like-minded people of the legitimacy of mass killing, selective extermination struggles to provide plausible justifications to others. Both the people who are themselves excluded and those who are not convinced by the fashion in which humanity is divided (in this case based in race) by such ideologies are unlikely to be persuaded that selective extermination provides sufficient grounds for mass killing. In this case, although opposition to mass killing in the colonial world was feint, owing to a basic consensus among governments and societies in Europe, criticism was evident in each of the three cases examined here and such criticism. As such, the capacity of selective extermination to deliver sufficient legitimacy was intimately connected to the material power of the states and societies that espoused it, because the doctrine was unable to persuade outsiders.

## CONCLUSION

My central claim in this chapter is that although the deliberate killing of civilians was not prohibited by international law, in some situations the moral principle of civilian immunity influenced responses to mass killing and exerted a restraining hand on perpetrators. With the notable exception of the colonized world, which was placed outside the protection of the moral rules governing civilized behaviour, perpetrators of mass killing were expected to provide special justification for mass killing. In particular, to secure sufficient legitimacy they were commonly required to be accepted as legitimate authorities and to demonstrate the necessity of atrocities and limit violence accordingly. When confronting insurgencies, governments could point to a legal tradition that placed insurgents and their civilian supporters outside the protection of the laws of war making them liable for reprisals. As the century progressed, emerging humanitarianism and the laws of war restricted these entitlements as necessity came to be understood as more constraining than enabling, culminating in the widespread condemnation of German reprisals in 1914 Belgium. This effectively marked the end of necessity as a vehicle for legitimising the mass killing of civilians.

The degree to which perpetrators succeeded in securing sufficient legitimacy for mass atrocities in the non-colonial world was primarily shaped by judgements about necessity and the relative legitimacy of the relevant actors. These two factors were linked. In general, the greater the degree of relative legitimacy enjoyed by the perpetrators immediately prior to the episode, the more anti-civilian violence it could expect to get away with by reference to necessity. The opposite was also true. Of course, in practice things were much more complicated than this and other contextual factors played important roles. For instance: British and French activism on Greece was driven more by geopolitical concerns about Russian expansionism than by public outrage at the massacre of Greeks and support for their cause, though this certainly helped; and US criticism of Spanish rule in Cuba was guided as much by self-interest as by anti-colonialism.

In some cases, as with French conduct in the Peninsular War and the repression of the 1848 uprising in Paris, the perpetrators' claims were validated. French conduct in the Peninsular War was seen as consistent with the customs of war and the suppression of 1848 was viewed as a legitimate law enforcement exercise against unruly mobs. By contrast, the French repression of the Paris Commune was tolerated rather than validated. In other cases, most notably the 1848 Vienna uprising and Cuba, governments confronting national self-determination movements found it difficult to sustain a claim to be the more legitimate actor. In a context of emergent popular sovereignty and perceiving that the rebels had legitimate grievances against their imperial rulers, external actors became sharply critical of government atrocities. Interestingly, in a third group of cases the relationship between actor-legitimacy and behaviour-legitimacy moved in the opposite direction. In these cases—most notably Greece and Armenia, but Congo to an extent as well—rather than a perpetrator's illegitimacy as an actor relative to other relevant actors affecting external judgements about the legitimacy of mass killing, perceptions that the perpetrator used unnecessary and disproportionate violence against civilians affected judgements about their right to rule a particular territory. In Greece and Armenia, the Ottomans and Turks demonstrably failed to satisfy the necessity condition, prompting foreign governments to cast doubt on their right to rule. In both these cases, the Ottoman/Turkish right to rule over Greece and Armenia was unchallenged at the outset of the respective crises but was called into question by the government's conduct. In these cases, contextual factors played a significant role in determining the effects of these legitimacy judgements: in the case of Greece, Britain, France, and Russia intervened to impose the establishment of an autonomous Greek state; in the case of Armenia, international society backed away from proposals to establish a protectorate for a combination of geopolitical concerns (relating to the need to support Turkey as a bulwark against the new Soviet Union) and domestic American political concerns.

All of this, however, applied only to the European world. Conduct towards non-European colonized peoples was judged according to a very different, and much more lenient, set of conditions shaped by an ideology of selective extermination that excluded those deemed to be uncivilized from moral and legal protection and sometimes valourized the use of force against them in the name of the 'civilizing mission'. This ideology was informed by a racist worldview widely shared among European and North American governments and societies. Mass killing was used to conquer and settle lands, suppress rebellions, extract profit, and more besides. Colonial terror recognized none of the limits evident in Europe. Except in the case of the Congo Free State, colonial atrocities were not widely criticized by European governments and in that case only after more than a decade of systematic violence committed under the authority of a private individual. However, it is important to stress that the colonial experience also exposed some of the weaknesses of selective extermination. Atrocities were sometimes criticized by Europe's liberals and socialists, particularly towards the end of the period, bearing witness to the emergence and spread of humanitarianism. Whilst Germany's conduct in South West Africa escaped international opprobrium, it was sharply criticized within Germany itself and the government there tried to rein in the excesses once it became aware of them.

Because each case is historically contingent and shaped by particular contextual factors, it is difficult to identify general trends and patterns as the wide variance in outcomes noted above attest. However, we can discern the emergence of two important transformations, both linked to the rise of liberalism. Together, they began to alter the manner and extent to which mass atrocities secured sufficient legitimacy. First, the bases of legitimate authority came under challenge and began to change. The old premise, that the authority to govern derived from God or personal lineage, was challenged by the doctrine of popular sovereignty—the notion that people have a right to choose their own government. This began to change the basis on which third parties evaluated the relative legitimacy of relevant actors, making it more difficult for multinational empires in Europe to claim a mandate to use violence against civilians in order to enforce the law or maintain order. As we noted earlier, even where the right to rule was not in doubt, such doubts could be created by the ineffective resort to mass atrocities against a national grouping. The second relevant aspect was the emergence and spread of humanitarianism, which heightened sensitivity to violations of civilian immunity. As the period progressed, serious questions were raised as to whether it was *ever* legitimate to deliberately kill civilians. In some contexts, such as the use of reprisals against civilians in insurgency warfare, a consensus had emerged by the turn of the twentieth century that the deliberate of killing civilians could not be justified by reference to necessity. In other contexts, however, the legitimation of mass killing remained an open question. This was especially true for the colonized world, which remained a spectator largely unaffected by these transformations.

# 3

# Totalitarian Mass Killing

This chapter explore debates about the legitimacy of mass killing by totalitarian states in the 1930s and 1940s and the principle of civilian immunity. The most prominent of the totalitarian states, Nazi Germany and the Soviet Union were 'immensely powerful, threatening and contagious dictatorships that... threatened to turn the world upside down'.[1] Totalitarian governments typically justified mass killing by reference to ideologies of selective extermination that shared important family resemblances to those espoused in the European colonial context. These ideologies removed entire nations, races, socio-economic classes, and other group types from basic moral protections and portrayed the killing of group members, and sometimes the extermination of whole groups, as a positive good—necessary for security or human progress.[2] Though there were important differences between them, genocides and mass atrocities unleashed by Stalin's Soviet Union and Hitler's Germany attempted to remould societies 'in the image of certain ascribed qualities' by annihilating class and racial enemies.[3]

The contention that there is a connection between the European colonial experience and the major totalitarian genocides and atrocities of the twentieth century—and especially between German genocidal killing in the Herero War (see Chapter 2) and the Holocaust—has provoked heated debate among

[1] Michael Geyer with Sheila Fitzpatrick, 'Introduction', in Michael Geyer and Sheila Fitzpatrick (eds), *Beyond Totalitarianism: Stalinism and Nazism Compared* (Cambridge: Cambridge University Press, 2009), p. 9.

[2] See Hannah Arendt, *The Origins of Totalitarianism* (London: George Allen and Unwin, 1951), p. 465. For a useful overview of debates about the definition of totalitarian terrorism, see Rosemary H. T. O'Kane, *Terror, Force and States: The Path from Modernity* (Cheltenham: Edward Elgar, 1996), pp. 1–27.

[3] Christopher R. Browning and Lewis H. Siegelbaum, 'Frameworks for Social Engineering: Stalinist Schema of Identification and the Nazi *Volksgemeinschaft*', in Geyer and Fitzpatrick (eds), *Beyond Totalitarianism*, p. 231. On differences, see Yoram Gorlizki and Hans Mommsen, 'The Political (Dis)orders of Stalinism and National Socialism', in Geyer and Fitzpatrick (eds), *Beyond Totalitarianism*, p. 73.

historians.[4] The basic proposition that there are structural similarities between the two experiences appears compelling. As Vinay Lal famously observed, 'from the standpoint of numerous Asian and Third World scholars, the Holocaust, alongside the killings of homosexuals, gypsies and the purportedly deranged, visited upon the people the violence that colonial powers had routinely inflicted on the "natives" all over the world for nearly five hundred years'.[5] But critics doubt the extent to which one directly influenced the other. They suggest—among other things—that in linking South West Africa to the Holocaust, this 'continuity thesis' comes close to rearticulating the discredited theory of 'German uniqueness', that it overstates evidence that German colonial experience influenced the Nazis, underplays significant variations between the two cases, and ignores the extent to which Nazism marked a radical break from Wilhemene Germany.[6] What is more, they point out that whilst genocidal practices were commonly practised by virtually all the major European colonizers, only the Germans went on to commit a Holocaust. The former could not, therefore, have caused the latter. Whilst the critics are right to claim that we cannot draw a straight line 'from Windhoek to Auschwitz'—and it is worth noting that leading proponents of the continuity thesis, such as Jurgen Zimmerer, do not suggest that we can—the structural similarities between the two sets of cases should not be ignored. Particularly significant for our purposes are structural similarities in the justifications employed.[7]

Though each was unique and rooted in its own context, the justifications and moral logics espoused by the totalitarian governments of the twentieth century nevertheless shared some important family resemblances. Some of these resemblances were rooted in the colonial logic of selective extermination. Whether consciously or not, these regimes drew on the colonial legacy and typically justified mass killing by reference to ideologies of selective

[4] The idea that the Holocaust had its roots in European imperialism was first touted by Hannah Arendt, *The Origins of Totalitarianism* (New York: Andre Deutsch, 1986 [1951]). More recently, see Shelley Baranowski, *Nazi Empire: German Colonialism and Imperialism from Bismarck to Hitler* (Cambridge: Cambridge University Press, 2011); Jurgen Zimmerer, 'The Birth of the *Ostland* out of the Spirit of Colonialism: A Postcolonial Perspective on the Nazi Policy of Conquest and Extermination', *Patterns of Prejudice*, 39 (2) 2005, pp. 197–219.

[5] Vinay Lal, 'Genocide, Barbaric Others and the Violence of Categories: A Response to Omer Bartov', *American Historical Review*, 103 (4) 1998, p. 1188.

[6] For instance, see Robert Gerwath and Stephan Malinowski, 'Hannah Arendt's Ghosts: Reflections on the Disputable Path from Windhoek to Auschwitz', *Central European History*, 42, 2009, pp. 279–300. For an overview of the debate, see Dan Stone, *Histories of the Holocaust* (Oxford: Oxford University Press, 2010), pp. 205–37; and Matthew P. Fitzpatrick, 'The Pre-History of the Holocaust? The *Sonderweg* and *Historikerstreit* Debates and the Abject Colonial Past', *Central European History*, 41, 2008, pp. 477–503.

[7] See David Furber, 'The Near as Far in the Colonies: The Nazi Occupation in Poland', *International History Review* 26 (3) 2004, p. 558; and Donald Bloxham, *The Final Solution: A Genocide* (Oxford: Oxford University Press, 2009), p. 283.

extermination which removed entire nations, races, or socio-economic classes from the basic moral protections afforded to humans. The genocide and mass atrocities unleashed by Stalin's Soviet Union and Hitler's Germany attempted to remould societies by annihilating class and racial enemies and both developed lines of argument that permitted or required the extermination of such groups.[8] But as with earlier colonial thinking, these ideologies appealed only to the perpetrators' own community and ideological sympathizers. In other words, just as colonialism was prefaced on a closed moral system that could not plausibly seek validation from outside the world of the colonizer, so too Stalinism and Nazism offered accounts of mass killing that appealed only to members of the 'in-group' and their sympathizers. This helped contain the ideology from restraints imposed by other moral and legal codes but limited their capacity to secure external legitimacy, making their very survival as working doctrines dependent upon the material power of their adherents. The ideas that underpinned Stalinism and Nazism were alike in many ways. Most importantly for our purposes, they attempted to make mass killing blameless by removing certain groups from moral protection and valourize it by making it appear necessary for securing cherished civilizational goals. When it came to justifying mass killing, therefore, the key difference between colonial versions of selective extermination and later totalitarian accounts lay not in the structure of their basic justificatory claims but in the place of races and nations within the historical struggle. They all rejected the idea that humans were endowed with inalienable rights in favour of a worldview that emphasized perpetual struggle, the survival of the fittest, and the privileging of the group over the individual. They differed on the foundations of differentiation, seen in biological terms by the Nazis and in principally socio-economic terms by the Stalinists, though nationality also played a role.[9]

But as with other forms of selective extermination, the totalitarian version appealed only to the perpetrator's own communities and ideological sympathizers. In other words, they espoused their own closed moral system that did not appeal to external validation. Whilst this certainly helped them evade moral limits imposed by the principles of necessity or civilian immunity, it also limited the extent to which mass killing could be legitimized outside that community, contributing to their ultimate demise. Although some of the basic racial, moral, and legal ideas from which Nazism and Japanese nationalism drew were widely held in early twentieth-century Europe, very few actors outside the totalitarians' own political or ideological community validated their justifications for mass killing. Indeed, even some governments within

[8] Richard Overy, *The Dictators: Hitler's Germany and Stalin's Russia* (London: Allen Lane, 2004), p. 214; and Henry Friedlander, *The Origins of Nazi Genocide: From Euthanasia to the Final Solution* (Chapel Hill: University of North Carolina Press, 1995), p. 142.

[9] Norman M. Naimark, *Stalin's Genocides* (Princeton, NJ: Princeton University Press, 2010).

the Axis orbit were reluctant to cooperate with Hitler's extermination of the Jews. For their part, liberal governments criticized both, waged war against the Nazis, and translated a wartime alliance with Stalin into a long 'Cold War'. Moreover, the totalitarian regimes were never wholly convinced that their own constituencies would find their ideological reasons for mass killing completely persuasive. Both the Stalinists and the Nazis sometimes tried to hide their violence from view, describing it through euphemisms principally because they were concerned about potential domestic opposition.

The Holocaust and the other totalitarian depredations of the period created a strong political imperative immediately after the Second World War to strengthen the principle of civilian immunity, remove the necessity exception and formalize the norm as an international legal rule (see Chapter 1). Matters are made more complex, though, by the fact that the Western allies also intentionally killed large numbers of civilians, principally through their strategic bombing campaigns. This is examined in the following chapter. This chapter focuses on totalitarian mass killing and proceeds in three parts. In the first, I briefly outline how ideas drawn from colonialism and Social Darwinism provided a moral framework onto which various totalitarian ideologies were grafted. The remaining sections focus on Stalin's Soviet Union and the Holocaust, examining how the perpetrators typically justified their behaviour, how those justifications were received by community members and outsiders, and what this tells us about civilian immunity.

## SELECTIVE EXTERMINATION AND THE TOTALITARIANS

Many of the basic ideas that underpinned Nazism and Stalinism in the 1930s and 1940s were alike, especially as they related to mass killing.[10] At their heart, they shared an ideology that permitted the wholesale extermination of enemies. Social Darwinism played a part in underwriting both. From Darwin, Hitler took the idea that human evolution was a perpetual struggle for survival between competing races. As he explained in a speech in 1928, 'life is only preserved because other living things perish through struggle.... In this

[10] For instance, Overy, *The Dictators*, George Watson, 'Was Hitler a Marxist? Reflections About Certain Affinities', *Encounter*, 63, December 1984, p. 19; and Ernst Nolte, 'Between Myth and Revisionism? The Third Reich in the Perspective of the 1980s', in H. W. Koch (ed.), *Aspects of the Third Reich* (New York: St. Martin's Press, 1985), p. 36. So numerous were the similarities that in 1934 Hitler proclaimed that 'there is more that binds us to Bolshevism than separates us from it', cited in Hermann Rauschning, *Hitler Speaks* (London: Thornton Butterworth, 1939), p. 134. On the key differences, see David Wedgwood Benn, 'On Comparing Nazism and Stalinism', *International Affairs*, 82 (1) 2006, pp. 189–94.

struggle the stronger, the more able, win, while the less able, the weak, lose. Struggle is the father of all things.... It is not by the principles of humanity that man lives or is able to preserve himself... but solely by the means of the most brutal struggle'.[11] Interestingly, communism was not widely seen as a potentially genocidal ideology until the Khmer Rouge unleashed its deadly rule over Cambodia in the 1970s yet almost from the outset, communist thinking was imbued with ideas relating to selective extermination.[12] Although the links between Social Darwinism, communism, and Stalinism are less clear than those between Social Darwinism and Nazism, Marx and Engels themselves sometimes endorsed basic Social Darwinist propositions. Where Hitler understood perpetual struggle as being one between nations and races, Marx and Engels typically conceived it as one between 'historical classes'.[13] Engels sometimes ran the two arguments together, claiming that some nations were inherently counter-revolutionary and thus impeded historical development. In one passage, published by Marx, Engels described counter-revolutionary nations as *Völkerabfall* (racial trash) and endorsed their extermination: 'until its complete extermination, or loss of national status, this racial trash always becomes the most fanatical bearer there is of counter-revolution... the next world war will cause not only reactionary classes and dynasties but also entire reactionary peoples to disappear from the earth. And that too is progress'.[14] Some prominent early British socialists expressed similar views.[15] Moreover, just as extreme nationalists dreamed of constructing biologically pure national bodies, so too Marxism espoused the idea that it was possible to construct a universal model man—*homo sovieticus*.[16] When it came to justifying mass killing, therefore, the key difference between the two ideologies lay not in the structure of their basic justificatory claims but in the place of race and nation within the historical struggle. As I observed earlier, Stalinism and Nazism rejected the idea that humans were endowed with certain inalienable rights in favour of a worldview that emphasized perpetual struggle, the survival of the fittest, and the priority of the community over the individual. Although such ideas were widespread in the intellectual

[11] Speech at Kulmbach, 5 February 1928, cited in Alan Bullock, *Hitler: A Study in Tyranny* (Harmondsworth: Penguin, 1962), p. 36.

[12] Helen Fein, *Genocide: A Sociological Perspective* (London: Sage, 1993), p. 77.

[13] Paul Johnson, 'Marxism vs. the Jews', *Commentary*, 77, April 1984, p. 32.

[14] Karl Marx and Fredreich Engels, *The Russian Menace to Europe: A Collection of Articles, Speeches, Letters and New Dispatches*, ed. Paul Blackstock and Bert Hoselitz (London: G. Allen 1953), pp. 61–2.

[15] See Mikhail Heller and Alexsandr Nekrich, *Utopia in Power: The History of the Soviet Union from 1917 to the Present*, trans. Phyllis Carlos (New York: Summit, 1986), p. 257; and Robert Conquest, *The Harvest of Sorrow: Soviet Collectivization and the Terror-Famine* (New York: Oxford University Press, 1986), pp. 308–21.

[16] Mark Levene, 'Why is the Twentieth Century the Century of Genocide?', *Journal of World History*, 11 (2) 2000, p. 321.

milieu of the early twentieth century, the Stalinists and Nazis 'actually believed it possible to eliminate forever what they perceived to be a disorienting and disturbing diversity of cultures and communities'.[17]

In the 1920s and 1930s, Social Darwinist propositions that human existence was a perpetual struggle in which only the fittest would survive and that races had inherent traits which determined the extent to which they could civilize were widely accepted in European and North American academic and political circles. As I noted in Chapter 2, mass killing in the non-European colonies was justified by reference to an ideology of selective extermination which held non-Europeans to be less capable than 'civilized' peoples and therefore outside normal legal and moral protection.[18] Indeed, among colonial theorists of the time, it was widely accepted that the least fit races would be exterminated by natural process.[19] By the late 1920s this way of thinking had spawned a pseudo-scientific discipline, 'eugenics', sterilization laws in America, and the academic field of 'racial hygiene' in Germany.[20]

The USA was the first country to legislate on the basis of eugenics, ruling that certain groups ought not to be permitted to reproduce. In 1907, Indiana passed a law authorizing compulsory sterilization of the mentally ill, people convicted of more than one sex-crime, those deemed 'feeble-minded' by IQ tests, 'morally degenerate' people, and epileptics. In 1927, the Supreme Court was required to assess a Virginia statute permitting the state to compulsorily sterilize handicapped patients diagnosed as suffering from hereditary 'imbecility'. The case involved a legal challenge to a compulsory sterilization order of a woman deemed 'feebleminded'. Council for the plaintiff argued that the order violated the women's constitutional right to bodily integrity. The Court rejected this argument by a margin of eight to four. Speaking on behalf of the majority, Oliver Wendell Holmes argued that: 'We have seen more than once that the public welfare may call upon the best citizens for their lives. It would be strange if it could not call upon those who already sap the strength of the State for these lesser sacrifices, often not felt to be such by those concerned, in order to prevent our being swamped with incompetence. It is better for all the

[17] Jorg Baberowski and Anselm Doering-Monteuffel, 'The Quest for Order and the Pursuit of Terror: National Socialist Germany and the Stalinist Soviet Union as Multiethnic Empires', in Geyer and Fitzpatrick (eds), *Beyond Totalitarianism*, p. 181.

[18] Arendt identified European imperialism as an essential stage in the genesis of Nazism. Arendt, *Origins of Totalitarianism*, p. 221.

[19] Thus, American anthropologist Robert Knox declared that 'extermination' was 'a law of Anglo-Saxon America' whilst British thinkers like Adam Smith, Thomas Malthus, and Thomas Lee argued simply that inferior races would become 'extinct'. See Traverso, *Origins of Nazi Violence*, trans. Janet Lloyd (New York: New Press, 1996), pp. 54–5.

[20] Stephen Jay Gould, *The Mismeasure of Man* (New York: W. W. Norton, 1981), pp. 113, 115 and 134. See Garland E. Allen, 'The Misuse of Biological Hierarchies: The American Eugenics Movement, 1900–1940', *History and Philosophy of the Life Sciences*, 5 (2) 1983, p. 122; and Friedlander, *The Origins of Nazi Genocide*, pp. 8–9.

world, if instead of waiting to execute degenerate offspring for crime, or to let them starve for their imbecility, society can prevent those who are manifestly unfit from continuing their kind. . . . Three generations of imbeciles are enough'. Eugenics began to lose ground in the West from the mid-1930s. Scientific discoveries cast serious doubts on its claims and there was a liberal backlash to repressive Nazi policies justified by reference to this pseudo-science.

In Germany, meanwhile, eugenics became the principal biological science. Opponents were removed from academic positions and many fled overseas. German eugenicists such as Karl Binding not only identified life they considered 'unworthy of life' because of hereditary 'feeblemindedness', criminality or incapacity, they also insisted on the importance of 'race hygiene', arguing that advanced races which interbred with less advanced became weaker and degenerate.[21] The Nazis put these ideas into practice, pledging to preserve 'the purity of German blood'. To accomplish this goal, the Nazis introduced 'racial social engineering' that began with the exclusion of Jews from public life and extermination of the handicapped and ended with the Holocaust.[22]

The Soviet Union also embraced eugenics, establishing a number of research institutes under the Commissariat of Health. Like the Nazis, the Stalinists had a utopian vision of society and an expressed interest in employing human biology to achieve it. But whereas Nazi eugenics focused on 'racial hygiene' and was generally pessimistic (fearing the degeneration of the Aryan race) and militaristic, Soviet eugenics focused on achieving the ascendancy of socialism. Drawing upon Marxist thinking about the role played by the environment, the Stalinist approach offered a more positive assessment that focused on improving the individual by reshaping the environment.[23] In the 1930s, Soviet eugenicists were forced by political demand to concede the paramouncy of the collective over the individual and the centrality of economic development. At the start of the 'Great Terror' the Soviet Union formally abandoned eugenics on the grounds that it was a fascist doctrine.[24] But the formal abandonment of eugenics did not mean the abandoning of eugenic thinking and the government remained committed to studying how to increase the birth-rate of certain classes and nation, whilst breeding out 'socially harmful' groups such as homosexuals. As Maxim Gorky put it: 'destroy the homosexuals—fascism will disappear'.[25]

[21] Friedlander, *The Origins of Nazi Genocide*, pp. 14–16.

[22] Friedlander, *The Origins of Nazi Genocide*, pp. 16–17.

[23] David L. Hoffman and Annette F. Timm, 'Utopian Biopolitics: Reproductive Policies, Gender Roles, and Sexuality in Nazi Germany and the Soviet Union', in Geyer and Fitzpatrick (eds), *Beyond Totalitarianism*, p. 102.

[24] Hoffman and Timm, 'Utopian Biopolitics', p. 102.

[25] Cited by Hoffman and Timm, 'Utopian Biopolitics', p. 111.

Although ideas connected with Social Darwinism were widespread in the early twentieth century, the totalitarian states put them into practice; Nazi Germany especially but also the Soviet Union.[26] This worldview provided a framework for justifying mass killing on the grounds that certain groups were somewhat less than human and therefore excluded from the realm of moral obligation.[27] Indeed, in the hands of some of the ideologues of totalitarianism, victim groups were portrayed as a biological threat to humanity. Having made mass killing blameless, these ideologies sometimes attempted to valourize it by portraying it as necessary for the long-term security of the race, nation, or people. The next sections of the chapter examine how these ideas were put into practice by the Stalinists and Nazis.

## STALINISM AND THE GREAT TERROR (1937–1938)

Until quite recently, Stalinist mass killing between 1933 and 1939, which reached a crescendo of violence in the 'Great Terror' of 1937–38, was portrayed as a systematic whole, an almost inevitable consequence of its underlying ideology.[28] Since the opening of Soviet archives, however, a consensus has emerged that there were peaks and troughs of violence, significant regional variations, and that although the terror was authorized at the highest levels, there was no overarching plan and plenty of local initiative.[29] As such, what is commonly described as the 'Great Terror' of 1937–38 is best understood 'not as a single phenomenon but as a number of related but discrete phenomena'.[30] Broadly, it is useful to distinguish two forms of terror: the 'public' repression of

[26] Rudolf Hess, for example, insisted that 'National Socialism [was] nothing but applied biology'. Cited by Joachim Fest, *Hitler* (Orlando, FL: Harcourt Brace, 1974), p. 91.

[27] Helen Fein, *Accounting for Genocide* (New York: Free Press, 1979).

[28] For Fainsod, Arendt, Brzezinski, and Solzhenitsyn, terror was an integral part of Stalinist government though for different reasons. Merle Fainsod, *How Russia is Ruled* (Cambridge, MA: Harvard University Press, 1953), p. 441; Arendt, *The Origins of Totalitarianism* and Zbigniew Brzezinski, *The Permanent Purge* (Cambridge, MA: Harvard University Press, 1956), esp. ch. 2. An alternative account holds that Soviet terror was a direct product of Stalin's personal paranoia. For instance, Roy A. Medvedev, *Let History Judge: The Origins and Consequences of Stalinism* (London: Macmillan, 1972), p. 191; and elsewhere and Robert C. Tucker, *Stalin as Revolutionary, 1879–1929* (New York: W. W. Norton, 1973). This view was derided by Solzhenitsyn. Aleksander I. Solzhenitsyn, *The Gulag Archipelago*, Vols I–III (New York: Harper and Row, 1974–8).

[29] J. Arch Getty, *The Origins of the Great Purges: The Soviet Communist Party Reconsidered, 1933–1938* (Cambridge: Cambridge University Press, 1985); and Robert W. Thurston, *Life and Terror in Stalin's Russia: 1934–1941* (New Haven: Yale University Press, 1996).

[30] Sheila Fitzpatrick, 'Varieties of Terror: Introduction to Part IV', in Sheila Fitzpatrick (ed.), *Stalinism: New Directions* (London: Routledge, 2000), p. 258. A view endorsed by Christian Gerlach and Nicolas Werth, 'State Violence—Violent Societies', in Geyer and Fitzpatrick (eds), *Beyond Totalitarianism*, p. 135.

elite members ('Old Bolsheviks', 'Trotskyists') characterized by the famous 'show trials' of 1936–38 and the 'hidden' mass repression of various marginalized groups in 1937–38.[31] The latter, which accounted for the vast majority of the killing, can be further categorized into two programmes that focused on different target groups: the first were those identified as being 'socially harmful elements' such as 'former Kulaks' (Kulaks were peasant farmers with smallholdings), 'former whites', 'former Tsarist bureaucrats' and the like, targeted by a programme authorized by Order No. 00447 (30 July 1937); the second were those caught up in various anti-national operations ('German operation', 'Polish operation', 'Finnish operation', etc.) that targeted people suspected of having contact with particular foreign countries.[32] Although the total number of victims remains contested, reports prepared for Soviet premier Nikita Khrushchev suggest that at least 682,000 people were executed in 1937–38 from a total of 800,000 arrested.[33] But because these figures exclude deaths under torture or during preliminary investigations, or what were described as 'non-ratified execution supplements', it is generally estimated that the number of people executed is likely to have been closer to 800,000.[34] Of these, the single largest victim group were those caught up by Order No. 00447. This group accounted for 320,000 of the recorded executions.[35] In addition, some seven million people were deported to the Gulags or 'special settlements' of whom around 1.8 million died unnatural deaths.[36] Many more died at the hands of the Stalinists during and immediately after the Second World War.

Selective extermination requires that specific groups be identified and placed outside moral and legal protection and that grounds be found to justify this exclusion. Stalinist mass killing was justified on the grounds that certain groups of people—such as Old Bolsheviks, Mensheviks, and Trotskyists accused of conspiracy, a wide variety of 'socially harmful elements', kulaks, and those in contact with foreigners—were guilty of crimes against the state and the people and that group members could therefore be legitimately executed.[37]

[31] Nicolas Werth, 'The Mechanism of a Mass Crime: The Great Terror in the Soviet Union, 1937–1938', in Robert Gellately and Ben Kiernan (eds), *Specter of Genocide: Mass Murder in Historical Perspective* (Cambridge: Cambridge University Press), p. 218.

[32] Werth, 'Mechanism of a Mass Crime', p. 218.

[33] Naimark, *Stalin's Genocides*, p. 109; and Werth, 'Mechanisms of a Mass Crime', p. 217.

[34] Werth, 'Mechanism of a Mass Crime', pp. 217–18.

[35] Werth, 'Mechanism of a Mass Crime', p. 225.

[36] See Nicolas Werth, 'The Crimes of the Stalin Regime: Outline for an Inventory and Classification', in Dan Stone (ed.), *The Historiography of Genocide* (London: Palgrave, 2008), p. 403. The most notorious of the Gulag prisons was the massive complex at Kolyma, where 'millions' are said to have died between 1932 and 1954. For a detailed account, see Nicolas Werth, *Cannibal Island: Death in a Siberian Gulag* (Princeton, NJ: Princeton University Press, 2007); and Robert Conquest, *Kolyma: The Arctic Death Camps* (London: Macmillan, 1978).

[37] Lynne Viola, 'The Second Coming: Class Enemies in the Soviet Countryside, 1927–1935', in J. Arch Getty and Roberta T. Manning (eds), *Stalinist Terror: New Perspectives* (Cambridge: Cambridge University Press, 1993), p. 66.

By the 1930s, there was a broad consensus among the Stalinist leadership that it was legitimate to kill, deport and/or imprison members of groups deemed 'enemies of the people'.[38] In 1929, Stalin paved the way for the mass terror by decreeing the liquidation of the kulaks as a class.[39] Beyond this, Stalinists argued amongst themselves about which groups to target, the grounds for targeting them, and whether all those placed outside moral and legal protection should be exterminated and whether some could be 're-educated' instead.[40] Whilst the open repression was aimed at changing the composition of the elite, the mass programmes attempted to eradicate 'all marginal strata of the population'.[41] As Paul Hagenloh points out, this mass terror was 'the culmination of a decade-long radicalization of policing practice against "recidivist" criminals, social marginals, and all manner of lower-class individuals who did not or could not fit into the emerging Stalinist system'.[42] Most of those caught up by the mass programmes were done so in police sweeps of urban areas and on the basis of information about a person's social background, rather than by escalating processes of denunciation and interrogation.[43]

Whilst the Soviet government clearly targeted groups, either in whole or in part, it often insisted upon demonstrations of individual guilt. Most obviously, in preparation for the show trials, the People's Commissariat for Internal Affairs (NKVD) and local police forces went to considerable lengths to secure confessions and denouncements—including the use of torture, threatening family members, constructing fanciful tales of exotic and complicated conspiracies, and the application of drugs. Although the demand for confessions was most obvious in the show trials, the mass repression was also heavily bureaucratized and pursued confessions. The mass repression of kulaks and 'socially harmful elements' was carried out under Order No. 00447 which provided a legal basis for individual executions by establishing local three-man tribunals (*troikas*) to identify suspects and determine their punishment (usually immediate execution)—though there were some significant regional variations. Each case was recorded, with records identifying the accused, the alleged crime, and the proposed punishment. These records were ratified by

[38] Paul R. Gregory, *Terror by Quota: State Security from Lenin to Stalin (An Archival Study)* (New Haven: Yale University Press, 2009), p. 258.

[39] Leo Kuper, *Genocide: Its Political use in the Twentieth Century* (New Haven: Yale University Press, 1981), p. 48.

[40] Manus Midlarksy, *The Killing Trap: Genocide in the Twentieth Century* (Cambridge: Cambridge University Press), p. 320; and J. Arch Getty and Oleg V. Naumov, *The Road to Terror: Stalin and the Self-Destruction of the Bolsheviks, 1932–1939* (New Haven: Yale University Press, 1999), p. 109.

[41] Werth, 'Mechanism of a Mass Crime', p. 219.

[42] Paul M. Hagenloh, '"Socially Harmful Elements" and the Great Terror', in Fitzpatrick (ed.), *Stalinism*, p. 286.

[43] Hagenloh, 'Socially Harmful Elements', p. 303.

the NKVD leadership. Similar bureaucratic systems were established for the various national operations, such as that mandated by Order No. 00439 (25 July 1937) which called for the arrest of all Soviet citizens with ties to Germany.[44] There are at least three explanations as to why, when it was clearly targeting individuals as members of groups, the regime insisted on eliciting confessions or creating the appearance of individual judicial proceedings and this tells us much about how and why the Stalinists tried to legitimize their mass killing.

First, Stalin and the NKVD leadership were genuinely concerned about international reactions and assumed that the other major powers would criticize and maybe punish them for repressing large numbers of Soviet citizens.[45] This concern was heightened by a belief that the Soviet Union's long-term security rested on allying with either Nazi Germany or the West, and that prospective alliances might be harmed by the expected illegitimacy of mass killing. Even in this unlikeliest of contexts, therefore, civilian immunity was doing some work in creating expectations about what could be plausibly legitimized. From this perspective, the Stalinists were attempting to secure sufficient legitimacy for mass violence by portraying their victims as enemies of the state individually guilty of crimes punishable by death—much as the French Revolutionary government had done. Selective extermination arguments were modified to some extent to claim that although certain groups could in theory be exterminated as such, the Soviet state only persecuted those guilty of actual crimes. Forced and fabricated confessions helped to justify the persecution of whole groups on the grounds that its members were party to anti-state conspiracies.

Second, it is sometimes contended that Stalin, his inner circle, and the NKVD leadership genuinely believed that they were threatened by subversion orchestrated by implacable opponents of communism.[46] The extraction of confessions provided clear proof that they were correct and pointed towards new conspiracies as torture victims were coerced into naming others. Confessions and the appearance of judicial proceedings made mass terror appear to be the legitimate exercise of state authority against criminals.

Third, the need for confession may have been rooted in communist ideology itself—and it is worth noting in this regard that both the Khmer Rouge in Cambodia and Maoist Chinese emphasized admissions of guilt to justify their own mass killing. According to Eric Weitz, communist ideology presumed that everyone should come to see the virtues of communism.[47] Because all

[44] Werth, 'Mechanisms of a Mass Murder', p. 232.

[45] Gregory, *Terror by Quota*, p. 258.

[46] See Thurston, *Life and Terror*, pp. 81–2; and Medvedev, *Let History Judge*, p. 282.

[47] Eric D. Weitz, 'The Modernity of Genocides: War, Race and Revolution in the Twentieth Century', in Gellately and Kiernan, *Specter of Genocide*, p. 69.

humans had the capacity to accept communism, those that refused to do so should be forced to confess their crimes so that they might find the path to communism and, we might add, to demonstrate that responsibility for deviance lay with the victim and not with the ideology.

The overall justification for Stalinist terror was grounded in the Soviet legal system and rested on the relationship between the state, the party, and the people in communist thinking. The basic idea that underpinned the Soviet legal system was that the interests of the state, the party, and the people were indistinguishable, that they justified whatever measure was necessary for their fulfilment, and that the good of the individual was subordinate to the good of the collective.[48] For example, in 1939 the president of the Soviet Supreme Court argued that the application of the law should be determined by the stages of communist development and that the repression of kulaks (for 'theft' of socialist property) and 'terrorists' witnessed in the 1930s were necessary, and thus lawful, elements of the second stage of socialist development. The first stage, he argued, required the 'liquidation' of the exploiting classes and the second eliminated the remaining capitalist classes and the inevitable opposition to socialist development.[49] Stalinist terror thus rested on a concept of 'revolutionary terror' that entailed the swift adjudication of cases and rapid execution of punishments under laws self-consciously biased against those thought individually or collectively guilty of opposing the state.[50] As the head of the NKVD, Nikolai Ezhov, explained, 'there will be some innocent victims in this fight against fascist agents. We are launching a major attack on the enemy; let there be no resentment if we bump someone with an elbow. Better that ten innocent people should suffer than one spy get away'.[51] For good measure, Stalin's victims were also sometimes portrayed as sub-humans capable of unspeakable evil and enemies of both the government and people.[52] Beyond that, Stalinists appealed to a traditional defence of state terror, arguing that their victims were 'criminals' and 'terrorists' and that mass killing was necessary to protect the people's will for communism in its historic battle against capitalism. All of these arguments helped support the claim that certain groups were not protected by moral or legal norms and that their killing was therefore blameless and necessary.

To justify excluding whole groups from the moral and legal protections usually owed to Soviet citizens, the Stalinists pointed to anti-regime

[48] Robert Conquest, *The Great Terror: A Reassessment* (London: Pimlico, 1992), pp. 13 and 115. This idea was even expressed by some communists who came to oppose Stalin, see Jonathan Haslam, 'Political Opposition to Stalin and the Origins of the Terror in Russia', *The Historical Journal*, 29 (2) 1986, p. 412.

[49] Thurston, *Life and Terror*, p. 125.

[50] Thurston, *Life and Terror*, p. 6.

[51] Cited by Medvedev, *Let History Judge*, p. 339.

[52] Thurston, *Life and Terror*, pp. 67–8.

conspiracies and foreign threats, explaining repression as a necessary response to these threats.[53] The Soviet leadership repeatedly argued that the communist state confronted existential threats that could only be stemmed by state terror.[54] For instance, in a 1973 interview, Molotov defended Stalin by arguing that 'it was necessary to beat the Rights, necessary to beat the Trotskyists, to give the order to punish them'. Molotov rejected the argument that the mass killing went too far, describing that claim as 'an oversimplification'. He continued, 'those who think so don't understand the situation in the country at that time. Of course, demands came from Stalin, of course things went too far, but I think that everything was permitted thanks to one thing: only to hold on to power'.[55]

This line of reasoning was most obvious in relation to the show trials and the elaborate—and sometimes contradictory—conspiracies unearthed. But as I mentioned earlier, the hidden mass repressions were also prefaced on the view that the state was threatened by conspiracy and that those subjected to punishment were guilty of crimes. This logic underpinned the issuing of quotas in relation to Order No. 00447. Order No. 00447 estimated the number of likely conspirators in each region (ostensibly based on past activities) and issued quotas detailing the number of people to be arrested for political crimes and the number to be executed. The quota system authorized the arrest of some 269,100 people and the execution of 75,950 people each year but regional leaders were permitted to request additional quotas.[56] The system created powerful incentives for local elites to kill members of targeted groups irrespective of individual guilt but also sparked a spiral of escalation in which quotas were overfulfilled. The over-filling of quotas occurred for different reasons in different regions, but the principal causes included: competition between different arms of government and factions within particular branches of local government to prove their determination to comply with the central government's intent; problems associated with identifying kulaks in the absence of a clear central government definition; the settling of local scores; and the 'cleansing' of particular towns and cities of 'social misfits'.[57] The inflation of executions relative to arrests was largely caused by prison overcrowding and the serious resource burdens imposed on local governments by large prison populations. Also important was the principle of collective responsibility with its escalatory logic. Collective responsibility was used to justify the

[53] Medvedev, *Let History Judge*, p. 190.

[54] Getty and Naumov, *The Road to Terror*, p. 447.

[55] Molotov interview with Chuev, 1973 cited in Getty and Naumov, *The Road to Terror*, pp. 545–6.

[56] Nevertheless, the Soviets remained resolute in their insistence that all those who it killed were criminals. See Document 90, in Getty and Naumov, *Road to Terror*, p. 292.

[57] Werth, 'Mechanism of a Mass Crime', pp. 226–30; and Hagenloh, 'Socially Harmful Elements'.

extermination or imprisonment of the family members, work colleagues, friends and acquaintances of convicted 'criminals' on nothing more than the assumption that they must have known about (and were therefore implicated in) perceived misdeeds.[58] Collective responsibility sometimes warranted the slaughter or deportation of families and whole groups not for what they had actually done, but for what they might do in the future.[59] This was formalized somewhat in 1935, when a new law expanded the death penalty to cover not only terrorists, spies, and 'parasites' (not specifically defined) but also to those who 'were aware of such activities and projects relating to them'.[60]

As I noted earlier, the Stalinists remained sensitive to the need to secure sufficient external legitimacy. On the one hand, the charade of the show trials, concoction of conspiracy theories and portrayal of victims as criminals were designed to legitimate mass killing by making it appear a carefully targeted and lawful response to existential threats. Although the terror was rationalized by reference to selective extermination, the show trials were the principle mechanism by which it was justified to the world. But elite purges accounted for only a small portion of the terror. In relation to the mass terror, the regime took steps to keep the extent and intensity of mass killing away from world attention—and, for that matter, from the attention of most Russians. Foreigners were not permitted to visit areas where mass killings, arrests, and deportations were occurring and neither was such action reported in the Soviet press.[61] Mass deportations were not publicized within the Soviet Union either and the NKVD was instructed to conduct executions secretely and with 'efficiency'.[62] Thus, whilst Soviet citizens undoubtedly knew about the purges, it is doubtful that they knew about the extent of the mass killing.

These two strategies—one open and one hidden—succeeded in securing sufficient external legitimacy for the Stalinists. Within the Soviet Union itself, the terror enjoyed a degree of popularity: the 'Old Bolsheviks' and established local officials were blamed for economic hardship and not much missed; the repression of marginalized groups was relatively popular among the masses; and foreign conspiracies were widely accepted as the cause of economic and social upheavals.[63] Key external actors such as the US and British governments were critical but generally tolerated Stalin's portrayal of the victims. The tendency to excuse Stalin's excesses became still more apparent after the

[58] Hélène Carrère d'Encausse, *Stalin: Order Through Terror* (London: Longman, 1981), p. 36.

[59] Simon Sebag Montefiore, *Stalin: The Court of the Red Tsar* (London: Weidenfeld and Nicolson, 2003), p. 169.

[60] Decree of 9 June 1935, cited in d'Encausse, *Stalin*, p. 35.

[61] Naimark, *Stalin's Genocides*, p. 8.

[62] Gerlach and Werth, 'State Violence—Violent Societies', pp. 172–4.

[63] Sheila Fitzpatrick, *Stalin's Peasants: Resistance and Survival in the Russian Village after Collectivization* (Oxford: Oxford University Press, 1994).

start of the Second World War when the West actually colluded in covering-up Soviet atrocities (see Chapter 6).

The repression was no secret in the West but international attention focused almost entirely on the elite-level purges and show trials. Not until the opening of archives after the collapse of the Soviet Union did the nature and scale of the mass terror come to light. At the time, it was widely known that thousands or tens of thousands of Stalin's opponents and others only loosely associated with them were being shot and imprisoned—though not many suspected that the toll ran into the hundreds of thousands.[64] Nevertheless, opinion polls taken in the USA prior to the Second World War showed a clear and consistent preference for Stalin over Hitler, despite the fact that the Stalinist terror had reached its peak whilst the Holocaust remained some years off. One Gallup poll, taken in 1938, reported that in the case of a war between the Soviet Union and Germany, 83 per cent of Americans preferred a Soviet victory.[65] This is not to say that Americans approved of communism or Soviet mass killing. The liberal and conservative media were consistently critical of Stalin, repeatedly drawing parallels between Soviet communism and Nazism.[66] Moreover, by 1940, literary works depicting and critiquing the purges, killings and gulags were beginning to appear.[67] Nevertheless, US opinion consistently judged Stalin's regime to be less unpalatable than Hitler's and this relative legitimacy mitigated against punishing the Soviet Union.

Within this context, the emerging chorus of public condemnation of Soviet crimes did not prevent President Franklin Roosevelt from unconditionally recognizing the Soviet government and, eventually, allying with it.[68] Also, despite being informed about the killings from as early as 1931, the State Department refused to assist civil society groups wanting to deliver aid.[69] The Administration's attitude was tempered by a combination of strategic considerations (viewing Hitler as a greater threat to world order than Stalin) and uncertainty about the facts, which was intentionally engineered and leveraged by the Soviets. Joseph Davies, the US Ambassador in Moscow noted important and troubling irregularities with the show trials and expressed doubts about

[64] Medvedev, *Let History Judge*, p. 251.

[65] William D. Rubinstein, *The Myth of Rescue: Why the Democracies could not have Saved more Jews from the Nazis* (London: Routledge, 1997), p. 58.

[66] See Thomas R. Maddux, *Years of Estrangement: American Relations with the Soviet Union 1933–1941* (Tallahassee: University Presses of Florida, 1980), pp. 76–7.

[67] Paolo Spriano, *Stalin and the European Communists* trans. Jon Rothschild (London: Verso, 1985), pp. 39–42.

[68] Wilson and Hoover had both refused to recognize the Soviet government largely on moral grounds and particularly because it had refused to endorse freedom of religion.

[69] W. Wayne Morris, *Stalin's Famine and Roosevelt's Recognition of Russia* (Lanham: University Press of America, 1994), pp. 103, 106, 115.

whether the accused were receiving true justice.[70] These suspicions prompted some first hand witnesses, such as George Kennan, to question the legitimacy of the Soviet regime and the US alliance with it.[71] But Davies also wrote that the trials had revealed a network of Nazi-related conspiracy to overthrow the Bolsheviks. Later, he commented that the trials had effectively destroyed pro-Nazi groups in the Soviet Union and obliterated prospective fifth columnists.[72] Kennan also observed that the US embassy was unable to prove the falsity of Soviet allegations.[73] Thus, although it knew that Stalin was undertaking political killings, the US Administration was probably not aware of the scale of mass killing and was inclined to accept Stalin's view that the Soviet regime was beset by internal and external enemies.[74] Certainly, most Russians seemed to believe that the show-trials were genuine and that their country was the victim of countless conspiracies.[75]

US calculations were directly influenced by the perceived threat posed by Hitler's Germany. According to Kennan, Roosevelt was primarily concerned about the perceived need to secure Soviet support against German and Japanese expansionism.[76] This also explains why the Administration repeatedly stressed its commitment to the principle of non-interference in relation to what it repeatedly described as domestic matters for the Soviet Union.[77] That rhetorical commitment to non-interference was a product more of perceived strategic interests than principled commitment was evidenced by the fact that the many prominent State Department officials, including Cordell Hull, who referred to non-interference in the Soviet case, did not follow this line in other

[70] Joseph E. Davies, letter to his daughter, 14 July 1937, reprinted in Joseph E. Davies, *Mission to Moscow: A Record of Confidential Dispatches to the State Department, Official and Personal Correspondence, Current Diary and Journal Entries, Including Notes and Comment up to October, 1941* (Sydney: Angus and Robertson, 1942), pp. 133–4. W. Averell Harriman, Roosevelt's special ambassador to Churchill and Stalin, later described Davies' view as 'utter nonsense . . . he never understood what was going on'. See George Urban, 'Was Stalin (the Terrible) Really a "Great Man"? A Conversation with W. Averell Harriman', *Encounter*, 57 (5) 1981, p. 24.

[71] George F. Kennan, *Memoirs: 1925–1950*, Vol. I (Boston: Atlantic-Little Brown, 1967), p. 57.

[72] Davies, 'The Fifth Columnists in Russia—a Study in Hindsight: 1941', in Davies, *Mission to Moscow*, p. 211.

[73] John Lewis Gaddis, *Russia, the Soviet Union and the United States: An Interpretive History* (New York: McGraw-Hill, 1990), p. 131.

[74] Davies argued that although 'horrifying', the terror was a legitimate response to the threats facing the Soviet regime. See Richard H. Ullman, 'The Davies Mission and United States–Soviet Relations, 1937–1941', *World Politics*, 9 (1) 1957, pp. 216–25.

[75] They also believed that those carted off to the 'gulags' were indeed 'criminals'. See Robert Thurston, 'Stalinism in Context and Perspective: Sources of Permission to Hate in Europe', in James Kaye and Bo Strath (eds), *Enlightenment and Genocide, Contradictions of Modernity* (New York: Peter Lang, 2000), pp. 186 and 211.

[76] George F. Kennan, *Russia and the West under Lenin and Stalin* (London: Hutchinson, 1961), p. 299. On the wider implications, see Morris, *Stalin's Famine*, p. 161.

[77] Morris, *Stalin's Famine*, p. 140; and Dennis J. Dunn, *Caught Between Roosevelt and Stalin: America's Ambassadors to Moscow* (Lexington: University Press of Kentucky, 1998), pp. 47–58.

cases. Most notably, Hull made representations to the German government in protest at the Nazis' treatment of the Jews.

The US Administration's attitude towards Stalin's terror was therefore shaped by a mixture of uncertainty about the facts of the case and strategic judgements about the relative merits of the Stalinists and the Nazis. These considerations helped to override the obvious moral concerns that were aired both within the Administration and outside. The US Administration and American public broadly accepted the view that although Stalin's behaviour was far from legitimate, the Soviet regime was less illegitimate than Hitler.

British opinion was also divided and similarly swayed by uncertainty and strategic preferences. Whilst the labour movement endorsed closer ties with the Soviet Union and supported Stalin, liberals and conservatives generally condemned the regime's excesses. The *Morning Post* denounced the Soviet regime as 'an implacable enemy of the Christian faith' and later labelled it 'the Red Devils of Moscow', whilst the *Daily Mail* described the Soviet leadership as a 'gang of thieves and assassins'.[78] Fitzroy Maclean, a British attaché in Moscow criticized the show trials as patently illegal and obviously false.[79] However, Winston Churchill—an ardent critic of totalitarianism and well known for his condemnation of Nazism—refused to accept that Stalin was simply killing his opponents, apparently because he believed claims about Nazi inspired anti-Soviet conspiracies. According to Churchill, there was a 'so-called military and Old-Guard Communist conspiracy to overthrow Stalin and introduce a regime based on a pro-German policy.... Thereafter there followed the merciless, but perhaps not needless, military and political purge in Soviet Russia, and the series of trials in January, 1937 ... played so masterful a part'.[80] Nevertheless, it appears that concerns about Stalin's treatment of his own population inhibited cooperation between Britain, France, and the Soviet Union prior to the outbreak of war though such inhibitions broke down quickly as strategic imperatives came to the fore.[81]

European intellectuals were similarly polarized. Some on the left, such as Lion Feuchtwanger, defended Stalin.[82] George Bernard Shaw praised the Soviet leader, arguing that Stalinist terror was inspired by socialist principle and was not as widespread as sometimes portrayed. Others shared their

[78] W. P. Coates and Zelda K. Coates, *A History of Anglo-Soviet Relations* (London: Lawrence and Wishart, 1944), p. 337.

[79] Fitzroy Maclean, *Eastern Approaches* (London: Jonathan Cape, 1949).

[80] Winston Churchill, *The Second World War* (London: Cassell and Co., 1948), Vol. 1, pp. 288–9.

[81] Adam B. Ulam, *Expansion and Coexistence: Soviet Foreign Policy, 1917–73* (New York: Praeger, 1974), pp. 241–2.

[82] Medvedev, *Let History Judge*, pp. 250–1. Likewise, prominent American communist, Hershel Meyer rejected evidence of the Stalinist terror as anti-Soviet propaganda, Hershel D. Meyer, *The Khrushchev Report and the Crisis of the American Left* (New York: Independence Publishers, 1956), p. 10.

government's ambivalence. Bertold Brecht chose not to believe reports about the mass killing and congratulated Feuchtwanger for his generally pro-Soviet account of the show trials. That changed in 1941 when Brecht visited the Soviet Union and learnt of the arrest of prominent anti-fascists and the shooting of a former teacher.[83] Italian socialist leader, Pietro Nenni exemplified European ambivalence when he argued that the mass killing represented a 'double degeneration': the degeneration of the Party into a repressive regime and the degeneration of the opposition into a criminal conspiracy. Critical of the oppression, Nenni nonetheless accepted that there was some legal justification for it.[84] Leading British communist, R. Palme Dutt, obfuscated on the show trials noting only that their validity was 'disputed'.[85]

Other intellectuals denounced the Stalinist terror and campaigned against it. Nobel laureates Irène Joliot-Curie, Frédéric Joliot-Curie, and Jean Perrin criticized Stalin and demanded the release of prisoners.[86] Albert Einstein wrote to Stalin protesting the arrest of prominent scientists. There was also disquiet among some communist sympathizers, prompting the Soviet ambassador to the UK to report that the terror was undermining support for socialism among European workers.[87]

Although Stalinist terror was widely criticized and there is little evidence that its account of selective extermination was emphatically endorsed outside its own circle, the Soviet Union acquired sufficient legitimacy for its mass killing thanks to the toleration of foreign governments. The toleration of external actors was primarily predicated on a combination of uncertainty, which was deliberately leveraged by the regime and assisted by the geographic remoteness of the Gulags and kulak populations, and judgements about the relative legitimacy of, and threats posed by, the Soviet and Nazi regimes. It was these contextual factors, rather than the merits of the justifications for mass killing proposed by the Stalinists that best explain why the Soviet terror generated much less criticism and punishment than other similar episodes around the same time.

## NAZISM AND THE HOLOCAUST

Mass murder reached its nadir with the Nazi Holocaust. The Nazis slaughtered around six million Jews, three million Russian prisoners of war, 500,000

[83] Medvedev, *Let History Judge*, p. 251.
[84] Medvedev, *Let History Judge*, p. 251.
[85] R. Palme Dutt, *The Internationale* (London: Lawrence and Wishart, 1964), p. 246.
[86] Letter reprinted in Alexander Weissberg, *The Accused* (New York: Simon and Schuster, 1951), pp. xviii–xix.
[87] Medvedev, *Let History Judge*, pp. 253–5.

German opponents and communists, around 70,000 handicapped Germans, thousands of homosexuals, as well as Roma, other marginalized groups, and those who showed sympathy for any of their other victims. The question of how widely Nazism was endorsed remains hotly contested and is difficult to determine with any degree of accuracy. The matter is made particularly complex by the fact that whilst much of the killing was done at the initiative of mid- and low-level functionaries without specific orders, other functionaries inhibited or slowed the killing. What is more, support for Nazi ideology was only one of the motivations that animated the perpetrators—others included material gain, peer pressure, and fear. In short, not all the killers were Nazis and not all the Nazis were killers.[88] Within Germany, Nazism and the elimination of the Jews found many willing supporters but also sites of opposition. In the wider Nazi orbit were willing executioners such as the Croatian *Ustashe* and the somewhat less enthusiastic such as the Hungarian government which willingly shipped some Jews to their death but in trying to protect Budapest's Jews argued that not all Jews posed a threat.[89] Others in Nazi occupied Europe, most notably the governments of Denmark and Bulgaria, rejected extermination in its entirety, arguing that it was morally wrong. As a result, Jewish populations in these two countries survived the war largely intact. Although there were significant pockets of anti-Semitism outside the Nazis' sphere of influence, most Western governments and their societies were resolutely critical, seeing Nazism as a greater evil than Stalinist communism. Thus, whilst the Nazi ideology of selective extermination secured sufficient legitimacy within its own orbit such that, as Dan Stone points out, the Holocaust would not have been conducted so effectively without widespread collaboration in several different countries, it failed to persuade many outsiders.

So-called 'intentionalists' argue that the Holocaust was a product of widely held anti-semitism and that thousands of individuals chose to participate because they agreed with Nazi ideology.[90] The contrary, 'structuralist', position argues that the Holocaust was a bureaucratic solution to an administrative problem and did not require any particular ideological commitment or heightened degree of racism.[91] The problem with the intentionalist account

[88] For instance, see Christian Gerlach and Nicolas Werth, 'State Violence—Violent Societies', in Geyer and Fitzpatrick (eds), *Beyond Totalitarianism*, pp. 134–5. The same was true in the Soviet Union.

[89] On the wide variation of local responses and high levels of collaboration, see Stone, *Histories of the Holocaust*, p. 17 ff.

[90] The best known, and most controversial, expression of the intentionalist position is Daniel J. Goldhagen, *Hitler's Willing Executioners: Ordinary Germans and the Holocaust* (New York: Knopf, 1996).

[91] E.g. Hannah Arendt, *Eichmann in Jerusalem: A Report on the Banality of Evil* (London: Penguin, 1994); Zygmunt Bauman, *Modernity and the Holocaust* (Ithaca: Cornell University Press, 1989), p. 17.

is that it downplays the role of the state and its bureaucracy in enabling, managing, and executing the Holocaust and cannot account for the participation of many 'ordinary' people who displayed little overt commitment to ideology or racism. The problem with the structuralist account is that it overlooks human agency and the deliberate Nazi policy of exterminating the Jews, as well as the handicapped, homosexuals, Roma, and others. These problems have persuaded some historians to move beyond the dichotomy by recognizing that Nazi violence had different perpetrators, features and motives in different times and places.[92] What I want to demonstrate in this discussion of how the Nazis' attempted to secure sufficient legitimacy for the Holocaust is that totalitarian mass killing, of which the Holocaust was exemplary, was predicated on an ideology of selective extermination that combined *both* a discriminatory ethic—which was accepted by millions of people—that afforded no value at all to the life of certain groups *and* the mobilization of the state to accomplish that goal.[93]

I argued earlier that Nazism was influenced by a colonial and Social Darwinist worldview which privileged the protection of the 'master race' and permitted the destruction of inferior races or groups, especially if—as with the Jews, handicapped, and homosexuals—they risked infecting or weakening the master race.[94] It hardly needs saying that the Nazis believed such groups to be well beyond the pale of moral protection and therefore liable for extermination. As early as 1923, Hitler argued that the Jews were not fully human. According to Hitler, '[t]he Jews are undoubtedly a race, but they are not human. They cannot be human in the sense of being in the image of God . . . Jews are the image of the devil. Jewry means the racial tuberculosis of the nations'.[95] This doctrine, and the logic of extermination that accompanied it, lay at the heart of Nazism from the outset. In 1919, Hitler argued that the goal of anti-Semitism must be 'the total removal of the Jews' and in *Mein Kampf* insisted that the defence of the civilized world depended on the destruction of the Jewish people. He wrote, 'If with the help of his Marxist creed, the Jew is victorious over the other peoples of the world, his crown will be the funeral wreath of humanity and this planet will, as it did millions of years ago, move through the ether devoid of men. Hence today, I believe, that I am acting in accordance with the will of the Almighty creator, by defending

[92] Christopher Browning, 'Beyond Intentionalism and Functionalism: The Decision for the Final Solution Reconsidered', in Christopher Browning, *The Path to Genocide: Essays on Launching the Final Solution* (Cambridge: Cambridge University Press, 1992), pp. 86–121.

[93] A position suggested by A. D. Moses, 'Structure and Agency in the Holocaust: Daniel J. Goldhagen and His Critics', *History and Theory*, 37 (2) 1998, pp. 194–219.

[94] See Peter J. Haas, *Morality After Auschwitz: The Radical Challenge of the Nazi Ethic* (Philadelphia: Fortress Press, 1988).

[95] Fest, *Hitler*, p. 365.

myself against the Jew'.[96] Indeed, the Nazis often insisted that Jews were responsible for plunging Europe into war, arguing that 'Europe cannot find peace until the Jewish problem has been solved' but that the result would be 'the annihilation of the Jewish race in Europe'.[97] Hitler also insisted that the Jews were collectively responsible for various wrongs done to the Aryans.[98] There is no evidence that at this early stage Hitler knew how he would affect his plans, but that the eventual extermination of the Jews was pivotal to Nazi ideology from the outset is absolutely clear.[99]

The extermination of Jews was supported within the Nazi movement itself and its broader 'Aryan' community.[100] According to one estimate, 25 per cent of adult Germans were directly involved in the killing or abuse of Jews in one form or another, though as mentioned earlier there were many reasons why people participated—ranging from ideological belief to financial reward and social pressure.[101] Historians generally agree that the Nazis did not coerce individuals (other than co-opted prisoners) to participate in the slaughter and there is no evidence that the agencies most responsible for the killing found recruitment difficult.[102] Understanding the *cause* of such sentiments is beyond the scope of this study. What is important for our purposes is that Nazism was underpinned by an ideology of selective extermination that removed whole groups from moral protection in order to make blameless their extermination and that this ideology secured sufficient legitimacy in many parts of Europe such that a large portion of German society as well as societies in Poland, Ukraine, the Baltic states, the Balkans, France, and even German occupied Britain either actively supported, willingly acquiesced, or remained indifferent to the transportation and killing of Jews. Many Ukrainians, Croats,

[96] Adolf Hitler, *Mein Kampf* trans. Ralph Mannheim (Boston: Houghton Mifflin, 1971), pp. 64–5.

[97] Adolf Hitler, speech to the Reichstag, 30 January 1939. Reproduced in J. Noakes and G. Pridham (eds), *Nazism 1919–1945*, Vol. 3: *Foreign Policy, War and Racial Extermination. A Documentary Reader* (Exeter: Exeter Studies in History, No. 13: 1988), p. 1049.

[98] See Michael Burleigh and Wolfgang Wippermann, *The Racial State: Germany 1933–1945* (Cambridge: Cambridge University Press, 1991), pp. 98–9.

[99] Potential alternatives to the Holocaust, such as deporting the Jews to Madagascar or housing them in Russia, all had in mind the same end state, the eventual destruction of the Jewish 'race'. See Burleigh and Wipperman, *The Racial State*, p. 99.

[100] Omer Bartov, 'Defining Enemies, Making Victims: Germans, Jews and the Holocaust', *The American Historical Review*, 103 (3) 1998, p. 783.

[101] Joachim Fest, *The Face of the Third Reich: Portraits of the Nazi Leadership* (New York: Weidenfeld and Nicolson, 1970). Michael Mann has identified nine principal sets of motives that prompt individuals to participate in 'Final Solutions', Mann, *The Dark Side of Democracy*, pp. 27–9.

[102] Goldhagen, *Hitler's Willing Executioners*, p. 179. Goldhagen's critics accept this basic proposition, but dispute its causes. See Alex Hinton, 'Why Did the Nazis Kill? Genocide and the Goldhagen Controversy', *Anthropology Today*, 14 (5) 1988, pp. 9–10; and Avishai Margalit and Gabriel Motzkin, 'The Uniqueness of the Holocaust', *Philosophy and Public Affairs*, 25 (1) 1996, pp. 69–70.

Hungarians, Poles, and Lithuanians were willing accomplices in the Holocaust. But so too was the British police in Jersey, which did not have to be coerced into transporting the handful of Jews there, and the Norwegian police.

On closer scrutiny, though, we find some marked variation in responses to Nazi ideology. The most notable cases of basic agreement with Nazism were the Antonescu regime in Romania and the *Ustashe* regime in Croatia.[103] For the purposes of illustration I focus only on the first, but it is important to stress that the Croatian *Ustashe* were enthusiastic adherents of Nazism and succeeded in eliminating virtually the entire Jewish population of Croatia and Bosnia in their first year.[104] After the Soviet Union seized Bessarabia and northern Bukovina from Romania in 1940, the retreating Romanian army massacred Jews, whom they blamed for Romania's defeat.[105] The killing continued after the German invasion of the Soviet Union.[106] Encouraged and supported by the SS, Romanian authorities began to deport the remaining Jews from Bessarabia and Bukovina into a newly occupied part of Ukraine labelled 'Transnistria'. Approximately 65,000 Jews were killed during the deportation and a further 130,000 died once in Transnistria.[107] There is little doubt that Antonescu's policy was influenced by sympathy towards Nazi anti-Semitism and its ideology of selective extermination.[108] On coming to power in September 1940, Antonescu insisted that 'I don't protect Jews, because they bear the blame for most of the disasters visited on this country'. Like the Nazis, Antonescu believed in a world Jewish conspiracy and argued that all those he deported were guilty of crimes against the Romanian people.[109] Antonescu outlined a Romanian version of Nazism whereby Romanian nationalists, identified and mobilized through Orthodox Christianity, would repudiate and destroy the 'Jewish morality' imbued with 'internationalism and humanism'.[110] But there were important anomalies in the Romanian case. Not only were the Jews of 'old Romania' (territory not involved in the 1940–42 land exchanges), Regat, and southern Transylvania not deported to Transnistria, but also the 60–70,000 Jews of Transnistria were not subsequently deported to

[103] Midlarsky, *Killing Trap*, p. 204.

[104] See Stevan K. Pavlowitch, *Hitler's New Disorder: The Second World War in Yugoslavia* (London: Hurst and Co., 2008), pp. 29–32.

[105] Radu Ionid, *The Holocaust in Romania: The Destruction of Jews and Gypsies Under the Antonescu Regime, 1940–1944* (Chicago: Ivan Dee, 2000), pp. 20–2.

[106] Raul Hilberg, *Destruction of the European Jews*, rev. edn (New York: Holmes and Meir, 1985), p. 771.

[107] This, according to Hilberg, made Romania second only to Germany in its massacre of Jews. Hilberg, *Destruction of the European Jews*, p. 759.

[108] Cited by Jean Ancel, 'Antonescu and the Jews', in Michael Berenbaum and Abraham J. Peck, *Holocaust and History: The Known, the Unknown, the Disputed, the Re-examined* (Bloomington: Indiana University Press with the US Holocaust Memorial Museum, 2002), p. 463.

[109] Ancel, 'Antonescu', p. 466.

[110] Ancel, 'Antonescu', p. 468.

Nazi killing centres. There is evidence that plans for their deportation existed as early as 1942, but Antonescu had a profound change of heart. Seeing the tide of war turning against the Nazis, he planned to switch sides. Roosevelt used diplomatic channels to warn the Romanian leader that he would be held accountable for the fate of the Jews. The principal cause of Antonescu's change of heart was therefore self-interested but it does suggest that the hold of Nazi ideology on the Romanian government was less strong than its hold on the other groups who continued to kill Jews to very end of the war.[111]

Other states and societies complied with the basic thrust of Nazi thinking but tried to moderate its effects. The Hungarian experience provides a good example of this type of response. Although the Hungarian government shared Antonescu's anti-Semitic standpoint, its policy towards the Jews was more complex. Anti-Semitism in Hungary was rooted in local history, augmented by the short-lived Communist dictatorship led by Béla Kun and other prominent Jews immediately after the First World War.[112] When Kun was overthrown, the counter-revolutionary terror that followed was marked with anti-Semitism.[113] According to Randolph Braham, only fear of Western intervention prompted the government to order a cessation of the pogroms.[114] Hungary was the first country outside Germany to pass anti-Jewish legislation and in 1939 all its Jews were registered.[115] In 1941, Hungary began transporting non-Hungarian Jews to Poland.[116] Between 18,000 and 23,000 Jews were killed immediately. Others were transported to the Eastern front to serve as forced labourers, and approximately 42,000 of them died in Ukraine. But the vast majority of Hungary's approximately 840,000 Jews were not transported during this period and their conditions might have actually improved.[117] Whilst this is partly explained by the fact that the Nazis did not apply pressure on Hungarian leader Miklos Horthy to deliver up Jews because he was considered an entirely reliable ally, it was also partly a product of differences in ideology. Whereas Nazis made no distinction between Jews, Hungarian nationalists distinguished between 'Magyarized' Hungarian Jews—inferior people but not deserving death—and 'alien' or foreign Jews liable for execution

[111] See Ancel, 'Antonescu', p. 476; Schechtman, 'Transnistria Reservation', *YIVO Annual of Jewish Social Sciences*, 8, 1953, p. 389; and Jean Ancel, 'German-Romanian Relations During the Second World War', in Randolph L. Braham (ed.), *Tragedy of Romanian Jewry* (New York: Columbia University Press, 1994), pp. 70–3.

[112] David Ceserani, *Genocide and Rescue: The Holocaust in Hungary 1944* (Oxford: Berg, 1977), p. 12; and Randolph L. Braham, 'Holocaust in Hungary', in Berembaum and Peck, *Holocaust and History*, p. 432.

[113] Midlarksy, *The Killing Trap*, p. 253.

[114] Randolph L. Braham, *The Politics of Genocide: The Holocaust in Hungary*, Vol. 1 (New York: Columbia University Press, 1981), pp. 18–19.

[115] Midlarksy, *The Killing Trap*, pp. 254–5.

[116] Midlarksy, *The Killing Trap*, p. 255.

[117] Braham, 'The Holocaust in Hungary', p. 433.

because they were vastly inferior people who threatened the nation. In 1944, Horthy told a conference of German and Hungarian officials: 'The Germans . . . want to deport the Jews. I don't mind. I hate the Galician Jews and the Communists. Out with them, out of the country! But you must see . . . that there are some Jews who are as good Hungarians as you and I. For example, here are little Chorin and Vida—aren't they good Hungarians? I can't allow these to be taken away. But they can take away the rest'.[118] When full-scale deportations to extermination camps began in April 1944, Jews were selected on this basis, with the most 'Magyarized' Jews of Budapest spared until later in the year.

On 7 July 1944, towards the end of the war, Horthy ordered a complete halt to the deportation of Hungarian Jews. Four factors played a role in influencing this decision. First, Horthy claimed that he came to believe that the Jews were being deported to extermination camps, rather than to work in factories (as the Germans had told him). Second, Roosevelt warned the Hungarian government that the persecution of Jews 'would not be tolerated'. The salience of this threat was reinforced on 2 July 1944, when the US Air Force bombed Budapest, an act that Horthy interpreted as retaliation for the deportation. Third, in late June 1944 (after the liberation of Rome in early June), Pope Pius XII appealed to Horthy to end the deportation. Fourth, the neutral Swedish government made a similar appeal in late June.[119] Retreating German forces responded by overthrowing Horthy. The deportations recommenced at a heightened rate.[120] In total, approximately 569,000 Jews were transported from Hungary to the extermination camps in three months in 1944—the fastest rate of deportation and killing in the Holocaust.[121]

The Hungarian case is full of perplexing contradictions. The fact that Hungarian Jews lived, relatively unscathed, in the geographic centre of the Nazi world until the very end of the war is indicative of the fact that whilst anti-Semitism may have been pervasive, this could not always be equated with support for Nazism. Horthy was undoubtedly a tyrant and a racist, but he did not share the Nazi worldview in its entirety. Hungarian nationalists considered only *some* Jews to be entirely beyond moral protection. But the fact that the authorities were able to transport so many people, so quickly, to a fate by then well-known, and in the knowledge that Germany's defeat was close at hand, led one commentator to argue that 'the destruction of the Hungarian

[118] Cited in Braham, *Politics of Genocide*, p. 61.

[119] See Hilberg, *The Destruction of the European Jews*, p. 856; Yehuda Baeur, *History of the Holocaust* (New York: Franklin Watts, 1982), pp. 58 and 318; and Leni Yahil, *The Holocaust: The Fate of European Jewry* (Oxford: Oxford University Press, 1987), p. 640.

[120] Hilberg, *Destruction of the European Jews*, p. 859.

[121] Midlarky, *Killing Trap*, p. 258.

Jewish community tells us how committed to their ethic' the Germans and their Hungarian functionaries were.[122]

There was more sustained resistance to the Nazis' ideology of selective extermination in other parts of the fascist world, most notably in Mussolini's Italy and Franco's Spain. Perhaps the most interesting case was that of Mussolini. According to some, Mussolini was a convinced anti-Semite.[123] Others, though, suggest that Italian fascism was not anti-Semitic, at least in its origins.[124] Before his alliance with Hitler, Mussolini's worldview differed markedly from Hitler's.[125] Mussolini believed in the superiority of Latin culture and the colonial 'civilizing mission', holding that most nations, including Slavs, Jews, and Ethiopians, could be socialized into Latin culture. In contrast to Hitler's biological determinism, Mussolini thought that fascist nations could be constructed through assimilation and the propagation of martial values.[126] Not only did Mussolini reject Hitler's interpretation of Social Darwinism as an eternal racial struggle, he also refused to single out the Jews as the source of all trouble.[127] Nonetheless, the Italian dictator introduced anti-Semitic legislation in the early 1930s though under little pressure from the Nazis to do so.[128] Even then, however, conditions for Jews in Italy were considerably better than in other parts of Europe.[129] It was with good reason that Jews, Serbs, communists, and other victims of *Ustashe* terror in the Balkans sought sanctuary in Italian held territory.[130] Mussolini also steadfastly refused to deport Jews from Italy. Before his fall in 1943 and the seizure of parts of Italy by the Nazis, *no* Italian Jews were deported to concentration camps or killing centres.[131] Although the Nazis soon got to work, two-thirds of Italy's Jews survived the Holocaust, one of the highest survival rates in Europe.[132]

[122] Haas, *Morality after Auschwitz*, p. 108.

[123] E.g. Rubinstein, *The Myth of Rescue*, p. 211.

[124] Norman Cantor, *The Sacred Chain: A History of the Jews* (London: Fontana, 1995), p. 338. According to Cantor, 'the advent of fascism made little difference to the old Jewish communities in Italy', a point disputed by Joshua D. Zimmerman (ed.), *The Jews of Italy Under Fascist and Nazi Rule, 1922–1945* (Cambridge: Cambridge University Press, 2005).

[125] In 1934 he remarked that Hitler's theories were so 'absurd' that if carried to their logical conclusion, the Laplanders could claim to be the 'bearers of the highest culture'. Cited by Esmonde Robertson, 'Race as a Factor in Mussolini's Policy in Africa and Europe', *Journal of Contemporary History*, 23 (1) 1988, p. 38.

[126] See Meir Michealis, *Mussolini and the Jews: German-Italian Relations and the Jewish Question 1922–1945* (Oxford: Oxford University Press, 1978), especially pp. 120–8.

[127] For this, there was no love lost between Mussolini and Nazi ideologues. See Michealis, *Mussolini*, pp. 39–41; and Robertson, 'Race', p. 39.

[128] See Joshua D. Zimmerman, 'Introduction' in Zimmerman (ed.), *Jews in Italy*, pp. 3–7.

[129] Cantor, *Sacred Chain*, p. 339.

[130] Pavlowitch, *Hitler's New Disorder*.

[131] But see James Walston, 'History and Memory of the Italian Concentration Camps', *The Historical Journal*, 40 (1) 1997, pp. 171–3.

[132] Cantor, *Sacred Chain*, p. 339.

Though it employed its own brand of totalitarian mass killing against communists and other opponents, Franco's Spanish fascism did not share the Nazi worldview. Virtually no Jews lived in Spain prior to the Second World War, but Franco permitted a small number of Jews fleeing from France to enter Spain and remain there.[133] In response, Germany pressured Franco into closing Spain's borders, a move which was criticized in April 1943 by Churchill.[134] In the face of this criticism, Franco reinstated the policy permitting Jewish and other refugees to enter Spain and remain there.[135]

Although opposition to deportation was more difficult in occupied Europe where the Nazis were able to exert direct pressure, there were many examples nevertheless—again indicating opposition to the Nazi worldview. In 1942, the Finnish government planned to deport its Jews but changed course after receiving a petition protesting the plan.[136] In 1943, German plans to deport Danish Jews were thwarted by concerted opposition from both the government and the people.[137] In response, the Nazis overthrew the government and ruled directly. This did not stop Danes from hiding Jews and many of the 475 who were captured and transported to Germany were later saved by the Danish government.[138] The Bulgarian government adopted relatively moderate anti-Jewish legislation in 1941, principally to cement its alliance with Germany and keep Bulgaria out of the war.[139] When Hitler stated his intention to exterminate Bulgaria's Jews, Bulgarian parliamentarians expressed their opposition.[140] The protests enabled King Boris, who opposed deportations, to argue against the plan by insisting that it could destabilize Bulgaria.[141] To appease the Nazis, the Bulgarian government moved the approximately 45,000 Jews of Sofia to other cities but no Bulgarian Jews were transported to killing centres. Although many factors contributed to saving Bulgaria's Jews,

[133] Haim Avni, *Spain, the Jews and Franco* (Philadelphia: Jewish Publication Society of America, 1982), p. 100.

[134] Avni, *Spain*, p. 104.

[135] Avni, *Spain*, pp. 100–4.

[136] See Tuomo Polvinen, *Between East and West: Finland in International Politics, 1944–1947*, ed. and trans. D. G. Kirby and Peter Herring (Minneapolis: University of Minnesota Press, 1986), pp. 280–4.

[137] Michael R. Marrus and Robert O. Paxton, 'The Nazis and the Jews in Occupied Western Europe, 1940–1944', *Journal of Modern History*, 54 (4) 1982, p. 688.

[138] Leni Yahil, 'The Uniqueness of the Rescue of Danish Jewry' in Yisrael Gutman and Efraim Zuroff (eds), *Rescue Attempts During the Holocaust* (Jerusalem: Yad Vashem, 1977), pp. 620–1; Midlarksy, *The Killing Trap*, pp. 282–4; Jean-Claude Favez, *The Red Cross and the Holocaust*, trans. John and Beryl Fletcher (Cambridge: Cambridge University Press, 1999), p. 74.

[139] There is broad consensus that Bulgaria's King Boris III passed the law for pragmatic reasons. See Frederick B. Chary, *The Bulgarian Jews and the Final Solution, 1940–1944* (Pittsburgh: University of Pittsburgh Press, 1972); and Tzvetan Todorov, *The Fragility of Goodness: Why Bulgaria's Jews Survived the Holocaust* trans. Arthur Denner (Princeton: Princeton University Press, 2001).

[140] Midlarksy, *The Killing Trap*, p. 327; and Todorov, *Fragility of Goodness*, p. 158.

[141] Midlarksy, *The Killing Trap*, p. 328.

including the country's relative remoteness, one important factor was that, as in Denmark, a significant proportion of the Bulgarian population rejected Nazism and were prepared to oppose it.[142]

What becomes clear from this discussion is that there were significant numbers of people within Nazi dominated Europe who did not accept its ideology. Sometimes, the differences were relatively small as in the Hungarian nationalists differentiated 'Magyarized' and 'alien' Jews; others, such as Mussolini, accepted the basic idea of racial hierarchy but not the practice of extermination; still others, including Franco's Spain and the Bulgarian government, deviated still further from Nazi ideology. In many of these cases, the Nazis were sometimes forced to coerce ostensible allies.

Evaluation of the Allies' response to the Holocaust is intimately related to the question of rescue. For some, the failure to rescue was a product of shared anti-Semitism on the part of the allies.[143] It is certainly true that decision-makers outside the Nazi-controlled world knew about the extermination of the Jews almost as soon as it began. At issue here though is not whether these actors could or should have done more to help the Jews, but the extent to which their failure to do so reflected a degree of sympathy with Nazi ideology. My basic contention here is that although there were obviously individuals who sympathized with the Nazis in both the governments and societies of the West, there was a large majority opinion that was deeply hostile to Nazism. This was most clearly expressed in the inter-allied statement of December 1942 condemning the genocide of Jews and promising retribution for those responsible.[144] To illustrate this, I will briefly consider American, British, and Catholic responses in turn.

Whilst Americans were informed about the extermination of Jews as early as 1941, there was some disbelief about the reports even among the Jewish community.[145] Anti-Semitic and far-right groups (such as *America First* and Father Coughlin's 'Union Party') were active in the USA and counted many prominent Americans among their number.[146] Perhaps the most infamous

[142] See Midlarsky, *The Killing Trap*, p. 330.

[143] E.g. David S. Wyman, *The Abandonment of the Jews* (New York: The New Press, 1984); William Perl, *The Holocaust Conspiracy: An International Policy of Genocide* (New York: Shapolsky, 1989); and Bernard Wasserstein, *Britain and the Jews of Europe* (Oxford: Oxford University Press, 1979). Others have pointed to the Catholic Church's collusion with the Nazis as evidencing its broad agreement with the Nazi policy. In particular, John Cornwell, *Hitler's Pope: The Secret History of Pius XII* (London: Viking, 1999).

[144] David Ceserani, 'Mad Dogs and Englishmen: Towards a Taxonomy of Rescuers in a "Bystander Country"', in David Ceserani and Paul A. Levine (eds), *Bystanders to the Holocaust: A Re-Evaluation* (London: Frank Cass, 2002), p. 36.

[145] A point demonstrated throughout Walter Laqueur, *The Terrible Secret: Suppression of the Truth about Hitler's 'Final Solution'*, new edn, (New York: Henry Holt and Co., 1998).

[146] Wayne S. Cole, *America First: The Battle against Intervention 1940–1941* (New York: Octagon Books, 1971).

was Charles Lindbergh.[147] Lindbergh held the Jews (along with the British and Roosevelt) responsible for the Second World War and argued that Jewish ownership of the American media and 'government' represented the 'greatest danger' to American society.[148] But Lindbergh's views were widely denounced. The 1940 Republican presidential candidate, Wendell Wilkie, described them as the 'most un-American talk' in living memory and Thomas Dewey, Republican candidate in 1944 and 1948, denounced Lindbergh's speeches as 'an inexcusable abuse of the right of freedom of speech'.[149] Indicators of American public opinion in the 1930s also suggest that the public was hostile to Nazism. Studies of the media and Gallup polling demonstrate a consistent and widely held hostility towards Nazi Germany and its policy towards the Jews. In one poll, taken in 1938, 94 per cent of respondents indicated that they 'disapproved' of Hitler's policy towards the Jews; 83 per cent said that they would rather the Soviet Union prevail over Germany should war breakout between them.[150] Deborah Lipstadt shows that American newspapers were almost universally hostile to Nazi Germany. Commenting on American media reports of *Kristallnacht*, she found that 'though the press may have offered differing explanations for the pogrom, there was little doubt about its revulsion at Germany'.[151]

The American government was also consistent in its condemnation of Nazism. Although it could certainly have adopted a more liberal refugee policy to aid the escape of European Jews in the 1930s, its restrictive policy was more a product of antipathy to refugees than an expression of sympathy with Nazi ideals.[152] There is little doubt that the Roosevelt administration was deeply opposed to Nazism. In addition to lying to Congress about the extent of US aid to anti-Nazi forces before Japan's attack on Pearl Harbour, Roosevelt publicly condemned the killing of Jews as soon as news of it began to appear in 1941 and in 1943–44 warned European leaders that they would be held accountable for their treatment of Jews.[153] Once engaged in the war, Roosevelt argued—not wholly implausibly—that the best way to save Europe's Jews was to win the

[147] Other famous anti-Semites and Nazi sympathizers include Henry Ford.

[148] See Wayne S. Cole, *Charles A. Lindbergh and the Battle against American Intervention in World War II* (New York: Harcourt Brace Jovanovich, 1971), pp. 171–3.

[149] Cole, *Lindbergh*, p. 175.

[150] Rubinstein, *Myth of Rescue*, pp. 46 and 55–8.

[151] Deborah E. Lipstadt, *Beyond Belief: The American Press and the Coming of the Holocaust 1933–1945* (New York: Free Press, 1986), p. 104.

[152] See Deborah E. Lipstadt, 'America and the Holocaust', *Modern Judaism*, 10 (3) 1990, pp. 286 and 291; and Midlarsky, *The Killing Trap*, pp. 243–4.

[153] See Cathal J. Nolan, '"Bodyguard of Lies": Franklin D. Roosevelt and Defensible Deceit in World War II', in Cathal J. Nolan (ed.), *Ethics and Statecraft: The Moral Dimension of International Affairs*, 2nd edn (Westport, CN: Praeger, 2004), pp. 35–58.

war as quickly as possible, rejecting specific military measures to rescue Jews as unlikely to succeed and risky diversions that might lengthen the war.[154]

British responses were similar. There were Nazi sympathizers and, as we noted earlier, prominent figures on both the right and left of politics endorsed the basic idea that the extermination of inferior or threatening groups was morally blameless. Most prominent in this respect was Sir Oswald Mosley and his 'British Union of Fascists'. But Mosley's organization was widely condemned by the British elite. Lloyd George described Mosley as 'a political maniac', insisting 'that all decent people must combine to kill his movement'.[155] There was a strong strain of anti-Semitism in the Conservative Party, with twenty-eight Tory MPs being members of right-wing organizations dedicated to improving relations between Britain and Nazi Germany.[156] This number, though, was fewer than the number of Jewish Conservative MPs. As in the USA, although anti-Semitism was undoubtedly alive in Britain, in the main British society was consistently hostile to Nazism. Andrew Scharf's study of the British media during this period shows that almost without exception the British press was sharply critical of the Nazis' treatment of the Jews.[157]

The British government—particularly under Churchill—was resolutely opposed to Nazism, choosing in 1939–40 to stand against Nazi Germany rather than sue for peace. Although much has been made of the fact that Britain did not enter the war in 1939 to save Jews or other persecuted groups, the fall of Chamberlain, rise of Churchill, and the decision to continue the war were, to some significant extent, moral decisions underpinned by revulsion towards Nazism.[158] Churchill's record conveys the point that it was both German aggression *and* the nature of the Nazi regime that compelled Britain to stand against it, the future Prime Minister condemning Hitler's treatment of the Jews as early as 1933.[159] In a message to America on 16 October 1938, Churchill insisted that: 'We are confronted with another theme. It is not a new theme; it leaps out upon us from the Dark Ages—racial persecution, religious intolerance, deprivation of free speech, the conception of the citizen as a mere soulless fraction of the State', he continued, 'people say we ought not to allow

[154] See Gerhard L. Weinberg, 'The Allies and the Holocaust' in Berembaum and Peck (eds), *The Holocaust and History*, pp. 489–90.

[155] Cited in Rubinstein, *Myth of Rescue*, p. 60. In June 1934, Mosley was banned from appearing on the BBC partially thanks to pressure from the Foreign Office. See Robert Skidelsky, *Sir Oswald Mosley* (London: Papermac, 1990), p. 371.

[156] Rubinstein, *Myth of Rescue*, p. 60.

[157] Andrew Scharf, *The British Press and the Jews Under Nazi Rule* (Oxford: Oxford University Press, 1964).

[158] Though the British government's opposition to Nazism certainly preceded Churchill. See Robert Shepherd, *A Class Divided: Appeasement and the Road to Munich, 1938* (London: Macmillan, 1988), p. 273.

[159] Churchill, *The Second World War*, Vol. 1: *The Gathering Storm*, p. 69.

ourselves to be drawn into a theoretical antagonism between Nazism and democracy; but the antagonism is here now.... Is this a call to war?... We need the swift gathering of forces to *confront not only military but moral aggression*'.[160] Indeed Hitler himself recognized the moral opposition of Churchill and his supporters.[161] In 1944, Churchill condemned the extermination of Jews in unequivocal terms as 'the greatest and most horrible single crime ever committed in the whole history of the world'.[162]

Some recent popular scholarship on the Catholic Church has concluded that not only did the Church remain silent in the face of the Holocaust, some clerics aided, abetted, and lent moral support to the Nazis. There is little doubt that many Catholic clerics did support the Nazis, but other clerics helped Jews and spoke out against Nazism.[163] The question therefore revolves around the Church's leadership, with debate focused on the depiction of Pope Pius XII as 'Hitler's Pope'. This label is based on three key charges: (1) that the Vatican did not speak out strongly enough against the Nazis; (2) that it did nothing to assist Italian Jews; and (3) that the aforementioned failings were caused by papal sympathy for Nazi anti-Semitism.[164] Whilst the Vatican could undoubtedly have done more to protect Jews, the evidence in relation to these charges is decidedly mixed.

In his Easter homily of 1940, Pius XII condemned the Nazi bombardment of defenceless citizens, the aged, and sick and innocent children. On 11 May 1940, he publicly condemned the invasions of Belgium and Holland and lamented 'a world poisoned by lies and disloyalty and wounded by excesses of violence'.[165] In June 1942, he spoke out against the deportation of Jews from Vichy France, instructing his *nuncio* in Paris to protest 'the inhuman arrests and deportation of Jews'. In his Christmas addresses of 1941 and 1942, the Pope criticized the Nazis and in his 1942 address expressed concern 'for those hundreds of thousands who, without any fault of their own, sometimes only by reason of their nationality or race, are marked down for death or progressive extinction'.[166] The Pope's critics argue that this fell far short of a denunciation

[160] Emphasis added. Winston Churchill, 'A Broadcast to the People of the United States', in Charles Eade (ed.), *The War Speeches of the Rt. Hon. Winston Churchill*, Vol. 1 (London: Cassell and Co., 1951), pp. 40–2.

[161] Adolf Hitler, speech at Saarbrucken, 9 October 1938, cited by Churchill, *Second World War*, Vol. 1 *The Gathering Storm*, p. 295.

[162] Michael J. Cohen, 'Churchill and the Jews: the Holocaust', *Modern Judaism*, 6 (1) 1986, p. 42 and n. 56.

[163] Meir Michealis, 'The Holocaust in Italy', in Berenbaum and Peck (eds), *The Holocaust*, pp. 453.

[164] Cornwell, *Hitler's Pope*.

[165] Cited by David G. Dalin, 'A Righteous Gentile: Pope Pius XII and the Jews', unpublished paper in the possession of the author, p. 2. The argument is developed in detail in David G. Dalin, *The Myth of Hitler's Pope: Pope Pius XII and His Secret War Against Nazi Germany* (New York: Regnery Publishing, 2005).

[166] Cited by Dalin, 'Righteous Gentile', p. 2.

of the Nazis and that Pius XII failed to excommunicate Nazis. At the time, however, Pius XII's comments were understood as a denunciation of the Nazis.[167] Indeed, there were many good reasons for the Pope's careful choice of words. Some Jewish leaders implored senior Catholics not to stridently condemn the Nazis, fearing reprisals. Moreover, there is no evidence to suggest that Papal denunciation would have constrained the Nazis, indeed just the opposite.[168] In Holland, Catholic Bishops issued a pastoral letter denouncing 'the unmerciful and unjust treatment meted out to Jews'. Comparatively speaking, the Dutch Jews fared worse than any others—around 80 per cent were murdered—and historians suggest a link between the rate of killing and vocal Dutch opposition. After learning about the fate of the Poles, Pius XII urged Catholic bishops to do all they could to save the victims. Finally, immediately after Mussolini's fall, the Vatican protected around 5,000 Jews from the Nazis. When Rome was liberated, Pius XII directed his diplomacy towards Catholic satellite states (the Hungarian case has already been mentioned), urging them not to deport Jews. In the final analysis, although the Pope could have condemned the Nazis more stridently and there is no doubt that individual clerics assisted and supported the Nazis, Pius XII's careful language was probably not a product of anti-Semitism but rather of an attempt to voice concern without drawing reprisals and it is unlikely that Jews might have been saved this way. Moreover, such a denunciation would have given the Nazis a pretext to attack the Church and seize the thousands of Jews that it protected.[169] There is little ground to suggest here that the institution of the Church validated Nazi thinking.

In summary, the Holocaust was justified by reference to an ideology of selective extermination based on a racist biological ethic that portrayed human existence as a struggle of annihilation between superior and inferior races. According to this ideology, the extermination of inferior races to protect the Aryan 'master race' was not only permissible, it was necessary. The Nazis identified Jews as the most pressing danger and set out to exterminate them. To what extent was this ideology legitimized? Nazism was certainly endorsed by a significant portion of German society, governments and societies in Romania, the Baltic states, Hungary, and Croatia, and sizeable groups elsewhere, including Ukraine. But even within the fascist world, there were many who rejected this ideology, often because they did not accept the legitimacy of its underlying logic of extermination. Beyond the fascist world, whilst there were notable anti-Semitic and pro-Nazi groups, European and North

[167] Dalin, 'Righteous Gentile', p. 2; and see Pinchas Lapide, *The Last Three Popes and the Jews* (London: Souvenir Press, 1967).

[168] Hitler considered deporting the Pope and the Vatican, in 1943, Hitler spoke of his desire to 'pack up that whole whoring rabble'. Dalin, 'Righteous Gentile', p. 4.

[169] Meir Michealis, 'The Holocaust in Italy', pp. 452–3.

American governments and societies were consistent in their denunciation of Nazism. The shock and trauma caused by the Holocaust created a powerful momentum for the principle of civilian immunity, propelling efforts to translate the moral principle into an international legal rule (see Chapter 1).

## CONCLUSION

The totalitarians examined in this chapter attempted to justify the mass killing of literally millions of civilians by reference to ideologies of selective extermination that shared important family resemblances with the earlier colonial varieties discussed in Chapter 2. Mass atrocities were justified by reference to ideologies which placed whole groups outside the realm of moral protection. This attempted to make the killing of group members appear blameless. Ideologies also helped present excluded groups as existential threats to the 'in-group', its interests and—in some cases—humanity and civilization themselves. For the Nazis, mass killing was thought necessary to protect the master race from infection by inferior races and to create spaces for German expansion. For the Stalinists, it was thought necessary to protect the revolution from its various class enemies—though nationality was also an important marker.

Each of these forms of totalitarianism won the support of significant portions of their own 'in-groups' and sympathetic outsiders, though this was helped by uncertainty about the nature and extent of mass killing, which was deliberately orchestrated by the two regimes. Usually, these groups shared the basic worldviews and ideological preferences of the perpetrators but just as often there were some important differences producing some interesting variations in the response of different in-groups. Inasmuch as the mass killing was not confronted with significant domestic opposition, we can conclude that these ideologies of selective extermination succeeded in securing sufficient internal legitimacy. But they both suffered serious external legitimacy deficits. Nazism failed to secure sufficient legitimacy, resulting in its failure to exterminate European Jewry and ultimate destruction. Stalinism, however, did secure sufficient legitimacy. This owed little to its practices or justifications and much to uncertainty about the facts of the case and Western judgements about the relative legitimacy of Stalinism and Nazism.

The great strength of selective extermination as a source of legitimacy for mass atrocities is also its greatest weakness. Selective extermination works by using the prejudices of a particular community to justify exorcising others from common moral protections. But because it is based on a closed moral system, its success as a legitimizing argument depends on the size and nature of the 'in-group' and the extent of prejudice within it. As a rule of thumb, the more powerful and ideologically homogenous the in-group, the more effective selective extermination is as a legitimating argument within it. The doctrine proved effective as a legitimizer of colonial genocides and mass atrocities whilst European governments were the world's great powers and whilst deep prejudices against non-whites prevailed. As European power waned and prejudices were challenged, selective extermination became less compelling as a source of legitimacy and less able to protect the perpetrators of mass killing from criticism. This basic point holds for the cases discussed in this chapter, too. Communist mass killing outlasted Nazi genocide only because of the size and power of its in-group, and the strategic preferences of outsiders, not because it was any more legitimate or less inhumane. I am not arguing here that colonialism made twentieth-century totalitarianism possible or inevitable—just that the basic moral framework developed to justify mass killing in colonial settings was modified and employed, whether consciously or not, to the same effect by later totalitarian states. And, that this being so, the capacity of colonialism, Stalinism, and Nazism to legitimize mass killing was shaped by similar sets of factors. Not only did the experiences described in this chapter diminish the capacity of selective extermination to justify mass killing, however, the moral anger generated by totalitarian excesses gave powerful momentum to the movement to translate civilian immunity from moral principle to international legal rule, making it more difficult in theory for would-be perpetrators of all stripes to get away with mass murder.

But the normative picture at the time was not quite so straightforward. Whilst condemning totalitarian mass killing as uncivilized and barbaric, the champions of liberalism—the USA and Britain—were deliberately killing very large numbers of German and Japanese civilians in strategic bombing campaigns. How they justified these obvious violations of civilian immunity and the implications for the norm are the subjects of the following chapter.

# 4

# Terror Bombing in the Second World War

In his dissenting opinion at the Tokyo war crimes trial that followed the Second World War, Justice Pal argued that the clearest case of direct orders to commit 'indiscriminate murder' during the Second World War might be found in 'the decision coming from the allied powers to use the atom bomb'.[1] A. C. Grayling described the British bombardment of Germany as a 'moral crime' according to the standards enumerated by the allies themselves in prosecuting German and Japanese soldiers as war criminals.[2] But there are still those who believe that the bombing was 'perfectly justified' or merely a consequence of the inevitable breakdown of the distinction between combatants and civilians in total wars.[3]

Between 300,000–600,000 German civilians and over 200,000 Japanese civilians were killed by allied bombing during the Second World War, most as a result of raids intentionally targeted against civilians themselves.[4] The path followed by the RAF and US Army Air Corps (USAAF) in the European and Pacific theatres respectively followed a similar trajectory. At the beginning of the war, both committed themselves to precision raids against military targets. But a combination of bombing inaccuracy, poor weather, high casualty rates, and strategic preferences persuaded the RAF (over Germany) and USAAF (over Japan) to adopt area bombing aimed at 'dehousing' workers and demoralizing enemy populations, thereby disrupting industrial production.

[1] Radhabinod Pal, *International Military Tribunal for the Far East, Dissentient Judgment* (Calcutta: Sanyal and Co., 1953), pp. 620–1.

[2] A. C. Grayling, *Among the Dead Cities: Was the Allied Bombing of Civilians in WWII a Necessity or a Crime?* (London: Bloomsbury, 2006).

[3] Robin Neillands, 'Facts and Myths about Bomber Harris', *RUSI Journal*, 146 (2) 2001, p. 69. The idea that the combatant/civilian distinction breaks down in total war is put forward by Melden E. Smith, 'The Strategic Bombing Debate: The Second World War and Vietnam', *Journal of Contemporary History*, 12 (1) 1977, p. 184. For an overview, see Igor Primoratz (ed.), *Terror from the Sky: The Bombing of German Cities in World War II* (New York: Berghahn Books, 2010).

[4] See Max Hastings, *Bomber Command* (New York: The Dial Press, 1979), pp. 226–7; and Richard B. Frank, *Downfall: The End of the Imperial Japanese Empire* (New York: Random House, 1999), p. 77 respectively.

Two important points for an understanding of the changing role of civilian immunity in this period emerge from the allied bombing experience during the Second World War. First, immediately prior to the war, whilst politicians and publics in Britain and the USA worried about the legitimacy of terror bombing and some lobbied for its prohibition, a consensus had emerged among strategists which held that area bombing was the most effective means of utilizing strategic air power and was morally preferable to the protracted slaughter of land-based warfare. This consensus persisted well into the Cold War and informed strategic arguments in favour of both area bombing and nuclear deterrence.[5] Second, despite this strategic consensus, neither the British nor American government was prepared to publicly justify their strategies of deliberately bombing civilians, primarily because they believed that they could not secure sufficient legitimacy and that this failure would weaken domestic support for the war. Instead, both governments maintained that they were not deliberately bombing civilians and that, as such, civilian casualties were the *unintended* consequence of attacks on military and industrial targets. There is some evidence to suggest that in order to sustain this case they mislead their own publics and even legislators. The adoption of this justificatory strategy in the midst of a world war in which both countries were victims of aggression suggests that liberal governments believed—rightly or wrongly—that the deliberate killing of civilians could not be legitimized at home by reference to anti-civilian ideologies or other arguments owing to the strength of civilian immunity as a dearly held moral principle within their societies. These considerations also point towards the emergence of a paradox in liberal thinking about civilian immunity: on the one hand, a belief in the strategic utility of terror bombing and, on the other, a commitment to the principle of civilian immunity which forbids such bombing. This paradox helped to shape debates in the West about aerial bombing and other forms of mass killing in the second half of the twentieth century. In the remainder of this chapter, though, I will consider RAF bombing of Germany and USAAF bombing of Japan respectively.

## THE RAF AND GERMANY

In the years immediately preceding the Second World War, the British government signalled its intent to comply with the principle of civilian immunity as it applied to aerial bombing. In 1938, Britain sponsored a League

[5] This consensus persisted well after the Second World War. See Ward Thomas, 'Victory by Duress: Civilian Infrastructure in Air Campaigns', *Security Studies*, 15 (1) 2006, pp. 1–33.

of Nations resolution declaring the intentional bombing of civilians to be illegal and insisting that belligerents target only military objectives.[6] In June of that year, Prime Minister Neville Chamberlain had set out rules to guide the Royal Air Force (RAF) Bomber Command's strategic planning. First, he insisted that 'it is against international law to bomb civilians as such and to make deliberate attacks on the civilian population'. Second, 'targets which are aimed at from the air must be legitimate military objectives and must be capable of identification'. Third, 'reasonable care must be taken in attacking those military objectives so that by carelessness a civilian population in the neighbourhood is not bombed'.[7] Later that same month, Chamberlain told the House of Commons that although terror bombing was not explicitly forbidden by the laws of war:

> We can strongly condemn any declaration on the part of anybody... that it should be part of a deliberate policy to try to win a war by the demoralization of the civilian population through the process of bombing from the air. This is absolutely contrary to international law, and I would add that, in my opinion, it is a mistaken policy from the point of view of those who adopt it, but I do not believe that the deliberate attack upon a civilian population will ever win a war for those who make them.[8]

At the beginning of the Second World War, both Britain and Germany responded positively to President Roosevelt's plea that they should avoid bombing each other's civilians. Evidently, the British government believed there to be a convention-dependent or 'weak' norm prohibiting terror bombing (see Chapter 1): a norm maintained by patterns of reciprocity and fear that the enemy might repay a terror attack in kind.[9]

But Britain's military thinkers had very different ideas. From their perspective, the Axis powers had exhibited little restraint in bombing campaigns during the Spanish Civil War and Italian invasion of Abyssinia. These experiences helped create expectations among Britain's military planners that in the event of war between the two countries, Germany would eventually target British cities.[10] At the very outset of the war, the *Luftwaffe* seemed to confirm expectations by bombing civilians in Warsaw (1939) and Rotterdam (1940).[11]

[6] Cited by Hans Blix, 'Area Bombardment: Rules and Reasons', in *British Yearbook of International Law* (Oxford: Clarendon Press, 1979), p. 36.

[7] In Sir John Slessor, *The Central Blue* (London: Cassell and Co., 1956), p. 44.

[8] Cited by Tom Harrison, *Living Through the Blitz* (London: Collins, 1962), p. 33.

[9] Ward Thomas, *The Ethics of Destruction: Norms and Force in International Relations* (Ithaca: Cornell University Press, 2001); and Jeffrey W. Legro, *Cooperation Under Fire: The Conduct of the Air War in the Second World War* (New York: St. Martin's Press, 1992).

[10] Manfred Messerschmidt, 'Strategic Air War and International Law', in Horst Boog (ed.), *The Conduct of the Air War in the Second World War* (Oxford: Berg, 1992), p. 303.

[11] Tami Davis Biddle, *Rhetoric and Reality in Air Warfare: The Evolution of British and American Ideas about Strategic Bombing, 1914–1945* (Princeton: Princeton University Press,

The expectation that the Axis powers would use terror bombing translated into a pervasive view amongst British strategists that the 'gloves' would come off eventually and that Britain would be compelled to reply to Nazi terror bombing in kind. Thus, only days after the declaration of war in 1939, a Memorandum from Bomber Command's Director of Planning called for an immediate relaxing of Chamberlain's bombing restrictions, insisting that 'it is of the utmost importance that, *when* we do initiate air action on a serious scale, *we must be allowed to do so in the most effective way and against those objectives which we consider will have the greatest effect in injuring Germany, unhampered by the inevitable fact that there is bound to be incidental loss, and possibly heavy loss of civilian life*'.[12]

Whatever the government's civilian leaders might have said about the legal and moral issues, area bombing was a cornerstone of British strategic thinking long before 1939. Since the First World War, strategists had argued that bombing enemy cities would reduce the overall level of killing in major wars by obviating the need for trench warfare.[13] In 1918, the Chief of the British Air Staff, Major-General Sykes, defended the strategic bombardment of cities to destroy enemy morale.[14] The first head of the RAF, Hugh Trenchard, was also a keen advocate of terror bombing. After the First World War, he argued that only a lack of resources had prevented him from destroying Germany's industrial centres.[15] Immediately before the Second World War, Trenchard argued that the RAF should be permitted to develop its capacity to strike enemy population centres, even at the expense of investment in other arms of the military.[16] He suggested that the use of air power against cities would enable a belligerent to prevail without having to defeat the enemy's army, a task that the First World War had demonstrated could only be achieved at a huge cost in lives.[17] The air force, he argued, should be deployed against the enemy's industrial and civilian centres in order to destroy production and morale.[18] This proposition found its way into a Staff College Manual in 1922

2002), p. 185. There is some evidence that extensive civilian damage in Rotterdam was accidental, but at the time it was widely seen as deliberate—a continuation of the path laid down at Guernica.

[12] PRO AIR 14 1939, p. 8. Emphasis in original.

[13] Though the architect of trench warfare and the bloody bayonet charges of the First World War, Sir Douglas Haig, continued to argue that infantry charges not tanks and aircraft were decisive. See Dan Diner, *Cataclysms: A History of the Twentieth Century from Europe's Edge*, trans. William Templer with Joel Golb (Madison: University of Wisconsin Press, 2008), p. 29.

[14] Sir Charles Webster and Noble Frankland, *The Strategic Air Offensive Against Germany 1939–1945*, Vol. I (London: HMSO, 1961), p. 46.

[15] Webster and Frankland, *Strategic Air Offensive*, p. 46.

[16] H. W. Koch, 'The Strategic Air Offensive Against Germany', *The Historical Journal*, 34 (1), 1991, p. 123.

[17] Webster and Frankland, *Strategic Air Offensive*, IV, p. 74.

[18] Philip S. Meilinger, 'The Historiography of Airpower: Theory and Decline', *The Journal of Military History*, 64 (2), 2000, p. 481.

and the *RAF War Manual* in 1935.[19] Brigadier General Groves heralded the new air power that replaced the 'war of lines' with the 'war of areas', praising the ability of strategic bombardment to exact a significant psychological effect on the enemy's population.[20] This basic proposition—that terror bombing could weaken enemy morale and shorten wars—reflected a wider consensus among strategists, including the period's leading theorist of air power, the Italian Giulio Douhet, and Britain's most prominent strategist Basil Liddell Hart.[21]

Trenchard was not unaware of the moral difficulties posed by the fact that terror bombing violated the moral principle of civilian immunity. Indeed, he accepted that it was 'contrary to the dictates of humanity [to engage in] the indiscriminate bombing of a city for the sole purpose of terrorising the civilian population'.[22] But in a refrain that became a staple justification for such bombing, he bypassed the norm by arguing that as a state's industrial capacity determined its ability to wage war, bombing aimed at 'dehousing' factory workers was legitimate and that 'moral effect' (breaking the will of the [civilian] people) was an 'inevitable result of a lawful operation of war'.[23] In other words, the 'moral effect' deemed essential to winning the war would be a secondary consequence of attacks aimed at legitimate military targets (factories and workers' houses). The death of the civilian workers whose houses were targeted was an unintended but not unhelpful byproduct. This line of thinking—which rests on the fallacy that it is possible to bomb a house without intending the kill the inhabitants—was first developed in 1928 when the heads of the British armed forces inquired into the legality of area bombing. The study found that attacks on industrial, economic, and military targets in German cities aimed at damaging the morale of German workers were 'perfectly legitimate objectives of air attack' that should be regarded as 'ordinary acts of war'.[24] In short, the problem of civilian immunity was evaded by

[19] Allan D. English, 'The RAF Staff College and the Evolution of British Strategic Bombing Policy', *Journal of Strategic Studies* 16 (3), 1993, pp. 408–31; and Richard Overy, 'Allied Bombing and the Destruction of German Cities' in Roger Chickering, Stig Förster, and Bernd Greiner (eds), *A World at Total War: Global Conflict and the Politics of Destruction, 1937–1945* (Cambridge: Cambridge University Press, 2005), p. 282.

[20] Brigadier General P. R. C. Groves, *Our Future in the Air: A Survey of the Vital Question of British Air Power* (London: Hutchinson, 1922).

[21] Giulio Douhet, *The Command of the Air* trans. Dino Ferrari (New York: Coward McCann, 1942), pp. 14, 54–8. There is evidence that Douhet's thinking was popular in Britain. See Louis A. Sigaud, *Douhet and Aerial Warfare* (New York: Putnam's, 1941). On Liddell-Hart, see Overy, 'Allied Bombing', p. 280; and Basil Liddell Hart, *Paris or the Future of War* (London: Garland, 1972 [1925]), pp. 28–9 and 40–2.

[22] Webster and Frankland, *Strategic Air Offensive*, IV, p. 74.

[23] Webster and Frankland, *Strategic Air Offensive*, IV, p. 74.

[24] In Overy, 'Allied Bombing', p. 281. In 1923 a Commission of Jurists had drafted rules to govern aerial warfare which prohibited 'aerial bombardment for the purposes of terrorizing the civilian population'. The draft regulations were rejected by all the main European powers. See

collapsing the distinction between soldiers and civilians, claiming that certain civilians were legitimate military targets, and supposing that civilian structures could be targeted without an intention to harm the civilians inside them. This basic justificatory strategy became a commonplace after the Second World War as perpetrators attempted to portray what was in effect the intentional killing of civilians as being consistent with civilian immunity.

By 1939, the RAF's strategic thinking was strongly predisposed towards the use of air power against industrial and civilian population centres, though the British government still insisted that it would not adopt this course of action. Although none of the British strategists mentioned above specifically called for the destruction of cities, each commended the psychological impact of such bombardment and advocated strategies that would deliver this effect. These psychological effects, Douhet observed, were brought about by the deliberate targeting of civilian population centres.[25] The British strategists justified their position through a mixture of prudential and legal arguments, though some of them recognized the moral problems associated with deliberately targeting civilians. They argued that bombing industrial centres—even working class residential areas—did not amount to terror bombing because the structures were legitimate military targets. They insisted that as inhumane as it might appear, area bombing was a lesser evil because it promised a short, sharp war with fewer overall casualties than could be expected if the enemy's armed forces had to be defeated in battle. Finally, they argued that bombing of this type was not illegal.[26]

It would be wrong, however, to suggest that this view was held across the government. The War Office and Admiralty were hostile to Trenchard's defence of area bombing, partly because of inter-service rivalry but partly because of moral and legal concerns. A memorandum drafted in response to Trenchard picked holes in the logic of collapsing the soldier–civilian distinction: 'Though the objective might be a given boot factory, the actual target would be the town in which the factory happened to be located . . . it is ridiculous to contend that the dropping of bombs would hit only the so-called military targets . . . *[through Trenchard's proposed doctrine] we are advocating what might be termed the indiscriminate bombing of undefended towns and of their unarmed inhabitants*'. It concluded that it was for the government alone, and not Bomber Command, to decide to adopt a strategy that amounted to 'unrestricted warfare' against the 'civilian population'.[27]

Frank E. Quindry, 'Aerial Bombardment of Civilian and Military Objectives', *Journal of Air Law*, 2 (4) 1931, pp. 474–509.

[25] Douhet, *Command of the Air*.

[26] A view not shared by other arms of government, see Telford Taylor, *Nuremberg and Viet Nam, an American Tragedy* (Chicago: Quadrangle, 1970), p. 89.

[27] Emphasis added. Webster and Frankland, *Strategic Bombing Offensive*, IV, pp. 81–2. For a discussion, see Geoffrey Best, *Humanity in Warfare: The Modern History of the International Law of Armed Conflict* (London: Weidenfeld and Nicolson, 1980), p. 275.

In the first months of the war both the RAF and *Luftwaffe* exhibited restraint. Both sides, however, were preparing to escalate to terror bombing.[28] In a story repeated in the Pacific theatre, it soon became clear that the RAF's precision bombing strategy was ineffectual and very costly.[29] As the tide of war continued to go against the British, Hitler brought forward plans for the invasion of Britain. In preparation, the *Luftwaffe* launched area attacks against British cities and initiated a massive air offensive aimed at destroying or substantially weakening the RAF. On 24 August 1940 German Bombers mistakenly bombed the centre of London. The RAF retaliated the following night by bombing Berlin. Outraged, on 2 September Hitler authorized a series of reprisal raids against London. The switch from attacking British airfields and air defences to attacking its cities unwittingly gave the RAF the time it needed to recoup its fighter strength and deny the *Luftwaffe* command of the air. Hitler was forced to indefinitely postpone the invasion of Britain and instead the *Luftwaffe* unleashed a blitz on London on other cities, ultimately killing around 50,000 British civilians.[30] This 'Battle of Britain' provoked public calls for harsh reprisals against Germany.[31]

The new Prime Minister, Winston Churchill, was more receptive to reprisals and terror bombing than his predecessor, though he initially resisted demands for reprisals against German cities.[32] From his experience in the First World War, Churchill had come to believe that area bombing was ineffective but in late 1940 arrived at the view that Britain had no other way of carrying the war to Germany.[33] In a note to Lord Beaverbrook, the Minister for War Production, on 8 July 1940, Churchill remarked that:

> When I look around to see how we can win the war I see that there is only one sure path. We have no Continental Army which can defeat the German military power. The blockade is broken and Hitler has Asia and probably Africa to draw from. Should he be repulsed here or not try an invasion, he will recoil eastward, and we have nothing to stop him. But there is one thing that will bring him back and bring him down, and that is an absolutely devastating, exterminating attack

[28] Tami Davis Biddle, 'Bombing by the Square Yard: Sir Arthur Harris at War: 1942–1945', *The International History Review*, 21 (3) 1999, p. 630; Webster and Frankland, *Strategic Air Offensive*, p. 78; and Messerschmidt, 'Strategic Air War', pp. 303–4.

[29] Biddle, *Rhetoric and Reality*, pp. 184–5.

[30] Barrie Paskins and Michael Dockrill, *The Ethics of War* (London: Duckworth, 1979), pp. 18–19.

[31] See Mark Connelly, 'The British People, the Press and the Strategic Air Campaign Against Germany, 1939–1945', *Contemporary British History*, 16 (2) 2002, p. 47.

[32] Harold Nicolson, *The War Years 1939–1945* (New York: Atheneum, 1967), pp. 121–2.

[33] In 1917, Churchill argued that it was 'improbable that any terrorization of the civil population which could be achieved by air attack would compel the Government of a great nation to surrender', H. A. Jones, *The War in the Air* (London: Oxford University Press, 1937), p. 79.

> by very heavy bombers from this country upon the Nazi homeland. We must be able to overwhelm him by this means, without which I do not see a way through.[34]

Sir Charles Portal, Chief of the Air Staff, advised that Bomber Command was unable to conduct effective precision attacks on military and industrial targets and—in line with the logic of convention-dependent norms (see Chapter 1)—that *Luftwaffe* attacks on British cities had released the RAF from its moral obligation to distinguish between combatants and civilians. On 23 October 1940, Portal argued that Bomber Command should begin targeting the 'will of the German people to continue the war'. The RAF, he argued, should use incendiary bombs to destroy as many buildings through fire as possible, creating 'generalised fear'.[35] Bomber Command launched its first large-scale area raid on 16 December 1940, against Mannheim.

Arthur Harris, undoubtedly the most strident public advocate of area bombing, was appointed chief of Bomber Command on 23 February 1942. For the record, this was *after* the decision was taken to bomb cities in night raids. Between late 1940 and early 1942, RAF raids over Germany were conducted exclusively at night to protect aircrews from German fighters and ground-fire. During this period the RAF continued to attack 'precision' targets but it targeted cities as well. At this stage, though, where cities were attacked, the aiming point was normally an industrial area rather than the city centre. In early 1942, the balance began to shift and the strategic bombing campaign adopted an almost exclusive focus on city centres. This was formalized on 14 February, when Bomber Command was issued a new directive insisting that bombing be 'focused on the morale of enemy civil population and in particular of the industrial workers'. In a memorandum to Bomber Command clarifying the order, Portal wrote that: 'Ref the new bombing directive: I suppose it is clear that the aiming points are to be the built-up areas, not, for instance the dockyards or aircraft factories. . . . This must be made quite clear if it is not already understood'.[36] Harris drew up a list of 100 cities that he thought necessary to destroy and proceeded to direct his crews to doing just that. For the rest of the war, Harris remained committed to achieving this target irrespective of progress in the war itself. In 1944, he sharply criticized instructions to divert bombers away from German cities to support the D-Day landings and in 1945, after the allies had assumed command of the skies and made vast improvements to bombing accuracy, he refused to abandon area bombing in favour of precision bombing.[37]

[34] Winston Churchill, *The Second World War*, II, p. 567.

[35] Public Record Office, 'Notes of a meeting held on 23 October 1940 to discuss bombing policy', AIR 9/443.

[36] Both documents cited in Webster and Frankland, *Strategic Air Offensive*, I, pp. 323–4.

[37] Webster and Frankland, *Strategic Air Offensive*, II, p. 84.

The British government offered no special justification for the switch to area bombing, instead opting to deny that any switch had been made or that it was intentionally targeting civilians. Whilst the February 1942 directive identified city centres as primary targets, government officials repeatedly argued that Bomber Command was only striking military and industrial targets and that the destruction of civilian areas was unavoidable collateral damage. In May 1942, Secretary for Air, Archibald Sinclair, told parliament that the raids on Lübeck and Rostock were directed at 'armament factories' not residential areas, though noting that 'it is impossible to distinguish in night bombing between the factories and the dwellings which surround them'.[38] On 31 March 1943, Richard Stokes (Labour MP for Ipswich) asked in the House of Commons whether 'instructions had been given to British airmen to engage in area bombing rather than limit their attention to purely military targets'. Salisbury replied that 'the targets of Bomber Command are always military, but night bombing of military objectives necessarily involves bombing the area in which they are situated'.[39] Even after the destruction of Dresden in early 1945, the government continued to insist that the RAF was not conducting attacks on the civilian population. In response to further criticism from Stokes, Sinclair opined, 'we are not wasting bombers or time on purely terror tactics. It does not do the Hon. Member justice to come here to this House and suggest that there are a lot of Air Marshals or pilots or anyone else sitting in a room trying to think how many German women and children they can kill'.[40]

This line of thinking was passed on to the British media and repeated throughout the war. According to Mark Connelly, throughout the war the media provided the British public with 'masses' of material supporting the bombing campaign and clouding the moral issues by holding to the line that only targets of military significance were attacked whilst simultaneously maintaining that the Germans were receiving their just desert.[41] Reporting the first raids on Berlin in September 1940, the *Daily Mail* argued that 'Berliners are learning that their city is no more immune than is London from large-scale bombing. The one difference is that our airmen select their targets and concentrate on objects of military value'. The *Daily Telegraph* peddled the same view, noting that Londoners: 'who have endured the frightfulness of persistent indiscriminate bombing night after night, with its wanton slaughter and torture of civilians will see in these effective attacks on the *military*

[38] Cited in Stephen Garrett, *Ethics and Airpower in World War II: The British Bombing of German Cities* (New York: St. Martin's Press), p. 31.

[39] Exchange recounted in Parker, *Struggle for Survival*, p. 164. In the House of Lords, Lord Robert Cecil, Secretary for Dominion Affairs, made precisely the same argument.

[40] Cited in Garrett, *Ethics and Airpower*, p. 119.

[41] Mark Connelly,'The British Debate', in Primoratz (ed.), *Terror from the Sky*, pp. 190–3.

*objectives* in Berlin, the most deadly form of counter-stroke'.[42] This editorial line was maintained throughout by all Britain's major news outlets. In September 1942, *The Times*' diplomatic correspondent argued that RAF bombing was targeting German industry not its cities and civilians.[43] In 1944 when George Bell, Archbishop of Chichester, used a speech in the House of Lords to challenge the air campaign's legitimacy (see below), the *Telegraph* replied that British bombing targeted military objectives and avoided revenge and pointless destruction.[44] Replying to Bell, the Marquess of Crewe argued that the RAF was doing all it could to avoid civilian casualties and Viscount Sanky argued that the government was best placed to judge the merits of individual missions.[45] Other Church leaders supported this line of thinking. Cyril Garbett, the Archbishop of York, wrote in *The Times* that German civilians were killed only unintentionally by the RAF.[46]

This line of justification raises the question of whether government denials were a self-conscious attempt to mislead or whether it actually believed its own arguments. According to Sir Charles Portal, Chief of the Air Staff, the targeting point was irrelevant. In response to public criticism of BBC war coverage which, some people complained, whitewashed the fact that the RAF was aiming at cities and not industrial targets, Portal wrote to his deputy, Sinclair, arguing that 'in order to make the matter clearer I have for some time been expounding that the whole of an industrial city is in itself a military target'.[47] But the clearest evidence that the government was deliberately misleading parliament and the public can be found in its response to a confidential note from the Marquis of Salisbury to Sinclair in November 1943. Arthur Harris' boasts about the destruction of German cities, Salisbury suggested, 'seem to bring us up short against the repeated Government declarations that we are bombing only military and industrial targets . . . there is a great deal of evidence that makes some of us afraid that we are losing moral superiority to the Germans. . . . Of course the Germans began it, but we do not take the devil as our example. Of course all these criticisms may be groundless, but if not, issue fresh confidential orders, I hope'. Sinclair asked colleagues to formulate a response supporting the government's claim that only military objectives were targeted. Sir Norman Bottomley, Deputy Chief of the Air Staff, responded to Sinclair's request, noting that 'to be strictly accurate, our primary object is the progressive destruction and dislocation of the German military, industrial and economic system and *the undermining of the morale of the*

[42] Emphasis added. Cited in Mark Connelly, 'The British Debate', in Primoratz (ed.), *Terror from the Sky*, p. 184.

[43] Connelly, 'The British People', p. 55.

[44] Connelly, 'The British Debate', p. 189.

[45] Connelly, 'The British Debate', p. 187.

[46] Connelly, 'The British Debate', p. 188.

[47] PRO, AIR 2/7852, Portal letter to Sinclair, 26 October 1943.

*German people.* There is no need to inform Lord Salisbury of the underlined [emphasized] phrase, since it will follow on success of the first part of the stated aim'.[48] In line with Bottomley's advice, Sinclair wrote to Salisbury advising him that Bomber Command 'adhered to the principle that we would attack none but military targets', omitting mention of 'morale bombing'—which was of course a clear reference to attacking the civilian population.[49]

Further evidence of deliberate dissembling can be found in debates between Arthur Harris and his superiors. Harris was sharply critical of the government's decision to deny that the RAF was engaged in area bombing. He defended such bombing on the grounds that it would shorten the war and save allied lives. Thus, he insisted that '[a]ttacks on cities like any other act of war are intolerable unless they are strategically justified. But they are strategically justified so far as they tend to shorten the war and to preserve the lives of Allied soldiers'.[50] Harris believed that government denials were bad for the morale of his crews. As he saw it, they were being ordered to risk their lives to implement the government's strategy whilst the government itself was not prepared to publicly defend it. Harris also had little time for those who expressed moral qualms. In October 1943, he wrote a memorandum responding to the government's public insistence that the RAF was only conducting precision attacks against military and industrial targets, in which he demanded that the public be told that the aim of the bomber offensive was 'the destruction of German cities, the killing of German workers and the disruption of civilised community life throughout Germany'. Directly contradicting the government, Harris insisted that:

> It should be emphasised that the destruction of houses, public utilities, transport and lives; the creation of a refugee problem on an unprecedented scale; and the breakdown of morale both at home and at the battle fronts by fear of extended and intensified bombing, are accepted and intended aims of bombing policy. *They are not by-products of attempts to hit factories.*[51]

In response, the Air Ministry advised Harris that the destruction of cities should not be portrayed as an end in itself but as 'the inevitable accompaniment of an all-out attack on the enemy's means and capacity to wage war'. Harris responded by suggesting that the distinction between intending the destruction of cities and accepting it as the inevitable consequence of area attacks was 'merely academic' and that 'the German economic system which I am instructed by my directive to destroy, *includes* workers, houses and public

[48] Emphasis in original. Documents cited and discussed in Hastings, *Bomber Command*, pp. 172–3.

[49] Hastings, *Bomber Command*, p. 173.

[50] Overy, 'Allied Bombing', p. 290. Also see, Garrett, *Ethics and Airpower*, p. 133.

[51] Emphasis added, in Overy, 'Allied Bombing', p. 290.

utilities, and it is therefore meaningless to claim that "wiping out German cities is "not an end in itself" . . . the cities of Germany including their working population, houses and public utilities are literally the heart of Germany's "war potential". That is why they are being attacked'. He went on to argue that the War Ministry's claim that the British public would not support such an overt admission of terror bombing was merely a sop to appease 'the sentimental and humanitarian scruples of a negligible minority'.[52] Clearly, as Mark Connelly claims, the British public was being 'fed a diet of truths, half-truths and outright lies' in relation to the strategic air campaign.[53] The added significance here, of course, is the evidence that the government withheld the truth about RAF targeting policy from the British public because it believed (rightly or wrongly) that the British public would not support terror bombing.

Harris was probably right to suggest that concerns about public opinion explained the government's decision to deny that the RAF was engaged in area bombing. Gallup polls taken during the war show that immediately after the blitz, only 46 per cent of respondents supported reprisal bombings on German cities; 48 per cent were opposed. As the war progressed, the level of support for reprisal bombing increased marginally to 53 per cent but at no time did fewer than 46 per cent of respondents oppose the terror bombing of German cities.[54] A report on the opinions of Londoners conducted for the *New Statesman* in 1944 found that six out of ten respondents supported the bombing campaign, two out of ten expressed moral qualms but believed the campaign necessary, one out of ten thought the campaign too awful in any conditions and the remainder were uncertain.[55] What is clear from these polls is that the British public was quite cautious about the morality of the strategic campaign and the widespread public support given to Bomber Command during and immediately after the war was partly based on a deliberately engineered misunderstanding about what the RAF was actually doing to Germany. It remains unclear though whether the public simply did not know about the terror bombing or whether it knowingly chose to accept the convenient fiction presented by the government. On the one hand, there certainly were pockets of dissent which provided clues as to the real nature of Bomber Command's strategy for those who wanted to listen. On the other hand though, the pockets were small and limited to sections of the elite and their arguments not widely disseminated in the popular press.[56] Matters came to a head, however, with the destruction of Dresden in February 1945.

[52] These documents all cited in Overy, 'Allied Bombing', pp. 290–1.
[53] Connelly, 'The British Debate', p. 198.
[54] See Connelly, 'The British Debate', p. 197; and Connelly, 'The British People', p. 55.
[55] Connelly, 'The British Debate', p. 198.
[56] Connelly, 'The British Debate', p. 198.

On 13–14 February 1945, Dresden was attacked by two waves of RAF bombers and a third wave of American bombers. A total of 800 RAF bombers, aiming for the city centre, dropped a mixture of incendiary bombs and high explosives designed to create a huge firestorm. Most estimates suggest that between 25,000 and 35,000 people were killed with other studies putting the figure nearer to 50,000 because of the high number of refugees in Dresden at the time.[57] In terms of sheer loss of life, the Dresden raid was smaller than American raids on Tokyo and Hiroshima and caused less damage to property than the 1943 attack on Hamburg.[58] What made Dresden stand out was not so much its sheer destructiveness, but its timing and the intent behind it: the attack came at the very end of the war, when victory was imminent; Dresden contained few targets of obvious military significance; and the raid was calculated to create misery for the approximately 100,000 refugees sheltering there.[59]

The raid was initially reported favourably by the British and American press and justified in the same way as earlier attacks.[60] That soon changed as information about the attack began to emerge. On 16 February, *The Times* reported that the RAF had unleashed 'a new and terrifying prodigy of airpower' and pointed to the attack's 'unprecedented fury'.[61] Most significantly, after a briefing from an RAF spokesman, the *Associated Press* filed a report stating that 'allied air commanders have made the long-awaited decision to adopt deliberate terror bombing of the great German population centres as a ruthless expedient to hasten Hitler's doom'.[62] The report caused alarm among the allies. In the USA, Secretary of War, Henry Stimson claimed that Dresden was attacked because it was a transportation hub, insisting that 'our policy never has been to inflict terror bombing on civilian populations'.[63] But American officials privately expressed grave concerns. The matter was also raised in the British parliament, prompting some rapid rethinking about the merits of area bombing and a 'sudden attack of conscience' on the part of Churchill.[64] On

[57] For a good overview, see Tami Davis Biddle, 'Sifting Dresden's Ashes', *The Wilson Quarterly*, 29 (2) 2005, p. 62.

[58] Martin Middlebrook, *The Battle of Hamburg: Allied Bomber Forces Against a German City in 1943* (London: Allen Lane, 1980).

[59] On the rationale behind it, see Biddle, 'Sifting Dresden's Ashes', p. 63.

[60] The *New York Times* emphasized Dresden's strategic position as an important industrial town and the centre of a major rail network. Biddle, *Rhetoric and Reality*, p. 255. The *Daily Express* told its readers that the destruction of Dresden had sowed confusion amongst Germans in the region. Connolly, 'The British People', p. 51.

[61] Biddle, *Rhetoric and Reality*, p. 255.

[62] Webster and Frankland, *Strategic Air Offensive*, III, p. 13.

[63] Cited by Mark Selden, 'A Forgotten Holocaust: US Bombing Strategy, the Destruction of Japanese Cities and the American Way of War from the Pacific War to Iraq', in Yuki Tanaka and Marilyn B. Young (eds), *Bombing Civilians: A Twentieth Century History* (New York: The New Press, 2009), p. 82.

[64] Connelly, 'The British Debate', p. 196.

28 March, Churchill wrote a memorandum to Portal observing that '[i]t seems to me that the moment has come when the question of the bombing of German cities for the sake of increasing the terror, should be reviewed.... The destruction of Dresden remains a serious query against the conduct of Allied bombing. I am of the opinion that military objectives must henceforth be more strictly studied...'.[65] Portal took exception to the minute, not least because the Cabinet itself had authorized the raid and successfully argued for the removal of the reference to 'terror'.[66] Harris was also angered by Churchill's remarks, telling Bottomley that the bombardment of German cities had achieved the strategic effect 'for which they were designed and from which the armies now profit'.[67] Nonetheless, the government turned its back on terror bombing and those that had been charged with implementing it, a position endorsed by the incoming Labour government in 1945. Bomber Command's contribution and the sacrifice of its crews were omitted from Churchill's victory speech, Harris was denied honours and the aircrews of Bomber Command denied awards commensurate with those of the other services.[68]

Although public criticism of area bombing was muted, in part because the public was so poorly informed and offered only the government's own interpretation, there were some notable pockets of dissent among the elite. In parliament, Alfred Salter and Richard Stokes repeatedly denounced the strategy and challenged the government to explain Bomber Command's activities.[69] Stokes persistently enquired about the bombing offensive, on one occasion asking Sinclair in Parliament whether the Air Ministry was simply afraid to admit that it was indiscriminatly attacking residential areas.[70] Outside parliament, the main forum for critical reflection on the bombing campaign was the Church. Although a majority within the Church viewed the campaign as a necessary evil, there were significant voices of dissent. One of the most prominent was George Bell, Bishop of Chichester. In 1943, Bell complained in his diocesan gazette that 'when a Minister of the Government speaks in exulting terms of a ruthless and destructive bombing of the German people... then we have real cause to grieve for a lowering of moral tone, and also to fear greatly for the future'.[71] In February 1944, he raised the matter in the House of Lords in a carefully written speech that distinguished between the unintended killing of civilians in attacks directed against military targets and

[65] Webster and Frankland, *Strategic Air Offensive*, III, p. 112.
[66] Biddle, 'Bombing by the Square Yard: Sir Arthur Harris at War', p. 655.
[67] Biddle, 'Bombing by the Square Yard: Sir Arthur Harris at War', p. 655.
[68] Garrett, *Ethics and Airpower*, pp. 34–7.
[69] Garrett, *Ethics and Airpower*, pp. 118–19.
[70] Garrett, *Ethics and Airpower*, p. 119.
[71] Garrett, *Ethics and Airpower*, p. 112; and Geoffrey Best, 'The Bishop and the Bomber', *History Today*, 33, September 1983, p. 31.

the terror bombing that, Bell observed, the RAF had unleashed on Germany. Argued Bell:

> I desire to challenge the Government on the policy which directs the bombing of enemy towns on the present scale, especially with reference to civilians who are non-combatants, and non-military and non-industrial objectives. I fully realise that in attacks on centres of war industry and transport the killing of civilians when it is the result of bona fide military activity is inevitable. But there must be a fair balance between the means employed and the purpose achieved. To obliterate a whole town because certain portions contain military and industrial establishments is to reject the balance. The Allies stand for something greater than power. The chief name inscribed on our banner is 'Law'. It is of supreme importance that we, who, with our Allies, are the liberators of Europe should so use power that it is always under the control of law.[72]

This view was shared by former Archbishop of Canterbury, Cosmo Lang, who argued in the House of Lords that the government had not adhered to its stated policy of attacking only military and industrial objectives and had instead embarked on a strategy of 'deliberate attempts to destroy whole cities'.[73] A third clerical opponent of terror bombing was John Collins, who briefly served as Chaplain to Bomber Command. Collins was disciplined on four occasions for his 'unorthodox' views and later described Bomber Command HQ as 'soul-destroying': 'For there, in contrast with the natural beauty of the surroundings, the evil . . . policy of the carpet bombing of German cities was planned'. On one occasion, Collins invited Sir Stafford Cripps to Bomber Command's High Wycombe HQ to give a talk on the question 'Is God my co-pilot?'. Cripps argued that officers should only send aircrew on missions that were morally as well as militarily justified. Harris responded by organizing a lecture by T. D. Weldon (Oxford University), who offered a counter argument under the title 'The ethics of bombing'. After the lecture, Collins stood and asked whether the title should have been 'The bombing of ethics'.[74]

Two of Britain's leading strategists also became critics of the bombing campaign. Liddell Hart, one of the earliest advocates of strategic bombing came to oppose the campaign over Germany on moral grounds. In 1942, he observed that 'it would be ironical if the defenders of civilisation depend for victory upon the most barbaric, and unskilled, way of winning a war'.[75] Likewise, J. F. C. Fuller described the 'worst devastations' of the Vandals, Huns, and Mongols as paling into insignificance 'when compared to the

72 In Garrett, *Ethics and Airpower*, p. 113.

73 Best, 'The Bishop and the Bomber', p. 31.

74 Jonathan Glover, *Humanity: A Moral History of the Twentieth Century* (London: Pimlico, 2001), p. 86.

75 Brian Bond, *Liddell Hart* (London: Cassell, 1979), p. 145.

material and moral damage now wrought' by Bomber Command.[76] Several prominent British academics and writers also questioned the campaign, including J. R. R. Tolkien (privately), Vera Brittain, and the Quaker, Condor Catchpool, whose 'Bombing Restriction Committee' had several thousand subscribers.[77]

There was virtually no public opposition to terror bombing in allied countries. In his meeting with Churchill in 1942, Stalin expressed support for the strategy. Indeed, Stalin was reportedly more impressed by the destruction of German cities than by the deployment of Allied forces in North Africa.[78] Soviet attitudes changed after the Iron Curtain fell across Europe, and the Dresden raid came to be characterized as an example of 'capitalist vengeance'.[79]

The US position was ambivalent. Although it did not publicly criticize its ally's strategy, the US Administration was careful not to endorse it. Government and military circles largely accepted that if it were militarily necessary to kill German civilians then that was a legitimate course of action. Indeed, the USAAF's initial bombing plan for Germany conceded that the air force might begin 'morale' attacks once German industry had begun to collapse. But there were concerns about the negative impact that terror bombing could have on domestic public opinion and support for the war. What is more, some US officials and strategists believed that such bombing was ineffective and that they had the technology to conduct precision raids. The US Air Commander in 1941, Henry Arnold, argued that humans were not 'priority targets' for the USA because attacks on civilians were an inefficient use of air power.[80]

Much has been made of American entreaties to the RAF to persuade it to divert resources away from area bombing, but it is important to stress that the US government was not primarily concerned with the moral questions involved. At the Casablanca conference in 1943, Air Force General Ira Eaker tried to persuade the British to adopt American-style precision bombing on the grounds that its heavy bombers had been designed for daytime precision raids and would draw out and destroy enemy fighters. Eaker's case against area bombing was entirely strategic. Eaker himself later told historians that neither he nor his colleagues objected to the RAF's campaign on moral grounds. As Eaker put it, 'I never felt that there was any moral sentiment among leaders of

[76] The editor of the *Evening Standard* refused to publish Fuller's article. See Anthony Trythall, *'Boney' Fuller* (London: Cassell, 1977), pp. 225–6.

[77] Letter from J. R. R. Tolkien to Christopher Tolkien, 23–5 September 1944 in Humphrey Carpenter (ed.), *The Letters of J. R. R. Tolkien* (London: Harper Collins, 1995), pp. 92–4; and see Garrett, *Ethics and Airpower*, pp. 122–3.

[78] W. A. Harriman and E. Abel, *Special Envoy to Churchill and Stalin* (London: Hutchinson, 1976), pp. 150–7.

[79] Connelly, 'The British Debate', p. 199.

[80] Richard Overy, *Why the Allies Won* (New York: W. W. Norton and Co., 1997), pp. 109–10.

the AAF [Army Air Force]. A military man has to be trained and inured to do the job. . . . The business of sentiment never enters into it at all'.[81] This attitude was shared by the US Air Commander, Henry Arnold. Shortly after Casablanca, Arnold made it clear to the air staff that American bombers would not spare German civilians on moral grounds. In a clear restatement of the strategy of bombing for morale effect, Arnold had an aide tell the air staff that, 'this is a brutal war and . . . the way to stop the killing of civilians is to cause so much damage and destruction and death that the civilians will demand that their government cease fighting'. Echoing the British government's justification of area bombing, Arnold continued: 'This doesn't mean that we are making civilians or civilian institutions a war objective, but we cannot "pull our punches" because some of them may get killed'.[82]

The US government also shared Britain's view that domestic public opinion would not support deliberate attacks on German civilians.[83] Concerns were indeed expressed outside military circles about the morality of area bombing. In March 1944, a group of anti-war clergymen and activists called upon Christians to 'examine themselves concerning their participation in this carnival of death'.[84] Such protests caused alarm among government officials. Whilst the Undersecretary of War, Robert Patterson, reproached the protestors for giving succour to the enemy, Robert Lovett, Assistant Secretary of War for Air, visited Europe to brief air force commanders on the problem of adverse publicity at home. Lovett told the Commander of US Strategic Air Forces in Europe that there was genuine sentiment in both the public and Congress about the immorality of indiscriminate bombing and advised 'utmost caution' if the air force pursued such a policy. He argued that it would be impossible for the government to publicly justify indiscriminate attacks if that became the avowed strategy of the USAAF.[85] As a result, the American air campaign over Europe was portrayed as being different and distinct from the RAF's, though it sometimes engaged in similar activities.

Overall, then, despite criticism from some parliamentarians, clerics, and strategists and a degree of US ambivalence, the British government succeeded in securing sufficient legitimacy for its area bombing campaign in Germany. Tellingly, it did so by arguing that it was not deliberately targeting civilians or attacking city centres and misleading those that asked questions about it. During the war itself, the strategy succeeded largely because censorship and

[81] Cited in Ronald Schaffer, 'American Military Ethics in World War II: The Bombing of German Civilians', *Journal of American History*, 67 (2) 1980, p. 321.

[82] Henry H. Arnold and Ira C. Eaker, *Winged Warfare* (New York: Harper and Brothers, 1941), p. 134; Heywood S. Hansell Jr, *The Air Plan that Defeated Hitler* (Atlanta: Higgins-McArthur, 1972), pp. 85–93; and Schaffer, 'American Military Ethics', p. 321.

[83] Schaffer, 'American Military Ethics', p. 322.

[84] Vera Brittain et al., 'Massacre by Bombing', *Fellowship*, 10, 1944, pp. 50–64.

[85] Schaffer, 'American Military Ethics', p. 323.

other restrictions limited reporting of RAF raids over Germany and because the context of war made the British public inclined to support its government. Reports about the bombing of Dresden threatened to unravel this consensus, however, prompting Churchill to order a change of strategy and to distance the government from area bombing in order to maintain the public's support.

## THE USAAF AND JAPAN

Debate about the legitimacy of the terror bombing of Japan followed similar contours and the issue remains controversial today.[86] As in the British case, the Americans displayed an initial preference for precision bombing. Finding this to be ineffective against mainland Japan, they turned in early 1945 to incendiary attacks on cities with civilians as the main targets. As in Britain, however, the US government never admitted that it was deliberately attacking civilians, arguing instead that it was bombing military objectives. As noted earlier, the American government thought it necessary to make this argument principally because it believed that a significant part of the American public would not support the deliberate targeting of civilians.

Before America joined the Second World War in earnest, its thinking on terror bombing was deeply divided. The US government had condemned the Japanese bombing of Chinese cities in the 1930s and, as I noted earlier, Roosevelt warned the British and Germans about its impermissibility.[87] At the same time, America's leading air strategist, Billy Mitchell, argued that in the event of a war with Japan, 'incendiary projectiles would burn the [Japanese] cities to the ground in short order'.[88] At a 'secret' press conference on the eve of war, on 15 November 1942, the Army Chief of Staff General George C. Marshall warned that 'if war with the Japanese does come, we'll fight

[86] See Barton J. Bernstein (ed.), *Politics and Policies of the Truman Administration* (Chicago: Quadrangle Books, 1970); and Barton J. Bernstein, *The Atomic Bomb: The Critical Issues* (Boston: Little, Brown, 1976); John Ray Skates, *The Invasion of Japan: Alternatives to the Bomb* (Columbia, SC: University of South Carolina Press, 1994); Ger Alperovitz, *Atomic Diplomacy: Hiroshima and Potsdam* (New York: Simon and Schuster, 1965); Jeffrey J. Roberts, 'Peering Through Different Bombsights: Military Historians, Diplomatic Historians and the Decision to Drop the Atomic Bomb', *Airpower Journal*, 12 (1) 1998; and Rufus E. Miles Jr, 'Hiroshima: The Strange Myth of Half a Million American Lives Saved', *International Security*, 10 (2) 1985, pp. 121–40.

[87] In addition, Secretary of State Cordell Hull condemned the 'aerial slaughter . . . at places near which there were no military establishments', Ronald H. Spector, *Eagle Against the Sun: The American War with Japan* (New York: The Free Press, 1985), p. 487. Two prominent military analysts, George Elliott and Ernest Dupuy, counselled that no 'country will consider it worthwhile to start so dreadful and unpredictable a cycle of slaughter', George Fielding Elliott and R. Ernest Dupuy, *If War Comes* (New York: Macmillan, 1937), p. 62.

[88] Cited in Michael S. Sherry, *The Rise of American Air Power: The Creation of Armageddon* (New Haven: Yale University Press, 1987), p. 58.

mercilessly. Flying fortresses will be despatched immediately to set the paper cities of Japan on fire. There won't be any hesitation about bombing civilians—it will be all out'.[89] The purpose of conducting an apparently oxymoronic 'secret' press conference was to convey a threat to the Japanese without being seen to be publicly endorsing terror bombing.[90] To air strategists, the physical structures and geographical layout of Japanese cities (buildings made largely of wood and paper and closely packed together) presented an opportunity for American air power to exact strategic effects that could not be achieved in Germany with area bombing.

In late 1942, air commanders requested that military intelligence provide them with a list of 'priority targets' of military and industrial objectives in Japan, in line with the doctrine of precision targeting. But in May 1943, the Chief of Planning also requested 'a study of the vulnerability of Japanese target areas to incendiary attack'.[91] In October 1943, the Intelligence Section handed down a report which advised that Japanese cities made much better targets than German cities.[92] The American air staff argued that area bombing in Japan could be highly effective with expected positive effects including high numbers of casualties among workers, the spreading of industrial inefficiency (echoes of the RAF's 'de-housing' strategy) and a reduction of public morale.[93] But the Committee of Operations Analysts argued that whilst there was a clear case for incendiary attacks on cities, such attacks should be delayed until a large enough air force with appropriate range and bomb capacity had been assembled in order to 'give maximum assurance of totally destroying the area attacked, the danger being that a small effort would merely create firebreaks against a later heavy attack'. In a memorandum of 9 May 1944, the committee recommended that if an adequate force could be assembled a 'general attack on Japanese urban industrial areas should be initiated in March of 1945 and concentrated during that month'.[94]

With the capture of the Marianas Islands in June 1944, the Japanese mainland came (barely) within the range of B-29 bombers. In November 1944, the USAAF commenced precision daytime raids against Japan's southern industrial targets. Like the first RAF raids on Germany, these proved ineffectual and expensive.[95] In January 1945, Curtis LeMay took command

[89] Larry Bland and Sharon Ritenour Stevens (eds), *The Papers of George Catlett Marshall*, II, (Baltimore: Johns Hopkins University Press, 1981), p. 678.

[90] See Thomas R. Searle, '"It Made a Lot of Sense to Kill Skilled Workers": The Firebombing of Tokyo in March 1945', *The Journal of Military History*, 66 (1) 2002, p. 116, n. 39.

[91] Searle, '"It Made a Lot of Sense"', p. 117.

[92] Searle, '"It Made a Lot of Sense"', p. 117.

[93] Searle, '"It Made a Lot of Sense"', p. 117.

[94] Searle, '"It Made a Lot of Sense"', p. 119.

[95] John Buckley, *Air Power in the Age of Total War* (Bloomington: Indiana University Press, 1999), pp. 193–4.

of the bombing effort and further territorial gains put mainland Japan squarely in range. Once the USAAF had the capacity to strike Japanese cities, it did so.

The firebombing of Tokyo in March 1945 killed between 80,000 and 100,000 people and injured over a million. In the months that followed, Nagoye, Kobe, Osaka, Yokohama, and Kawasaki suffered the same fate. In June 1945 alone, over 40 per cent of the urban areas of these cities were levelled.[96] Whilst LeMay's bombers were exacting a heavy toll on Japan's cities and war production, advances on the ground were coming only at a very heavy price.[97] Thus, when atomic weapons became available for use, the US delivered two bombs on the cities of Hiroshima and Nagasaki, killing around 100,000 people, mostly civilians.

Like the British, the American leadership denied that civilians were the intended targets of these attacks. They insisted that only military and industrial targets were subject to attack but that the dispersed nature of Japan's war industry and condensed nature of its cities made unintended civilian deaths inevitable. As LeMay put it in his memoirs:

> We were going after military targets. No point in slaughtering civilians for the mere sake of slaughter. Of course there is a pretty thin veneer in Japan, but the veneer was there. It was their system of dispersal of industry.... I'll never forget Yokohama. That was what impressed me: drill presses. There they were, like a forest of scorched trees and stumps, growing up throughout the residential area. Flimsy construction all gone... everything burned down or up, and drill presses standing like skeletons.[98]

That this basic claim (civilian deaths were unintended) was a deliberate fiction has been demonstrated by the release of planning documents and by some of LeMay's less guarded comments. Impressed by the devastation wrought by terror bombing, LeMay reflected that 'I was not happy, but neither was I particularly concerned about civilian casualties on incendiary raids' because, he wrote later, 'we knew how the Japanese had treated the Americans—both civilian and military—that they'd captured in places like the Philippines'.[99] Released documents have revealed that air force planners used three criteria to select targets. In order of importance, they were: (1) 'congestion/inflammability' of the city; (2) incidence of war industry; (3) incidence of transportation facilities.[100] Despite public claims to the contrary, therefore, the planners clearly chose cities themselves as targets and primarily on the basis of the

[96] Buckley, *Air Power*, p. 143.

[97] Miles, 'Hiroshima' and Henry L. Stimson, 'The Decision to Use the Atomic Bomb', *Harper's Magazine*, February 1947, pp. 97–107.

[98] Frank, *Downfall*, p. 67.

[99] Thomas B. Allen and Norman Polmar, *Code-Name Downfall: The Secret Plan to Invade Japan—and Why Truman Dropped the Bomb* (New York: Simon & Schuster, 1995), p. 90.

[100] Frank, *Downfall*, p. 150.

likely destruction that could be wrought, with the presence of war industries a secondary consideration to the potential for destroying cities congested with civilians. The presence of military facilities was apparently not a major factor in target selection.

Although there was more debate about whether to use the atom bombs than there was about the area bombing of Japanese cities, the decision was taken remarkably quickly and with few signs of dissent. Indeed, Truman inherited the view that if the USA acquired atomic capabilities, it would use them from his predecessor.[101] The validity of this opinion was widely endorsed. Chief of the Manhattan project, General Leslie Groves told a Congressional hearing after the war that 'the aim from the start was to produce an atomic bomb at the earliest date to bring the war to a successful conclusion'. Truman agreed, recalling in his memoirs that 'I regarded the bomb as a military weapon and never had any doubt that it should be used'.[102]

It is important to stress that the decision to use the atom bomb did not involve breaking a moral threshold—after all, the allies had been deliberately targeting German and Japanese civilians for years.[103] It was not thought necessary, therefore, to develop novel justifications for its use and at the time the US justification mirrored broader allied arguments about the legitimacy of strategic bombing. Truman resolutely maintained that whilst the aim of the atomic attacks was to shorten the war and save American lives by avoiding the need to invade the Japanese mainland—implying a necessity-based justification—the bombs were dropped on military and industrial targets. Truman never departed from this argument.[104] During the Potsdam conference in July 1945, before the atomic attacks, Truman wrote:

> This weapon is to be used against Japan between now and August 10. I have told the Sec[retary] of War, Mr. Stimson to use it so that military objectives and soldiers and sailors are the target and not women and children. Even if Japs are savages, ruthless, merciless and fanatic, we as the leader of the world for the common welfare cannot drop this bomb on the old capital [Kyoto] or the new [Tokyo]. He and I are in accord. The target will be a purely military one.[105]

When he announced the bombing of Hiroshima, Truman began by stressing that the bomb had been aimed at a military target: 'Sixteen Hours Ago an

[101] Barton J. Bernstein, 'Truman and the A-Bomb: Targeting Noncombatants, Using the Bomb, and His Defending the "Decision"', *Journal of Military History*, 62 (3) 1998, p. 549.

[102] Cited by Stephen Harper, *Miracle of Deliverance: The Case for the Bombing of Hiroshima and Nagasaki* (London: Sidgwick and Jackson, 1985), p. 205. The earliest discussions about how to use the bomb included potential military uses. See Lawrence Freedman and Saki Dockrill, 'Hiroshima: Strategy of a Shock', in Gordon Martel (ed.), *The World War Two Reader* (New York: Routledge, 2004), p. 67.

[103] Selden, 'Forgotten Holocaust', p. 85.

[104] Bernstein, 'Truman and the A-Bomb', p. 563.

[105] Cited in Bernstein, 'Truman and the A-Bomb', p. 558.

American airplane dropped one bomb on Hiroshima, *an important Japanese Army base*'. The speech also contained a threat of worse to come, but this too was prefaced by the claim that any future targets of A-bomb attacks would be military in nature: 'We are now prepared to obliterate more rapidly and completely every productive enterprise the Japanese have above ground in any city. We shall destroy their docks, their factories, and their communications. Let there be no mistake; we shall completely destroy Japan's power to make war'.[106] This line of argument—that Hiroshima and Nagasaki were legitimate military industrial objectives, that the killing of workers was licit and that of surrounding women and children unintended—was almost identical to the British justification for bombing German cities.[107]

In a famous article for *Harper's Magazine* in 1947, Henry Stimson emphasized the necessity of 'this deliberate premeditated destruction' as 'our least abhorrent choice'.[108] But this claim came some eighteen months after the bombing and only after it had become abundantly clear that the original argument, that Hiroshima and Nagasaki were military targets, was not supported by evidence from the two cities—a point which generated sharp criticism of the decision to use the bomb (see below). Stimson's article was a direct response to post-war criticism of the bombing.[109] His use of necessity in this article does not detract from the central point that at the time of the bombing, and for the duration of the war, the US administration argued that it only targeted military objects. What is more, though pointing to necessity, Stimson did not concede that civilians were the intended targets of attack, maintaining the fiction that their deaths were unavoidable collateral damage.

Evidence suggests, however, that decision-makers understood that the target was not primarily military. Truman had received advice about the bomb from various quarters. A 'Targeting Committee' comprising scientists and military officers held its first meetings in April and May 1945. The committee's deliberations were shaped by a shared belief that the decisive factor in ending the war would be 'the will of the people'. It worked from the principle that targets should exert the maximum effect on enemy morale and that this would be achieved by maximizing the devastation wrought by the atom bomb. In one of the opening meetings, Groves set out the parameters of the decision:

> I had set out as the governing factor that the targets chosen should be places the bombing of which would adversely affect the will of the Japanese people to

[106] Statement by the President Announcing the use of the A-Bomb at Hiroshima, 6 August 1945. Emphasis added.

[107] Frank, *Downfall*, p. 257.

[108] Stimson, 'Decision to Use the Atomic Bomb'.

[109] Robert P. Newman, 'Hiroshima and the Trashing of Henry Stimson', *The New England Quarterly*, 71 (1) 1998, p. 20.

> continue the war. Beyond that, they should be military in nature, consisting of either important headquarters or troop concentrations, or centers of production of military equipment or supplies. To enable us to assess accurately the effects of the bomb, the targets should not have been previously damaged in air raids. It was also desirable that the first target be of such size that the damage would be confined within it, so that we could definitely determine the power of the bomb.[110]

The first meeting agreed that the preferred targets would be 'large urban areas of not less than three miles in diameter existing in the larger populated areas'. The second meeting, chaired by Oppenheimer, focused on the question of how to maximize the bomb's psychological impact. The experts agreed that tying the weapon's use to purely military objectives would diminish its psychological impact. The minutes show that little attention was paid to moral considerations. It was quickly agreed that the target should be 'a much larger area' than a military target in order to accomplish the desired psychological objectives.[111] The meeting then drew up a target list of Kyoto, Hiroshima, Yokohama, and the Kokura arsenal. Kyoto was placed at the top of the list because of its size (over a million inhabitants), the fact that it had not been attacked previously (because of its cultural status), and the argument that its status as an intellectual and cultural centre would maximize the psychological effects of the attack. Thus, the original concern that the planners find a *military* target was quietly sidestepped in the face of the primacy of maximizing psychological impact. A third meeting, on 28 May, firmed up the two priority targets of Kyoto and Hiroshima and agreed that the aiming point should be the city centres rather than a military or industrial target to ensure that maximum damage was caused even if the bombs missed their targets.[112] Groves himself favoured Kyoto because the city was large enough for the blast to 'run out within the city' and thus provide a 'firm understanding' of its destructive power.[113] Stimson and Truman were reticent about destroying Kyoto because of its cultural heritage.

The remit of an 'Interim Committee' created by Stimson to plan for war's end, included future atomic policy, bringing it into the targeting debate. One of the committee's scientific advisors, Arthur Compton, argued that the bomb introduced 'the question of mass slaughter, really for the first time in history'.[114] Other members questioned whether the bomb would have the desired psychological and political effects, given that its immediate effects would be indistinguishable from conventional incendiary attacks. Oppenheimer countered that if used appropriately, the bomb would have tremendous visual and destructive impact and the committee concluded 'that we could not

110 Frank, *Downfall*, p. 254.
111 Frank, *Downfall*, p. 255.
112 Frank, *Downfall*, p. 255.
113 Freedman and Dockrill, 'Hiroshima', p. 67.
114 Frank, *Downfall*, p. 256.

give the Japanese any warning, that we could not concentrate on a civilian area, but that we should seek to make a profound psychological impression on as many Japanese as possible [and] that the most desirable target would be a vital plant employing a large number of workers and closely surrounded by workers' houses'.[115] Like the targeting committee, therefore, the Interim Committee maintained the chimera of selective targeting whilst in effect endorsing the use of atomic weapons against civilians.

Two other important contributors to the discussion raised questions about the use of the bomb but did little to shake the consensus. Some Manhattan Project scientists argued either against the use of the bomb outright or in favour of demonstrating its power in a non-lethal or limited fashion.[116] Leo Szilard, a prominent member of the Manhattan Project, secured 150 signatures against the bomb's use from scientists working on the project.[117] Others argued that a demonstration alone would compel Japan to surrender. They raised the idea of a 'non-military demonstration of the bomb's effects'.[118] Possible options included inviting Japanese observers to the USA to witness a test explosion, dropping the bomb on an uninhabited part of Japan, or issuing a clear warning about when and where the bomb would be dropped to permit evacuation. A number of strong objections were raised, however. It was argued that a general warning had already been issued to Japan at the Potsdam conference, which had demanded unconditional surrender and threatened severe consequences if Japan failed to comply. Senior military figures such as George Marshall argued that a demonstration of the A-bomb would undermine the weapon's psychological impact.[119] A further problem was that the scientists were unsure whether the bomb would actually work, making publicizing a demonstration a risky strategy. Finally, military figures argued that any mission over Japan was risky because the aircraft might be downed over Japan, giving the Japanese access to the bomb. Given the risk, they argued that the bomb should only be used in a manner that guaranteed maximum effect.[120]

A second source of critical reflection was the military itself. Some military figures argued that conventional bombing alone could end the war. LeMay and Arnold believed that Japan had a high 'pain threshold' and that only increased

[115] In Frank, *Downfall*, p. 257.

[116] Other scientists, of course, supported its use. See Frank, *Downfall*, p. 260.

[117] William Lanouette, 'The 17th Petition of the Manhattan Project Scientists', in Kai Bird and Lawrence Lifschultz (eds), *Hiroshima's Shadow* (Stony Creek, Conn: Pamphleteer's Press, 1998), p. 213; and Leo Szilard, 'A Personal History of the Atomic Bomb', *Roundtable*, no. 601, 25 September 1949, pp. 14–15.

[118] Freedman and Dockrill, 'Hiroshima', p. 73; and Frank, *Downfall*, p. 258.

[119] L. Giovannitti and F. Freed, *The Decision to Drop the Bomb* (London: Methuen, 1967), p. 36.

[120] See McGeorge Bundy, *Danger and Survival: Choices About the Bomb in the First Fifty Years* (New York: Random House, 1988), pp. 172–7.

conventional attacks would force Japan's surrender. LeMay saw the atomic bombs as a mere supplement to conventional weapons and argued that they would not be decisive.[121] Generals Eisenhower and MacArthur are also reported to have expressed 'distaste' at the use of bomb and both later distanced themselves from the decision to use it, though there is little evidence that they openly voiced their concerns prior to the bombings.[122]

Overall, then, within American decision-making circles there was very little opposition to the use of the bomb. For the most part, opposition was couched in pragmatic rather than moral terms and, where moral concerns were expressed, they were easily overridden by strategic considerations.

In the immediate aftermath, the bombing was widely applauded. Churchill insisted that 'the decision whether or not to use the atomic bomb to compel Japan to surrender was never even an issue. There was unanimous, automatic, unquestioned support'.[123] Churchill famously referred to the bomb's 'miracle of deliverance': 'Now all this nightmare picture had vanished. In its place was the vision—fair and bright indeed it seemed—of the end of the whole war in one or two violent shocks.... To avert a vast, indefinite butchery, to bring the war to an end, to give peace to the world, to lay healing hands upon its tortured peoples by a manifestation of overwhelming power at the cost of a few explosions, seemed, after all our toils and perils, a miracle of deliverance'.[124] The Australian *Standard* newspaper argued that 'the use of atomic bombs against this atrocious race... [which] trained their soldiers as thoroughly in lust as in arms... is fully justified'.[125] Opinion polls in the USA showed a majority of 54 per cent in favour of dropping the bombs, with 23 per cent arguing that more bombs should have been dropped.[126] Indeed, Democratic Senator Richard Russell telegraphed Truman on 7 August calling for harsher terms against Japan and further atomic attacks.[127] Another poll taken two months after the bombing showed that fewer than 5 per cent of Americans disapproved as a matter of principle of the military use of a bomb '1,000 times' as powerful as its predecessors.[128] The rapid Japanese capitulation seemed to support the view that the bomb had saved lives by obviating the need for a ground invasion.[129] In line with the view of civilian immubity as a convention-

[121] Richard Rhodes, *The Making of the Atomic Bomb* (London: Simon & Schuster, 1986), p. 627.

[122] Freedman and Dockrill, 'Hiroshima', p. 69.

[123] In Harper, *Miracle of Deliverance*, p. 205.

[124] Winston S. Churchill, *The Second World War*, Vol. VI: *Triumph and Tragedy* (Boston: Houghton Mifflin, 1953), pp. 638–9.

[125] Christopher Thorne, *The Issue of War: States, Societies and the Far Eastern Conflict of 1941–1945* (London: Hamish Hamilton, 1985), p. 130.

[126] Harper, *Miracle of Deliverance*, p. 202.

[127] Bernstein, 'Truman and the A-Bomb', p. 556.

[128] 'The Fortune Survey', *Fortune*, December 1945, p. 305.

[129] Harper, *Miracle of Deliverance*, p. 202.

dependent norm, some Americans also argued that the norm had been thoroughly discredited by the Germans and Japanese and was therefore no barrier to American action.[130]

As with the British reaction to Bomber Command, however, American attitudes towards the bombing began to change after war's end—at least in part because it became clear that the targets had not been military. Although a majority continued to voice their support, some Church leaders criticized the attacks. Two weeks after Hiroshima, thirty-four Protestant clerics wrote to Truman protesting the attacks and expressing revulsion at the killing of non-combatants. In March 1946, a committee of Protestant theologians, including the noted realist thinker Reinhold Niebuhr, issued a report that found the attacks on Japan 'morally indefensible' due to the 'indiscriminate slaughter of non-combatants'.[131] Other prominent writers, such as Lewis Mumford and A. J. Muste, pointed to the contradiction between the allies' declaration on war crimes committed by the Axis powers and commitment to prosecute those responsible for 'killing the innocent' with the mass slaughter of civilians by the allies.[132]

Like the British, therefore, the US government began the Second World War intending to avoid area bombing and limit its strategic campaign to precision bombing. In practice, although the USAAF made a point of not endorsing the RAF's German strategy and pursuing its own, precision-based, alternative, it too engaged in area bombing. From the outset of the Pacific War, American planners advocated incendiary attacks on Japanese cities and early restraint was mainly a product of limited capacity. Once the USA secured airfields close enough to permit the strategic bombardment of Japanese cities, the USAAF launched some limited 'precision' daylight raids. Finding these to be costly and ineffective, it switched to terror bombing. Also like the British, the US Administration maintained that it targeted only military and industrial targets and not civilians whereas in reality civilian areas and city centres were often the intended targets. This was made clear by the decision-making process behind the use of the atomic bomb and the selection of targets designed to produce the greatest psychological effect by killing as many civilians as possible. These claims were widely accepted by Americans and other allied governments during the war, but later, as information about the devastation wrought on these two cities was disseminated, opposition began to grow. As in the British case, the US Administration opted to mislead the public about its targeting strategy largely because it believed—rightly or

[130] Sahr Conway-Lanz, *Collateral Damage: Americans, Noncombatant Immunity and Atrocity after World War II* (New York: Routledge, 2006), p. 14.

[131] Both cited in Conway-Lanz, *Collateral Damage*, p. 15.

[132] See Lewis Mumford, 'Atom Bomb', *Air Affairs*, 2 (3) 1948, pp. 326–45; and A. J. Muste, *Not by Might: Christianity, the Way to Human Decency* (New York: Harper, 1947), pp. 5–17.

wrongly—that terror bombing would be seen by some to be an immoral breach of civilian immunity, carrying with it the potential for weakening public support for the war. That public criticism did indeed increase after the war, as information about the bomb's effects became clearer, suggests that the administration might have been correct in its judgement.

## CONCLUSION

The key point in this chapter is not so much that the Second World War allies intentionally killed large numbers of German and Japanese civilians—though that certainly muddies the water in terms of interpreting the war's effects on civilian immunity—but that the British and American governments believed that even in the midst of this epic struggle, a significant portion of their publics would not support such killing. Despite clearly intending to bomb cities and kill civilians—the aiming point for both RAF attacks on German cities and the USAAF attacks on Tokyo, Hiroshima, and Nagasaki were city centres not industrial or military centres—the British and American governments consistently argued that they were attacking only military and industrial targets. Civilian casualties, they repeatedly claimed, were an unintended consequence though such casualties were actually pivotal to securing the campaigns' strategic effects. The governments adopted this line largely because they believed that significant parts of their domestic constituencies would not support terror bombing, even in the face of compelling necessity. In other words, they believed that for a significant part of their public, when it came to judging the validity of military operations civilian immunity trumped almost everything else. As a result, the allies consistently argued that the bombing campaigns targeted only military and industrial objectives and that the killing of civilians was a secondary—unintended—effect. During the war itself, Britain and the USA secured sufficient legitimacy because a majority of people in allied countries seemed prepared to accept this argument, at least partly because they were misled about the real nature of the strategic campaigns but also because they supported the war's aims and accepted a convenient fiction in order to resolve their own cognitive dissonance. The closest either came to losing that legitimacy was in the aftermath of the Dresden raid, and it is telling that Churchill called for a change in approach soon after. Once the war was over, public support for the air campaigns dwindled as the intent behind them and their effects became clearer.

For the West, the lessons of the Second World War and what they meant for civilian immunity were decidedly mixed. On the one hand, Japan's rapid surrender especially seemed to confirm the strategists' view that killing large numbers of civilians quickly could play a decisive role in modern war. The importance of this was augmented by three shocking discoveries: (1) totalitarian states were prepared to wage almost unlimited war in pursuit of their ideological utopias; (2) these states were prepared to exterminate literally millions of people, including entire groups; (3) in the nuclear age these states were likely to at some point become capable of equipping themselves with the means of achieving both these goals. In the wake of the Second World War, these three concerns created a powerful strategic rationale for disregarding civilian immunity as a factor in defence planning.

On the other hand, however, Axis war crimes and the Holocaust created a powerful impetus for the strengthening of protections for civilians and Prisoners of War. At the Nuremberg and Tokyo trials, Axis leaders were held legally accountable for some of their crimes. In 1948, states agreed to punish the perpetrators of genocide and commit to its prevention and a year later the Geneva Conventions demanded that all non-combatants be treated humanely (see Chapter 1). As Conway-Lanz argued, 'the killing of innocent civilians would become the international epitome of evil and symbolize the cruelty of an enemy that the Allies had sacrificed so much to defeat'.[133] Over the next forty years, ever greater progress was made in making civilian immunity an international legal rule, closing potential loopholes, and giving effect to this rule. In addition to the various contextual factors described in Chapter 1, debates in the West about civilian immunity and the legitimacy of mass killing during the Cold War were shaped by this paradox: the perceived utility of mass killing in the face of serious threats and its moral and legal prohibition.

For the communists, however, the lessons were quite different. Stalin and his ideology of selective extermination emerged strengthened by the Second World War. New communist regimes were estbablished throughout Eastern Europe and parts of Africa and Asia. Some, such as Mao's China and the thankfully short-lived Khmer Rouge in Cambodia, proved just as bloody as Stalin. These, and other, communist regimes presented their own versions of communist selective extermination and paid little, if any, attention to norms being developed outside their ideological orbit though they did sometimes appeal to the norms in order to criticize the West.

Although civilian immunity was translated from moral principle to international norm and legal rule after the Second World War, it was immediately challenged by a belief among some Western militaries in the strategic utility of killing civilians in some circumstances and by the persistence of communist ideologies of selective extermination. The Cold War struggle between these strategic and ideological forces and the new legal rule of civilian immunity is examined in the following two chapters.

[133] Conway-Lanz, *Collateral Damage*, p. 15.

# 5

# The Cold War Struggle (1): Capitalist Atrocities

This chapter is the first of two to investigate the relationship between mass killing and civilian immunity during the Cold War. The post-Second World War period saw the gradual transformation of civilian immunity from shared moral norm to international legal rule and embedded (though not necessarily internalized) norm. While both sides of the emerging Cold War divide committed themselves to the new rules, countervailing beliefs, assumptions, and interests pulled governments and militaries away from compliance and limited the extent to which the norm became embedded. These countervailing forces were driven by the Cold War protagonists' belief that they were engaged in an existential struggle for the future. As Mark Mazower put it, the Cold War 'played an enormous role in creating a climate of mutual hostility and paranoiac suspicion between and within the two great power blocs that divided the world'.[1] In his 12 March 1947 address to Congress, President Truman signalled America's readiness to defend freedom wherever it was menaced by totalitarianism and warned that the world was being riven by a conflict between two ways of life: one managed by self-chosen institutions; the other governed by a small elite for its own interests. Every nation, Truman warned, would have to choose between these two alternatives.[2] The Soviet Union replied in kind. Having disbanded Comintern to curry favour with its wartime allies in the West, the Soviet Union established Cominform in 1947 to promote the global spread of revolutionary communism.

These ideological antagonisms were sharpened by recent experience: Soviet losses in the Second World War exceeded twenty million civilians; in the West, revelations about the Holocaust and Soviet brutality (see Chapter 6) brought home the deadly potential of totalitarianism. For both sides, then,

[1] Mark Mazower, 'Violence and the State in the Twentieth Century', *The American Historical Review*, 107 (4), 2002, p. 1172.

[2] Dan Diner, *Cataclysms: A History of the Twentieth Century from Europe's Edge* trans. William Templer with Joel Golb (Madison: University of Wisconsin Press, 2008), p. 200.

defeat in this new struggle was viewed in apocalyptic terms. Some have seen in US foreign policy after the Second World War the idea of a duty to intervene abroad whenever American interests were threatened by communism.[3] Within this context, the emerging international consensus that civilian immunity should be transformed into an international legal rule and embedded norm sat uneasily with prevailing beliefs that societies confronted supreme threats to their ways of life and must do whatever was necessary to protect themselves. This chapter focuses on the use of mass atrocities in this struggle by the West and its allies. The following chapter focuses on atrocities committed by communists.

For the West and its allies, the norm of civilian immunity sometimes stood in tension with the grave necessity of preventing communist expansion. Very few actors in the West were prepared to reject civilian immunity out of hand, but neither were military and political leaders prepared to forgo the utility associated with the deliberate killing of civilians in certain circumstances. As a result, atrocities were used, supported, excused, or tolerated in many different settings but never justified as such. In addition to the cases examined in this chapter (Korea, Indochina, Indonesia, and El Salvador), actors in the West supported, tolerated, or excused the governments in Argentina and Chile as they suppressed communist movements by killing, torturing, and kidnapping civilians, killing between 14,000–30,000. What is more, the following chapter shows that some Western and Asian governments tolerated and delivered political and material support to the genocidal Khmer Rouge, responsible for the deaths of some two million civilians in Cambodia.

Whilst the fact that atrocities were so widely employed, excused, or tolerated shows that civilian immunity was not wholly *internalized* in the West, this does not mean that it was irrelevant. For the West, at least, the norm became *embedded*—a crucial (though not wholly determinative) factor in the way states and societies evaluated each others' behaviour that had to be taken into account by policy-makers. Continuing the pattern set by the Western allies during the Second World War, perpetrators typically refrained from openly justifying the deliberate killing of civilians and instead attempted to portray their behaviour as being consistent with the norm of civilian immunity by using rhetorical techniques to create and leverage uncertainty. This clear preference for portraying behaviour as being consistent with the norm and forgoing the use of anti-civilian ideologies is evidence that many non-communists believed that civilian immunity trumped anti-civilian ideologies and that open violations would be regarded as illegitimate and might provoke the imposition of costs and punishments. As such, much hinged on how contextual factors shaped the interpretation of events by external actors and

[3] Gabriel Kolko, *Confronting the Third World: United States Foreign Policy, 1945–1980* (New York: Pantheon Books, 1988), pp. 5–6.

the consequences that they believed should flow from this. Particularly important factors were the dissemination of timely and accurate reports about massacres, the position of the perpetrators and victims relative to the superpowers, and the perceived interests of those powers and their allies. For much of the Cold War, these factors played a critical role in shaping how international society judged mass killing and the consequences that flowed from those judgements. Typically, perpetrators secured sufficient legitimacy through the support or toleration of ideological allies when the dissemination of information was limited and where the perpetrator's purposes corresponded with those of significant outsiders. Where information about massacres was more widely disseminated, even ardent ideological supporters found it difficult to protect perpetrators from criticism though they could usually protect them from punishment. Thus, domestic opposition forced the Nixon Administration to end its bombardment of Cambodia and Laos and the staunchly anti-communist Reagan Administration found itself criticizing its allies in El Salvador and Guatemala and calling on them to exercise restraint.

This chapter focuses on the Cold War's two major 'hot wars' in Korea and Indochina before examining two quite different cases from the Cold War's margins—the Indonesian killings of 1965–66 and the counter-insurgency in El Salvador. The story that unfolds is one of an uneven and gradual but nevertheless profound shift in the centrality of civilian immunity to judgements about the legitimacy of violence and in the role played by contextual factors in shaping the politics of legitimation and punishment. By the end of the period, it had become more difficult—but still not impossible—for non-communist perpetrators of mass killing to secure sufficient legitimacy for their deeds.

## THE KOREAN WAR (1950–1953)

The Korean War provided the first major test for the new rules governing war in which the requirements of civilian immunity and perceived military necessity repeatedly came into conflict.[4] In the early days of the war, American politicians refused to authorize the targeting of civilians on the grounds that it was legally prohibited (although the USA did not ratify the Geneva Conventions until 1956), would aid North Korea's propaganda effort, and undermine the war's legitimacy. But as the war progressed, commanders gradually privileged military necessity over civilian immunity and authorized the indiscriminate

[4] Though 'Americans discussed the Korean war as if a contradiction did not exist between US war-fighting methods and non-combatant immunity', Sahr Conway-Lanz, *Collateral Damage: Americans, Noncombatant Immunity and Atrocity after World War II* (New York: Routledge, 2006), p. 83.

bombardment of North Korean cities, towns, and villages.[5] As in the Second World War, the intentional killing of civilians was never justified as such and there was not much recognition that US strategy involved targeting civilians. The USA maintained that its airforce attacked only military and industrial targets and that civilian casualties were unintended by-products of these attacks. Thanks largely to a combination of public support for the war, tight media censorship, and limited reporting of civilian casualties these claims were widely accepted in the USA. Elsewhere in the West and among some non-aligned governments, these factors helped to create sufficient legitimacy for terror bombing but this was partially eroded by concerns about the potential use of atomic weapons and the emergence of evidence of civilian destruction. This prompted some of the war's supporters to question the legitimacy of strategic bombing.

The Korean War was initially understood as a limited war to restore the status quo by forcing the North Korean army to retreat behind the 38th parallel. US leaders wanted to wage it in a limited fashion to protect its legitimacy, avoid Chinese or Soviet intervention, and not overstretch US forces.[6] Pulling against this, however, was the widely held assumption that the stakes were much higher than the fate of Korea alone and view that the normal rules of war did not apply in Asia.[7] General Lawnton Collins told the *New York Times* that the Korean War involved 'a reversion to old-style fighting—more comparable to that of our own Indian frontier days than to modern war'.[8]

Although the President and the Joint Chief of Staff (JCS) favoured compliance with civilian immunity, the newly independent US Air Force (USAF) firmly believed that the bombing of Japanese cities had won the Second World War and anticipated that it could do 'even better' against 'primitive Asiatic armies' in Korea.[9] Air force commanders therefore advocated the use of 'overwhelming' force against North Korea.[10] General 'Rosie' O'Donnell (commander

[5] Robert F. Futrell, *The United States Air Force in Korea, 1950–1953*, rev. edn (Washington, DC: Government Printing Office, 1983), p. 187; and Ward Thomas, *The Ethics of Destruction: Norms and Force in International Relations* (Ithaca: Cornell University Press, 2001), p. 149.

[6] J. Caridi, *The Korean War and American Politics: The Republican Party as a Case Study* (Philadelphia: University of Pennsylvania Press, 1968), pp. 29–30.

[7] John W. Spanier, *The Truman–MacArthur Controversy and the Korean War* (Cambridge, Mass: Harvard University Press, 1959), pp. 23–4; Max Hastings, *The Korean War* (London: Michael Joseph, 1987), p. 101; Clay Blair, *The Forgotten War: America in Korea, 1950–1953* (New York: Times Books, 1987), p. 659; David Rees, *Korea: The Limited War* (Oxford: St. Martin's Press, 1964), p. 143; and Paul G. Pierpaoli, *Truman and Korea: The Political Culture of the Early Cold War* (Columbia, Missouri: University of Missouri Press, 1999), p. 29.

[8] *New York Times*, 27 December 1950, cited in Bruce Cumings, *Korea's Place in the Sun: A Modern History* (New York: W. W. Norton and Co., 1997), p. 271, n. 63.

[9] James Gavin, *War and Peace in the Space Age* (New York: Harper, 1958), p. 130.

[10] Conrad C. Crane, 'Raiding the Beggar's Pantry: The Search for Airpower Strategy in the Korean War', *Journal of Military History*, 63 (4) 1999, pp. 889–90.

of the Strategic Air Command's Fifteenth Air Force) and Curtis LeMay proposed a massive strategic bombing campaign.[11] They selected five target areas on the basis of richness of targets (Konan, Wonsan, Pyongyang, Seishin, and Rashin) and proposed their destruction by incendiary attacks.[12] The USA should declare its intention, they insisted, and this announcement would also constitute a warning to civilians—in their minds satisfying the demands of civilian immunity.[13] Though sympathetic, MacArthur rejected the plan but authorized the destruction of military and industrial targets within the designated areas.[14]

A few days later, MacArthur issued an instruction through the commander of the Far Eastern Air Force (FEAF), General George Stratemeyer, forbidding raids on 'urban areas' but authorizing attacks on 'specific military targets' within urban areas. Stratemeyer wrote that 'reasonable care' should be taken 'to avoid providing a basis for claims of "illegal" attack upon population centres'.[15] Bomber pilots were instructed to engage targets only if they made visual contact. In July 1950, MacArthur imposed further restrictions on the strategic air campaign, prohibiting radar guided attacks on Seoul's railway yards to limit the accidental killing of civilians.[16]

It is clear from Stratemeyer's directive that concerns about the legality of targeting civilians played some part in the Administration's decision-making at this stage in the war.[17] But evidence from a key meeting of the National Security Council (NSC) on 29 June 1950 and Truman's own account suggest that this was primarily driven not by fidelity to the norm itself but by a desire to avoid giving the Chinese or Soviets a pretext for intervention.[18] Both Truman and Secretary of State Dean Acheson argued in favour of limiting the air campaign to avoid provoking the Soviets.[19] Indeed, Acheson reported that the Soviet Ambassador to the UN had already expressed concerns about the potential bombing of North Korean cities. Limiting attacks to 'purely military' targets was therefore seen as critical to maintaining the war's legitimacy,

[11] Conrad C. Crane, 'Raiding the Beggar's Pantry', p. 889.

[12] Crane, 'Raiding the Beggar's Pantry', p. 889. Also see Crane, *American Airpower Strategy in Korea, 1950–1953* (Lawrence: University Press of Kansas, 2000), p. 23; and Futtrell, *The United States Air Force in Korea*, p. 186.

[13] Crane, 'Raiding the Beggar's Pantry', p. 889.

[14] Crane, 'Raiding the Beggar's Pantry', p. 889.

[15] Sahr Conway-Lanz, *Collateral Damage: Americans, Noncombatant Immunity and Atrocity after World War II* (New York: Routledge, 2006), p. 86.

[16] Conway-Lanz, *Collateral Damage*, p. 86.

[17] Futrell, *The United States Air Force in Korea*, pp. 41–2.

[18] See Conway-Lanz, *Collateral Damage*, p. 247, n. 3; and Marilyn B. Young, 'Bombing Civilians: From the Twentieth to the Twenty-First Centuries', in Yuki Tanaka and Marilyn B. Young (eds), *Bombing Civilians: A Twentieth Century History* (New York: The New Press, 2009), p. 162.

[19] Conway-Lanz, *Collateral Damage*, p. 85.

which was itself important for denying the Chinese and Soviets a pretext for intervention.[20]

But bombing restraint proved short-lived. With the war proving more difficult than expected, the JCS advised MacArthur that it considered it 'highly desirable to undertake mass air operations' against 'industrial targets' in North Korea. Envisaging that this widening would increase the danger to civilians, the JCS directed that warnings be issued in areas scheduled for attack.[21] On 31 July 1950, 500 tonnes of napalm was dropped on the city of Hungnam. On 6 August, the army requested that several towns near the front be 'obliterated'. Ten days later, B-29s dropped napalm on a wide rectangular area including these towns.[22]

Chinese military intervention in the winter of 1950 raised the stakes still further, prompting MacArthur to lift the restraints on bombing almost entirely.[23] In early November, after the first reports of engagements with Chinese forces, Stratemeyer requested permission to 'burn' the city of Sinuiju, close to the Chinese border. The principal aim of the attack would be to send a 'salutary warning' to the Chinese and undermine communist morale. MacArthur initially rejected the request because he planned to use the city after the war, but was sympathetic to the basic idea of burning urban areas. So, when Stratemeyer proposed Kanggye (considered a communist communications hub) as an alternative target, MacArthur reportedly replied: 'burn it if you so desire. Not only that, Strat, but burn and destroy as a lesson any other of those towns that you consider of military value to the enemy'.[24] Later that same evening, possibly after MacArthur had been informed of the massing of Chinese troops near the border, the commander authorized the burning of Sinuiju as well. Stratemeyer noted that his new orders were that 'every installation, facility, and village in North Korea now becomes a military and tactical target', with the only exceptions being the hydroelectric plants and the city of Rashin.[25] Just as in the Second World War, the USA argued that it was attacking only military targets but the category 'military target' was defined so broadly as to encompass almost every human-made structure in North Korea.

On 5 November, 65 per cent of Kanggye's built up area was destroyed by incendiaries. Stratemeyer argued that the 'entire city . . . was a virtual arsenal and tremendously important communications centre' and therefore a legitimate military target.[26] This argument was repeated to justify other attacks, but

[20] Conway-Lanz, *Collateral Damage*, p. 85; and Futrell, *The United States Air Force*, p. 198.

[21] Crane, 'Raiding the Beggar's Pantry', p. 891.

[22] Bruce Cumings, *The Origins of the Korean War*, Vol. II: *The Roaring of the Cataract, 1947–1950* (Princeton, NJ: Princeton University Press, 1990), p. 706.

[23] Crane, *American Airpower Strategy*, p. 46.

[24] Conway-Lanz, *Collateral Damage*, p. 105.

[25] Conway-Lanz, *Collateral Damage*, p. 105.

[26] Cited by Crane, *American Airpower Strategy*, p. 46.

the reality was that MacArthur had ordered the destruction of physical structures irrespective of whether they were military or civilian in character.[27] By the end of the month, Manpojin (95 per cent), Hoeryong (90 per cent), Namsi (90 per cent), Chosan (85 per cent), Sakchu (75 per cent), Huichon (75 per cent), Koindong (90 per cent), and Uiji (20 per cent) had suffered the same fate.[28] The objective, MacArthur told American Ambassador Muccio, was to create a 'desert' between UN lines and the Chinese border.[29] At the end of December, the FEAF set about destroying Pyongyang. Incendiary attacks on 3–5 January 1951, aimed at 'burning the city to the ground with incendiary bombs' according to General Ridgway, destroyed 35 per cent of Pyongyang's built up area.[30] Pyongyang was visited several more times and virtually the whole city was levelled.[31] On 11 July 1952, thousands of gallons of napalm were dropped on North Korea's capital.[32] Towards war's end, with the FEAF advising that there were no targets left to attack in North Korea, the FEAF attacked the formerly off limits hydroelectric plants and irrigation system, destroying the rice crop and placing North Korean civilians in serious danger of starvation.[33] It also resurrected the idea of 'morale bombing'.[34] General Smart, the FEAF's deputy operations commander, called for attacks 'against targets of military significance so situated that their destruction will have a deleterious effect upon the moral of the civilian population'.[35] These attacks, whose targets included 'the pitiable civilian population of Pyongyang... flattened what was left' of the North Korean capital.[36]

It is difficult to estimate the cost of the bombing campaign on North Korea's civilian population because of scarce information. According to one study, North Korea's population declined by 1.3 million during the war and it is widely thought that around 1 million of its casualties were civilians and that a

[27] Crane, *American Airpower Strategy*, p. 47.

[28] Conway-Lanz, *Collateral Damage*, Crane, *American Airpower Strategy*, pp. 48 and 63.

[29] Sahr Conway-Lanz, 'Beyond No Gun Ri: Refugees and the United States Military in the Korean War', *Diplomatic History*, 29 (1) 2005, p. 67.

[30] Crane, *American Airpower Strategy*, p. 63 and Conway-Lanz, *Collateral Damage*, p. 106. Ridgway quote, Cited in Cumings, *Origins of the Korean War*, II, p. 753.

[31] Blair, *The Forgotten War*, p. 969.

[32] There are large differences as to how many gallons, precisely, were dropped. Rees argues that it was 23,000: Rees, *Korea*, p. 379. This position is shared by Steven Hugh Lee, *The Korean War* (New York: Longman, 2001), p. 88. However, Callum McDonald puts that figure at 2,300. See Callum McDonald, *Korea: The War Before Vietnam* (London: Macmillan, 1986), p. 156. The FEAF itself admitted to dropping 10,000 gallons.

[33] Crane, 'Raiding the Beggar's Pantry', p. 917; and Rees, *Limited War*, p. 381.

[34] Robert A. Pape, *Bombing to Win: Air Power and Coercion in War* (Ithaca: Cornell University Press, 1996), p. 160.

[35] Crane, 'Raiding the Beggar's Pantry', p. 912.

[36] Blair, *The Forgotten War*, p. 969.

large proportion of those were killed by aerial bombing.[37] Marilyn Young puts the death toll from bombing higher still, at between two and three million.[38] Writing for the Hoover Institution in 1973, Joseph Chang concluded that by the end of the war, North Korea's industrial production was 'virtually zero':[39] 8,700 industrial plant were destroyed; 600,000 homes; 5,000 schools; 1,000 hospitals and clinics; and 260 theatres.[40]

As in the Second World War, the USA and its allies maintained that civilians were not the object of attack. Indeed, General Ridgway, MacArthur's replacement as allied commander, ordered that civilians not be deliberately targeted whilst simultaneously ordering attacks directly aimed at the civilian population, such as the destruction of towns and villages to deny shelter to enemy forces.[41] The FEAF was exceptionally vague about the nature of its targets, presenting such a wide definition of 'military target' that almost any physical structure could be classified thus. In addition to structures actually used by the enemy, structures that could be so used in the future were also considered fair game. Referring to target lists that included 'cities', 'towns', and 'villages', Stratemeyer insisted that 'under present circumstances all such have marked military potential and can only be regarded as military installations'.[42] This effectively designated everything in North Korea as a military target, collapsing the distinction between soldiers and civilians upon which civilian immunity depends.[43] There is also evidence that on at least one occasion, military commanders misled the public about the campaign in order to preserve the convenient fiction that civilians were not intentionally targeted. Before one raid on Pyongyang in 1951, the Joint Chiefs stressed that no publicity should be given to the 'mass' nature of the attack. The raid should be reported as 'a normal operation against persistent enemy build up'.[44]

In addition to arguments portraying civilian deaths as unintended by-products of attacks on military targets, the USA and its allies used warnings as evidence of their compliance with civilian immunity. The FEAF dropped leaflets instructing civilians that their towns and villages would be attacked and advising them to leave. The US Administration argued that the warnings demonstrated the FEAF's intention to avoid civilian casualties. But far from emanating from genuine concern for civilians, the warnings were intended to

[37] Byung Chul Koh, 'The Effects of the Korean War on North Korea', in Chae-Jin Lee (ed.), *The Korean War: 40-Year Perspectives* (Claremont, CA: Keck Center for International and Strategic Studies, 1991), p. 100.

[38] Young, 'Bombing, p. 157.

[39] Joseph Chang, *The North Korean Economy: Structure and Development* (Stanford, CA: Hoover Institution Press, 1973), p. 86.

[40] Byung Chul Koh, 'Effects of the Korean War', p. 99.

[41] Conway-Lanz, 'Beyond No Gun Ri', p. 69.

[42] Cited in Crane, 'Raiding the Beggar's Pantry', p. 895.

[43] Crane, *American Airpower Strategy*, p. 67.

[44] McDonald, *Korea*, p. 235.

disrupt North Korean production, lower civilian morale, create a 'favourable world press' and respond to communist criticism of the 'indiscriminate' bombing of North Korea. US commanders also hoped that the North Korean government would be blamed for civilian casualties.[45] Warnings also reinforced the collapsing of the distinction between soldiers and civilians by allowing the USA to argue that it was fair to assume that those who ignored them and remained in threatened areas were combatants and therefore legitimate targets. In reality, it is doubtful that civilians paid much attention to the leaflets and there is little evidence to suggest that they helped protect civilians.[46]

As with the Second World War, there was very little public protest at the bombing in the USA itself—a product of Korea's geographical remoteness, government control of the media which limited reporting of civilian casualties, and a climate of anti-communism spearheaded by McCarthyism.[47] Outside the USA, the bombing was condemned by communists, and communist propaganda—not all of it untruthful—helped inform international debate as well. For instance, *Pravda* reported that attacks on railyards near Pyongyang had killed a considerable number of civilians. Carrying communist reports into the West, London's *Daily Worker* accused the Americans of 'indiscriminate bombing'. In a letter to the UN, the North Korean government complained of 'the inhuman slaughter of peaceful citizens'.[48] The Russian Orthodox Church 'resolutely condemned . . . the inhuman destruction of the peaceful population of Korea by American aircraft'.[49]

Public discussion in the West was constrained by heavy censorship, itself enabled by Korea's geographic isolation and the fact that very few journalists travelled into North Korean held territory. One effect of censorship was that contemporaneous reports about the use of napalm on civilians were released from embargo only in 1969.[50] As such, public debate in the West—such as it was—began in earnest only towards the end of the war, sparked by the very obvious destruction of North Korea's hydroelectric plants in June 1952. This attack created what one commentator described as an 'uproar' in Paris, prompting the French Foreign Minister to warn US Secretary of State Dean Acheson of the 'unfavourable public and legislative opinion' of the campaign in France and urge a more restrained approach. Norway also expressed profound disquiet at the civilian casualties, arguing that this alone created

[45] McDonald, *Korea*, p. 235; and Conway-Lanz, *Collateral Damage*, p. 87.

[46] McDonald, *Korea*, p. 235. For an example, see Austin Stevens, 'US Counters Red Charges Napalm is Used on Civilians', *New York Times*, 19 August 1952, p. 1.

[47] Young, 'Bombing Civilians', pp. 160–1.

[48] Conway-Lanz, *Collateral Damage*, p. 87.

[49] 'End Aggression in Korea: Demand by Russian Orthodox Church', *The Times*, 24 August 1950, p. 3.

[50] Rene Cutforth, 'A Generation Ago', *The Listener*, 11 September 1969, p. 343.

reason enough to seek an immediate peace.[51] Perhaps the most significant indicators of the impact of the bombing on the war's legitimacy, however, were the British and Indian responses. Both initially supported the war, but concerns about the potential use of atomic weapons and reported civilian casualties led both to express grave doubts about the campaign: Britain remained committed to the campaign but concerns about its legitimacy pushed the government to urge the USA to show greater restraint and led many parliamentarians to call for its termination; India allowed concerns about civilian casualties to shift its position from one of supporting the war to one of opposing it.

In the wake of the Second World War, both sides of British politics had moved to publicly distance themselves from the terror bombing of German cities, heaping blame for the excesses on functionaries such as Arthur Harris. So although the British government and its military leaders privately accepted the strategic logic of bombing North Korea, they were eager to present the campaign as limited and restrained in order to avoid potential analogies with Germany. The British government's doubts about the bombing were first aired in the context of the US decision to issue warnings. British officials worried that far from protecting civilians, the leaflets would provide a pretext for saturation bombing and would be seen as an admission of the allies' intention to kill civilians. They believed that this perception would damage support for the war in Asia especially.[52] Similar views were expressed in the British media, with both *The Times* and the *News Chronicle* speculating that the warnings might generate negative reactions in Asia.[53] Although some British parliamentarians endorsed saturation and atomic bombing—Conservative MP Peter Roberts called for an atomic bomb to be dropped 'on the capital of North Korea'[54]—the appearance of terror bombing and potential for an atomic escalation caused alarm in the government. In a state of 'grave perturbation', Attlee hastened to Washington to clarify America's position on the use of atomic weapons.[55] The British Prime Minister sought written assurances that the bomb would not be used, but received only a verbal promise from Truman. Briefing the French prime minister about his meeting, Attlee lamented that the atomic threat would reinforce the view that 'Europeans and Americans have a low regard for the value of Asiatic lives'.[56]

[51] See Blair, *Forgotten War*, p. 969; Thomas, *Ethics of Destruction*, p. 150; 'French Views on Raids', *The Times*, 26 June 1952, p. 8; and Spanier, *The Truman–MacArthur Controversy*, p. 181.

[52] Crane, *American Airpower Strategy*, p. 42.

[53] Conway-Lanz, *Collateral Damage*, p. 88.

[54] Rees, *Korea*, p. 143.

[55] William Stueck, *Rethinking the Korean War: A New Diplomatic and Strategic History* (Princeton, NJ: Princeton University Press, 2002), p. 125.

[56] Cumings, *Origins of the Korean War*, p. 749. Also see Bruce Cumings, 'American Airpower and Nuclear Strategy in Northeast Asia Since 1945', in Mark Selden and Alvin Y. So (eds), *War*

Attlee was right to be concerned because even without atomic escalation, the bombing campaign provoked strong criticism from his own backbenchers, the Church of England, and other prominent Britons.[57] After Attlee's fall in the 1951 election, new Prime Minister Winston Churchill expressed doubts about the legitimacy of the bombing in Korea and especially about the use of napalm but continued to support the war.[58] The bombing issue was raised in the House of Commons several times during 1952, and criticisms were repeated. Of course, some MPs supported the strategy. Fitzroy Maclean (Conservative) defended the campaign 'against important military targets', maintaining that it was necessary to convince the communists that 'aggression does not pay'. But most parliamentarians were critical, seeing through the fiction that the targets were military in nature. Chuter Ede described it as 'unnecessary force' that jeopardized the likelihood of peace, whilst T. Driberg condemned it as 'crazy irresponsible and wicked'.[59] A number of prominent Labour politicians including future ministers Barbara Castle and R. H. S. Crossman took their argument to the public, writing: 'we have been deeply disturbed by the continued use of bombs containing napalm . . . and to the indifference of the Governments concerned to the widespread disquiet which this form of warfare has evoked'. They continued, 'more serious . . . than the barbarity of the weapon itself is the abundant evidence from non-Communist sources that it has been, and is being, indiscriminately used against inhabited places, with appalling results. It is a measure of the deterioration of our values that an international organization set up to defend the rule of law should conduct itself in this manner. We do not accept the argument that because a Power has been declared an aggressor its civilian subjects thereby become legitimate targets for unrestricted warfare'.[60] The bombing of North Korea's hydroelectric plants in 1952 drew strong criticism from Attlee himself.[61]

As a critically important post-colonial state, India provides a useful barometer of wider reactions to the bombing. India initially supported UN intervention in Korea.[62] From the outset, though, Prime Minister Nehru expressed

*and State Terrorism: The United States, Japan, and the Asia-Pacific in the Long Twentieth Century* (Lanham: Rowman & Littlefield Publishers, 2004), p. 71.

[57] McDonald, *Korea*, p. 156; and 'American Weapons in Korea: Dr Barnes's Criticism', *The Times*, 3 March 1952, p. 4.

[58] Gavan McCormack, *Cold War, Hot War: An Australian Perspective on the Korean War* (Sydney: Hale and Iremonger, 1983), p. 132; and Crane, 'Raiding the Beggar's Pantry', p. 913.

[59] 'Comments on Bombing: Speakers' Conflict of Views', *The Times*, 30 June 1952, p. 4.

[60] Marjory Allen of Hurtwood et al., 'Napalm Bombs', *The Times*, 8 July 1952.

[61] Thomas, *Ethics of Destruction*, p. 150.

[62] Spanier, *The Truman–MacArthur Controversy*, p. 171.

concerns about the deliberate targeting of civilians. He worried that allied strategy might cause unnecessary damage and kill innocent people, arguing that the bombing was ineffective and would cause 'problems' in the future.[63] The Indian media repeatedly argued that the destruction of civilians proved that Americans placed more value on European than Asian life.[64] The restrictions placed on American bombing at the beginning of the war were in part a response to precisely this sort of concern which, the State Department feared, threatened the war's legitimacy in Asia. As the bombing restrictions were lifted, Indian criticism increased. In 1952, Nehru criticized 'horrible things called napalm bombs', called on other states to condemn chemical and bacteriological weapons, and criticized the escalation of US bombing.[65] India also criticized the UN (which Nehru labelled a 'protector of colonialism') and called for an immediate end to the war.[66]

US concerns that the appearance of civilian destruction would weaken the war's legitimacy and provide a pretext for Soviet or Chinese intervention demonstrate the growing sensibilities associated with civilian immunity. Although those sensibilities were overcome by perceived strategic imperatives—a move not widely criticized in the USA itself—the switch to terror bombing came at the cost of a degree of lost legitimacy. Some aspects of the bombing campaign were criticized by allies who nevertheless continued to support the war partly because they judged defeating communists to be more important than protecting civilians, whilst in the eyes of at least one prominent non-aligned country (India), the bombing campaign helped transform a legitimate war into an illegitimate one. Growing concerns about the legitimacy of bombing contributed to the erosion of international support for the Korean War and although the US continued to secure *sufficient* legitimacy—evidenced by the fact that it did not suffer punishment—the loss of legitimacy reinforced the momentum behind the principle of a negotiated truce. Thus, whilst civilian immunity did not prevent the deliberate targeting of civilians, spark public protest in the USA, or cause allies to defect, it encouraged the USA to show initial restraint and take measures to create the appearance of compliance. As the campaign escalated and high profile civilian targets such as the hydroelectric plants were attacked, American claims to be complying with civilian immunity became less plausible, resulting in a reduction of legitimacy that increased the costs of continuing to fight.

[63] Conway-Lanz, *Collateral Damage*, p. 88.

[64] Conway-Lanz, *Collateral Damage*, pp. 88–9. E.g. Futrell, *The United States Air Force*, p. 198.

[65] 'UN Criticized by Mr Nehru', *The Times*, 13 June 1952, p. 6; and 'Mr Nehru "Aghast"', *The Times*, 27 June 1952, p. 6.

[66] 'UN Criticized by Mr Nehru', *The Times*, 13 June 1952, p. 6.

## INDOCHINA

This struggle between strategic interests and civilian immunity, and the role of contextual factors in shaping debates about the legitimacy of killing civilians, were also evident in relation to America's campaigns in Indochina between 1961 and 1975. In the strategic bombing of North Vietnam, there was strong evidence of increased sensitivity towards civilian immunity amongst the political and military leadership in the USA.[67] Despite this, these campaigns were widely and sharply condemned both in the USA and internationally.[68] Whilst the criticism demonstrates the growing relevance of civilian immunity, it was also a product of more general opposition to the war itself. Other aspects of the wars, notably elements of the counter-insurgency strategy employed in South Vietnam and the air campaigns over Laos and Cambodia, demonstrated the limits of civilian immunity as a restraint on behaviour and influence on legitimation when set against contextual factors such as perceived strategic interests, alliance politics, geographic remoteness, and limited information. As in Korea, American leaders believed that the stakes extended well beyond Indochina and exhibited what one commentator described as 'moral infallibility'—a sure conviction that the political end of stopping the spread of communism justified the military means that were applied.[69] Also like Korea, the USA tried to portray its behaviour as consistent with civilian immunity by employing a variety of techniques ranging from actually restraining the use of force to collapsing the distinction between combatants and civilians.[70] The adoption of these multiple and varied justificatory strategies suggest that whilst civilian immunity was still not internalized in the USA, military and political leaders recognized that it was embedded in international society and shaped external expectations about appropriate behaviour. They understood that legitimacy required at least the appearance of compliance with civilian immunity in situations where actual compliance was thought counter-productive to good strategy. That civilian immunity was not internalized but was rather seen as an external constraint embedded in international society was evidenced by the fact that campaigns waged beyond the international media's gaze bore all the hallmarks of disregard for civilians displayed in Japan and Korea. Most notably, the USAF conducted massive indiscriminate bombing campaigns over Laos and Cambodia. More tons of

[67] Thomas, *Ethics of Destruction*, p. 152. Also see Pape, *Bombing to Win*, pp. 175–208.

[68] See Guenter Lewy, *America in Vietnam* (Oxford: Oxford University Press, 1978), p. 400. This criticism was acknowledged by Henry Kissinger, *The White House Years* (Boston: Little, Brown & Co., 1979), p. 1446.

[69] Frances Fitzgerald, *Fire in the Lake: The Vietnamese and Americans in Vietnam* (Boston: Little, Brown and Co., 1972), p. 368.

[70] See William V. O'Brien, *The Conduct of Just and Limited War* (New York: Praeger, 1981), p. 99.

explosive ordinance (2.75 million) were dropped on Cambodia than were dropped by the allies in the Second World War (2.1 million) and Laos suffered a similar fate (2 million tons).[71] Conservative estimates suggest that a little fewer than one million civilians in Laos and Cambodia were killed by American bombing.

As a permanent member of the UN Security Council, the USA was never likely to face international punishment for its behaviour. Moreover, the great ideological divide meant that whilst the USA faced stinging criticism from the communist bloc, many of its friends in the capitalist bloc—including the UK, Australia, and frontline Southeast Asian governments such as Thailand, Indonesia, and the Philippines—were prepared to at least tolerate or excuse American non-compliance with civilian immunity. As a result, although American operations in Indochina confronted a perennial legitimacy deficit, the USA was able to secure sufficient legitimacy for long periods, though some individual campaigns such as *Linebacker II* failed to do so. Where sufficient legitimacy was secured, this was often largely due to limited independent reporting, geographic remoteness, and confusion about the situation. This explains why the largely discriminate air attacks on North Vietnam attracted more international criticism than the largely indiscriminate campaigns over Laos and Cambodia.

Although complex and occasionally paradoxical, the story that emerges from the Indochina wars is largely consistent with the idea of a widening and deepening international consensus on the norm of civilian immunity and our understanding that the norm's impact on legitimacy and the consequences that flow from this are influenced by contextual factors. Where intentional civilian killings were reported, they were widely criticized—damaging the perpetrators' legitimacy. Recognizing the embeddeness of civilian immunity, in circumstances where the deliberate killing of civilians was likely to be reported US policy-makers and military leaders tried to reduce civilian casualties and comply (or at least create the appearance of compliance) with civilian immunity. Civilian immunity had much less impact on behaviour when the same actors believed that civilian casualties would not be extensively reported. This section begins by considering the bombing of North Vietnam and America's counter-insurgency campaign in the south before discussing the bombing campaigns in Laos and Cambodia.

## Vietnam

The US conducted three major bombing campaigns against North Vietnam: *Rolling Thunder*, *Linebacker*, and *Linebacker II*.[72] *Rolling Thunder* (March

[71] Taylor Owen and Ben Kiernan, 'Bombs over Cambodia', *The Walrus*, October 2006, p. 67.

[72] A fourth campaign, *Freedom Train*, will not be discussed.

1965 to October 1968) attempted to interrupt the supply of people and material into South Vietnam and to coerce the North into peace negotiations.[73] This involved striking dual-use (military and civilian) targets—especially the transport infrastructure (railways, ports, roads) and North Vietnam's industrial capacity. The JCS wanted to target civilian morale as the best way of coercing the North to the negotiating table.[74] But as in Korea, this initial proposal was rejected by the Administration on the grounds that civilian destruction might provide the Chinese and/or Soviets with a pretext for intervention and weaken domestic support for the war.[75] Bombing restraint was not therefore a product of normative fidelity to civilian immunity but of a belief that it would be difficult to legitimize civilian devastation in the face of an embedded norm of civilian immunity and that illegitimacy might generate serious material costs.

With these concerns in mind, the Johnson Administration imposed tight limits on *Rolling Thunder.* The Hanoi and Haiphong areas were declared 'restricted' and proposed strikes there required White House approval. The USAF was instructed to avoid targeting populated areas without White House approval and missile sites located in populated areas could be attacked only if they were in the process of firing. When attacks on restricted targets were permitted, the White House typically imposed further limitations to reduce civilian damage. These included orders that: the attacks proceed only in the event of good weather conditions and high visibility; they employ experienced pilots; the need to avoid civilian casualties be stressed to all pilots; the direction of attack avoid populated areas; and attacks employ high-precision munitions.[76] The bombing restrictions were gradually eased during the course of the campaign, though not to the same extent as in Korea.[77] Indeed, President Johnson continued to insist that the bombing should avoid 'excessive civilian casualties'.[78] These restrictions persuaded most lawyers and expert commentators

[73] See Pape, *Bombing to Win*, p. 175; and Thomas, *Ethics of Destruction*, p. 152.

[74] Hamilton DeSaussure and Robert Glasser, 'Methods and Means of Warfare', in Peter D. Trooboff (ed.), *Law and Responsibility in Warfare: The Vietnam Experience* (Chapel Hill: University of North Carolina Press, 1975), p. 120; and Mark Clodfelter, *The Limits of Airpower: The American Bombing of North Vietnam* (New York: Free Press, 1989), p. 128.

[75] DeSaussure and Glasser, 'Methods and Means', p. 120; and James P. Harrison, 'History's Heaviest Bombing', in Jayne S. Werner and Luu Doan Huynh (eds), *The Vietnam War: Vietnamese and American Perspectives* (New York: M. E. Sharpe, 1993), p. 136; and Michael Krepon, 'Weapons Potentially Inhumane: The Case of Cluster Bombs', *Foreign Affairs*, 52 (3) 1974, p. 605.

[76] W. Hays Parks, 'Rolling Thunder and the Law of War', *Air University Review*, January–February 1982, p. 14.

[77] Lewy, *America in Vietnam*, p. 403.

[78] Parks, 'Rolling Thunder', p. 10.

that *Rolling Thunder* was conducted lawfully.[79] Its legitimacy was more in doubt.

Despite the restrictions, there were a significant number of civilian casualties. The USA estimated that 17,900 civilians were killed between March 1965 and September 1966, climbing to 52,000 by the time the operation ended in 1968. In total, around 80 per cent of all casualties were civilians, the majority killed by attacks on 'targets of opportunity' such as trucks, cars, and trains, where aiming, accuracy, and the correct identification of targets was less precise.[80] Nonetheless, as Robert Pape argues, this was a rate of killing significantly lower than the Second World War and Korea.[81] This fact notwithstanding, civilian casualties attracted criticism both at home and abroad, much of which (incorrectly) accused the USA of using indiscriminate force and thereby violating civilian immunity.

In the USA, domestic opinion was loudly and sharply divided but opinion polls reveal that although a vocal minority opposed the campaign, a large majority supported it—giving the Administration the domestic legitimacy it needed. Opposition to *Rolling Thunder* was spearheaded by Bertrand Russell's mock 'War Crimes Tribunal' which, after hearing one-sided evidence and no plausible defence, unanimously found the USA guilty of 'the deliberate, systematic and large-scale bombardment of civilian targets, including civilian populations, dwellings, villages, dams, dykes, medical establishments, leper colonies, schools, churches, pagodas, historical and cultural monuments'.[82] Harrison Salisbury, assistant managing editor of the *New York Times* visited North Vietnam in 1966–67 and issued dispatches that, according to Guenter Lewy, 'left the impression that the US was wilfully bombing non-military targets'.[83] Another prominent American critic was the writer Daniel Berrigan, who in 1968 accused the USA of waging a 'monstrous and intentionally genocidal air war'.[84] Although certainly vocal, opposition to the bombing was a minority view. The mainstream media tended not to criticize the campaign for indiscriminate bombing. When *US News & World Report* and

[79] Parks described it as 'one of the most constrained military campaigns in history'. Parks, 'Rolling Thunder', p. 21. Telford Taylor, described the campaign as 'virtually impeccable', Telford Taylor, *Nuremberg and Viet Nam: An American Tragedy* (New York: Times Books, 1970), p. 142.

[80] Raphael Littauer and Norman Uphoff, *The Air War Indochina*, rev. edn (Boston: Beacon Press, 1971), pp. 38–9 and 48.

[81] Pape, *Bombing to Win*, p. 190.

[82] John Duffet (ed.), *Against the Crime of Silence: Proceedings of the International War Crimes Tribunal* (New York: Simon and Schuster, 1970), pp. 308–9.

[83] Lewy, *America in Vietnam*, p. 400. Telford Taylor replied that Harrison Salisbury had graphically described the damage caused by American bombing but 'fell far short of demonstrating any intent to cause civilian casualties'.

[84] Cited in Lewy, *America in Vietnam*, p. 405.

*Newsweek* criticized *Rolling Thunder* they cited its ineffectiveness.[85] For its part, *Time* supported *Rolling Thunder*, a view that was very much in step with American public opinion at the time.[86] A July 1967 Harris poll revealed that 72 per cent of respondents supported *Rolling Thunder*, whilst some 40 per cent supported increased military pressure on North Vietnam.[87]

Outside the USA, attitudes towards *Rolling Thunder* were generally more critical. However, the campaign enjoyed sufficient legitimacy because the USA blocked the UN path to censure and enjoyed the support of key regional allies including Australia, Thailand, Malaysia, the Philippines, and South Korea. These governments privileged the strategic necessity of defeating communism, judged the USA and South Vietnam to be the more legitimate belligerents and largely accepted American justifications. Several of them, including Malaysia, Thailand, and the Philippines believed that North Vietnamese advances motivated their own communist insurgents to expand their revolutionary activities, giving them a shared interest in stemming the communist tide.[88] Unsurprisingly, just as US allies privileged strategic concerns over civilian immunity, the communist bloc exaggerated the extent to which the USA was violating civilian immunity in order to score political points. North Vietnam decried the campaign as a 'war crime', a position later endorsed by the Iranian Ayatollah.[89] Elsewhere, China argued that the raids near Hanoi and Haiphong established grounds for legitimate intervention; government-sponsored demonstrators in Warsaw denounced the Americans as 'murderers and fascists'; and the Soviet news agency *Tass* described the raids as 'unprecedented barbarity'.[90]

A middle ground was occupied by some key European governments. Though they supported the bombing campaign itself, the governments of France and Britain criticized some attacks as disproportionate or insufficiently compliant with civilian immunity. Along with India they criticized the 1966 raids on oil storage areas in Hanoi and Haiphong and the 1967 raids on power plants.[91] In Britain, Harold Wilson's Labour government faced a backbench revolt against its support for the US war in Vietnam and was forced to issue a statement insisting that 'we believe that the value of each application of force must be judged not merely in terms of the military needs which it is designed

[85] James Landers, *The Weekly War: Newsmagazines and Vietnam* (Columbia: University of Missouri Press, 2004), pp. 124–6.

[86] 'The Fighting American', *Time*, 23 April 1965, pp. 22–5; and 'Wishing, Still Nothing', *Time*, 17 February 1967, pp. 17–18.

[87] Clodfelter, *Limits of Air Power*, p. 142.

[88] Odd Arne Westad, *The Global Cold War: Third World Interventions and the Making of Our Times* (Cambridge: Cambridge University Press, 2007), p. 191.

[89] Parks, 'Rolling Thunder', p. 1.

[90] 'Mixed Reaction to Raids', *The Times*, 1 July 1966, p. 11.

[91] Clodfelter, *Limits of Air Power*, p. 142.

to meet but also in terms of the additional suffering and distress which it inflicts upon innocent people'.[92] Norway indicated that it 'deplored' the bombing, whilst Canada urged against escalation.[93] The European media also tended towards criticizing US strategy, focusing on civilian casualties: *Le Monde* condemned the killing of civilians and the populist right-wing *Sun* demanded that the British Prime Minister oppose the campaign.[94] Whilst European governments stopped well short of demanding that the USA change its Indochina policy or imposing costs on the USA, the perceived illegitimacy of the campaign strengthened the reluctance of America's European allies to make a meaningful contribution to the war effort. This, in turn, placed the burden of war and all its costs squarely on the USA.

In relation to this aspect of the war, concerns about civilian immunity restrained American behaviour and shaped judgements about the legitimacy of *Rolling Thunder* to a greater extent than had been the case in the Second World War and Korea. Not only did the USA publicly commit not to deliberately target civilians and act accordingly, it also took measures to avoid unintentional killing—though some of these restrictions were eventually relaxed. The minimization of civilian casualties helped shore up domestic support for the campaign, but outside the USA only those governments that actively supported America's role in Vietnam were prepared to defend or excuse the campaign. Neutral governments and those, like Britain, that supported the war aims but were reluctant to commit troops, tended to criticize particular raids because of their apparently limited compliance with civilian immunity. These attitudes hardened during the *Linebacker* campaigns of 1972.

President Johnson brought *Rolling Thunder* to an end in October 1968 on the understanding that North Vietnam would refrain from using agreed demilitarized zones and that the Viet Cong would not attack major cities in the south.[95] But in late March 1972, the North launched a major offensive. The Nixon Administration responded with what became known as *Linebacker I*. In Christmas 1972, continuing North Vietnamese violations prompted Nixon to authorize a bombing resumption, known as *Linebacker II*.

The *Linebacker* campaigns were guided by many of the restrictions that had characterized *Rolling Thunder*.[96] Indeed, Ward Thomas notes that additional precautions were taken to minimize harm to civilians. Most notably,

[92] 'Mr Wilson Deplores Vietnam Bombing' *The Times*, 30 June 1966, p. 1. The USA responded by dismissing Wilson's concerns and insisting that civilian casualties had been 'minimal'. 'British Fears over Hanoi Bombing Dismissed', *The Times*, 1 July 1966, p. 11.

[93] Kim McQuaid, *The Anxious Years: America in the Vietnam–Watergate Era* (New York: Basic Books, 1989), p. 72.

[94] Lewy, *America in Vietnam*, p. 400.

[95] Lyndon B. Johnson, *The Vantage Point* (New York: Holt, Rinehart and Winston, 1971), pp. 515–29; and Walt W. Rostow, *Diffusion of Power* (New York: Macmillan, 1972), pp. 522–3.

[96] Thomas, *Ethics of Destruction*, p. 154.

precision-guided munitions (PGMs) were to be used for attacks near populated areas, reducing the likelihood of collateral damage, and there were stricter requirements for bomb damage assessment.[97] However, targeting guidance procedures were relaxed to give pilots and forward air controllers greater freedom of action. Moreover, whereas the *Rolling Thunder* directive ordered that all injury to the civilian population be avoided, the JCS now instructed operational commanders only to exercise 'reasonable precautions to avoid incidental damage' to civilian life.[98]

The *Linebacker I* campaign killed approximately 13,000 North Vietnamese civilians, and the shorter *Linebacker II* campaign accounted for approximately 1,600 civilians.[99] To put these figures in context, during these campaigns the USAF dropped over 155,000 tons of munitions and inflicted more damage on North Vietnam's lines of communication than all earlier bombing campaigns combined.[100] The relatively low number of civilian casualties in *Linebacker II* was at least in part a product of their evacuation from Hanoi prior to the campaign.[101] All this did not, however, prevent widespread condemnation at home and abroad. Civilian casualties were extensively reported, as the North Vietnamese provided graphic details and invited American journalists to view the damage and the casualties first hand.[102]

With opinion polls showing domestic support for the war below 30 per cent, American opinion was a little more critical of the *Linebacker* operations that it had been of *Rolling Thunder* when approval for the war was much higher. Significatly, the issue of civilian casualties was more prominent. Kissinger himself recognized that 'the moral indignation rose with each day', continuing, 'charges of immorality and deception were thrown about with abandon; "barbaric" was a favourite adjective'.[103] According to Kissinger, the Administration was accused of 'deliberately slaughtering civilians in a purposeless campaign of terror', a charge that he claims went largely 'unchallenged' in the media.[104] But although criticism was sharper and more prominent than before, opinion polls suggest that the campaign itself was seen more favourably than the war as a whole and that a majority of Americans did not

97 Thomas, *Ethics of Destruction*, p. 154.

98 W. Hays Parks, 'Linebacker and the Laws of War', *Air University Review*, 34 (2) 1983, p. 5.

99 Pape, *Bombing to Win*, p. 208; Thomas, *Ethics of Destruction*, p. 154.

100 Clodfelter, *Limits of Air Power*, p. 167.

101 Casualty figures would likely have been much higher had civilians not been evacuated. See Thomas, *Ethics of Destruction*, p. 154.

102 Though reporting was still very limited by later standards. See Philip Knightly, *The First Casualty: The War Correspondent as Hero, Propagandist, and Myth Maker from the Crimea to Vietnam* (London: Andre Deutsch, 1975), p. 383.

103 Henry Kissinger, *Ending the Vietnam War: A History of America's Involvement in and Extrication from the Vietnam War* (New York: Simon & Schuster, 2003), p. 413.

104 Kissinger, *Ending the Vietnam War*, p. 413. Nixon anticipated the criticism. See Kissinger, *White House Years*, p. 1446.

view it as particularly immoral. Harris polling during the *Linebacker* campaigns showed that fewer than half of the respondents believed the bombing to be 'inhuman and immoral' and 71 per cent believed it to be no worse than anything the communists had done during the war.[105]

Elite level criticism of *Linebacker* was much sharper than its criticism of earlier campaigns. *Newsweek*, which had been critical of *Rolling Thunder*, criticized the *Linebacker* operations but this time on the grounds that they exacted a heavy toll on civilians.[106] *Time*, which had supported *Rolling Thunder*, was strident in its denunciation of *Linebacker*, focusing its attention squarely on civilian casualties. Repudiating its earlier claim that the American air force bombed with supreme accuracy, it held that 'since April 6 [1972], when Nixon officially reinstated mass bombing of the North, aerial attacks on civilian targets have become all too common'. It continued, 'American jets in search of visible targets have destroyed countless hospitals, churches and even cathedrals, as well as residential suburbs'.[107] Likewise, the *New York Times* argued that the bombing amounted to the 'massive, indiscriminate use of the United States' overwhelming aerial might', best described as 'terrorism on an unprecedented scale' and 'Stone Age barbarism'.[108] The *Washington Post* described it as 'the most savage and senseless act of war ever visited... by one sovereign people on another'.[109] Forty-one religious leaders wrote an open letter criticizing the campaign and calling for peace. Cardinal Krol—President of the National Conference of Catholic Bishops—expressed 'grief' and 'dismay' at the 'massive bombing', the Massachusetts Council of Churches described the bombing as 'savage and cynical' whilst fourteen Catholic Bishops labelled *Linebacker II* a 'hideous contradiction of the Christmas spirit of peace'.[110] Some foreign policy experts also criticized the bombing.[111] In the legislature, Democrats lined up to denounce the campaign. Senator Edward Kennedy insisted that the raids 'should outrage the conscience of all Americans' and Representative Don Riegle called the bombing a 'monstrous

[105] William M. Hammond, *Military and the Media 1962–1968* (Washington, DC: US Army Centre of Military History, 1988), p. 610.

[106] 'Diplomacy by Terror', *Newsweek*, 8 January 1973, pp. 10–12; and 'What Went Wrong?', *Newsweek*, 1 January 1973, pp. 8–12.

[107] 'Vietnamization: A Policy under the Gun', *Time*, 17 April 1972, pp. 34–9; 'Living Inside a Bull's Eye', *Time*, 23 October 1972, p. 42. The transformation of *Time*'s position was driven by commercial factors (the war was increasingly unpopular) and recognition of the damage to America's image overseas. Landers, *Weekly War*, p. 130.

[108] 'Terror from the Skies', *New York Times*, 22 December 1972, p. 30.

[109] Cited by Stanley Karnow, *Vietnam: A History*, rev. edn (New York: Viking Penguin, 1991), p. 667; and Thomas, *Ethics of Destruction*, p. 157.

[110] 'Urge End to War', *New York Times*, 23 December 1972, pp. 6–7.

[111] Writing in the *New York Times*, Leslie Gelb and Anthony Lake described the campaign as American 'barbarities abroad'. Leslie H. Gelb and Anthony Lake, 'And is this to be America's Hell?', *New York Times*, 24 December 1972, p. E9.

outrage'.[112] Even some Republicans expressed concerns. Republican Senator Javits supported moves to restrain the White House by cutting-off funds and Senator William Saxbe argued that Nixon had 'taken leave of his senses'.[113] Counter-arguments insisted simply that critics had exaggerated the level of civilian damage and that the USA was not intentionally targeting civilians.[114]

Attitudes to *Linebacker* were more hostile outside the USA. Once again, civilian casualties played an important part in shaping legitimacy judgements. Not surprisingly, the strongest criticism came from the communist bloc. Both China and the Soviet Union called for an immediate halt to the bombing, the former labelling it 'a new barbarous crime'.[115] Trying to maximize international sympathy, North Vietnam agued that the campaign was indiscriminately targeting civilians.[116] Most notable, however, was the strongly critical stance adopted in Western Europe where governments condemned the resumption to bombing and what they saw as the unnecessary killing of civilians. Finnish Foreign Minister, Ahti Karjalainen declared that 'it is especially difficult to understand on what arguments the vast bombardment of the North Vietnamese territory has been based', the Danish government issued a formal protest whilst Sweden's foreign minister, Krister Wickman, described the bombing as 'blind and brutal'. Wickman was joined by Sweden's Prime Minister, the well-respected Olaf Palme, who argued that the bombing was an outrage to be listed with Nazi massacres in the Second World War. Palme insisted that 'what is happening today in Vietnam is a form of torture. There are no military grounds for the bombing'. *Expressen*, Scandinavia's biggest selling newspaper, insisted that 'the outrage against Nixon's ordering for attack is deepening'.[117] The bombing campaign was criticized by the Pope and described as a 'crime against humanity' by one German newspaper.[118] In France, *Le Figaro*, which had—until then—supported the war, condemned *Linebacker*.[119]

Whereas British opinion had tended to tolerate (if critically) earlier US campaigns, it became sharply critical of *Linebacker*. On the left, *The Mirror*

[112] Clodfelter, *Limits of Air Power*, pp. 191–2; and Kissinger, *Ending the Vietnam War*, p. 413.

[113] Kissinger, *Ending the Vietnam War*, pp. 413–14.

[114] John W. Finney, 'Hanoi is Blamed: Lack of Seriousness at Paris Charged—4th B-52 Lost', *New York Times*, 21 December 1972, p. 1. Also, Parks, 'Linebacker and the Laws of War', p. 11.

[115] Cited in Kissinger, *Ending the Vietnam War*, p. 414.

[116] John W. Finney, 'Hanoi is Blamed: Lack of Seriousness at Paris Charged—4th B-52 Lost', *New York Times*, 21 December 1972, p. 1.

[117] 'In Capitals, Bombing Draws Protests, Some Support', *New York Times*, 21 December 1972, p. 16; 'Much European Criticism', *New York Times*, 21 December 1972, p. 16; and Alvin Shuster, 'Europe Reacts to Bombing With Increasing Protests', *New York Times*, 24 December 1972, p. 1. This led Kissinger to surmise that 'not one NATO ally supported us or even hinted at understanding our point of view', Kissinger, *Ending the Vietnam War*, p. 414.

[118] Karnow, *Vietnam*, p. 667; and Thomas, *Ethics of Destruction*, p. 157.

[119] Alvin Shuster, 'Europe Reacts to Bombing With Increasing Protests', *New York Times*, 24 December 1972, p. 1.

described the operation as a 'crude exercise in the politics of terror' and *The Guardian* asked whether 'Mr Nixon wants to go down in history as one of the most murderous and bloodthirsty of American presidents'. At the other end of the political spectrum, *The Times* suggested that the bombing had 'a particular horror because of its massive scale [and] its indiscriminate character'.[120] The British Labour Party despatched its chairman—Bill Simpson—to the US Embassy to seek assurances that 'terror bombing would no longer be applied as a tactic by the United States government'. The delegation also presented a resolution from the party's National Executive Committee protesting the 'slaughter' of Vietnamese civilians.[121] Despite this chorus of criticism, the Conservative government continued to offer cautious support for the US, though without furnishing much in the way of material aid. In this, it was supported by conservative voices such as the *Daily Telegraph*, which argued that the bombing was conducted for a 'just cause'.[122]

Even as the legitimacy of its campaign dwindled in European eyes, the USA was still able to protect itself from punishment by keeping the UN out of the conflict and preservinmg an albeit diminished degree of legitimacy based on support from allies in Southeast Asia, many of whom were themselves engaged in bloody campaigns against communists. The Lon Nol military dictatorship in Cambodia described the bombing as 'necessary to force North Vietnam to adopt a more conciliatory stance in the peace talks' and Indonesia's foreign minister, Adam Malik, insisted that both sides were equally to blame for the escalation of violence.[123]

Despite these pockets of support and although Nixon and Kissinger favoured the use of air power to coerce North Vietnam to the negotiating table, the stinging domestic and international criticism ultimately forced Nixon to accept that continued bombing was not a 'viable option' owing to the costs associated with illegitimacy.[124]

There were a number of reasons why criticism of *Rolling Thunder* and *Linebacker* was so prevalent and why it became sharper. Perhaps more so than in relation to any other campaign up to this time, legitimacy judgements were shaped by shared expectations that civilians be immune from attack. Against the backdrop of these shared expectations, contextual factors shaped legitimacy judgements. Most notably, doubts about the legitimacy of the war itself and hence the relative merits of the American and North Vietnamese positions,

[120] Cited in Alvin Shuster, 'Europe Reacts to Bombing with Increasing Protests', *New York Times*, 24 December 1972, p. 1.

[121] 'Labour Seeks US Pledge Over "Terror Bombing"', *The Times*, 6 January 1973, p. 5.

[122] Alvin Shuster, 'Europe Reacts to Bombing With Increasing Protests', *New York Times*, 24 December 1972, p. 1.

[123] 'In Capitals, Bombing Draws Protests, Some Support', *New York Times*, 21 December 1972, p. 16.

[124] Cited in Clodfelter, *Limits of Air Power*, p. 192.

widespread reporting of civilian devastation in North Vietnam—much of it based on information provided by the North Vietnamese themselves, and the targeting of dual-use facilities which created the appearance of indiscriminacy, made many outside observers sceptical of American arguments. Together, shared expectations about civilian immunity and these contextual factors meant that even though the bombing campaigns in North Vietnam were more discriminate than earlier campaigns over Korea, Japan, and Germany, they were seen as less legitimate and received more criticism.

A combination of domestic support for the war and much greater support for bombing campaigns, US institutional power vis-à-vis the UN, and a shared interest in preventing communist expansion which gave the USA the support of key Asian and some European governments, granted sufficient legitimacy to the bombing campaigns for a number of years. Over time, however, the erosion of domestic support (principally a function of American casualties) and increase in international criticism diminished the campaign's legitimacy to the point where the Nixon Administration was forced to abandon it—despite its clear preference for this strategy—on the grounds that it was counter-productive politically. In other words, the Nixon administration judged that it could no longer secure sufficient legitimacy for the bombing of North Vietnam.

## Aspects of a Ground War: Free-Fire Zones

In South Vietnam, the Viet Cong employed classic insurgency tactics against American forces and their allies. They used booby-traps and ambushes, wore civilian clothing, hid amongst the civilian population and launched attacks from ostensibly peaceful villages.[125] To engage this enemy, the USA first used a strategy based on the French theory of *Guerre Revolutionaire* which assumed that the local population based decisions about which side to support on calculations of interest. The aim was to raise the costs of supporting insurgents and, in the process, separate the insurgents from the local population.[126] This lent itself to 'search-and-destroy' tactics—painstaking village-by-village operations seeking out and destroying Viet Cong units with the South Vietnamese army conducting follow-on operations to pacify and hold secured territory.[127] This approach failed, partly because the South Vietnamese proved incapable

[125] Eric M. Bergerud, *The Dynamics of Defeat: The Vietnam War in Hau Nghia Province* (Boulder: Westview, 1991), p. 174.

[126] Richard Shultz, 'Breaking the Will of the Enemy During the Vietnam War: The Operationalization of the Cost–Benefit Model of Counterinsurgency Warfare', *Journal of Peace Research*, 15 (2) 1978, p. 111.

[127] George McT. Kahin, *Intervention: How American Became Involved in Vietnam* (New York: Alfred Knopf, 1979), p. 405.

of holding pacified ground.[128] Additionally, 'search-and-destroy' missions employed American ground troops in areas of high Viet Cong activity, resulting in heavy US losses. They also caused significant civilian casualties, making it more difficult to win the support of the local population.[129]

To address these problems, the commander of US ground forces—General William Westmoreland—developed a new approach between late 1965 and 1967. Westmoreland wanted to increase the amount of firepower that could be brought to bear on the Viet Cong and reduce American casualties. Referred to as 'territorial denial', the new strategy had much in common with British counter-insurgency strategy used against the Boers and the US ground strategy during the Korean War. Certainly, the underlying theory was identical: because insurgents live among the rural population and are difficult to distinguish from civilians, the best solution is to remove the population, leaving only the insurgents behind.[130] Civilians were encouraged to evacuate areas of Viet Cong activity, sometimes through leaflet drops and sometimes forcibly.[131] Once cleared of civilians, these areas could be designated as 'free-fire/strike zones'. Structures, inhabitants, means of sustaining life, and natural cover could then be systematically destroyed without the need to worry about distinguishing civilians from soldiers or place US forces in harm's way.[132] Designated areas could be systematically destroyed by air and artillery bombardment before troops were sent it. Having been duly warned, Vietnamese inside the zones were assumed to be combatants and therefore legitimate targets.[133]

Westmoreland argued that this strategy protected civilians by removing them from the battlefield. As he put it, this '[w]as one of the reasons for evacuating civilians from villages where they were intermixed with the Viet Cong, for forcing them to endure the indignity and hardship of refugee camps, for creating much-maligned "free-fire zones" where anybody who remained had to be considered an enemy combatant'.[134] The key problem, he later told a

[128] Kahin, *Intervention*, p. 405.

[129] O'Brien, *The Conduct of Just and Limited Wars*, p. 104.

[130] Taylor, *Nuremberg and Viet Nam*, p. 145.

[131] Taylor, *Nuremberg and Viet Nam*, p. 144. As in Korea, the use of leaflets 'whenever there's time' was the primary means by which US forces 'keep from hurting as many civilians as we can', Jonathan Schell, *The Real War: The Classic Reporting on the Vietnam War* (New York: Pantheon Books, 1987), p. 341.

[132] Kahin, *Intervention*, p. 407; Marilyn B. Young, *The Vietnam Wars, 1945–1990* (New York: Harper Perennial, 1991), pp. 173–7.

[133] Taylor, *Nuremberg and Viet Nam*, p. 146. According to one study, US soldiers preferred 'free-fire zones' to working in 'pacified areas' because soldiers were entitled to fire without first ascertaining the identity of the target and were permitted to make more liberal use of fire support from artillery. Robert J. Graham, 'Vietnam: An Infantryman's View of Our Failure', *Military Affairs*, 48 (3) 1984, p. 133.

[134] General William C. Westmoreland, *A Soldier Reports* (New York: Dell, 1976), p. 375. Also see, Thomas O. Schlesinger, 'The Army and the Guerrilla: The Strategy of the Expedient', *Polity*, 4 (3) 1972, p. 333.

Congressional committee, was that 'enemy forces were intermingled with the civilian populace' and could not be engaged without inflicting civilian casualties.[135] Evacuation and 'free-fire zones' enabled US forces to engage the insurgents without having to carefully distinguish between soldiers and civilians whilst claiming to be complying with the norm of civilian immunity.[136] Within the zones, 'harassment and interdiction' fire could be employed indiscriminately and much of this firepower fell on the civilian population.[137] Nevertheless, the strategy was supported by a number of leading American intellectuals. Ethicist William O'Brien judged that 'it was, on the whole, legitimate to clear civilians from areas in which enemy combat forces operate'.[138] Prominent political scientist, Samuel Huntington, defended the use of free-fire zones on the grounds that civilian casualties were the unintended consequences of legitimate measures against insurgents.[139]

The military's principal method for evaluating operational effectiveness was the body count. This was prefaced on the assumption that, like conventional mechanized wars, counter-insurgency warfare was attrition-based. The key to success, in other words, lay in killing the enemy and destroying its means of fighting.[140] To measure progress, individual units were required to report enemy 'kills' and were rewarded for kills with leave or other bonuses. According to O'Brien, this system encouraged a degree of 'insensitivity' to distinguishing the enemy's military dead from civilian dead.[141] In fact, by rewarding 'kills' based upon self-assessments the system did much more than this: it established incentives for killing civilians.[142] Where curfews were imposed, soldiers sometimes assumed that anyone caught outside could be regarded as *prima facie* enemy combatants and killed.[143] Sometimes, they imposed arbitrary exclusion zones around hamlets and shot civilians found outside. Some assumed that they could use force against any Vietnamese who fled from them

[135] General William Westmoreland, House Committee on Armed Services, Armed Services Investigating Subcommittee, *Investigation of the My Lai Incident: Hearings of the Armed Services Investigating Subcommittee of the Committee on Armed Services*, 91st Cong., 2nd session, 1970, pp. 834–6.

[136] See Westmoreland, *A Soldier's Report*, p. 375; and W. Hays Park, 'The Law of War', in David L. Anderson (ed.), *Facing My Lai: Moving Beyond the Massacre* (Lawrence: University Press of Kansas, 1998), pp. 128–31.

[137] James William Gibson, *The Perfect War: The War we Couldn't Lose and How We Did* (New York: Random House, 1988), p. 136.

[138] O'Brien, *Conduct of Just and Limited War*, p. 100.

[139] Samuel P. Huntington, 'The Bases of Accommodation', *Foreign Affairs*, 46 (4) 1968, pp. 650–3.

[140] See Michael D. Sallah and Mitch Weiss, 'Rogue GIs Unleashed Wave of Terror in Central Highlands', *Toledo Blade*, 22 October 2003.

[141] O'Brien, *The Conduct of Just and Limited Wars*, p. 100.

[142] For e.g. see Michael D. Sallah and Mitch Weiss, 'Rogue GIs Unleashed Wave of Terror in Central Highlands', *Toledo Blade*, 22 October 2003, p. 1.

[143] Gibson, *The Perfect War*, p. 142.

on the assumption that flight was a sign of combatancy. Across the theatre, troops did little to distinguish soldiers from civilians. Within the free-fire zones, artillery and airpower was employed without discrimination. Perhaps the clearest evidence of how widespread the practice of killing civilians was is provided by the dramatic gap between reported body counts and the number of weapons recovered. To take just one of many such examples, in 1968 the Ninth Infantry Division conducted *Operation Speedy Express* in the Mekong Delta. The Army claimed that it had killed 11,000 Viet Cong, yet it captured only 748 weapons. At the time, this significant discrepancy went unquestioned but a little discussed *Associated Press* report in 1969 noted complaints about the inclusion of civilian deaths in the official body count.[144] In 1972, *Newsweek* reported that one American official had estimated that, of the 11,000 reported kills in *Speedy Express*, at least 5,000 were civilians.[145]

The role of the body count in enabling (indeed, incentivizing) the killing of civilians emerged clearly at the trial of Lieutenant Duffy, who was tried by court martial for killing a civilian prisoner in 1969. Duffy was charged with ordering or permitting one of his sergeants to shoot the prisoner. Duffy's defence was that the 'body count' policy was the Army's official measure of success and that by killing the prisoner he was simply adhering to policy. Four other lieutenants testified that they were under instructions to take no prisoners, insisting that their orders emphasized the primacy of the body count. In response, the Pentagon insisted that the killing of prisoners was tantamount to murder. But having first convicted Duffy of murder, the military court changed its verdict to involuntary manslaughter and sentenced the defendant to just six months confinement. This led Telford Taylor to conclude that the judges must have found some substance in the defence—demonstrating a clear link between strategy, the body count, and the killing of civilians.[146]

Some see a direct connection between the 'free-fire' strategy, body counts, and the notorious My Lai massacre.[147] Indeed, the link was stressed by the commanding officer at My Lai, Lt. Calley. On trial for his role in the massacre of around five hundred civilians, Calley insisted that he was following orders that he had no reason to doubt because they were consistent with the overall strategy for dealing with a hostile population.[148] The Peers Commission, established to investigate the massacre, found senior officers culpable for

[144] Knightly, *First Casualty*, p. 399.

[145] The actual number of civilian deaths is likely to have been higher than this. Knightly, *The First Casualty*, pp. 399–400.

[146] Taylor, *Nuremberg to Viet Nam*, p. 151.

[147] Schlesinger, 'The Army and the Guerrilla, p. 334; and Jonathan Glover, *Humanity: A Moral History of the Twentieth Century* (London: Pimlico, 2001), pp. 58–61. This was disputed by Nixon, see Taylor, *Nuremberg to Viet Nam*, p. 126.

[148] Tom J. Farer, 'The Laws of War 25 Years After Nuremberg', *International Conciliation*, No. 583, May 1971, p. 29.

either implicitly ordering or failing to prevent war crimes. Peers also found that senior Army officers had conspired to cover up the massacre.[149] My Lai was the most notorious atrocity, but it was part of a wider pattern of killing. Indeed, the dead civilians of My Lai were originally counted as part of the 10,000 'enemy combatants' reported killed in *Operation Wheeler Wallawa*.[150] Only when witnesses complained—against the wishes of their commanding officers—was the case examined in more detail.[151] Although My Lai became the iconic image of American atrocities in Vietnam, it was not unique. In 2006, documents released by the Pentagon revealed that some 320 cases involving the mistreatment of civilians had been substantiated; including seven massacres and seventy-eight other major attacks.[152] The papers confirmed that abuses were committed by every division operating in Vietnam. The Army logged a further 500 alleged atrocities.[153]

The US military argued that civilian casualties were unintentional and caused by the Viet Cong's insurgency tactics. It sometimes claimed that most 'civilians' actively aided the enemy and were therefore properly described as combatants.[154] Civilians were targeted for being 'related' to insurgents or for providing them with supplies, shelter, and intelligence.[155] Whilst some—probably many—civilians in South Vietnam played these roles, this rationale was sometimes used to designate entire villages and hamlets as Viet Cong and all their inhabitants as combatants. Some American Just War theorists sympathized with the US military, arguing that blame for civilian casualties should lay with the Viet Cong because it was responsible for eroding the distinction between combatants and civilians.[156]

Public discussion of 'free-fire zones' was much more limited than debate about the bombing of North Vietnam. In the early phases of the war, the American news media tended to downplay civilian casualties at the hands of the army. In 1965, among the weekly news magazines, *Newsweek* was alone in sporadically reporting civilian casualties. *Time* still considered civilian casualties to be a 'minor consequence' of the war, whilst *US News & World Report*

[149] Lt. Gen. W. R. Peers, *The My Lai Inquiry* (New York: W. W. Norton and Co., 1979); and Herbert C. Kelman and V. Lee Hamilton, *Crimes of Obedience: Toward a Social Psychology of Authority and Responsibility* (New Haven: Yale University Press, 1989), p. 9.

[150] Herman and Chomsky, *Manufacturing Consent*, p. 197.

[151] W. R. Peers, *The My Lai Inquiry* (London: W. W. Norton and Co., 1979), p. 129.

[152] E.g. see Nick Turse and Deborah Nelson, 'Civilian Killings Went Unpunished: Declassified Papers Show US Atrocities Went Much Further than My Lai', *Los Angeles Times*, 6 August 2006.

[153] Nick Turse and Deborah Nelson, 'Civilian Killings Went Unpunished: Declassified Papers Show US Atrocities Went Much Further than My Lai', *Los Angeles Times*, 6 August 2006.

[154] Graham, 'Vietnam', p. 134.

[155] Neil Sheehan, *Bright Shining Lie: John Paul Vann and America in Vietnam* (New York: Vintage, 1989), pp. 110–11.

[156] E.g. Paul Ramsey, *The Just War: Force and Political Responsibility* (Lanham: Rowman and Littlefield, 2002), pp. 435–6; and O'Brien, *The Conduct of Just and Limited War*, p. 100.

believed reports of civilian deaths to be 'overblown'.[157] With the exception of *Newsweek*, the magazines typically rejected stories of civilian casualties as communist propaganda. When they initially reported the 'free-fire' policy, they understated its impact on the civilian population.[158] This attitude was reflected in the television media. One study of network newscasts from 1965 to the 1973 peace treaty found that civilian casualties were rarely reported and where they were, they were often portrayed as unintended but necessary consequences of war caused by the Viet Cong's insurgency. For instance, one NBC report on an air strike on a village ended with the comment that 'there was no discriminating one house from another. There couldn't be, and there did not need to be. The whole village had turned on the Americans so the whole village was being destroyed'.[159]

Some concerns were raised in the US media in 1966–67 but only after 1968, following the Tet offensive and My Lai massacre, did the media become more uniformly critical. At this point, *US News & World Report* and the *New York Times* began to routinely criticize the use of indiscriminate force.[160] But even after My Lai, public criticism of the 'free-fire zones' was tempered by disbelief about the reported civilian casualties (one poll found that 48 per cent of respondents did not believe reports about My Lai) and a widely held assumption that they were unintended.[161] Some commentators offered excuses for My Lai. Kenneth Crawford contrasted the aberration at My Lai with the 'systematic massacre' that the communists would unleash on Vietnam if the USA withdrew; the *Wall Street Journal* reminded its readers that the communists employed terrorism against civilians; and John Wheeler pointed out that the communists had murdered some 3,000 civilians at Hue during the Tet offensive.[162] After the trial and conviction of Lt. Calley, polls revealed that only 9 per cent of respondents approved of his prosecution, whilst 80 per cent objected.[163] Although support for Calley declined over time, a poll taken two months after his conviction found that 45 per cent of respondents supported the view that 'it is unfair to send a man to fight in Vietnam and then put him

[157] Landers, *Weekly War*, p. 121.

[158] 'Assault on the Iron Triangle', *US News & World Report*, 23 January 1967, p. 39. Contrast with Jonathan Schell, 'The Village of Ben Suc', *New Yorker*, 15 July 1967. See Landers, *Weekly War*, p. 135.

[159] Edward S. Herman and Noam Chomsky, *Manufacturing Consent: The Political Economy of the Mass Media* (New York: Pantheon, 1988), p. 203.

[160] E.g. 'Why US Isn't Winning a War', *US News & World Report*, 1 April 1968, pp. 44–8; 'An American Nightmare', *New York Times*, 22 November 1969, p. 36; James Reston, 'Washington: The Massacre of Songmy: Who Is to Blame?', *New York Times*, 26 November 1969, p. 44.

[161] William M. Hammond, *Reporting Vietnam: Media and Military at War* (Lawrence: University Press of Kansas, 1998), p. 191.

[162] Hammond, *Reporting Vietnam*, p. 190.

[163] Joanna Bourke, *An Intimate History of Killing: Face-to-Face Killing in Twentieth Century Warfare* (London: Granta Books, 1999), pp. 194–5.

on trial for doing his duty'.[164] Nixon recorded that immediately after Calley's trial, the White House received 5,000 telegrams, 'running 100 to 1 in favor of clemency'.[165] Similar sentiments were evident among some of America's allies. Polling in Australia found that two-thirds believed that the soldiers responsible for My Lai should go unpunished.[166] In the end, Calley was the most senior officer prosecuted for the massacre, serving only three years before being released on the President's orders.[167]

Although Vietnamese civilian deaths were widely accepted by the US public as unintended but necessary consequences of military operations, the rising toll became a core feature of anti-war agitation. In February 1971, the Vietnam Veterans against the War (VVAW) hosted hearings at which one hundred veterans and sixteen civilians provided testimony about civilian casualties.[168] John Kerry famously testified before a Congressional Committee that 'we learned the meaning of free fire zones, shooting anything that moves, and we watched whilst America placed cheapness on the lives of Orientals'. He continued, 'we watched the US falsification of body counts, in fact the glorification of body counts'.[169] Concerns were also raised about the legality of the 'free-fire' strategy. Telford Taylor, America's chief prosecutor at the Nuremberg trials, argued that the 'free-firing' part of the strategy was patently unlawful.[170] This view was shared by another prominent lawyer, Tom Farer, who argued that the targeting standards employed within free fire zones, 'manifested a large indifference to principles of proportionality and discrimination'.[171]

International opinion was more consistently critical of US strategy, though it did not reach the peaks of denunciation associated with the air campaign—partly because the civilian devastation was not reported to the same degree. Even in allied countries, such as Britain, the media was almost uniformly critical of the free-fire strategy. In 1969, the conservative *Times* described how evacuated civilians had lived 'in caves and bunkers for many months' because 'heavy American bombing and artillery and naval shelling' had destroyed their

[164] Bourke, *Intimate History*, p. 195.

[165] Richard Nixon, *The Memoirs of Richard Nixon*, volume 1 (New York: Warner Books, 1978), p. 449.

[166] Bourke, *Intimate History*, p. 195.

[167] Herbert C. Kelman and V. Lee Hamilton, *Crimes of Obedience: Toward a Social Psychology of Authority and Responsibility* (New Haven: Yale University Press, 1989), p. 12.

[168] Nick Turse and Deborah Nelson, 'Civilian Killings Went Unpunished: Declassified Papers Show US Atrocities Went Much Further than My Lai', *Los Angeles Times*, 6 August 2006.

[169] John Kerry, 'Transcript: Kerry Testifies Before Senate Panel, 1971', 22 April 1971, p. 2. Transcript made available by National Public Radio at http://www.npr.org/templates/story/story.php?storyId=3875422 last accessed 26 March 2012.

[170] Taylor, *Nuremberg to Viet Nam*, p. 146.

[171] Tom Farer, 'Remarks by Tom Farer' in Richard Falk (ed.), *Vietnam War and International Law: Volume 4 The Concluding Phase* (Princeton, NJ: Princeton University Press, 1976), p. 376.

homes. Two years later, it maintained that My Lai was a direct consequence of US strategy, which valued force protection above that of civilians. *The Times* described the US as an 'indiscriminate war machine'.[172]

A combination of legal concerns, its evident capacity to enable atrocities, and its negative impact on the campaign to win 'hearts and minds', persuaded the USA to abandon the free-fire strategy in the late 1960s.[173] Subsequent US thinking on counter-insurgency has tended to emphasize the importance of complying with International Humanitarian Law in order to win the trust and support of the local population, although these assumptions were tested once more during the occupation of Iraq after 2003.

In summary, the free-fire strategy had much in common with counter-insurgency strategies employed by the French in Spain, Prussians in France, British in South Africa, Spanish in Cuba, and the US and its allies in Korea. Like those before it, the USA confronted a dilemma of how to separate the civilian population from the insurgents and responded with a strategy of evacuating civilians from areas of insurgent activity and then assuming that all those who remained were combatants. This assumption got around civilian immunity by collapsing the distinction between soldier and civilian. It enabled indiscriminate firing in areas that were in reality not free of civilians whilst allowing the perpetrators to claim that their behaviour was consistent with civilian immunity. The promulgation of formal rules forbidding the mistreatment of civilians, the trial and conviction of Lt. Calley, the issuing of warnings and the evacuation of civilians provide evidence of growing recognition of the need to comply with civilian immunity in order to secure legitimacy. But the lenient sentence given to Calley, the public support he received, the all-too evident practice of ignoring rules prohibiting the killing of civilians, the impunity this practice enjoyed, and the tactic of indiscriminate bombardment of civilian-populated areas demonstrate a continuing tendency to accept the privileging of military necessity over civilian immunity where limited information and clever arguments persuade people to collapse the soldier–civilian distinction. In other words, civilian immunity was embedded but not internalized. On the whole, whilst the killing of civilians was criticized by anti-war protestors, the liberal media and foreign governments, the free-fire strategy received less criticism than the bombing of North Vietnam. This was largely because the body counts created uncertainty about the identity of the victims and front-line reporting was difficult and information uncertain. Where the strategy's effects were most obvious—as in the My Lai massacre—domestic and international reactions were sharpest. But even here legitimacy judgements were

[172] Herman and Chomsky, *Manufacturing Consent*, p. 196; and Louis Heren, 'Lieut. Calley, a Cog in a War Machine', *The Times*, 1 April 1971, p. 6.

[173] Lewis M. Simmons, 'Free Fire Zones', in Roy Gutman and David Rieff (eds), *Crimes of War: What the Public Should Know* (New York: W. W. Norton, 1999).

influenced by prior judgements about the relative legitimacy of the actors and of the war itself. These judgements evidently influenced the extent to which massacre reports were believed by different communities. Governments and individuals who supported the war and regarded the Viet Cong as illegitimate communist invaders tended to dismiss massacre reports as exaggerated. Those who held contrary views about the war and the relative legitimacy of the belligerents tended to draw different conclusions. Ultimately, though, the strategy's ineffectiveness (which was in part due to the fact that it alienated the local population) and doubts about its legality were sufficient to prompt a strategic rethink in the late 1960s.

## The Bombardment of Laos and Cambodia

The US bombardment of Laos and Cambodia confirms my argument that American sensitivity towards civilian casualties in North Vietnam was prompted more by concerns about maintaining sufficient legitimacy that by principled fidelity to civilian immunity. In other words, although the norm was not internalized in the USA, policy-makers there recgonized that civilian immunity was embedded in international society. These cases also lend weight to the argument that external judgements about the legitimacy of killing civilians were influenced by contextual factors, in these cases especially prior judgements about the relative legitimacy of the actors involved and the dissemination of accurate information. As it had done in the Second World War and Korea, the USA denied that it was indiscriminately killing civilians in Laos and Cambodia. Indeed, for many years it refused to admit that it was bombing these two countries at all. Although this argument sufficed for a number of years, a massive escalation of bombing after 1969 made outright denial less tenable, prompting the US Administration to claim that it was attacking only military targets. For a number of years, these justificatory arguments succeeded in securing sufficient legitimacy and the assaults on Laos and Cambodia attracted relatively little criticism either at home or internationally. This was principally because Western journalists had very limited access to Laos and Cambodia and were mainly confined to the respective capitals, often a long way from where most of the bombing was being conducted. This allowed the USA to maintain a veil of secrecy over its bombing activities in Laos and Cambodia, shielding these largely indiscriminate campaigns from the withering international criticism that accompanied the much more discriminate campaigns in North Vietnam. As that veil began to lift, the US Administration found it much more difficult to maintain sufficient legitimacy. Not only did the bombing attract international criticism, but widespread domestic opposition prompted Congress to sever funding in May 1973. To demonstrate these points, this section begins with a brief discussion of the campaigns in Laos before moving on to Cambodia.

US military involvement in Laos began in earnest in 1964 and was guided by three objectives: interdicting Viet Cong/North Vietnamese logistics lines; assisting the government of Laos against communist insurgents (the Pathet Lao); and preventing the spread of Chinese communist influence.[174] US activities gradually escalated into a massive air campaign aimed at defeating the Pathet Lao insurgency by destroying the physical setting in which it operated and the social infrastructure that it used.[175] Recognizing that it was impossible to directly engage and defeat insurgents from the air, the bombing campaign (May 1964–June 1973) attempted to separate the insurgents from the people and deny the communists the ability to sustain life in two critical regions—northeast Laos including the Plain of Jars and the frontier with North Vietnam, and southeast Laos. To accomplish these ends, the US pursued a strategy labelled 'demoralization, deprivation and destruction': demoralize the civilian population and raise the costs of supporting the communists; deprive the Pathet Lao of rice, vegetables, livestock, civilian supporters, and natural cover; destroy communist forces, commerce, and trade.[176] Even some of the campaign's supporters tacitly recognized that this amounted to an indiscriminate campaign against civilians.[177]

Between May 1964 and October 1966, bombing was sporadic, chiefly conducted by Laotian aircraft and directed against Pathet Lao targets. The second phase (October 1966–early 1968) saw an increase in the use of US aircraft and a change in the target profile, with villages and towns in rebel affected areas being targeted. In early 1968, the air war escalated once again. The US and Lao government forces issued warnings and evacuated civilians from regions that were then systematically destroyed from the air. The final phase coincided with a bombing pause in North Vietnam. From 1969, bombing was almost continuous and napalm was used extensively. The target list was widened to include not only towns and villages but physical structures of any kind, livestock, and forested areas. The rules of engagement were relaxed almost entirely during this phase.[178] During this phase the USA conducted on average 300–400 daily sorties over Laos.[179]

Because of the secrecy that accompanied this campaign, there is little reliable information about the level and nature of the destruction. Indeed,

[174] Fred Branfman, 'Presidential War in Laos, 1964–1970', in Nina S. Adams and Alfred W. McCoy (eds), *Laos: War and Revolution* (New York: Harper & Row, 1970), p. 214.

[175] Branfman, 'Presidential War', p. 213.

[176] Branfman, 'Presidential War', p. 232.

[177] See Littauer and Uphoff, *Air War in Indochina*, p. 84.

[178] Branfman, 'Presidential War', p. 233; and Littauer and Uphoff, *Air War in Indochina*, p. 81.

[179] Robert Shaplen, 'Our Involvement in Laos', *Foreign Affairs*, April 1970.

there are no firm estimates as to how many civilians lived in the targeted areas before the bombing (up to 1 million civilians is the most common estimate).[180] We do know that the USAF dropped 2,092,900 tonnes of explosives on Laos, more than three-quarters of it after the escalation in 1969. This amounted to two-thirds of a tonne for every person in Laos and two tonnes for every person living in areas controlled by the Pathet Lao.[181] Around 3,500 towns and villages were controlled by the Pathet Lao and reports concur that almost all of them were destroyed. One air force officer wrote simply that 'there just aren't any villages in northern Laos any more' and another, responsible for analysing reconnaissance photographs, observed that 'the countryside in the photographs . . . looked like a bombers' test range'.[182] In 1960, approximately 150,000 people lived on the Plain of Jars. After a decade of bombing and forced evacuations, only 9,000 remained. Most had fled or been forcibly relocated but a conservative estimate would suggest that at least 30,000 had been killed by the bombing.[183] The *New York Times* estimated that, in total, approximately 350,000 people—mostly civilians—were killed in Laos by US bombing.[184] If true, this would amount to 10 per cent of the country's pre-war population.[185]

Victim and witness testimony is remarkably consistent in its portrayal of an increasingly indiscriminate bombing campaign exacting a heavy toll on civilians. Ronald Rickenbach, a former relief officer for USAID, told a Senate Committee in 1970 that 'if the truth is to be known, more havoc and meaningless destruction (rather than military advantage), has been wrought by what can in many cases only be characterized as indiscriminate bombing of civilian population centres'.[186] Referring specifically to the Plain of Jars, George Chapelier, a UN official, reported that the bombing had destroyed all organized life. 'By 1968', he claimed, 'the intensity of the bombings was such that no organized life was possible in the villages. The villages moved to the outskirts and then deeper and deeper into the forest as the bombing reached its peak in 1969 when jet planes came daily and destroyed all stationary structures. Nothing was left

[180] Branfman, 'Presidential War', p. 231, n. 19.

[181] Arnold R. Isaacs, *Without Honor: Defeat in Vietnam and Cambodia* (Baltimore: Johns Hopkins University Press, 1983), p. 161.

[182] Both cited in Isaacs, *Without Honor*, p. 162.

[183] Isaacs, *Without Honor*, p. 162. Some of those displaced were Hmong—US allies abandoned to a terrible, some would say genocidal fate. See Jane Hamilton-Merritt, *Tragic Mountains: The Hmong, The Americans, and the Secret Wars for Laos, 1942–1992* (Bloomington: Indiana University Press, 1993).

[184] Nicole Barrett, 'Holding Individual Leaders Responsible for Violations of Customary International Law: The US Bombardment of Cambodia and Laos', *Columbia Human Rights Law Review*, 32, 2001, p. 434.

[185] Isaacs, *Without Honor*, p. 162.

[186] Statement of Ronald J. Rickenbach to the Subcommittee to Investigate Problems Connected with Refugees and Escapees of the Committee of the Judiciary United States Senate, 7 May 1970, p. 26.

standing. The villagers lived in trenches and holes or in caves. They only farmed at night. [Each] of the informants [refugees from the area], without any exception, had his village completely destroyed. In the last phase, bombings were aimed at the systematic destruction of the basis of the civilian society'.[187] There are countless other testimonies that confirm this view of the campaign.[188] Taken together, they point to the complete breakdown of the distinction between combatants and civilians and the waging of a massive indiscriminate bombing campaign against parts of Laos.[189]

Rather than justify the campaign, the US government went to considerable lengths to deny it. Between May 1964 and March 1970, when Nixon finally acknowledged that the USA was bombing Laos, American officials denied that the military was engaged there. Instead, they insisted that bombing was confined to the Ho Chi Minh trail and 'North Vietnamese supply routes'.[190] The Administration deliberately misled both Congress and Senate on this point.[191] Once complete denial became untenable, the Administration misled legislators about the nature of US involvement, arguing that the campaign was limited, discriminate, and focused on North Vietnamese (not Pathet Lao) targets. In October 1969, the Senate held closed hearings during which senior officials testified that the bombing was limited and discriminate. Former Ambassador Sullivan testified that 'the Lao, of course, placed restrictions on those strikes that would go into populated areas . . . the United States Air Force contribution was limited to striking at the logistic routes, or what were Allied check points on those routes or at points of concentration which fed into the area where the actual ground battling was taking place . . . it was the policy not to attack populated areas'. Likewise, Air Attaché Tyrrell testified that 'villages, even in a free drop zone, would be restricted from bombing'.[192] Given the aforementioned evidence, this testimony was clearly inaccurate. After being forced to admit the campaign's existence, the Administration repeatedly argued that the bombing campaign was carefully targeted. Nixon insisted that it was directed exclusively against North Vietnamese targets and scrupulously avoided civilian casualties.[193] In late 1971, Air Force Secretary Robert Seamans issued a statement noting 'I have seen no evidence of indiscriminate

[187] Cited in Walter Haney, 'A Survey of Civilian Fatalities Among Refugees from Xieng Khouang Province, Laos', US Senate Sub-Committee on Refugees and Escapees, 9 May 1972, p. 5.

[188] E.g. see Gibson, *Perfect War*, pp. 393–4.

[189] Fred Branfman, *Voices from the Plain of Jars: Life Under an Air War* (New York: Harper & Row, 1972), p. 26.

[190] Branfman, 'Presidential War', p. 268.

[191] Littauer and Uphoff, *Air War in Indochina*, p. 76.

[192] US Congress, Senate, Subcommittee on United States Security Agreements and Commitments Abroad of the Committee on Foreign Relations, *Hearings*, Vol. 1, Part 2: *Kingdom of Laos*, 91st Cong., 1st sess., 21 October 1969, p. 500.

[193] Branfman, *Voices from the Plain of Jars*, p. 6.

bombing'.[194] The claim was supported by publication of rules of engagement instructing that attacks be carefully targeted and directed by forward air controllers.[195] In reality, the rules were complex, barely ever followed, and relaxed entirely in 1968.[196] The clear discrepancy between the published rules and the evident destruction inflicted on Laos was noted by a Senate Foreign Relations Committee researcher.[197]

Given the geographic isolation of the targeted areas and an elaborate strategy of denial and dissembling, it is perhaps unsurprising that neither the American nor international media discussed the bombardment of Laos much before Nixon made it public in 1970. Indeed, even once reports began to emerge in 1968/9 and the campaign itself escalated massively, the American media generally accepted the Administration's claim that the targets were North Vietnamese combatants using Laotian territory because it had little evidence of its own to the contrary.[198] Only after Nixon's public announcement did the press begin to report the campaign and even then usually only to confirm the Administration's version of events.[199] Gradually, though, evidence of indiscriminate targeting began to emerge and to attract criticism. The most senior and outspoken domestic critic was Democrat Senator Edward Kennedy, chair of the Senate's Subcommittee on Refugees and Escapees which conducted extensive hearings on the campaign's impact. Kennedy issued a strong denunciation of Nixon's campaign in Laos.[200]

International reporting was understated but consistently critical. Foreign newspapers carried the observations of T. D. Allman before the US media carried his reports in 1971. In 1970, Allman wrote in the *Far Eastern Economic Review* that 'air bombings during the last year have mutilated the economic and ethnographic map of Laos'.[201] Reporting on the Plain of Jars in late 1971, Allman argued that 'it is empty and ravaged' by American napalm and heavy bombs which had clearly been 'used in an attempt to extinguish all human life in the target area'.[202] Three years earlier, Jacques Decornoy had painted a similar picture in *Le Monde*.[203] Decornoy wrote of 'a world without noise, for the surrounding villages has disappeared, the inhabitants themselves living

[194] Cited by Herman and Chomsky, *Manufacturing Consent*, p. 258.
[195] Gibson, *Perfect War*, p. 390.
[196] Gibson, *Perfect War*, p. 391.
[197] Gibson, *Perfect War*, p. 391.
[198] Herman and Chomsky, *Manufacturing Consent*, p. 256.
[199] Herman and Chomsky, *Manufacturing Consent*, p. 256.
[200] Refugee and Civilian War Casualty Problems in Laos and Cambodia: Hearing Before the Subcommittee to Investigate Problems Connected with Refugees and Escapees of the Senate Committee on the Judiciary, 91st Cong. 1, 1970, opening statement of Senator Kennedy.
[201] T. D. Allman, 'Laos: The Labyrinthine War', in *Far Eastern Economic Review*, 12 March 1970.
[202] Herman and Chomsky, *Manufacturing Consent*, p. 258.
[203] Herman and Chomsky, *Manufacturing Consent*, pp. 255–6.

hidden in the mountains'. Directly challenging American claims that population centres had not been bombed, Decornoy described the provincial centre of Sam Neua district, first bombed by the USA in February 1965, as being 'razed to the ground', observing that the town's buildings had been demolished. Up to thirty kilometres outside this town, 'no house in the villages and hamlets had been spared'. Decornoy's writings helped turn *Le Monde* into a focal point for opposition to America's bombing in Laos, taking French opinion with it.[204]

By and large, however, American denials and attempts to create and leverage uncertainty limited criticism and preserved a degree of legitimacy for the campaign. Extremely limited reporting combined with geographic isolation, the consent of the host government, and a shared Western and Southeast Asian interest in stemming communist expansion coalesced to enable the USA to secure sufficient legitimacy for a number of years with largely implausible claims. But as the veil of uncertainty began to lift, concerns about the indiscriminate bombing of civilians combined with wider opposition to Nixon's strategy in Indochina fuelled criticism and encouraged Congress to take the unusual step of severing funds. A similar pattern played out in relation to Cambodia.

Cambodian territory was used by the Viet Cong for supply routes and to house safe bases from which to attack South Vietnam. In 1966, US forces were permitted to fire artillery into Cambodia but only after receiving fire themselves. Involvement was extended the following year to include intelligence gathering and commando raids. President Johnson rejected repeated military requests to escalate the war in Cambodia on the grounds that it would damage international support, weaken the legitimacy of Sihanouk's fragile government, and provide China with a pretext for intervention.[205] The Nixon Administration was not so cautious. In March 1969, the JCS proposed a single 'short-duration, concentrated' attack by forty-two B-52s on an area of Cambodia suspected of housing the communists' mobile military headquarters, known as COSVN (it later transpired that the much-sought COSVN did not actually exist, at least not in the form of a fixed military headquarters).[206] Nixon duly authorized the assault, which gradually escalated into a wider campaign.[207]

As in Laos, the campaign against Cambodia was initially cloaked in secrecy. Neither Congress nor the public were notified and the Administration engaged in an elaborate game to hide the campaign under a veil of uncertainty. Military commanders falsified documents. Kissinger even argued that the

[204] Herman and Chomsky, *Manufacturing Consent*, pp. 255–6.

[205] Isaacs, *Without Honor*, p. 193; and Seymour M. Hersh, *The Price of Power: Kissinger in the Nixon White House* (New York: Summit Books, 1983), p. 54.

[206] Isaacs, *Without Honor*, p. 194; and Hersh, *Price of Power*, p. 55.

[207] Nixon, *Memoirs*, Vol. 1, p. 471.

pilots themselves should be misled about the locations they were bombing.[208] A complex targeting system was developed, partly to make it difficult to prove that Cambodia was being bombed without overtly misleading the aircrews.[209] In these early raids, pilots were directed in their pre-mission briefings to coordinates inside Vietnam but then redirected mid-flight into Cambodia by forward air controllers. Only given coordinates, aircrews were often unaware that they were bombing Cambodia and not Vietnam. Spokesmen were instructed on how to evade questions and misdirect the media.[210] General Wheeler advised his media team that: 'In the event press enquiries are received following the execution of the Breakfast Plan [the first bombing of Cambodia] as to whether or not US B-52s have struck in Cambodia, US spokesmen will confirm that B-52s did strike on routine missions adjacent to the Cambodian border but state that he has no details and will look into this question. Should the press persist in its inquiries or in the event of a Cambodian protest concerning US strikes in Cambodia, US spokesmen will neither confirm nor deny reports of attacks on Cambodia but state it will be investigated. After delivering a reply to the Cambodian protest, Washington will inform the press that we have apologized and offered compensation'.[211]

Between 1970 and 1973, the war in Cambodia intensified as the Khmer Rouge grew in strength and the Cambodian government struggled to find troops. In 1970, American and South Vietnamese forces invaded Cambodia, prompting a more general escalation into civil war there. The USA bombed sporadically until the end of *Linebacker II* presented it with military capacity to dramatically escalate in Cambodia.[212] As mentioned earlier, declassified documents reveal that the USAF dropped 2.7 million tonnes of ordinance on Cambodia, the large majority in the campaign's final year—a total significantly greater than the tonnage dropped during the Second World War. On 1 April 1973, the *Boston Globe* reported that, 'refugees swarming into the capital from target areas report dozens of villages, both east and south-west of Phnom Penh, have been destroyed and as much as half their population killed or maimed in the current bombing'.[213] According to Ben Kiernan, within days of this report, the level of bombing stood at 3,600 tons *per day* (this compares to 3,900 tons dropped in the massive allied raid on Dresden in 1945).[214]

[208] Hersh, *Price of Power*, p. 60.

[209] Hersh, *Price of Power*, p. 54.

[210] Isaacs, *Without Honor*, p. 195.

[211] William Shawcross, *Sideshow: Kissinger, Nixon and the Destruction of Cambodia* (New York: Simon and Schuster, 1979), p. 22. Explanatory parentheses added.

[212] Ben Kiernan, *How Pol Pot Came to Power: Colonialism, Nationalism, and Communism in Cambodia, 1930–1975* (New Haven: Yale University Press, 2004), p. 349; and Shawcross, *Sideshow*, p. 264.

[213] Cited in Kiernan, *How Pol Pot Came to Power*, p. 350.

[214] Kiernan, *How Pol Pot Came to Power*, p. 350.

The bombardment of Cambodia was largely indiscriminate, focusing in general on rural areas where the communists were thought active. These areas were effectively treated as free-fire zones. Even before the 1973 escalation, the campaign had inflicted a heavy toll on the civilian population.[215] Ben Kiernan has documented more than a dozen attacks on civilians between 1970 and 1972. In 1971, 67 per cent of displaced Cambodians indicated that aerial bombardment was the principal cause of their flight.[216] The level of civilian destruction increased when the bombing escalated in 1973, culminating in the carpet-bombing of south-west Cambodia in August. Because this area was much more populous than other parts of rural Cambodia, the civilian casualty toll soared in this period.[217] It is difficult to know precisely how many civilians were killed by US bombing. The Kampuchea Inquiry Commission, set up in 1980 with the support of the Finnish government, concluded that out of a total pre-war population of seven million people, the war between 1969 and 1973 was responsible for 600,000 deaths and that a further two million were forced from their homes. The overwhelming majority of these casualties were civilians.[218] The Commission's figures are considered conservative by most analysts. Karl Jackson puts the figure up to 700,000 casualties before the Khmer Rouge's victory and Ben Kiernan argues that the refugee toll was much higher than two million, placing it at 3,389,000.[219] All agree that US bombing accounted for a large portion of this but precisely how much remains unclear. Kiernan suggests that in a private memo for Kissinger, the US Defence Department itself acknowledged 50,000 civilian deaths as a result of its bombing campaign and that this is probably the lower limit of an estimated range of 50,000–150,000 civilian deaths.[220]

As in Laos, the US Administration preferred secrecy and denial to public justification. In his memoirs, Nixon candidly noted that the campaign was kept secret to protect it from anticipated domestic and international protests.[221] According to one White House insider, Nixon delayed the bombing several times because of concerns about potential protests overseas. The president reportedly worried that 'a leak of plans to bomb Cambodia may have triggered serious anti-war demonstrations abroad'.[222]

[215] Kiernan, *How Pol Pot Came to Power*, p. 350.

[216] Reported by Kiernan, *How Pol Pot Came to Power*, p. 350.

[217] Isaacs, *Without Honor*, p. 217.

[218] Kimmo Kiljunen, 'Power Politics and the Tragedy of Kampuchea During the Seventies', *Bulletin of Concerned Asian Scholars*, 17, 1985, esp. p. 49.

[219] Karl Jackson is cited in Barrett, 'Holding Individual Leaders Responsible', p. 438, n. 33. Ben Kiernan in Ben Kiernan and Chanthou Boua (eds), *Peasants and Politics in Kampuchea, 1942–1981* (London: Zed Books, 1982), p. 282.

[220] Kiernan, *How Pol Pot Came to Power*, 2nd ed, p. xxiii.

[221] Nixon, *Memoirs*, Vol. 1, p. 472.

[222] Jeffrey Kimball, *Nixon's Vietnam War* (Lawrence: University Press of Kansas, 1998), p. 133.

When the veil of secrecy was lifted, the USA employed four arguments to justify its actions. First, that bombing was a legitimate means of protecting Americans in South Vietnam.[223] Second, that there were very few civilian casualties. US military commanders, citing information gathered from Cambodian government commanders, argued that civilian casualties were minimal. In addition, the US embassy in Phnom Penh advised journalists that there were 'almost no civilian casualties'.[224] Later, responding to William Shawcross' claim that the bombing inflicted heavy civilian casualties, Kissinger claimed 'there is no evidence of massive civilian casualties'.[225] Third, that communist artillery rather than US airpower was responsible for civilian deaths. Kissinger argued that US aircraft only bombed areas that were uninhabited by civilians because the civilian population had been forced out by the communists. Casualties were therefore either communist insurgents or civilian victims of communist violence.[226] Fourth, when American responsibility for a specific attack could not be denied, the communists were blamed for making it impossible to distinguish between combatants and civilians.[227]

When the campaign in Cambodia became public knowledge with the launching of the land invasion in 1970, it provoked a storm of domestic protest largely among those already associated with the anti-war movement. On 4 May 1970, members of the Ohio National Guard opened fire on students protesting the bombing and land incursions into Cambodia, killing four and wounding nine others. A few days later, around 100,000 protesters marched in Washington, DC to protest the killing of unarmed students. But these staunchly anti-war attitudes were not majority opinion in the USA. A Gallup poll taken immediately after the Kent State killings found that 58 per cent of respondents believed that the students were responsible, 31 per cent were unsure, and only 11 per cent blamed the national guardsmen.[228] Other polls found that over 50 per cent of respondents supported the President's assault on Cambodia.[229]

Wider domestic criticism was circumscribed by the fact that the bombing of Cambodia and the level of civilian casualties were not widely reported, even after the campaign itself became public knowledge. The US Administration played an active role in limiting the dissemination of information. For

[223] A justification that Congress inserted into every proviso from October 1970 onwards. See Barrett, 'Holding Individual Leaders Responsible', p. 456. Also see Henry Kissinger, *The White House Years: Volume II: Years of Upheaval* (New York: Little Brown and Co., 1982), p. 36.

[224] Isaacs, *Without Honor*, p. 217.

[225] Kissinger, *Ending the Vietnam War*, p. 571.

[226] Kissinger, *White House Years*, p. 240.

[227] Kiernan, *How Pol Pot Came to Power*, p. 350. Such claims were not always unfounded.

[228] David Lawrence, 'Campus Unrest Linked to Drugs', *Palm Beach Post*, 28 May 1970, p. A.14.

[229] Samuel Lipsman and Edward Doyle, *Fighting for Time* (Boston: Boston Publishing Co., 1983), p. 182.

instance, when *Newsweek*'s Sylvana Foa reported that the USA was still conducting bombing operations in 1973 despite assurances to the contrary and provided evidence to visiting Senators that contradicted the Administration's claims that the reports were 'ridiculous', she was expelled from Cambodia at the request of the US Embassy.[230] One survey of American media reporting found that as a result of various restrictions—not all of them government imposed—in the first five months of 1972, with the bombing escalating massively, 'in terms of war casualties, the focus in the *New York Times* and *Time* was on military-related deaths and almost always on those that occurred in Vietnam. . . . During the winter and spring of 1972, the war in Cambodia and Laos was ignored . . . *Time*, in fact, had more coverage on civilian casualties in Northern Ireland during the first half of 1972 than it did [on Cambodia]'.[231] Where civilian casualties in Cambodia were reported, the tenor was usually critical. Two reporters covered the consequences of the American bombing in detail and filed highly critical reports. In 1973, the *New York Times*' Sydney Schanberg reported 'extensive' destruction of 'a whole series of villages' caused by the bombing.[232] In 1970, Richard Dudman of the *St. Louis Post-Dispatch* was captured by the Khmer Rouge and released a little over a month later. In a series of reports about what he witnessed during that time, Dudman painted a vivid picture of civilian suffering at the hands of American bombing.[233] Reporting Dudman's work in the *New York Times*, Anthony Lewis issued a damning condemnation of American strategy in Cambodia: 'the American government has decided that Cambodians are better off dead than red. For sheer colonial arrogance, that rivals the best that Cecil Rhodes and Cortés could produce'.[234]

There was also dissent within government. Some 250 State Department officials signed a letter of protest to the Secretary of State and Democrat Congresswomen Elizabeth Holtzman and four Air Force officers launched an ultimately unsuccessful lawsuit to stop the bombing.[235] Criticism increased in the wake of the Paris Peace Agreement of January 1973 which ended the war with North Vietnam. With the Administration showing no sign of ending

[230] Mort Rosenblum, *Coups and Earthquakes: Reporting the World for America* (New York: Joanna Cotler, 1979).

[231] Howard R. Elterman, 'The State, the Mass Media, and Ideological Hegemony: United States Policy Decisions in Indochina, 1974–75: Historical Record, Governmental Pronouncements and Press Coverage', New York University Dissertation, (1978), p. 335.

[232] Schanberg's work is summarized in Herman and Chomsky, *Manufacturing Consent*, p. 279.

[233] Anthony Lewis, 'Better Dead Cambodians Than Red', *New York Times*, 27 June 1970, p. 24.

[234] Lewis, 'Better Dead Cambodians', p. 24; and Anthony Lewis, 'The Civilian Tragedy in Indo-China', *The Times*, 3 April 1971, p. 5.

[235] Young, *The Vietnam Wars*, pp. 247–8; and Stephen M. Millett, 'The Air Force, the Courts and the Controversial Bombing of Cambodia', *Air University Review*, July–August 1976, pp. 1–7.

the bombing despite the loss of its *casus belli* (the protection of US forces in South Vietnam), Congress resolved to terminate funding for the mission—forcing Nixon to bring it to a close. In September 1973, departing US Ambassador to Cambodia, Emory Swank, described the campaign as 'Indochina's most useless war'. California Congressman Pete McLosky went further, arguing that what the USA had 'done to the country is greater evil than we have done to any country in the world, and wholly without reason, except for our own benefit to fight against the Vietnamese'.[236]

At the time, international criticism was muted by the veil of secrecy, uncertainty as to the nature of the US campaign and the apparent consent of the Cambodian government. In relation to the latter, Kissinger repeatedly claimed that the bombing enjoyed Prince Sihanouk's consent, although there is evidence to the contrary.[237] In fact, before its overthrow by the US-backed General, Lon Nol, the Royalist Cambodian government filed over one hundred formal protests about US attacks with the UN between July 1968 and March 1970.[238] The Cambodian government complained that the USA had attacked villages, peasants working in the fields, and fishermen.[239] Sihanouk's government publicly condemned the killing of civilians: in March 1969, it condemned attacks on 'the Cambodian population living in the border regions . . . almost daily by US aircraft', claiming them to be directed against 'peaceful Cambodian farmers'. In the same month, Sihanouk rejected American reports that he 'would not oppose US bombing, the victims of which were Khmer peasants, women and children in particular'. He issued an appeal to the world's media: 'I appeal to you to publicize abroad this very clear stand of Cambodia—that is, I will in any case oppose all bombings on Cambodian territory under whatever pretext'.[240] Sihanouk later described the bombing of 'Khmer peasants' as 'a scandal and a crime'.[241] The Lon Nol regime that ousted Sihanouk in 1970 was much more supportive of American bombing and expressed little concern for the fate of Cambodian civilians. As one Lon Nol official put it in 1973, 'we do worry about the effect of the bombing on the people, but when you have a cancer on your skin and you take out the bad cells

[236] Both cited in William Blum, *Killing Hope: US Military and CIA Interventions since World War II* (London: Zed Books, 2003), p. 139.

[237] Kissinger, *Ending the Vietnam War*, p. 68.

[238] Barrett, 'Holding Individual Leaders Responsible', p. 439.

[239] Barrett, 'Holding Individual Leaders Responsible', p. 439.

[240] Herman and Chomsky, *Manufacturing Consent*, p. 270, citing *Bombings in Cambodia*, Hearings Before the Committee on Armed Services, US Senate, 93rd Cong. 1st sess., July/August 1973, pp. 158–60.

[241] Cited in Joseph B. Treaster, 'Big Bombing Toll in Cambodia Seen', *New York Times*, 6 April 1973, p. 1.

some good cells must go along and you will probably have a scar on your skin. It is the same with the bombing and we think we must accept this'.[242]

Although international criticism was muted by the veil of secrecy, profound uncertainty and apparent Cambodian consent, privately Western diplomats were highly critical of the bombing campaign. In mid-April, unnamed diplomats expressed their belief that the campaign was being conducted on the basis of 'inadequate intelligence and often imprecise control, causing high civilian casualties'. One was quoted as lamenting that 'the Americans are throwing air support around like a mad woman. They don't know what effect it's having'.[243] International media commentators were almost uniformly critical. After being evacuated from Phnom Penh after its fall to the Khmer Rouge in 1975, British journalist Jon Swain reported in the conservative *Sunday Times* that: 'The United States has much to answer for here.... The War damage here, as everywhere else we saw, is total. Not a bridge is standing, hardly a house. I am told most villagers have spent the war years living semi-permanently underground in earth bunkers to escape the bombing.... The entire countryside has been churned up by American B-52 bomb craters, whole towns and villages razed. So far I have not seen one intact pagoda'.[244] Overall, though, as with Laos, contextual factors such as limited reporting, geographic remoteness, putative government consent, and shared strategic interests coalesced to limit reporting and thus criticism of the bombing of Cambodia, shielding the perpetrators from some of the material and reputational costs associated with illegitimacy. Where the bombardment was reported, responses were almost uniformly critical of the indiscriminate killing of civilians.

## Summary

The Indochina case is consistent with the view that during the Cold War civilian immunity became embedded in international society as it was transformed from a shared norm to legal rule, but that it was not internalized within US political and military circles and among some of its allies. It is significant that American leaders recognized that indiscriminate attacks were unlikely to be legitimized, either domestically or internationally, and that anti-civilian ideologies did not offer a pathway to legitimacy. These beliefs

[242] Joseph B. Treaster, 'Big Bombing Toll in Cambodia Seen', *New York Times*, 6 April 1973, p. 1.

[243] Joseph B. Treaster, 'Big Bombing Toll in Cambodia Seen', *New York Times*, 6 April 1973, p. 1.

[244] Jon Swain, 'Diary of a Doomed City', *Sunday Times*, 11 May 1975, pp. 15–19. See Jon Swain, *A River of Time: Memoir of Vietnam and Cambodia* (Oxford: St. Martin's Press, 1997).

encouraged restraint in relation to the bombing of North Vietnam and led them to impose rules of engagement to protect civilians, investigate and prosecute some individuals responsible for abusing civilians, and go to considerable lengths to deny and create uncertainty about the indiscriminate bombing and civilian casualties. The widespread and often pronounced domestic and international criticism that some aspects of the US wars in Indochina attracted suggests that they were right to suppose that they could not sufficiently legitimize the intentional killing of civilians.

But these experiences also point to some of the limits on the capacity of civilian immunity to influence behaviour. Although concerned about potential international criticism, American leaders were still prepared to indiscriminately kill large numbers of civilians when military necessity seemed to dictate and contextual factors allowed them to pull veils of secrecy and uncertainty over their actions. There is little evidence that moral concern about civilian casualties played a role in the key decision-making moments. When set against military necessity, the protection of Indochinese civilians was simply not an issue. Where restraints were introduced, they were done so to secure domestic and international legitimacy. For a number of years the amount of legitimacy that the USA needed for sufficiency was relatively low: its institutional power prevented the mobilization of the UN as a source of criticism (much less, punishment); shared interest in limiting communist expansionism encouraged some key European and Asian governments to at least tolerate and sometimes actively support the USA; significant variation in the level and degree of media reporting impacted on the level of domestic and international attention paid to different aspects of the campaigns and the extent of concern for civilian casualties; and perceptions and debates were framed by Cold War politics—communists, socialists, and other leftists tended to reject American arguments and exaggerate American crimes; anti-communists did the reverse. Centrists sometimes sat on the fence—endorsing campaigns whilst criticizing some aspects of them. Over time, however, the reporting of civilian casualties made it more difficult for the USA to secure sufficient legitimacy and in the end even Nixon and Kissinger were forced to relent and end their use of coercive strategic bombing.

## KILLING TO KEEP THE WORLD FREE FROM COMMUNISM

The remainder of this chapter considers two other cases (Indonesia and El Salvador) in which governments and their allies deliberately killed civilians in struggles against communists. It finds that, in each case, the politics of legitimacy followed the basic paths identified in relation to Korea and Indochina. Perpetrators employed or enabled mass atrocities because they believed it strategically prudent but tried to portray their behaviour to the outside world as consistent with civilian immunity. Typically, they denied the fact of atrocities and collapsed the distinction between soldiers and civilians by claiming that proven victims were collaborating with communist insurgents. Where denial was not possible, they claimed, among other things, that the perpetrators were rogue elements of the armed forces, militias operating beyond government control or the communists themselves. By denying rather than justifying the killing of civilians, perpetrators exhibited awareness of shared expectations of appropriate behaviour based on civilian immunity. Contextual factors such as limited reporting, shared interests, and positive relations with influential outsiders sometimes helped perpetrators to secure sufficient legitimacy and mitigate the potential costs associated with illegitimacy. In the case of Indonesia this was enough for the army and its allies to literally get away with mass murder. In the case of El Salvador, however, sufficient legitimacy rested on the toleration of a single government—the USA. In these protracted cases, as reporting of atrocities increased so too did international criticism. As legitimacy was called into question, both the perpetrators and some of their external supporters were prompted to modify their behaviour to bring it more obviously into line with civilian immunity.

Whilst the cases studied here stand out as among the worst state atrocities committed during anti-communist campaigns, they were not the only cases. The rightist military regime in Argentina (1976–80) killed between 9,000 and 20,000 suspected leftists, the Pinochet regime in Chile (1973–76) killed up to 20,000 suspected leftists and the government of Guatemala killed over 100,000, including 80,000 Mayans in a campaign many have judged genocidal. It was not just states that committed atrocities against their communist enemies. Non-state groups, such as the Contras in Nicaragua, RENAMO in Mozambique, and UNITA in Angola, perpetrated massacres during their violent struggles against communist or socialist governments. Such groups were commonly supported by the USA, its allies, and/or South Africa.

## Indonesia (1965–1966)

In late September 1965, a small group of Indonesian officers linked to the Communist Party (PKI), kidnapped and killed six senior army officers in an attempted coup in support of Indonesia's increasingly left-leaning President, Sukarno. The army, led by General Suharto, quickly suppressed the revolt and eliminated those suspected of association with what became known as the '30 September movement'. With the coup suppressed, the army then set about violently destroying the PKI. Between October 1965 and March 1966, around

500,000–600,000 civilians were killed by the army and allied militia, religious youth groups, and mobs.[245] Although justifications varied, perpetrators typically saw themselves as purging the country of communists who were attempting to overthrow the state, destroy traditional life, and impose an alien ideology. Coming in the midst of escalating tension in Indochina, the massacres received very little international attention and the violent destruction of Indonesian communism was welcomed by US officials, although some moral concerns were raised. The muted response was mainly a product of limited international reporting, widespread acceptance of the army's claim that the killings were a spontaneous societal response to the attempted coup and the view, particularly evident in the USA and Southeast Asia, that the mass killing of communists was excusable because it removed the communist threat from a strategically important country.

The background to the crisis lies in President Sukarno's system of 'guided democracy' centred upon an uneasy relationship between nationalist (PNI) and communist (PKI) parties and the army. The principal antagonism in this relationship was between the PKI and the army. In the early 1960s, Sukarno began to lean towards the communists, establishing closer ties with China and withdrawing from the UN.[246] The PKI became increasingly assertive, with some of its propaganda calling for the 'eradication' and 'extermination' of opponents.[247] The attempted coup was apparently intended to weaken the army and strengthen Sukarno's hand.

Responding quickly to the coup attempt, General Suharto deployed loyal units and crushed the rebellion within twenty-four hours.[248] With the immediate danger past, Suharto then used units with strong anti-communist credentials—KOSTRAD (reservists under Suharto's command) and RPKAD (elite units, staunchly anti-communist)—to begin a wider campaign against PKI members and sympathizers. Initially led by local Muslim groups, the massacre of communists began in Aceh in early October, and with the army's

[245] An army fact finding commission put the figure at 78,500, but this has widely been criticized as being too low. Some estimates put the death toll at 2 million. Another official report, by KOPKAMTIB, estimated that 800,000 had been killed in central and eastern Java and another 100,000 in both Bali and Sumatra, putting the total at 1 million. See Robert Cribb, 'Problems in the Historiography of the Killings in Indonesia', in Robert Cribb (ed.), *The Indonesian Killings 1965–1966: Studies From Java and Bali* (Melbourne: Centre of Southeast Asian Studies, Monash, 1990), p. 7; and Arnold C. Brackman, *The Communist Collapse in Indonesia* (New York: W. W. Norton, 1969), p. 115.

[246] Rex Mortimer, *Indonesian Communism under Sukarno: Ideology and Politics, 1959–1965* (Ithaca: Cornell University Press, 1974), p. 375.

[247] Brackman, *Communist Collapse in*, p. 63.

[248] Michael van Langenberg, 'Gestapu and State Power in Indonesia', in Cribb (ed.), *The Indonesian Killings 1965–1966*, p. 45; Robert Cribb and Colin Brown, *Modern Indonesia: A History since 1945* (London: Longman, 1995), pp. 97–9; and Ulf Sundaussen, *The Road to Power: Indonesian Military Politics 1945–1967* (Kuala Lumpur: Oxford University Press, 1982), pp. 207–12.

assistance rapidly spread to central and east Java and other provinces.[249] Suharto argued that the PKI as a whole was responsible for the coup attempt and called for an 'absolutely essential cleaning out' of communists.[250] Rationalizing that the PKI's network of grassroots followers made it a persistent threat to the regime, he encouraged the establishment of local militias and offered them the political authority, training, arms, and logistical support they needed to conduct mass killings.[251]

Although much of the killing was not done by the army itself, in most (though not all) cases militias, youth groups, and mobs did not start committing atrocities until elite military units arrived to direct, encourage, and enable violence by instructing and arming the perpetrator groups.[252] In October 1965, the army worked hard to whip up a 'near hysterical anti-communist pogrom'. One of the survivors of the 30 September plot, General Nasution—whose daughter had been killed during the attempt to kidnap him—urged that, 'all of their [PKI] followers and sympathisers should be eliminated, otherwise the incident will recur'. The PKI, he argued, should be exterminated 'down to its very roots'.[253] Nasution insisted that 'they must be immediately smashed' because 'they have committed treason'.[254] As Sarwo Edhie, commander of RPKAD, reportedly explained, in order to 'clean-out' communists, 'we decided to encourage the anti-communist civilians to help with the job . . . we gathered together the youth, the nationalist groups, the religious organisations. We gave them two or three days training, then sent them out to kill the communists'.[255] Another army officer, Dinas Sejarah wrote that 'the RPKAD gave military training . . . as part of a general programme of cooperation between the army and the people to crush the remnants of G30S/PKI'.[256]

249 Robert Cribb, 'Genocide in Indonesia, 1965–1966', *Journal of Genocide Research*, 3 (2) 2001, p. 233; van Langenberg, 'Gestapu and State Power', in Cribb (ed.) *Indonesian Killings 1965–1966*, p. 49. In a few districts, the killing began before the army arrived, as in Pasuruah (Central Java). See Robert W. Hefner, *The Political Economy of Mountain Java: An Interpretive History* (Berkeley: University of California Press, 1990), p. 210. This fact is used by Christian Gerlach to argue that the army played less of a role than hitherto thought in directing the killing. See Christian Gerlach, *Extremely Violent Societies: Mass Violence in the Twentieth-Century World* (Cambridge: Cambridge University Press, 2010), pp. 17–91.

250 Brackman, *Communist Collapse*, p. 119; Cribb and Brown, *Modern Indonesia*, p. 100.

251 Cribb, 'Problems in the Historiography', in Cribb (ed.) *Indonesian Killings 1965–1966*, p. 21.

252 Cribb, 'Problems in the Historiography', p. 21; and Cribb, 'Genocide in Indonesia', p. 233 and pp. 235–6.

253 Cited by Brackman, *Communist Collapse*, p. 117.

254 Cited by John Hughes, *Indonesian Upheaval* (New York: D. McKay Co., 1967), p. 189.

255 Cited in Hughes, *Indonesian Upheaval*, p. 151.

256 Sejarah, 'TNI AD: Crushing the G30S/PKI in Central Java', in Cribb (ed.) *Indonesian Killings 1965–1966*, p. 165.

Studies of individual massacres confirm that killing was often initiated by the military and then continued by others at the military's urging.[257] It seems clear, therefore, that although patterns of killing and levels of centralized control were uneven, the massacres were orchestrated by the army with the intention of eliminating the PKI.[258] By March 1966, the atrocities had achieved the army's objective of eliminating the PKI and it moved to restrain the militia, end the killing, and restore order.[259] The deal was sealed by the elevation of General Suharto to the presidency.

Although the killing was encouraged, enabled, and sometimes perpetrated by the army, the military enlisted the help of many other organizations and sometimes whole communities. This enabled it to support its claim that it was not complicit in the massacres. Indeed, some report that the army went to considerable lengths to make them appear spontaneous.[260] Given that the nature of the killing and identity of the perpetrators differed from region to region, it is unsurprising to find not one, but many different types of justification. Certainly, in the different ideological arguments relating to the guilt of the communists in the coup plot and religious arguments about their godlessness we can see traces of selective extermination thinking helping to place the victims outside the universe of moral obligation.[261] Rather than repeat these justifications to the outside world, however, the army and Indonesia's new military government claimed that whilst the elimination of communism was a great deed, it was not itself responsible for atrocities.[262]

The army—a secular organization—sometimes employed religious arguments to incite others to commit mass atrocities. Army propagandists insisted that 'the sword cannot be met by the Koran . . . but must be met by the sword. The Koran says that whoever opposes you should be opposed as they oppose you'.[263] Sometimes, the army forced or simply fabricated confessions from PKI leaders intimating a deep plot to take over the country and impose

[257] E.g. see Kenneth Orr, 'Schooling and Village Politics in Central Java in the Time of Turbulence', in Cribb (ed.), *The Indonesian Killings 1965–1966*, pp. 182–91; and Robert Cribb, 'Bali' in Cribb (ed.), *The Indonesian Killings*, p. 243; and Geoffrey Robinson, 'Post-Coup Massacre in Bali', in Daniel S. Lev and Ruth McVey (eds), *Making Indonesia: Essays on Modern Indonesia* (Ithaca: Cornell University Press, 1996) pp. 124–40.

[258] Julie Southwood and Patrick Flanagan, *Indonesia: Law, Propaganda and Terror* (London: Zed, 1983), p. 73.

[259] Robert Cribb, 'Nation: Making Indonesia', in Donald K. Emmerson (ed.), *Indonesia Beyond Suharto: Polity, Economy, Society, Transition* (Armonk: ME Sharpe, 1999), p. 33.

[260] Hilmar Farid, 'Indonesia's Original Sin: Mass Killings and Capitalist Expansion, 1965–1966', *Inter-Asia Cultural Studies*, 6 (1) 2005, p. 4.

[261] Helen Fein, 'Revolutionary and Anti-Revolutionary Genocides: A Comparison of States Murders in Democratic Kampuchea, 1975 to 1979, and in Indonesia, 1965 to 1966', *Comparative Studies in Society and History*, 35 (4) 1993, p. 815.

[262] Brackman, *Communist Collapse*, p. 116.

[263] Robinson, 'The Post-Coup Massacre in Bali', p. 124.

communism.[264] It also concocted lurid stories about the torture, humiliation, and mutilation of the six generals who were killed and claimed that naked female communists danced over the generals' bodies. Images portraying these horrific scenes were frequently broadcast on television.[265] The communist assault on Indonesia's way of life and their perverted brutality required a thorough 'cleansing' and the killing was often described in this way by the army and its allies.[266] Indeed, the army made a point of portraying the communists as denigrating traditional Indonesian beliefs, be they Islamic, Buddhist, Hindu, Christian, or nationalist.[267] In some places, this helped generate demands for a holy war against communists. In Bali, nationalist party (PNI) leaders allied with the army incited the Hindu population to violence by arguing that God approved of killing communists.[268] Some Hindus in Bali described mass killing as 'purification' in 'fulfilment of a religious obligation to purify the land'. Islamist radicals portrayed the killing as a holy war (*Jihad*), whilst the Muslim group, *Muhammediyah* issued a *fatwah* (religious decree) pronouncing the extermination of the PKI a religious duty.[269]

The extermination of Indonesia's communists and suspected communists elicited very little international attention and still less criticism. Within Indonesia itself, criticism of the killing was mute—for obvious reasons. One notable critic was President Sukarno himself. Sukarno accused the people of 'running amok like monkeys caught in the dark' and heaped blame on the Muslim community, opining that Indonesians were 'killing, shooting and slandering each other'.[270]

Internationally, two contextual factors inhibited criticism and delivered sufficient legitimacy to the perpetrators. First, the massacres were barely reported and academics paid little attention to them. Here, the veil of secrecy was helped by the rapidity of the killing: the entire episode lasted only six months. During that time, there was little international media interest and little scope for investigative journalism. As such, very few international commentators questioned the government's claims that the killings were a spontaneous popular revolt against communism. The idea that a lack of reporting might have contributed to the general absence of criticism is circumstantially supported by the fact that even Western leftists who, at the time, were

[264] Dinas Sejarah, 'TNI—Angkatan Darat—Crushing the G30S/PKI in Central Java', in Cribb (ed.), *The Indonesian Killings 1965–1966*, p. 165.

[265] Mortimer, *Indonesian Communism*, p. 389.

[266] Cribb, 'Problems in the Historiography', pp. 24 and 30.

[267] See Robinson, 'The Post-Coup Massacre in Bali', p. 124.

[268] Robinson, 'The Post-Coup Massacre in Bali', p. 141.

[269] Hughes, *Indonesian Upheaval*, p. 192; Robinson, 'Post-Coup Massacre in Bali', p. 140; Hefner, *The Political Economy of Mountain Java*, p. 210.

[270] Brackman, *Communist Collapse*, p. 115 and Harold Crouch, *The Army and Politics in Indonesia* (Ithaca: Cornell University Press, 1978), pp. 156–7.

animated by the situation in Indochina were relatively mute in their criticism.[271] To be sure, there was some criticism from the left but no concerted protests or demonstrations. In the UK, *The Guardian* condemned the massacres and Bertrand Russell insisted that 'the massacres in Indonesia demand international investigation'.[272] To the extent that it was reported at all, Chomsky and Herman claim that the killing was portrayed as a 'benign bloodbath' in the West.[273] There were three main reasons for the lack of reporting. First, there were very few international journalists and academics inside Indonesia at the time of the massacres and the regime made access difficult. Second, in the aftermath of the coup, the government cracked down on local press freedom, deterring the Indonesian media from reporting the killings. Finally, the continuing repression of communism in Suharto's Indonesia made Indonesians deeply reluctant to provide information about the killings.[274]

The second factor influencing the world's response to the Indonesia killings relates to strategic interests and perceptions about the relative legitimacy of the actors involved. Western governments (especially the US), non-communist Asian governments, and even some informed commentators tacitly accepted that massacres were excusable in the name of destroying Indonesian communism.[275] One article that reported the massacres, noted the very high casualty rates, and recognized the army's culpability, nevertheless described the suppression of the PKI as 'the West's best news for years in Asia'.[276] Likewise, the *New York Times* noted that 'the US is heartened by Red setback in Indonesia'.[277] Reflecting on the massacres in June 1966, James Reston reported in the same newspaper that the 'savage transformation' of Indonesia cast 'a gleam of light in Asia'.[278] In the UK, *The Times* ran a series of articles on the massacres without criticizing the authorities.[279]

Some journalists and academics lent credence to the army's claim that the killing had been spontaneous and communal. Most famously, the noted anthropologist, Clifford Geertz, argued that the killings were not products of state violence.[280] Likewise, writing in 1969, Arnold Brackman concluded that

[271] Cribb, 'Problems in the Historiography', p. 4.
[272] Both cited in Brackman, *Communist Collapse*, p. 121.
[273] John Roosa, *Pretext for Mass Murder: The September 30th Movement and Suharto's Coup d'Etat in Indonesia* (Madison, WI: University of Wisconsin Press, 2006), p. 15.
[274] Cribb, 'Problems in the Historiography', p. 4; and Brackman, *Communist Collapse*, p. 125.
[275] Cribb, 'Problems in the Historiography', p. 5.
[276] 'Vengeance with a Smile', *Time*, 15 July 1966, p. 26.
[277] Cited by Roosa, *Pretext for Mass Murder*, p. 16.
[278] Cited by Roosa, *Pretext for Mass Murder*, p. 16.
[279] Brackman, *Communist Collapse*, p. 121.
[280] Clifford Geertz, *After the Fact: Two Countries, Four Decades, One Anthropologist* (Cambridge, MA: Harvard University Press, 1995).

'what happened in Indonesia . . . was more akin to civil war than mass murder . . . it was a peasant affair settled in a peasant fashion'. The massacre, he argued, 'was more of a spontaneous reaction to the PKI's involvement in the murder of the generals than an organised affair'.[281] Taking a slightly different tack, Ulf Sundhaussen found that it would 'be difficult to prove' that Suharto had planned the killing, that even if he had it could not be proved that the killing was supported by the officer class, and that the army had nothing to gain from the killing.[282] Historian Theodore Frend and the *New Yorker* also insisted that the killings were spontaneous.[283] Others simply wrote the massacres off as products of Asian backwardness. Writing in the *New York Times*, C. L. Sulzberger suggested that the killings were hardly unusual given that in Asia, 'life is cheap'. In similar vein, Dan Moser wrote in *Life* that Indonesians were engaged in 'mass hysteria' and an 'orgy of cruelty'. The point was made most emphatically by Robert Shaplen, who commented that it was unfair for 'the rest of the rational world to expect the Indonesians to feel that they had done anything wrong because the Indonesians were able to explain the bloodbath, at least to their own satisfaction, in ancient terms of catharsis and the eradication of evil'.[284] Together, these arguments and perceptions reduced the Indonesian army's culpability, protecting it from criticism and potential legitimacy costs.

The US Administration did little to discourage the massacres and, once it was clear that Sukarno would not be able to stage a comeback, actively colluded with the army.[285] At the very least, the USA helped to create an enabling environment which left the perpetrators free to go about their bloody business with impunity.[286] At the beginning of the slaughter, US officials gave the Indonesian army the green light to proceed. In early October, Ambassador Green advised the Administration to support the Indonesian army through covert efforts to 'spread the story of the PKI's guilt, treachery and brutality'.[287] A few days later, Green was instructed to communicate that the US was 'as always, sympathetic to the Army's desire to eliminate Communist influence'.[288] On 4 November 1965, the US Embassy informed the State Department that American officials in Indonesia had 'made clear that Embassy and US

[281] Brackman, *Communist Collapse*, p. 117.

[282] Ulf Sundhaussen, *Road to Power: Indonesian Military Politics 1945–1967* (Kuala Lumpur: Oxford University Press, 1982), p. 218.

[283] Cited in Roosa, *Pretext to Mass Murder*, p. 27.

[284] Cited in Roosa, *Pretext to Mass Murder*, p. 27.

[285] Robinson, 'Post-Coup Massacre in Bali', p. 127.

[286] A point raised by Fein, 'Revolutionary and Anti-Revolutionary Genocides', pp. 802–4.

[287] Cited in H. W. Brands, 'The Limits of Manipulation: How the United States Didn't Topple Sukarno', *The Journal of American History*, 76 (3), 1989, p. 802.

[288] Cited by Brands, 'Limits of Manipulation', p. 802.

generally sympathetic with and admiring of what Army doing'.[289] Later, US officials reported that the campaign to destroy the PKI was 'moving fairly swiftly and smoothly', Green cabled in mid-December that 'the elimination of the communists continues apace' and the CIA reported that 'the era of Sukarno's dominance has ended . . . the army has virtually destroyed the PKI'.[290] The diplomatic support was well-received by the army. General Nasution's aide told US officials in early October 1965 that US assistance 'was just what we needed by way of assurances that we weren't going to be hit from all angles as we moved to straighten things out'.[291]

Neither President Johnson nor Secretary of State Dean Rusk commented publicly on the mass killing, claiming that information about the number of people killed was too sketchy to justify public comment and that condemning the massacre would have constituted interference in Indonesia's domestic affairs.[292] Johnson did, however, privately welcome the 'break' in Indonesian politics.[293] A 1966 State Department report on the attempted coup noted that whilst the US Administration adopted a quiet public posture, it had indicated privately that it stood ready to offer material support to the new leaders (i.e. Suharto) when the time was right.[294] US Ambassador to Indonesia, Marshall Green, later argued that the killings were an understandable product of national antagonism towards communism: 'the bloodbath visited on Indonesia can be largely attributed to the fact that communism, with its atheism and talk of class warfare, was abhorrent to the way of life of rural Indonesia, especially in Java and Bali, whose cultures place great stress on tolerance, social harmony, mutual assistance . . . and resolving controversy through talking issues out in order to achieve an acceptable consensus solution'.[295] The US embassy in Jakarta provided the Indonesian army with a list of 5,000 names of suspected PKI members. It is reported that the army used the list to identify some of its victims.[296] The US Administration was also quick to recognize the new Suharto regime, provided a small but symbolically significant amount of covert military aid, and assisted the army with propaganda.[297] Privately, embassy and CIA staff applauded the Indonesian army, with one intelligence

[289] Original cable sent by Deputy Chief of Mission Galbraith is cited by Frederick Bunnell, 'Low Posture Policy Towards Indonesia in the Months Leading up to the 1965 Coup', *Indonesia*, 50, 1990, p. 60.

[290] Cited by Brands, 'Limits of Manipulation', p. 803.

[291] Cited in Robinson, 'Post-Coup Massacre in Bali', p. 126.

[292] Brackman, *Communist Collapse*, p. 122.

[293] Robinson, 'Post-Coup Massacre in Bali', p. 127; Robert McNamara argued in 1967 that the PKI's destruction mitigated against the need to expand the war in Indochina. McNamara is cited in John Roosa, *Pretext for Mass Murder*, p. 15.

[294] Robinson, 'Post-Coup Massacre in Bali', p. 127.

[295] Robinson, 'The Post-Coup Massacre in Bali', p. 120.

[296] Cribb, 'Problems in the Historiography', p. 4.

[297] Robinson, 'Post-Coup Massacre in Bali', p. 126; Bunnell, 'Low Posture Policy', p. 59.

officer reportedly expressing concern that it might not go far enough in its destruction of the PKI.[298]

Within the USA, the only prominent voice of condemnation was that of Robert Kennedy who in January 1966 declared that: 'the slaughter of thousands in Indonesia, like the jailing of intellectuals in the USSR and racial discrimination in New York or Cape Town are differing evils [but] are the common works of man [and] call upon different qualities of conscience and indignation'. He continued, 'we have spoken out against the inhuman slaughters perpetrated by the Nazis and the Communists. But will we speak out also against the inhuman slaughter in Indonesia, where over 100,000 alleged Communists have not been perpetrators, but victims?'[299] Beyond that, one has to scour the letters pages of newspapers for critical commentary in the USA.[300]

Just as Cold War politics encouraged antipathy in the West, among communist states it encouraged sharp criticism of the massacres. The Chinese press was initially cautious but became gradually more vociferous in its condemnation.[301] The Chinese government deplored what it described as 'heinous and diabolical crimes . . . unprecedented in history'.[302] Yugoslav diplomats also criticized the killing, one commenting that: 'even assuming the guilt of the politburo [PKI leadership], which I do not, does this justify genocide? Kill the Central Committee, but do not kill 100,000 people who did not know and had no part in it [the 30 September plot]'.[303] North Korea later denounced the Suharto government as a 'military fascist regime'.[304] For the Soviet Union, Andrei Sakharov labelled the killing a 'tragic event', describing it as 'an extreme case of reaction, racism and militarism', but otherwise the Soviet response was relatively muted.[305]

These criticisms did not have much impact on the world stage. UN officials, including Secretary-General U Thant, studiously avoided commenting on the killings and when Suharto returned Indonesia to the UN, it was warmly welcomed back with only Albania and a lone protestor sounding a note of

[298] Robinson, 'Post-Coup Massacre in Bali', p. 126.

[299] Cited in Arthur Schlesinger, *Robert Kennedy and his Times* (New York: Random House, 1978), p. 790.

[300] Brackman, *Communist Collapse*, p. 123.

[301] J. A. C. Mackie, 'Anti-Chinese Outbreaks in Indonesia, 1959–1968', in J. A. C. Mackie, *The Chinese in Indonesia: Five Essays* (Melbourne: Thomas Nelson in conjunction with the Australian Institute of International Affairs, 1976), p. 114.

[302] Brackman, *Communist Collapse*, pp. 115 and 120. Indonesia's relations with China soured significantly. See Michael Leifer, *Indonesia's Foreign Policy* (London: George Allen and Unwin for the Royal Institute of International Affairs, 1983), p. 126.

[303] Cited in Brackman, *Communist Collapse*, p. 115.

[304] Brackman, *Communist Collapse*, p. 120.

[305] Brackman, *Communist Collapse*, p. 120.

criticism.[306] And the massacres did not affect Indonesia's standing in the Non-Aligned Movement either. Despite criticism from Yugoslav diplomats, Yugoslavia joined India and the United Arab Republic in despatching a goodwill mission to welcome the new regime into the fold. Moreover, regional neighbours Thailand, the Philippines, Malaysia, Singapore, and Australia moved quickly to establish ties with the new government, prompting foreign minister Adam Malik to report diplomatic results 'beyond expectations'.[307]

The Indonesia case therefore confirms a number of points about the norm of civilian immunity. Although barely spoken about directly, the norm was clearly at work in shaping expectations among the Indonesian army leadership that it was not likely to be able to legitimize mass atrocities. Rather than proclaim its destruction of Indonesian communists to the world, the army attempted to make the massacres appear spontaneous and disorganized to support claims that it was not culpable. With extremely limited reporting, largely inaccurate analysis, and interpretations sharply divided along Cold War ideological lines, the Indonesian army succeeded in securing sufficient legitimacy and establishing a 'new order' without Indonesia's communists.

Information scarcity was also a major consideration in the case of El Salvador but three other factors meant that Western leaders could not so easily avoid difficult questions about mass killing and civilian immunity in this case. First, the episode was much more protracted, which meant that more information became available and interest groups were able to mobilize and apply pressure. Second, the flow of information was aided by the proximity of El Salvador to the USA. Third, as the Cold War progressed into its final stages and the global threat of communism receded, some governments and publics began to privilege civilian immunity over other concerns, facilitating its internalization.

## El Salvador (1977–1991)

In El Salvador, social unrest following a fraudulent election in 1977 was met with state terror (killings, disappearances, torture). This prompted the unification of five opposition groups into a leftist guerrilla organization, the *Farabundo Marti National Liberation Front* (FMLN).[308] In late 1980, the FMLN launched an insurgency campaign to which the government responded with a brutal counter-insurgency almost identical in form to that in South

[306] Brackman, *Communist Collapse*, p. 117.

[307] Brackman, *Communist Collapse*, p. 120.

[308] See Thomas Carothers, *In the Name of Democracy: US Policy Towards Latin America in the Reagan Years* (Berkeley: University of California Press, 1991), p. 14 and Tommie Sue Montgomery, *Revolution in El Salvador: From Civil Strife to Civil Peace*, 2nd edn (Boulder: Westview Press, 1995), pp. 25–80.

Vietnam (and Guatemala for that matter). Having received some initial support from external allies, principally the USA, El Salvador gradually came under mounting international pressure to change its behaviour, which it did after 1983. Violence escalated once more in 1989 when the FMLN launched a major offensive. The government's response this time was more restrained, but the killing of six Jesuit priests by an elite army unit prompted the USA to withdraw its support, coercing the government into negotiations that brought the war to an end in 1991.[309] Between 75,000–100,000 people were killed in the war—the majority of them civilians killed by government forces.[310] A further 750,000 were internally displaced and1 million fled to the USA.[311]

El Salvador's civil war had three main phases. The first (1977–80) was a 'dirty war' in which the opposition conducted sporadic attacks and the government responded with political murders, disappearances, and occasional massacres—the latter usually conducted by 'death squads'.[312] During this period, almost any form of non-rightist political organization was considered a front for the rebels and therefore a legitimate target.[313] In May 1980 the army massacred between 300 and 600 women and children at Sumpul River (the border with Honduras) and a death squad murdered Archbishop Oscar Romero—a champion of the poor and powerful critic of violence on both sides.[314] Archbishop Romero had called on President Carter to suspend military aid to the government and his murder was only the most prominent of a wave of priest-killings that were part of an orchestrated campaign against the Church.[315] The violence escalated sharply in the early 1980s. In 1979, over

[309] For an overview of war termination, see Edelberto Torres-Rivas, 'Insurrection and Civil War in El Salvador', in Michael W. Doyle, Ian Johnstone, and Robert C. Orr (eds), *Keeping the Peace: Multidimensional UN Operations in Cambodia and El Salvador* (Cambridge: Cambridge University Press, 1997), pp. 209–24.

[310] Christine Wade, 'El Salvador: The Success of the FMLN' in Jerden de Zeeuw (ed.), *From Soldiers to Politicians: Transforming Rebel Movements after Civil War* (Boulder: Lynne Rienner, 2008), p. 33. El Salvador's Truth Commission found that around 85 per cent of civilian deaths were caused by government forces, El Salvador Truth Commission, *From Madness to Hope: The 12-Year War in El Salvador*, Part IV, chapter 1.

[311] Mario Lungo Ucles, *El Salvador in the Eighties: Counterinsurgency and Revolution* (Philadelphia: Temple University Press, 1996), p. 194; and Peter Sollis, 'Displaced Persons and Human Rights: The Crisis in El Salvador', *Bulletin of Latin American Research*, 11 (1) 1992, pp. 49–67.

[312] Joan Didian, *Salvador* (New York: Simon and Schuster, 1983); and Mark Danner, *The Massacre at El Mozote: A Parable of the Cold War* (New York: Vintage, 1994), p. 27.

[313] Cathy McIlwaine, 'Contesting Civil Society: Reflections from El Salvador', *Third World Quarterly*, 19 (4) 1998, pp. 659–60.

[314] Tommie Sue Montgomery and Christine J. Wade, 'El Salvador', in Howard J. Wiarda and Harry F. Kline (eds), *Latin American Politics and Development*, 6th edn (Boulder: Westview, 2007), p. 487.

[315] Robert Armstrong and Janet Shenk, *El Salvador: The Face of Revolution* (Boston: South End Press, 1982), p. 61.

800 people were killed by the government and its supporters. In 1980, approximately 10,800 people were killed by the security forces.[316] Assassinations by the FMLN and other leftists totalled approximately 1,200 in the same year. In 1981, around 9,825 civilians were killed by the security forces.[317]

In the second phase (late 1980–83), the war became a counter-insurgency characterized by a combination of 'search and destroy' and 'free-fire' methods.[318] To use Mao's terminology, government strategy involved destroying the 'fish' (guerrillas) by draining the 'water' (civilian population) by depopulating whole regions.[319] Government forces attacked areas of FMLN activity, forcing the guerrillas to disperse, concentrating the remaining population in a small area, and then deploying the elite Atlacatl Brigade to eliminate those who remained—the vast majority of them civilians.[320] Within the 'red zones' (the equivalent of 'free-fire zones' in Indochina), everyone was assumed to be an insurgent.[321] In the early stages, the army focused on killing specific people associated with the opposition but as the offensives widened, the killing became more random and whole villages or groups were targeted.[322]

Government forces conducted twenty-one such operations in 1981.[323] The most notorious was 'Operation Rescue' in December 1981, a sweep through Morazan province, which contained many FMLN bases. The army used regular units to force rebels and civilians from their houses and hideouts and the Atlacatl brigade to eliminate them. As in other cases, everyone who remained inside the target area was regarded as a combatant and treated accordingly. On 11 December 1981, at El Mozote, Atlacatl brigade soldiers massacred up to 900 captured civilians, including women and children.[324] One mass grave exhumed in 1991 contained 143 skulls, all but twelve of which were of children under twelve years of age. The brigade conducted a similar massacre at El Calabozo in August 1982, where over 200 civilians were killed.[325]

During its third phase (1984–91), the war settled into a pattern of lower level violence punctuated with sporadic escalations. The FMLN adopted a

[316] William Stanley, *The Protection Racket State: Elite Politics, Military Extortion and Civil War in El Salvador* (Philadelphia: Temple University Press, 1996), p. 178; Armstrong and Shenk, *El Salvador*, p. 161.

[317] Torres-Rivas, 'Insurrection and Civil War', p. 220.

[318] Armstrong and Shenk, *El Salvador*, p. 195.

[319] Armstrong and Shenk, *El Salvador*, p. 195.

[320] Danner, *The Massacre at El Mozote*, pp. 41–2; Philippe Bourgois, 'The Power of Violence in War and Peace: Post Cold War Lessons from El Salvador', *Ethnography*, 2 (1) 2001, p. 9.

[321] Danner, *Massacre at El Mozote*, p. 42.

[322] Danner, *Massacre at El Mozote*, p. 59.

[323] Hugh Byrne, *El Salvador's Civil War: A Study of Revolution* (Boulder: Lynne Rienner, 1996), p. 81.

[324] Peter W. Van Arsdale, *Forced to Flee: Human Rights and Human Wrongs in Refugee Homelands* (New York: Lexington Books, 2006), p. 99.

[325] Danner, *Massacre at El Mozote*, p. 140.

more patient attrition-based strategy designed to gradually wear down the government and the government refined its tactics.[326] Attacks on civilians persisted, though by 1985–86 it had returned to 1980 levels—much lower than the 1981–83 level but still significant.[327] Ultimately, the end of US patronage in the late 1980s paved the way for a negotiated end in 1991.[328]

The government of El Salvador denied that its forces were intentionally killing civilians. Where massacres perpetrated by the armed forces were reported, as at El Mozote, the government simply rejected reported deaths as communist propaganda. Denial was often augmented with arguments collapsing the distinction between soldiers and civilians and attempts to avoid responsibility by subcontracting killing out to clandestine 'death squads'. In relation to the counter-insurgency, fighters, supporters, sympathizers, and bystanders situated in the 'red zones' were collectively labelled 'rebels' or 'communists' and identified as combatants and thus as legitimate targets.[329] In relation to the 'dirty war', a wide range of opposition figures were labelled 'communists' and identified as legitimate targets for assassination on the grounds that they supported armed opposition to the state.[330]

The most significant external audience for these claims was the US government, which remained largely sympathetic for long periods. US patronage protected El Salvador from international punishment and provided a steady stream of material support. This support was out of step with international opinion, which was more uniformly critical, but proved sufficient owing to America's material and institutional power. US support was therefore the difference between sufficient legitimacy and costly illegitimacy.

There were important differences of tone between the Carter Administration—which was initially reluctant to support the government of El Salvador but was gradually convinced to set aside its human rights concerns and privilege strategic interests—and the Reagan Administration, which made a political virtue out of this prioritization. However, both administrations and sections of the American public bought into El Salvador's justifications to an extent. For example, both administrations and the US media tended to accept El Salvador's denials and obfuscations over the identity of human rights abusers. For example, in 1979 the *Washington Post* and *Miami Herald* argued—against strong evidence to the contrary—that the identity of Archbishop Romero's killer could not be ascertained, suggesting that the killers could have just as easily been leftist extremists as

[326] James Dunkerley, *The Long War: Dictatorship and Revolution in El Salvador* (London: Junction Books, 1982).

[327] Stanley, *Protection Racket State*, p. 230; and Van Arsdale, *Forced to Flee*, p. 106.

[328] James Dunkerley, *The Pacification of Central America: Political Change in the Isthmus, 1987–1993* (London: Verso, 1994), p. 66.

[329] Danner, *Massacre at El Mozote*, p. 13; and Sollis, 'Displaced Persons and Human Rights', pp. 52–60.

[330] Armstrong and Shenk, *El Salvador*, p. 154.

government-linked death squads.[331] In the same year, the murder of opposition leaders was condemned as 'an unspeakable crime' by the US Ambassador who nonetheless ascribed them to nameless 'extremists'. After three American nuns were raped and murdered, Carter despatched an investigator who concluded that there was no direct evidence to link the murder to the military, despite witness evidence to the contrary.[332] US officials and sections of the media also rejected reports of a massacre at El Mozote as communist propaganda. The State Department and US Embassy poured cold water on initial massacre reports by questioning their source. Responding to a request for information from the National Council of Churches, the State Department insisted that there was no evidence of a massacre and that the reports had come from the FMLN and was therefore unreliable. Around one month after the massacre, the *New York Times* despatched a reporter to El Mozote who provided photographic evidence of the massacre. Once again, the Administration responded that there was no evidence of 'government excesses' and the government of El Salvador chimed in that the reports were 'Marxist propaganda'. US officials criticized organizations such as Americas Watch and Amnesty International that investigated and verified the atrocity. Thomas Enders, Assistant Secretary of State, denounced the two organizations for spreading communist propaganda, arguing that there was 'no evidence to confirm that government forces systematically massacred civilians in the operations zone'.[333] This rhetorical offensive was taken up by sections of the media. The *Wall Street Journal* criticized the massacre story and decried the *New York Times* for conducting what it described as a propaganda war favouring the Marxists.[334]

The Carter Administration pursued a somewhat contradictory twin-track strategy of promoting political reform whilst supporting El Salvador's military.[335] Before the *Sandinista* victory in Nicaragua in 1979, human rights concerns were given higher priority than military aid. Both Congress and the Administration were critical of El Salvador's human rights record, with Congress holding hearings on the matter in 1977.[336] In the same year, the USA strongly criticized the El Paisnal massacre and disappearances, delayed the appointment of an ambassador, despatched a State Department human rights officer to assess the situation, and withheld approval of a $90 million

[331] Armstrong and Shenk, *El Salvador*, p. 153.

[332] Six soldiers were later charged but never brought to trial.

[333] Cited by Danner, *Massacre at El Mozote*, p. 126.

[334] Danner, *Massacre at El Mozote*, pp. 132–60.

[335] Montgomery and Wade, 'El Salvador', p. 489.

[336] Susan Burgerman, 'First Do No Harm: US Foreign Policy and Respect for Human Rights in El Salvador and Guatemala, 1980–1996', in Debra Liang-Fenton (ed.), *Implementing US Human Rights Policy* (Washington, DC: USIP, 2004), p. 281; and Armstrong and Shenk, *El Salvador*, p. 90. The hearings were led by Representatives Drinan, Harkin and (Ted) Kennedy.

Inter-American Development Bank loan on human rights grounds.[337] But the *Sandinista* victory in Nicaragua elevated concerns about communist expansion in Latin America, forcing human rights down the list of priorities. This change of emphasis was signalled by incoming ambassador, Frank Devine, when he advised that 'we believe that any government has the full right and obligation to use all legal means at its disposal to combat terrorism'.[338] The Carter Administration still prevaricated: though a 1979 State Department human rights report ranked El Salvador alongside Nicaragua as 'the most serious violators of individual freedoms' in the region but other arms of the administration channelled aid to government forces.[339] In 1980, the US delivered $55 million of military aid (transport, communications, and intelligence), justifying it as necessary to combat communism.[340]

The in-coming Reagan Administration displayed none of Carter's qualms about human rights. It saw the situation in El Salvador squarely in Cold War terms and as a key test of its resolve.[341] Reagan decided to 'draw a line' in El Salvador by backing anti-communist forces to the full. At stake in El Salvador, Reagan argued, was US national security itself.[342] To back this view, in 1981 the State Department issued a White Paper which it claimed provided definitive evidence that the FMLN was armed by the Soviet Union and Cuba as part of a broader regional strategy.[343] Within this context, according to UN Ambassador Jeanne Kirkpatrick, the US faced a choice between supporting rightist authoritarians or accepting the proliferation of communist dictatorships on its doorstep.[344] Financial aid increased to an annual peak of $897 million in 1986. The Administration also despatched military advisors who oversaw a massive expansion of El Salvador's armed forces.[345] During this period, some Embassy officials endorsed the El Salvadorian army's view that civilians living in combat zones were legitimate targets because of their support for the FMLN.[346] Some State Department officials claimed that most atrocities were committed by leftists.[347]

337 Armstrong and Shenk, *El Salvador*, p. 95; and Stanley, *The Protection Racket State*, p. 181.

338 Armstrong and Shenk, *El Salvador*, p. 98.

339 Armstrong and Shenk, *El Salvador*, p. 98.

340 Armstrong and Shenk, *El Salvador*, p. 139.

341 Byrne, *El Salvador's Civil War*, p. 75.

342 Carothers, *In the Name of Democracy*, p. 28.

343 Van Arsdale, *Forced to Flee*, p. 98; and William M. LeoGrande, 'A Splendid Little War: Drawing the Line in El Salvador', *International Security*, 6 (1) 1981, p. 27.

344 Cited by Carothers, *In the Name of Democracy*, p. 17.

345 Torres-Rivas, 'Insurrection and Civil War', p. 222; Carothers, *In the Name of Democracy*, p. 20. For a more detailed account, see Cynthia Arnson, *El Salvador: A Revolution Confronts the United States* (Washington, DC: Institute for Policy Studies, 1982).

346 Burgerman, 'First Do No Harm', p. 272.

347 LeoGrande, 'Splendid Little War', pp. 46–7.

The Reagan Administration overplayed its enthusiastic support for the El Salvador government and soon faced public criticism, especially after the murder of American nuns by government-linked militia. This episode caught the attention of Congress, the Churches (especially the Catholic Church), and human rights organizations, all of whom lobbied the Administration to temper its support for El Salvador. On 3 May 1981, 25,000 people protested in Washington, DC, against the Administration's position. Members of Congress—including some Republicans—expressed displeasure at the Administration's position but were reluctant to block aid to EL Salvador outright. Instead, they made assistance conditional on the Administration certifying improvements in human rights at six-monthly intervals.[348] In itself, this was an empty gesture because Reagan proved willing in 1982 and in 1983 issued re-certification certificates even in the face of clear evidence of human rights abuse. The President terminated the process by pocket veto in 1983 in part because human rights organizations were using it to highlight atrocities and embarrass the Admiunistration. Where it acknowledged atrocities by rightists, the Administration argued that these crimes were perpetrated by death squads operating outside government control.[349]

The Reagan Administration was not impervious to domestic criticism, however, and from 1983 gradually increased pressure on El Salvador whilst continuing to deny reported massacres. A good barometer of the pressure that the Administration was under is provided by the 1984 report of the President's bipartisan Commission on Central America led by Henry Kissinger. The Commission's criticism of the El Salvador government was blunt:

> There is, of course, a darker side as well in El Salvador. The United States obviously cannot accept, let alone support, the brutal methods practiced by certain reactionary forces in Central America. Some of these actions are related to counter-insurgency. Their common denominator is the systematic use of mass reprisals and selective killing and torture to dissuade the civil population from participating in the insurgency or from providing any help to the insurgents. . . . Other violence has in fact nothing to do with insurgency at all. It is designed to terrorize opponents, fight democracy, protect entrenched interests, and restore reactionary regimes.
>
> Whatever their aims, these methods are totally repugnant to the values of the United States.[350]

[348] Van Arsdale, *Forced to Flee*, p. 98.

[349] Carothers, *In the Name of Democracy*, p. 23. In 1983, Reagan terminated the process by pocket veto. Burgerman, 'First Do No Harm', p. 283.

[350] *The Report of the President's National Bipartisan Commission on Central America* (New York: Macmillan, 1984), p. 113.

This view echoed 1983 comments by Ambassador Thomas Pickering that the US could no longer ignore the 'terrorism of the right'.[351] To appease the critics, Vice-President George H. W. Bush visited El Salvador to warn the government to disassociate itself from the death squads.[352]

US support for the government in El Salvador was supported by the continent's other rightist governments—many of them military dictatorships. Among the government's key supporters were Argentina, Venezuela, and anti-Castro Cubans in Florida. Outside this relatively small circle, however, world opinion was uniformly critical. In 1977, the OAS Human Rights Commission documented and criticized the commission of torture and other abuses.[353] Three years later, the UN General Assembly condemned the human rights violations (Resolution 36/155).[354] This was followed a year later by a Resolution—sponsored by states from both sides of the Cold War divide (France, Greece, Algeria, Yugoslavia, and West Germany)—condemning the government (Resolution 38/101).[355] In 1984, the General Assembly adopted a further resolution expressing 'deep regret' at the civilian casualties caused by the government (Resolution 39/119). The USA and Turkey were the only NATO members to vote against the resolution. Outside the UN, Mexico was a particularly vocal critic of both the El Salvador government and US support for it.[356] In 1981, Mexico and France issued a joint declaration labelling the FMLN a 'representative political force'.[357] The USA responded by organizing a counter-declaration by key regional allies Guatemala, Chile, Argentina, Paraguay, Venezuela, Bolivia, Colombia, and the Dominican Republic that criticized Mexico and France for interfering in El Salvador's domestic affairs.

Churches and major international civil society groups were almost uniformly critical of El Salvador. Provoked by the government's killing and abuse of priests and especially by the murder of Archbishop Romero, the Catholic Church was outspoken in its criticism and demanded that the USA sever its ties with El Salvador.[358] In a 1981 report, the World Council of Churches condemned the 'insidious repression' in El Salvador and argued that government violence against the civilian population deserved the label 'genocide'.[359] Amnesty International issued a long line of reports documenting abuses against civilians and criticizing the perpetrators.[360] Likewise, in

[351] Cited in Burgerman, 'First Do No Harm', p. 287.

[352] Van Arsdale, *Forced to Flee*, p. 97; and Stanley, *Protection Racket State*, p. 229.

[353] Armstrong and Shenk, *El Salvador*, p. 106.

[354] Armstrong and Shenk, *El Salvador*, p. 171.

[355] Armstrong and Shenk, *El Salvador*, p. 199.

[356] LeoGrande, 'A Splendid Little War', p. 40.

[357] Armstrong and Shenk, *El Salvador*, p. 198; Byrne, *El Salvador's Civil War*, p. 90.

[358] Byrne, *El Salvador's Civil War*, p. 90; Burgerman, 'First Do No Harm', p. 271.

[359] Commission of the Churches on International Affairs, *El Salvador: One Year of Repression* (Geneva: World Council of Churches, 1981), pp. 1 and 28.

[360] Armstrong and Shenk, *El Salvador*, p. 120.

1984 the ICRC documented and criticized the repeated bombardment of civilian villages by government forces.[361] In January 1982, Americas Watch and the American Civil Liberties Union issued a joint report which documented the 'mass killing of peasants' by government forces.[362]

As more information about atrocities began to emerge and domestic and international criticism of both the government of El Salvador and the USA mounted, denial became a less plausible justificatory strategy. The US Administration came under increasing domestic from Congress, human rights groups, the Churches, and foreign governments to withdraw its patronage. Although it did not actually withdraw aid until 1989, the Administration was persuaded to demand improvements to human rights and reduce its assistance, helping to push the government of El Salvador to move away from the mass atrocities of 1980–83.

The El Salvador case therefore lends further weight to the basic story of this chapter. Whilst none of the governments most directly involved had internalized civilian immunity, they recognized that it was an embedded norm in inrernational society that shaped legitimacy judgements. As such, both the perpetrators and their main supporters tried to portray their behaviour as being consistent with the norm. A combination of weak international reporting, the ideological support of several external states, and the institutional and material weight of a superpower patron afforded the perpetrators sufficient legitimacy for a period. But over time, the emergence of clear evidence of atrocities made denial less plausible, reducing the legitimacy of both the perpetrators' actions and that of their foreign patrons, encouraging both to gradually moderate their behaviour.

## CONCLUSION

For the Western world, during the Cold War there was a tension between fidelity to civilian immunity, the political imperative of preventing communist expansion, and lingering beliefs about the necessity of sometimes violating the former to achieve the latter. In none of the cases discussed in this chapter was civilian immunity found to be internalized—hardly surprising given my focus on the commission of mass atrocities. Governments and militaries were repeatedly prepared to employ, tolerate, excuse, or support mass atrocities. But civilian immunity played a role in shaping events by guiding legitimacy judgements. The potential for civilian immunity to influence legitimacy and

361 Stanley, *Protection Racket State*, p. 230.

362 Americas Watch and American Civil Liberties Union, *Report on Human Rights in El Salvador* (New York: Vintage Books, 1982).

the invalidity of anti-civilian ideologies was tacitly recognized by the perpetrators, suggesting that it had become an embedded norm in international society. Perpetrators were not prepared to publicly justify the intentional killing of civilians but instead denied responsibility for massacres and portrayed their behaviour as consistent with civilian immunity. To achieve this, they creatively employed a rich variety of rhetorical strategies, including: blanket denial of civilian deaths; portraying such deaths as the unintended consequence of legitimate military activities; collapsing the distinction between soldiers and civilians; re-labelling civilians as insurgency-supporters; subcontracting the killing out to non-state actors including death squads, criminal gangs, youth groups, religious groups, and local militia; misleading and misdirecting publics and parliaments about the nature of military operations; misdirecting soldiers themselves; blaming undeniable atrocities on 'rogue elements' and issuing token punishments; questioning the reliability of massacre reports; questioning the motives of those who provided such reports; and simply blaming opponents for civilian deaths. These, and other tactics were intended to protect the orchestrators and perpetrators of violations of civilian immunity from the expected costs. This suggests that perpetrators believed that civilian immunity was a factor—an embedded international norm—that weighed heavily on the judgements of others and that there remained no plausible avenues by which to justify violating this norm. Repeated attempts to present non-compliant behaviour as compliant provide counter-factual validity to the norm itself.

When perpetrators try to secure sufficient legitimacy by denying that they are violating a shared norm rather than by invoking other norms, contextual factors play an important role in determining the extent of legitimation and the consequences that flow from this. Uncertainty about the facts of a case, provoked by factors such as geographic remoteness, a paucity of accurate and timely reporting, and the deliberate creation and leveraging of uncertainty by perpetrators and their allies, sometimes made denial a plausible strategy. Factors such as the ideological predispositions of outsiders, their perceived strategic interests and priorities, and their prior relations with the actors involved informed judgements about the relative legitimacy of those actors and, in turn, the extent to which reports and denials were accepted. Anti-communists were more likely to believe justifications and tolerate, excuse, and sometimes (though notably very rarely in public) endorse mass atrocities than those who were less committed to the ideological fight. But, as exemplified by the gradual softening of Reagan's position on Latin America, even ideological zealots were persuaded to at least nod in the direction of civilian immunity when confronted with incontrovertible evidence of extensive violations.

Of these contextual factors, the supply of information was particularly crucial and shaped both what the perpetrators could plausibly argue and the level and type of aid that sympathetic outsiders could legitimately offer. Where mass killing was kept away from public attention, civilian immunity exhibited very little restraining effect on either the perpetrators or their allies. The clearest examples of this were the US bombing campaigns over Laos and Cambodia and the massacre of Indonesian communists. Thanks to a combination of geographic isolation, contexts of armed conflict, and government censorship, these episodes were not accurately or extensively reported at the time and the perpetrators exhibited very little concern for civilian immunity. But where it was anticipated that civilian casualties would be reported, potential perpetrators were sometimes inhibited and chose to restrain their behaviour. Sometimes, external patrons found it increasingly difficult to sustain their support for governments associated with mass atrocities in the face of domestic and international criticism. In some cases, therefore, the gradual accumulation of information about violations of civilian immunity and criticism of those violations brought pressure to bear on both the perpetrators and their supporters: President Nixon ultimately backed away from bombing North Vietnam; the US Congress stepped in to end the bombing of Cambodia; and the government of El Salvador was encouraged to moderate its behaviour.

Clearly then, although not yet widely internalized inasmuch as few governments were unwilling to jettison the use or toleration of mass atrocities altogether as a policy option worth considering, civilian immunity was embedded in international society and played a significant though complex and varied part in the politics of mass killing during the Cold War. The question now is whether these sensibilities were apparent only in the capitalist world and whether anti-civilian ideologies continued to offer an alternative to civilian immunity in the communist world.

# 6

# The Cold War Struggle (2): Communist Atrocities

Communist regimes massacred millions of civilians during the Cold War. A conservative estimate would put the number of civilians deliberately killed by communist regimes after the Second World War between 6.7 million and 15.5 million, with the real figure probably much higher. Communist governments in the Soviet Union, China, and Cambodia initiated programmes of radical social transformation and killed, tortured, or allowed to starve whole groups thought hostile to change or simply unworthy of life. In these and other communist countries, including Albania, North Korea, East Germany, Romania, Bulgaria, Ethiopia, Vietnam, and Yugoslavia, governments employed violence against civilians to deter and defeat actual and imagined opponents and/or exact revenge for wrongs committed during the Second World War.[1] Where communist rule was challenged, governments exhibited little concern for civilian immunity, as evidenced by the Soviet assaults on Hungary and Afghanistan and North Korea's conduct in the Korean War. Communism also spawned violent non-state actors, such as the Red Brigades in Italy, the Baader-Meinhof gang in West Germany, the Shining Path in Peru, and FARC in Colombia, all of which intentionally killed civilians.[2]

But it is not simply the number of victims that distinguishes communist from non-communist atrocities in the Cold War. In none of the major cases of

[1] See, *inter alia*: Stephane Courtois, Nicolas Werth, Jean-Louis Panne, Andrzej Paczkowski, Karel Bartosek, and Jean-Louis Margolin, *The Black Book of Communism: Crimes, Terror, Repression* (Cambridge, MA: Harvard University Press, 1999); Andargachew Tiruneh, *The Ethiopian Revolution 1974–1987: A Transformation from an Aristocratic to a Totalitarian Autocracy* (Cambridge: Cambridge University Press, 1993).

[2] See, *inter alia*: Robert C. Meade Jr, *Red Brigades: The Story of Italian Terrorism* (London: Macmillan, 1990); Yonah Alexander and Kenneth A. Myers (eds), *Terrorism in Europe* (London: Croom Helm, 1982); Yonah Alexander and Dennis A. Pluchinsky (eds), *Europe's Red Terrorists: The Fighting Communist Organizations* (London: Frank Cass, 1992); Steve Stern (ed.), *Shining and Other Paths: War and Society in Peru 1980–1995* (Durham, NC: Duke University Press, 1998); and James J. Brittain, *Revolutionary Social Change in Colombia: The Origin and Direction of the FARC-EP* (London: Pluto, 2010).

communist mass killing did leaders weigh up the pros and cons of killing civilians or take steps to either reduce civilian devastation or create the appearance of reducing such devastation. Often guided by ideologies of selective extermination, communist perpetrators rarely even acknowledged the moral questions raised by their policies of sometimes systematic extermination, let alone recognize that such behaviour was prohibited by international law or a norm embedded in international society. Ideological solidarity prompted communist governments to support one another, often enabling communist perpetrators of mass killing to secure sufficient legitimacy. Where solidarity broke down, as in did in relation to Vietnam and Cambodia after 1977, this was usually the result of political disputes not related to mass killing and only occasionally exposed perpetrators to punishment. Where there was criticism, it almost always came from outside the communist world. Even this was often heavily conditioned by contextual factors.

I argued earlier that ideologies of selective extermination have trouble securing legitimacy outside the political communities from which they arise. Their capacity to secure sufficient legitimacy is therefore dependent on things such as the material power of their hosts and the role played by contextual factors. The Soviet Union was arguably the first communist government to move away from selective extermination, Stalin's successors recognizing that the doctrine bred political instability, imposed significant economic costs, and inhibited social development. This did not stop others, particularly the communist regimes in China and Cambodia, from developing and employing Stalinist thinking, but they too found the going tougher towards the end of the Cold War: communist China turned its back on selective extermination after Mao's death for very similar reasons to those of the Soviet Union, and having been ejected from power by Vietnam in 1979, external support for the Khmer Rouge dwindled as Cold War hostilities lessened. Although the Soviet and Chinese transitions away from selective extermination were largely domestic affairs, they were certainly helped by changes to the international context. In particular, the fragmentation of global communist solidarity reduced the level of legitimacy available within the communist world and opened up the potential for alliances between communists and non-communists (e.g. US and Chinese cooperation against the Soviet Union in Afghanistan); the stagnation of communist economies made regimes more aware of the costs associated with mass repression and more vulnerable to external ideational influences; the reduction of global strategic competition brought about by détente and accelerated by Gorbachev's reforms in the late 1980s increased the relative priority afforded by international society to human rights; and the strengthening of global communications made it more difficult (though not impossible) for perpetrators to avoid external scrutiny or create and leverage uncertainty.

But although communist governments moved away from selective extermination and became more sensitive about international reactions to violations of civilian immunity, they did not internalize civilian immunity. Indeed, both the Soviet Union (in Afghanistan) and China (in the 1989 Beijing massacre) committed atrocities after abandoning selective extermination. In both cases they opted to create and leverage uncertainty in order to secure sufficient legitimacy, employing arguments similar to those utilized by non-communist regimes (see Chapter 6). But in sharp contrast to their relative success in securing sufficient legitimacy prior to the late 1970s, neither the Soviet nor Chinese governments secured sufficient legitimacy in these later cases by leveraging uncertainty—although for very different reasons. International denunciation of Soviet atrocities was conditioned by opposition to the invasion of Afghanistan itself. The world's response to the Beijing massacre was conditioned by the recently changed international context and the work of three contextual factors especially—the first hand presence of international media which resulted in detailed real-time reporting, the relative legitimacy of the victims vis-à-vis the regimes, and the absence of countervailing policy concerns, which helped to elevate human rights as an international priority. Perhaps learning from China's experience, since the end of the Cold War, the remaining communist regimes have been no more likely to commit mass atrocities than non-communists, suggesting that the end of the Cold War took with it the communist ideology of selective extermination.

This chapter focuses on three major communist perpetrators of mass atrocities after 1945—the Soviet Union (1945–89), China (1945–89) and Cambodia (1975–79)—all of whom were repeat offenders. I argue that at different points, the Soviet Union and China moved away from selective extermination (the Soviets in the 1950s, and the Chinese in the 1970s), opting instead to leverage uncertainty in order to secure sufficient legitimacy for their more recent atrocities. All three regimes, I argue, found it more difficult to legitimize mass killing in the Cold War's final decade than in earlier decades. In both the Chinese and Cambodian cases, we can trace this shift to changes in the role of contextual factors, especially the availability of reliable and timely information and the decline of countervailing interests that had earlier inhibited external actors from prioritizing the punishment of gross violations of civilian immunity. Because strategic and political concerns played such a large role in shaping international reactions to Soviet atrocities in Afghanistan, we cannot say definitively that responses were determined by the changed impact of contextual factors on the norm of civilian immunity, but it is clear that they played a role. This experience confirms the argument that it was more difficult to legitimize mass killing at the end of the Cold War than it had been at the beginning and that this was due to the widening and deepening of normative support for civilian immunity and the changing role played by contextual factors. After examining the three regimes at the height of the Cold War, the final part of the chapter focuses on the late Cold War cases of Afghanistan and the Beijing massacre.

## SOVIET UNION (1940–1953)

This section continues the story of totalitarian terror in the Soviet Union, focusing on the period during and immediately after the Second World War. Although not reaching the heights of the 'great terror' of 1937–38, the Stalinist regime continued to employ mass terror against groups considered politically suspect. Despite this, it largely succeeded in avoiding international criticism thanks mainly to perceptions about the relative legitimacy of Stalin and Hitler and—after the War—the presence of countervailing concerns such as the safe return of Western Prisoners of War from Soviet occupied areas, the avoidance of armed hostilities, and international crises such as the Korean War and Suez crisis. Moreover, Western governments calculated that they had little influence over Soviet Union behaviour within its sphere of influence.[3]

At the time of his death in 1953, Stalin was fermenting a major crackdown against the Jewish community and a new purge of the communist leadership. Afterwards, the Soviet leadership quickly moved away from the systematic use of terror and in 1956, Stalin's successor, Nikita Khrushchev, denounced Stalinist terror.[4] Although this signalled a shift away from selective extermination as a routine part of state policy, it did not indicate the internalization of civilian immunity. In the same year, the Soviet Union brutally repressed the reformist regime in Hungary, killing 1,000–2,000 civilians in the process and executing up to 400 others afterwards. In the 1980s, Soviet armed forces employed mass atrocities as part of their counter-insurgency campaign in Afghanistan (see below).

During the Second World War itself, Soviet forces repeatedly showed contempt for civilians but the West prioritized alliance cohesion and turned a blind eye to Soviet atrocities. At home, Stalin worried that national minorities situated in strategically important regions harboured treasonous intentions and would aid the enemy if given the chance.[5] Between 1941 and 1944, he ordered the forcible deportation of Finns, Germans, Kalmyks, Karachays, Chechens, Ingush, Balkars, Crimean Tartars, Crimean Greeks, Meskhetian

[3] Jack F. Matlock Jr, 'US Policy on Human Rights in Relations with the USSR, 1961–91', in Debra Liang-Fenton (ed.), *Implementing US Human Rights Policy: Agendas, Policies and Practices* (Washington, DC: United States Institute of Peace Press, 2004), p. 246.

[4] E. A. Rees, 'Stalin as Leader, 1937–1953: From Dictator to Despot', in E. A. Rees (ed.), *The Nature of Stalin's Dictatorship: The Politburo, 1924–1953* (London: Palgrave, 2004), p. 229.

[5] Chris Ward, *Stalin's Russia*, 2nd edn (London: Arnold, 1999), p. 195.

Turks, Kurds, and Khemeshils from their homelands and their resettlement in Siberia and Kazakhstan.[6] Up to two million people were forcibly removed and forced to endure conditions similar to those of the *kulaks* in the 1930s.[7] The violence of their forced removal, long train journeys in cramped coaches, the utter desolation of their destinations, and forced labour had resulted in the death of 309,100 deportees by 1948. The death rate varied by national groups, with the Volga Germans, for example, faring reasonably well (3.5 per cent death rate). Worse hit were the Ingush and Chechens, with Soviet records showing that 144,704, almost a quarter (23.7 per cent) of those transported, had died by 1948.[8] Worst hit of all, though, were the Tartars who lost some 46 per cent of their pre-deportation population.[9] In line with Stalin's general ideology of selective extermination, the deportations were justified on the basis of the collective responsibility of these national groups for crimes against the Soviet Union, including spying, espionage, harbouring foreign agents, and acts of insurrection.[10] Additionally, some 'nations' were portrayed as products of capitalism and the welfare of these 'reactionaries' deemed irrelevant.[11] Deportations were conducted with the utmost secrecy both to minimize resistance and prevent international criticism. Soviet publications made no mention of the deportations and deported groups were simply deleted from national records, maps, and publications. Use of their names and languages were prohibited.[12] Only after the Second World War did evidence of the deportations begin to emerge outside the Soviet Union.[13] It is this complete absence of reporting that best explains the lack of international criticism.

The same cannot be said, however, of the Soviet massacre of Polish officers at Katyn or the mass killing and imprisonment of Soviet citizens and other groups forcibly repatriated by the allies between 1944 and 1947. In the Katyn case, Western governments publicly accepted the Soviet Union's implausible denial. Forced repatriation, meanwhile, was conducted under a cloud of secrecy to prevent widely anticipated public opposition in the West.

[6] See Robert Conquest, *The Nation Killers: The Soviet Deportation of Nationalities* (London: Macmillan, 1970).

[7] Indeed, sometimes in the so-called 'special settlements' they occupied 'camps' left vacant by Kulaks who had either died or in the intervening years built themselves better shelters. See Aleksandr M. Nekrich, *The Punished Peoples: The Deportation, and Fate of Soviet Minorities at the end of the Second World War* (New York: W. W. Norton and Co., 1978), pp. 98–9.

[8] J. Otto Pohl, *Ethnic Cleansing in the USSR, 1937–1949* (Westport: Greenwood Press, 1999), p. 8; on the reasons, see pp. 96–8.

[9] According to Conquest, *Nation Killers*, pp. 161–2.

[10] See Pohl, *Ethnic Cleansing*, pp. 35 and 85.

[11] Conquest, *Nation Killers*, p. 112. Also see p. 118.

[12] Conquest, *Nation Killers*, p. 67.

[13] Conquest, *Nation Killers*, p. 95.

In spring 1940, approximately 14,500 Polish officers and policemen taken prisoner by the Soviet Union during its September 1939 invasion of eastern Poland were executed in what became known as the Katyn massacre, after the Katyn forest where the first mass graves were discovered.[14] After being captured by the Red Army, the prisoners of war were held at camps in Koselsk, Ostashkov, and Starobelsk. On 5 March 1940, the Politburo ordered their execution on the grounds that they were 'hardened and uncompromising enemies of Soviet authority'.[15] After the German invasion of the Soviet Union in 1941, Poland was permitted to raise an army to combat the Nazis. The Polish government-in-exile in London soon realized, however, that around half of the entire officer corps was missing. Polish authorities made repeated requests for information. The Soviets responded with a wall of silence and misinformation. On one occasion they claimed that the officers had escaped to Manchuria and on another insisted that they had been released.[16] In April 1943, the German government announced that it had discovered mass graves containing the remains of several thousand Polish officers in Katyn forest, near Smolensk. Describing the accusation as 'fascist slander', the Soviets immediately blamed the Germans for the massacre, arguing that the Poles had fallen into German hands in 1941.[17] The Polish government remained unconvinced by Soviet entreaties and requested that the International Committee of the Red Cross (ICRC) investigate. In a move calibrated to sow distrust among the allies, Germany also requested a Red Cross investigation, prompting the Soviet Union to break diplomatic ties with the Polish government-in-exile, claiming that it was collaborating with the Germans. The ensuing German-led investigation, which was monitored by Polish observers, revealed sufficient forensic and photographic evidence to persuade the Poles that the Soviet Union, not the Germans, had been responsible for the massacre. In 1944, the Soviets established their own commission of enquiry which fabricated evidence pointing to German guilt. In 1946, the chief Soviet prosecutor at the Nuremberg Tribunal tried to indict German officers for the Katyn massacre but dropped the case after the USA and UK refused to support it and

[14] See Anna M. Cienciala, Natalia S. Lebedeva, and Wojciech Materski (eds), *Katyn: A Crime Without Punishment* (New Haven: Yale University Press, 2007); J. K. Zawodny, *Death in the Forest: The Story of the Katyn Forest Massacre* (Notre Dame, IN: University of Notre Dame Press, 1972); and Polish Cultural Foundation, *The Crime of Katyn: Facts & Documents* (London: Polish Cultural Foundation, 1965).

[15] Cienciala, Lebedeva, and Materski, *Katyn*, p. 121. Quote is translation of the Politburo order, in Allen Paul, *Katyn: Stalin's Massacre and the Seeds of Polish Resurrection* (Annapolis, MD: Naval Institute Press, 1996), pp. 353–4.

[16] Zawodny, *Death in the Forest*, pp. 9–10.

[17] Personal and Secret Message from Premier J. V. Stalin to the Prime Minister, Mr W. Churchill, 21 April 1943 available at http://www.revolutionarydemocracy.org/Stalin/corrv1_1943.htm accessed 26 March 2012.

the German defence team promised to bring forward strong evidence of Soviet guilt.[18]

Initially, the British and American governments publicly accepted the Soviet version of events. Indeed, the British joined the Soviet Union in opposing the ICRC investigation, which Churchill told Stalin 'would be a fraud, and its conclusions reached by terrorism'.[19] On the one hand, both governments were predisposed to believe the Soviet government over the Nazis. As Anthony Eden bluntly told the head of the Polish government-in-exile, General Sikorski, 'first of all, the British government did not believe the Germans'.[20] Likewise, the Madden Congressional Committee in the USA found that the Roosevelt Administration had also refused to believe that the Soviets were responsible. The President himself was quoted as saying, '. . . this is entirely German propaganda and a German plot. I am absolutely convinced that the Russians did not do this'.[21] On the other hand, even where serious doubts were expressed about the Soviet version of events, British and American leaders were reluctant to jeopardize the alliance by questioning Stalin's account. Churchill candidly told Sikorski that he could certainly believe Soviet guilt but warned that the issue should not be pursued publicly lest it damage relations with the Soviet Union. Eden advised that Britain 'could not estrange such a powerful ally'.[22] To counter German propaganda, both the British and American governments suppressed media coverage of Katyn between 1943 and 1945.[23] Matters began to change in the 1950s, when the emerging Cold War switched the political imperative and prompted new efforts to discover the truth about Katyn. In 1953, the aforementioned Madden Congressional Committee called for the Soviet perpetrators to be tried at the United Nations. That move failed to secure bipartisan support because Democrats associated the Madden committee with the McCarthy communist witch-hunt and the Eisenhower administration needed Soviet cooperation over Korea. Meanwhile, Khrushchev made no mention of Katyn in his secret denunciation of Stalin's crimes and ordered the destruction of thousands of files relating to the massacre.[24]

[18] See Zawodny, *Death in the Forest*, pp. 49–76.

[19] Personal and secret message from the Prime Minister, Mr Winston Churchill, to Marshal J. V. Stalin, 24 April 1943.

[20] Cienciala, Lebedeva, and Materski, *Katyn*, p. 219.

[21] *The Katyn Forest Massacre: Final Report of the Select Committee to Conduct an Investigation and Study of the Facts, Evidence and Circumstances on the Katyn Forest Massacre*, 22 December 1952, p. 6, available at http://archive.org/stream/katynforestmassa04unit/katynforestmassa04unit_djvu.txt accessed 26 March 2012.

[22] Cited in Cienciala, Lebedeva, and Materski, *Katyn*, pp. 217 and 219.

[23] Cienciala, Lebedeva, and Materski, *Katyn*, pp. 235–6.

[24] Cienciala, Lebedeva, and Materski, *Katyn*, pp. 239–40.

Equally notorious—though only since the 1970s—was the forced repatriation of Soviet Prisoners of War and groups (such as the Cossacks) who had fled the Soviet Union after the 1919–20 civil war.[25] Having endured brutal treatment at the hands of the Nazis in concentration and detention camps, many Soviet Prisoners of War donned German uniforms either as members of labour battalions or as armed units. Some did so enthusiastically but others were forced to do so. From the very beginning of *Operation Overlord*, Soviet citizens in German uniforms and Soviet civilians fell into the hands of the allies. Although some were eager to return to the Soviet Union, most expressed a wish to not return, fearing for their lives and believing that the British and Americans would not turn them over to Stalin.[26] The Soviet leadership was keen to secure their return as quickly as possible. The presence of so many Soviet citizens in German uniforms was a major source of embarrassment for the regime and it was eager to exact its revenge.[27] Initially, the British government proposed granting amnesty to Russians who surrendered, but this option was rejected by Molotov who, in what was widely seen at the time as a lie, argued that there were very few Russians collaborating with the Germans and therefore no reason to give them special treatment.[28] Foreign Secretary Anthony Eden favoured rapid repatriation, but was opposed by Lord Selbourne who argued that it would be 'inhumane' to send back 'many thousands of men to die, either by execution or in Siberia'.[29] Churchill wavered, recognizing the validity of Selbourne's position and the fact that most of the prisoners had joined the German army only after experiencing severe privations and that most had not actively fought the allies. The matter was settled in a closely guarded secret agreement at Yalta when the allies agreed to forcibly repatriate all Soviet citizens that fell into their hands. Driving this agreement were British and Americans concerns about the quick return of British and American Prisoners of War who had fallen into Soviet hands. US Secretary of State, Henry Stimson detected a thinly veiled threat behind the Soviet negotiating position: 'to refuse to return those claiming Soviet citizenship to the Soviet Government, even against their express

[25] Moving in the other direction were up to three million Germans expelled from Soviet occupied eastern Europe under the terms of the Potsdam agreement. Article 13 of the Potsdam Treaty insisted that 'the transfer to Germany of German populations, or elements thereof remaining in Poland, Czechoslovakia and Hungary will have to be undertaken'. For details of the expulsion of Germans, see Steffen Prauser and Arfon Rees (eds), 'The Expulsion of the "German" Communities from Eastern Europe at the End of the Second World War', European Union Institute, Working paper 2004/1, 2004.

[26] Nicholas Bethell, *The Last Secret: Forcible Repatriation to Russia 1944–47* (London: Andre Deutsch, 1974), p. 5.

[27] Nikolai Tolstoy, *Victims of Yalta* (London: Hodder and Stoughton, 1977), p. 48.

[28] Tolstoy, *Victims of Yalta*, p. 44.

[29] Cited in Tolstoy, *Victims of Yalta*, p. 53.

desires, might result in the retention of our released prisoners of war in their custody'.[30] These concerns were repeatedly echoed in the media.[31]

British and American politicians, officials, and soldiers were under few illusions about the ultimate fate of many of the returnees.[32] Most of the 2.8 million surviving Prisoners of War were arrested and interrogated by the NKVD. Many were shot as traitors and most of the others were despatched to the gulags. Only around one-fifth of returnees were allowed home.[33] A similar fate befell the 5.5 million civilian returnees—Soviet citizens who had fallen into allied hands at the end of the war and been compulsorily returned under the terms of the Yalta agreement. Some were found guilty of collaboration and shot; around 3 million were sent to labour camps.[34] Stalin also demanded that the allies return civilians who had fled the Soviet Union before the war, many during and immediately after the Russian civil war. Because most were not Soviet citizens in 1939, the allies were under no obligation to comply, yet did so largely because they were unsure about what else to do. Most notoriously, in May and June 1945, the British forcibly repatriated 50,000 Cossack soldiers and civilians. Many committed suicide prior to deportation and the fate of those who were deported remains uncertain.[35] Certainly all of the officers were executed almost instantly and the remainder despatched to the gulag. There were few, if any, reported survivors.

Some were prepared to argue that the returnees, especially those that had collaborated with the Nazis, deserved their fate. The *New York Times* at one point referred simply to '100,000 to 150,000 Russians traitors who are being held as prisoners and presumably will ultimately face Soviet justice' whilst General Omar Bradley caustically commented that 'I don't believe these people have much of a future'.[36] Prominent British Marxist, John Strachey

[30] Cited in Bethell, *The Last Secret*, p. 28.

[31] E.g., 'Russia's War Prisoners', *New York Times*, 5 January 1949; 'Moscow Refuses Data on Prisoners', *New York Times*, 3 October 1950; and 'UN Has a Mystery in War Prisoners', *New York Times*, 5 August 1951.

[32] Gaddis suggests that the shipping of prisoners to labour camps was done 'much to the horror' of the Americans who had forcibly repatriated them, implying that the US government was surprised about this development. See John Lewis Gaddis, *Russia, the Soviet Union, and the United States: An Interpretive History*, 2nd edn (New York: McGraw Hill, 1990), p. 190. However, both Tolstoy and Bethell demonstrate that allied government leaders and officials, as well as the soldiers who carried out the policy, expected returnees to be mistreated.

[33] Norman Lowe, *Mastering Twentieth-Century Russian History* (London: Palgrave, 2002), section 7.3.

[34] Lowe, *Russian History*, section 7.3.

[35] Nikolai Tolstoy, *Stalin's Secret War*, ch. 17; Tolstoy, *Victims of Yalta*, chs 7 and 8; Bethnell, *The Last Secret*. The Soviet Union was not alone in massacring political groups forcibly returned by the allies. The allies forcibly returned between 50,000–100,000 Croats who had fled to Austria back to communist Yugoslavia. Whilst some in this group were undoubtedly guilty of grave crimes perpetrated by the fascist wartime Croatian state, others were ordinary soldiers and a majority were probably civilians. All were massacred by the communists at Bleiburg in 1945.

[36] Cited in Bethell, *The Last Secret*, p. 68.

described the prisoners as quislings who 'deserved everything that was coming to them'. These comments aside, however, it seems that the British and American governments were correct in their belief that, if made public, the Yalta agreement and forced repatriation programme would be sharply criticized at home. For one thing, senior figures in both governments expressed grave doubts about the morality of the policy. In the USA, Henry Stimson observed that 'I think we are unnecessarily running into danger by turning over German prisoners of Russian origins to the Russians. First thing, you know, we will be responsible for a big killing by the Russians'. Attorney-General Robert H. Jackson advised that 'I gravely question the legal basis or authority for surrendering the objecting individuals to representatives of the Soviet government', prompting Stimson to argue that returns be made conditional on Soviet guarantees of good treatment.[37] As a limited amount of information about the deportations began to emerge in mid-1945, the media in both countries became hostile to the policy. The *Manchester Guardian* insisted that 'unless these wretches are accused of some definite crime against the Soviet, they should be given the same free choice as other displaced persons'. The *New York Herald Tribune* reported disquiet amongst the soldiers charged with implementing the policy and observed that senior officers had called for revisions to the Yalta agreement. The *Christian Science Monitor* reported 'plenty of apprehension over the kinds of men and tactics that may be employed' by the Soviets.[38] On 20 February 1946, Pope Pius XII issued an allocution against 'the repatriation of men against their will and the refusal of the right of asylum'. Vatican officials told the media that the Yalta policy was 'a betrayal of the morality and ideals for which the Allies fought' and 'against humanity and justice'.[39] The Bishop of Chichester joined Lord Selbourne in denouncing the forcible return of 'fugitives from tyranny'.[40] On the ground, soldiers sometimes disobeyed orders to forcibly return prisoners. General Alexander, for example, questioned the legality of using force to return prisoners against their will and there were many cases of detainees being allowed to escape. Almost half of the Cossack prisoners in one convoy escaped and were not pursued by the soldiers guarding them.

With the war now over and under growing public pressure, the American government halted forced repatriations from the USA itself but along with Britain continued to return prisoners held in Europe. The final deportations took place in central Europe under a cloud of secrecy and deception. Clearly, had the full scale of the forced repatriation, details about the high rate of suicide among the returnees, the facts that a good many of the detainees had

[37] Cited in Bethell, *The Last Secret*, p. 27.
[38] All cited in Bethell, *The Last Secret*, pp. 179–80.
[39] Cited in Bethell, *The Last Secret*, p. 192.
[40] Cited in Tolstoy, *Victims of Yalta*, p. 64.

either not collaborated with the Germans, were not Soviet citizens, or whilst formally collaborating had never lifted a finger against the West whom they considered natural friends, the conditions in which they were deported, the use of deception and violence in the deportation, and the fate that awaited them upon their return—all of which was known to the authorities but suppressed from public view until the 1970s—been known to Western publics at the time, the degree of opposition would have been much sharper and more widespread in the Soviet Union itself.

Victory in the Second World War gave new domestic legitimacy to the Stalinist regime.[41] Terror therefore persisted as a staple of state policy. At the end of the war, nationalists in the Baltic states, Moldova, and Poland launched insurgencies against the Soviets. To prevent the discontent from spreading—and as punishment for wartime collaboration with the Nazis—the Soviets deported or imprisoned approximately 300,000 people from western Ukraine and manipulated food distribution, causing a famine which ravaged rebellious parts of Ukraine and claimed the lives of between 75,000 and 100,000 people.[42] In addition, the Soviets deported 95,000 'kulaks and nationalists' from the Baltic states and conducted or supported mass killings and imprisonment in Bulgaria, Romania, and Poland.[43]

Soviet policy also became distinctly anti-Semitic after the war, with Stalin observing that 'every Jew is a potential spy'.[44] In January 1948, Stalin ordered the building of new prison camps for 'Trotskyites'—by which he meant Jews.[45] In January 1948, Solomon Mikhoels, a well known Jewish playwright was killed on Stalin's orders. Later that year, the Jewish Anti-Fascist Committee was disbanded and its leaders arrested. Jewish schools and libraries were closed, Jewish publications were banned, Jews were removed from professional positions, and were arrested on the slightest pretence.[46] Victims were tortured to force confessions for crimes including spying and conspiring. Most were executed or sent to prison camps. Almost none were acquitted.[47] The dictator's final purge was the imprisonment of the Kremlin's mainly

[41] A point made by Moshe Lewin, *Russia/USSR/Russia* (New York: The New Press, 1995), p. 237; and Ward, *Stalin's Russia*, p. 214. On the Second World War death toll, see Richard Overy, *Russia's War: A History of the Soviet War Effort 1941–1945* (Harmondsworth: Penguin, 1998), pp. 287–9.

[42] Lowe, *Russian History*, section 7.3.

[43] See Andrej Paczkowski, 'Poland, the "Enemy Nation"' and Karel Bartosek, 'Central and Southeastern Europe', both in Courtois et al., *Black Book of Communism.*

[44] Cited by Iakov Etinger, 'The Doctor's Plot: Stalin's Solution to the Jewish Question', in Yaacov Ro'I (ed.), *Jews and Jewish Life in Russia and the Soviet Union* (London: Frank Cass, 1995), p. 104. On the anti-Semitic turn, see Robert J. Brym, *The Jews of Moscow, Kiev and Minsk: Identity, Antisemitism, Emigration* (New York: New York University Press, 1994), p. 13.

[45] Lewin, *Russia*, p. 238.

[46] Lowe, *Russian History*, section 7.3.

[47] Nora Levin, *The Jews of the Soviet Union since 1917: Paradox of Survival* (New York: New York University Press, 1990), pp. 393–4, 477–9, and 512–24.

Jewish doctors. They were accused of plotting to assassinate leaders and were tortured to extract confessions.[48] At this time, Stalin openly talked of rounding up all Jews and deporting them to Siberia. In February 1953, the Soviet Union broke diplomatic ties with Israel.[49] Thankfully for the Sovet Union's Jews, Stalin died later that year, bringing the persecution to a close and forestalling a widely anticipated pogrom. Nonetheless, Stalin's death was greeted with an outpouring of public grief in the Soviet Union, which even the country's critics admit was a genuine reflection of the deceased leader's esteem.[50]

Stalin's death signalled the beginning of the Soviet Union's move away from selective extermination. Having outmanoeuvred his opponents and secured his place as Stalin's successor, in 1956 Nikita Khrushchev denounced Stalinist terror in a secret speech to the Twentieth Communist Party Congress. According to Khrushchev, 'Stalin . . . used extreme methods and mass repressions'. He 'originated the concept "enemy of the people"', which 'made possible the usage of the most cruel repression, violating all norms of revolutionary legality, against anyone who in any way disagreed with Stalin, against those who were only suspected of hostile intent, against those who had bad reputations'. 'There were', Khrushchev continued, 'often no sufficiently serious reasons for their physical annihilation'. Referring to the deportation of national groups, he noted: '[a]ll the more monstrous are the acts whose initiator was Stalin and which are rude violations of the basic Leninist principles of the nationality policy of the Soviet state'.[51] There are various explanations as to why Khrushchev took this extraordinary step, all of them pointing to domestic factors unrelated to civilian immunity. These include, an interest in delegitimizing Stalin loyalists such as Beria and Molotov, protecting the senior leadership from future purges, the new leader's intention to assert his authority and present a sanitized historic account that absolved the new leadership of moral blame, and recognition that the terror imposed massive economic costs and retarded development.[52] Almost immediately, around half of the prisoners held in gulags were released.

Although Soviet reform saw the regime move away from employing the language of selective extermination, change was limited and fell far short of internalizing civilian immunity, though the Soviets were sensitive to the fact

[48] Lewin, *Russia*, p. 239. For an excellent first hand account of the so-called 'doctor's plot', see Etinger, 'The Doctors Plot', pp. 103–24.

[49] Lowe, *Russian History*, section 7.3.

[50] See Robert Thurston, 'Stalinism in Context and Perspective: Sources of Permission to Hate in Europe', in James Kaye and Bo Strath (eds), *Enlightenment and Genocide, Contradictions of Modernity* (New York: Peter Lang, 2000), p. 186.

[51] Nikita Khriushchev, Secret Speech to the Twentieth Communist Party Congress, 24–25 February 1956, reprinted in Frank Chalk and Kurt Johanssohn, *The History and Sociology of Genocide: Analyses and Case Studies* (New Haven: Yale University Press, 1990), pp. 301–3.

[52] Rees, 'Stalin as Leader', pp. 229–30; and Nicholas Werth, 'The Exit from Stalinism' in Coutois et al., *The Black Book of Communism*, p. 251.

that external actors might use civilian immunity to judge their actions. When Hungarian workers and students rebelled in 1956, the Soviets intervened militarily and imposed a new communist government. Refraining from wholesale slaughter, Soviet forces did occasionally employ indiscriminate force, killing around 1,500 civilians.[53] In the worst incident, Soviet tanks opened fire on protestors in Salgotajan, killing 190 and injuring many more.[54] Having suppressed the uprising, the new Soviet-backed regime executed between 350–400 civilians. This response was justified on the grounds that the uprising had been orchestrated by NATO, had unleashed a 'white terror' of mob violence, and that the Hungarian government had requested Soviet help.[55]

Unsurprisingly, international reactions reflected Cold War divisions. The Soviet invasion was generally supported within the communist world, including by China and Yugoslavia, and although it was criticized in the West, the USA in particular made it clear that it had no intention of assisting the Hungarian rebels. The USA recognized that Hungary was in the Soviet Union's sphere of influence and, along with the UK and France, was preoccupied by the Suez Crisis in the Middle East.[56] Western engagement was therefore limited to making entreaties to the UN. With the Security Council route blocked by Soviet veto (interestingly, Yugoslavia abstained on a draft resolution condemning the Soviet invasion), the matter was taken up by the General Assembly. Between 1956 and 1962, the Assembly issued annual resolutions demanding the withdrawal of Soviet troops and recognition of Hungary's right to independence and self-determination. The first resolution was passed by 50 to 8 (Soviet bloc), with 15 abstentions. In 1957, the Assembly convened a five nation (Australia, Ceylon [Sri Lanka], Denmark, Tunisia, and Uruguay) committee to examine the circumstances of the invasion. Its report, based largely on witness testimony, was a damning indictment of the Soviet Union which concluded that the post-1956 Hungarian government had been imposed by force by the Soviet Union.[57] The Assembly condemned the Soviet invasion by a large majority in 1957, but thereafter support for the Hungarian cause began to dwindle as the Soviet Union succeeded in winning allies among newly decolonized states and the issue was pushed to the backburner by

[53] Charles Gati, *Failed Illusions: Moscow, Washington, Budapest and the 1956 Hungarian Revolt* (Stanford: Stanford University Press, 2006), p. 5.

[54] Paul Lendvai, *One Day that Shook the Communist World: The 1956 Hungarian Uprising and its Legacy* (Princeton, NJ: Princeton University Press, 2006), pp. 189 and 215.

[55] See Nikita Khrushchev, 'Restoring Order in Hungary', in Edward Crankshaw (ed.), *Khrushchev Remembers*, trans. Strobe Talbott (London: Sphere Books, 1971), pp. 379–92.

[56] Landvai, *One Day*, p. 134.

[57] See *Report of the Special Committee on the Problem of Hungary*, UN General Assembly, A/3592, 1957. Especially, General Assembly Resolutions 1004 (4 November 1956), 1005 (9 November 1956), and 1006 (9 November 1956).

decolonization and various crises in the Middle East. In 1962, the West agreed to take the matter off the Assembly's agenda in return for a general amnesty.[58]

In summary, under Stalin's leadership the Soviet Union continued to employ mass terror and to justify this by reference to selective extermination both during and immediately after the Second World War. Not only did the Stalinists largely escape international opprobrium, in some instances the West even cooperated in covering up atrocities (the Katyn massacre) or delivering new victims (post-war deportations). A number of contextual factors were at play in shaping these responses. Most notably, the internal deportations of nationalities during the Second World War were conducted in secret and not reported until much later; a combination of the relative legitimacy of the Soviets and Nazis, alliance politics, and the leveraging of uncertainty muted the response to the Katyn massacre; and concerns about the timely return of Western Prisoners of War overrode worries about the fate of Soviets citizens and others handed over to the Soviets. This took place in a context in which the West recognized a Soviet sphere of influence and believed (probably correctly) that it had little diplomatic leverage. Stalin's death precipitated a rapid shift in Soviet thinking away from selective extermination. Recognizing that the doctrine imperilled leaders, inhibited economic development, strained the country's resources, and fostered instability, Khrushchev denounced the terror and reversed some of its worst elements. This did not amount to internalizing civilian immunity but it did increase recognition of an embedded international norm that encouraged restraint. Thus, although Soviet forces did fire indiscriminately on civilians during the 1956 uprising in Hungary, they refrained from the wholesale slaughter of civilians and although opposition figures were executed afterwards, these were counted in the hundreds not in the hundreds of thousands. In essence, the ousting of Stalin brought the Soviet Union into line with the USA on the question of civilian immunity. Though no longer able to justify wholesale extermination, the Soviet regime was not prepared to renounce the killing of civilians altogether. Instead, as became clear during the Afghanistan War (below), the Soviet leadership attempted to secure sufficient legitimacy by leveraging uncertainty in much the same way as the USA did during this period.

But although the Soviet Union abandoned selective extermination in the 1950s, other communist regimes—in China and Cambodia especially, but also Albania and Ethiopia—did not follow suit. Communist solidarity often shielded these governments from international criticism or punishment, sometimes with the help of Western governments that prioritized strategic interests over civilian protection. The next sections examine China and Cambodia respectively.

[58] See Janos Radvanyi, *Hungary and the Superpowers: The 1956 Revolution and Realpolitik* (Stanford: Stanford University Press, 1972).

## CHINA (1949–1988)

Excluding regime-induced famine, the Maoist regime in China killed somewhere between three million and thirty-five million people, with most estimates coming in somewhere between four and a half million and nine million.[59] Although the highest figure may seem outlandish, the low figures are widely thought too conservative and new accounts based on local county records are pushing fatality estimates upwards.[60]

Chinese communists had committed bloody purges before assuming power.[61] On coming to power, they instigated a country-wide programme of land reform and counter-revolutionary terror in which individual villages were instructed to identify, humiliate, and often execute 'land-owners'. Where there were no land-owners in a village, former collaborators with the Japanese or nationalist armies, new arrivals, or people unpopular for whatever reason were sometimes killed instead.[62] Less than a decade after redistributing land to peasants, the communists took it back in a massive programme of collectivization that paved the way to the so-called 'Great Leap Forward'. Between thirty and forty-five million people died in the ensuing regime induced famine, but much less well known is that at least two and a half million people were summarily killed or tortured to death.[63] In 1950, China invaded Tibet and in 1959 crushed a rebellion there, killing around 50,000 civilians in post-rebellion reprisals. In the 1960s, Mao unleashed the Cultural Revolution to win back and 'purify' the party. Between 1 million and 20 million people were killed, most in pitched battles between rival Red factions or were humiliated and tortured until they committed suicide. Another path-breaking study based on local government records reveals that at least 250,000 people were killed by the regime in mass killings in 1967–68 alone.[64] As European communism crumbled in 1989, the Chinese army massacred between 1,000 and 3,000 protestors in Beijing and hundreds of others elsewhere in the country. Although this massacre was small by Chinese communist standards, it elicited more international opprobrium than all the others

[59] For the high end, see R. J. Rummel, *China's Bloody Century: Genocide and Mass Murder since 1900* (New Brunswick: Transaction, 1991). The lower range is in Jean-Louis Margolin, 'Mao's China: The Worst Non-Genocidal Regime?', in Dan Stone (ed.), *The Historiography of Genocide* (London: Palgrave, 2008), p. 438.

[60] See Frank Dikotter, *Mao's Great Famine: The History of China's Most Devastating Catastrophe, 1958–1962* (London: Bloomsbury, 2010); and Yang Su, *Collective Killings in Rural China During the Cultural Revolution* (Cambridge: Cambridge University Press, 2010).

[61] Jean-Louis Margolin, 'Mao's China', pp. 446 and 455.

[62] See Philip C. C. Huang, 'Rural Class Struggle in the Chinese Revolution: Representational and Objective Realities from the Land Reform to the Cultural Revolution', *Modern China*, 21 (1) 1995, pp. 105–43.

[63] Dikotter, *Mao's Great Famine*, p. xi.

[64] Yang Su, *Collective Killings in Rural China*.

combined—signalling the end of communism's potential to secure sufficient legitimacy for mass killing through ideologies of selective extermination. This last massacre is examined at the end of the chapter.

Like the Stalinists and the Khmer Rouge in Cambodia, Maoist communists justified mass killing by reference to a doctrine of selective extermination but also denied and tried to keep secret the full extent of the killing in order to maintain support among those who might not be wholly persuaded by the ideology. The Maoist version of selective extermination drew on the basic communist theme that individuals and groups deemed to threaten the revolutionary order could be legitimately eliminated. What it added, was a potent mixture of biological determinism (children born to politically problematic parents, identified as 'black elements', or the 'four types', were thought likely to be counter-revolutionary) and arbitrariness (people accused of 'wrong thoughts' could be killed; what constituted a 'wrong thought' changed arbitrarily) in the selection of victims.[65] Until the international outcry that accompanied the 1989 massacre in Beijing, however, communist China avoided serious international criticism and punishment. Although solidarity from within the communist world is not surprising, the West's reticence to condemn communist China is more puzzling. Of the pre-1989 episodes, the killings in Tibet received more attention than the other episodes, although the death toll there was much lower. This relative silence cannot be attributed to the prioritization of strategic or political interests over humanitarian concerns, because the major episodes ('land reform killings', 'Great Leap Forward', and the 'Cultural Revolution') occurred *before* China's rapprochement with the USA. In the 1950s and 1960s, the West considered communist China a major threat and was therefore unlikely to have willingly forgone the propaganda opportunities provided by communist atrocities. The key explanation, therefore, lies in the supply of information. Simply put, Chinese mass atrocities were not widely condemned because they were not widely reported. Foreign reporters and diplomats enjoyed very limited access, only a few people managed to escape from communist China, and China was diplomatically isolated—it was not a member of the UN until 1971. In comparison, the Beijing massacre in 1989 triggered international outrage primarily because it was reported in almost real-time. The Chinese experience, therefore, is a case study in the role played by information in shaping the legitimation of mass atrocities. This section begins by examining Maoism as

[65] See Xiaoxia Gong, 'The Logic of Repressive Collective Action: A Case Study of Violence in the Cultural Revolution', in Kam-yee Law (ed.), *The Chinese Cultural Revolution Reconsidered: Beyond Purge and Holocaust* (London: Palgrave, 2003), pp. 120–1; and Shaoguang Wang, 'Between Destruction and Construction: The First Year of the Cultural Revolution', in Law (ed.), *Chinese Cultural Revolution*, p. 36.

an ideology of selective extermination before exploring the land reform massacres, Tibet, the Great Leap Forward, and the Cultural Revolution.

Maoist thinking contained all the critical elements of an ideology of selective extermination and shared much with Stalinism.[66] Most commentators agree that Mao was genuinely committed to the radical transformation of Chinese society at almost any cost. He advocated action and struggle above all else and believed that (carefully directed) violent mass struggle could reform both China and the world.[67] According to Margolin, Mao's utopianism had five components. First, an 'utter contempt' for social institutions. Second, a commitment to the destruction of structures and individuals associated with them. Third, a belief that nothing was immoral when done with the aim of achieving revolutionary utopia and, we might add, a view that violence was both a necessary and desirable aspect of the revolutionary ideal. As Mao himself opined in 1927: 'A revolution is not a dinner party, or writing an essay, or painting a picture, or doing embroidery; it cannot be so refined, so leisurely and gentle, so temperate, kind, courteous, restrained and magnanimous. A revolution is an insurrection, an act of violence by which one class overthrows another'.[68] The fourth aspect of Mao's utopianism, Margolin contends, was a Manichean view of society that rendered certain groups 'irredeemable' on the basis of their socio-economic status. The fifth element was the centrality of the 'revolutionary party'. Combined, these elements produced an approach to government that was often divorced from reality and prepared to tolerate almost any cost incurred in the pursuit of its utopian vision.[69] For the Maoists, the first three elements justified the rapid and forcible adoption of radical measures to impose the will of the party and transform the county. The fourth element was critical in identifying individuals and groups that constituted threats to the people and could therefore be justly eliminated.

The durability and significance of 'class struggle' was a cornerstone of Maoist thinking.[70] Mao believed that communist societies should maintain something approximating a permanent struggle against class enemies, lest they become infected with capitalist thought.[71] Thus, Mao saw Khrushchev's repudiation of Stalin as evidence of resurgent capitalist thought. According to Mao, 'in socialist

[66] Byung-joon Ahn, *Chinese Politics and the Cultural Revolution: Dynamics of Policy Processes* (Seattle: University of Washington Press, 1976), p. 27.

[67] Margolin, 'Mao's China', p. 441.

[68] Cited in Craig Dietrich, *People's China: A Brief History*, 2nd edn (New York: Oxford University Press, 1994), p. 187.

[69] Simon Leys, *The Chairman's New Clothes: Mao and the Cultural Revolution* (London: Allison and Bushby, 1977), p. 14.

[70] Yang Su, 'Mass Killing in the Cultural Revolution', p. 115.

[71] Cited by Dietrich, *People's China*, p. 157. Also see Roderick MacFarquhar, 'Mao's Last Revolution', *Foreign Affairs*, 45, 1966–7, p. 114.

society, the overthrown bourgeoisie and other reactionary classes... sneak into the... cultural and educational institutions so as to resist or usurp the leadership of the proletariat.... In the ideological, cultural and educational fields, they counterpose the bourgeois world outlook to the proletarian world outlook and try to corrupt the proletarian and other working people with bourgeois ideology'.[72] Maoists argued that existential threats were actively encouraged by imperialists who, the *People's Daily* insisted in 1965, had 'evil designs' for China's youth.[73] Elsewhere, capitalists were likened to 'snakes' and 'poison'.[74] Maoism held that the line between 'the people' and their class enemies was clear and that the former could be kept on track with regular doses of criticism and self-criticism, whereas the latter could only be suppressed through force—'killing at a blow' as Lu Tang-yi, director of the Propaganda Department, put it in 1956.[75] The regime's rhetoric abounded with exhortations to 'eliminate' class enemies.[76]

Like other totalitarian regimes, Maoist China classified individuals to identify those who should be privileged and protected and those to be removed from the state's protection and subjected to repeated bouts of persecution.[77] In a seminal work on the subject, Lynn White described the process of social classification that took place in early 1950s Shanghai. The process took three years (1951–54) and involved labelling every individual into pre-designated groups based on their family's social origins, their profession, and/or their political affiliation.[78] At the bottom of the pile were four groups labelled the 'four black elements' or 'four types': landlords, 'rich' peasants, reactionaries, and so-called 'bad elements'. As the implacable enemies of the proletariat, the 'four types' were ostracized and subjected to recurrent persecution.[79] At the top of the pile—the Reds—were industrial workers, poor and lower-middle peasants, and 'revolutionary heroes' (members of the People's Liberation Army and other communists). 'Intermediates'—those with capitalist traits but thought reformable—included upper-middle peasants, (some) capitalists,

[72] Cited by Dietrich, *People's China*, p. 163. Also see Byung-joon Ahn, *Chinese Politics*, p. 224.

[73] Jean Esmein, *The Chinese Cultural Revolution*, trans. W. J. F. Jenner (New York: Anchor Press, Doubleday, 1973), p. 94.

[74] A. Doak Barnett, *Communist China: The Early Years, 1949–1955* (London: Pall Mall, 1964), p. 155.

[75] Cited by Byung-joon Ahn, *Chinese Politics*, pp. 18–19. Mao wrote similar things. See Dietrich, *People's China*, p. 163.

[76] Margolin, 'Mao's China', p. 458.

[77] See Lu Xiuyuan, 'A Step Towards Understanding Popular Violence in China's Cultural Revolution', *Pacific Affairs*, 67 (4) 1994–5, p. 552.

[78] Lynn T. White III, *Policies of Chaos: The Organizational Causes of Violence in China's Cultural Revolution* (Princeton, NJ: Princeton University Press, 1989). This formula was based on a 1933 paper written by Mao. Huang, 'Rural Class Struggle', p. 112.

[79] See White, *Policies of Chaos*, pp. 86–93; Y. Zheng, *Scarlet Memorials: Tales of Cannibalism in Modern China* (Boulder: Westview Press, 1996), p. 42; and L. Zhang and C. MacLeod, *China Remembers* (Hong Kong: Oxford University Press, 1999), p. 168.

and (some) intellectuals. The composition of these groups changed over time. During the Cultural Revolution, for example, 'intermediates' were incorporated into the 'four types', a category which was expanded to include twenty-three distinct groups. In practice, the lines were often much more ambiguous and the ideology interpreted differently in different times and places to justify the persecution and killing of a wide range of people. Individuals or families were sometimes categorized arbitrarily, or categorized as 'four types' because they had supported the nationalists or Japanese, because of other 'bad behaviour' (such as sexual promiscuity), or because they were ostracized outsiders or the enemies of local activists.[80] Sometimes they were erroneously assigned.[81] As elsewhere in the communist world, the central government sometimes imposed pre-determined quotas which encouraged local cadres to inflate the numbers of 'four types'.[82] In a 1955 directive, Mao spelled out that 5 per cent of the members of every organization were 'bad elements and should be purged'.[83] The fear of retribution made local leaders determined to fill their quotas.[84]

Maoist thinking about selective extermination, therefore, had much in common with Stalinism. Like Stalinism, Maoism elevated the proletariat, identified implacable class enemies, insisted that class struggle was permanent and that enemies were constantly, and secretly, at work, aided by foreign forces. As the party of the proletariat, the Chinese communists insisted that they were entitled to eliminate their enemies and that all measures adopted with this end in mind were legitimate.

Mao's first atrocities were perpetrated against his own supporters. In 1930, a purge was launched against 'Anti-Bolsheviks' in the small area of southern China controlled by the communists known as the Soviet Republic of Jiangxi. It is estimated that between 10 and 20 per cent of the area's population were killed or fled during three years of terror.[85] During the civil war with the nationalists (1947–49), the communists tried to win over 'intermediates' by presenting themselves as moderates.[86] So successful were they that some US diplomats reported that they did not believe the communists to be true communists at all.[87] In reality, though, the Chinese communists continued

[80] Huang, 'Rural Class Struggle', pp. 116–20.

[81] Reassignment was very difficult and in one reported case took more than twenty years. Huang, 'Rural Class Struggle', p. 124.

[82] Margolin, 'Mao's China', p. 454.

[83] Cited in Rummel, *China's Bloody Century*, p. 241.

[84] Rummel, *China's Bloody Century*, p. 241.

[85] S. C. Averill, 'The Origins of the Futian Incident', in Tony Saich and Hans J. van de Ven (eds), *New Perspectives on the Chinese Communist Revolution* (London: M. E. Sharpe, 1995), pp. 79–115.

[86] Edward L. Dreyer, *China at War, 1901–1949* (London: Longman, 1995), p. 313.

[87] James E. Sheridan, *China in Disintegration: The Republican Era in Chinese History, 1912–1949* (New York: The Free Press, 1975), p. 274.

to perpetrate atrocities. These were probably overlooked at the time because atrocities were a recurrent feature of war in China, perpetrated by both the nationalists and the Japanese before them as well as by the communists. Indeed, US diplomats described the nationalists as 'repugnant' owing to their mistreatment of civilians, a judgement that contributed to the US government's decision to reduce its aid to them.[88] But the communists probably killed many more civilians than the nationalists during the civil war.[89] In 'liberated' areas they launched an 'Anti-Traitor Accusation Movement' in which activists encouraged local communities to identify, 'try', and often execute those found guilty of collaborating with the Japanese and nationalists, profiteering from the war, acting as 'spies', 'puppets' or 'agents' of unfriendly forces, or being 'counter-revolutionaries'. 'Counter-revolutionary' became a ubiquitous label, effectively representing any groups or individuals that local activists wanted to eliminate. When the largely Christian town of Siwantzu was 'liberated', Christianity was taken as a sign of counter-revolutionary sentiment and all the inhabitants (most of them 'poor peasants' in communist terminology) were massacred.[90] In addition to revenge killings and the elimination of 'suspect' groups, the communists also launched a programme of violent land reform in 'liberated' zones, providing a foretaste of what was to come. Each 'liberated' village was encouraged to identify landowners and 'evil' 'rich' peasants at mass rallies organized by local cadres.

Quite how many civilians were massacred during the civil war it is impossible to know. Rummel suggests between 1.1 million and 2.3 million but these are unreliable figures based on extrapolations from a handful of recorded cases. Although we cannot know the precise number, clearly the killing was extensive because it drew the public attention of the party leadership. In a speech in 1950, then party vice-chairman Liu Shaoqi admitted that in 1946–47 the land reform programme had produced 'indiscriminate beating and killing'.[91] There is other evidence that the communist leadership was uneasy with the level of indiscriminate violence but their reasoning was more pragmatic than principled. Mao himself criticized the bloodletting: 'we must insist on killing less and must strictly forbid killing without discrimination. To advocate killing more or killing without discrimination is entirely wrong;

[88] This, of course, did not mean that the USA wanted anything other than a nationalist victory. See Sheridan, *China in Disintegration*, p. 280.

[89] Rummel estimates twice as many. Rummel, *China's Bloody Century*, p. 189. It is worth noting, though, that nationalist atrocities predate the Japanese invasion of China. See Sheridan, *China in Distintegration*, p. 274.

[90] Raymond de Jaegher and Irene Corbally Kuhn, *The Enemy Within: An Eyewitness Account of the Communist Conquest of China* (New York: Doubleday, 1952), pp. 293–4.

[91] Cited in Franz Schurmann, *Ideology and Organization in Communist China* (Berkeley: University of California Press, 1966), p. 435.

*this would only cause our Party to forfeit sympathy, become alienated from the masses and fall into isolation*'.[92]

None of this attracted much in the way of international opprobrium. Whilst it took the communists several decades to persuade the rest of the world to accept them as the legitimate government of China, this legitimacy gap was related more to regime type than its use of atrocities. Indeed, contemporary reports in the West tended to compare communist behaviour favourably with the ignoble nationalists and, to this day, to the extent that they are mentioned at all, communist reprisal killings and atrocities associated with the first stages of land reform are not widely discussed in accounts of the civil war. Given the sense of impunity this would have created, it is hardly surprising that, having prevailed in the civil war, the communists repeatedly used mass violence to impose their authority.

The first round of atrocities in communist ruled China were committed under the auspices of land reform, the 1951 'Anti Campaign' aimed at corruption, waste, and bureaucracy within the party, and the 1952 'Five Antis-Campaign' aimed at 'capitalists'. These campaigns were eventually unified into the 'suppression of counter-revolutionaries campaign'.[93] Of these, land reform was the bloodiest. Between 1949 and 1953, between two million and five million people were killed.[94] Mao himself, who we noted earlier sometimes urged restraint and could therefore be expected to downplay it, estimated that 700,000 landlords were killed or 'liquidated'.[95] Teng Tzu-hui, Vice Chairman of the Central South Military and Administrative Council reported that 10 per cent of the peasants were landlords and rich peasants, and that 15 per cent of those were executed.[96]

The land reform campaign, which began during the civil war and was extended to the whole country afterwards, started with the classification of individuals described earlier. The centre advised that around 5 per cent of the membership of any organization should be identified as class enemies ('four types'/'bad elements'). In instructional materials on 'agrarian reform', Mao informed cadres that 'one-tenth of the peasants would have to be destroyed', a

[92] Mao Tse-tung, *Selected Works of Mao Tse-tung* (Beijing: Foreign Languages Press, 1967), vol. 4, pp. 185–6.

[93] Byung-joon Ahn, *Chinese Politics*, p. 14.

[94] Julia C. Strauss, 'Paternalist Terror: The Campaign to Suppress Counterrevolutionaries and Regime Consolidation in the People's Republic of China, 1950–1953', *Comparative Studies in Society and History*, 44 (1) 2002, pp. 87–8; and Dietrich, *People's China*, p. 69.

[95] The precise translation of this quote is contested, 'liquidated' might not have meant 'killed'. See Harold S. Quigley, *China's Politics in Perspective* (Minneapolis: University of Minnesota Press, 1962), p. 142; and Nick Eberstadt, 'Introduction', in Iosif G. Dyadkin (ed.), *Unnatural Deaths in the USSR, 1928–1954*, trans. Tania Deruguine (New Brunswick, NJ: Transaction,1983), p. 11.

[96] Extrapolated to the whole country, this would put the death toll at 7.5 million. See Rummel, *China's Bloody Century*, pp. 222–3.

figure repeated by other senior party members.[97] Landlords in particular were marked out for 'liquidation'.[98] In every village, a 'class struggle' was organized 'conducted as a great moral drama pitting the revolutionary forces of good against the class enemies' forces of evil, almost in the manner of village operas'.[99] A directive instructed the local cadre to, '[a]dopt every possible measure to incite the hatred of the people and excite them into frenzy and hysterical animosity against landlords. The high-ranking cadre responsible for the Land Reform Movement must not hesitate to allow the Land Reform Squads a free hand in executing landlords'.[100] Those identified as class enemies were publicly humiliated, beaten, and tortured until forced to confess their class crimes, which then often justified a further round of persecution. Many were executed, sometimes *en masse*.[101] The communist press reported some of these executions, though probably only a fraction of the total. In Shenyang in 1951, over 400 suspected 'counter-revolutionaries' were brought to a stadium in which 60,000–70,000 people called for their execution. After recounting forced confessions, they were condemned by the crowd and shot. Similar mass gatherings and executions were held in Nanking, Shanghai, and Tietsin. There were several such gatherings in Beijing—at one, 199 people were shot, at another 221 were killed, and at another 237.[102]

There were some (though not many) contemporaneous reports about the killing. In Hong Kong, one commentator noted in 1951 that those coming out of China, 'refer to, though they fail in attempting to describe, this constant haunting fear'.[103] The *New York Times* reported Zhou Enlai's claim that counter-revolutionaries were engaged in sabotage that must be 'firmly prevented and punished' and later reported 'thousands of arrests' as part of a 'reign of terror'.[104] It also reported the establishment of 'people's tribunals' empowered to pass the death sentence on land-owners and counter-

[97] Cited in Rummel, *China's Bloody Century*, p. 223.

[98] Barnett, *Communist China*, pp. 172–3.

[99] Huang, 'Rural Class Struggle', p. 18.

[100] Cited by Ching-wen Chow, *Ten Years of Storm: The True Story of the Communist Regime in China* (New York: Holt, Rinehart and Winston, 1960), p. 104.

[101] Probably between 500,000 and 1 million people were killed in 1951 alone during this campaign. See Dietrich, *People's China*, pp. 71–2, Theodore H. E. Chen, *The Chinese Communist Regime: Documents and Commentary* (New York: Frederick A. Praeger, 1967), pp. 210–15; and Suzanne Labin, *The Anthill: The Human Condition in Communist China* (New York: Praeger, 1960), pp. 51–2.

[102] Rummel, *China's Bloody Century*, pp. 224–5. All of these cases were reported by the Chinese media. Also see Margolin, 'Mao's China', p. 432. Many more were imprisoned in forced labour and other camps, which had high death rates. See Jean-Louis Margolin, 'China: A Long March into the Night', in Courtois et al., *Black Book of Communism*, p. 497 ff.

[103] Cited in Richard L. Walker, *China under Communism: The First Five Years* (New Haven: Yale University Press, 1955), p. 214.

[104] '200,000 Fight Reds in China, says Chou [Zhou]', *New York Times*, 4 October 1950 and 'Mao's China-Wide Purge Claiming Many Victims', *New York Times*, 18 May 1951.

revolutionaries.[105] But in most Western media reports of the land reform and anti-counter-revolutionaries programmes, executions were mentioned only in passing, if at all.[106] Compounded by the West's preoccupation with events in Tibet and Korea, this limited reporting was insufficient to generate a diplomatic response. In 1957, Mao's admission that 700,000 people may have been killed in the 'Red Terror' was widely reported in the West, and US intelligence agencies were quoted as suggesting that this figure was a 'gross understatement' and that not fewer than ten million people had indeed been killed. But even this did not translate into international condemnation or even much public discussion of the killing.[107]

Chinese forces invaded Tibet in 1950 and imposed an autonomy ('Seventeen Points') agreement on the Dalai Lama. Acting without the Dalai Lama's support, in 1956 nomadic Khampas launched a revolt.[108] Things came to a head in 1959 when (false, as it turned out) rumours that the Chinese planned to kidnap the Dalai Lama prompted a full-scale rebellion in Lhasa. After some fierce fighting, the Chinese army suppressed the revolt. The Dalai Lama fled to exile in India and the Chinese conducted a purge.[109] An investigation by the International Commission of Jurists found that 'acts of genocide had been committed in Tibet in an attempt to destroy the Tibetans as a religious group' based on evidence that the Chinese had killed Tibetans who refused to renounce their Buddhist faith, targeted monasteries and religious leaders, and forcibly transferred children.[110] The US Permanent Representative to the UN, Henry Cabot Lodge, lauded the report, maintaining that 'it seems that there is no reason whatsoever for doubting one single fact that the Dalai Lama has stated'—a view broadly supported by the media in the USA.[111] Two

[105] Henry R. Lieberman, 'Chinese Reds Press their Fight on Landlords in Reform Program', *New York Times*, 24 October 1950; and Henry R. Lieberman, 'Peiping's Reform Linked to Unrest', *New York Times*, 29 December 1950.

[106] Executions are also mentioned in Henry R. Lieberman, 'Inside Mao's China: Clues to a Mystery', *New York Times*, 5 April 1953; and 'struggle sessions' by Henry R. Lieberman, 'Peiping is Pushing Land Revolution', *New York Times*, 17 February 1952. Another report noted large scale arrests, but not executions: 'Millions Tried in China', *New York Times*, 15 May 1953.

[107] 'Victims of Chinese Terror Far Exceed Mao's Figure: But Still Peiping Regime is Believed to be Facing Serious Unrest', *New York Times*, 30 June 1957. For a more detailed contemporary report of Mao's speech, see 'Mao Text Shows Reds "Liquidated" 800,000 since "49"', *New York Times*, 13 June 1957.

[108] See Dawa Norbu, *China's Tibet Policy* (London: Curzon, 2001), p. 217. On the revolt's precursors, see pp. 218–21.

[109] For accounts of the uprising, see Tsering Shakya, *The Dragon in the Land of Snows: A History of Modern Tibet since 1947* (New York: Columbia University Press, 1999), pp. 181–222; and A. Tom Grunfeld, *The Making of Modern Tibet*, rev. edn (Armonk, NY: M. E. Sharpe, 1996), pp. 132–46.

[110] International Commission of Jurists, *Tibet*, pp. 13–15.

[111] Cited in Grunfeld, *Making of Modern Tibet*, p. 146. Both the *New York Times* and *Los Angeles Times* endorsed the report, see B. K. Shrivastava, 'American Public Opinion on the Tibetan Question', *International Studies*, 10 (4), 1968, p. 596.

years later, in 1961, the USA used a speech in the UN General Assembly to accuse China of perpetrating the 'systematic eradication' of the Tibetan people and their way of life.[112] Today, the charge of genocide is not widely supported.[113] Far from eradicating Buddhism, the Chinese had cooperated with the Dalai Lama and rescinded Tibet's autonomy only after he fled into exile. Although the communists certainly hoped to persuade the Tibetans to give up Buddhism, there is little evidence that they pursued its systematic destruction.[114] It is also important to stress that the level of state sanctioned killing in Tibet was probably lower than in most other parts of China at the time.[115] Whether genocidal or not, though, there is little doubt that Chinese communists employed mass atrocities to punish communities for their resistance to Chinese rule and to assert Chinese authority.

As ever with Cold War China, precise casualty figures are hard to come by.[116] The Commission of Jurists painstakingly documented atrocities committed by China between 1956 and 1959, which together accounted for approximately 10,374 civilian lives. The Dalai Lama, meanwhile, reported that between 1955 and 1959, 65,000 Tibetans were killed in the Chinese crackdown (presumably including rebel soldiers) and a further 10,000 children deported.[117] Rummel, meanwhile, notes that Radio Lhasa itself reported 87,000 executions in 1959–60 alone.[118] We can say, then, that at least 10,000 and maybe as many as 87,000 people were killed by the communists during and immediately after the 1959 uprising.

Tibet's plight in 1959 received more international attention than China's other Cold War massacres, largely because China's 1950 invasion had itself proven controversial, Tibetan exiles reported atrocities to the outside world, and their cause was taken up by civil society groups in the West.[119] India, the USA, and the UK had expressed grave concern at the 1950 invasion and wanted to persuade the UN to apply pressure. Ultimately, though, none of them were prepared to take the initiative. The British view was especially instructive. Britain favoured a UN General Assembly or Security Council resolution condemning China for invading Tibet but some officials observed

[112] 'US Assails Peiping in the UN on Tibet', *New York Times*, 20 December 1961.

[113] See Bill Brugger, *China: Liberation and Transformation 1942–1962* (London: Croom Helm), pp. 199–200.

[114] See George Ginsburgs and Michael Mathos, *Communist China and Tibet: The First Dozen Years* (The Hague: Martinus Nijhoff, 1964).

[115] The higher figure is taken from Jamyang Norbu, 'The Tibetan Resistance Movement and the Role of the CIA', in Robert Barnett (ed.), *Resistance and Reform in Tibet* (London: Hurst and Co., 1994), p. 189.

[116] These difficulties are noted in Grunfeld, *Making of Modern Tibet*, p. 133.

[117] Hugh E. Richardson, *Tibet and its History*, revised and updated (Boulder: Shambhala, 1984), p. 242.

[118] Rummel, *China's Bloody Century*, p. 240.

[119] See B. K. Shrivastava, 'American Public Opinion on the Tibetan Question', p. 597.

that Tibet's legal status was 'uncertain', that because China was not a member of the UN a resolution calling for the withdrawal of its troops could not be enforced and was therefore unlikely to alter the course of events, and that Tibet was a 'very secondary consideration' compared with Korea.[120] It was also noted that as the Soviet Union supported China's position, it would be impossible to persuade the Security Council to adopt binding measures.[121]

After China's invasion of Tibet, the USA was eager to use Tibet to strengthen its anti-communist propaganda.[122] But it was reluctant to take the lead publicly, fearing that this might create a backlash from India for 'bringing the Cold War to the Himalayas'.[123] Instead, the USA provided clandestine support to the Khampa rebellion—inadvertently furnishing the Chinese with evidence to support their claims that internal unrest was agitated by foreign powers. In 1956, John Foster Dulles declared that communism in China was a 'passing phase' and that Americans would 'do all that we can to contribute to that passing'. The USA stepped up its aid to the nationalists in Taiwan and provided some support to the Khampa rebellion.[124] The material support was negligible however, amounting to a small degree of training, some radio equipment, and a dozen or so air drops of arms.[125]

Both the revolt and crackdown in Tibet were more widely reported in the international media at the time than the earlier episodes of mass killing in China.[126] But reports lacked clarity about the course of events and editorials in the USA at least were more or less united in arguing that there was very little that external actors could do to shape events in Tibet.[127] Where the uprising was reported in the West, the reporting was uniformly critical. Typical was an article in the *Washington Post* which endorsed the International Commission of Jurists' findings and, whilst conceding that bringing the report to the UN would be unlikely to have much effect, observed that an objective presentation of the facts would 'demolish the image of respectability which China seeks to create and thereby serve as some possible restraint'.[128]

Unusually, and probably because of the international attention, China offered some specific justifications for its actions in Tibet. When the Dalai

[120] See Shakya, *The Dragon in the Land of Snows*, pp. 51–63. For a strong rebuttal to the British view, see Charles Henry Alexandrowicz-Alexander, 'The Legal Position of Tibet', *American Journal of International Law*, 48 (2) 1954, pp. 265–74.

[121] Shakya, *The Dragon in the Land of Snows*, p. 57.

[122] Norbu, *China's Tibet Policy*, p. 264.

[123] Shakya, *The Dragon in the Land of Snows*, p. 73.

[124] Shakya, *The Dragon in the Land of Snows*, pp. 170–1. Details are provided in Norbu, *China's Tibet Policy*, pp. 269–70.

[125] See Graham Hutchings, *Modern China: A Guide to a Century of Change* (Cambridge, MA: Harvard University Press, 2001), p. 432.

[126] B. K. Shrivastava, 'American Public Opinion on the Tibetan Question', p. 585.

[127] Shrivastava, 'American Public Opinion', p. 597.

[128] Shrivastava, 'American Public Opinion', p. 597.

Lama first complained about the military suppression, the Chinese responded that Tibet was *de jure* part of China and that the military action was a justified response to an unlawful and violent rebellion by Tibetan reactionaries who were opposed the emancipation of the serfs.[129] Mao argued that the Tibetan ruling class was a historical enemy of the [Tibetan] people and that the rebellion presented an opportunity to 'resolve the problem through war'.[130] General Tan Guansan, Political Commissar of the Tibet Military District, further explained the Chinese position in a letter to the Dalai Lama shortly before the uprising in Lhasa:

> The traitorous activities of the reactionary clique of the upper strata in Tibet have grown into intolerable proportions. . . . The Central People's Government had long adopted an attitude of magnanimity . . . but the Local Government of Tibet has all along adopted an attitude of feigning compliance while actually helping them [the reactionaries] with the result that things have now come to a grave impasse'.[131]

These basic themes were reiterated in the official Chinese version of the Lhasa uprising:

> These traitors have used their legal status . . . to muster reactionary forces among the upper strata, collaborated with the external enemy [referring specifically to Taiwan here] and actually directed some of the most reactionary owners . . . to organise armed rebel forces. . . . Their rebellion was engineered by the imperialists, the Chiang Kai-shek bands [nationalists] and foreign reactionaries. Most of their arms were brought in from abroad.[132]

China therefore argued that foreign—especially Indian and American—criticism of its crackdown was simply an extension of these countries' support for the rebels. It accused its critics of interference in its domestic affairs, which it described as an 'imperialist trick'.[133]

Whilst the communist bloc tended to back China, one notable—though only partial—dissenter was Yugoslavia. The Yugoslav media, relatively free by communist standards, carried reports about the situation in Tibet and argued that the uprising had been caused by China's misunderstanding of Marxist ideology on national identity. Without repudiating these reports, the Yugoslav

129 Norbu, *China's Tibet Policy*, pp. 219 and 222.

130 Communique issued by Mao on 22 January 1959, cited in Chen Jian, 'The Tibetan Rebellion of 1959 and China's Changing Relations with India and the Soviet Union', *Journal of Cold War Studies*, 8 (3), 2006, p. 69.

131 Cited in Grunfeld, *Making of Modern Tibet*, pp. 135–6.

132 Cited in Grunfeld, *Making of Modern Tibet*, p. 138.

133 The 'imperialist trick' quote is from Werner Levi, 'Tibet Under Chinese Communist Rule', *Far Eastern Survey*, 23 (1) 1954, p. 3. On the non-interference argument, see Shakya, *The Dragon in the Land of Snows*, p. 222.

government held the line that Tibet was an internal issue for China.[134] It is also worth noting that although the Soviet Union supported China at the UN, the Tibet incident contributed to the souring of Sino-Soviet relations, with the Soviets expressing concerns about its impact on Indian attitudes towards the communist bloc.[135]

The West's response was delayed by the complex politics surrounding the issue. On 28 March 1959, the State Department expressed its 'profound sympathy with the people of Tibet in the face of barbarous intervention of the Chinese communist imperialists'.[136] A few days later, Australia's external affairs minister Richard Casey called for the issue to be brought before the UN. The USA argued that it was important that an Asian country propose any prospective resolution on Tibet. As in 1950, Britain remained cautious about using the UN and argued against pushing the matter on the grounds that (1) many states, including the UK, acknowledged Chinese suzerainty over Tibet; (2) bringing the matter to the UN would raise the thorny question of Chinese representation at the UN; (3) it would create further political difficulties for India and would therefore not be well received; (4) raising the matter might generate parallels between Tibet and other non-self governing territories and create a unwelcome precedent (the UK was especially worried about Northern Ireland in this regard); (5) China was not likely to comply with any UN resolution.[137] Australia accepted this line of reasoning and dropped the matter. The case against bringing the matter to the UN was also endorsed by the Chinese nationalists. Fearing that the issue could bring the question of Chinese representation at the UN to the fore, the nationalists endorsed the communist view that Tibet was an internal matter.[138] This did not, however, prevent an outpouring of anger and condemnation in Taiwan, where one group of legislators argued that the 'time was ripe for a Nationalist invasion of the mainland'.[139] The UN's apparent ambivalence on Tibet drew criticism from public commentators and the media, especially in the USA. In response, Secretary-General Dag Hammarskjöld told the British that he expected the organization to be seen to be acting on Tibet, but ruled out what he described as 'political' action and carefully limited any potential UN role to the provision of humanitarian relief.[140]

Momentum gradually gathered around the idea that the UN General Assembly should adopt a resolution on Tibet. Nehru's cautious stance, the product of an effort to show concern for Tibet and maintain friendly relations

[134] Shakya, *The Dragon in the Land of Snows*, p. 212.
[135] Chen Jian, 'The Tibetan Rebellion of 1959', p. 55.
[136] Shakya, *The Dragon in the Land of Snows*, p. 213.
[137] Shakya, *The Dragon in the Land of Snows*, p. 221.
[138] Shakya, *The Dragon in the Land of Snows*, p. 221.
[139] 'Nationalists Call to Action', *New York Times*, 2 April 1959.
[140] Shakya, *The Dragon in the Land of Snows*, p. 222.

with China, drew sharp criticism both at home and in the US media, creating pressure for him to take a tougher position.[141] Still eager not to draw Chinese ire, Indian diplomats privately instructed their foreign counterparts that although India could not sponsor a UN resolution on Tibet, it would not oppose a resolution.[142] India also indicated that it was prepared to use diplomatic channels to help the Tibetans, but would not countenance intervention or support independence.[143] The push was supported by the release of the aforementioned International Commission of Jurists report on 5 June.[144] A few months later, the Dalai Lama wrote to Hammarskjöld, pleading 'in view of the inhuman treatment and crimes against humanity and religion to which the people of Tibet are being subjected, I solicit immediate intervention of the United Nations'.[145] Hammarskjöld transmitted the letter and a list of alleged human rights violations to UN member states.

In this context, Ireland and Malaya came forward as co-sponsors of a resolution on Tibet. They argued that 'there exists *prima facie* evidence of an attempt to destroy the traditional way of life of the Tibetan people . . . as well as systematic disregard for . . . human rights and fundamental freedoms'. 'In such circumstances', they continued, 'the UN has both a moral obligation and a legal duty to discuss the situation'.[146] The USA urged the UK and France to support the resolution, but both declined, citing Article 2(7) of the UN Charter, which prohibits interference in the domestic affairs of states and the danger of setting an unwelcome precedent. The USA had more luck gathering support from Latin America. Unsurprisingly, communists supported the Chinese view that Tibet was an internal affair. Other Asian governments adopted a cautious stance and expressed concern that because Tibet was a 'Cold War issue', the adoption of a resolution might hinder progress towards peace.[147]

When the draft resolution was debated, the Soviet Union vociferously rejected allegations of human rights abuse in Tibet, arguing that if anything had indeed happened there it was only the suppression of reactionaries who had attempted to prevent the emancipation of oppressed serfs.[148] The Soviet Union and Albania alleged that the Tibetan elite were guilty of 'inhuman tortures' and exploiting the serfs, and that China was simply attempting to halt

[141] Mahendra Kumar, 'Sino-Indian Relations 1950–1959', *International Studies*, 1963, 5 (1–2); Chen Jian, 'The Tibetan Rebellion', p. 85; and Shrivastava, 'American Public Opinion', p. 586.
[142] Shakya, *The Dragon in the Land of Snows*, p. 226.
[143] 'Nehru Explores Way to Aid Tibet', *New York Times*, 1 April 1959.
[144] Shakya, *The Dragon in the Land of Snows*, p. 223.
[145] Shakya, *The Dragon in the Land of Snows*, p. 226.
[146] Shakya, *The Dragon in the Land of Snows*, p. 228.
[147] McCandlish Phillips, 'Push Due in UN for Tibet Debate', *New York Times*, 28 September 1959.
[148] See Richardson, *Tibet and its History*, p. 219.

these abuses.[149] Playing on Asian concerns, the Soviets argued that the draft resolution was a 'clumsy manoeuvre designed to bring the United Nations back into the dark period of the Cold War' and criticized Malaya and Ireland as 'tools' of the West.[150] Cabot Lodge dismissed these allegations, arguing that the Tibetan case 'obviously' fell under the purview of the UN. Asian opinion was divided—Nepal worried that a resolution would 'imperil' friendly relations in the region, but Pakistan backed the resolution, as did Indonesia which argued that 'China is working overtime to alienate those who have championed her over the years. It was an evil day when China felt the need to use force in Tibet. Now Peking must do some serious thinking if she does not want uncommitted Asia to range itself with the anti-Communist nations against her'.[151] The West was also divided. Several governments—including Finland, Belgium (sensitive about its position in the Congo), and France (sensitive about its position in Algeria)—argued that although they were deeply troubled by the human rights situation in Tibet, Article 2(7) took precedence and prohibited the UN from taking a stance on this issue. One of the resolution's keenest supporters, New Zealand, criticized these positions as self-interested, maintaining that it would be 'an abdication of responsibility' for the General Assembly to not take action on Tibet because of 'illusory arguments of expediency'.[152] In the end, the resolution was passed with 45 in favour, 9 against and 25 abstentions.[153] Given the various political sensitivities, the vote represented a reasonably clear statement that international society considered that China had violated important norms in Tibet. But those political sensitivities meant that the resolution stopped short of demanding that China engage in a political process or withdraw its troops and there was no question of the matter being referred to the Security Council for enforcement. As was widely anticipated, this resolution—and two subsequent resolutions in 1960 and 1961—imposed no additional costs on the Chinese and had no discernible impact on their behaviour. The Tibetans tried to push the issue further, calling on the General Assembly to appoint a mediator and endorse Tibet's right to self-determination. Although this won sufficient support to secure resolutions in the General Assembly, Indian, British, French, and communist opposition prevented their implementation.[154]

149 Richardson, *Tibet and its History*, p. 219. Soviet support for China did begin to cool in 1959, see Grunfeld, *Making of Modern Tibet*, p. 145.

150 Lindesay Parrott, 'Full Tibet Airing is Urged by Lodge', *New York Times*, 21 October 1959.

151 Lindesay Parrott, 'Full Tibet Airing is Urged by Lodge', *New York Times*, 21 October 1959. Indonesia quote cited in Tillman Durdin, 'Asia Deeply Stirred by Tibet Repression', *New York Times*, 19 April 1959.

152 Shakya, *The Dragon in the Land of Snows*, p. 230.

153 Lindesay Parrott, 'UN Vote Assails Tibet Repression', *New York Times*, 22 October 1959.

154 Shakya, *The Dragon in the Land of Snows*, pp. 231–5.

The rebellion and crackdown in Tibet occurred concurrently with the beginning of the Great Leap Forward—a disastrous attempt to propel the Chinese economy through mass collectivization and industrialization.[155] The government abolished all forms of private food production, forced peasants into communes, over-supplied cities and party cadre with food, and exported food in the face of domestic shortages.[156] Peasants were forced to eat communally and household goods including kitchen utensils were appropriated.[157] The process was driven forward by relentless violence, much of it targeting the 'four types' groups and those opposed to communalization. Using local government records and Chinese media reports, Frank Dikotter estimates that as many as half of all cadre regularly employed violence. 4,000 of 16,000 villagers forced to work on the Huangcai reservoir project in 1959–60 were kicked and beaten; 400 died as a result.[158] A detailed study of Xinyang in Henan revealed that 67,000 people were beaten to death in 1960 alone.[159] In Luoding commune, half the cadre beat the villagers and 100 died. A committee reported to Zhou Enlai that in Hunan province, not thought to be one of the most violent, people were beaten to death in eighty-two of the eighty-six counties and cities.[160] They found that at least 6 per cent and in some counties as much as 17 per cent of the total fatalities were caused by beatings and other abuses.

A Hong Kong Study Commission estimated that in total 15.7 million people were executed during the 'Great Leap Forward' and Walter Robertson (former US Assistant Secretary of State for Far Eastern Affairs) put the figure at 18 million.[161] Dikotter's research suggests that at least 2.5 million people were summarily killed or tortured to death during the Great Leap Forward.[162] Available witness testimony confirms that people were routinely killed for such misdemeanours as accurately reporting production figures when they should have been inflated.[163] In 1959, *Honan Peasant's Daily*, a provincial

[155] O. Edmund Clubb, *20th Century China*, 3rd edn (New York: Columbia University Press, 1978), p. 355; and Frederick C. Teiwes with Warren Sun, *China's Road to Disaster: Mao, Central Politicians, and Provincial Leaders in the Unfolding of the Great Leap Forward 1955–1959* (Armonk, NY: M. E. Sharpe, 1999).

[156] Vaclav Small, 'China's Great Famine: Forty Years On', *British Medical Journal*, 18–25 December 1999, p. 1619.

[157] Paul J. Bailey, *China in the Twentieth Century* (Oxford: Wiley-Blackwell, 2001), p. 172.

[158] Dikotter, *Mao's Great Famine*, p. 294.

[159] Dikotter, *Mao's Great Famine*, p. 294.

[160] Dikotter, *Mao's Great Famine*, p. 295.

[161] Jonathan Fenby, *The Penguin History of Modern China: The Fall and Rise of a Great Power 1850–2009* (London: Penguin, 2008) pp. 396–439. The other estimates are cited in Rummel, *China's Bloody Century*, p. 243.

[162] Dikotter, *Mao's Great Famine*, p. xi.

[163] Jung Chang, *Wild Swans: Three Daughters of China* (London: Flamingo, 1992), p. 297.

newspaper, reported that around 50,000 people in three regions had died of exhaustion.[164]

Whilst diplomats agonized over how to respond to the situation in Tibet, international society remained largely indifferent to the destruction caused by the Great Leap Forward. Eyewitness reports from the few refugees who managed to flee into Hong Kong were often dismissed and seldom reported.[165] Still not widely acknowledged, let alone recounted and explained, the terror that produced the Great Leap attracted almost no international criticism—though the Soviet premier, Nikita Khrushchev, criticized China's communes.[166]

The Great Leap Forward sowed the seeds for the next Maoist cataclysm: the Cultural Revolution. Judged the architect of the Great Leap failure, Mao was forced to relinquish some of his power, with Liu Shaoqi replacing him as President of the Republic. The Party's retreat from Great Leap policies sowed in Mao's mind a belief that he was being sidelined by conservatives (or 'capitalist roaders' as Mao described them) and that only a massive and radical about-turn would revive the country's revolutionary fortunes.[167] The official line that emerged during the Cultural Revolution attributed the failings of the Great Leap to the 'rightist deviations' of Liu Shaoqi and his supporters.[168] Liu Shaoqi was humiliated, tortured, beaten, and imprisoned, and died in prison a broken man in 1969.

The Cultural Revolution was launched in 1966 and endured for a decade, though most of the killing took place between 1966 and 1968. To regain his status and renew the revolution, Mao launched an attack on the state and party themselves, calling on Chinese youths to overthrow established institutions and 'purify' them of rightist tendencies. Driven to acquiesce by Mao, the Central Committee insisted that 'our objective is to struggle against and crush those persons in authority who are taking the capitalist road, to criticize and repudiate the reactionary bourgeois academic "authorities" and the ideology of the bourgeoisie and all other exploiting classes'.[169]

Some eleven million youths organized themselves into 'Red Guards' militia. They ransacked homes and public buildings, burnt books, and destroyed historical artefacts deemed bourgeois. So-called 'rightists' were publicly

[164] Rummel, *China's Bloody Century*, p. 247.

[165] Indeed, to this day there remains only one significant book-length account of the famine, based largely on testimonies from the Hong Kong refugees, J. Becker, *Hungry Ghosts* (New York: Free Press, 1996).

[166] Bailey, *China in the Twentieth Century*, p. 174.

[167] Bailey, *China in the Twentieth Century*, p. 166.

[168] William A. Joseph, 'A Tragedy of Good Intentions: Post-Mao Views of the Great Leap Forward', *Modern China*, 12 (4) 1986, p. 441.

[169] Central Committee, Program for the Cultural Revolution, cited by Clubb, *20th Century China*, p. 406.

humiliated, beaten, and tortured, and often killed.[170] Mao urged the Red Guards on, telling them to 'dare to be violent', that 'to rebel is good' and instructing them to 'sweep away monsters and demons'.[171] Mao directed them to root out and eliminate the 'four olds': old ideas, habits, customs, and culture, giving the young rebels a very wide mandate for violence.[172] Inciting violence, the *People's Daily* repeated the exhortation to 'sweep away all monsters and demons'. It offered favourable reports of the violence, such as this editorial from 1 June 1966: 'the Great Proletarian Cultural Revolution is advancing with great rapidity and intensity. One group of monsters and demons after another has been exposed, and one reactionary bastion after another has been shattered . . . '.[173] Maoists provided some Red Guards groups with militia training and weapons.[174]

Estimates of the total number of people who died unnatural deaths as a result of the Cultural Revolution vary considerably. After Mao's death, the 'Gang of Four' allies of Mao who were behind the cataclysm were prosecuted for their crimes. During their trial, prosecutors alleged that up to 35,000 people had been 'persecuted to death'.[175] This seems a gross underestimate. The Party's Central Committee allegedly estimated 400,000 casualties between 1966 and 1969 alone; in 1980 the Governor of Kwangtung estimated that 400,000 people had been killed in his province alone; Mao's successor, Deng Xiaoping suggested that a million people had been killed by mob violence; and foreign minister Chen Yi claimed that 400,000 party cadres were 'liquidated' in 1966.[176] From this, it seems fair to estimate that the total number of casualties was between 1 million and 2 million people.[177] Although much of this violence targeted the party itself, the large majority of people who were killed were members of the 'four types' groups. Thus, whilst the Cultural Revolution was portrayed to China and the world as a largely communist affair, most of its victims were not party members. They were members of groups targeted in the past by the communists.[178]

170 Hutchings, *Modern China*, pp. 90–1.

171 Cited by Lu Xiuyuan, 'A Step Towards Understanding Popular Violence', p. 534.

172 Clubb, *20th Century China*, pp. 408–9.

173 Cited in Dietrich, *People's China*, p. 183. Other officials joined in with the incitement of violence, see Donald S. Sutton, 'Consuming Counterrevolution: The Ritual and Culture of Cannibalism in Wuxuan, Guangxi, China, May to July 1968', *Comparative Studies in Society and History*, 37 (1) 995, p. 139.

174 Esmein, *Chinese Cultural Revolution*, p. 98. As Anne Thurston concludes, by inciting the violence the regime created the context which enabled it. See Anne F. Thurston, 'Urban Violence During the Cultural Revolution: Who is to Blame?', in Jonathan N. Lipman and Stevan Harrell (eds), *Violence in China: Essays in Culture and Counterculture* (New York: State University of New York Press, 1990), pp. 149–71.

175 See Joseph, 'A Tragedy of Good Intentions', p. 420.

176 All cited in Rummel, *China's Bloody Century*, p. 262.

177 A higher estimate is offered by Rummel, *China's Bloody Century*, p. 255.

178 Huang, 'Rural Class Struggle', p. 131; and Margolin, 'Mao's China', p. 454.

There were three main stages of violence during the Cultural Revolution. During the first, sometimes labelled the period of 'red terror', Red Guards and other factions employed mob violence against selected individuals and groups. The violence began with forty-four days of terror in Beijing in which Red Guards, aided and abetted by the Minister of Public Security, searched 33,600 homes, displaced 85,000 people and beat 1,700 people to death.[179] The Guards then dispersed into the countryside at the urging of a *People's Daily* editorial which called on them to seize power from below.[180] During the second stage, local party elites, their children, and workers in several regions mobilized their own factions to combat the Red Guards, provoking pitched battles that claimed thousands of lives. There were violent rebellions in twenty-one provinces during this period.[181] The most serious was in Wuhan where workers established a coalition called the 'One Million Heroic Troops' which closed down factories and attacked Red Guards and other radical factions. The army was eventually called in to restore order.[182] The Wuhan incident shook Mao's faith in the Red Guards movement and in September 1967, Mao—having reasserted his authority over the party—changed course. He criticized the Red Guards, instructed the army to restore order, and called for the establishment of 'Revolutionary Committees'.[183] The Red Guards militia were dismantled and members either persecuted or forced to become agricultural labourers.[184] Although this brought the worst of the mob violence to an end, it ushered in a new wave of killing. This third stage, much less reported but more central to our purposes, involved mass executions organized by state officials. In many regions, local authorities—now organized into Revolutionary Committees—attempted to seal their legitimacy and head off potential opposition by encouraging and sometimes perpetrating the mass killing of 'enemies'.[185] A conservative estimate based on the government's own reports of these incidents suggests that at least 250,000 people were killed in mass executions in 1967–68 alone, and this figure is likely to be an underestimate.

Although the general violence associated with the Cultural Revolution was reported to a greater extent than that of previous cases with the exception of Tibet, these mass executions were not widely reported outside China.[186] What we do know is largely the product of path-breaking research by Yang Su.[187]

[179] Rummel, *China's Bloody Century*, p. 258.
[180] Clubb, *20th Century China*, p. 409.
[181] Rummel, *China's Bloody Century*, p. 260.
[182] Dietrich, *People's China*, pp. 193–4.
[183] Dietrich, *People's China*, p. 195.
[184] Leys, *The Chairman's New Clothes*, p. 13. Also see Dietrich, *People's China*, p. 199.
[185] On the Revolutionary Committees, see Esmein, *Chinese Cultural Revolution*, chs 7 and 8.
[186] Margolin, 'China: A Long March', pp. 513–15.
[187] Yang Su, 'Mass Killing in the Cultural Revolution: A Study of Three Provinces', in Joseph W. Easherwick, Paul G. Pickowicz, and Andrew G. Walder (eds), *The Chinese Cultural*

Based on official county gazettes from three provinces (Guangxi, Guangdong, and Hubei), Yang Su shows that mass killings were relatively common between late 1967 and 1969—the period in which radical organizations were suppressed and Revolutionary Committees established. He identifies three basic types of mass killing. The first targeted members of the 'four types'. To give one example, here is a record from Quanzhou county, Guangxi, cited by Yang Su:

> October 3 [1967]. In Sanjiang Brigade, Dongshan Commune, the militia commander Huang Tianhui led [the brigade militia] to engage in a massacre. They pushed off a cliff and killed seventy-six individuals of the brigade—former landlords, rich peasants and their children—in snake-shaped Huanggu'an canyon.... From July to October, [another] 850 individuals [in the county]—the four type elements (landlords, rich peasants, counterrevolutionaries, and bad elements) and their children—were executed with firearms.[188]

By 1971, the county gazette had reported some 2,156 similar 'unnatural deaths'. The second type of mass killings were the result of 'political witch-hunts'. Unlike the first type, which ostensibly targeted well-established enemy groups, the second type focused on groups thought guilty of more recent political crimes associated with the first stages of the Cultural Revolution. Once again, however, the largest single group of victims were people identified as 'four types'. To quote another gazette:

> In the name of 'cleansing the class ranks' and 'mass dictatorship', indiscriminate killings took place across the county. Between mid-June and August [1968], 1,991 people were killed as members of 'Assassination Squads', 'Anti-Communist Army of Patriots', and other 'black groups'. Among them were 326 cadre, 79 workers, 53 students, 68 ordinary urban residents, 547 peasants, and 918 four-type elements and their children. Among the 161 [of the county], only Wenquan in Huixian and Dongjiang in Wantian did not indiscriminately detain and kill.

The third type of mass killing was the summary execution of captives. Yang Su finds that most of the killing was concentrated into a period of a few months and mostly occurred outside major towns—in regions where state control was weakest, confirming his assessment that the killing was associated with the formation of Revolutionary Committees and their efforts to secure legitimacy and assert authority. None of the three types of killing was spontaneous. It was almost always organized by government authorities, usually militia leaders.

*Revolution as History* (Stanford: Stanford University Press, 2006); and Yang Su, *Collective Killings in Rural China.*

[188] Cited in Yang Su, 'Mass Killings in the Cultural Revolution: A Study of Three Provinces', in Joseph W. Easherwick, Paul G. Pickowicz, and Andrew G. Walder (eds), *The Chinese Cultural Revolution as History* (Stanford: Stanford University Press, 2006), p. 99.

Outside China, the Cultural Revolution was received with a mixture of confusion and apprehension. Generally, only Red Guards atrocities were reported.[189] The systematic mass executions detailed above went largely unnoticed outside China. Significantly, when witness testimony pointed towards the commission of large scale atrocities, such reports tended to be dismissed as unreliable. Thus, analysts in Washington, DC, were reported as saying they have 'no evidence of large scale killings in the current political upheaval in China'.[190] Whilst accepting that the Red Guards had caused deaths, they estimated the total number as being in the 'hundreds' and 'certainly not more than one thousand'.[191] Governments and commentators were by and large more concerned about China's intransigent foreign policy than by its domestic tumult and at the time there was little in the way of direct protest about the killings.[192] China's intransigence only deepened its international isolation—a problem not helped by the recalling of Chinese diplomats and cessation of international flights—further shielding it from international reporting.[193] Although it is difficult to measure the impact this had on communist China's international standing, the number of states voting against the communists taking China's UN seat increased from nationalists increased from forty-seven in 1965 to fifty-seven in 1966.[194] Two notable exceptions to the general silence were Hong Kong and the Soviet Union. In Hong Kong, nationalist agitation and refugee reports prompted an outpouring of anger against the communists, manifested in a wave of anti-communist strikes, riots, and bombings.[195] The Soviet Union was highly critical of the Red Guards on ideological grounds, though it did not specifically criticize the killings.[196]

After Mao's death, the Chinese Communist Party quickly moved to repudiate the Cultural Revolution and back away from selective extermination for reasons very similar to those underpinning the Soviet Union's shift a few decades earlier: many members of the new leadership had suffered personally during the Cultural Revolution and wanted to put leadership on a surer footing; many in the party recognized that bouts of massive instability threatened the country's cohesiveness; and there was some acknowledgement

[189] E.g. 'Pravda Pours Scorn on Red Guards', *The Times*, 17 September 1966.

[190] 'China's Red Guard Drive Reported Costly in Lives', *New York Times*, 25 September 1966.

[191] 'US Analysts Sceptical', *New York Times*, 24 September 1966.

[192] Andrew G. Walder, 'Cultural Revolution Radicalism: Variations on a Stalinist Theme', in William A. Joseph, Christine P. W. Wong, and David Zweig (eds), *New Perspectives on the Cultural Revolution* (Cambridge, MA: Harvard University Press, 1991), p. 42.

[193] Bailey, *China in the Twentieth Century*, p. 183; and Rosemary Foot, *Rights Beyond Borders: The Global Community and the Struggle Over Human Rights in China* (Oxford: Oxford University Press, 2000), p. 60.

[194] Foot, *Rights Beyond Borders*, p. 60.

[195] Rafe De Crespigny, *China this Century* (Melbourne: Oxford University Press, 1992), p. 259.

[196] 'Pravda Pours Scorn on Red Guards', *The Times*, 17 September 1966.

that massive repression inhibited economic development. As I noted earlier, the 'Gang of Four' were prosecuted and the party's official line declared that the Cultural Revolution was 'responsible for the most severe setback and the heaviest losses suffered by the Party, the state and the people since the founding of the People's Republic'.[197] As in the Soviet Union, communist China's shift away from selective extermination had relatively little to do with either civilian immunity or external pressure and—as I will demonstrate in the final section—did not amount to the internalization of civilian immunity.

In summary, the Maoist regime unleashed repeated waves of mass killing, against those it loosely defined as class enemies. Basing their approach on Stalinist precepts, Mao and his allies argued that by conspiring against the people, 'class enemies' were the enemies of the people and therefore outside the protection of the state. Identifying and eliminating these enemies—collectively labelled, among other things, 'four types', 'bad elements', or 'monsters and demons'—was portrayed as a virtue, though the party occasionally tried to limit the extent of the violence. Throughout the period, China had relatively little trouble in securing sufficient legitimacy. Given the scale and repetitiveness of the killing, there was surprisingly little criticism by international society and virtually no discussion of punishment. Tibet was the exception in this regard because international disquiet with China's invasion of the province in 1950 and the dissemination of information by exiled Tibetans provoked a storm of protest and an accusation of genocide in response to the crackdown in 1959. Even in this case, though, whilst there was sharp criticism there was little serious discussion of punishment. In part this was because the regime was protected by communist solidarity but other contextual factors played a part as well. In particular, the UK and France worried about setting a dangerous precedent, India worried about its long-term relations with China, and—whilst certainly pushing for tough criticism of China—the USA was more interested in other matters.

In relation to the other, much bloodier, cases there was virtually no international response. The West's relative silence on the question of Chinese massacres seems hard to explain at first. Certainly, the slience between 1971 and 1989 could be explained by reference to the strategic partnership between China and the USA established in 1972, which was prefaced on a common interest in containing the Soviet Union. This partnership certainly helped shield China from scrutiny and created expectations among some in the West that—left to its own devices—it would gradually reform and abandon communism.[198] But this

[197] Party line declared in 1981. Cited by Dietrich, *People's China*, p. 202.

[198] Andrew Nathan, for instance, points to the widely held view that the US practised 'double standards' when it came to the issue of human rights in China, applying different—and more lenient—moral criteria. See Andrew J. Nathan, *China's Crisis: Dilemmas of Reform and Prospects for Democracy* (New York: Columbia University Press, 1990), p. 82. The role of the strategic partnership in shielding China from human rights criticism is also emphasized by Foot, *Rights*

cannot explain Western responses to the cases of mass killing examined here, because they occurred prior to the 1972 rapprochement. Prior to 1972, the West had every reason to find grounds for condemning Chinese communism. Indeed, the USA had direct confrontations with China over Taiwan in 1954 and 1958.[199] Nor can we simply say that human rights in China were a 'non-issue' in China's relations with the world because in relation to Tibet it was very much an issue.[200] These problems point us to some of the other contextual factors, in particular the facts that the mass killing went largely unreported in the West, that Western governments believed there were no plausible alternatives to the communists and that they had little leverage, and that Chinese domestic affairs were a relatively low policy priority especially when contrasted with international problems such as Korea and Indochina where China had the potential to cause major trouble.[201] In the case of Tibet, where the first of these factors was not present, the absence of plausible leverage mechanisms and the relative priority given to other situations (especially decolonization and Korea) limited the scope of criticism and potential for punishment. The partial opening up of China in the 1980s and especially its opening to foreign news media, the emergence of pro-democracy groups with high international (or, at least, Western) legitimacy, and the decline of countervailing policy concerns as a result of the completion of decolonization and reduction of Cold War tensions stand out as the most important factors dictating the world's very different responses to the comparatively small Beijing massacre in 1989, as I will demonstrate below.

## CAMBODIA (1975–1979)

The Khmer Rouge, which governed Cambodia from 1975 to early 1979, attempted to radically transform Cambodian society, but in the end managed only to destroy it.[202] They emptied the cities, abolished money, markets, and private property down to the level of cooking utensils and clothes, collectivized

*Beyond Borders*, p. 84; and James D. Seymour, 'Human Rights in Chinese Foreign Relations', in Samuel S. Kim (ed.), *China and the World: Chinese Foreign Policy Faces the New Millennium* (Boulder: Westview Press, 1998), p. 220.

[199] Judith F. Kornberg and John R. Faust, *China in World Politics: Policies, Processes, Prospects* (Vancouver: University of British Columbia Press, 2005), pp. 132–3; and Steven I. Levine, 'Sino-American Relations: Practicing Damage Control', in Kim (ed.), *China and the World*, p. 94.

[200] A claim advanced by Ming Wan, *Human Rights in China's Foreign Relations: Defining and Defending National Interests* (Philadelphia: University of Pennsylvania Press, 2001).

[201] See Levine, 'Sino-American Relations', p. 93.

[202] Kurt Jonassohn with Karin Solveig Bjornson, *Genocide and Gross Human Rights Violations in Comparative Perspective* (New Brunswick: Transaction, 1999), p. 60.

agriculture, closed monasteries and destroyed Buddhism, eradicated the free press, cleared hospitals, abolished schools, and burned books. Families were displaced and separated. People were forced to eat in communal mess halls. Human communication almost disappeared.[203] The overall death toll will never be known, but approximately 1.5 million people were shot, hacked, beaten, drowned, tortured, starved, and worked to death.[204] The Khmer Rouge dubbed its victims 'subpeople' or 'microbes' who had to be purged for the good of the people.[205] The communist world supported the regime, until its solidarity was split by Vietnam's intervention. Whilst the West condemned Khmer Rouge atrocities, some governments calculated that the Cambodian communist offered a bulwark against Vietnamese (and hence Soviet) influence in Indochina, restraining international activism against it. This contextual factor was assisted by Cambodia's geographic remoteness, isolation from the world, and leftist sympathy towards the Khmer Rouge propelled by opposition to US bombing (see Chapter 5). Combined, they meant that Western governments were not seriously challenged to take a moral stand against the Khmer Rouge's atrocities. As such, the USA publicly criticized the Khmer Rouge whilst privately signalling its preparedness to cooperate with it. Others, such as Canada, the UK, France, and Norway criticized the killing but limited their activism to presenting documents to the UN Human Rights Commission in 1978. For its part, ASEAN recognized the Khmer Rouge regime. After Vietnamese intervention drove the Khmer Rouge from power, strategic interests again overrode fidelity to civilian immunity. Vietnam, not the Khmer Rouge, was condemned and punished with sanctions. The USA, the UK, Thailand, and some others even provided clandestine military aid to the Khmer Rouge—perpetrators of one of the twentieth century's bloodiest genocides—on the grounds that they were waging a guerrilla war against Soviet-backed Vietnam.[206]

[203] Ben Kiernan, *The Pol Pot Regime: Race, Power, and Genocide in Cambodia under the Khmer Rouge, 1975–79* (New Haven: Yale University Press, 1996), pp. 8–9; and Hurst Hannum, 'International Law and Cambodian Genocide: The Sounds of Silence', *Human Rights Quarterly*, 11 (1) 1989, p. 85.

[204] The estimate of 1.5 million is from Kiernan. Most writers put the toll anywhere between 1 million and 3 million, so 1.5 million is probably a conservative estimate. For a survey, see Ben Kiernan, 'The Demography of Genocide in Southeast Asia: The Death Tolls in Cambodia, 1975–79, and East Timor, 1975–80', *Critical Asian Studies*, 35 (4) 2003, pp. 585–97. R. J. Rummel, for example, puts the figure at 2.4 million. See R. J. Rummel, *Death by Government* (New Brunswick: Transaction Publishers, 1994), p. 160.

[205] Chalk and Jonassohn, *The History and Sociology of Genocide*, p. 405.

[206] See Nicholas J. Wheeler, *Saving Strangers: Humanitarian Intervention in International Society* (Oxford: Oxford University Press, 2000), pp. 78–110. I share Kiernan's view that the Khmer Rouge committed genocide, especially in their destruction of Buddhism, the Muslim Cham, ethnic Chinese and—most especially—in their almost complete annihilation of the ethnic Vietnamese who remained in Cambodia. Cf. Hurst Hannum, 'International Law and Cambodian Genocide, pp. 82–138; and (opposing this view) Alain Destexhe, *Rwanda and Genocide in the Twentieth Century* (New York: New York University Press 1999), pp. 18–19.

The roots of the Cambodian genocide are found in the Indochina described in the previous chapter, and need not detain us much here.[207] After its defeat at Dien Bien Phu in 1954, France withdrew from Indochina and colonial rule in Cambodia was replaced by autocratic royal rule under Prince Norodom Sihanouk. But colonial rule had already inspired the creation of a pro-independence militia ('Issarak'), which by 1954 numbered around 5,000 and counted the Vietnamese communists among their allies.[208] The new government responded with purges which only fuelled further resistance. This in turn drew more government abuses, including atrocities against civilians. Militia were routinely tortured and summarily executed and there were several documented massacres of civilians.[209] But by itself, this relatively small resistance movement could never have mustered the support needed to displace the government.[210] Two factors helped change this: the overthrow of Sihanouk by Lon Nol and the destruction of the Cambodian countryside by US bombardment. Together, these factors shattered Cambodian society and boosted support for the communists. Having fatally weakened the government, in 1973 the USA ceased its military operations in Cambodia. Government forces—hollowed out by years of corruption and confronting a large, angry, battle-hardened (though rather disparate) enemy—collapsed. Phnom Penh fell to the communists in April 1975.

What came next was something of a surprise even to those that had been paying attention to the Khmer Rouge's brutal tactics. As a result of its fractious history involving alliances with Issaraks, Sihanoukists, Vietnamese, and other anti-government forces, there were significant regional differences in communist thinking. The mass displacement, torture, killing, and other abuse, though, was dictated from the party centre, run by Pol Pot, Ieng Sary, and Kheiu Samphan and one of its principal aims was the imposition of the party centre's authority.[211] The pattern of killing was complex and regionally differentiated, but for our purposes we can distinguish three main phases and an additional component—the elimination of national and religious minorities.[212]

The first phase saw the evacuation of towns and cities.[213] This was also the most widely reported element of the campaign because a number of Western

[207] See Ben Kiernan, *How Pol Pot Came to Power: Colonialism, Nationalism and Communism in Cambodia, 1930–1975*, 2nd edn (New Haven: Yale University Press, 2004).

[208] Kiernan, *Pol Pot Regime*, pp. 11–13.

[209] Rummel, *Death by Government*, p. 164.

[210] Serge Thion, *Watching Cambodia: Ten Paths to Enter the Cambodian Tangle* (Bangkok: White Lotus, 1993), p. 215.

[211] Michael Vickery, *Cambodia 1975–1982* (Sydney: Allen and Unwin, 1984), p. 85.

[212] Hannum, 'International Law', p. 90, though I have added the fourth element: the destruction of national and religious minorities.

[213] Kimmo Kiljunen (ed.), *Kampuchea: Decade of the Genocide: A Finnish Inquiry* (London: Zed, 1984), p. 10.

journalists were in Phnom Penh when the city fell and witnessed the events. Within hours of taking the city, communist soldiers began ordering people to leave. Amidst the chaos, there was little advice as to where city residents should go and little time for them to collect their belongings.[214] No one (except Western journalists holed up in the French embassy) was spared—even hospitals were emptied. Many of those who refused to go or were too ill to walk were killed. As the cities were evacuated, the communists identified former Lon Nol soldiers, government employees, teachers, journalists, and members of religious groups or ethnic minorities and thousands were executed immediately.[215] Over 10,000 others are likely to have perished on the trek.[216] At the time, the Khmer Rouge told evacuees that the deportations were temporary and meant to protect them from American airstrikes; to international society, they argued that the evacuation was humanitarian and aimed at directing the population to where food was in order to prevent urban famine caused by the cessation of US food aid.[217] The reality was that the evacuation of the cities was intended to destroy the urban classes for both ideological and more mundane self-interested reasons. Ideologically, the cities were viewed as unproductive centres of foreign influence and corruption. Evacuations allowed the 'cleansing' of non-Khmers and foreign influences.[218] They also made urban areas easier to control and eliminated an important potential source of opposition.[219] In the minds of the party centre, the evacuation also created a large population of Khmers that could be resettled in traditional Khmer territory (Khmer Krom) in South Vietnam once the regime there had collapsed and the land been seized by the Khmer Rouge.[220]

Once the evacuation was completed, the level of killing subsided temporarily.[221] The Khmer Rouge divided the population into two groups: 'base people' were peasants who lived in areas controlled by the Khmer Rouge prior to 1975;

[214] See Ben Kiernan, 'The Cambodian Genocide: Issues and Responses', in George J. Andreopoulos (ed.), *Genocide: Conceptual and Historical Dimensions* (Philadelphia: University of Pennsylvania Press, 1997), pp. 194–6.

[215] None of Cambodia's university professors or lecturers who remained in the country in 1975 survived. Ben Kiernan, 'Coming to Terms with the Past: Cambodia', *History Today*, September 2004, p. 17.

[216] Kiernan, *Pol Pot Regime*, p. 48.

[217] See Chalk and Jonassohn, *The History and Sociology of Genocide*, p. 403. It was repeated by some Western analysts. See G. C. Hildebrand and G. Porter, *Cambodia: Starvation and Revolution* (New York: Monthly Review Press, 1976).

[218] Chalk and Jonassohn, *History and Sociology of Genocide*, p. 404.

[219] Kiernan, *Pol Pot Regime*, pp. 63–4.

[220] Kiernan, *Pol Pot Regime*, pp. 63–4.

[221] See David P. Chandler, 'Introduction and Translation of "Report of Activities of the Party Center According to the General Political Tasks of 1976"', in David P. Chandler, Ben Kiernan, and Chanthou Boua (eds), *Pol Pot Plans the Future: Confidential Leadership Documents from Democratic Kampuchea, 1976–1977* (New Haven: Yale University Southeast Asia Studies, 1988), pp. 177–8.

'new people'—so-called because of their recent arrival to the revolution, were former city and town dwellers.[222] Generally speaking, 'new people', considered the lowest group in the new social system, were given less food, harder labour, treated with suspicion, and subjected to higher levels of arbitrary violence.[223] Some of the highest death rates were among 'new people' sent into undeveloped forested regions in the northwest to clear and plant the land and build irrigation systems. Forced to work long hours in harsh conditions and dependent entirely on rice supplied by other regions, malnutrition, disease, and illness exacted an exceptionally heavy toll.[224] 'Base people' did not escape the regime's brutality, however. In different parts of the country, but especially in the north which was considered a Lon Nol bastion, the Khmer Rouge purged populations of people thought to be enemies, often only by association.[225] Thousands of 'base people' and party cadre, including children, suspected of harbouring oppositionist tendencies were despatched to the notorious Tuol Sleng (S-21) prison, where confessions were extracted under torture and carefully documented before the victims were executed.[226] Others were tortured and killed elsewhere.[227]

The new regime enforced its ban on religion vigorously. The Khmer Rouge determined that Buddhism was a repressive influence, so temples and pagodas were destroyed and monks who refused to disrobe, disobeyed orders, or exhibited Buddhist tendencies, were executed. Before 1975 there were around 60,000 monks in Cambodia. In late 1979 barely 1,000 remained. In three and a half years, the Khmer Rouge had completely destroyed Buddhism as an organized religion and had killed almost all of its leading practitioners.[228]

The purges came to a bloody crescendo in the regime's third and final phase. Convinced that cadre in the eastern zone, known for their close links with Vietnam, were plotting against the regime, the party centre stepped up its repression, despatching thousands of suspect party members and their families to Tuol Sleng. Predictably, repression fermented opposition, which erupted into outright rebellion in 1978. The party centre responded with a

[222] Jean-Louis Margolin, 'Cambodia: The Country of Disconcerting Crimes', in Courtois et al., *The Black Book of Communism*, p. 583.

[223] For instance, see Ben Kiernan and Chanthou Boua, *Peasants and Politics in Kampuchea, 1942–1981* (London: Zed, 1982), pp. 345–6; and Loung Ung, *First They Killed My Father: A Daughter of Cambodia Remembers* (New York: HarperCollins, 2000), p. 62; and Kiljunen, *Kampuchea*, p. 15.

[224] Vickery, *Cambodia*, p. 85.

[225] Vickery, *Cambodia*, p. 85.

[226] See David Chandler, *Voices from S-21: Terror and History in Pol Pot's Secret Prison* (St. Leonards, UNSW: Allen and Unwin, 1999); and Elizabeth Becker, *When the War Was Over: Cambodia and the Khmer Rouge Revolution*, rev. edn (New York: Public Affairs, 1998), pp. 271–96. Up to 20,000 people died at Tuol Sleng, and there were only ten survivors.

[227] Craig Etcheson, 'The Number—Quantifying Crimes Against Humanity in Cambodia', Documentation Centre of Cambodia, 1999, p. 2.

[228] Hannum, 'International Law and Cambodian Genocide', p. 88.

campaign of 'purification', forced displacement, and mass killing. Khmer Rouge soldiers and party members who had trained in Vietnam, as well as their families and associates, were singled out for execution. Easterners were even required to wear blue scarves to mark themselves out.[229] Estimates suggest that at least 100,000, and more probably 250,000, 'base people' were killed in these purges during the regime's final six months.[230]

Alongside these three phases of destruction, the Khmer Rouge targeted national and religious minorities. The regime denied the existence of minorities and then attempted to make Cambodian society reflect its own 'truth' through 'forced Khmerisation'.[231] This policy was first applied to the Vietnamese, who faced what Ben Kiernan aptly described as 'systematic racial extermination'.[232] Around half of Cambodia's 400,000 Vietnamese had been expelled by Lon Nol, and several thousand killed in nationalist pogroms. The Khmer Rouge first attempted to expel all the remaining Vietnamese, whom Pol Pot believed had 'secretly infiltrated' Cambodia and were 'hidden, mixed with the population'.[233] Around 150,000 Vietnamese were expelled within months. But in mid-1976, the regime changed course and decreed that no more Vietnamese would be permitted to leave.[234] The approximately 50,000 ethnic Vietnamese who remained in Cambodia were identified, arrested, and executed.[235] By the time that the Khmer Rouge was defeated in early 1979, there were virtually no Vietnamese survivors.[236] The Muslim Cham fared somewhat better than the Vietnamese, but even so more than a third of the entire pre-1975 Cham population of 250,000 died in the proceeding three and a half years. The party centre decided that they were bourgeois or independent fishermen and therefore not part of the Khmer peasantry.[237] As such, they were targeted for being 'new people' and as members of a religious group. In 1976, the Khmer Rouge imposed a policy of Khmerisation, banning religion,

[229] Ben Kiernan, 'The Cambodian Genocide 1975–1979', in Samuel Totten and William S. Parsons (eds), *Century of Genocide: Critical Essays and Eyewitness Accounts* (London: Routledge, 1997), p. 349.

[230] Kiernan, *Pol Pot Regime*, pp. 404–5; Vickery, *Cambodia*, p. 137.

[231] Becker, *When the War Was Over*, p. 243.

[232] Kiernan, 'Cambodian Genocide', p. 198. Nayan Chanda described the extermination as a 'final solution' to Cambodia's Vietnamese problem. Nayan Chanda, *Brother Enemy: The War After the War* (New York: Harcourt Brace Jovanovich, 1986), p. 86.

[233] Cited in Liai Duong, 'Racial Discrimination in the Cambodian Genocide', Genocide Studies Program, Yale University, Working Paper No. 34, 2006, p. 8.

[234] Kiernan, *Pol Pot Regime*, p. 267.

[235] For evidence of specific instructions to exterminate Vietnamese, see Alexander Laban Hinton, *Why Did They Kill?* (Berkeley: University of California Press, 2005), p. 219.

[236] Kiernan reports that a year's research in Cambodia after 1979 failed to turn up a single Vietnamese person who had survived in the country from 1970–79. Kiernan, 'Cambodian Genocide', p. 198.

[237] See Ben Kiernan, 'Orphans of Genocide: The Cham Muslims of Kampuchea under Pol Pot', *Bulletin of Concerned Asian Scholars*, 20, 1988, p. 7.

forcing the Chams to violate their religious beliefs by eating pork, and dispersing them across the country to accelerate their assimilation. Later, dispersal was replaced with mass killing. Some Chams resisted Khmerisation and were then targeted for extermination instead; others were killed simply because they belonged to a minority group.[238] Finally, ethnic Chinese were targeted and almost half the Chinese population died between April 1975 and December 1978.[239] Given that most Chinese were merchants, it is difficult to know what portion of this destruction was due to their ethnicity and what portion due to their socio-economic status.[240] Nevertheless, there is evidence that ethnic Chinese were specifically singled out for abuse and execution.[241]

The Khmer Rouge's reign of terror was brought to an end by Vietnamese intervention. In 1977–78, the Khmer Rouge increased its anti-Vietnamese rhetoric and launched raids into Vietnam proper. In one incident, in September 1977, Khmer Rouge forces attacked Tay Ninh province in Vietnam and killed hundreds of civilians.[242] Vietnam responded with an armed incursion that failed to stem the violence or force the Khmer Rouge into negotiations. Lessons learned from that experience helped Vietnam develop a more effective military strategy. On Christmas Day 1978, around 150,000 Vietnamese troops and 15,000 Cambodian rebels, mainly comprised of former eastern zone Khmer Rouge, invaded Cambodia. Crippled by internal purges, outgunned, and outmanoeuvred, the Khmer Rouge army crumbled and Phnom Penh fell on 9 January. The Khmer Rouge leadership and some of its army escaped into Thailand, from where they launched a protracted insurgency. As they retreated, the Khmer Rouge burned granaries, worsening Cambodia's food crisis.[243]

To justify its mass killing, the Khmer Rouge combined Khmer chauvinism with ideas borrowed from elsewhere (especially Maoism and Stalinism) into a theoretically unsophisticated but politically powerful ideology of selective extermination. This ideology helped identify victim groups, remove them from the universe of moral obligation, and justify the use of extreme violence against them.

[238] Vickery contends that the forced eating of pork was simply to alleviate famine, whilst Philip Short argues that the dispersal of Chams cannot be regard an act of racial discrimination. Neither is convincing. See Vickery, *Cambodia*, p. 182; and Philip Short, *Pol Pot: The History of a Nightmare* (London: John Murray, 2004), p. 585. For a detailed account, see Duong, 'Racial Discrimination', pp. 11–23.

[239] Ben Kiernan, 'Kampuchea's Ethnic Chinese Under Pol Pot: A Case of Systematic Social Discrimination', *Journal of Contemporary Asia*, 16, 1986, p. 18.

[240] Duong, 'Racial Discrimination', p. 25.

[241] Duong, 'Racial Discrimination', p. 26.

[242] Grant Evans and Kelvin Rowley, *Red Brotherhood at War: Vietnam, Cambodia and Laos Since 1975* (London: Verso, 1984), p. 106.

[243] Kiernan, *Pol Pot Regime*, p. 453.

Khmer Rouge ideology borrowed three ideas from outside. The first, taken from Mao and expressed by intellectuals like Frantz Fanon, was the notion that only violence could free colonized peoples of colonial rule and foreign imposed mindsets.[244] Second, and also from Mao, they took the vision of a 'pure communist' society that could be achieved in a very short space of time by radical policies supported by extreme violence.[245] Pol Pot was profoundly influenced by China's 'Great Leap Forward' and the belief that radical transformation could be rapidly achieved, even if at great cost. Ignoring the fact that China's 'Great Leap' was a monumental failure and brushing off warnings from the Chinese themselves, the Khmer Rouge leadership reckoned that they could achieve a pure communist society more quickly than China, through a *super* great leap forward.[246] Third, from Stalinism they took the idea that the best means of achieving their great leap was extreme violence and secrecy. Karl Jackson has identified four key similarities between Stalin's tactics and those used by the Khmer Rouge: (1) brutal swiftness in collectivizing agriculture; (2) the rapid extermination of whole classes; (3) a narrow definition of protected people; (4) extensive purges of party cadre.[247] In addition, the Khmer Rouge took secrecy to new lengths, hiding behind the term *Angkar* ('the organization') and only revealing the existence of the Communist Party itself in 1976.[248]

The ideology's indigenous aspects were rooted in Khmer chauvinism. The Khmer Rouge created an historical mythology that venerated the ancient Angkor Kingdom. According to the Khmer Rouge, Angkor civilization demonstrated Khmer superiority but was coveted by other powers, ultimately destroying the Khmer kingdom and impoverishing the Khmer people. The Khmer Rouge portrayed themselves as heirs of this ancient heritage and branded opponents enemies of the people whose lives were of no value and whose eradication was necessary for the rekindling of Khmer civilization. Mass killing was often portrayed as purification or cleansing, weeding out foreigners and the foreign influences that had corrupted Cambodian society.[249] Loyal Cambodian peasants were venerated and the reclaiming of their former greatness was the centrepiece of Khmer Rouge thinking.

[244] Chalk and Jonassohn, *History and Sociology of Genocide*, p. 400.

[245] Karl D. Jackson, *Cambodia 1975–1979: Rendezvous with Death* (Princeton, NJ: Princeton University Press, 1992), p. 219.

[246] Norodom Sihanouk, *War and Hope: The Case for Cambodia* (New York: Random House, 1980), p. 86. On plans for a 'super' great leap forward, see David P. Chandler, Ben Kiernan, and Chanthou Boua (eds), *Pol Pot Plans the Future*, pp. 169, 171, and 327.

[247] Jackson, *Cambodia 1975–1979*, p. 235.

[248] Ben Kiernan, 'External and Indigenous Sources of Khmer Rouge Ideology', Yale Cambodian Genocide Project, accessed 15 March 2010.

[249] Joan D. Criddle and Teeda Butt Mam, *To Destroy You is No Loss* (New York: Anchor, 1987), p. 164.

All those who fell outside this venerated group were regarded as actual or potential enemies who could be legitimately exterminated.[250] Members of these groups (which included Sihanoukists, Lon Nol loyalists, national minorities, religious groups, urban classes, and Vietnamese influenced communists) were considered to be beyond redemption. As Pol Pot explained in 1975, they 'are not to be regarded as being our people. They are to be regarded as enemies of Democratic Kampuchea'.[251] The party enjoined people to 'pull up the grass, dig up the roots' and use the bodies of city people and other enemies as 'fertiliser'.[252] 'New people' were likened to animals to justify them being treated as such.[253] Perceived enemies and their associates were referred to as 'microbes' and 'pests buried within' that needed to be identified and eradicated to cleanse Khmer society, or as a 'sickness' or 'infection' that should be 'treated' or 'cut out'.[254] Radio Phnom Penh announced that 'what is infected must be cut out, what is rotten must be removed, what is too long must be shortened and made the right length'.[255] This was nothing short of an attempt to implement an ideological vision of humankind by literally eliminating all of those that did not fit the desired stereotype.[256]

The Khmer Rouge therefore justified mass atrocities through an ideology of selective extermination that valourized a particular group (Khmer peasants) and explained its malaise by reference to degenerative foreign influences. 'Carriers' of foreign influence would have to be sought out and destroyed. This was morally defensible because it was necessary for restoring Khmer supremacy and because the lives of members of these groups were considered to be without value. Like other totalitarians before them, the Khmer Rouge swept civilian immunity away by arguing that it did not apply to groups it placed outside the universe of moral obligation.

Contextual factors connected with the Cold War played a significant role in shaping international responses to the Cambodian genocide. In the West and Southeast Asia especially, early condemnation driven by reported atrocities gave way to the realization that the Khmer Rouge were no friends of the Vietnamese and were therefore a useful counter to Vietnam's regional

250 See Jackson, *Cambodia 1975–1978*, pp. 50–1.

251 Cited in Jackson, *Cambodia 1975–1978*, p. 56.

252 Cited by Kiernan, 'External and Indigenous Sources', p. 7.

253 Alexander Laban Hinton, 'A Head for an Eye: Revenge in the Cambodian Genocide', *American Ethnologist*, 25 (3) 1998, pp. 365–6.

254 Ben Kiernan, 'Twentieth-Century Genocides: Underlying Ideological Themes from Armenia to East Timor' in Samuel Totten and Paul R. Bartrop (eds), *The Genocide Studies Reader* (London: Routledge, 2009), p. 245; and Alexander Laban Hinton 'Agents of Death: Explaining the Cambodian Genocide in Terms of Psychosocial Dissonance', *American Anthropologist*, 1996, 98 (4), p. 824.

255 Cited in Chalk and Jonassohn, *History and Sociology of Genocide*, p. 404.

256 Francois Ponchaud, *Cambodia Year Zero*, trans. Nancy Amphoux (Harmondsworth: Penguin, 1978), p. 60

hegemony. The communist world tended to defend the Khmer Rouge until Vietnam's intervention in 1978. The intervention split the communist bloc with the Soviet Union and its allies switching their allegiance to Vietnam, whilst China and North Korea continued to support the Khmer Rouge. But even the unfriendly communist governments preferred not to criticize the Khmer Rouge for killing civilians. Indeed, there is little evidence to suggest that any interested government prioritized the protection of Cambodian civilians above the pursuit of its own interests. Without Vietnam's intervention—itself a response to Khmer Rouge irredentism, not its genocide—international society would have permitted the Khmer Rouge to remain in power well beyond 1979.

Because the Khmer Rouge shrouded its activities in secrecy, it was some time before a clear picture of what was happening in Cambodia emerged but even when it did, Cambodia did not attract much international media attention. Reports were often sketchy and disputed.[257] The first reports, written mainly by Western journalists in Phnom Penh at the time of its fall, focused on the evacuation of the cities but once the journalists were evacuated, reporting dried up. In the summer of 1975, Bruce Loudoun in *The Times* and Henry Kamm in the *New York Times* reported widespread executions, based on testimony from refugees. But other reports cast doubt on atrocity stories, including some published in *Newsweek* (late 1975), the *Sunday Times*, the *Far Eastern Economic Review*, and *Der Speigel.* William Shawcross reports that it was not until *Le Monde* published excerpts of Francois Ponchaud's first-hand account of atrocities in 1977 that they came to be generally accepted as valid.[258]

The evacuation of the cities in 1975 was sharply criticized by the West. Henry Kissinger—whose views were discredited by his now well-established reputation for lying about Indochina—condemned what he described as an 'atrocity of major proportions'.[259] The day after the Khmer Rouge seized Phnom Penh, he warned that the communists would 'try to eliminate all potential opponents' and in early May the US Administration presented 'hard intelligence' showing the commission of atrocities.[260] Democratic Senator, George McGovern, an opponent of the Indochina wars, was one of the Khmer Rouge's loudest critics on Capitol Hill and called for military

[257] William C. Adams and Michael Joblove, 'The Unnewsworthy Holocaust: TV News and Terror in Cambodia', in William C. Adams (ed.), *Television Coverage of International Affairs* (Norwood, NJ: Ablex, 1982), p. 217.

[258] William Shawcross, 'Cambodia: Some Perceptions of a Disaster', in David P. Chandler, Ben Kiernan, and Chanthou Boua (eds), *Revolution and its Aftermath in Kampuchea: Eight Essays* (New Haven: Yale University Southeast Asian Studies), pp. 238–9.

[259] 'Kissinger Sees Atrocity in Events in Cambodia', *New York Times*, 14 May 1975.

[260] Samantha Power, *A Problem from Hell: America and the Age of Genocide* (New York: Flamingo, 2003), p. 107.

intervention.[261] The *Wall Street Journal* denounced McGovern's position as 'truly mind-boggling'.[262] In 1976, another Democrat, Stephen Solarz, described the Khmer Rouge's record as one of 'barbarous butchery which is surpassed in recent history only by the Nazi atrocities' and expressed his amazement that so little had been done to investigate or condemn the atrocities.[263] Along with Senator Claiborne Pell, Solarz and McGovern persuaded the House to hold hearings on Cambodia in 1977, but not much else.[264] In the US media, conservative columnist William Buckley called for military intervention against the Khmer Rouge.[265] Other columnists such as William Safire (*New York Times*) and a prominent NGO, the International Rescue Committee, condemned the Khmer Rouge and demanded international action.[266]

Blinded by a pervasive suspicion of the US government (which, to be fair, had lied repeatedly about Cambodia) and an almost unlimited faith in leftist governments, some prominent members of the Western left rejected reported massacres as fictions cooked up by anti-communists. The charge was led by Noam Chomsky and Edward Herman who questioned the motives of witnesses, rubbished the sources of massacre reports, and argued that the reports served Western interests. They insisted that reports of massacres were exaggerated.[267] They also complained that the Western media had embarked on a 'vast and unprecedented propaganda campaign' against the Khmer Rouge.[268] This view was supported by the 'Indochina Resource Centre', an anti-war group led by George Hildebrand and Gareth Porter, which issued a report in September 1975 claiming that the evacuation of Phnom Penh was not an atrocity but a reasonable attempt to save the people from famine. The following year, they published a book which dismissed atrocity reports and argued that the evacuation of cities would improve the lives of Khmer civilians.[269] In 1977, Porter denounced the 'wild exaggeration and wholesale falsehood' of alleged Khmer Rouge atrocities, arguing that it was a 'myth' that more than a million Cambodians had been slaughtered.[270] But it was not just individual leftists that denied atrocity reports. Before deciding to support calls for a UN

[261] See Kiljunen, *Kampuchea*, p. 122.

[262] Power, *A Problem from Hell*, p. 133.

[263] Cited in Power, *A Problem from Hell*, p. 128.

[264] On Solarz and McGovern, see Christopher Brady, *United States Foreign Policy Towards Cambodia, 1977–1992: A Question of Realities* (London: Macmillan, 1999), pp. 33–5.

[265] See Power, *A Problem from Hell*, p. 123. Also, *International Herald Tribune*, 10 January 1979.

[266] Power, *A Problem from Hell*, p. 130.

[267] Noam Chomsky and Edward Herman, *After the Cataclysm: Postwar Indochina and the Reconstruction of Imperial Ideology* (Cambridge, MA: South End Press, 1979).

[268] Chomsky and Herman, *After the Cataclysm*, p. 140.

[269] For discussion, see Jamie Frederic Metzl, *Western Responses to Human Rights Abuses in Cambodia, 1975–1980* (New York: St. Martin's Press, 1996), p. 56.

[270] Power, *A Problem from Hell*, p. 128.

investigation into human rights in Cambodia in 1978, Amnesty International poured cold water on reported atrocities. In September 1975 it argued that atrocity reports were 'impossible to substantiate' and based on 'flimsy evidence and second-hand accounts'. A year into the genocide, its annual report dedicated a little over one page to Cambodia. Almost two years after the Khmer Rouge seized power, an internal Amnesty document argued that refugee testimony accusing the regime of grave abuses was biased.[271]

There was, however, widespread criticism elsewhere in the West, though not much before 1977. Israel was the first country to raise the Cambodia issue at the UN, its ambassador warning of the commission of 'auto-genocide' in May 1977.[272] In April 1978, the Canadian parliament passed a motion denouncing what it described as genocide.[273] Writing in the UK's *Daily Mirror*, John Pilger described the 'echoes of Auschwitz' at Tuol Sleng, though without much discernible effect on public opinion.[274] *The Economist* denounced 'brutality that would make Hitler cringe'. Writing in *The Times* in February 1977, Bernard Levin opined that '[e]ven in a century which has gorged itself on atrocities until it has become almost too replete to swallow more, the horrors which accompanied and have followed the fall of Cambodia to the communists are exceptional both in their peculiarly barbaric nature and in the colossal scale on which they have been carried out'.[275]

Behind this public condemnation, however, key Western governments opted to privilege strategic interests over putative concern for Cambodians.[276] Despite closed doors, the US Administration sent positive signals to the Khmer Rouge. When Kissinger met Thai foreign minister, Chatichai Choonhavan in November 1975, he indicated that the USA was prepared to adopt a friendly posture towards the Khmer Rouge, which it saw as a balance to Vietnamese hegemony, and that US interests trumped concern about communist atrocities. Kissinger informed his interlocutor that, '[y]ou should also tell the Cambodians that we will be friends with them. They are murderous thugs, but we won't let that stand in our way. We are prepared to improve relations with them. Tell them the latter part, but don't tell them what I said before'.[277] He advised the foreign minister that 'you should tell them that we bear no hostility towards them. We would like them to be independent as a

[271] Power, *A Problem from Hell*, p. 113.

[272] Power, *A Problem from Hell*, p. 125.

[273] Motion of the Canadian Parliament, 'Condemnation of Communist Atrocities in Kampuchea', 7 April 1978, UN document, E/CN.4/Sub.2/414/Add.1, p. 2.

[274] Cited by Shawcross, 'Cambodia, p. 230.

[275] Bernard Levin, 'Communism Shows its Brutal Face Once More', *The Times*, 2 February 1977.

[276] Michael Haas, *Cambodia, Pol Pot, and the United States: The Faustian Pact* (New York: Praeger, 1991), p. 15.

[277] Department of State, Memorandum of Conversation, 26 November 1975. Kissinger instructed that these minutes not be published for thirty years.

counterweight to North Vietnam'.[278] The following week, President Ford gave the same basic message to President Suharto of Indonesia: 'there is . . . resistance in Cambodia to the influence of Hanoi. We are willing to move slowly in our relations with Cambodia, hoping perhaps to slow down the North Vietnamese influence although we find the Cambodian government very difficult'.[279] Kissinger put it more bluntly: 'The Chinese want to use Cambodia to balance off Vietnam . . . We don't like Cambodia, for the government in many ways is worse than Vietnam, but we would like it to be independent. We don't discourage Thailand or China from drawing closer to Cambodia'.[280] Ben Kiernan notes that almost immediately after these exchanges, press sources close to the US Administration began to shift towards a more favourable attitude towards the Khmer Rouge. For instance, writing in the *Readers Digest*, conservative columnist Joseph Alsop described the Khmer Rouge as 'passionate nationalists', defended the evacuation of Cambodian cities, and raised fears about Vietnamese expansionism.[281] In September 1977, the CIA reported a decrease in the level of killing in Cambodia and claimed that most killing was linked to preventing people crossing the Thai border and in-fighting within the communist party.[282]

Although the Carter Administration stepped up criticism of the Khmer Rouge, it also continued to prioritize strategic concerns. In 1978, President Carter maintained that the Khmer Rouge were 'the world's worst violators of human rights' and that 'it is an obligation of every member of the international community to protest the policies of this or any nation which cruelly and systematically violates the rights of its people'. Deputy Secretary of State Warren Christopher condemned the 'systematic terror and grinding down of the Cambodian people'.[283] But in practice the administration pursued the same policy as its predecessor. Kissinger's replacement as National Security Advisor, Zbigniew Brzezinski, recalled that in 1979 'I encouraged the Chinese to support Pol Pot. Pol Pot was an abomination. We could never support him, but China could'.[284] According to Brzezinski, after the Vietnamese

[278] Department of State, Memorandum of Conversation, 26 November 1975.

[279] Cited in Ben Kiernan, 'Documentation Delayed, Justice Denied: The Historiography of the Cambodian Genocide', in Stone (ed.), *The Historiography of Genocide*, p. 479.

[280] Cited in Kiernan, 'Documentation Delayed', p. 479.

[281] Kiernan, 'Documentation Delayed', p. 479. By 1977, however, *Readers Digest* had changed tack, publishing a book on what it labelled 'communist genocide' in Cambodia.

[282] CIA, 'Memorandum: Human Rights Violations in Cambodia', 21 September 1977. It maintained this line even after the Khmer Rouge's fall from power, publishing a 'demographic report' in May 1980 which denied that the Khmer Rouge was guilty of any killings in 1977–78—ironically, the two bloodiest years of its rule. The CIA concluded that the 'final executions' of the Khmer Rouge period had been in 1976. CIA, *Kampuchea: A Demographic Catastrophe*, National Foreign Assessment Centre, May 1980.

[283] Cited by Adams and Joblove, 'The Unnewsworthy Holocaust', p. 221.

[284] Cited by Kiernan, 'Documentation Delayed', p. 480.

intervention the USA 'winked semi-publicly' at Chinese and Thai aid to Khmer Rouge forces, whilst the USA worked through the UN and other agencies to provide aid through the refugee camps on the Thai border.

This pattern was repeated elsewhere in the non-communist world. The case of Thailand is instructive. When the Khmer Rouge seized power, Thailand was undergoing democratic reform. Viewing Vietnam as the greater threat, the Thai government recognized the new regime in April 1975. In 1976, the Thai government was overthrown by a military coup and the new regime adopted a more hardline anti-communist view that was deeply critical of the Khmer Rouge. But once it became clear from 1977 that the Khmer Rouge was not a Vietnamese ally, the Thai government's attitude became more accommodating towards it. Indeed, Thailand provided sanctuary to the Khmer Rouge after their 1979 defeat. To justify this stance, Thai officials and academics downplayed Khmer Rouge atrocities, challenged the evidence, and portrayed killings as responses to Vietnamese hegemony.[285] The Thai position was shared by most other ASEAN governments.[286]

Communist opinion was also primarily shaped by strategic interests. Before Vietnam's intervention, communist governments and media uniformly defended the Khmer Rouge. After the intervention, communist opinion bifurcated into Soviet support for Vietnam and Chinese support for the Khmer Rouge. The Khmer Rouge's staunchest ally, China, never wavered. In 1977, the Chinese *People's Daily* reported a visit by journalists to Cambodia, telling its readers that: 'We were full of wonder at seeing their heroic deeds in defending and building the country. The cadres were closely in contact with the troops and refused sleep and food. The troops were changing nature night and day'.[287] Initially, the Soviet Union also backed the Khmer Rouge. The matter was not widely discussed in public but in 1977, the state newspaper *Novoje Vremja* refuted Western allegations of mass killing.[288] The Soviet position changed immediately when Vietnam invaded. In January 1979, *Pravda* reported that three million people had been killed by the Khmer Rouge, whilst *Novoje Vremja* explained its earlier positive attitude to the Cambodian government by claiming that the Khmer Rouge had been skilled in hiding its misdeeds.[289] Yugoslav journalists were permitted to enter Cambodia and whilst official pronouncements toed the communist line that all was well, a series of reports published by *Politika* in 1978 told a different story. Writing in

[285] Puangthong Rungswasdisab, 'Thailand's Response to the Cambodian Genocide', Yale University Genocide Project, 2010, pp. 21–2.

[286] Shawcross, 'Cambodia', p. 243.

[287] *Xinhua*, 17 April 1977.

[288] Juri Antoshin in *Novoje Vremija*, no. 9, 1979.

[289] *Pravda*, 14 January 1979; Juri Tavrovski in *Novoje Vremija*, no. 9, 1979.

his own name, Dragoslav Rancic argued that the Cambodian revolution had gone sour.[290]

Western ambivalence and communist support resulted in only limited international efforts to restrain the genocide. Debate in the UN was limited to the Human Rights Commission. Backed by Amnesty International (which had earlier cast doubt on the atrocities) and the International Commission of Jurists, in 1978 Canada, Norway, the UK, the USA, and Australia presented material on the situation in Cambodia and called for an investigation. The USA expressed its 'concern about the reported flagrant abuses of human rights'; the UK documented 'alleged abuses and upheaval, which has involved the forcible evacuation of the cities, wide-scale executions, and the destruction of much of the traditional Kampuchean way of life'; and Canada noted that all evidence pointed to the systematic 'violation of human rights in Cambodia'.[291] In response, the Khmer Rouge denounced its critics as 'imperialists' and 'expansionists' guilty of waging a campaign of 'denigration and calumny'.[292] The communist bloc supported the Khmer Rouge, citing the principle of non-interference in the domestic affairs of states, but were unable to prevent the passage of a resolution calling for an investigation.[293] After 1979, the Commission's focus turned to Vietnamese occupation and the demand for immediate withdrawal. The Khmer Rouge (which still held Cambodia's seat), China, and Vietnam repeatedly presented material accusing each other of massacres and human rights abuses. In 1980 and 1981, the Commission passed cautious resolutions, stressing Cambodia's right to self-determination and condemning past human rights violations in generic terms.[294]

Vietnam's December 1978 intervention was stridently condemned by international society. For some, the intervention violated the principle of non-interference which was privileged over the protection of civilians from mass atrocities. In the UN Security Council, China described the intervention as a 'great mockery of and insult to the United Nations and its member states' and sponsored a resolution condemning Vietnam's 'aggression'. The United States agreed. Its ambassador argued that the international community could not

[290] Dragoslav Rancic, *Politika*, 19(3), 20(3), 25(3), 28(3), and 31(3), 1978.

[291] Respectively, Submission from the Government of the United States, E/CN.4/Sub.2/414/Add.4, 14 August 1978; Submission from the Government of the UK, E/CN.4/Sub.2/414/Add.3, 17 August 1978, and further submission from the Government of Canada, E/CN.4/Sub.2/414/Add.7, 8 September 1978. Norway's submission is at E/CN.4/Sub.2/414/Add.2, 18 August 1978.

[292] Letter from Ministry of Foreign Affairs, Democratic Kampuchea to the UN Commission on Human Rights, Sub-Commission on Prevention of Discrimination and Protection of Minorities, E/CN.4/1295, E/CN.4/Sub.2/418, 13 June 1978. For a discussion, see Kiljunen (ed.), *Kampuchea*, pp. 104–5.

[293] See William Shawcross, *The Quality of Mercy: Cambodia, Holocaust and Modern Conscience* (New York: Simon and Schuster, 1984), pp. 65–7.

[294] Kiljunen (ed.), *Kampuchea*, p. 105.

allow Vietnam's violation of Cambodian sovereignty to 'pass in silence' as this 'will only encourage Governments in other parts of the world to conclude that there are no norms, no standards, no restraints'.[295] President Carter praised Thailand for 'preparing and permitting a haven' for people fleeing the Vietnamese advance—a significant number of them Khmer Rouge cadres and soldiers.[296] Some other states tried to balance their concerns about Cambodian sovereignty and human rights, but clearly prioritized the former. France argued that 'the notion that because a regime is detestable foreign intervention is justified and forcible overthrow is legitimate is extremely dangerous. That could ultimately jeopardize the very maintenance of law and order'. Norway admitted to 'strong objections to the serious violation of human rights committed by the Pol Pot government. However the domestic policies of that government cannot—we repeat cannot—justify the action of Viet Nam'.[297] With only a handful of exceptions (such as William Buckley, above) the Western media supported their governments' stance. The *International Herald Tribune* condemned both Khmer Rouge atrocities and Vietnamese intervention, arguing that human rights abuse did not create a licence for intervention.[298] In France, *Le Monde* argued that the intervention threatened regional stability.[299] Vietnam's allies (USSR, Cuba, Czechoslovakia, East Germany, Hungary, Mongolia, Poland, and Bulgaria) defended the intervention pointing, among other things, to the grave abuses of human rights by the Khmer Rouge—although their earlier support for the regime strongly suggests that political not human rights concerns were at the fore.

Whilst remaining ambivalent about their potential return to power, over the next decade several Western governments provided political and material support to the Khmer Rouge. The US encouraged Thailand to establish havens and permit aid to reach Khmer Rouge cadres and soldiers, provided much of that aid itself, and encouraged and assisted armed opposition to the Vietnam-backed government in Phnom Penh.[300] There is also evidence that CIA former deputy director, Ray Cline, a confidant of the Reagan administration, visited the Khmer Rouge inside Cambodia.[301] British Special Forces provided training (including in the use of land mines) and arms to the Khmer Rouge.

[295] Both cited by Wheeler, *Saving Strangers*, pp. 90–1.

[296] Cited in Brady, *United States Foreign Policy*, p. 28.

[297] Both cited by Simon Chesterman, *Just War or Just Peace? Humanitarian Intervention and International Law* (Oxford: Oxford University Press, 2001), p. 80.

[298] *International Herald Tribune*, 18 January 1979.

[299] *Le Monde*, 10 January 1979.

[300] Brady, *United States Foreign Policy*, p. 44.

[301] 'Thais Furious at Cambodians for Disclosing Visit by Reagan Aide', *Los Angeles Times*, 5 December 1980.

The legitimacy of this support was challenged by the emergence of reports-about Khmer Rouge atrocities, which created an international outcry—especially in the West.[302] To mitigate this problem, some attempted to rehabilitate the Khmer Rouge. The CIA published research which denied that the communists had committed mass atrocities in 1977–78. In addition, Douglas Pike, a US government analyst, played down Khmer Rouge crimes. Pike argued that Pol Pot was the 'charismatic' leader of a 'bloody but successful peasant revolution with a substantial residue of public support' and that 'on a statistical basis, most of them [Khmers] . . . did not experience much in the way of brutality'.[303] Stephen Heder, a former US intelligence officer, argued that Khmer Rouge atrocities were not premeditated.[304]

Another tactic was to provide political cover to the Khmer Rouge by establishing a united opposition to Vietnamese occupation comprising the former communist and Sihanoukist governments, and a third group the Khmer People's National Liberation Front (KPNLF) led by Son Sann. Thailand played a key role in brokering this deal, with US support.[305] Pol Pot was encouraged to step aside, allowing Khieu Samphan to assume the Khmer Rouge leadership. In this way, assistance to the Khmer Rouge was disguised and indirectly funnelled through Thailand, allowing the USA and its allies to provide support to the Khmer Rouge without having to justify this policy to their publics.[306]

In terms of political support, throughout the 1980s the West continued to recognize the Khmer Rouge as the government of Cambodia and holder of the country's seat at the UN. The USA also rejected an Australian plan to investigate and prosecute the Khmer Rouge for genocide and crimes against humanity.[307] By the late 1980s, however, the reduction of Cold War tensions gave new prominence to human rights issues, making it both more difficult to justify even indirect support to the Khmer Rouge and less apparently necessary to provide such support. The US Administration began to change its

[302] See Ben Kiernan, 'Introduction', in Ben Kiernan (ed.), *Genocide and Democracy in Cambodia: The Khmer Rouge, the United Nations and the International Community* (New Haven: Yale University Southeast Asian Studies Monograph, No. 41, 1993), pp. 10–11; and George Chigas, 'The Politics of Defining Justice After the Cambodian Genocide', *Journal of Genocide Research*, 2 (2) 2000, pp. 247–8.

[303] *St. Louis Post Despatch*, 29 November 1979 and *Christian Science Monitor*, 4 December 1979.

[304] Cited in A. Barnett, 'Democratic Kampuchea: A Highly Centralised Dictatorship', in David Chandler Ben Kiernan, and Anthony Barnett (eds), *Revolution and its Aftermath in Kampuchea: Eight Essays* (New Haven: Yale University Southeast Asian Studies, 1983), p. 228.

[305] Puangthong Rungswasdisab, 'Thailand's Response to the Cambodian Genocide', p. 17.

[306] A point recognized by Zbigniew Brzezinski, *Power and Principle* (London: Weidenfeld and Nicolson, 1983), p. 440.

[307] Kiernan, 'Documentation Delayed', p. 482.

position and Congress passed a law instructing it to use all appropriate means to prevent the Khmer Rouge from returning to power.[308]

In summary, the Khmer Rouge genocide was justified by reference to an ideology of selective extermination that combined elements of Khmer chauvinism, Maoism, and Stalinism. Groups that carried foreign influences or showed oppositionist tendencies were viewed as implacable opponents of the Khmer people and beyond redemption. Placed outside the Khmer community, their lives were seen as having no value and their destruction as essential for Khmer rejuvenation. Khmer Rouge ideology received little—if any—international support. But the widespread rejection of the Khmer Rouge's justifications did not strip the regime of sufficient legitimacy or generate punishment. Were it not for its local dispute with Vietnam, the Khmer Rouge would in all probability have continued to govern for many more years. Communist governments publicly accepted the Khmer Rouge's case. Western governments acknowledged concerns about the Khmer Rouge's behaviour but privileged strategic concerns over worries about massive violations of civilian immunity. Many in the West saw the Khmer Rouge as a useful barrier against Vietnamese hegemony and were prepared to tolerate the regime. Toleration morphed into clandestine support to some extent after the Khmer Rouge was toppled by Vietnam. Motivated by Cold War politics, this stance was enabled by contextual factors such as the geographic and political isolation of Cambodia, relatively little and unclear media reporting, and leftist scepticism about atrocity reports which limited the extent to which Western governments were called upon to oppose Khmer Rouge atrocities. Thus, although there is little evidence of direct sympathy for the Khmer Rouge or acceptance of its justificatory arguments, the regime was able to secure (barely) *sufficient* legitimacy which in the absence of the dispute with Vietnam would have protected it from punishment for its mass atrocities. Vietnam, nonetheless, was criticized and punished by international society for invading Cambodia. The public condemnation of Khmer Rouge atrocities lends further weight to the argument that civilian immunity had become an embedded norm in international society during the Cold War, and it is difficult to argue that the Khmer Rouge legitimized its atrocities. The normative power of civilian immunity forced the USA, the UK, and Thailand to disguise their assistance to the Khmer Rouge after 1979. But this case also serves as a powerful lesson about the limits of civilian immunity when confronted with powerful strategic interests and the capacity of interests and contextual factors to shape how norm violations are interpreted and the consequences that flow from this.

[308] US Public Law 100–502, 18 October 1988.

## THE WANING COLD WAR: AFGHANISTAN AND BEIJING

I argued earlier that the death of Stalin in 1953 and that of Mao in 1976 prompted the Soviet Union and China to abandon selective extermination for strikingly similar reasons. Leaders in both countries recognized that massive repression retarded economic development, destabilized society, and imperilled members of the elite. But although it encouraged these governments to recognize civilian immunity as an embedded norm of international society, the abandonment of selective extermination did not amount to the internalization of civilian immunity as the two cases discussed in this section demonstrate. In these cases—the Soviet war in Afghanistan and the 1989 Beijing massacre—the Soviet Union and China respectively perpetrated mass atrocities and attempted to secure sufficient legitimacy by leveraging uncertainty in a manner not dissimilar to that of non-communist perpetrators of mass atrocities. Ultimately, both failed to secure sufficient legitimacy and were criticized and punished for their behaviour. Although the source of these failures and types of punishment were different, these cases lend further weight to the argument levelled in the previous chapter that contextual changes in the late Cold War period—especially improved global communications, reduced Cold War tensions that elevated civilian immunity as a political priority, and heightened humanitarian activism—made it more difficult for even powerful states to secure sufficient legitimacy for mass killing.

### The Soviet War in Afghanistan (1979–1988)

The Soviet Union invaded Afghanistan in December 1979, deposing the brutal and unpopular communist government headed by Hafizullah Amin and installing a new government it hoped would prove more popular. The invasion was widely condemned, and the UN General Assembly passed a string of resolutions with large majorities calling for an immediate withdrawal. To make matters worse, the new government proved no more popular than the old and the Soviets soon faced concerted *mujahadeen* resistance. Unable to defeat the insurgents in conventional battle, the Soviets employed counterinsurgency tactics similar to those used against communist insurgents in Indochina and Latin America, utilising indiscriminate air power and artillery to terrorize the civilian population and drive them from their homes. But not only did the Soviet Union adopt tactics similar to those employed against communist insurgents elsewhere, they also offered similar justifications attempting to create and leverage uncertainty. This confirms both the shift away from selective extermination and Soviet recognition of civilian immunity as an embedded norm in international society. The illegitimacy of both the invasion and Soviet tactics encouraged several states, including the USA, Pakistan, the UK, China, Saudi Arabia, and the United Arab Emirates to provide material support to the rebels. The *mujahadeen* also committed atrocities—torturing and executing Soviet prisoners, although they tended to treat Afghan conscripts more leniently.[309]

Inadequate reporting and the difficulty of distinguishing intended from battle-related civilian deaths make it difficult to determine precisely how many civilians were intentionally killed by the Soviet army and their Afghan allies.[310] Most humanitarian agencies, the UN, the Soviet government, and the *mujahadeen* put the total number of Afghans killed in the period between the Saur revolution (1978) and Soviet withdrawal (1989) at between 1.3 million and 2 million.[311] It is commonly estimated that 80 per cent of these casualties were civilians, suggesting that between 1 million and 1.6 million civilians were killed in total. Up to 50,000 civilians were killed in the months immediately before the Soviet invasion. Of the remaining casualties, it is impossible to know precisely what proportion died as a direct result of attacks on the civilian population but the limited number and small scale of battles between the armed belligerents—a consequence of the insurgents' strategy—means that relatively few civilians are likely to have been killed in crossfire. Indeed, when the Special Rapporteur to the UN's Human Rights Commission, Felix Ermacora, argued that 35,000 civilians were killed in 1985 alone, he noted that the majority were killed by indiscriminate bombing and shelling and massacres.[312] On this basis, we can suggest with some confidence that at least 500,000 Afghan civilians were killed by indiscriminate bombardment, shelling, booby traps, summary executions, and massacres perpetrated by the Soviet Union and that the actual number might be closer to 1 million. According to the UNHCR, by the late 1980s, some 5.5 million Afghan civilians had fled to Pakistan and Iran and another 2 million were internally displaced.

The background to the crisis lay in Soviet efforts to support an unpopular communist regime in Afghanistan. With the regime in danger of collapsing, the Soviet leadership began examining the merits of intervention in 1978. Some senior military figures and Politburo members were concerned that

[309] Harry S. Bradsher, *Afghan Communism and Soviet Intervention* (Oxford: Oxford University Press, 1999), p. 140. The issue of Islamist atrocities is considered in Chapter 11.

[310] See Helen Fein, 'Discriminating Genocide from War Crimes: Vietnam and Afghanistan Reconsidered', *Denver Journal of International Law and Policy*, 29, 1993–94, p. 56; and Jeri Laber and Barnett R. Rubin, *A Nation is Dying: Afghanistan under the Soviets 1979–87* (Evanston, IL: Northwestern University Press, 1988), p. 10.

[311] See Bradsher, *Afghan Communism*, pp. 177–9. Larry Goodson puts the death toll at 'nearly two million'. See Larry P. Goodson, *Afghanistan's Endless War: State Failure, Regional Politics, and the Rise of the Taliban* (Seattle: University of Washington Press, 2001), pp. 92–3.

[312] Felix Ermacora, *Report on the Situation of Human Rights in Afghanistan*, E/CN.4/1986/24, 17 February 1986, p. 17.

invasion lacked a solid legal basis and would damage the country's international reputation.[313] But as the situation in Afghanistan deteriorated, Brezhnev prevailed on the Politburo to agree to the invasion on the basis of the Brezhnev doctrine of using force to support communist governments, pointing to the seriousness of the threat in Afghanistan, his belief that the tide of the Cold War had swung decisively in the communists' favour, and calculation that a new Afghan government could defeat the rebels with Soviet help.[314]

But rather than being cowed by Soviet firepower and wooed by the new government, Afghans rallied against the foreign invader.[315] Mass desertions almost halved the size of the Afghan army.[316] Sensitive about their own casualties and unable to defeat the growing *mujahadeen* in conventional battle, the Soviet and Afghan governments developed a counter-insurgency strategy based on indiscriminate force.[317] In the countryside, they tried to separate the insurgents from the civilian population by depopulating troublesome regions. In the cities, the notorious secret police (KhAD) used detention, torture, and summary executions to eliminate those suspected of supporting the resistance.

According to Felix Ermacora, Special Rapporteur to the UN Human Rights Commission, 'the main types of action which have caused deaths and casualties, in particular among the civilian population of Afghanistan are bombardments, shelling and massacre in reprisal, acts of brutality committed by armed forces, and the use of anti-personnel mines and booby-trap toys'.[318] Soviet strategy employed airpower, mines, and booby traps to terrorize the population, followed up with ground-based sweeps to eliminate insurgents and further terrorize the civilian population—a strategy later employed in Chechnya in the 1990s.[319] Several valleys (including the Panjshir, Paghman, Kunar, and Logar valleys) were devastated and virtually their whole civilian population displaced.[320] According to Larry Goodson, at least half of Afghanistan's 24,000 villages were destroyed by Soviet airpower and artillery.[321] This

[313] Angelo Rasanayagam, *Afghanistan: A Modern History* (New York: I. B. Tauris, 2005), pp. 85 and 87.

[314] Bradsher, *Afghan Communism*, pp. 38–9 and, on military scepticism, p. 49; Rasul B. Rais, *War Without Winners: Afghanistan's Uncertain Transition after the Cold War* (Oxford: Oxford University Press, 1994), pp. 77–8.

[315] Nabi Misdaq, *Afghanistan: Political Frailty and External Interference* (London: Routledge, 2006), pp. 143–7.

[316] Boulouque, 'Communism', in Courtois et al., *Black Book of Communism*, p. 715.

[317] Goodson, *Afghanistan's Endless War*, pp. 60 and 94; and William Maley, *The Afghanistan Wars* (London: Palgrave), pp. 47, 49–50.

[318] Ermacora, *Report on the Situation of Human Rights in Afghanistan*, p. 17.

[319] E.g. Claude Malhuret (Executive Director of MSF), 'Report from Afghanistan', *Foreign Affairs*, 62, 1983–1984, pp. 427–9.

[320] Scott Ray McMichael, *Stumbling Bear: Soviet Military Performance in Afghanistan* (London: Brassey's, 1991), p. 54.

[321] Goodson, *Afghanistan's Endless War*, p. 95.

strategy was predicated on a general acceptance that civilians would be intentionally targeted, and testimony from Soviet soldiers repeatedly emphasized the army's culture of impunity towards killing civilians.[322] Ermacora identified thirty-two separate incidents involving the bombardment, shelling, or massacre of civilians in 1985 alone.[323] The strategy succeeded in its immediate aim of driving off the population, but failed to destroy the *mujahadeen*'s rural support bases, not least because the insurgents had access to foreign support and havens in Pakistan.[324]

Typically, the first line of assault was indiscriminate airpower or artillery fire.[325] Michael Barry documented a series of air raids on civilian settlements between 1980 and 1982.[326] Sometimes, as in Laghman province in 1985, air power was employed against villages and civilian structures with the intention of denying them to the insurgents—much as the USA had done in Korea and with much the same effect on the civilian population.[327] Homes, fields, orchards, and mosques were targeted. In provincial towns, marketplaces and residential districts were subjected to aerial bombardment.[328] At other times, armoured personnel carriers positioned themselves on the outskirts of a village, blockaded exit points and fired indiscriminately into the village. After the initial bombardment, soldiers entered the village ostensibly to root out insurgents. To terrorize the civilian population, Soviet soldiers sometimes committed summary executions, raped women, committed random acts of violence, and looted goods.[329]

Massacre reports were not slow to emerge. The Permanent Peoples' Tribunal in Stockholm, a follow-on to the 'Russell Tribunal' established to investigate US conduct in Vietnam, despatched a team of investigators. They returned with clear eyewitness, photographic, and forensic evidence of a massacre of 105 civilians in Padkhwab-e Shana (Longar province) on 13 September 1982. When the village was attacked by Soviet forces, the villagers hid in an underground irrigation canal and were burned alive with a combination of gasoline, pentrite, and trinitrotoluene (TNT), which they piped into the canal.[330] Amnesty International reported that 100 villagers in Khasham

[322] See Anna Heinamaa, Maija Leppanen, and Yuri Yurchenko, *The Soldiers' Story: Soviet Veterans Remember the Afghan War* (Berkeley: University of California, International and Area Studies, 1994).

[323] Ermacora, *Report of the Situation*, p. 17.

[324] McMichael, *Stumbling Bear*, p. 54.

[325] Rais, *War Without Winners*, p. 99.

[326] Michael Barry, 'Statement to the Bar Association, January 28, 1983', *World Affairs*, 145 (3), 1982/83, p. 308.

[327] Boulouque, 'Communism', p. 719.

[328] Laber and Rubin, *A Nation is Dying*, p. 11 and see pp. 12–16.

[329] Laber and Rubin, *A Nation is Dying*, pp. 18–20, 35–42; and Boulouque, 'Communism', p. 718.

[330] Michael Barry, 'Statement to the Bar Association', p. 300.

Kalar, also in Longar province, suffered the same fate.[331] On 13 October 1983, the Soviets responded to an attack on a convoy near Kandahar by killing 126 civilians—mostly women and children—in the villages of Timur Qalachi, Kolchabad, and Muchkizai. Fifty of the victims were women aged between twenty and thirty-two and twenty-six were children.[332] Amnesty International also documented the massacre of twenty-three civilians in a reprisal attack in Raudzi in 1983 (Ghazni province).[333] Another study listed in first-person detail no fewer than 8,152 cases of atrocities committed in 1983 alone.[334] The massacres continued in 1984 and 1985. Laber and Rubin detail the March 1985 massacre of around 120 civilians in Darra-e-nur, a massacre of 250 civilians in Kunduz (December 1984/January 1985), and the April 1985 massacre of 500 civilians in Laghman province.[335] Reprisal bombings against villages in the vicinity of rebel attacks were described as 'frequent' by one analyst, whilst Barnett Rubin concluded that 'the Soviets have a clear and consistent policy of taking reprisals against civilians for military actions by the Resistance'.[336] Soviet forces devised other cruel ways of terrorizing the population. Targeting children, they dropped booby trapped clocks and toys, designed to detonate when touched.[337] Booby traps were also placed under mattresses during house searches.

A different strategy was used to eliminate opponents in urban areas. A Soviet journal reported that in government-controlled territory, the secret police (KhAD) 'used the tools of Stalin's great terror'.[338] In his 1985 report to the UN Human Rights Commission, Ermacora described the KhAD as an 'immense torture machine'.[339] A month after the KhAD's main prison, Pol-e-Charki, was captured by the *mujahadeen* a mass grave was uncovered nearby with the remains of an estimated 12,000 people.[340] Mohammed Hassan Kakar estimated that up to 50,000 people were executed there.[341]

[331] Amnesty International, *Annual Report 1983* (London: Amnesty International, 1983), p. 227.

[332] Boulouque, 'Communism', p. 719. These massacres were also documented by UN Human Rights Commission's Special Rapporteur for Afghanistan, Felix Ermacora.

[333] Amnesty International, *Annual Report 1984* (London: Amnesty International, 1984), p. 222.

[334] National Committee for Human Rights in Afghanistan, *Russia's Barbarism in Afghanistan*, three volumes, 1984, 1985, 1986 respectively.

[335] Laber and Rubin, *A Nation is Dying*, pp. 22–34.

[336] McMichael, *Stumbling Bear*, p. 82; and Barnett R. Rubin, 'Human Rights in Afghanistan' in Rosanne Klass (ed.), *Afghanistan: The Great Game Revisited* (New York: Freedom House, 1990), p. 351; and Laber and Rubin, *A Nation is Dying*, pp. 17–22

[337] Barry, 'Statement to the Bar Association', p. 301; Malhuret, 'Report from Afghanistan', p. 426; and Laber and Rubin, *A Nation is Dying*, pp. 45–6.

[338] Cited by Bradsher, *Afghan Communism*, p. 137.

[339] Felix Ermacora, *Report on the Situation*, p. 11.

[340] Boulouque, 'Communism', p. 723.

[341] Cited by Bradsher, *Afghan Communism*, p. 139.

The Soviet Union justified its invasion of Afghanistan by arguing that a popular uprising had ousted Amin, installed a new communist government, and requested Soviet assistance.[342] In relation to the killing of civilians, the Soviet Union attempted to secure sufficient legitimacy by creating and leveraging uncertainty. As *The Times* editorialized in 1985, 'it is hard but not impossible to discover the truth of Soviet atrocities in Afghanistan. Obviously, stifling the flow of information to the outside world has been one of the Soviet Union's highest priorities: hardly for Moscow the daily disadvantage of television bulletins showing Migs strafing villages and mines or booby traps blowing the legs off children and livestock. Consequently, revelations about Soviet atrocities are spasmodic but each successful foray into the mountains only confirms a deepening brutality and cynicism in the conduct of the war'.[343] At its most basic, the strategy entailed challenging the validity of atrocity reports. To do this, the Soviets refused to grant access to foreign journalists and humanitarian agencies, severely limiting the degree of first-hand reporting and allowing them to deride atrocity reports as fabrications.[344] In January 1980, the ICRC was authorized to send delegates to Afghanistan to assist 'political and security prisoners' and prisoners of war, but in June, as the violence escalated, the delegates were instructed to leave. The ICRC requested permission to return, but these requests were rejected until the final stages of the conflict. At one point, the Soviet Union argued that the ICRC should not be concerned about Soviet compliance with International Humanitarian Law in Afghanistan because it was not engaged in combat operations there.[345] When foreign humanitarian organizations operating in Afghanistan provided witness to atrocities, they were sometimes attacked—both verbally and physically. Médecins sans Frontières reported that six clearly marked hospitals that it operated were attacked by helicopter gunships in 1980 and 1981, retribution—it believed—for bearing witness to Soviet atrocities.[346]

When faced with criticism by the UN Human Rights Commission's Special Rapporteur, Felix Ermacora, the Soviet Union tried to discredit the author—a tall order given that it had welcomed Ermacora's earlier reports on Chile, Israel, and South Africa.[347] Presented with evidence from the People's Tribunal concerning the massacre at Padkhwab-e Shana, Afghan authorities simply denounced the Tribunal as an instrument of imperialism (despite earlier communist endorsements of its findings on Vietnam) and denied the

[342] Bradsher, *Afghan Communism*, p. 107.

[343] 'Blood on their Hands', *The Times*, 19 February 1985, p. 13.

[344] *The Times*, for example, accused the Soviets of 'skilfully shielding' the atrocities from world opinion. See 'Blood on their Hands', *The Times*, 19 February 1985, p. 13.

[345] W. Michael Reisman and James Silk, 'Which Law Applies to the Afghan Conflict?', *American Journal of International Law*, 82 (3) 1988, p. 479.

[346] Malhuret, 'Report from Afghanistan', pp. 431–2.

[347] Bradsher, *Afghan Communism*, p. 141.

accusation, arguing that the ceilings in the water pipes were too small for humans to hide inside.[348] Soviet news agency *Tass* simply rejected the reported massacre at Kerala, denouncing it as 'anti-Soviet propaganda' and 'monstrous misinformation'.[349] Other governments within the Soviet bloc adopted a similar line. When it assumed the presidency of the UN General Assembly in 1982, Hungary broke long-standing protocol by using a presidential speech to claim that 'the killings in Afghanistan are largely exaggerated' and insist that the 'extermination' of Palestinians by Israel be given greater attention.[350] On the few occasions where it did admit that its forces had committed crimes, the Soviet government argued that individual crimes were perpetrated by rogue soldiers who were duly punished. Indeed, some 2,500 Soviet soldiers were imprisoned for crimes committed in Afghanistan, but the majority of these were for crimes against Soviet property or other members of the armed forces. Very few were imprisoned for crimes against Afghans.[351]

Soviet censorship, restrictions on travel within Afghanistan, the difficult Afghan terrain, security problems, and the clandestine nature of US support to the resistance, limited international reporting of the Afghan war for a time.[352] There was some initial scepticism about reported atrocities, primarily because they were difficult to verify and survivors were generally unwilling to speak publicly for fear of retribution against family members.[353] Despite this, international society was quick and consistent in its condemnation of the Soviet Union, with only the Soviet-bloc defending its conduct.

From the outset, the USA strongly opposed the Soviet occupation of Afghanistan, which it described as 'dirty and brutal'.[354] Worried about the negative precedent that might be established if the Soviet Union prevailed, President Carter stated that 'we are the other superpower on earth and it became my responsibility . . . to take action that would prevent the Soviets from [accomplishing] this invasion with impunity'.[355] On 28 December, the President labelled the invasion 'a clear threat to peace . . . [that] could mark a

[348] Boulouque, 'Communism', p. 717.

[349] Linda Charlton, 'Moscow Scorns US Press Reports About a "Massacre" in Afghanistan', *New York Times*, 6 February 1980.

[350] Bernard D. Nossiter, 'UN Official Assails Killings in Lebanon, not in Afghanistan', *New York Times*, 24 September 1982, p. A4.

[351] Bradsher, *Afghan Communism*, p. 203.

[352] Several writers make this point. E.g. Boulouque, 'Communism', p. 716.

[353] See 'Editor's Note', 'Atrocities and Violations of Human Rights and International Law in Afghanistan', *World Affairs*, 145 (3), 1982/83, p. 299.

[354] As the State Department's Regional Director for Pakistan and Afghanistan (1982–84), Harmon Kirby, put it, 'the United States strongly opposes the Soviet occupation of Afghanistan and seeks an end to the terrible agony it has brought to the Afghan people'. See Harmon E. Kirby, 'US Policy on Afghanistan', in Ralph H. Magnus (ed.), *Afghan Alternatives: Issues, Options and Policies* (New Brunswick: Transaction Books, 1988), p. 143.

[355] Cited by Bradsher, *Afghan Communism*, p. 101.

fundamental and long-lasting turning point in our relations'.[356] The USA stepped up its criticism as the conflict continued, and it became common for Reagan Administration officials and politicians from both parties to accuse the Soviet Union of committing genocide. In 1985 Deputy Assistant Secretary of State, Arnold Raphael noted that 'we've seen increased bombing there in the past year—carpet bombing of villages, napalming of civilians—and this continuation of genocide against the Afghan people'. Pushed to explain the genocide claim, he argued that 'more than one third of the Afghan people are refugees.... The Soviets, for example, use mines which are disguised as toys, which children pick up, doing great damage to the children and great harm to the people. It is in every sense of the word genocide'.[357] Democrat Senator Bill Bradley also labelled the killing as 'genocide' and opined that 'indiscriminate carpet bombing has levelled entire villages; whole populations have been massacred', noting 'this is not the first time that the Soviet Union has resorted to genocide to secure its political ends'.[358] This view was also aired by the Independent Council on International Human Rights, which found 'considerable evidence' to support this view.[359]

Recognizing that there was little chance of the Soviet Union heeding US advice and withdrawing unilaterally, Carter directed his officials to develop policies to 'make Soviet involvement as costly as possible'.[360] The Administration delayed ratification of the SALT II arms control treaty, placed an embargo on grain exports to the Soviet Union, restricted the sale of high-technology products, withdrew fishing privileges, and boycotted the 1980 Moscow Olympics.[361] These measures had little direct effect but drew sharp criticism from the Soviet leadership. In addition, though, Carter also decided that the US had a 'moral obligation' to assist the Afghan resistance. The CIA briefed Congress on a $30 million plan to arm the rebels and, there being no objections, began shipments in January 1980. By the end of the year, the administration had doubled military aid to $60 million, working with Saudi Arabia, China, Egypt, Israel, and Pakistan to purchase and supply inconspicuous Soviet-made weapons.[362] The level of US aid increased dramatically under Reagan. In 1984, Congress allocated $250 million to the programme and agreed

[356] Cited by Bradsher, *Afghan Communism*, p. 101. Also see, President Carter speech to the University of Virginia, 4 January 1980; and Rasanayagam, *Afghanistan*, p. 91.

[357] Arnold Raphael in 'Afghanistan: War Without End?', The MacNeil/Lehrer News Hour, 27 December 1985.

[358] Bill Bradley, 'Captive Afghanistan, 6 Years Later: Fighters Need US Aid', *New York Times*, 27 December 1985, p. A31.

[359] Paul Lewis, 'UN Urges Soviet to Pull Forces From Afghanistan', *New York Times*, 11 November 1987, p. A12; and see Michael Reisman and C. H. Norchi, 'Genocide and the Soviet Occupation of Afghanistan', Institute for the Study of Genocide News, 1988.

[360] Bradsher, *Afghan Communism*, p. 102. See Brzezinski, *Power and Principle*, pp. 427–30.

[361] Bradsher, *Afghan Communism*, p. 103; and Rasanayagam, *Afghanistan*, p. 91.

[362] Bradsher, *Afghan Communism*, pp. 215–16.

to equip the resistance with high-technology Stinger missiles to counter the threat from Soviet helicopters and aircraft. Soviet air losses increased from an average of twenty per year to over two hundred per year as a result.[363]

Most West European governments also condemned Soviet behaviour.[364] The British government's stridently anti-Soviet stance was echoed by sections of the press there. *The Times*, for inastance, complained that 'Soviet tactics in Afghanistan would seem to violate every canon of international law'.[365] Britain joined the USA in delivering clandestine military assistance to the *mujahadeen*, supplying Blowfish anti-aircraft missiles, SAS trainers, and around $17million worth of military aid per year.[366] West Germany stopped short of imposing economic sanctions but boycotted the 1980 Olympics and channelled financial assistance to the rebels, at a level the Soviets believed to be double that of British aid.[367]

The West's view was broadly in step with that of most of the rest of the world. The invasion immediately reversed deteriorating US–Pakistani relations and the military regime in Pakistan lined up squarely with the USA in denouncing the Soviets and supporting the *mujahadeen*. Pakistan's position was shaped by various factors including the fact the regime in Kabul employed Pashtun nationalist rhetoric and questioned the demarcation of the Afghan–Pakistan border; deep concerns about Soviet hegemony, especially given Moscow's friendly relations with India; ties between the Afghan regime and rebels in Pakistan's Baluchistan region; the major flow of refugees into Pakistan caused by Soviet intervention (which reached two million by 1985); and the potential to leverage the situation to secure political, financial, and military assistance from the USA.[368]

Fearing the extension of Soviet hegemony in Asia, China also denounced the Soviet Union and applauded the US response.[369] It cooperated with the USA in the clandestine delivery of military aid to the *mujahadeen*. Saudi Arabia and the United Arab Emirates were also staunch opponents of the Soviet invasion. Between them, they probably channelled more assistance to the *mujahadeen* than the USA did.[370] Iran joined Pakistan in offering sanctuaries to the rebels.[371] In late January 1980, the Organization of the Islamic

[363] Rais, *War Without Winners*, p. 207.

[364] Bradsher, *Afghan Communism*, p. 106.

[365] 'Blood on their Hands', *The Times*, 19 February 1985, p. 13.

[366] Bradsher, *Afghan Communism*, p. 219.

[367] Bradsher, *Afghan Communism*, p. 219.

[368] This list is a compilation of factors identified by Rasanayagam, *Afghanistan*, pp. 102–5; and Rais, *War Without Winners*, p. 168.

[369] See A. Z. Hilali, 'China's Response to the Soviet Invasion of Afghanistan', *Central Asian Survey*, 20 (3) 2001, pp. 323–51.

[370] The Soviet Union certainly thought so, estimating that in 1985 these two countries supplied $320 million of assistance to the rebels. See Bradsher, *Afghan Communism*, p. 219.

[371] Rais, *War Without Winners*, pp. 212 and 236–8.

Conference (OIC) condemned the invasion as 'a flagrant violation of international law' and demanded an immediate withdrawal. The OIC also suspended Afghanistan's membership, awarding its seat to the *mujahadeen* and calling on others to not recognize the 'illegal regime' installed there.[372]

The invasion was hotly debated by Non-Aligned Movement foreign ministers at a conference in New Delhi in February 1981. India, which had adopted a neutral position that reflected its generally good relations with the Soviet Union and interest in weakening Pakistani influence, offered an even-handed draft resolution that did not demand the withdrawal of foreign forces from Afghanistan. Pakistan responded with its own more strongly worded draft which expressed 'particular concern' about Afghanistan and 'urgently called' for a withdrawal. The Pakistani draft prevailed.[373]

All this translated into a relatively strong stance by the UN, with the General Assembly condemning the invasion and expressing concern at the plight of civilians. With the UN Security Council blocked by Soviet veto, the Council could only refer the matter on to the General Assembly by a procedural resolution (Resolution 462, 9 January 1980).[374] By a very large majority (104 for, 18 against, 18 abstentions [including, India, Iraq, Syria, Yemen, Ethiopia, and others with close ties to the Soviet Union]), the General Assembly issued a resolution that 'strongly deplor[ed]' the invasion and called for the immediate and unconditional withdrawal of all foreign (i.e. Soviet) forces (ES-6/2, 14 January 1980). As well as condemning the invasion itself, the General Assembly 'expressed its deep concern at the severe consequences for the civilian population of indiscriminate bombardments and military operations aimed primarily at the villages and the agricultural structure'. The resolution also expressed the Assembly's 'deep concern that the Afghan authorities, with heavy support from foreign troops, are acting with great severity against their opponents and suspected opponents without any respect for the international human rights obligations which they have assumed'.[375] Firmly placed on the Assembly's agenda, the demand for an immediate withdrawal was reiterated each year throughout the 1980s and continued to command its large majority. In 1987, the year before the Geneva Peace Accords provided for Soviet withdrawal, 123 countries voted in favour, 19 against, and 11 abstained.[376] Not only did these repeated heavy defeats undermine the Soviet Union's international reputation, by the late 1980s they also stood in the way of the regime's interest in using the UN to resolve

[372] Misdaq, *Afghanistan*, p. 156.

[373] Bradsher, *Afghan Communism*, p. 105.

[374] Maley, *Afghanistan Wars*, p. 77.

[375] General Assembly Resolution 40/137, 13 December 1985, paras. 3 and 4.

[376] Paul Lewis, 'UN Urges Soviet to Pull Forces From Afghanistan', *New York Times*, 11 November 1987, p. A12.

a number of regional conflicts (e.g. Cambodia, Mozambique).[377] The Soviets did succeed, however, in securing UN credentials for the new regime, but only because that matter was resolved prior to the General Assembly's emergency session on the issue.[378]

The Soviet Union therefore paid a high price for its behaviour in Afghanistan: its forces suffered significant material and credibility losses; the conflict placed a heavy drain on the Soviet economy; the government's domestic standing was damaged by the evident inaccuracy of its propaganda; and its international reputation was badly affected.[379] These costs ultimately forced the Soviet Union to negotiate a withdrawal that paved the way for a *mujahadeen* victory in 1992.[380] The new Soviet leader, Mikhail Gorbachev described the war as a 'bleeding wound' and shortly after the Soviet withdrawal, the Foreign Ministry declared that the war had been an, 'oppressive moral and material burden . . . [it] was actually seen in most countries . . . as a bid to expand our sphere of influence by taking advantage of a regional conflict. The presence of Soviet troops in Afghanistan not only froze our relations with many countries . . . but called in question what had been accomplished in the years of détente'.[381]

The Soviets claimed that the invasion was legitimate because it was requested by the Afghan government and leveraged uncertainty to deny that it was targeting civilians, arguing that the victims were insurgents and not civilians, that civilian deaths were unintended, that some massacre reports were fabrications or that individual crimes were committed by rogue soldiers who were duly punished. None of this helped to legitimize the war or its conduct and the Soviet Union paid a heavy price for its illegitimacy. With significant external support, the Afghans sustained and then escalated armed resistance, inflicting significant casualties and financial costs upon the Soviet Union, ultimately forcing its withdrawal. Mounting casualties (14,500 Soviet soldiers were killed by 1989) facilitated by external support for the rebels provoked domestic opposition to the regime, which certainly played a part in the final collapse of Soviet communism. But although it was the invasion itself that sparked the outpouring of international condemnation, concerns about civilian devastation were also evident. Thus, Soviet justifications were neither tolerated nor endorsed outside the Soviet bloc in part because of the illegitimacy of the invasion (and hence the relative illegitimacy of the Soviets

[377] Maley, *Afghanistan Wars*, p. 77.

[378] Maley, *Afghanistan Wars*, p. 77.

[379] On the damage to reputation, see Tom Rogers, *The Soviet Withdrawal from Afghanistan: Analysis and Chronology* (Westport: Greenwood Press, 1992), p. 8; and Maley, *Afghanistan Wars*, pp. 160–1.

[380] There are many accounts of the ending of the Soviet-Afghanistan War. See, for example, Rais, *War Without Winners*, p. 118 ff; Rogers, *Soviet Withdrawal*.

[381] Cited by Bradsher, *Afghan Communism*, p. 253.

vis-à-vis the *mujahadeen*) and in part because its attempts to excuse its conduct appeared implausible in the face of evidence of widespread violations of civilian immunity. That it was these two factors (relative legitimacy of the actors and plausibility of the Soviet claim to be complying with civilian immunity) working together that generated the all-too evident illegitimacy and not simply the latter is demonstrated by the fact that a few years later, the Russian Federation was able to secure sufficient legitimacy for mass killing in Chechnya with equally implausible arguments.

## The Beijing Massacre (1989)

In what was perhaps the final communist atrocity of the Cold War, on 4 June 1989 the Chinese army forcibly broke up a demonstration centred on Tiananmen Square in Beijing. In the process, they massacred between 1,000 and 3,000 civilians. Although it certainly portrayed its victims as 'class enemies' or 'criminals' who deserved their fate, the Chinese government's primary justificatory argument was to deny that a massacre had taken place. But although the government went to greater lengths than ever before to try to justify the killing of civilians to international society, it received sharp international criticism and was punished with economic sanctions. This was in marked contrast to earlier cases, when the Chinese government killed many more people but received much less (if any) criticism and punishment, despite not bothering to offer much in the way of justification. The key factors in explaining this difference were the flow of credible and timely information and judgements about the relative legitimacy of the regime and the protestors.

The protests that led to the massacre were prompted by the death of Hu Yaobang on 15 April 1989.[382] Hu's death and funeral brought students out onto Tiananmen Square to demand government reform. Over time, they were joined by other groups, including workers' organizations and established a permanent presence on the Square. In late May, they erected a statue to the 'Goddess of Liberty'. Thanks to Soviet leader Mikhael Gorbachev's landmark visit to Beijing in April, the city was full of foreign journalists, many of whom stayed to cover the protests. This fixed the world's attention firmly on Beijing. In early May, US Congress held hearings in which a US State Department Official warned China that 'non-peaceful' repression would have a 'deleterious' effect on US–China relations. Harry Harding (Brookings Institution) advised that the USA should support political reform, and Pei Minxin advised

[382] On the origins of the protest, see Anita Chan, 'The Social Origins and Consequences of the Tiananmen Crisis', in David S. G. Goodman and Gerald Segal (ed.), *China in the Nineties: Crisis Management and Beyond* (Oxford: Clarendon Press, 1991), pp. 105–30.

that Congress should warn the Chinese government to not use force.[383] Students in the USA, the UK, Germany, and France mobilized in support of the Beijing protests and the Western media also backed the protestors.[384]

In mid-May, martial law was imposed on Beijing and troops moved into the city.[385] On 2 June, an unarmed military assault on the square was stopped in its tracks and some soldiers were beaten by the protestors. Hope that the protestors had succeeded proved short-lived, however, as the following day the army launched another attack on the square, this time using live ammunition, personnel carriers, and tanks. Confronting barricades and an angry crowd at Muxidi on the road into the square, the troops opened fire and strafed surrounding buildings. Protestors responded by attacking tanks and soldiers, and the violence continued into the night. The army reached Tiananmen at around 4 a.m. and following tense negotiations, the student leaders decided to evacuate peacefully to avoid further bloodshed. Sporadic violence continued for several days as civilians in Beijing continued to attack isolated soldiers and tanks and the army responded with occasional indiscriminate violence.[386]

The total number of casualties from the events surrounding 4 June remains hotly contested. It was initially reported that a source at the Chinese Red Cross had claimed that 2,600 protestors had been killed, but the Red Cross quickly denied this. In a detailed report on the incident, Amnesty International put the figure at 'at least' 1,000 whereas the government admitted that 300 people had died and 400 were missing, including soldiers. Most other estimates place the death toll at between 1,000 and 3,000, but almost all agree that despite the event's popular epithet, very few—if any—students were intentionally killed on Tiananmen Square itself.[387] Protests in other parts of the country were also crushed, sometimes violently. In Chengdu around 400 protestors were killed when the army stepped in to restore order.[388]

[383] All these statements were noted by the Chinese government itself. Reported in Zhang Ling, *The Tiananmen Papers*, edited by Andrew J. Nathan and Perry Link (New York: Public Affairs, 2001), p. 120.

[384] Zhang Ling, *Tiananmen Papers*, p. 120.

[385] Craig Calhoun, *Neither Gods nor Emperors: Students and the Struggle for Democracy in China* (Berkeley: University of California Press, 1994), pp. 111–12.

[386] More detailed accounts of the events are offered in: Calhoun, *Neither Gods nor Emperors*; Nathan, *China's Crisis*, pp. 171–92. For reproductions of reports provided by the authorities themselves, see Zhang Ling, *Tiananmen Papers*.

[387] See Hutchings, *Modern China*, pp. 421–2; and Colin Mackerras, Pradeep Taneja, and Graham Young, *China Since 1978: Reform, Modernisation and 'Socialism with Chinese Characteristics'* (New York: St. Martin's Press, 1993), p. 63. Two weeks after the event, Nicholas Kristof put the figure at between 400–800, though he acknowledged that it was likely higher and that this estimate did not include those who died on the days after 4 June. See Nicholas Kristof, 'A Reassessment of How Many Died in the Military Crackdown in Beijing', *New York Times*, 20 June 1989.

[388] Colin Mackerras, Kevin Bucknall, and Russell Trood, 'The Beijing Tragedy: Implications for China and Australia', Centre for the Study of Australia-Asia Relations, Griffith University, research paper no. 51, 1989.

To justify the crackdown, on 1 June, the hardliner Li Peng had circulated a report entitled 'On the True Nature of the Turmoil'. The use of the phrase 'turmoil' (sometimes translated as 'chaos') is particularly noteworthy as, after the death of Mao, this was the term used to describe and criticize the Cultural Revolution. The report argued that 'a tiny minority has organized and plotted turmoil and has made continuous occupation of the Square an important political tactic'. The protestors were intent on 'provoking conflicts, exacerbating conflict, and trying to cause bloodshed in order to make a national and even international impact'. The report argued that the protest had secured 'a large amount of spiritual support and material aid' from 'various hostile forces, organizations and individuals at home and abroad'. It recommended that the state 'take swift and decisive measures immediately to suppress the counterrevolutionary turmoil in Beijing'.[389] On the same day, the Beijing Party Committee circulated a report in which it argued that the protests were backed by Western capitalists, and especially the USA, as part of their campaign to infiltrate and undermine Chinese communism.[390] Claiming that the very future of communism in China was a stake, this report concluded: 'the international monopoly capitalists and hostile, reactionary forces have not abandoned for a moment their intent to destroy us. It is now clear that murderous intent has always lurked behind their protestations of peace and friendship. When the opportunity arises they will remove the façade and reveal their true colours. They have only one goal: to annihilate socialism'.[391]

The following day (2 June), party elders (including Deng Xiaoping) agreed to order the army to clear the square. Deng suggested that it would be best if the Square was peacefully cleared but the meeting's general emphasis was firmly focused on doing whatever it took to clear the square. Wang Zhen, for example, argued:

> Those goddam bastards! Who do they think they are, trampling on sacred ground like Tiananmen for so long? They're really asking for it! We should send the troops right now to grad those counterrevolutionaries.... What's the People's Liberation Army for anyway? What are martial law troops for? They are not supposed to just sit around and eat. We've got to do it or we'll never forgive ourselves.... Anybody who tries to overthrow the Communist Party deserves death and no burial!

Deng Xiaoping supported the Li Peng line. He argued that the West had provided material support and propaganda to the protests, describing

[389] This report is reproduced in Zhang Ling, *Tiananmen Papers*.

[390] The paranoid belief that the USA was behind the protests was apparent across the leadership. Deng Xiaoping himself was a keen subscriber to this view. See Joseph Fewsmith, *China Since Tiananmen: From Deng Xiaoping to Hu Jintao* (Cambridge: Cambridge University Press, 2008), p. 43.

[391] This report is reproduced in Zhang Ling, *Tiananmen Papers*.

protestors as 'the scum of the Chinese nation', and that China's economic and political development depended on a speedy resolution to the crisis. He proposed that 'martial law troops begin tonight to carry out the clearing plan and finish it within two days. As we proceed with the clearing, we must explain it carefully to all the citizens and students, asking them to leave and doing our very best to persuade them. *But if they refuse to leave, they will be responsible for the consequences*'.[392]

Later that day, these instructions were translated into military orders to clear the square. Troops were instructed to clear the Square by 6 a.m. on 4 June and that 'no delays will be permitted'. The order read: 'if blocking occurs, soldiers may clear it using any and all self-defensive means that may be required'. Commanders were told to instruct their troops only 'to open fire as a last resort' and 'only if everything else fails', though the objective of clearing the Square by 6 a.m. overrode all other considerations. On a direct order from Deng, troops were instructed that there was to be 'no bloodshed within Tiananmen Square—period'. The order continued, 'What if thousands of students refuse to leave? Then the troops carry away thousands of students on their backs! No one must die in the Square'.[393] In the event, the troops followed their orders to the letter. While the mission was poorly executed, largely because the troops were trained for conventional combat not riot control, there is no evidence that indiscipline contributed to the bloodshed. As instructed, troops used all means necessary to reach the Square and then cleared it without violence before 6 a.m. on 4 June.[394]

The Chinese government used three basic arguments to justify its crackdown. First, it denied that there had been a massacre by pointing to the fact that no students were killed on the Square itself.[395] On 7 June, the military commissar of the 27th Group Army told television viewers that not a single student had been killed during the operation to clear Tiananmen Square. This is probably true if one only considers the Square itself, but overlooks the fact that the 27th Group Army fired on protestors at Muxidi and elsewhere when it found its way to the Square blocked.[396] Second, the government argued that force was only used as a last resort and in self-defence and that the government had pursued a peaceful path, demonstrating patience in the face of extreme provocation. Those deaths that were acknowledged were judged to have been

[392] Emphasis added. Minutes are reproduced in Zhang Ling, *Tiananmen Papers.*

[393] Reproduced in Zhang Ling, *Tiananmen Papers.*

[394] Michael T. Byrnes, 'The Death of a People's Army', in George Hicks (ed.), *The Broken Mirror: China after Tiananmen* (London: Longman, 1990), pp. 140–1.

[395] Calhoun, *Neither Gods nor Emperors*, pp. 140–1.

[396] Richard Baum, *Burying Mao: Chinese Politics in the Age of Deng Xiaoping* (Princeton: Princeton University Press, 1994), p. 292.

the result of clashes provoked by protestors (labelled 'ruffians' and 'rioters').[397] To emphasize this point, the government repeatedly showed graphic images of the bodies of soldiers killed by the protestors.[398] As the mayor of Beijing, Chen Xitong put it, 'among the non-military casualties were rioters who deserved the punishment, people accidentally injured, and doctors and other people who were carrying out their various duties on the spot. The government will do its best to deal with the problems arising from the latter two kinds of people'.[399] Third, the government argued that it was legitimate to forcibly disperse protestors because they constituted a threat to the people. Left unchecked, the protests would have spread turmoil, stymieing China's economic development.[400]

Confronted by graphic real-time reporting of the killing of protestors, Western governments unanimously condemned China, and the USA and several European countries imposed sanctions. In the immediate aftermath, President Bush expressed 'deep regret' over the use of force and Secretary of State James Baker described events as 'most unfortunate'. Members of Congress were less diplomatic and offered 'sanctuary' to Chinese students studying in the USA. Stephen Solarz, chair of the Asia-Pacific sub-committee of the House Foreign Relations Committee urged the recall of the US Ambassador and the cessation of military cooperation and commercial exchange. Under pressure from Congress, on 5 June President Bush announced the adoption of five measures, some of them punitive: (1) a temporary halt to weapons sales and commercial exports; (2) suspension of military exchanges and visits; (3) consideration of student requests to extend their stays in the USA—a position that resulted in the granting of extended visas to 45,000 Chinese students; (4) the provision of humanitarian relief to the victims through the Red Cross; and (5) a review of bilateral agreements.[401] These measures won rapid and unanimous support from both the House of Representatives and the Senate, with the latter also voting unanimously to demand that the President adopt further measures. On 20 June, the USA urged its Western allies to support the suspension of multilateral loans to China, and a few days later the World Bank announced that its loans would indeed be suspended.

[397] In formal statements to the UN, China stated that it acted to prevent 'a handful of people from violating the law'. Cited by Foot, *Rights Beyond Borders*, p. 121.

[398] Some soldiers were indeed killed, including one who was pulled from an APC and literally torn to pieces. However, these killings probably occurred only *after* the soldiers had opened fire on the protestors. See Calhoun, *Neither Gods nor Emperors*, p. 128; and Baum, *Burying Mao*, p. 292.

[399] Cited by Calhoun, *Neither Gods nor Emperors*, p. 144.

[400] See the quotes set out in Foot, *Rights Beyond Borders*, p. 138.

[401] Kornberg and Faust, *China in World Politics*, p. 140; and Foot, *Rights Beyond Borders*, pp. 116–17. On domestic pressure on Bush, see Ming Wan, *Human Rights in China's Foreign Relations*, pp. 42–3.

The mood was little different elsewhere in the West. British Prime Minister Margaret Thatcher said she was 'appalled by the indiscriminate shooting of unarmed people', and the Labour Party also condemned the killings.[402] French President François Mitterrand expressed his 'shock and outrage' and argued that a government which opens fire on its young has no future. French Foreign Minister, Roland Dumas expressed his 'dismay' at the 'bloody repression'. Sweden also condemned the use of force, calling it a 'giant step backward' in China's development. Germany and Italy condemned the use of force and called for the adoption of punitive measures.[403] Britain and Germany cancelled planned ministerial visits and most Western European countries imposed economic sanctions.[404] Australia and New Zealand followed suit. It is estimated that, in total, the Beijing massacre cost China $11 billion over four years.[405]

Closer to home, in Hong Kong, up to a million people marched in protest at the massacre.[406] There were also demonstrations in Macao and Taipei.[407] Japan issued a sharply worded protest, recalled bank staff from China, froze two major loans, and imposed restrictions on Chinese imports. Though couching their responses in more conciliatory terms, South Korea, Thailand, the Philippines, and Indonesia all expressed concern.[408] Elsewhere, Brazil expressed regret, whilst El Salvador communicated to the UN that it 'strongly condemns the bloody general repression carried out by the Beijing regime'.[409] Costa Rica issued a statement to the UN which, 'in view of the bloody events in mainland China, expresses its grave concern at, and strongest condemnation of, the repressive action'.[410]

Not even the remaining communist bloc rallied to China's cause. The Soviet Union expressed 'regret' over the use of force. Foreign Ministry Spokesman, Gennadi Gerasimov told reporters that the Soviet Union was 'extremely dismayed' at China's actions and surprised by the brutality of the crack-

[402] Robert McFadden, 'The West Condemns the Crackdown', *New York Times*, 5 June 1989.

[403] Zhang Ling, *Tiananmen Papers* and Robert McFadden, 'The West Condemns the Crackdown', *New York Times*, 5 June 1989.

[404] In addition to those mentioned in this paragraph, Belgium, Portugal, Greece, Austria, Netherlands, Denmark, Finland, and Switzerland imposed sanctions. Zhang Ling, *Tiananmen Papers*. Also see, Richard Bernstein, 'Beijing Orders its Ambassadors Home for a Meeting', *New York Times*, 29 June 1989; and Ming Wan, *Human Rights in Chinese Foreign Relations*, p. 68.

[405] Foot, *Rights Beyond Borders*, p. 117.

[406] Hutchings, *Modern China*, p. 426.

[407] Robert McFadden, 'The West Condemns the Crackdown', *New York Times*, 5 June 1989.

[408] On Thai concerns, see Steven Erlanger, 'Turmoil in China; Asian Diplomats Express Concern', *New York Times*, 8 June 1989.

[409] Letter from the Permanent Mission of El Salvador to the UN Economic and Social Council, A/44/325, 15 June 1989.

[410] Letter from the Permanent Representative of Costa Rica to the UN Secretary-General, A/44/466, 17 August 1989.

down.[411] Poland, Hungary, and Yugoslavia expressed their concern, whilst the Vietnamese foreign ministry flatly denied Western reports that it supported China's actions, describing such views as 'pure fabrications'.[412]

This sharply critical international response surprised the Chinese leadership and prompted it to restrain its post-demonstration crackdown somewhat. Martial law was terminated in January 1990 and by June 1990, 881 people arrested for their participation in the protests had been released. China also permitted the noted dissident, Fang Lizhi, who had sought refuge in the US embassy immediately after the massacre, to leave the country.[413] Recognizing the damage done to its international reputation, China also began to acknowledge the importance of human rights. In 1991, China issued a White Paper defending a conception of human rights, albeit one that prioritized economic and group rights over political rights. In January 1992, Premier Li Peng told the UN that, 'China values human rights and stands ready to engage in discussion and cooperation . . . on the question of human rights'.[414] The early 1990s also saw a general expansion of human rights studies in China, as the government tried to understand and assertively engage with the standards to which it was now being held.[415]

One of the key diplomatic battles came at the the UN Human Rights Commission. In sharp contrast to its earlier strategy of simply denouncing or ignoring human rights diplomacy, in the wake of the Beijing massacre, China actively and aggressively engaged in multilateral diplomacy to press its case.[416] The catalyst was a 6 June report by the UN's Special Rapporteur on Summary and Arbitrary Executions, which called on China to 'curb its excesses'. This report, and the attention attracted by the massacre, brought Chinese human rights to the top of the agenda of the UN's sub-commission for summary and arbitrary executions. Led by the International Commission of Jurists and International League for Human Rights, several NGOs lobbied for a resolution criticizing China. They also arranged for Li Lu, a student protestor who had fled to France, to present testimony. China responded

[411] 'Turmoil in China; Kremlin Dismayed, Aide says', *New York Times*, 10 June 1989.

[412] Zhang Ling, *Tiananmen Papers.*

[413] Baum, *Burying Mao*, p. 291.

[414] According to Ann Kent, the White paper asserted China's view of a 'hierarchy of rights'. See Ann Kent, *Between Freedom and Subsistence: China and Human Rights* (Hong Kong: Oxford University Press, 1993), p. 222. For an earlier account of Chinese views about human rights, see R. Randle Edwards, Louis Henkin, and Andrew J. Nathan, *Human Rights in Contemporary China* (New York: Columbia University Press, 1986), pp. 21–9. Li Peng is cited in Andrew J. Nathan, 'China and the International Human Rights Regime', in Elizabeth Economy and Michel Oksenberg (eds), *China Joins the World: Progress and Prospects* (New York: Council on Foreign Relations, 1999), p. 137; and Seymour, 'Human Rights in Chinese Foreign Relations', pp. 221–2.

[415] Yongjin Zhang, *China in International Society since 1949* (London: Macmillan, 1998), p. 181.

[416] The following section draws on Foot, *Rights Beyond Borders*, p. 118 ff.

by branding Li a 'criminal' and furiously lobbying sub-commission members. In the end, by fifteen votes to nine, the sub-commission passed a resolution expressing 'concern' about 'events which took place recently in China' and calling upon the Secretary-General to submit a report. The resolution also referred to matter to the Human Rights Commission. As requested, the Secretary-General issued a report detailing human rights abuses in China and the Commission's Western members began to draft a critical resolution. China responded with a furious diplomatic offensive, despatching its foreign minister to Geneva and privately telling many states that they would lose Chinese support and assistance if they supported a motion criticizing China. Pakistan then introduced a motion barring a resolution on China, which passed by a narrow margin (17 for, 15 against, 11 abstentions). Although China won the day, it had been forced to expend significant diplomatic capital to secure a narrow procedural victory.

Ultimately, countervailing concerns meant that punishment of China was short-lived.[417] In the USA, although Congress dictated a tough response, President Bush was reluctant to isolate China completely, fearing that this would encourage the Chinese to reverse a decade of political and economic reform and weaken strategic cooperation. In July 1989, Bush despatched his national security adviser, Brett Scowcroft and Lawrence Eagleburger, the deputy Secretary of State, on a secret mission to Beijing to reassure China that no serious and permanent damage had been done to relations and to emphasize that the sanctions were relatively moderate. The two officials returned to Beijing for a public visit in December 1989.[418] The trend towards normalization of relations between China and the West was reinforced by Iraq's invasion of Kuwait in late 1990. The invasion sidelined the furore over the 1989 massacre and gave China important diplomatic leverage over the West, because the USA wanted the UN Security Council to authorize a coalition to use force against Iraq.[419] In a classic example of diplomatic horse-trading, the USA dropped its remaining economic sanctions in return for a Chinese abstention on Kuwait. Other key Western governments, especially the European Community and Japan, followed Bush's lead and relaxed sanctions.[420]

How can we explain why the world reacted so much more sharply to the killing of less than 3,000 civilians than it had over the previous decades to much larger violations of civilian immunity? The strength of civilian immunity and its internalization in parts of the West cannot alone explain the radical difference, because the West had condemned abuses of civilians in Tibet in the

[417] Foot, *Rights Beyond Borders*, pp. 116–17.
[418] Kornberg and Faust, *China in World Politics*, p. 140.
[419] Foot, *Rights Beyond Borders*, p. 114.
[420] Foot, *Rights Beyond Borders*, pp. 123–9.

1950s. Nor, for the same reason, is it the case that human rights in China was simply a 'non-issue' or that it was shielded by non-membership of the UN and non-participation in the international human rights regime.[421] As I noted earlier, between 1959 and 1961 the USA and others had been particularly strident in their condemnation of Chinese behaviour in Tibet. None of this would have happened had civilian immunity been a factor only in 1989 and not in 1959.

Just as the paucity of information, legitimacy of the perpetrators relative to other relevant actors, and the foreign policy priorities of external actors were crucial in dampening criticism of China's violation of civilian immunity in relation to the land reform killings, Great Leap Forward, and Cultural Revolution, so these three factors had the reverse effect in this case. First, because dozens of foreign journalists were in Beijing, the massacre was graphically reported around the world and global attention 'sharply focused on human rights violations in China'.[422] It is also important to note in this regard, that Western human rights NGOs had not reported on China until Amnesty International did so in 1978.[423] The government's problems were compounded by the gradual unfolding of the drama in the weeks preceding the massacre. One poll noted that 75 per cent of Americans were 'closely' following events in Beijing prior to the massacre and US officials later confirmed that media coverage had prompted them to develop contingency plans for sanctions in the event of the Chinese government using force.[424] In contrast to earlier atrocities which were barely reported, the open reporting of events in 1989 exposed the implausibility of Chinese denials. The evident dissonance between Chinese arguments and the reported facts of the case exposed the massacre as a blatant violation of civilian immunity, producing an outpouring of international condemnation and punishment. Like some capitalist governments before it, China found that once it became unable to control the dissemination of information it was also unable to secure sufficient legitimacy, forcing it over time to moderate its behaviour to make it more consistent with the norm of civilian immunity.

The relative legitimacy of the relevant actors was also important in shaping the international response. The crisis was framed by the Western media as one of pro-democracy students representing a silent majority of Chinese people against an outdated authoritarian regime unwilling to reform.[425] Thus, the Chinese government was widely viewed as being less legitimate than the

[421] As suggested, among others, by Nathan, 'China and the International Human Rights Regime', p. 146; and Ming Wan, *Human Rights in Chinese Foreign Relations*, p. 4.

[422] Foot, *Rights Beyond Borders*, p. 113.

[423] Foot, *Rights Beyond Borders*, pp. 86–7. Human Rights Watch/Asia also reported on China from the late 1970s. See Seymour, 'Human Rights in Chinese Foreign Relations', p. 220.

[424] Foot, *Rights Beyond Borders*, p. 115.

[425] Foot, *Rights Beyond Borders*, p. 115.

protestors, making outside observers less likely to accept Chinese arguments and more likely to accept massacre reports.

Finally, the reduction of Cold War tensions in Europe and Indochina eliminated the shared interest in containing the Soviet Union that had underpinned China's relationship with the West since 1971.[426] Combined with the end of European imperialism and the resolution of the Chinese representation issue at the UN, this removed many of the countervailing foreign policy concerns that had tempered criticism of Chinese communist mass killing in the past, elevating China's norm violation briefly to the top of the international agenda and exerting pressure on governments—especially the US—to punish China. Post-1971 concerns relating to the promotion of reform through engagement, as well as the more immediate need for Chinese acquiescence with the use of force to remove the Iraqi army from Kuwait explains why the punishment of China was so short-lived.

## CONCLUSION

Ideologies of selective extermination persisted in the Communist world well after the Second World War, given renewed legitimacy by Stalin's role in the victory over fascism and communist victory in the Chinese Civil War. Although they differed from place to place, communist ideologies tended to place individuals and sometimes whole socio-economic, national or religious groups outside the universe of moral obligation on the grounds that they constituted an actual or potential threat to the regime and the people. Such arguments were widely accepted by other governments inside the communist bloc, helping to secure sufficient legitimacy for the perpetrators of some of the century's bloodiest episodes of mass killing and protect them from censure and punishment. But Stalinist Soviet Union and Maoist China were also aided by contextual factors which moderated the degree of criticism they received from outside the communist world. In the Soviet case, favourable comparisons to Hitler, the Second World War alliance, and post-war concerns about the safe and speedy return of allied Prisoners of War who had fallen into Soviet hands produced a degree of Western toleration and acquiescence with renewed bouts of Stalinist terror. Other aspects of this new terror, such as the deportation of nationalities, were carefully hidden from view. The absence of reporting was also critical in helping Maoist China avoid opprobrium for its recurrent bouts of mass killing. When information was more readily available, as in the aftermath of the 1959 uprising in Tibet, communist China was

[426] Levine, 'Sino-American Relations', p. 95.

subjected to criticism and had to largely rely on communist solidarity to prevent censure through the UN. But the existence of other strategic priorities on the part of the West, notably Korea and decolonization, also played a role in shaping responses in a way generally favourable to the Maoists.

The deaths of Stalin and Mao were the catalysts for the Soviet and Chinese moves away from ideologies of selective extermination. The underlying reasons for the shifts were grounded in domestic politics and not related to civilian immunity. Among other things, new leaders worried about the costs of mass repression, the instability, and the terror it enjoined within the ever-imperilled elite. In Cambodia, however, where the Khmer Rouge combined elements of Stalinism, Maoism, and local nationalism, selective extermination taken to genocidal extremes was restrained only by armed intervention. Here again, contextual factors played the major role in shaping the world's response. Before Vietnam's intervention, the Khmer Rouge benefited from global communist solidarity which was riven apart by that intervention. The Khmer Rouge's antagonistic relationship with Vietnam persuaded the USA and some of its European and Southeast Asian allies to tolerate the genocidal regime and even provide its remnants with political and material support in a further example of political interests trumping civilian immunity.

Towards the end of the Cold War, communist perpetrators began to find it more difficult to sustain sufficient legitimacy for mass atrocities. This was largely a result of changes to the global context, most notably the enhancement of global communications which improved the speed and quality of information dissemination, the reduction of Cold War tensions which elevated civilian immunity and human rights more generally up the list of international policy priorities, and the material decline of the communist bloc relative to the capitalist world. The alignment of political interests and concerns for civilian immunity proved particularly powerful in the case of Afghanistan, prompting many states to furnish military assistance to anti-Soviet forces. As evidenced by the Soviet experience in Afghanistan and the Beijing massacre, major communist regimes still resorted to atrocities when they believed it necessary but, like their capitalist counterparts, preferred to create and leverage uncertainty rather than point to doctrines of selective extermination and found it more difficult to avoid criticism and punishment. In both of these cases, the perpetrators were criticized and materially punished, forcing both to moderate their behaviour somewhat.

For much of the Cold War, therefore, civilian immunity co-existed alongside doctrines of selective extermination within the communist world, suggesting that for communists, at least, civilian immunity was not as much of an embedded international norm as it was for the West. Selective extermination was overcome not by the power of civilian immunity but by a combination of unrelated domestic concerns. The shift away from selective extermination helped embed civilian immunity as a norm within both the communist and non-communist parts of international society, but did not signify its internalization. Civilian immunity clearly shaped how the non-communist world responded to mass killing—evidenced by domestic criticism of the West's cooperation with Stalin over prisoner returns, criticism of Chinese behaviour in Tibet, and Western determination to keep its aid to the Khmer Rouge secret—but norm-based responses require information about norm violations (which was often scarce) and are conditioned by contextual factors. Until the last few years of the Cold War, the frequent lack of credible and timely reporting and the presence of competing interests tempered criticism and punishment of communist atrocities, allowing the perpetrators to secure sufficient legitimacy more often than not. As in the previous chapter, though, changes in the global context made the legitimation of mass killing more difficult. This trend continued after the Cold War as it became still more difficult—but, crucially, not impossible—to secure sufficient legitimacy for mass atrocities.

# 7

# Atrocities and the 'Golden Age' of Humanitarianism

It is has become common to read that the end of the Cold War brought with it renewed concern for humanitarianism and the protection of people from mass violence. According to this view, international debate about mass atrocities focused no longer on whether or not atrocities were legitimate but instead on questions of how to respond to protect the victims.[1] As the UN Secretary-General, Perez de Cueller put it in 1991, 'it is now increasingly felt that the principle of non-interference with the essential domestic jurisdiction of States cannot be regarded as a protective barrier behind which human rights could be massively or systematically abused with impunity'.[2] In post-Cold War era, mass atrocities in Angola, Bosnia, Somalia, Rwanda, East Timor, Kosovo, Sierra Leone, Liberia, the Democratic Republic of the Congo (DRC), and Darfur, were condemned by an international society which invariably adopted some measures aimed at helping the victims or punishing the perpetrators.[3] In practice, however, responses sometimes proved deficient largely because of disagreements about how to respond and reluctance on the part of governments to commit troops and other resources to the protection of foreign populations.[4] For our purposes, though, more important is the fact that although perpetrators of mass atrocities were more likely to face international criticism and punishment after the end of the Cold War than before it, responses were not

[1] Thomas G. Weiss, 'The Sunset of Humanitarian Intervention? The Responsibility to Protect in a Unipolar Era,' *Security Dialogue* 35 (2), 2004, p. 135.

[2] Javier Perez de Cuellar, *Report of the Secretary-General on the Work of the Organization*, 1991, p. 12.

[3] Martin Binder, 'Humanitarian Crises and the International Politics of Selectivity', *Human Rights Review*, 10, 2009, pp. 327–48.

[4] There is a vast and growing literature on the litany of political and operational problems during the 1990s. See, for example, Mats Berdal and Spyros Economides (eds), *United Nations Interventionism, 1991–2004* (Cambridge: Cambridge University Press, 2007); Trevor Findlay, *The Use of Force in UN Peace Operations* (Oxford: Oxford University Press for SIPRI, 2002); Lise Morje Howard, *UN Peacekeeping in Civil Wars* (Cambridge: Cambridge University Press, 2008); and Thomas G. Weiss, *Civil–Military Interactions* (Oxford: Rowman and Littlefield, 1999).

uniformly critical. In at least two significant cases (Russia's wars in Chechnya and post-genocide massacres by the Rwandan Patriotic Front (RPF) in Rwanda and the DRC) perpetrators of mass atrocities were still able to secure sufficient legitimacy and avoid condemnation and punishment.

Continuing the argument developed in the previous two chapters, this chapter suggests that it was shifts in the global context rather than new found commitments to human rights or civilian immunity which propelled changes that became evident in the 1990s.[5] This also explains why that transformation was less radical than sometimes suggested. Whilst there was a greater propensity on the part of international society to condemn massacres and adopt measures against the perpetrators, the legitimation of mass atrocities and the consequences that flowed from this were still conditioned by contextual factors, making it possible—even in this new era of humanitarianism—to sometimes secure sufficient legitimacy for mass atrocities.

Of course, in most post-Cold War cases mass atrocities were condemned by international society, which debated how to punish the perpetrators and protect the victims. In these debates, states weighed up the relative importance of civilian immunity, the norm of non-interference, prudential concerns and political considerations in deciding whether to back-up condemnatory words with protective or punitive action.[6] After a number of heated debates and false starts, in 2005 the world's largest ever gathering of heads of state and government agreed that all states had a responsibility to protect their populations from genocide, war crimes, ethnic cleansing and crimes against humanity and that the principle of non-interference did not automatically shield states from collective enforcement measures when they violated civilian immunity.

Some of the trends that made this possible were evident before the end of the Cold War. The improvement of global communications increased the degree, depth, and speed with which mass killing was reported. Although significant uncertainty often remained about the details, the fact of mass killing was widely reported. The effects of this were clear in the later stages of the war in El Salvador, the Soviet war in Afghanistan and the 1989 Beijing massacre. During the Cold War (and indeed before it), clear reporting of massive violations of civilian immunity had generated criticism and sometimes public pressure for governments to 'do something'. Indeed, in the three aforementioned cases, perpetrators were prompted by international criticism

[5] It is commonplace to argue that the rapid spread of 'human rights norms' post-1989 contributed to the transformation. See, for example, Peter Viggo Jakobsen, 'The Transformation of United Nations Peace Operation in the 1990s', *Cooperation and Conflict*, 37 (3) 2002, p. 274.

[6] This book touches on the relationship between intervention and non-interference but only tangentially. For more detailed analysis, see Nicholas J. Wheeler, *Saving Strangers: Humanitarian Intervention in International Society* (Oxford: Oxford University Press, 2000); and Simon Chesterman, *Just War or Just Peace? Humanitarian Intervention and International Law* (Oxford: Oxford University Press, 2001).

to either modify or abandon strategies of mass killing. But the improvement of global communications did not resolve questions about how reports should be *interpreted*. Much hinged on how information was interpreted: should mass killing in Rwanda be viewed as genocidal or tribal killing? To what extent were all Bosnia's warring parties responsible for mass atrocities? To what extent did Chechen rebels provoke Russian reprisals? Judgements about how to interpret information were informed by prior judgements about the relative legitimacy of relevant actors which influenced whose accounts were more likely to be believed. Moreover, whilst the so-called 'CNN effect' might have begun to drive international criticism of mass atrocities, it had a more limited influence in shaping how governments responded, affecting policy only when there was uncertainty about how to respond and where the range of policy options were relatively limited and inexpensive.[7] In other words, when it came to punishing perpetrators, the media's effect was greater when the costs to the punisher were lower, and vice versa.[8] It is also important to acknowledge that media coverage remained patchy, granting some perpetrators much greater leeway than others. Conflicts in Angola and the DRC, for instance, received little international reportage—and the perpetrators more impunity—than those in the Balkans. In other cases, such as Rwanda, reporting was delayed and unclear. The patchiness of reporting sometimes helped perpetrators to create and leverage uncertainty.

The decline of Cold War tensions impacted on the prioritization of civilian immunity relative to strategic interests, judgements about the relative legitimacy of relevant actors in episodes of mass killing, and the disposition of institutional power. As Cold War hostilities receded, so too did the various strategic reasons for supporting regimes and non-state groups that perpetrated mass killing, shifting the balance between political interests and humanitarianism in favour of the latter and enabling cooperation between the two former Cold War blocs. Perhaps the clearest evidence of this can be seen in the use of the veto in the UN Security Council. Between 1990 and 2002, only twelve draft resolutions were vetoed, compared to 238 vetoes between 1945 and 1990, an average of forty-three per decade.[9]

Although the general trend of this period was squarely towards the criticism and punishment of perpetrators of mass atrocities, contextual factors sometimes pulled in the other direction and helped to protect perpetrators. Governments that condemned the indiscriminate bombardment of Sarajevo and punished the Bosnian Serbs chose to neither condemn Russia for its much

[7] Piers Robinson, *The CNN Effect: The Myth of News, Foreign Policy and Intervention* (London: Routledge, 2002), p. 123.

[8] Robinson, *CNN Effect*, p. 124.

[9] Alex J. Bellamy and Paul D. Williams, *Understanding Peacekeeping*, 2nd edn (Cambridge: Polity, 2010), p. 95.

larger indiscriminate bombardment of Grozny nor punish it. Likewise, governments that condemned the Rwandan genocide, ignored post-genocide massacres perpetrated by the RPF.

With these cases in mind, this chapter argues that it became more difficult but not impossible to secure sufficient legitimacy for mass atrocities in the post-Cold War era. First, I examine the world's response to atrocities in post-Gulf War Iraq, which were seen as a watershed on the question of humanitarian intervention but which, on closer scrutiny, supports the view that contextual factors remained crucial and that the end of Cold War did not produce a sharp break from late Cold War practice. The general claim that these contextual changes made it more difficult for perpetrators to secure sufficient legitimacy is supported by briefly noting two cases—one in which the world failed to respond decisively (Rwanda, 1994) and the other where a regional alliance intervened militarily to stop mass atrocities (Kosovo, 1999). Having shown the general trend, the second part of the chapter examines two cases (post-genocide massacres by the RPF and Chechnya) that defy the trend, showing that even in the post-Cold War period it was not impossible to secure sufficient legitimacy for mass atrocities.

## A NEW POLITICS? IRAQ 1991

The variation between the international response to Iraq's 'Anfal' campaign against Kurdish separatists and civilians between 1986 and 1988 and the response to Kurdish and Shi'ite uprisings following its 1991 Gulf War defeat is instructive in terms of understanding the transformation of the politics of mass atrocities in the post-Cold War period.[10] During the Iran–Iraq War (1980–88), Iran funnelled military aid to Kurdish separatist groups (the Patriotic Union of Kurdistan (PUK) and Kurdish Democratic Party (KDP)) to support guerrilla attacks on the Iraqi army.[11] In 1983, the KDP and Iranian forces conducted a joint operation against Iraqi forces in Haj Omran. Iraq responded with chemical weapons and the interning or killing of 8,000 Barzani men.[12] In 1987, an Iranian counter-offensive against Iraq began to

[10] As Wheeler argues, there is a 'stark contrast' in the international response to the two cases. See Wheeler, *Saving Strangers*, p. 140.

[11] Weiss, *Civil–MilitaryInteractions*, p. 46.

[12] Human Rights Watch, *Iraq's Crime of Genocide: The Anfal Campaign Against the Kurds*, Human Rights Watch, 1993, pp. 26–7; and Joost R. Hilterrmann, 'Outsiders as Enablers: Consequences and Lessons from International Silence on Iraq's Use of Chemical Weapons During the Iran–Iraq War', in Lawrence G. Potter and Gary G. Sick (eds), *Iran, Iraq and the Legacies of War* (New York: Palgrave, 2004), p. 153.

falter and the USA increased material support to Iraq.[13] Emboldened by its stronger position, Iraq moved decisively against its Kurdish opposition, escalating to a counter-insurgency characterized by the systematic destruction of Kurdish villages.[14]

The offensive was stepped up during the eight 'Anfal' campaigns in 1988. The regime employed chemical weapons to 'smoke out' guerrillas from their bases and separate them from the civilian population.[15] It also attempted to make the countryside inhospitable by destroying villages to deprive rebels (and, of course, civilians) of shelter and food. In the most notorious single attack of the campaign, in March 1988, the Iraqi air force dropped chemical weapons on Halabja, killing approximately 5,000 people—mostly civilians. Elsewhere, civilians and prisoners in fallen villages were lined up near mass graves, shot and then buried by bulldozers.[16] In total, between 50,000–200,000 Kurds were killed (most estimates put the figure around 70,000–100,000), the vast majority of them civilians.[17] In addition 3,000–4,000 villages were destroyed, 800,000 civilians were internally displaced and a further 100,000 fled into Turkey. Only one-quarter of Kurdish villages were left intact; one-third of the territory of Iraqi Kurdistan was depopulated.[18] But Iraq's reach only extended to low-lying villages. The regime could only attack the rebels' mountain strongholds with air power. These were declared to be 'prohibited zones'—effectively 'free-fire zones' open to indiscriminate aerial bombardment.[19]

The Iraqi regime argued that it was conducting legitimate military operations against Kurdish 'saboteurs' and denied using chemical weapons. It also claimed that the Halabja massacre was fabricated by the Kurds.[20] To support these claims it used an October 1987 census process to collapse the distinction between combatants and civilians. It argued that Kurds who did not register themselves at government-run displacement camps or 'collective towns' would be considered guerrillas and treated accordingly. Unsurprisingly,

[13] See Joost R. Hiltermann, *A Poisonous Affair: America, Iraq and the Gassing of Halabja* (Cambridge: Cambridge University Press, 2007), pp. 238–9.

[14] Jane E. Stromseth, 'Iraq' in Lori Fisler Damrosch, *Enforcing Restraint: Collective Intervention in Internal Conflicts* (New York: Council on Foreign Relations Press, 1993), p. 81.

[15] Human Rights Watch, *Iraq's Crime of Genocide*, pp. 39–49.

[16] Reported by Kanan Makiya, 'The Anfal: Uncovering an Iraqi Campaign to Exterminate the Kurds', *Harper's Magazine*, May 1992, pp. 57–61. This version of events is supported by Middle East Watch and Physicians for Human Rights, *Unquiet Graves: The Search for the Disappeared in Iraqi Kurdistan* (New York, 1992).

[17] Human Rights Watch estimated '70–100,000' killed and Amnesty International estimated '100,000' deaths. Joost Hiltermann, suggests a maximum of 70,000 deaths. See Hiltermann, *A Poisonous Affair*, pp. 134–5.

[18] Weiss, *Civil–Military*, p. 47.

[19] Hiltermann, *A Poisonous Affair*, pp. 81–103; and Middle East Watch, *Genocide in Iraq: The Anfal Campaign Against the Kurds.*

[20] See Michael J. Kelly, 'The Tricky Nature of Proving Genocide Against Saddam Hussein Before the Iraqi Special Tribunal', *Cornell International Law Journal*, 38, 2005, pp. 989–99.

most rural Kurds chose to not submit themselves to the Iraqi government. The regime then claimed that all Kurds who remained at large in the countryside were guerrillas and therefore legitimate targets.[21] On the basis of this assumption, Ali Hasan al-Majid—appointed by Saddam Hussein to lead the campaign—ordered that chemical weapons be employed in the 'prohibited areas', that all those who were found in these areas should be detained, and that men aged between 15–70 should be separated from the rest and killed once information had been extracted from them.[22]

Iraq's use of chemical weapons against civilians was reported at the time. US State Department officials later told Samantha Power that they had good and reliable information about what was happening, including satellite imagery of destroyed villages. The Department's unclassified human rights report in 1987 described 'widespread destruction and bulldozing of Kurdish villages, mass forced movements of Kurds, and exile of Kurdish families into non-Kurdish parts of Iraq'.[23] In public, though, massacre reports were sometimes either ignored or dismissed as Kurdish propaganda.[24]

The combination of Iraqi justifications and this leveraging of uncertainty helped limit international condemnation and prevent punishment. As an example of the effect of the combination of Iraqi arguments and uncertainty, in September 1987 the *New York Times* reported the destruction of some 500 villages as simply a product of a 'ruthless drive to deny sanctuary to Kurdish guerrillas'.[25] The US administration took a similar line in its public discourse, with Assistant Secretary of State Murphy arguing that 'the Iraqi military campaign, brutal as it was, sought to reclaim territories occupied for years by rebels closely allied with, and financed, armed and reinforced by, Iran'.[26]

However, there were some very specific massacre reports, which forced Western governments to at least criticize Iraqi actions, if not punish them. French President Mitterrand and the Reagan administration condemned Iraq's use of chemical weapons, but the condemnation was low-key and

[21] Human Rights Watch, *Iraq's Crime of Genocide*, pp. 56–60.

[22] Human Rights Watch, *Iraq's Crime of Genocide*, pp. 52–6.

[23] Cited by Samantha Power, *A Problem from Hell: America and the Age of Genocide* (New York: Basic Books, 2002), p. 186.

[24] *Agence France Presse* reported the massacre immediately, and the *New York Times* did so the following day. Iran flew journalists into Halabja two days after the attack. These journalists, including David Hirst of *The Guardian*, began reporting the massacre from 22 March; *Washington Post* and *Los Angeles Times* started running the story on 24 March. See Joost Hiltermann, 'Elusive Justice: Trying to Try Saddam', *Middle East Report*, no. 215, summer 2000, n. 2 p. 35. On the dismissal or downplaying of atrocity reports, see Susan Meiselas, *Kurdistan: In the Shadow of History* (New York: Random House, 1997), p. 312.

[25] Reported by Power, *Problem from Hell*, p. 187.

[26] Cited by Power, *Problem from Hell*, p. 225.

neither pressed for punishment.[27] The US Senate Foreign Relations Committee received a detailed report on the use of chemical weapons by Iraq in October 1988, which sparked a protracted but ultimately fruitless debate about the imposition of sanctions.[28] Indeed, the Reagan administration lobbied other governments against sanctioning Saddam's regime.[29] The tepid US response was no doubt helped by uncertainty cast on the facts of the case. In 1990, a former CIA analyst citing information released by the US Defence Intelligence Agency argued that Iran, and not Iraq, was responsible for the gassing of Halabja.[30] Other American opponents of imposing sanctions on Iraq pointed to uncertainty about the identity of the perpetrators.[31] The Administration leveraged this uncertainty by, for instance, noting that chemical weapons canisters had not been retrieved from the site of the attacks and suggesting that there were genuine question marks about the versacity of massacre reports—a line of argument that was supported by Turkey.[32]

For its part, the UN became engaged on the issue of chemical weapons during the Iran–Iraq War in August 1983. The Security Council was forced by Iran's repeated requests to despatch an investigatory team in March 1984.[33] Chemical attacks continued regardless, prompting the UN Secretary-General, Javier Perez de Cuellar to call upon both sides to refrain from attacking purely civilian population centres—though to little avail.[34] In 1987 and 1988, the UN despatched chemical weapons experts to Iraq to investigate further allegations. Among other things, the experts reported that Kurdish civilians in Iraq were indeed the victims of chemical attacks.[35] In August 1988, the UN Security

[27] Stromseth, 'Iraq', p. 81. After his defeat and capture Saddam was later tried for the Anfal massacres, but was executed before the completion of his trial on these particular charges. See Michael J. Kelly, 'The Anfal Trial Against Saddam Hussein', *Journal of Genocide Research*, 9 (2) 2007.

[28] US Senate Committee on Foreign Relations, *Chemical Weapons Use in Kurdistan: Iraq's Final Offensive*, staff report, October 1988. This report was written by Peter Galbraith, see Power, *Problem from Hell*, pp. 179–85.

[29] Susan J. Schuuman, 'An "Inconvenient Atrocity": The Chemical Weapons Attack on the Kurds of Halabja, Iraq', thesis, University of New Mexico, 2007.

[30] See Stephen Pelletiere, *The Iran–Iraq War: Chaos in a Vacuum* (New York: Praeger, 1992), discussed in Hiltermann, *A Poisonous Affair*, pp. 183–205. Pelletiere repeated and extended his claim in *Iraq and the International Oil System—Why America Went to War in the Gulf.* These claims were the subject of a heated debate in the 'Notes and Comments' section of *International Journal of Middle Eastern Studies*, 35, 2003, pp. 211–14.

[31] Power, *Problem from Hell*, p. 212.

[32] Power, *Problem from Hell*, p. 208.

[33] David M. Malone, *The International Struggle over Iraq: Politics in the UN Security Council 1980–2005* (Oxford: Oxford University Press, 2006), p. 31. The investigators and Council stopped short of singling out Iraq for particular criticism. According to Sweden's Jan Eliasson, 'reacting weakly and meekly to the use of chemical weapons may have been the single most objectionable feature of the international community's response to Saddam Hussein's aggression and foreshadowed his further depredations through chemical weapons in 1988'. Cited by Malone, *International Struggle*, p. 32.

[34] Malone, *International Struggle*, p. 32.

[35] Discussed at length in Hiltermann, 'Outsiders as Enablers'.

Council unanimously condemned the use of chemical weapons by both sides and threatened 'appropriate and effective measures' in the event of their future use of chemical weapons (Resolution 620, 26 August 1988). There were no moves to apply this decision to northern Iraq.

Given that the atrocities were reported at the time, how do we explain international society's failure to forcefully condemn or punish Iraq? On the Western side, two concerns weighed against punishing Iraq. First, Saddam was still seen by the West as a useful counter to the Islamic regime in Iran, which was viewed as a threat to the Persian Gulf.[36] Second, Kurdish separatism enjoyed little international support because the Kurds also laid claim to tracts of eastern Turkey (a strategically important member of NATO) and Western governments believed that supporting the Kurds in Iraq would embolden the separatists in Turkey. In addition, Iraq was reasonably well regarded by a number of key countries, for different reasons. It was a major purchaser of French arms and whilst its relations with the Soviet Union had become strained as a result of Saddam's support for the *mujahadeen*, Iraq had been a Soviet ally since the Baathists seized power in 1968 and remained one of the Soviet Union's main customers for arms.[37] Moreover, Iraq's neighbours were not prepared to condemn or punish the regime: Turkey had a common interest with Iraq in seeing the suppression of the Kurds; whilst Iran was prepared to offer arms and sanctuary to Iraq's Kurds, it too was concerned about exacerbating its own Kurdish problem.[38] Thus, whilst there was certainly sympathy for the Kurds and disquiet about Iraq's conduct, these proved insufficient to override countervailing interests and judgements about the relative illegitimacy of Kurdish separatist claims. Although these concerns remained in evidence three years later, a changed context produced a very different international reaction to another round of Iraqi atrocities.

On 2 August 1990, Iraq invaded and overran Kuwait. The UN Security Council responded with a string of resolutions demanding an immediate withdrawal (Resolution 660), imposing economic sanctions (Resolution 661), and declaring the invasion to be illegal (Resolution 662). In Resolution 678, the Council demanded that Iraqi forces withdraw by 15 January 1991 and authorized the use of force to eject them if they failed to comply. A US-led coalition defeated Iraqi forces and forced their withdrawal from Kuwait. The USA decided against regime change in Baghdad, believing that this would rupture the international coalition and draw the USA into a civil war it was keen to avoid. Instead, President Bush suggested that Iraq's repressed Kurds and Shi'ites should take the opportunity presented by Saddam's

36 Schuuman, 'An "Inconvenient Atrocity"'.
37 Stromseth, 'Iraq', pp. 81–2.
38 Stromseth, 'Iraq', p. 82.

weakness to rebel and overthrow the dictator.[39] Taking these comments as a statement of US support, the Kurds in the north and Shi'ites in the south rebelled in early March. Amidst the chaos of post-war Iraq, both rebellions scored significant early gains but the tide soon turned. Iraq had not committed Republican Guard elements to the war in Kuwait and these divisions were now employed against the rebels with devastating effect. Utilizing the brutal tactics employed during the Anfal campaigns, the Iraqi army targeted rebels and civilians alike.[40] At the peak of the crisis, between 400 and 1,000 displaced Kurdish civilians were dying every day as a result of Iraqi attacks, exhaustion, hypothermia, and disease.[41] Around 1 million Kurds in total were displaced in the mountains of northern Iraq close to the Turkish border. In the south, Iraqi forces committed mass executions of religious leaders and other civilians in Najaf and Karbala, forcing around 70,000 Shi'ites to seek refuge in Iran, 30,000 to flee to coalition occupied territory and leaving between 500,000–850,000 trapped in the southern marshlands.[42] In total, between 20,000 and 100,000 people were killed in the uprisings, with most estimates suggesting that at least 30,000 civilians were killed.[43] As in 1988, Iraq argued simply that it was engaged in legitimate counter-insurgency operations against armed rebels.[44]

France condemned the atrocities but this time argued that international society had a duty to step in. In this, it was supported by Turkey and Iran, both of which feared a mass influx of Kurds across their borders. They wrote to the Security Council, requesting international assistance.[45] In early April, France tried unsuccessfully to persuade the Council to insert a paragraph condemning Iraqi massacres of Kurds into Resolution 687 setting out the terms of the Gulf War ceasefire.[46] President Mitterrand argued that failing to protect the Kurds would severely weaken the Council's 'political and moral authority'. The President's wife also chipped in, criticizing the lack of international action and maintaining that she was 'totally appalled by the repression', that the Kurds were 'being exterminated', and that nobody could claim to not know what was happening.[47] Foreign Minister, Roland Dumas

[39] Barton Gellman, 'Kurds Contend US Encouraged Rebellion via "Voice of Free Iraq"', *Washington Post*, 9 April 1991, p. A17.

[40] Middle East Watch, *Endless Torment: The 1991 Uprising in Iraq and Its Aftermath* (New York, 1992), pp. 29–66.

[41] Wheeler, *Saving Strangers*, p. 141; Weiss, *Civil-Military Interactions*, p. 50.

[42] Weiss, *Civil-Military*, p. 51.

[43] See Weiss, *Civil-Military*, p. 50; and Taylor Seybolt, *Humanitarian Military Intervention: The Conditions for Success and Failure* (Oxford: Oxford University Press for SIPRI, 2007), p. 47.

[44] Seybolt, *Humanitarian Military Intervention*, p. 192.

[45] See letter to the President of the UN Security Council from Turkey (S/22435, 2 April 1991) and Iran (S/22447, 4 April 1991).

[46] Wheeler, *Saving Strangers*, p. 141.

[47] Quoted in Wheeler, *Saving Strangers*, p. 142.

went further, calling for the Council to recognize a duty of intervention in cases of massive violations of human rights.[48] In the Security Council, France argued that 'the violations of human rights such as those now being observed become a matter of international interest when they take on such proportions that they assume the dimension of a crime against humanity' and that the Council 'would have been remiss in its task had it stood idly by without reacting to the massacres of entire populations, the extermination of civilians, including women and children'.[49] French demands initially received little support. The British thought that the French had overreached by articulating a 'duty of intervention' that would be seen as a violation of the principle of non-interference.[50]

A compromise came in the form of UN Security Council Resolution 688, which identified the displacement of people across borders as a threat to international peace and security, called for humanitarian assistance and demanded the cessation of hostilities. The resolution was passed with ten affirmative votes, three negative votes (Cuba, Yemen, Zimbabwe) and two abstentions (China and India). China and India argued that whilst they sympathized with the Kurds' plight, they were deeply concerned about the extension of the Security Council's authority to human rights matters.[51] But because it did not specifically initiate or license intervention to protect Kurds, the resolution proved insufficient to resolve the crisis or satisfy increasingly vocal Western publics.

Having incited the Kurds and Shi'ites to rebellion, the Bush Administration was deeply reluctant to intervene. But public and political opinion in the USA was sharply against Iraq. Congressman Lee Hamilton accused Iraqi helicopters of 'creating a bloodbath'.[52] In the face of such arguments, the Bush Administration argued that the situation was best characterized as a 'civil war' and that the USA should not allow itself to be drawn in.[53] But the USA also came under diplomatic pressure from Turkey and Saudi Arabia to ensure that Iraq not break up, with Turkey worried about the implications for its own Kurdish secessionists and Saudi Arabia fearful of Iranian hegemony. Nicholas Wheeler shows that in the face of these concerns, the administration completely reversed its position in the space of two weeks and agreed to the deployment of military forces to protect safe havens in Iraqi Kurdistan.[54]

[48] Wheeler, *Saving Strangers*, p. 141.

[49] Quoted in Wheeler, *Saving Strangers*, p. 145.

[50] On the British position, see Wheeler, *Saving Strangers*, p. 142, n. 8.

[51] S/PV.3105, pp. 6–7.

[52] Cited by Wheeler, *Saving Strangers*, p. 147.

[53] Cited by Wheeler, *Saving Strangers*, p. 147. Elsewhere Bush focused on the risk of US casualties: 'I do not want one single soldier or airman shoved into a civil war in Iraq that's been going on for ages', President Bush, remarks at Maxwell Air Force Base, 13 April 1991, see Malone, *International Struggle*, p. 89.

[54] Wheeler, *Saving Strangers*, pp. 147–8.

This dramatic about-face was prompted by two factors. First, the mounting press coverage of the crisis generated public attention and created domestic pressure to act. Western media not only reported the humanitarian crisis, it also editorialized strongly in favour of intervention.[55] Claiborne Pell, chairman of the Senate Foreign Relations Committee, declared that the USA had 'a moral obligation to do what we can to stop Saddam from killing those who have the courage to resist' and Senator Sam Nunn described the killing as 'genocide'.[56] In addition, the Gulf War had established public expectations that international society should assume some responsibility for Iraq's oppressed national groups—expectations heightened by Bush's incitement to rebellion.[57] Western publics and many politicians demanded action to protect the Kurds and Shi'ites, and US public opinion swung rapidly to support for a continued military presence in Iraq.[58] In the face of mounting evidence of atrocities and suffering, Bush's view of the crisis as a 'civil war'—a view shared by British Prime Minister John Major—became untenable.[59] Major was criticized by his predecessor Margaret Thatcher for allowing 'legal niceties' to inhibit decisive action to protect the Kurds.[60]

Second, Iraq's neighbours called for international intervention to prevent wider regional instability. Confronted with a massive humanitarian emergency, Turkey was forced to partially open its border with Iraqi Kurdistan. It was reluctant to open its borders fully, fearing that a massive influx of Iraqi Kurds would strengthen its own Kurdish separatists.[61] Some US officials shared Turkey's concern about potential long-term instability.[62] On 7 April 1991, the Turkish President argued that the best way of protecting the Kurds was to authorize the UN to secure territory and deliver aid inside Iraq.[63] This idea was picked up by John Major, who believed it offered a workable solution to

[55] See Martin Shaw, 'Global Voices' in Tim Dunne and Nicholas J. Wheeler (eds), *Human Rights in Global Politics* (Cambridge: Cambridge University Press, 1999), p. 229; James Mayall, 'Non-Intervention, Self-Determination and the "New World Order"', *International Affairs*, 67 (3), 1991, p. 426; Weiss, *Civil–Military*, p. 52; Malone, *International Struggle*, p. 85.

[56] Both cited in Wheeler, *Saving Strangers*, pp. 150–1.

[57] Adam Roberts, for example, was adamant that it was this post-Gulf War context that made international intervention possible. See Adam Roberts, 'Humanitarian War: Military Intervention and Human Rights', *International Affairs*, 69 (3), 1993, p. 437. A view broadly shared by Robert Jackson, see Robert J. Jackson, 'Armed Humanitarianism', *International Journal*, 48, 1993, p. 594.

[58] Malone, *International Struggle*, p. 85.

[59] A point made by Wheeler, *Saving Strangers*, p. 150.

[60] Wheeler, *Saving Strangers*, p. 149.

[61] Lawrence Freedman and David Boren, '"Safe Havens" for Kurds', in Nigel S. Rodley (ed.), *To Loose the Bands of Wickedness* (London: Brassey's 1992), pp. 49–50.

[62] Indeed, one US diplomat described this as 'our main concern', cited in Seybolt, *Humanitarian Military Intervention*, p. 146, n. 20.

[63] Weiss argues that there were also strong humanitarian reasons for favouring repatriation to Iraq over settlement in Turkey, but clearly political considerations were at the fore. See Weiss, *Civil–Military*, p. 55.

the humanitarian problem that did not require the deployment of coalition forces into Iraq proper.[64] Major proposed the establishment of a safe haven in the north, protected for a time by coalition forces. The ensuing *Operation Provide Comfort* involved the deployment of approximately 10,000 American, British, French, and Dutch troops to northern Iraq to protect Kurds and facilitate the delivery of military aid.

The variation in international response to Iraqi atrocities against Kurds in 1988 and 1991 is best explained by changes to two key contextual factors. First, detailed reporting and interventionist editorializing made the leveraging of uncertainty less persuasive, creating public pressure in the West for decisive international action that was absent in 1988. The impact of this factor was heightened by the unique sense of responsibility generated by the Gulf War context and President Bush's incitement to rebellion. Second, the 'safe havens' strategy—not contemplated in 1988—offered a way of balancing humanitarian concern for the Kurds with an interest in regional stability, especially in relation to Turkey. Support for the claim that it was these contextual factors rather than enhanced international commitment to civilian immunity that were ciritcal can be found by contrasting the establishment of safe havens in Iraqi Kurdistan with the much less robust response to the catastrophe that befell Iraq's Shi'ites.

Though no less grave than the situation in the north, the humanitarian crisis in Iraq's south was much less well reported, resulting in much less pressure for Western leaders to act decisively there.[65] In this context, concerns that supporting the Shi'ites with safe havens would strengthen Iranian hegemony in the region were privileged over humanitarian concerns.[66] In the south, therefore, the coalition limited itself to imposing a no-fly zone in August 1992 (*Operation Southern Watch*) which did little to prevent atrocities against the Shi'ites.[67] In June 1991, Britain warned Iraq that military action against the Shi'ites would contravene Resolution 688 and be punished. On behalf of the UN, Sadruddin Aga Khan visited the area and proposed the establishment of a UN humanitarian centre to provide aid to civilians and deter further attacks. Iraq rejected the UN proposal, prevented the delivery of UN aid to the Shi'ites and blockaded the marshlands in which they sought refuge (it would later drain the marshes to deny sanctuary and subsistence).[68]

[64] Seybolt, *Humanitarian Military Operations*, p. 146, n. 20.

[65] Wheeler, *Saving Strangers*, p. 167; Weiss, *Civil-Military*, p. 52. The problem was exacerbated by the fact that Iraq was able to maintain much tighter control of reporters and access in the south than it was in the north. See Stromseth, 'Iraq', p. 115, n. 137.

[66] Malone, *International Struggle*, p. 86.

[67] Malone, *International Struggle*, p. 98.

[68] The UN finally succeeded in persuading Iraq to accept the establishment of a humanitarian centre in Nasariyah in March 1992, but it was closed down in September 1993. See Stromseth, 'Iraq', p. 111, n. 111.

The following month, Special Rapporteur to the UN Human Rights Commission, Max van der Stoel, reported that displaced Shi'ite civilians were subjected to indiscriminate artillery attacks and that Iraqi generals had been instructed to 'wipe out' Shi'ite tribes in the marshlands.[69] Belgium persuaded the Security Council to consider van der Stoel's report and although the Council condemned Iraq's repression of the Shi'ites, it stopped short of punishing it or adopting measures to protect civilians. An Iranian request that the Council authorize a safe haven in the south won very little support, primarily due to Western and regional fears that it might be used to strengthen Iran's regional hegemony.[70] Instead, it was not until almost a year later that the USA, the UK, and France imposed a no-fly zone. They responded to criticism of the weakness of their response, by maintaining that this was the limit of what was legally permissible.[71] Moreover, although the number of refugees that fled to Iran was up to three times higher than the number that fled to Turkey, Iran received less than half the amount of humanitarian and financial assistance that Turkey received.[72] Thus, despite being no less critical of Iraqi atrocities in the south, in the absence of media attention, public pressure, and a policy that could effectively balance humanitarian concerns with strategic priorities, the West did much less to protect Shi'ites than it did to protect the Kurds.

Comparing the two cases of Iraqi atrocities that straddled the ending of the Cold War shows that it was changes in the role played by contextual factors, not the level of international commitment to civilian immunity per se, that best explains the very different reactions. Actors involved in the 1991 intervention condemned both the 1988 and 1991 atrocities. But in 1988 the limited amount of independent reporting left doubt about the veracity of atrocity reports and political concerns further limited the options that seemed available to Western governments. Intriguingly, both the US and the UK initially responded in the same way in 1991, describing the atrocities as a 'civil war' in order to reduce pressure for intervention. But persistent and clear media reporting of atrocities and Kurdish suffering made this position untenable and Turkey's argument in favour of delivering aid inside Iraq presented a way of delivering humanitarian assistance without emboldening Kurdish separatists outside Iraq. That these two factors played an especially influential role was confirmed by comparing the international response to the Kurdish problem with its response to the mass killing of Shi'ites. Less well reported and lacking a viable humanitarian strategy, the West did less to protect the Shi'ites than it did the Kurds.

[69] Cited by Wheeler, *Saving Strangers*, p. 160.
[70] See Wheeler, *Saving Strangers*, p. 161.
[71] Wheeler, *Saving Strangers*, p. 163.
[72] Weiss, *Civil–Military*, p. 59.

Significantly, where there was international opposition to Western intervention in northern Iraq, this focused on the legitimacy of the intervention rather than on the right of the Iraqi government to mistreat its population. As a result, international debate focused on the world's response to what was widely agreed to be illegitimate Iraqi behaviour. This basic pattern was also evident in reactions to crises elsewhere. For illustrative purposes, I will briefly examine the cases of Rwanda (1994) and Kosovo (1999).

## RWANDA (1994)

Confronted with reports about genocide in Rwanda, international society exhibited concern and condemned the perpetrators but lacked the political will to take decisive action. For our purposes, what is important is that few—if any—external actors were prepared to excuse or tolerate the genocide and that debates about intervention floundered on prudential and self-interested arguments rather than principled ones.

After years of recurrent civil war, Rwanda's mainly Hutu regime led by Habyarimana concluded a power-sharing agreement with the mainly Tutsi RPF. The UN established a small peacekeeping force to observe compliance with the ensuing Arusha Accords. But radical Hutus opposed the deal and, possibly after killing the president, unleashed a genocide.[73] *Interahamwe* and *Impuzamugambi* militia had been prepared in advance to slaughter the Tutsi population and Hutu sympathisers. When the President's plane was shot down, Hutus were called to arms by Radio Television Libre des Mille Collines (RTLMC). Among the first victims were potential Hutu opponents and ten Belgian peacekeepers, tortured and killed in a bid to force the Belgians to withdraw. Over the next 100 days, around 800,000 people were slaughtered in the genocide.

Inside Rwanda, the *genocidaires* employed the language of selective extermination to justify their behaviour and incite others to participate. This rhetoric was guided by a Hutu nationalist account of history articulated in a report for the government written in 1991 by Colonel Theoneste Bagosora—one of the genocide's key figures. According to Bagosora's paper, the Tutsi posed a major threat to Rwanda; they were by nature, 'dictatorial, proud, cruel, arrogant, clever and sneaky' but had never had a country of their own and so were intent on stealing Rwanda.[74] This jaundiced account of history made

[73] See Gerard Prunier, *The Rwanda Crisis: History of a Genocide* (London: Hurst and Co., 1997); Linda Melvern, *Conspiracy to Murder: The Rwandan Genocide* (London: Verso, 2004); and Fergal Keane, *Season on Blood: A Rwandan Journey* (London: Penguin, 1995), p. 27.

[74] See Linda Melvern, *A People Betrayed: The Role of the West in Rwanda's Genocide* (London: Zed, 2000), pp. 61–2.

Tutsis collectively responsible for past and present wrongs and thereby justified their extermination. In 1993 and 1994 Hutu propagandists dehumanised Tutsis by calling them 'cockroaches' and collectively portrayed them as members of the RPF and therefore guilty of treason and subject to punishment by death.[75] RTLMC described Tutsi soldiers as devils who killed their victims by 'extracting various organs . . . for example by taking the heart, the liver, the stomach . . . the cruelty of the inyenzi [cockroach] is incurable, the cruelty of the inyenzi can only be cured by their total extermination'.[76] The radio station urged Hutus to see all Tutsis as a threat and demanded a merciless war against them. As a 1993 article in the Hutu nationalist magazine *Kangura* put it in an article headed 'A Cockroach Cannot Give Birth to a Butterfly': 'A cockroach gives birth to another cockroach . . . . The history of Rwanda shows us clearly that a Tutsi stays always exactly the same, that he has never changed. The malice, the evil are just as we knew them in the history of our country'.[77] The radio station broadcast direct instructions to the *genocidaires*, such as 'you have missed some of the enemies in this or that place. Some are still alive. You must go back there and finish them off' and 'The graves are not yet quite full. Who is going to do the good work and help us fill them completely?'[78]

The Rwandan government gave a quite different account of events to international society. In international venues, it argued that the initial violence was a spontaneous response to the president's death and that subsequent violence was simply the resumption of civil war in which all sides were committing atrocities and where responsibility for individual massacres was either unknown or most likely to rest with the RPF. The minister for foreign affairs, Jerome Bicamumpaka sent a letter to the UN Security Council claiming that the violence was a 'spontaneous' response against those 'under suspicion' of killing the president but that the government was now restoring order.[79] Its diplomacy was helped by the coincidence that Rwanda was a non-permanent member of the Security Council at the time, giving the perpetrators a voice in international deliberations about how to respond. On 28 April, Bagosora told the US Deputy Assistant Secretary of State for African Affairs that the armed forces were working hard to bring an end to the violence but that 'it is very difficult to end these hatreds'. On 13 May Bicamumpaka told the Security Council that the problem was one of 'ethnic disturbance' that had 'unleashed the animal instincts of a people afraid of being enslaved again'.[80]

[75] Melvern, *A People Betrayed*, p. 57.

[76] Cited by Melvern, *A People Betrayed*, p. 155.

[77] Cited by Ben Kiernan, *Blood and Soil: A World History of Genocide and Extermination from Sparta to Darfur* (New Haven: Yale University Press, 2007), pp. 558–9.

[78] Cited by Prunier, *Rwanda Crisis*, p. 224. For other RTLMC quotes, see Kiernan, *Blood and Soil*, p. 566.

[79] Melvern, *Conspiracy to Murder*, p. 202.

[80] Both quotes from http://www.trumanwebdesign.com/~catalina/western.htm

He insisted that the death toll reported in the media was 'exaggerated' and that the Council should understand that the violence was caused by the 'age-old history of the nation'. What Rwanda was experiencing, Bicamumpaka claimed, was not genocide but an 'inter-ethnic war of unbelievable cruelty'.[81] Back in Rwanda, Bicamumpaka was a leading extremist—a founding member of the Hutu nationalist Coalition pour la Defense de la Republique (CDR) and shareholder of RTLMC. The foreign minister incited the killing of Tutsis at public rallies and supervised *Impuzamugami* roadblocks.[82]

The world's reaction focused on how to interpret the situation and on the appropriate response. Widespread—if sometimes confused—reporting of the bloodshed and a general absence of countervailing interests placed the emphasis of international debate squarely on the atrocities themselves. Although there were some pre-conflict alignments which undoubtedly affected the international reaction—most notably French support for the Hutu-led regime—these were not as influential as the Cold War tensions that had shaped the politics of mass atrocities for several decades.[83] Few, if any, governments were prepared to excuse the Rwandan regime and no state argued that the government should be protected from outside interference. As such, when France belatedly requested a Security Council mandate to establish safe areas, it received the Council's endorsement despite some deep misgivings about French motives.[84] Moreover, in November 1994, the Council established the International Criminal Tribunal for Rwanda (ICTR) to prosecute individuals for grave breaches of International Humanitarian Law committed in Rwanda in 1994.

The international response was not primarily characertized by debates about the legitimacy of what the regime and its allies were doing—there was a general consensus on its illegitimacy—but by debates about how best to respond, doubts about the nature of the situation, a sense that there were few viable options, and a widely shared reluctance to sacrifice soldiers to protect Rwandans. At the beginning of the genocide, Belgium withdrew its peacekeepers not because it was unconcerned with the killing but because it was unwilling to sacrifice its own soldiers to stop it. Likewise, in April 1994 the UK and the USA argued for downsizing rather than reinforcing UNAMIR on the grounds that there was no peace to keep and no government willing to send its troops to fight a war in Rwanda.[85] When the Security Council agreed to

[81] Cited by Melvern, *Conspiracy to Murder*, p. 239.

[82] Melvern, *Conspiracy to Murder*, p. 239.

[83] On the French role in the Rwandan genocide, see Daniela Kroslak, *The Role of France in the Rwandan Genocide* (London: Hurst and Co., 2007).

[84] See Chesterman, *Just War or Just Peace?*, p. 146; and Wheeler, *Saving Strangers*, pp. 236–7.

[85] Wheeler, *Saving Strangers*, p. 221; and Melvern, *A People Betrayed.* On Somalia, see John L. Hirsch and Robert B. Oakley, *Somalia and Operation Restore Hope: Reflections on Peacemaking and Peacekeeping* (Washington, DC: United States Institute of People, 1995).

reinforce UNAMIR in May 1994, member states were unwilling to provide the necessary troops and equipment.[86]

These concerns were enabled and given some credibility at the time by uncertainty at the beginning of the genocide about what was happening. During the first few days of the genocide, the Rwandan government was not alone in characterizing the violence as spontaneous, chaotic, and born of civil strife. Some Western media outlets, including the *New York Times*, blamed the RPF for the violence.[87] The first to caricature the situation as genocide was the left-wing French newspaper *Liberation* on 11 April, but this paper lacked influence and it was more than a week before this interpretation of events was repeated in the English-speaking world. The problem was confounded by the fact that most foreign NGOs understandably withdrew their staff from Rwanda when the violence erupted and it was not until 19 April that NGOs began labelling the situation as genocide.[88] For his part, the UN Secretary-General ignored advice from the UNAMIR commander, Romeo Dallaire, about the one-sided nature of the violence and advised the Council that the crisis was rooted in the breakdown of the Arusha peace agreement.[89] Only gradually did a clearer picture of genocide emerge and even then, it lacked clarity owing to the simultaneous eruption of fighting between the RPF and government forces. It is clear though that as the genocide progressed and evidence of its nature was confirmed, many states continued to portray the violence as civil war in order to avoid public pressure for them to act.

## KOSOVO (1998–1999)

Although the outcome was very different, international society's reaction to the commission of mass killing was similar during the wars of Yugoslav dissolution (1992–95 and 1998–99). Even governments positively inclined towards the groups responsible for most of the mass atrocities (the government of Serbia and the Bosnian Serbs), criticized the intentional killing of

[86] See Michael Barnett, *Eyewitness to a Genocide: The United Nations and Rwanda* (Ithaca: Cornell University Press, 2002), p. 161.

[87] See Walter C. Soderlund and E. Donald Briggs, 'Rwanda, 1994: UNAMIR I, UNAMIR II and Operation Turquoise', in Walter C. Soderlund, E. Donald Briggs, Kai Hilderbrandt, and Abdel Salam Sidahmed (eds), *Humanitarian Crises and Intervention: Reassessing the Impact of Mass Media* (Stirling, VA: Kumarian Press, 2008), p. 113.

[88] See Gregory Stanton, 'Could the Rwandan Genocide have been Prevented?', *Journal of Genocide Research*, 6 (2) 2004, pp. 211–28.

[89] Boutros Boutros-Ghali, *Special Report of the UN Secretary-General on UNAMIR*, S/1994/470, 20 April 1994. For Dallaire's account, see Lt. Gen. Romeo Dallaire, *Shake Hands with the Devil: The Failure of Humanity in Rwanda* (London: Arrow Books, 2004).

civilians and accepted the need for some kind of international response.[90] Pronounced disagreements related to the balance of guilt (were all parties equally blameworthy?) and the most appropriate responses. Kosovo is a particularly instructive case precisely because deep divisions about the legitimacy of unilateral armed intervention did not preclude agreement about the illegitimacy of the Yugoslav government's behaviour. Indeed, the Kosovo case provides evidence of a strong international consensus on the illegitimacy of mass atrocities.

The Kosovo crisis had its roots in the late 1980s when the new nationalist regime in Serbia rescinded the province's autonomy and created an apartheid-style system that privileged the minority Serbs. The Kosovar Albanians responded with a campaign of non-violent resistance. When that proved ineffective, radicals launched an armed insurrection in 1998. The Serb authorities responded with campaigns of indiscriminate violence, massacres, and ethnic cleansing, ultimately killing between 5,000–10,000 civilians.[91]

Yugoslavia's President, Slobodan Milosevic, tried to secure sufficient legitimacy by leveraging uncertainty. First, he tried to cloud the situation by arguing that all the parties were equally guilty of targeting civilians, that his government was not directly responsible for ethnic cleansing, and that he had condemned such practice.[92] Where Serbs committed atrocities they did so as members of non-state groups and were duly punished, he claimed. Describing the charge that government forces were engaged in ethnic cleansing as 'a big lie', he continued: 'we are not angels. Nor are we the devils you have made us out to be. Our regular forces are highly disciplined. The irregular forces are another matter. Bad things happened, as they did to both sides during the Vietnam War. We have arrested those irregular self-appointed leaders'.[93] Second, Milosevic attempted to make the Serb authorities appear more legitimate than their Kosovar Albanian rivals by referring to the Kosovo Liberation Army (KLA) as 'terrorists' and portraying Yugoslav military and police activities as counter-terrorism operations. The KLA, he argued, had not engaged in regular battle with Yugoslav forces and focused their violence on civilians.[94] They were 'murderers, rapists, kidnappers, who terrorise not only Serbs and other non-Albanian population in Kosovo . . . . They also terrorise Albanians. I have to tell you that the situation of Albanians in Kosovo . . . is

[90] For a useful overview, see Alex Danchev and Thomas Halverson (eds), *International Perspectives on the Yugoslav Conflict* (London: Macmillan, 1996).

[91] See Tim Judah, *Kosovo: War and Revenge* (London: Yale University Press, 2000); and Alex J. Bellamy, *Kosovo and International Society* (London: Palgrave, 2002).

[92] Slobodan Milosevic, transcript of interview the *Washington Post*, 16 December 1998.

[93] Arnaud de Borchgrave, interview with Slobodan Milosevic for UPI, 30 April 1999. He reiterated this view in an interview he gave to Fox News from his cell in The Hague, 24 August 2001.

[94] Arnaud de Borchgrave, interview with Slobodan Milosevic for UPI, 30 April 1999.

tragic. They are being manipulated. They are being terrorised. By those murderers and kidnappers, those rapists and drug dealers'.[95] Third, he claimed that the almost one million Kosovar Albanian refugees who fled the Serb onslaught in 1999 were fleeing not from Serbian ethnic cleansing as they claimed but from NATO's aerial bombing.[96]

In a context of extensive and relatively accurate independent reporting about the situation on the ground, these arguments had little palpable effect on the legitimacy judgements reached by external actors. Although there was some debate about the part played by the KLA, no significant international actors disputed the fact that Serb forces were using violence against civilians in Kosovo. From the outset, the European response, if somewhat indecisive, was based on the presumptions that ethnic cleansing and other grave human rights abuses were illegitimate and that external actors had a legitimate role to play in bringing abuses to an end, protecting vulnerable civilians, and holding the perpetrators to account. Whilst US Secretary of State, Madeleine Albright immediately intimated the possibility of military intervention, German Foreign Minister Klaus Kinkel advocated a multi-pronged approach that involved strengthening NATO's presence in Macedonia and the WEU's (Western European Union) mission in Albania and embarking on a joint EU–OSCE (Organization for Security and Co-operation in Europe) peace process.[97] Kinkel's proposed diplomatic route prevailed and European efforts were supported UN Security Council Resolution 1160 (31 March 1998).

Resolution 1160 was adopted under Chapter VII of the Charter, recognizing that the emerging conflict in Kosovo posed a 'threat to international peace and security'. The resolution called for an end to the violence, imposed an arms embargo on Yugoslavia, voiced support for the non-violent opposition movement in Kosovo, and called upon both sides to cooperate with international efforts to broker a negotiated settlement. The significance of Resolution 1160 lay in its recognition that the situation in Kosovo warranted international engagement owing to the commission of atrocities. The Resolution's adoption at a relatively early stage in the crisis caused significant unease within the Russian and Chinese governments in particular, both of which abstained arguing that the situation in Kosovo was a domestic matter that fell within Yugoslavia's jurisdiction.[98] China argued that Security Council intervention in internal matters such as this was likely to set a negative precedent for the future. However, a clear majority of Council members believed that human

[95] Ronald Hatchet, interview with Slobodan Milosevic, KHOU television, 21 April 1999.

[96] Ronald Hatchet, interview with Slobodan Milosevic, KHOU television, 21 April 1999.

[97] In Alex J. Bellamy, 'Geopolitics and Solidarity on the Borders of Europe: The Yugoslav Wars of Succession', in J.-M. Coicaud and N. J. Wheeler (eds), *National Interest and International Solidarity: Particular and Universal Ethics in International Life* (Tokyo: UN University Press, 2008), p. 246.

[98] S/PV.3868, 31 March 1999.

rights abuse in Kosovo constituted a threat to regional peace and security.[99] Although Russia expressed concerns about international engagement in what it saw as a domestic matter, its position began to change after the passage of Resolution 1160 leaving China isolated as the only Council member arguing against Council activism on the grounds of domestic jurisdiction.

Immediately after the passage of Resolution 1160, Russia attempted to negotiate a peaceful settlement and Slobodan Milosevic assured Russian diplomats that Serbian Interior Ministry forces had been withdrawn from Kosovo as requested by the Security Council.[100] Russia still formally opposed international mediation on the grounds that the Kosovo conflict was a domestic matter, but by engaging in diplomacy that linked the lifting of sanctions with Yugoslav compliance with Council demands, Russia was tacitly accepting the idea that a state's domestic behaviour could be a legitimate international concern. It soon became clear, however, that despite its assurances to the Russian government, Yugoslavia was not complying with the Security Council's requests.[101] Western governments responded by demanding tougher sanctions and armed intervention, forcing Russian President Boris Yeltsin to engage in direct diplomacy to persuade Milosevic to comply with Resolution 1160. Yeltsin persuaded Milosevic to comply with three of the Council's four demands; Milosevic agreed to withdraw paramilitary forces from Kosovo only once the KLA ceased violent attacks.[102] At one level, this was a major diplomatic coup that outmanoeuvred the West. At another level, though, this move represented a deepening of Russian acceptance of the legitimacy of international activism to stem mass atrocities.

Yeltsin's diplomatic triumph was short-lived. Having promised to restrain Yugoslav forces in Kosovo, Milosevic permitted the Yugoslav army to reinforce its positions in the province and within a month tanks were being employed against villages on the outskirts of the province's capital, Pristina.[103] In response, the Russian position hardened against Yugoslavia, demonstrated by its vote in support of a tougher UN Security Council Resolution, 1199 (23 September 1999), which was passed with fourteen votes in favour and a Chinese abstention. Resolution 1199 demanded (rather than requested) a cessation of hostilities and required the leadership of both sides take urgent

[99] See Wheeler, *Saving Strangers*, p. 259; and Jennifer Welsh, 'The Security Council and Humanitarian Intervention', in V. Lowe, A. Roberts, J. Welsh, and D. Zaum (eds), *The United Nations Security Council and War: The Evolution of Thought and Practice since 1945* (Oxford: Oxford University Press, 2008), pp. 548–9.

[100] 'Statement by the Spokesman of the Ministry of Foreign Affairs of the Russian Federation', 2 April 1998; and 'Memorandum by the Russian Federation', 14 April 1998.

[101] *European Union Report on the Situation in Kosovo*, Annex to United Nations Press Release (S/1998/361), 21 April 1998.

[102] See Tim Youngs, 'Kosovo: The Diplomatic and Military Options', *House of Commons Research Paper 98/93*. 1998, p. 28.

[103] *The Times*, 30 June 1998.

steps to 'avert the impending humanitarian catastrophe'. The Council also insisted that it would consider further measures in the event of non-compliance.[104] China was now alone in arguing that it could not support the resolution and felt the need to supplement its argument that the crisis in Kosovo was a domestic matter with the pragmatic argument that threatening punitive measures 'would adversely affect the possibilities of a peaceful settlement to the conflict'.[105]

The key point here is that prior to NATO's intervention in Kosovo there was a broad international consensus that Yugoslavia was not entitled to violate civilian immunity. Specifically, Resolution 1199 imposed on Yugoslavia obligations to 'cease hostilities', 'take immediate steps to improve the humanitarian situation' and made the Yugoslav authorities accountable to the Security Council by deciding that further measures would be considered in the case of non-compliance. Of course, as in the case of Rwanda this did not translate into agreement on the most appropriate means for ensuring Yugoslav compliance. Both points were apparent in the debate that followed the launch of NATO's intervention in March 1999.

On 24 March 1999, a day after NATO began its air campaign against Yugoslavia, Russia introduced a draft resolution demanding an immediate cessation of hostilities. The draft resolution limited itself to criticizing NATO's use of force as a breach of Article 2(4) of the Charter and recalling the Council's primacy on matters of international peace and security. It did not take a position sympathetic to Yugoslavia's actions in Kosovo.[106] Nonetheless, the draft resolution was heavily defeated by 3–12, with only Russia, China, and Namibia voting in favour. Among the states voting against the resolution were Argentina, Bahrain, Brazil, Gabon, Gambia, and Malaysia. Whilst the vote cannot be understood as retrospective authorization for the intervention, it was indicative of a broader sentiment regarding Yugoslavia's behaviour and the illegitimacy of its mistreatment of Kosovo's Albanian population.

Russia's position rested on two arguments which focused on the intervention, rather than the legitimacy of Yugoslavia's case. First it argued that NATO did not have the authority to make determinations about when to use force. Only the UN Security Council had that authority, Russia complained.[107] Stressing that it did not condone 'violations of international humanitarian law by any party', Russia's second argument was that military intervention was likely to worsen the crisis in Kosovo.[108] This basic claim—that it was the fact of unilateral armed intervention and not sympathy for Yugoslavia and its

[104] S/PV.3930, 23 September 1998.
[105] S/PV.3930, 23 September 1998.
[106] S/1999/328, 26 March 1999.
[107] S/PV.3988, 24 March 1999; and S/PV.3989, 26 March 1999.
[108] S/PV.3988, 24 March 1999.

treatment of the Kosovar Albanians that was the nub of the problem—was further emphasized by Namibia, who joined China in supporting Russia's draft resolution. Indeed, Namibia's argument opened with a restatement of the claim that the Yugoslav government was behaving illegitimately: 'the current crisis in the Serbian province of Kosovo . . . is a source of great concern to us. The degree of brutality perpetrated on the civilian population, the massacre of women, children and the elderly, the displacement of people from their homes, kidnappings and the wanton destruction of property continue to take place in Kosovo'.[109] Others, such as India and Belarus, made broadly similar points.[110]

Among NATO's chief critics, only China continued to question the legitimacy of international engagement in what it saw as an essentially 'domestic' matter. Even it, however, stopped well short of excusing Yugoslav behaviour. Indeed, China argued that any political settlement should guarantee 'the legitimate rights and interests of all ethnic groups in the Kosovo region'.[111]

It goes without saying that NATO and its allies defended the intervention by arguing that widespread and systematic violations of civilian immunity by government forces established a moral imperative to intervene. Interestingly, though, many of the non-aligned states that participated in the Security Council debates also referred to Yugoslavia's failure to protect its population from mass atrocities. Argentina argued that states have an 'obligation to protect and ensure respect' of the fundamental legal norms of international humanitarian law;[112] Gambia plainly stated that 'it is the responsibility of any Government to protect its citizens' and that 'we cannot remain indifferent to the plight of the murdered people of Kosovo';[113] Malaysia insisted that '[s]uch a tragic situation calls for appropriate and prompt action by the international community'.[114] Although the Non-Aligned Movement opposed NATO's use of force without Security Council authorisation, the Organization of the Islamic Conference (OIC) issued a letter to the Security Council condemning the ethnic cleansing of Kosovar Albanians, demanding an immediate cessation of hostilities, and insisting that the Yugoslav government accept the terms of an international peace plan.[115] A significant number of other states, including Mexico, South Africa, and India, also expressed concerns about the Yugoslav government's conduct in Kosovo.[116]

[109] S/PV.3988, 24 March 1999.
[110] S/PV.3988, 24 March 1999; and S/PV.3989, 26 March 1999.
[111] S/PV.3988, 24 March 1999.
[112] S/PV.3989, 26 March 1999.
[113] S/PV.3988, 24 March 1999.
[114] S/PV.3989, 26 March 1999.
[115] S/1999/394, 7 April 1999.
[116] Albrecht Schnabel and Ramesh Thakur (eds), *Kosovo and the Challenge of Humanitarian Intervention: Selective Indignation, Collective Action, and International Citizenship* (Tokyo: UN University Press, 2000).

In short, the international furore caused by NATO's intervention in Kosovo masked an international consensus around the norm of civilian immunity. Few, if any, governments excused Yugoslavia's conduct and all except one member of the Security Council (China—itself a serial offender) emphasized the immorality of targeting Kosovar Albanian civilians. Moreover, the majority accepted that it fell to the Security Council to adopt measures to end the violence although states disagreed on what those measures might be. As with Rwanda, therefore, the underlying international debates in 1999 were not primarily concerned with the legitimacy of the Yugoslav government's behaviour—there was very little disputing that it was illegitimate—but with questions about the most appropriate international response. This confirms the proposition that changes to the global context had made it more difficult for perpetrators to secure sufficient legitimacy for mass atrocities and helps create the impression that in the post-Cold War period, the condemnation of mass atrocities by international society had become an almost default response—suggesting perhaps that the norm had gone from being embedded in international society to internalized among its members. But this would only be part of the story. Because context played such a large role in shaping responses to mass atrocities, we have to remain attuned to the prospect that these same contextual factors might sometimes work in the opposite direction and allow perpetrators to secure sufficient legitimacy. The remainder of this chapter examines two such cases from the 1990s: the first Russian war in Chechnya and post-genocide massacres committed by the RPF.

## LEGITIMIZING MASS KILLING IN THE HUMANITARIAN ERA

### First Chechen War

Chechnya is an obvious exception to post-Cold War international society's rhetorical (though always material) defence of civilian immunity. Between 1994 and 1996 ('First Chechen War') and again in 1999–2000 ('Second Chechen War'), Russia waged counter-insurgency campaigns characterized by the indiscriminate bombardment of cities, towns, and villages, occasional massacres of civilians and captured rebels, and the widespread commission of other war crimes such as rape, torture, and looting.[117] As Matthew Evangelista argues, 'from the first days of the first invasion, the Russian armed

[117] The literature on the Chechen wars is unanimous in its assessment that the Russian military committed war crimes and violated the principle of civilian immunity. E.g. Emma Gilligan, *Terror in Chechnya: Russia and the Tragedy of Civilians in War* (Princeton, NJ:

forces... violated the laws of war on a vast scale'.[118] Despite repeated violations of civilian immunity, Russia avoided international condemnation almost entirely during the First Chechen War. It was only moderately censured for very similar conduct during the second war, which will not be examined here. Russia's capacity to secure sufficient legitimacy for military campaigns characterized by widespread violations of civilian immunity stands in stark contrast to the experiences discussed in the first part of this chapter. The significant variation between the international response to Chechnya and responses to other contemporaneous atrocities was largely a product of two contextual factors: key external actors had powerful countervailing interests and they regarded the Russian regime as more legitimate than its Chechen rivals.

When the Soviet Union collapsed in 1991, a nationalist movement headed by former air force general, Jokhar Dudayev, seized power in Chechnya.[119] Dudayev declared Chechnya's independence from Russia, to which the Russian *Duma* responded by declaring the presidency and the declaration invalid. A few days later, Russia imposed a state of emergency but was unable to enforce it. The political crisis ended with a negotiated settlement that saw Russian troops withdraw from Chechnya. An uneasy truce persisted until 1994 during which time Russia provided arms and assistance to anti-Dudayev groups.[120] This undeclared war culminated in a disastrous assault on Grozny in November 1994, in which Russian-backed anti-Dudayev forces tried and failed to oust the government. This embarrassing failure persuaded the Russian government to confront Chechnya head-on, believing that a 'small victorious war' would not only resolve the Chechnya problem but also restore President Yeltsin's flagging domestic popularity.[121]

The war began badly for the Russians. Armoured columns entered Chechnya in mid-December and were greeted with mass (largely unarmed) civilian opposition. Throughout Chechnya, Russian columns were prevented from advancing by crowds of civilians. Russian bases were besieged. Sometimes the confrontations became violent—protestors smashed windows and hurled rocks; troops responded by firing into the crowds. Yeltsin compounded the problem by issuing contradictory orders, instructing the army to protect Chechen civilians from civil war whilst removing the Dudayev regime and

Princeton University Press, 2010), p. 1; and Emil Soulemanov, *An Endless War: The Russia–Chechnya War in Perspective* (Frankfurt: Peter Lang, 2007).

[118] Matthew Evangelista, *The Chechen Wars: Will Russia Go the Way of the Soviet Union?* (Washington, DC: The Brookings Institution, 2002), p. 8.

[119] Carlotta Gall and Thomas de Waal, *Chechnya: Calamity in the Caucuses* (New York: New York University Press), p. 99; Anatol Lieven, *Chechnya: Tombstone of Russian Power* (New Haven: Yale University Press, 1999), pp. 57–8.

[120] Lieven, *Chechnya*, p. 67; and Lila Shevtsova, *Yeltsin's Russia: Myth and Reality* (Washington, DC: Carnegie Endowment for International Peace, 1999), p. 111.

[121] Gall and de Waal, *Chechnya*, pp. 159–60.

restoring 'constitutional order'.[122] Unsure of both the legality and substance of their orders, some columns halted, others turned back. Dozens of officers refused to instruct their troops to advance on Grozny, Lt. General Eduard Vorobyov arguing that 'I consider it criminal to use the army against my own people'.[123] As a result, although some 40,000 Russian troops had entered Chechnya (an area slightly smaller than Wales), Grozny remained firmly in Dudayev's hands as 1994 drew to a close.

Russia commenced sporadic air attacks on Grozny in mid-December. This campaign escalated dramatically on 22 December with the launch of indiscriminate daytime raids. On New Years Eve, Russian armoured columns entered the city but were destroyed by the Chechen defenders. Dozens of tanks and armoured cars were soundly defeated and approximately 1,500 Russian soldiers killed or injured.[124] Russian forces retreated and reverted to indiscriminate aerial and artillery bombardment aimed at terrorizing the civilian population and blasting the rebels from their hiding places.[125] Russian forces destroyed buildings to prevent the rebels using them as cover, employed fuel-air and other incendiary bombs to force the rebels into the open and torched whole streets. Russian soldiers indiscriminately shot people they found on the streets.[126] Civilians bore the brunt of the attack and approximately 20,000–27,000 were killed during the assault on Grozny.[127] The Chechens held the Presidential Palace until it was struck by a massive penetration bomb on 19 January which destroyed its cellars, and then retreated southwards.[128] At this point, with the Chechens still holding about half of the city, Russia opened up what has been described as the most intensive bombardment since the Second World War. Russian aircraft, artillery, and tanks mounted an indiscriminate round-the-clock attack on Grozny's southern districts. One observer counted 4,000 detonations in a single hour. This compared to 3,500 detonations *each day* at the peak of the bombardment of Sarajevo in Bosnia.[129]

The assault on Grozny was only the first phase of the war. After the city's fall, the conflict became a guerrilla war 'in which virtually the entire civilian

[122] Gall and de Waal, *Chechnya*, p. 175; and Shevtsova, *Yeltsin's Russia*, p. 113.

[123] Quoted in Soulemanov, *Endless War*, p. 101; and Lieven *Chechnya*, p. 103. In total, some 557 officers were sacked or disciplined for refusing orders to invade Chechnya or resigned in protest.

[124] Gall and de Waal, *Chechnya*, p. 16; and Lieven, *Chechnya*, pp. 110–11.

[125] Lieven, *Chechnya*, pp. 43, 111 and (on the intent to terrorize civilians) 107.

[126] Lieven, *Chechnya*, p. 47.

[127] Gall and de Waal suggest 27,000 dead civilians, whereas Lieven puts the figure at 'not in excess of' 20,000. Lieven, *Chechnya*, p. 108. Juan Gaytisolo argues that 'experts' agree that 40,000 were killed. Juan Gaytisolo, *Landscapes of War: From Sarajevo to Chechnya* (San Francisco: City Lights, 2000), p. 185.

[128] Lieven, *Chechnya*, p. 111.

[129] Frederick Cuny, 'Killing Chechnya', *New York Review of Books*, 6 April 1995. The scale of the assault is also said to have dwarfed that of Beirut during the Lebanese civil war. See Lieven, *Chechnya*, p. 43.

population of Chechnya came to be seen as the enemy'.[130] Rather than retreat to the mountains, the rebels harried Russian forces, forcing them to fight village by village.[131] Wherever they met resistance, Russian forces resorted to the tactics employed in Grozny—retreat and indiscriminate bombardment followed by a *zachistka* ('mop-up' or, more literally, 'cleansing') operation. Médecins sans Frontières reported that attacks followed a familiar pattern: villages would be surrounded and threats issued; Russian troops would demand bribes; Chechen men would be arrested and despatched to filtration camps; goods looted and houses burned.[132] Chechnya's second city, Gudermes, suffered a similar fate to the capital. Argun, a small town near to Grozny held out until 23 March but succumbed after being completely devastated by Russian bombardment. To the south, the village of Bamut held out for twelve months.[133] Sometimes, *zachistka* operations turned into massacres. In April 1995 Russian forces killed between 100–120 civilians after taking the village of Samashki.[134] This pattern of events was repeated in Novogroznensky in January 1996, where 40 per cent of the town's houses were destroyed.[135] Things did not improve much once Russian forces assumed control of an area.[136] Chechen civilians were subjected to arbitrary violence at roadblocks and during building searches, and sexual violence and looting were common.[137] Chechen males of fighting age were sent to 'filtration camps' ostensibly to weed out insurgents. Up to 1,000 were killed in the camps and many more experienced random beatings and torture.[138]

Although the Chechens managed to hold out for several months against the Russian army, in April 1995 Dudayev was killed and by June 1995 the rebels were facing defeat.[139] Insurgents led by the radical, Shamir Baseyev, stormed

[130] Gail W. Lapidus, 'Dynamics of Secession in the Russian Federation: Why Chechnya?', in Mikhail A. Alexseev (ed.), *Center-Periphery Conflict in Post-Soviet Russia* (New York: St. Martin's Press, 1999), p. 64.

[131] Lieven, *Chechnya*, p. 121.

[132] Médicins sans Frontières report cited by Lieven, *Chechnya*, 133.

[133] Lieven, *Chechnya*, p. 121.

[134] One report says 'all except four' were civilians, another 93 victims were confirmed to be civilians. On the former, see Gall and de Waal, *Chechnya*, p. 242. The Red Cross initially put the figure at 250 and commented that the true figure was likely higher because they had been prevented from entering the village for a week after the massacre. Soulemanov, *Endless War*, pp. 110–11.

[135] Lieven, *Chechnya*, p. 127.

[136] Lieven, *Chechnya*, p. 127.

[137] Lieven maintains that there were 'innumerable' cases of violence against civilians at checkpoints or in house searches, see Lieven, *Chechnya*, p. 131. Lapidus records the 'extreme brutality' of Russian forces towards the civilian population. See Lapidus, 'Dynamics of Secession', p. 64.

[138] The OSCE's conservative figures suggested that 2,000 were captured and that 'hundreds' were killed. Lieven, *Chechnya*, p. 132. For testimonies and interviews, see Valery Tishkov, *Chechnya: Life in a War-Torn Society* (Berkeley: University of California Press, 2004), pp. 135–40.

[139] Lieven, *Chechnya*, p. 123.

the Russian town of Budyonnovsk, seizing 2,000 civilians at the hospital and demanding an immediate cessation of violence. After two botched attempts to storm the hospital, Prime Minister Viktor Chernomyrdin agreed to call a ceasefire in Chechnya and provide the rebels safe passage.[140] Following a basic pattern of Chechen attacks and Russian bombardment, punctuated by periodic ceasefires and peace plans, the war continued until 1996, when the rebels retook Grozny in an audacious assault and forced the Russians to agree to withdraw from Chechnya.

The Yeltsin government justified its Chechnya campaign as an exercise in law enforcement. As Vladimir Lukin, Russia's former Ambassador to the USA and chair of the *Duma*'s foreign relations committee, put it, 'using the army inside the country in extreme situations, when threats to the state appear, is the norm in democratic states'.[141] Between 1992 and 1994, hardliners in the Kremlin had repeatedly referred to Dudayev's government as a 'criminal regime'. Internal Affairs Minister Anatolly Kulikov argued that the separatists wanted to build a 'militaristic, totalitarian, extremist, criminal state that is absolutely anti-Russian'.[142] Yeltsin emphasized this line of argument in his televised address of 27 December 1994, arguing that Russian troops were defending Russia's integrity and constitution: 'no territory has the right to leave Russia', he maintained. He told Russians that the decision to intervene had been a difficult but necessary one because Chechnya had become a 'breeding ground' for crime and a threat to Russia's national security. He embellished his argument with the patently false claim that Grozny was 'awash' with 10,000 foreign mercenaries and painted a grossly inaccurate picture of the tactical situation, claiming that Russian forces had already blocked all the 'armed bands' and that they were doing a good job.[143] The Kremlin also insisted that the war would be short and victorious—a 'bloodless blitzkrieg', Kozyrev predicted.[144]

When it came to justifying the war's conduct, Russian authorities simply denied the use of indiscriminate violence or the commission of atrocities and tried (unsuccessfully) to create and leverage uncertainty. According to Evangelista, Yeltsin lied about the war from start to finish, and his lies were often transparent.[145] When they were called to account for civilian casualties, the Russian army and government commonly blamed the insurgents for making it impossible to distinguish between soldiers and civilians and for

140 Gall and de Waal, *Chechnya*, pp. 257–9; Lieven, *Chechnya*, 124.
141 Cited by Shevtsova, *Yeltsin's Russia*, p. 118.
142 Cited by Lapidus, 'The Dynamics of Secession', p. 61.
143 Cited by Gall and de Waal, *Chechnya*, pp. 200–1.
144 Lapidus, 'Dynamics of Secession', p. 63.
145 Evangelista, *Chechen Wars*, p. 39.

using civilians as 'human shields'.[146] Typically, it argued that civilian casualties were unintended consequences of the fighting.[147] Faced with accusations about the massacre at Samashki, the Interior Ministry denied that there had been any civilian casualties and argued that all of the dead were insurgents. Indeed, Russian military logs recorded all of the casualties at Samashki as 'fighters'.[148] The Military Prosecutor's Office accepted this explanation and found there to be insufficient evidence to bring charges against those accused of killing civilians. A parliamentary commission reached a similar conclusion.[149] The very obvious gap between government claims and media reports about what was actually happening in Chechnya badly damaged the government's domestic legitimacy—though it did not have much effect on its international position (see below).

The government denied bombarding Grozny in December 1994 and when the New Years Eve assault went badly wrong, reported only a 'Russian victory' arguing that the bombardment had ended and that 'normalization operations' had begun.[150] On 2 January, as fighting in Grozny continued, Defence Minister Grachev argued that 'mopping up' operations would be over within a week and that displaced residents would be able to return.[151] Five months later, Yeltsin assured Germany's Chancellor Kohl that 'the classic military campaign in Chechnya' was over.[152]

In sharp contrast to the chorus of condemnation that greeted Iraqi atrocities against the Kurds or Serbian atrocities in Bosnia and Kosovo, the international response to the indiscriminate killing of civilians in Chechnya was limited and ambivalent.[153] Where there was any criticism, it was usually mild. There was little, if any, serious discussion of punishment. The pattern was set in December 1994 when, despite the escalating violence in Chechnya, the issue was barely discussed at an OSCE summit. Russia insisted that Chechnya was an internal matter outside the organization's mandate and most other members were prepared to accept that view.[154] Western governments expressed some

[146] Gall and de Waal, *Chechnya*, p. 247.

[147] Lieven, *Chechnya*, p. 131.

[148] Gall and de Waal, *Chechnya*, p. 245.

[149] Gall and de Waal, *Chechnya*, p. 246.

[150] Lieven, *Chechnya*, p. 111.

[151] Grachev had a notoriously tenuous grasp on reality. See Lapidus, 'Dynamics of Secession', p. 64.

[152] Cited by Dmitri V. Trenin and Aleksei V. Malashenko, *Russia's Restless Frontier: The Chechnya Factor in Post-Soviet Russia* (Washington, DC: Carnegie Endowment for International Peace, 2004), p. 22.

[153] See Andrei Shoumikhin, 'The Chechen Crisis and the Future of Russia', *Contemporary Strategy*, 15, 1996, p. 6; and Dmitri Trenin, *The End of Eurasia: Russia on the Border Between Geopolitics and Globalization* (Washington, DC: Carnegie Endowment for International Peace, 2002), p. 324.

[154] Gall and de Waal, *Chechnya*, p. 186. Also see Greg Hansen and Robert Seely, 'War and Humanitarian Action in Chechnya', War and Humanitarian Action Project Occasional Paper No. 26, 1996, pp. 23–4.

concern about the 'excessive' use of force but generally endorsed Russia's characterization of the conflict as an 'internal matter'.[155]

The USA did not respond directly until 13 February 1995, when Clinton called Yeltsin to—in the words of the White House Press Secretary—note international concern about the humanitarian situation in Chechnya and 'reiterate the importance of an end to the bloodshed and the start of a process leading to a peaceful settlement of the dispute'.[156] Secretary of State, Warren Christopher, hinted at the reason for the soft line when he commented that 'Russia is operating in a democratic context' so the USA should 'not rush to judgment'.[157] US criticism increased somewhat after Yeltsin was re-elected in 1996, but remained guarded. On one occasion, when Russian commanders responded to the rebels' recapture of Grozny by instructing residents to leave within forty-eight hours or face 'massive military operations', Clinton wrote to Yeltsin indicating his 'deep concern' about the escalation of violence and insisting that the cycle of violence be brought to an end.[158] But at no point did the USA condemn Russia's behaviour or consider anything more than informal diplomatic pressure. Suggestions that the IMF and World Bank make future lending conditional on improved human rights in Chechnya were dismissed out of hand. This proved controversial, as critics complained that the IMF was effectively bankrolling the war.[159] Even entirely symbolic sanctions were rejected. For instance, in June 1995 Clinton joined Yeltsin in Moscow for Victory in Europe day parades despite the ongoing violations of civilian immunity in Chechnya.[160]

The EU also chose not to condemn Russia's conduct in Chechnya or consider using economic leverage to encourage restraint, though an EU–Russia trade accord was deferred. The European Bank for Reconstruction and Development (EBRD) never even discussed the possibility of withholding financial assistance from Moscow.[161] The Parliamentary Assembly for the Council of Europe (PACE) criticized the Russian campaign, persuading the Council to delay consideration of Russia's application for admission. Russia was admitted in February 1996, but the Council decided to establish an ad hoc Committee on Chechnya to monitor and report on the situation there.[162]

[155] For example, in January 1995, German Chancellor Helmut Kohl described the offensive as 'sheer madness' and called on Yeltsin to resolve the conflict peacefully. Cited by Shevtsova, *Yeltsin's Russia*, p. 122.

[156] Gall and de Waal, *Chechnya*, p. 186.

[157] Cited by Evangelista, *Chechen Wars*, p. 145.

[158] Gall and de Waal, *Chechnya*, p. 352.

[159] See Hansen and Seely, 'War and Humanitarian Action', p. 57.

[160] Lapidus, 'Dynamics of Secession', p. 77.

[161] Lapidus, 'Dynamics of Secession', p. 77. Critics argue that the financial aid forwarded to Moscow by the EBRD, World Bank, and IMF helped finance the war.

[162] Hansen and Seely, 'War and Humanitarian Action', p. 57.

In January 1995, the OSCE's Permanent Council issued a chairman's statement describing the humanitarian situation as 'catastrophic'.[163] The organization despatched a small team led by Hungarian diplomat Istvan Gyarmati to investigate the situation. Members of the mission reported that they were 'appalled by the magnitude of destruction and compared the condition of Grozny with that of Stalingrad during World War II'.[164] But under pressure to take a soft line on Russia, whose consent the OSCE needed in order to operate in the region, Gyarmati's report criticized Russia's use of 'disproportionate and indiscriminate military force' in Chechnya but insisted that both sides were equally responsible for atrocities—a conclusion not supported by the evidence.[165] Reassured that the OSCE would not take a stridently critical line and under diplomatic pressure from the USA and EU, Russia permitted the establishment of a six-person mission to Grozny in April 1995 led by another Hungarian, Sandor Meszaros.[166] The mission was given the somewhat contradictory mandate of facilitating peace talks and reporting on human rights abuses. Critics argued that it focused too heavily on the peace talks and neglected to sufficiently condemn Russian atrocities.[167]

The UN was largely silent on the issue. Secretary-General Boutros-Ghali intimated his 'anguish' at the war but stopped short of criticizing Moscow, seeking a role in mediation, or coordinating a humanitarian response.[168] For this, the Secretary-General was criticized by Human Rights Watch which accused him of failing to 'uphold the human rights principles set out in the UN Charter'.[169] The UN responded 'angrily' to the accusations, pointing out that the Secretary-General had no mandate to intervene.[170]

Ironically, criticism of the war inside Russia itself was much sharper.[171] In May 1999 a simple majority of the *Duma* voted to impeach Yeltsin for launching what they described as an 'illegitimate war' against Chechnya in 1994.[172] Sixty per cent of Russians polled at the height of the conflict said that they opposed the use of force and 25 per cent said that they were prepared

[163] Hansen and Seely, 'War and Humanitarian Action', p. 30.

[164] Evangelista, *Chechen Wars*, p. 144.

[165] Indeed, Gall and de Waal describe the OSCE's finding of moral equivalence as 'ludicrous', Gall and de Waal, *Chechnya*, p. 279.

[166] Hansen and Seely, 'War and Humanitarian Action', p. 30.

[167] Lieven, *Chechnya*, p. 122.

[168] Chechnya did not rate a mention in Boutros-Ghali's subsequent account of his time as UN Secretary-General suggesting that little thought was given to the issue. See Boutros Boutros-Ghali, *Unvanquished: A US–UN Saga* (New York: Random House, 1999).

[169] Cited by Hansen and Seely, 'War and Humanitarian Action', p. 55.

[170] Hansen and Seely, 'War and Humanitarian Action', p. 55.

[171] Some, it should be noted, criticized the war for being too soft on the Chechens, see e.g. Gall and de Waal, *Chechnya*, p. xii.

[172] The resolution did not accuse Yeltsin of war crimes and fell 17 short of the two-thirds majority needed to impeach him. See John Russell, 'Obstacles to Peace in Chechnya: What Scope for International Involvement?', *Europe-Asia Studies*, 58 (6) 2006, p. 958.

to accept Chechen independence.[173] Criticism was led by Russia's Human Rights Commissioner, the former dissident Sergei Kovalyov.[174] Kovalyov visited Grozny in December 1994 and witnessed first hand the escalation of indiscriminate bombardment. Kovalyov telegrammed Yeltsin directly, calling on the president to stop 'this crazy massacre' and pull the country 'out of this vicious circle of despair and bloodstained lies'.[175] The Human Rights Commissioner catalogued civilian casualties and repeatedly called upon Yeltsin to end the bombing, lamenting that 'these pilots and gunners do not know where they are aiming'.[176] He later accused Russian forces of committing war crimes.[177] His criticism was not only reserved for the Russians, however. Kovalyov was also strident in his denunciation of the West and its preference for 'senseless negotiations' over meaningful pressure on Russia.[178] Another key domestic source of opposition was the human rights group, Memorial. Among other things, Memorial documented testimonials given by Chechens who had been imprisoned, abused, and tortured in Russian run 'filtration centres'. The testimonies revealed a pattern of arbitrary detention and violence, torture, and killings. The filtration system failed to elicit meaningful intelligence, Memorial found, but was 'the beginnings of a system of mass terror'.[179]

How do we explain the world's ambivalent response to Chechnya? The sharp variation between the response to this case and other contemporaneous cases rests in the role played by contextual factors. The first thing to note in this regard is that there was no shortage of available information about Russia's use of indiscriminate force, especially in Grozny. Russian authorities did very little to limit media access to the war or to 'spin' the news.[180] There were 'hundreds' of foreign journalists in Grozny at the time of the initial assault, which was reported in the West—although interest evaporated after the city's fall.[181] There was also blanket coverage of the war in Russia itself.[182] Nor did the government conduct a persuasive campaign of creating and leveraging uncertainty. As I noted earlier, its battlefield reports and denials

[173] Lapidus, 'Dynamics of Secession', p. 64.

[174] Media tycoon Boris Berezovsky was another key critic. On Berezovsky, see Trenin and Malashenko, *Russia's Restless Frontier*, p. 23.

[175] Cited by Gall and de Waal, *Chechnya*, p. 200.

[176] Cited by Gall and de Waal, *Chechnya*, p. 197.

[177] David Remnick, *Resurrection: The Struggle for a New Russia* (New York: Random House, 1997), p. 264.

[178] Gall and de Waal, *Chechnya*, p. 187.

[179] Cited by Gall and de Waal, *Chechnya*, p. 232.

[180] Leading some journalists to dub the conflict 'the great drive in war'. Lieven, *Chechnya*, pp. 119–20.

[181] Gall and de Waal, *Chechnya*, p. 198; Daniel Heradstreit, 'Nationalism and Ethnic Nationalism in the Caucuses: Past and Present', in Ole Horis and Sefa Martin Yurukel (eds), *Contrasts and Solutions in the Middle East* (Aarhus: Aarhus University Press, 2011), pp. 391–2.

[182] Gall and de Waal, *Chechnya*, p. 183.

were not viewed as credible by Russians who noted the sharp difference between the government's version of events and what they could see on television.[183] It was not only the Russian government that was irritated by the media, though. In a remarkable outburst, in December 1994 the US State Department criticized the media for raising the conflict's international profile in a manner the USA found unhelpful.[184]

The ambivalent response cannot therefore be explained by reference to uncertainty about the facts of the case. Instead, perceptions about the relative legitimacy of the various relevant actors (especially Russia vis-à-vis the Chechens and Yeltsin vis-à-vis other aspirants for the Russian presidency) and the presence of significant countervailing interests best explain the international reaction.

First, there was little international support for Chechen independence and few actors gave credence to the Chechens' political claims. As a result, foreign governments accepted the view that the crisis was a domestic matter beyond serious international scrutiny.[185] This point was expressed very clearly by President Clinton in April 1995. Asked whether the USA should have been more critical of Russia, Clinton replied 'I think it depends. Do you think that Chechnya is a part of Russia or not?' He went on to compare the Chechen War to the US Civil War and, implicitly, Yeltsin with Abraham Lincoln: 'I would remind you that we once had a civil war in our country in which we lost on a per capita basis far more people than we lost in any of the wars of the twentieth century over the proposition that Abraham Lincoln gave his life for, that no state has a right to withdrawal from our Union'.[186] This line of argument was accepted by UN Secretary-General Boutros-Ghali. Challenged to explain why the UN was not more engaged, the Secretary-General retorted 'we are bound by the UN Charter'.[187]

Second, the West was concerned that criticism of Yeltsin would strengthen his parliamentary opponents, principally the communists and nationalist radicals.[188] This, it was thought, would inhibit Russia's domestic reform programme without improving conditions in Chechnya.[189] Western leaders and diplomats repeatedly emphasized this point and the USA continued to provide aid to Yeltsin's government in the interests of protecting the reform

[183] Lieven, *Chechnya*, p. 120.

[184] Lapidus, 'Dynamics of Secession', p. 76.

[185] Lapidus, 'Dynamics of Secession', p. 75.

[186] David Hoffman, 'Yeltsin Turns to Clinton for Help in Chechen War', *International Herald Tribune*, 22 April 1996.

[187] Cited by Lapidus, 'Dynamics of Secession', p. 73.

[188] Trenin and Malashenko, *Russia's Restless Frontier*, p. 25.

[189] On 26 February 1993, Warren Christopher argued that Europe's long-term interest was best served by supporting democratic reformists in Russia, principally Yeltsin. See Lapidus, 'Dynamics of Secession', p. 75.

programme.[190] Ernst Muehlemann, a Swiss general who chaired the Council of Europe's Chechnya committee, responded to criticism from Kavalyov by emphasizing the importance of protecting Yeltsin from the communists.[191] Support for Yeltsin was not just a product of concern for domestic political reforms, though. A wide range of international issues thought important in the West, including nuclear non-proliferation (START II), responding to the war in Bosnia, and NATO enlargement, required Russian cooperation and it was widely thought that not only was Yeltsin more likely to cooperate than a communist or nationalist president but also that applying pressure over Chechnya would force him into a less cooperative stance on these issues. Given that most Western governments saw Chechnya as a marginal issue in an obscure region, they saw little value in this.[192]

Third, Western leaders were concerned about the potential Balkanization of Russia—a threat talked up by the Kremlin despite the fact that Chechnya was the country's only secessionist republic.[193] The West worried that if Chechnya was allowed to secede others would be encouraged to follow. The US State Department voiced this concern on 14 December 1994, its spokesman stating that 'we have no interest and the world has no interest in seeing a splintering or dismembering of the Russian Federation. That would be enormously destabilizing. It would produce the possibility of large-scale refugee flows'. A high level US official agreed, telling the press that 'I accept Yeltsin's argument that if Chechnya breaks away others will follow suit . . . it's very important for our long-term security that Russia remain a unitary state that remains stable. We have an obvious interest in the stability of their armed forces [and] nuclear forces'.[194]

Thus judgements about the relative legitimacy of the belligerents and the presence of countervailing interests allowed Russia to avoid criticism and punishment despite violating civilian immunity in Chechnya. The Russian position was helped by the lack of international support for Chechen independence and concerns about protecting Yelstin's reformist regime from its communist and nationalist opponents, worries about potential caused by the potential Balkanization of Russia, and the need for Russian cooperation on several pressing international issues. This latter point speaks to an additional consideration—Russia's material and institutional power. The former limited international expectations about what might be achieved through coercive pressure whilst the latter closed off the principal potential institutional avenue for addressing mass

[190] For which Clinton was criticized by conservative Republicans. See Lapidus, 'Dynamics of Secession', p. 75.

[191] Gall and de Waal, *Chechnya*, p. 316.

[192] Lapidus, 'Dynamics of Secession', pp. 76 and (on the obscurity of the region) 78.

[193] As one Russian politician put it, 'we've got Chechnya everywhere'. Cited by Trenin and Malashenko, *Russia's Restless Frontier*, p. 1.

[194] Both cited by Lapidus, 'Dynamics of Secession', p. 74.

atrocities—the UN Security Council. As such, whilst some governments and regional bodies expressed concern about the indiscriminate use of force against civilians, they typically refrained from condemning Russia and steered clear of calling for punishment.

## Post-Genocide Massacres in the African Great Lakes Region

We might be tempted to think that Russia's ability to avoid censure and punishment owed more to its power than anything else. But a second example from the 1990s shows that relatively weak states—Rwanda (governed by the Rwandan Patriotic Front (RPF)—and its ally, Joseph Kabila's Alliance des Forces Democratiques pour la Liberation du Congo-Zaire (ADFL)—could also avoid criticism and punishment for violations of civilian immunity in the right context.[195] In the years following the 1994 Rwandan genocide, the RPF perpetrated several massacres inside Rwanda—including the killing of over 4,000 displaced persons at a camp patrolled by UN peacekeepers—and with its Congolese allies hunted down and killed around 230,000 Hutu refugees. Not only did this killing go unpunished, barely a word of condemnation was uttered by international society. Indeed, the UN and USA actively suppressed reports detailing the massacres in order to protect the perpetrators.

During the 1994 Rwandan genocide, the Rwandan Patriotic Front (RPF) waged a civil war against the Hutu led Rwandan Army (FAR) and the Hutu militia (*interahamwe* and *inpuzamugambi*). It was the RPF's victory that brought the genocide to an end, but during the war the RPF itself committed atrocities against Hutu and Tutsi civilians. At the end of the genocide, the Rwandan government and Hutu militia fled in the wake of the RPF advance, taking up to two million Hutu civilians with them. Some of these civilians fled voluntarily and some were forced to flee by their political leaders. Given the RPF's record of atrocities, Hutu civilians had very good reason to flee the advancing RPF and although there is no doubt that ex-FAR soldiers and *genocidaire* militia were among them, a large number of those that fled were genuine refugees.[196] As early as 1992, Africa Watch had accused the RPF of committing serious human rights abuses and the following year it reported a pattern of summary executions, pillaging, and forced deportation.[197] According to Filip Reyntjens, between the resumption of civil war in April 1994 and

[195] The military wing of the RPF is the Rwandan Patriotic Army (RPA). It was the RPA that was responsible for committing the massacres, but under the instructions of the RPF leadership. As such, I refer only to the RPF but this should be taken as denoting both RPF and RPA.

[196] Fiona Terry, *Condemned to Repeat? The Paradox of Humanitarian Action* (Ithaca: Cornell University Press, 2002), p. 173.

[197] Africa Watch, *Rwanda: Talking Peace and Waging War. Human Rights Since the October 1990 Invasion,* 27 February 1992.

September 1994, the RPF massacred up to 100,000 civilians.[198] The killing continued after the end of the war, the most famous episode being the Kibeho massacre in April 1995. RPF forces surrounded the camp in an attempt to intimidate the displaced persons into returning home. When some displaced people attempted to flee in panic, the RPF opened fire with guns and mortars.[199] Australian medics, there as part of UNAMIR, counted at least 4,000 bodies before the RPF instructed them to stop counting. Most estimates put the number of massacred civilians at between 4,000 and 8,000. The government blamed the confused situation and argued that only 300 civilians were killed, accusing UN staff of falsifying the casualty figures.[200] UNAMIR actually assisted the cover up by embargoing a report which showed that the RPF removed and destroyed bodies. The report was leaked anyway, but UNAMIR headquarters refused to confirm its existence and contents.[201] An Independent Commission of Inquiry, hastily convened by the Rwandan government, investigated the massacre and broadly supported the RPF's explanation, revising downwards the UN's casualty estimates to 2,000 and apportioning responsibility evenly among the RPF, UNAMIR, NGOs, and armed elements inside the camp.[202] This obviously flawed report was widely endorsed. In a 'Lessons Learned' report, the UN's Department for Peacekeeping Operations (DPKO) attributed the loss of life to poor coordination among the peacekeepers and a stampede—the RPF's use of force against civilians received barely a mention:

> One instance when the coordination mechanism of the integrated operations center failed was in the Kibeho camp for internally displaced people in late April 1995. The government's decision to close the camp, by force if necessary, resulted in a stampede in which many people lost their lives. Some of those interviewed stated that if the government, UNAMIR, and the humanitarian community had coordinated well with each other by providing transportation and allowing sufficient time to those who were willing to return to their home communes, some lives could have been saved.[203]

Even the UN's Human Rights mission in Rwanda deflected responsibility for the Kibeho massacre away from the RPF. Its deputy chief, Mark Frohardt, commented that the massacre was caused by the inability of relief

[198] Filip Reyntjens, 'Rwanda, Ten Years On: From Genocide to Dictatorship', *African Affairs*, 103, 2004, p. 194. This estimate is also accepted by Garard Prunier. Also see Philip Verwimp, 'Testing the Double-Genocide Thesis for Central and Southern Rwanda', *Journal of Conflict Resolution*, 47 (4) 2003, pp. 423–43.

[199] James Orbinski, *An Imperfect Offering: Dispatches from the Medical Frontline* (Melbourne: Text Publishing, 2008), p. 261.

[200] See Arthur J. Klinghoffer, *The International Dimensions of Genocide in Rwanda* (New York: New York University Press, 1998), p. 64.

[201] Orbinski, *An Imperfect Offering*, p. 262.

[202] See Terry, *Condemned to Repeat*, pp. 209–10.

[203] *Comprehensive Report on Lessons Learned from United Nations Assistance Mission for Rwanda (UNAMIR), October 1993–April 1996*, p. 35.

organizations to close displaced persons camps in a timely fashion.[204] Médecins sans Frontières was almost alone in trying to publicize the massacre and demand that the perpetrators be brought to justice. The Rwandan government responded by expelling the organization's entire French section.[205] Having enjoyed impunity at Kibeho, the sporadic killing of senior Hutu figures and massacres of groups of unarmed people continued between 1995 and 1997.[206]

The presence of up to two million refugees in eastern DRC in the immediate wake of the Rwandan genocide prompted a massive humanitarian operation, with UN agencies led by the UNHCR and Western NGOs supplying the camps with food, shelter, and medical aid. This inflow of aid posed a major problem for the RPF because it risked giving the ex-FAR (the FAR had fled Rwanda virtually intact) and genocidaire militia the space and resources they needed to regroup.[207] With the support of Zaire's President Mobutu, most of the refugees settled in camps in eastern Zaire, close to the Rwandan border. Many camps came under the control of the former Rwandan government, army, and militia, which used them as bases from which to attack Rwanda.[208] Hutu militia in the camps also attacked local Tutsis (*Banyamulenge*) with the aim of driving them from their homes and establishing a 'Hutuland' from which to launch attacks into Rwanda.[209] The *Banyamulenge* resisted and many joined the RPF, appealing to the new Rwandan government for assistance. Given this, it was clear that the ex-FAR and militia presence in eastern Zaire therefore posed a clear threat to post-genocide Rwanda, and the RPF-led government pressed for their immediate repatriation—whilst planning a military solution.[210]

In August 1996, the RPF's leader, Paul Kagame, privately informed the US State Department that Rwanda would forcibly remove the refugees from the border region if the UN failed to do so. He later claimed that the USA agreed to acquiesce.[211] In early 1996, Kagame and Ugandan president Yoweri Musaveni approached Joseph Kabila to be the acceptable Congolese face of an

[204] Cited in Philip Gourevitch, *We Wish to Inform You that Tomorrow we will be killed with our families: Stories from Rwanda* (London: Picador, 2000), p. 205.

[205] Orbinski, *An Imperfect Offering*, p. 262.

[206] Filip Reyntjens, 'Post 1994 Politics: Problematising "Liberation" and "Democratisation"', *Third World Quarterly*, 27 (6) 2006, p. 1105.

[207] Terry, *Condemned to Repeat?*, p. 156.

[208] Kisangani N. F. Emizet, 'The Massacre of Refugees in Congo: A Case of UN Peacekeeping Failure and International Law', *Journal of Modern African Studies*, 38 (2) 2000, p. 165; Gerard Prunier, *Africa's World War: Congo, the Rwandan Genocide, and the Making of a Continental Catastrophe* (Oxford: Oxford University Press, 2009), pp. 25–9; and Thomas Turner, *The Congo Wars: Conflict, Myth and Reality* (London: Zed Books, 2007), pp. 124–5.

[209] Emizet, 'Massacre of Refugees in Congo', p. 168.

[210] On the security situation, see Severine Autusserre, *The Trouble with the Congo: Local Violence and the Failure of International Peacebuilding* (Cambridge: Cambridge University Press, 2010), p. 60.

[211] Emizet, 'Massacre of Refugees in Congo', p. 172.

alliance to close the camps and remove Zaire's President Mobutu.[212] In September 1996, the RPF and *Banyamulenge* militia began attacking refugee camps near Uvira, forcing 100,000 refugees to flee. Rwanda denied any involvement, but France called for the deployment of a multinational force to protect the refugee camps, and disarm and repatriate the militia. By November, the ADFL–RPF alliance had taken control of Bakuvu and Goma in eastern Zaire and threatened camps around Goma, which now housed some 800,000 refugees, ex-FAR, and militia.

Although the USA remained unenthusiastic about international intervention, momentum gathered behind the French proposal for a multinational force and Canada agreed to provide the military leadership. Although badged as a mission to save the refugees, the main intention of those behind the plan—especially France and Francophone African governments—was to save Mobutu from what looked like impending defeat.[213] Rwanda opposed intervention whilst the USA—motivated by a desire to support Kagame and remove Mobutu—dragged its feet, accepting the idea in principle and committing 1,000 troops on paper—but doing little to further its advancement.[214] On 15 November, the Security Council authorized the deployment of a multinational force to protect the refugees and secure the delivery of humanitarian aid (Resolution 1080). By then, however, the situation on the ground had changed dramatically.

On 8 November, ADFL–RPF forces attacked the Mugunga camps near Goma—a move that prompted UN Secretary-General Boutros-Ghali to throw his support behind the proposed intervention but which ultimately provided the grounds for not intervening. Whilst the West debated what to do, ADFL–RPF forces shelled and stormed the camps, leaving a gap in their offensive line to allow refugees to flood back into Rwanda. Over the next few days between 600,000–700,000 refugees returned to Rwanda. This allowed the Rwandan government and its new allies in the West to argue that the refugee problem had been solved because the majority of genuine refugees had been repatriated. The RPF argued that the mass repatriation obviated the need for a multinational force and claimed that reports of hundreds of thousands of refugees fleeing deeper into Zaire were inaccurate.[215] This position was supported by the USA, its ambassador to Kigali, Robert Gribben rejecting the UN's claims that several hundred thousands of refugees remained in Zaire and writing that 'most of the refugees still in Zaire are either Zairian or Burundians and the number of Rwandese refugees are nothing like those put forward by aid agencies.... They are in the twenties of thousands rather than these vast

[212] Prunier, *Africa's World War*, pp. 115–16.
[213] Prunier, *Africa's World War*, p. 119.
[214] Prunier, *Africa's World War*, p. 120.
[215] Cited by Prunier, *Africa's World War*, p. 123.

numbers'.[216] A US press conference on 23 November provided aerial photos which, when combined with other evidence, the USA claimed, demonstrated that most of the displaced people remaining in Zaire were ex-FAR and *interahamwe* fighters and their families.[217] Aid agencies, such as Médecins sans Frontières that continued to argue that there were hundreds of thousands of refugees facing great peril inside Zaire were denounced for 'crying wolf', being 'hysterical', and for being duped by the *genocidaires.*[218]

With US support, the view that the mass return of refugees obviated the need for a multinational force was welcomed by other members of the UN Security Council, which annulled its earlier decision to intervene.[219] In reality, however, some 500,000–600,000 refugees had fled away from Rwanda and were in grave peril. Included in that number were between 50,000–65,000 ex-FAR and Hutu militia members.[220] Between October 1996 and September 1997, the ADFL–RPF hunted down the remaining refugees as they fled westwards and southwards. A mapping exercise conducted for the UN High Commissioner on Human Rights and published in 2010 shows that during this period, the RPF and its Congolese allies committed at least two hundred massacres of unarmed civilians.[221] In what came to be known as 'bait and kill' operations, RPF–ADFL forces encouraged NGOs to set up feeding stations and medical facilities to lure the refugees out of the forest and then denied access to the agencies for a few days. Access was only restored after the refugees had disappeared and a large number massacred.[222] RPF–ADFL forces chased the survivors over one thousand kilometres. One of the final massacres was perpetrated in Mbandaka, in the far west of Zaire. Up to 1,000 refugees were singled out and gunned down as they tried to flee across the river into Congo-Brazzaville.

Because the precise number of refugees involved, the number of *genocidaires* hiding amongst them, and the final whereabouts of the survivors are not known, it is impossible to know exactly how many civilians were massacred.

[216] Cited by Prunier, *Africa's World War*, p. 123.

[217] Orbinski, *An Imperfect Offering*, p. 269.

[218] Orbinski, *An Imperfect Offering*, pp. 270–1. Howard Adelman uses the term 'hysterical' to describe the humanitarian response. This is particularly lamentable because at the time Adelman was writing (2001–02), plenty of evidence of RPF–ADFL massacres was available. Howard Adelman, 'Use and Abuse of Refugees in Zaire', in Stephen John Stedman and Fred Tanner (eds), *Refugee Manipulation: War, Politics and the Abuse of Human Suffering* (Washington, DC: Brookings Institution Press, 2003), p. 120.

[219] Emizet, 'Massacre of Refugees in Congo', p. 169 and Prunier, *Africa's World War*, p. 123.

[220] Emizet, 'Massacre of Refugees in Congo, p. 165.

[221] Office of the United Nations High Commissioner for Human Rights, *Report of the Mapping Exercise Documenting the Most Serious Violations of Human Rights and International Humanitarian Law Committed Within the Territory of the Democratic Republic of Congo between March 1993 and June 2003*, August 2010, pp. 78–150.

[222] Human Rights Watch, *Casualties of War: Civilians, Rule of Law, and Democratic Freedoms*, report no. 11, February 1999.

The UN Human Rights Commission's mapping exercise found that it was unable to confidently estimate the number of victims in around half of all the reported massacres and also observed that the number of massacres reported was probably much smaller than the number of actual massacres. The task of documenting the crimes was made more difficult by the fact that the perpetrators sometimes went to great lengths to hide and destroy evidence. The Special Rapporteur to the UN Human Rights Commission, Human Rights Watch, and Médecins sans Frontières all reported efforts to destroy evidence by burning corpses, intimidating witnesses, and 'cleansing' massacre sites. The RPF even established disposal areas to which corpses were transported for incineration.[223] These efforts were intensified when the UN began investigating alleged massacres. One study used estimated ranges for the number of refugees and controlled for expected mortality rates, concluding that approximately 233,000 refugees were massacred by the RPF and its allies.[224] This figure is endorsed by the respected historian Gerard Prunier and appears broadly consistent with what the UN was able to document.[225]

When Rwanda began its assault on the refugee camps in eastern Zaire, the RPF denied that Rwandan forces were operating inside Zaire and argued that the violence was entirely local. Rwandan radio reported that 'the foreign media continue to implicate Rwanda in the eastern Zaire crisis.... But we must stress that the current conflict ... involves Zairians fighting against Zairians'.[226] This line of argument lacked credibility given overwhelming evidence that the RPF was operating inside Zaire. Once the prospect of a multinational force receded, Kagame changed his justificatory arguments and admitted that the Rwandan government had led a military campaign against the refugee camps to prevent them from being used by the *genocidaires* for attacks on Rwanda and that the removal of Mobutu was a secondary objective.[227] At this point, the RPF argued that it was acting in self-defence against *genocidaires* operating from the refugee camps.[228] Mobutu's regime was a legitimate target, the RPF maintained, because it had supported armed incursions into Rwanda.

The RPF always denied that its forces massacred civilians in either Rwanda or the DRC—claiming that the victims at Kibeho and in the DRC were armed former *genocidaires* and not civilians.[229] Where civilian deaths were

[223] Prunier, *Africa's World War*, p. 17.

[224] Emizet, 'Massacre of Refugees in Congo, pp. 163–202.

[225] Prunier, *Africa's World War*.

[226] Cited by Prunier, *Africa's World War*, p. 117.

[227] See J. Pomfret, 'Rwandans Led Revolt in Congo', *Washington Post*, 9 July 1997.

[228] Emizet, 'Massacre of Refugees in Congo', p. 186.

[229] Rene Lemarchand, 'Genocide in the Great Lakes: Which Genocide? Whose Genocide?', *African Studies Review*, 41 (1) 1998, p. 8. These arguments, Lemarchand maintains, betray 'utter disregard for the evidence'. As Prunier put it, 'the RPF never boasted about its violence, even indirectly, and it denied any responsibility unless caught red-handed. And then excuses were made, often quite convincingly'. See Prunier, *Africa's World War*, p. 21.

acknowledged at all, the RPF argued that the victims were collectively responsible for the 1994 genocide and were killed in isolated revenge attacks rather than as part of a systematic campaign. For example, responding to charges of civilian killings made by the UN human rights observation mission in 1997, Rwandan presidential adviser Claude Dusaidi argued that 'if civilians had been killed, they were accomplices, people who sympathised with these armed men [ex-FAR and Hutu militia]'.[230] In December 1997, Prime Minister Rwigema made the same basic argument when he maintained that 'whoever acts in connivance with them [the Hutu rebels] will suffer a fate similar to theirs'. President Kagame reportedly made similar claims in early 1998.[231] Kagame told the very sympathetic journalist Philip Gourevitch that the *genocidaires* were responsible for the deaths of the civilians they fled with, saying 'they are not genuine refugees.... They're simply fugitives, running away from justice after killing people in Rwanda'.[232] All this led Prunier to conclude that 'the RPF vision of the Hutu masses seems to have been that of a permanent danger to be kept at bay by random mass killings to instil fear and to be defanged by neutralizing real or potential leaders'.[233] For the RPF, Hutus and *genocidaires* were considered to be basically synonymous.[234] The RPF's critics—both domestic and international—were labelled revisionists and accused of supporting the *genocidaires*. Kagame argued that his critics preferred to support the Hutu over the Tutsi in order to mask their own guilt for failing to halt the genocide.[235] In reality, the opposite was true—feelings of guilt encouraged international society to turn a blind eye to RPF massacres.

Evidence of massacres was not slow to emerge, but most foreign governments and the UN secretariat did not publicly attribute responsibility to the RPF or criticize Rwanda's new government.[236] As I noted earlier, plans for the deployment of a multinational force were abandoned when the RPF attacked the camps and the UN Security Council eagerly accepted the claim that it had successfully repatriated Hutu refugees, despite an abundance of evidence that several hundreds of thousands remained unaccounted for. The killing of refugees was greeted with international silence—there were few public protests and most governments shied away from condemning the massacres. Indeed, the UN, Western governments, and several aid agencies suppressed

[230] Cited by Reyntjens, 'Rwanda, Ten Years On', p. 195.

[231] Reyntjens, 'Rwanda, Ten Years On', p. 195.

[232] Gourevitch, *We Wish to Inform You*, p. 338.

[233] Prunier, *Africa's World War*, p. 20.

[234] Turner, *Congo Wars*, p. 155. The tendency to collectively label Hutu as *genocidaires* was also identified by Lemarchand, 'Genocide', p. 8.

[235] Gourevitch, *We Wish to Inform You*, p. 339.

[236] The first rumours about the killing of refugees emerged soon after the assault on the camps. The Dutch newspaper *De Standaard* published accounts of massacres on 20 October 1996. See Prunier, *Africa's World War*, p. 124.

information about atrocities and played down the allegations. Where massacres were acknowledged, few actors were willing to openly acknowledge the RPF's responsibility—even sometimes preferring to blame themselves rather than the actual perpetrators, as in the case of the DPKO's lessons learned report on the Kibeho massacre discussed earlier. Even some of the most outspoken aid agencies were reluctant to identify the RPF as the perpetrators of massacres. For example, Refugees International called for international society to 'immediately act in concert to stop Zaire from executing ethnic cleansing', wrongly attributing the principal threat as emanating from Mobutu rather than Kagame.[237] As evidence of massacres in eastern Zaire mounted, it became more difficult for international actors to avoid discussing them. But public figures still assiduously avoided naming the RPF among the perpetrators. The EU's Commissioner for Humanitarian Affairs, Emma Bonino, accused Laurent Kabila of having turned eastern Zaire into a 'veritable slaughterhouse'—without mentioning Kabila's erstwhile Rwandan ally, whose forces were virtually indistinguishable from the ADFL during this campaign.[238]

This pattern was set in the immediate aftermath of the Rwandan genocide when the UN secretariat and international society failed to react to RPF massacres inside Rwanda. The USA even provided military training to the RPF before, during, and after Rwanda's invasion of Zaire.[239] In 1995, as tensions between Zaire and Rwanda mounted, evidence of splits emerged between the US State Department and Defense Department. The State Department preferred a cautious approach and asked defence officials to communicate a warning to Rwanda to not allow its forces to cross the border. The Defense Department refused to convey the message, preferring to tacitly support Kagame's military solution, and the State Department eventually fell into line. As such, when Assistant Secretary of State for African Affairs, Susan Rice, returned from a trip to the region, a member of her staff told the press that 'Museveni and Kagame agree that the basic problem in the Great Lakes is the danger of a resurgence of genocide and they know how to deal with that. The only thing we have to do is look the other way'.[240] That is precisely what the USA and most of the rest of international society did.

The first attempt to systematically document the situation in post-genocide Rwanda was a report by a three person team for the UNHCR, led by consultant Robert Gersony. In August and September 1994, the team conducted around two hundred interviews in ninety-one different locations. Evidence of widespread and systematic massacres perpetrated by the RPF was

[237] Prunier, *Africa's World War*, p. 117.
[238] Cited by Turner, *Congo Wars*, p. 157.
[239] Prunier, *Africa's World War*, p. 126.
[240] Cited by Prunier, *Africa's World War*, p. 339.

overwhelming. Although some incidents could be written off as revenge killings, many were highly organized and involved the use of ruses designed to bring civilians into one place to be killed. Gersony reported to the UNHCR that between 25,000 and 45,000 civilians had been massacred by the RPF between April and August 1994. The UNHCR was shocked by the findings and passed the report on to the UN Secretary-General, Boutros-Ghali. Under pressure from the USA to support the RPF, Boutros-Ghali indicated that the report would be embargoed so as not to destabilize the new Rwandan government. A later Joint Evaluation of Emergency Assistance to Rwanda concluded that the Gersony report was suppressed because, 'had it been officially released at the time it would have reduced the legitimacy of the new government and severely jeopardized efforts by UN agencies and many of the donor organizations to assist the new government to establish an effective administration'.[241] UNHCR officials briefed the Rwandan government on the report's contents but also indicated that it would not be released. The report has remained embargoed since and its findings were discredited by UN officials.[242] A spokesman for the UN Rwanda Emergency Office said that the report provided no physical or forensic evidence to support its claims, stating that 'these are sensitive allegations to make without proof'.[243] Some UNHCR officials even denied that the report existed—the UNHCR wrote to the UN Human Rights Commission's Special Rapporteur, Robert Garreton, advising that the Gersony report 'does not exist'.[244] Afterwards, the UNHCR proved very reluctant to raise the issue of massacres with the Rwandan government. In January 1995, the UNHCR's country director prevented historian Gerard Prunier from visiting the site of a suspected RPF massacre at Kibungo, accusing him of 'wanting to create problems with the government'.[245] Member states were equally reluctant to take heed of Gersony's report. Most notably, the US government judged it counter-productive to publicize the report's findings and tasked Under-Secretary of State Tim Wirth with undermining its credibility. Wirth reassured the RPF, 'hinted at a Hutu conspiracy', and briefed against the report. Lacking good background knowledge on the region, the international media largely accepted this line and either expressed its disbelief at the alleged massacres or explained them away as revenge killings.[246] The UN Secretary-General then passed the report on to the UN

[241] Cited by Terry, *Condemned to Repeat*, p. 208, n. 170.

[242] Alison des Forges, *Leave None to Tell the Story: Genocide in Rwanda* (New York: Human Rights Watch, 1999), pp. 726–31; and Prunier, *Africa's World War*, p. 17.

[243] Terry, *Condemned to Repeat*, p. 174, n. 63.

[244] Terry, *Condemned to Repeat*, p. 174, n. 64.

[245] Prunier, *Africa's World War*, p. 19.

[246] The media response is documented by Prunier, *Africa's World War*, p. 377, n. 124. Some academics writing years after the events when plenty of information to the contrary was available continued to write off the massacres as revenge killings. See, for example, Adelman, 'Use and Abuse', p. 113.

Human Rights Commission which conducted a brief fact-finding mission before concluding that whilst there was some evidence of 'killings by Tutsi elements of Hutu individuals' these limited killings did not constitute genocide and therefore warranted no further investigation.[247]

In March 1997, the UN's High Commission for Human Rights instructed its special rapporteur for the Democratic Republic of Congo (DRC, formerly Zaire), Robert Garreton, to investigate the alleged massacre of refugees. Garreton's team was obstructed every step of the way by the Kabila-led DRC government and the Rwandan government, which among other things demanded that the UN pay $1.7 million per day to cover its costs. Kabila was particularly concerned about the team investigating the alleged massacre of up to 1,000 refugees in Mbandaka on 13 May 1997—four days before his forces seized Zaire's capital Kinshasa. As Howard French commented in the *New York Times* the following year:

> An investigation in Mbandaka was particularly threatening. Killings in the east, near Rwanda, could perhaps be written off as random acts of overzealous or vengeful Tutsi soldiers. But for Hutu refugees to be tracked down and killed at the opposite end of this huge country, when Kabila's victory in the war was already assured, would strongly suggest deliberate extermination.[248]

Obstructions notwithstanding, Garreton documented evidence of forty massacres committed by the ADFL and RPF in North and South Kivu provinces in eastern DRC. The report also provided evidence of the direct involvement of Rwandan soldiers, their intent to destroy the refugees, and the removal of bodies and evidence.[249] Garreton labelled the massacres acts of genocide owing to the obvious intent to find and exterminate Hutu refugees and called for further investigations and criminal prosecutions.[250] He found that the killing of refugees was an intentional and carefully planned exercise, which began with the destruction of the camps in eastern Congo and ended with the final massacres of survivors in the country's west.[251]

In response, Kabila sought—and secured—Garreton's removal.[252] In April 1998, the UN Secretary-General stepped in to terminate the human rights

[247] Prunier, *Africa's World War*, p. 31.

[248] H. W. French, 'Reports Point to Mass Killing of Refugees in Congo', *New York Times*, 27 May 1998, p. A21.

[249] Evidence of direct Rwandan involvement in the massacres was also provided by Human Rights Watch. See S. Campbell, 'What Kabila is Hiding: Civilian Killings and Impunity in Congo', *Human Rights Watch*, 9, 5a, October 1998.

[250] 'Report on the Situation of Human Rights in Zaire, Prepared by the Special Rapporteur, Mr. Roberto Garreton in Accordance with Commission Resolution 1996/77', UN Commission on Human Rights, 1997.

[251] Cited by Emizet, 'Massacre of Refugees in Congo' p. 179. Prunier's research uncovered the same practice. See Prunier, *Africa's World War*, p. 17.

[252] Emizet, 'Massacre of Refugees in Congo', p. 170.

mission on the grounds that the DRC government was refusing to cooperate.[253] The Secretary-General then instigated his own investigation which also found that 'elements' of the RPF were responsible for crimes against humanity and possibly genocide in the DRC, and that up to 200,000 refugees remained 'unaccounted for'.[254] Although the report was circulated to the UN Security Council there was no follow-up.

Rwanda responded vociferously to these, and other, attempts to hold it to account. In 1997, UN High Commissioner for Human Rights, Mary Robinson, condemned serious human rights violations in Rwanda. The government responded by strenuously rejecting Robinson's claims and accusing her of being influenced 'by informants whose aims are to mislead international public opinion on the situation in Rwanda'. The government then refused to admit a field office of the High Commissioner to conduct human rights monitoring and in 2001 successfully lobbied African governments to support Rwanda's removal from the Commission's agenda.[255]

Perhaps the biggest challenge that the RPF faced was from Carla del Ponte, the former chief prosecutor for the International Criminal Tribunal for Rwanda (ICTR), established by the Security Council in 1994 (Resolution 955, 8 November). In 2000, del Ponte informed Kagame that she intended to investigate crimes allegedly committed by the RPF. The Rwandan president responded that Rwanda had already punished those responsible for isolated crimes and launched an ultimately successful campaign to prevent the investigation.[256] The government issued a new law on travel documentation which impeded witnesses from travelling to the tribunal in Arusha (Tanzania). This was followed by a concerted campaign against del Ponte herself. The RPF's liaison with the tribunal lamented that 'we don't think the prosecutor is qualified to venture into this area when she hasn't even brought the prosecutors of genocide to justice' and Kagame himself cast doubt on the credibility of the tribunal:

> They [the international community] simply ran away from responsibility and left people to be killed in the thousands. They have no moral authority whatsoever. We cannot be lectured by them. If they are so concerned about human rights why

[253] Garreton was recalled by Kabila in January 1999, after a rift between him and the RPF-backed *Banyamulenge* escalated into rebellion, giving the DRC leader an interest in delegitimizing the Rwandans. See Emizet, 'Massacre of Refugees in Congo', p. 172.

[254] 'Report of the Investigative Team Charged with Investigating Serious Violations of Human Rights and International Humanitarian Law in the Democratic Republic of Congo', S/1998/581, 29 June 1998.

[255] Reyntjens, 'Rwanda, Ten Years On', p. 203.

[256] But in fact, as Human Rights Watch documented, only one RPF soldier was prosecuted and was convicted for the killing of 30 civilians. He was released on appeal. See Jennifer L. Petersen 'Rwanda's Leveraging of Moral Authority in the International Realm', unpublished paper, 2010, p. 13.

> did they allow hundreds of thousands of people to die here during the genocide, when they knew it was going to happen? Even when it was happening they ran away from it. Afterwards, they did not come forward in a tangible way to help Rwanda. So what moral authority do they have?[257]

The campaign to undermine del Ponte persuaded the UN Secretary-General Kofi Annan to remove the prosecutor from her post on the grounds that the tribunals for the former Yugoslavia and Rwanda should have different prosecutors.

How do we explain international society's failure to condemn the RPF's role in the killing of around 230,000 people? The response needs to be seen in the context of international society's failure to prevent or halt the 1994 genocide. Because of the role it played in ending the genocide, the RPF enjoyed unparalleled international legitimacy—described as a 'genocide credit' by Filip Reyntjens.[258] Having failed to protect Rwandans, very few governments were now prepared to criticize the group that had brought the 1994 genocide to a close. In the USA, for example, the Jewish lobby voiced strong support for the new RPF government and President Clinton's top Africa advisers—Susan Rice, John Prendergast, and Richard Bogossian—shared the president's unease at having failed to halt the genocide and a simplified view of the post-genocide situation that portrayed the RPF as 'good' and the Hutus as more or less collectively responsible for genocide.[259] This helped produce an outpouring of international sympathy for Rwanda's new regime, evidenced to some extent by the tenor of some of the early books on the genocide.[260] General Joulwan, head of NATO, went so far as to describe Kagame as 'a visionary'.[261]

The RPF's strong international legitimacy relative to other relevant actors—borne from its role in ending the genocide, unease about international society's failure in that regard, and a simplistic understanding of the situation—made criticizing it appear illegitimate. This shielded it from international opprobrium.[262] The product was an extraordinary degree of self-censorship on the part of various UN agencies and governments. In a context where major powers had few other strategic concerns, this relative legitimacy allowed the RPF to enjoy 'total impunity'.[263] As a result, when the RPF began shelling

[257] Cited in Petersen 'Rwanda's Leveraging of Moral Authority in the International Realm', p. 12.

[258] Reyntjens, 'Post-1994 Politics in Rwanda', p. 1103; Reyntjens, 'Rwanda, Ten Years On', p. 199; and Prunier, *Africa's World War*, p. 23.

[259] Prunier, *Africa's World War*, p. 34.

[260] See Emizet, 'Massacre of Refugees in Congo', p. 183. Most notable in this regard was Philip Gourevitch's award winning book. See Gourevitch, *We Wish to Inform You*, pp. 188–94.

[261] Quoted by Prunier, *Africa's World War*, p. 119

[262] A point made by Reyntjens, 'Post-1994 Politics', p. 1104.

[263] Reyntjens, 'Post-1994 Politics', p. 1114. On the future consequences of impunity, see Eugenta Zorbas, 'Reconciliation in Post-Genocide Rwanda', *African Journal of Legal Studies*, 1 (1) 2004, p. 41.

the refugee camps in eastern DRC, the UN's decision-making bodies were extremely reluctant to criticize it. As the AFP's correspondent in New York put it, 'there are enormous inhibitions among [Security] Council members due to a feeling of guilt towards Rwanda. Very few delegates are willing to criticize Kigali, at least openly'.[264] This pattern of thought persisted for several years.

The idea that the RPF was the most legitimate relevant actor translated into an equally widely held belief that it held the key to regional stability. Some UN agencies, NGOs, and governments believed that criticizing the Rwandan government would weaken its legitimacy and impair their ability to stabilize the humanitarian situation and assist in restoring order and building an effective administration. In the absence of a credible alternative, many international actors believed that they had little alternative but to support the new Rwandan government.[265]

Other factors also impacted upon the international response. The new Rwandan regime was especially skilled at controlling and manipulating the flow of information and at exploiting its relative legitimacy to leverage uncertainty and avoid condemnation. With a few exceptions—most notably the Kibeho massacre—the RPF and its allies were careful to minimize publicity, usually committing massacres only after areas were closed to outsiders to prevent reporting. As Kagame himself explained to Nick Gowing: 'we used communication and information warfare better than anyone. We have found a new way of doing this.... I learned from the field that the media and NGOs would be a problem. For a specific amount of time these people have to be kept out. We managed to keep them out. They leaked information. They were very damaging.... They are not neutral as many claim to be. To allow a free hand will not bring us the best results'.[266] As I noted earlier, the RPF was also careful to destroy evidence of mass killing—burning bodies and moving mass graves. In addition, journalists, diplomats, and aid agencies that publicized the RPF's mistreatment of civilians were threatened with expulsion and reprisals against local staff and their families. Gerard Prunier was accused of being 'indirectly responsible for the 1994 genocide' because he wrote about the RPF's massacres; Reuters correspondent Christian Jennings was expelled in 1997 probably because he quoted Kagame saying that it was legitimate to divert international aid money to Rwanda's war in Zaire; and Stephen Smith, a journalist for the French newspaper *Liberation*, was expelled for criticizing the regime.[267] The intimidation of aid agencies was more pronounced. The offices of both Médecins sans Frontières and American Refugee International

264 Cited by Prunier, *Africa's World War*, p. 117.
265 Terry, *Condemned to Repeat*, p. 208.
266 Cited by Orbinski, *An Imperfect Offering*, p. 299.
267 Reyntjens, 'Rwanda, Ten Years On', p. 202.

were raided and robbed, with tear gas used against the former.[268] In January 1997, the Médecins sans Frontières compound in Kigali was attacked with grenades and three Spanish aid workers working for Médicos del Mondo killed. Their Rwandan security guard was arrested by the RPF and beaten to death.[269] The RPF sometimes cultivated good relations with friendly NGOs (those willing to overlook the regime's misdeeds) and bugged the communications of other NGOs.[270] This helped create what two researchers for Médecins sans Frontières called a 'law of silence' among NGOs: 'closed eyes and mouths are a condition for the perpetuation of these crimes. Apart from the political and juridical impunity automatically offered by states, the authorities thus benefit from the moral and media impunity resulting from the resignation of the witnesses'.[271]

The RPF also exploited its victim status to legitimize its own wrongdoings and undermine its accusers.[272] It denounced a 2001 report by Amnesty International as 'an unsupportable insult to the memory of more than a million victims of the 1994 genocide'.[273] Other Amnesty reports were denounced as 'misinformation' and the International Crisis Group was accused of waging an 'anti-Rwanda misinformation campaign'.[274] When an international panel of eminent persons criticized the RPF for committing atrocities in a report to the OAU, the Rwandan government accused the panel of partiality and of being 'cheated' by 'revisionists'.[275] This strategy was largely successful in a post-genocide context characterized by an influx of journalists, aid workers, academics, and diplomats unfamiliar with the region and ready to accept a simplistic portrayal.[276]

As in the Chechnya case, the relative legitimacy of the relevant actors played a significant role in shielding the perpetrators of mass atrocities from condemnation and punishment. Not only did international society fail to condemn the RPF, some international bodies and governments actively suppressed evidence of mass killing to protect the perpetrators. The principle reason for this was that in the immediate aftermath of the 1994 Rwandan

[268] Orbinski, *An Imperfect Offering*, p. 285.

[269] Orbinski, *An Imperfect Offering*, pp. 290–1.

[270] Reyntjens, 'Rwanda, Ten Years On', p. 199.

[271] Cited in Reyntjens, 'Rwanda, Ten Years On', p. 198.

[272] See Mahmood Mamdani, *When Victims Become Killers: Colonialism, Nativism and Genocide in Rwanda* (Princeton, NJ: Princeton University Press, 2002), pp. 234–63; and M. van Leeuwen, 'Rwanda's *Imidugudu* Programme and Earlier Experiences with Villagisation and Resettlement in East Africa', *Journal of Modern African Studies*, 39, 2001, pp. 623–44.

[273] The report was, Amnesty International, *Democratic Republic of Congo: Rwandese-Controlled East: Devastating Human Toll*, London, 19 June 2001. For the response, see Reyntjens, 'Rwanda, Ten Years On', p. 200.

[274] Reyntjens, 'Rwanda, Ten Years On', p. 200.

[275] Reyntjens, 'Rwanda, Ten Years On', p. 200.

[276] See Johan Pottier, *Re-Imagining Rwanda: Conflict, Survival and Disinformation in the late Twentieth Century* (Cambridge: Cambridge University Press, 2002).

genocide, few governments or international organizations were prepared to condemn the group responsible for ending the genocide. This pervasive belief in the relative legitimacy of the RPF, combined with the group's skilful manipulation of information and use of argumentation, a tendency to view the situation in simplified terms, and belief that the RPF was pivotal to regional stability, helped the new Rwandan government avoid condemnation for its direct role in the massacre of around 230,000 people.

## CONCLUSION

In addition to the demise of the communist doctrine of selective extermination, charted in Chapter 8, the ending of the Cold War was associated with two important changes to the global social context in which mass atrocities were debated by international society—both of which were evident prior to the fall of the Berlin Wall. Between them these changes made it more difficult—though not impossible—for actors to secure sufficient legitimacy to enable the commission of mass atrocities. First, improved global communications made it more difficult to conceal mass atrocities, making it harder for perpetrators to create and leverage uncertainty to secure sufficient legitimacy. Improved reporting increased the capacity of external actors to judge for themselves the validity of the perpetrators' arguments by reference to reported facts. This, in turn, made it more difficult to conceal massacres and easier for external actors to identify implausible arguments. Second, the relaxing and eventual displacing of Cold War tensions and the strategic interests they generated elevated the standing of civilian immunity relative to other interests. In most post-Cold War cases, there were few countervailing interests sufficiently strong to mitigate the condemnation of violations of civilian immunity. The commission of mass atrocities was therefore much more likely to receive generalized condemnation than previously. As a result, international debates tended to concentrate more on *how* to protect the victims and (less often) punish the perpetrators than on *whether* to do so. There were very few instances of mass killing in the post-Cold War era that elicited no condemnation or international action of some type.[277]

But it would be premature to herald the victory of civilian immunity. The post-Cold War context made it difficult—but not impossible—to secure sufficient legitimacy for mass atrocities. In two important cases—Russia's wars in Chechnya and post-genocide massacres in Rwanda and Zaire—international society failed to condemn, let alone punish, the perpetrators of mass

[277] Binder, 'Humanitarian Crises and the International Politics of Selectivity'.

atrocities. In the case of Chechnya, international society privileged the protection of democratic reform in Russia from nationalist and communist recidivism, the preservation of Russia's territorial stability, and maintenance of friendly international relations with a powerful state over concerns about violations of civilian immunity. Thus, whilst Bosnian Serbs were sanctioned, bombed, and subjected to international trials for the bombardment of Sarajevo, Russians avoided criticism or punishment for the heavier bombardment of Grozny, which resulted in a higher number of civilian casualties. In the Rwandan case, the relative legitimacy acquired by the RPF as a consequence of its role in ending the 1994 genocide, its skilful use of information and argumentation to create and leverage uncertainty and cast doubt on the credibility of its critics, and the pervasive view that regional stability depended on the RPF, pushed international society to not only fail to condemn or punish the perpetrators of mass atrocities, but to collude in the suppression of information about the atrocities.

The triumph of civilian immunity in the post-Cold War period was therefore less complete than is sometimes suggested. Whilst it was certainly more difficult to secure sufficient legitimacy for mass atrocities after the Cold War than at any other point charted in this book, it was by no means impossible. What is more, at the beginning of the twenty-first century even this progress was challenged by the rise to prominence of a doctrine of selective extermination in the form of radical Islamism and the articulation of new necessity based arguments to justify actions that skirted the edges of civilian immunity as part of the so-called War on Terror. These new challenges are examined in the following chapter.

# 8

# Radical Islamism and the War on Terror

The end of European imperialism brought an end to the colonial doctrine of selective extermination. The defeat of Germany and Japan in the Second World War closed the book on fascist selective extermination. The deaths of Stalin and Mao enabled the Soviet Union and China to abandon communist selective extermination. In the immediate post-Cold War period one might have been forgiven for thinking that civilian immunity had finally triumphed over the major ideologies of selective extermination. Whilst new episodes of mass killing continued to erupt, there was little question of perpetrators avoiding international opprobrium by employing anti-civilian ideologies (necessity or selective extermination) as so many had done before. But it would have been premature to think that no more ideologies of selective extermination would emerge to challenge the embedded norm of civilian immunity. Indeed, one such doctrine, rooted in radical Islamism, was emerging in the Middle East and North Africa throughout the 1990s and was thrust to the fore of world politics on 11 September 2001.

This chapter examines the radical Islamist ideology of selective extermination espoused by Al Qaeda.[1] At its most basic, the doctrine holds that civilian immunity does not apply to non-believers or apostates and that members of these groups may be legitimately killed either as collective punishment for perceived wrongs inflicted on the Muslim world or as a necessary part of a war to establish a world Islamic state (caliphate). Like all such ideologies, the radical Islamist variant appeals only to members of a specific group (mainly Sunni Muslims) and can therefore only hope to secure a limited degree of global legitimacy. Rejected by most of the world's non-Muslims, the ideology is also hotly disputed within the Muslim world itself. It is this relative lack of legitimacy and material capacity, rather than any limitations on violence contained within the ideology itself that explains why radical Islamism has

[1] Although this chapter focuses only on Al Qaeda, it is important to recognize that Al Qaeda is by no means the only the radical Islamist group to espouse selective extermination. See John L. Esposito, *Unholy War: Terror in the Name of Islam* (Oxford: Oxford University Press, 2002), p. 91.

thus far killed so many fewer people than colonialism, fascism, and communism.

The second part of the chapter briefly examines aspects of the US-led response to radical Islamism. Although the USA and its allies have, in the main, attempted to comply with the norm of civilian immunity, the Bush Administration was repeatedly confronted by the tension between compliance and necessity evident during the Cold War.[2] Partly as a result, some aspects of the War on Terror were conducted in ways that appeared to privilege necessity over civilian immunity. This section briefly examines some of the arguments advanced by the Administration in relation to the treatment of prisoners before considering the 2004 assaults on Fallujah in Iraq, which appeared to privilege necessity over civilian immunity. In Fallujah, the USA expressed an intention to comply with civilian immunity but the available evidence suggests that it fell short in practice, establishing a case for thinking that civilians might have been subjected to indiscriminate violence. The combination of practice with the return of necessity based arguments is important because were they to be legitimized this would constitute a direct challenge to civilian immunity by resurrecting necessity as a potentially plausible justification for killing civilians.

In their own way, therefore, both Al Qaeda terrorism and aspects of the US-led 'War on Terror' challenged the norm of civilian immunity: the former represents a new incarnation of selective extermination, the latter nods towards the resurrection of necessity. Ironically, the two challenges support one another because the legitimation of one form of behaviour that is inconsistent with civilian immunity makes it easier to commit and validate the other by weakening the norm that inhibits both. Together, radical Islamism and the War on Terror threatened to reverse the progress charted in the previous chapters. Fortunately, civilian immunity has thus far proven resilient to these challenges: Al Qaeda was widely condemned as were civilian casualties at the hands of the USA and its allies. In a clear contrast to the Cold War, therefore, countervailing strategic concerns have generally failed to trump concerns about civilian immunity in the War on Terror.

## RADICAL ISLAMISM AND AL QAEDA

Radical Islamists identify themselves as the 'vanguard' of Islam, blessed by God to destroy deviation, corruption, and unbelief. They believe that Islamic

[2] Described as the 'restraint-annihilation paradox' by Colin H. Krahl, 'In the Crossfire or the Crosshairs? Norms, Civilian Casualties, and US Conduct in Iraq', *International Security*, 32 (1) 2007, pp. 7–46.

law is not just a matter of religious faith but a comprehensive system of living that must be realized through the establishment of an Islamic state on earth. The ultimate purpose of Islamic radicalism and the violent struggle in its name is not therefore destruction for destruction's sake. It is rather the establishment and imposition of an Islamic state to govern all of humanity under the rule of Shari'a.[3]

The roots of the ideology of selective extermination that accompanies some variants of radical Islamism lay in the work of theorists such as Mawlana Mawdudi, Hasan al-Banna, and Sayyid Qutb, and violent struggles against secular governments in Egypt and Afghanistan in the 1970s and 1980s. According to John Esposito, 'it is almost impossible to exaggerate the direct and indirect influence of these three men'.[4] They sowed the seeds of radical Islamism by blaming Muslim decline—epitomized by the birth of the state of Israel, successive Arab military defeats, and the emergence of secular government in Egypt—on Western imperialism and Muslim deviation from Islamic law. As a remedy, they pointed to Islamic law. Mawdudi and al-Banna influenced Qutb, and Qutb's ideas informed those of Al-Qaeda ideologue, Ayman al-Zawahiri and Osama Bin Laden. This is a largely Sunni line of thinking, though there are prominent Shi'ite adherents as well.[5]

As set out by Al Qaeda's leadership, the main elements of the radical Islamist ideology of selective extermination are very similar to earlier secular doctrines. They are: (1) a Manichean/Darwinian concept of the world characterized by perpetual struggle between forces of good and evil; (2) a deep seated belief in the singular rightness of their ideology and beliefs; (3) a method of categorizing social groups, identifying those unworthy of life because they (a) tarnish or infect the 'in-group' and/or (b) challenge its purposes; (4) a belief that ultimate good can only be achieved through the subjugation or destruction of these degenerate groups.[6]

Writing mainly between the late 1930s and early 1970s, Mawdudi was principally animated by the decline of Muslim rule in South Asia and the rise of secular Hindu nationalism—both of which he attributed to European colonialism.[7] He rejected as a diversion from Islamic orthodoxy the emerging

[3] John Kelsay, *Arguing the Just War in Islam* (Cambridge, MA: Harvard University Press, 2007), p. 159.

[4] Esposito, *Unholy War*, p. 50. This chain of influence is also noted by Kelsay, *Arguing the Just War in Islam*, p. 96.

[5] Richard Bonney, *Jihad: From Qur'an to bin Laden* (London: Palgrave, 2004), p. 369.

[6] According to David Zeidan, Islamism exhibits (1) a view of life as a perennial battle between Islam and its principal enemies—Jews, Christians, and secularists; (2) an absolutist vision of morality and revulsion at relativism or pluralism; (3) thriving commitment to conspiracy theories. See David Zeidan, 'The Islamic Fundamentalist View of Life as a Perennial Battle', *Middle East Review of International Affairs*, 5, 2001, pp. 47–8.

[7] Bonney, *Jihad*, pp. 201–2; and Esposito, *Unholy War*, p. 51. The very idea of nationalism, he believed, was an alien import.

idea that violent *jihad* was incompatible with Islam as a religion of peace, arguing instead that *jihad* was a call to (violent) world revolution. As such, Mawdudi was one of the first contemporary writers to call for a global *jihad* to establish something akin to a world Islamic state.[8] As he explained in 1939:

> ... the objective of the Islamic *Jihad* is to eliminate the rule of an un-Islamic system, and establish in its place an Islamic system of state rule. Islam does not intend to confine this rule to a single state or to a handful of countries. The aim of Islam is to bring about a universal revolution. Although in the initial stages, it is incumbent upon the members of the Party of Islam to carry out a revolution in the state system in the countries to which they belong, their ultimate objective is none other than a world revolution.[9]

Although Mawdudi accepted that the Qur'an forbade the use of force to convert people to Islam, he argued that violence was essential to liberate humanity from injustice and oppression. Once liberated, individuals would be free to choose Islam and to live according to Islamic law. In effect, this was an injunction for Muslims to wage violent struggles to topple governments everywhere, a point stated bluntly and frequently by Mawdudi himself:

> ... in order to eradicate evil and prevent wrong, Islam has prescribed that by systematic endeavour, *jihad*—and if the necessity should befall, by war and bloodshed—all such [non-orthodox Muslim] governments should be wiped out. In their place a just and equitable system of government should be erected which is founded upon the fear of God and based upon the canons He ordained.[10]
>
> Islam is not merely a religious creed or a name for a collection of a few acts of worship. It is a comprehensive system which seeks to annihilate all evil and tyrannical systems in the world, and enforce its own programme of reform, which it deems best for the well-being of mankind.[11]

Thus, Mawdudi argued that *jihad* enjoined Muslims to demolish—violently if necessary—un-Islamic forms of government.[12]

As a God-given system, Mawdudi believed that Islam provided a perfect form of law. Muslims could not live under a non-Islamic government and those that did committed acts of 'continuous sin'. Believers, he maintained, could not live under two systems simultaneously and true belief was demonstrated by the struggle to destroy false systems of rule regardless of the prospects for success. Non-Muslims, he argued, must be forced to live in the Islamic state and be prevented from imposing their 'spurious laws' on

[8] A. G. Noorani, *Islam & Jihad: Prejudice Versus Reality* (London: Zed, 2002), p. 71.

[9] Sayyid Abul A'la Mawdudi, *Jihad fi Sabillah: Jihad in Islam*, trans. Khurshid Ahmad and ed. Huda Khattab (Birmingham: UK Islamic Mission Dawah Centre, 1995), p. 12.

[10] Cited in Bonney, *Jihad*, p. 203.

[11] Cited in Bonney, *Jihad*, p. 204.

[12] Though he argued on prudential grounds that armed insurrection should not be employed to topple governments. See Bonney, *Jihad*, pp. 210–11.

Muslims and fermenting 'evil and strife'.[13] The Islamic state (caliphate) would be authoritarian in form, enjoying sweeping coercive powers to enforce Islamic law and an exclusive right to interpret that law. It would be 'all-embracing', knowing no distinction between public and private affairs and moulding all areas of human activity to its purpose.[14]

Mawdudi pioneered the idea of a violent *jihad* to destroy non-Islamic governments and impose an Islamic state. Although he did not specifically endorse the killing of civilians, at least two aspects of his thinking pointed decisively in that direction: he excused past cases of mass killing and enslavement perpetrated by Muslim armies and denounced 'Western' laws of war, proclaiming the superiority of Islamic laws that privileged the moral purposes of war over its ethical conduct.[15]

Hasan al-Banna, founder of the Muslim Brotherhood in Egypt, shared many of these views but preferred a more incremental approach.[16] Like Mawdudi, al-Banna maintained that *jihad* was firmly connected with war-fighting. God ordained *jihad*, he maintained, not as a tool of oppression or to satisfy selfish ends but rather 'as a defence for the mission [of spreading Islam], a guarantee of peace, and a means of implementing the supreme message'.[17] He also believed that Islam provided a comprehensive system of government and that all Muslims had a duty to struggle for the Islamic state. However, uniquely among these radical thinkers, al-Banna found a concept of mercy within *jihad* which granted immunity to 'the peaceful who offer no resistance', especially women, children, old men, the wounded, monks, and hermits. The Egyptian government banned the Muslim Brotherhood in 1948 and placed al-Banna under house arrest. Shortly afterwards, the Egyptian prime minister, Mahmud Pasha, was assassinated and despite repudiating the killing, al-Banna was himself killed by government agents in February 1949.[18]

Mawdudi was described as 'the great Muslim scholar' by Sayyid Qutb, an Egyptian radical whose writings directly influenced Al Qaeda's chief ideologue, Ayman al-Zawahiri.[19] The assassination of Hasan al-Banna and the

[13] See Ishtiaq Ahmed, *The Concept of an Islamic State: An Analysis of the Ideological Controversy in Pakistan* (London: Pinter, 1987), p. 104.

[14] Not surprisingly, Mawdudi acknowledged that there were important similarities between the Islamic state he envisaged and the fascist and communist dictatorships of his time. Bonney, *Jihad*, pp. 206–7.

[15] Ahmed, *Concept of an Islamic State*, p. 105.

[16] At the time of his assassination, the Brotherhood boasted 2,000 branches and 600,000 members. Noorani, *Islam and Jihad*, pp. 69–70.

[17] C. Wendell (ed.), *Five Tracts of Hasan al-Banna, 1906–1949* (Santa Barbara, CA: University of California Press, 1978), p. 151.

[18] Bonney, *Jihad*, p. 215.

[19] Sayyid Qutb, *In the Shade of the Qur'an*, trans. and ed. Adil Salahi (Leicester: Islamic Foundation, 2004), VII, p. 25. See Karen Armstrong, *The Battle for God* (New York: Alfred A. Knopf, 2000).

'happy and joyous reception' that it received in the USA was a second important influence on Qutb. The third was his revulsion at American society, which he expressed very clearly:

> Look at this capitalism with its monopolies, its usury . . . at this individual freedom, devoid of human sympathy and responsibility for relatives except under force of law; at this materialistic attitude which deadens the spirit; at this behaviour, like animals, which you call 'free mixing of the sexes'; at this vulgarity which you call 'emancipation of women'; at this evil and fanatic racial discrimination.[20]

Qutb joined the Muslim Brotherhood and in 1951 began to set out his radical agenda. He maintained that the Islamic mission was to liberate mankind from unjust rule and impose a true peace. For Qutb, this meant the violent exporting of Islamism to the non-Muslim world. Islam, he believed, was a revolutionary ideology which demanded the destruction of all governments that strayed from its law. Islam was a universal religion, he believed, that should govern all humanity.[21] True peace meant that Muslims could not accept 'superficial' peace treaties with non-Muslim countries that imposed un-Islamic laws upon their own people. Thus, no matter where they lived, it was a religious duty for Muslims to oppose un-Islamic governments, dislodge unbelievers from positions of power, and force them to submit to the Islamic system.[22] For Qutb, *jihad* was a perpetual struggle against the forces of unbelief and injustice.[23] There could be no coexistence, he maintained, between the house of Islam (*Dar al-Islam*) and the rest of the world (*Dar al-Harb*). Where Islam did not govern, there could only be perpetual war.[24] Qutb made this point clearly when he argued that:

> Islam is a general declaration of the liberation of man on earth from subjugation to other creatures, including his own desires, through the acknowledgement of God's Lordship over the universe and all creation . . . this declaration signifies a total revolution against assigning sovereignty to human beings, whatever forms, systems and situations such sovereignty may take. There are two essential prerequisites for this great goal. The first is to put an end to all oppression and persecution which targets the followers of this religion who declare their own liberation from human sovereignty and submit themselves to God alone. . . . The second prerequisite is the destruction of every force that is established on the basis of submission to human beings in any shape or form.[25]

[20] Sayyid Qutb, *Milestones* (Stuttgart: Ernst Klett Printers, 1978), p. 261.
[21] Bonney, *Jihad*, p. 218.
[22] Bonney, *Jihad*, p. 218.
[23] Bonney, *Jihad*, p. 217.
[24] A. S. Moussalli, *Moderate and Radical Islamic Fundamentalism: The Quest for Modernity, Legitimacy and the Islamic State* (Gainesville, FL: University of Florida Press, 1999), p. 154.
[25] Qutb, *In the Shade of the Qur'an*, VII, pp. 133–4.

Qutb intimated that Islam was a religion of peace but heavily qualified this claim insisting that this 'must be based on saving all mankind from submission to anyone other than God' and that the ultimate aim must be to 'destroy all forces that stand in its way of liberating mankind from any shackle that prevents the free choice of adopting Islam'.[26] It would continue, 'until the satanic forces are put to an end and the religion is purified for God *in toto*'.[27] 'Aggressive' war against those in the *Dar al-Harb* was justified—indeed, required as a religious duty—because non-believers committed an original aggression against God's law. Those who refused to participate in the *jihad* were the enemies of God who could be excommunicated and killed.[28] Like communist and fascist apologists for mass murder, Qutb argued that 'enemies' were plotting and mobilizing against Islam. He maintained that 'atheists' and the 'religious enemies of Islam' were cooperating to support un-Islamic regimes, such as those in Turkey and his own Egypt, in a bid to complete the task begun in the eleventh century by the crusades.[29]

Like Mawdudi, Qutb did not specifically endorse the killing of civilians. But he did reject the imposition of moral or legal restraints on violent *jihad* and insisted that because the struggle between the *Dar al-Harb* and *Dar al-Islam* was eternal, co-existence was impossible, and *jihad* a religious duty. There could be no restraint other than those imposed by strategy.

To many disaffected Muslims, Mawdudi, al-Banna, and Qutb offered both an appealing explanation of Islamic malaise, which placed the blame squarely on Western imperialists and their apostate collaborators in Muslim lands, and a putative solution in the form of an Islamic state wrought by violent *jihad*. But although each contemplated violent *jihad*, and two of the three left the door open for the mass killing of civilians, they all warned against armed struggle in the near term on prudential grounds. What changed this assessment and gave the next generation of thinkers led by Ayman al-Zawahiri and his patron, Osama Bin Laden, reason to think that armed insurrection and terrorism could topple even the most powerful state was the *mujahadeen* experience in Afghanistan and the establishment of the Taliban regime there four years after the Soviet withdrawal. Victory over the superpower Soviet Union—albeit secured with significant American assistance—affirmed among Islamist radicals a belief that persistent violent struggle could succeed against even the most powerful. The subsequent establishment of an Islamic state by the Taliban seemed to prove the effectiveness of the violent path and gave radicals like Bin Laden both a laboratory in which to test their radical ideas and a base from

[26] Cited by A. S. Moussalli, *Radical Islamic Fundamentalism: The Ideological and Political Discourse of Sayyid Qutb* (Beirut: American University of Beirut, 1992), pp. 205–10.

[27] Cited by Natana DeLong Bas, *Wahhabi Islam: From Revival and Reform to Global Jihad* (New York: Oxford University Press, 2004), p. 264.

[28] Esposito, *Unholy War*, pp. 60–1,

[29] Bonney, *Jihad*, p. 220.

which to launch their global *jihad* inspired by the words of Qutb and his predecessors.[30]

It is difficult to pin down precisely when Al Qaeda was established or which terrorist attacks it was directly responsible for.[31] It is commonly thought that it was responsible for the World Trade Centre bombing in 1993, the bombing of a Philippines Airlines flight in 1994, and the murder of two German nationals in Libya in 1994.[32] As well as the 11 September 2001 (9/11) attacks on New York and Washington, DC, in which around 3,000 civilians were killed, Al Qaeda was also certainly responsible for the 1998 bombing of the US embassies in Nairobi and Dar-es-Salaam, and the 2000 attack on the *USS Cole* in Yemen, and a plan to simultaneously destroy eleven US aircraft over the Pacific and assassinate the Pope.[33] The US-led intervention into Afghanistan in late 2001 effectively destroyed Al Qaeda as a terrorist actor in its own right and since then it has developed into a complex and loosely knit movement or network.[34] Since 9/11, many attacks, most notably the 11 March 2004 Madrid train bombing, the May 2004 attack on Western workers in the Khobar Towers, Saudi Arabia, and the 7 July 2005 bombings in London have been claimed by Al Qaeda affiliates or ad hoc groups inspired by the network. Al Qaeda also contributed to the Taliban insurgency in Afghanistan, conducted or supported a wave of terrorist attacks in Pakistan, and an affiliate launched an insurgency in Iraq, bombing the UN headquarters in 2003 and conducting a bloody campaign against Shi'ites and secular Sunnis there.[35] In all of these various manifestations, the name Al Qaeda has become synonymous with the intentional killing of civilians.[36]

[30] On the significance of Afghanistan, see Esposito, *Unholy War*, pp. 9–18. Bin Laden repeatedly argued that Taliban-ruled Afghanistan was a model Islamic state. See Christopher M. Blanchard, 'Al Qaeda: Statements and Evolving Ideology', Congressional Research Service report, 9 July 2007, p. 4.

[31] Compare Rohan Gunaratna, *Inside al-Qaida* (London: Hurst, 2002) and Jason Burke, *al-Qaeda: Casting a Shadow of Terror* (London: IB Tauris, 2003); David J. Whittaker, *Terrorism: Understanding the Global Threat* (London: Longman, 2002), p. 100; and Marc Sageman, *Leaderless Jihad: Terror Networks in the Twenty-First Century* (Philadelphia: University of Pennsylvania Press, 2008), pp. 29–46.

[32] Yossef Bodansky, *Bin Laden: The Man Who Declared War on America* (New York: Random House, 2001), pp. 225–6. Also see Montasser Al-Zayyat, *The Road to Al-Qaeda: The Story of Bin Laden's Right Hand Man* (London: Pluto Press, 2004), pp. 68–70.

[33] See Burke, *Al-Qaeda*, pp. 7–22.

[34] Thomas Hegghammer, 'Global Jihadism After the Iraq War', *Middle East Journal*, 60 (1) 2006, p. 4.

[35] See Blanchard, 'Al Qaeda', pp. 7–8.

[36] See Louis P. Pojman, 'The Moral Response to Terrorism and Cosmopolitanism', in James P. Sterba (ed.), *Terrorism and International Justice* (New York: Oxford University Press, 2003), p. 138.

In 1998, Bin Laden established 'the World Islamic Front for *Jihad* against Jews and Crusaders'—later modified to 'World Islamic Front'. Among its first actions was the issuing of a religious decree (*fatwa*) insisting that it was a religious duty for Muslims to kill Americans and their allies, including civilians. The 1998 *fatwa* is worth quoting at length because it is a clear and specific injunction to kill civilians:

> The ruling to kill the Americans and their allies—civilians and military—is an individual duty for every Muslim who can do it in any country in which it is possible to do it, in order to liberate the al-Aqsa Mosque and the holy mosque from their grip, and in order for their armies to move out of all the lands of Islam, defeated and unable to threaten any Muslim. This is in accordance with the words of Almighty God: 'and fight the pagans all together as they fight you all together', 'and fight them until there is no more tumult or oppression', and there prevail justice and faith in God...
>
> ...We—with God's help—call on every Muslim who believes in God and wishes to be rewarded to comply with God's order to kill the Americans and plunder their money wherever and whenever they find it...[37]

In much the same way as Mawdudi, al-Banna, and Qutb had done, the 1998 *fatwa* used the principles of defensive *jihad*, based on the putative need to 'liberate' Muslim lands, to justify an aggressive campaign against Westerners and apostates.[38] The *fatwa* also clearly demonstrates Al Qaeda's commitment to the extermination of 'Americans and their allies—military and civilian'. But on what grounds was it issued? When we look at the specific arguments used by Bin Laden and Al Qaeda's chief theorist, Ayman al-Zawahiri, to defend the *fatwa* and the deliberate killing of civilians, the influence of the three radical writers examined above becomes clear. Simply put, Americans, their allies, and apostates in the Muslim world were held responsible for the various ills facing Muslims and their destruction was portrayed as essential for reversing Muslim fortunes and establishing an Islamic state. Because the imposition of Islamic law was considered God's will, the destruction of enemies was divinely sanctioned and this sanction recognized no distinction between soldiers and civilians for all were equally blameworthy.

Beyond that, Al Qaeda appears to have had three principal objectives. First, it sought to remove all governments within the land of Islam (*Dar al-Islam*) that did not govern according to its own fundamentalist interpretation of Shari'a law. According to Bin Laden and al-Zawahiri, Western influence in the Islamic world had corrupted and divided the region's governments, making

[37] The *fatwa* is reproduced in full in Isaac Cronin (ed.), *Confronting Fear: A History of Terrorism* (New York: Thunder's Mouth Press, 2002), pp. 402–5.

[38] On the centrality of perceived American aggression which legitimized defensive *jihad* in Al Qaeda's justification, see James Turner Johnson, *The War to Oust Saddam Hussein: Just War and the New Face of Conflict* (Lanham: Rowman and Littlefield, 2005), pp. 14–16.

Muslims subservient to the West. This was the product of a 'new crusade led by America against the Islamic nations' that would trigger a civilizational conflict between Islam and the West.[39] Al Qaeda aimed to overthrow these corrupt governments, especially in Saudi Arabia, and replace them with an Islamic caliphate.[40]

Second, Al Qaeda wished to end what it saw as the American oppression of Muslims worldwide. This, Bin Laden and al-Zawahiri argued, justified the targeting of Americans and their allies anywhere in the world. According to Bin Laden, 'America and its allies are massacring us in Palestine, Chechnya, Kashmir and Iraq. The Muslims have a right to attack America in reprisal' he continued, 'for over half a century, Muslims in Palestine have been slaughtered and assaulted and robbed of their honour and of their property'.[41] Elsewhere he argued that 'the call to wage war against America was made because America has spearheaded the crusade against the Islamic nation'.[42] Al-Zawahiri wanted to take the battle beyond the *Dar al-Islam*, arguing 'we must move the battle to the enemy's grounds to burn the hands of those who ignite fire in our countries'.[43]

But these demands were merely the first stage of a project whose ultimate goal was the establishment of the Islamic state envisaged by Qutb and his predecessors—dubbed the 'pious caliphate' by Bin Laden.[44] Like the radicals that preceded them, Bin Laden and al-Zawahiri argued that divisions between Muslims and non-Muslims were irreconcilable and that the former could not tolerate societies that were not governed by Islamic law.[45] According to al-Zawahiri in 2005, the Islamic revolution was prefaced on three principles: Islamic law (Shari'a) as the only law under which Muslims may live, the expulsion of all non-Muslims from the *Dar al-Islam*, and the freedom of all Muslims to run their own affairs by promoting virtue and preventing vice.[46] These principles, al-Zawahiri argued, could only be achieved through violent

[39] Blanchard, 'Al Qaeda, p. 3.

[40] Yonah Alexander and Michael S. Swetnam, *Usama Bin Laden's al-Qaida: Profile of a Terrorist Network* (New York: Transnational Publishers, 2001), p. 2; Paul L. Williams, *Al-Qaeda: Brotherhood of Terror* (New York: Alpha Press, 2002), p. 82; and Roland Jacquard, *In the Name of Osama Bin Laden: Global Terrorism and the Bin Laden Brotherhood* (Durham: Duke University Press, 2002), pp. 93–8.

[41] Esposito, *Unholy War*, pp. 22–3.

[42] Amira Sonbol, 'Norms of War in Sunni Islam', in Vesselin Popovski, Gregory M. Reichberg, and Nicholas Turner (eds), *World Religions and Norms of War* (Tokyo: United Nations University Press, 2009), p. 299.

[43] Bonney, *Jihad*, p. 386.

[44] Blanchard, 'Al Qaeda', p. 3.

[45] As Bin Laden told the BBC, 'under no circumstances should we forget this enmity between us and the infidels. For the enmity is based on creed . . . '. 'Bin Laden Rails Against Crusaders and UN', 3 November 2001, reproduced in Robert O. Marlin IV (ed.), *What Does Al-Qaeda Want? Unedited Communiques* (Berkeley, CA: North Atlantic Books, 2004), p. 35.

[46] Cited in Kelsay, *Arguing the Just War in Islam*, p. 160.

struggle, which should start with the expulsion of all non-Muslims from the 'lands of Islam':

> I would also like to stress that the expulsion of the invading Crusaders and Jews from the lands of Islam will not be accomplished merely through demonstrations and hoarse throats in the streets. Reform and expelling of invaders from the lands of Islam will only be accomplished by fighting for the sake of God . . .[47]

As was made abundantly clear by his *fatwa* against the American people, Bin Laden expressly advocated the killing of civilians. He repeatedly argued that the American people as a whole, their supporters and apostates in the Muslim world were responsible for the various woes that afflict Muslims.[48] Americans, he argued, could be held collectively responsible because they elect their government.[49] As Bin Laden explained:

> It is a fundamental principle of any democracy that the people choose their leaders, and as such, approve and are party to the actions of their elected leaders. . . . By electing these leaders, the American people have given their consent to the incarceration of the Palestinian people, the demolition of Palestinian homes and the slaughter of the children of Iraq. This is why American people are not innocent. The American people are active members in all these crimes'.[50]

Bin Laden made a point of describing the USA and its Western allies as 'crusaders', portraying their role in the contemporary Middle East as simply the latest instalment of an aggressive anti-Muslim war which began in the eleventh century.[51] Drawing a distinction between 'commendable' and 'reprehensible' terrorism, he insisted that Al Qaeda's struggle fell into the 'commendable' bracket because 'it is directed at the tyrants, the traitors who commit acts of treason against their own countries and their own faith. . . . Terrorising those and punishing them are necessary measures to straighten things and make them right'.[52] Finally, all of this was supported by the claim that Al Qaeda terrorism enjoyed a divine mandate. Bin Laden reportedly told an ABC reporter that 'Allah is the one who created us and blessed us with this religion, and orders [us] to carry out our holy struggle—jihad—to raise the word of Allah above all the words of unbelievers'.[53]

[47] Cited by Kelsay, *Arguing the Just War in Islam*, p. 160.

[48] Esposito, *Unholy War*, p. 24.

[49] Esposito, *Unholy War*, pp. 23–4.

[50] Cited by Blanchard, 'Al Qaeda', n. 17, pp. 4–5.

[51] Robert A. Pape, *Dying to Win: The Strategic Logic of Suicide Terrorism* (New York: Random House, 2005), pp. 120–2.

[52] Bin Laden cited by Esposito, *Unholy War*, pp. 24–5.

[53] ABC interview cited by Williams, *Al-Qaeda: Brotherhood of Terror*, p. 135.

Similar messages were aired by al-Zawahiri. Extolling the 7/7 bombings in London, al-Zawahiri sent a clear message to the 'crusader coalition' in a statement issued on 4 August 2005:

> As for the English, I say to them: Blair has brought destruction upon you, to the center of London, and he will have more of it, God willing. Oh peoples of the Crusader coalition! We have offered you, at least [the opportunity] to stop your aggression against the Muslims.... The lion of Islam, the struggle, Shaykh Usama bin Ladin, may God protect him, offered you a truce, so that you will leave the lands of Islam. Did Shaykh Usama bin Ladin not tell you that you could not dream of security before we live it as a reality in Palestine and before all infidel armies leave the land of Muhammed? But you have made rivers of blood in our countries, so we blew up volcanoes of rage in your countries. Our message to you is clear and unequivocal: You will not be saved unless you withdraw from our land, stop stealing our oil and our resources, and cease your support of the corrupt [Muslim] rulers.[54]

Ideologies of selective extermination are meant to garner legitimacy for mass killing within a particular community. Bin Laden and al-Zawahiri repeatedly claimed to be speaking on behalf of Islam as a whole, though their message was primarily directed at Sunnis.[55] As such, Al Qaeda's justifications were never likely to win support and legitimacy outside the Muslim world and it is not surprising that non-Muslims were almost uniformly hostile. Equally unsurprising, given the organization's direct attack on the lone remaining superpower, overt endorsement of mass atrocities, lack of powerful allies, and absence of mitigating contextual factors, its illegitimate behaviour has been severely punished. Since 2001, a US-led coalition comprising more than forty states and enjoying the support or acquiescence of most others and the UN Security Council, has conducted a military campaign to destroy Al Qaeda's bases in Afghanistan and Pakistan. No major power opposed or criticized the violent toppling of the Taliban regime from power in Afghanistan in 2001 or the killing of Bin Laden ten years later. These attitudes were reflected outside government where among the major news corporations only the Arabic *al Jazeera* criticized the invasion of Afghanistan.[56]

The UN Security Council's interest in, and condemnation of, Al Qaeda terrorism predated 9/11. Responding to the 1998 US embassy bombings, President Clinton had dedicated his entire address to the plenary session of the UN General Assembly that year to the need for urgent international action against terrorism.[57] The following year, the UN Security Council passed

[54] Cited by Kelsay, *Arguing the Just War in Islam*, p. 157.

[55] Sonbol, 'Norms of War', p. 300.

[56] Walid Phares, *The War of Ideas: Jihadism Against Democracy* (London: Palgrave, 2007), p. 176.

[57] Jeffrey Laurenti, 'The United Nations and Terrorism', in Leonard Weinberg (ed.), *Democratic Responses to Terrorism* (New York: Routledge, 2008), p. 72.

Resolution 1267 (15 October 1999) which condemned the bombings and imposed sanctions on the Taliban regime as punishment for providing safe haven to Al Qaeda's leaders.[58] This was followed up by a more comprehensive approach in Resolution 1269 (19 October 1999), in which the Council unanimously condemned 'all acts, methods and practices of terrorism as criminal and unjustifiable, regardless of their justification' and recognized that terrorism constituted a threat to international peace and security.[59] Among other things, the resolution demanded that states prevent and suppress terrorist acts, deny safe haven to terrorists, and cooperate with one another against terrorism. Given this track record, it was not surprising that the Council reacted swiftly and strongly to the 9/11 atrocity. On the day after the attack, it passed a resolution condemning the perpetrators and recognizing that the victims had a right to use force in self-defence.[60] A little over two weeks later, the Council passed a further resolution (1373 (2001)) requiring all states to adopt specific measures to suppress terrorist financing, ensure that national territory could not be used by terrorists, and cooperate by exchanging information and assisting criminal investigations by other states. This resolution, which was also passed unanimously, placed clear legal obligations on all states and was relatively specific about the counter-terrorism tasks it expected them to undertake.[61] Among its many provisions, the resolution called for the establishment of a Counter Terrorism Committee (CTC) to monitor compliance reports from states.[62] By 30 September 2005, all UN member states had submitted a first report, 169 states had followed up with a second report and 622 reports had been submitted in total.[63] This was an unparalleled level of compliance with Security Council demands for reporting.[64]

These resolutions and the work of the CTC demonstrate the unusual degree of international solidarity generated by Al Qaeda and the determination of a significant portion of international society to destroy the organization. All the aforementioned resolutions were adopted unanimously and encountered little diplomatic resistance. Moreover, this shared hostility towards Al Qaeda has

[58] See Jane Boulden and Thomas Weiss (eds), *Terrorism and the UN: Before and After September 11* (Bloomington: Indiana University Press, 2004).

[59] Jane Boulden, 'Terrorism', in Thomas G. Weiss and Sam Daws (eds), *The Oxford Handbook on the United Nations* (Oxford: Oxford University Press, 2007), p. 430.

[60] Resolution 1368, 12 September 2001.

[61] Jane Boulden, 'The Council and Terrorism', in Vaughn Lowe, Adam Roberts, Jennifer Welsh, and Dominik Zaum (eds), *The United Nations Security Council and War: The Evolution of Thought and Practice since 1945* (Oxford: Oxford University Press, 2008), p. 612. Indeed, some go so far as to suggest that in adopting the resolution, the Security Council took upon itself the role of international legislator. See Paul C. Szasz, 'The Security Council Starts Legislating', *American Journal of International Law*, 96 (4) 2005, pp. 901–5.

[62] Boulden, 'Council and Terrorism', p. 614,

[63] Boulden, 'Council and Terrorism', p. 615.

[64] See Laurenti, 'The United Nations and Terrorism', p. 76.

been maintained over time in the Council despite significant differences over issues such as the definition of terrorism and the 2003 Iraq War.[65]

Given that we expect to find opposition to selective extermination among outsider groups, the critical point here is that Al Qaeda's illegitimacy proved highly consequential. Extensive coverage of Al Qaeda atrocities, the relative illegitimacy of the terrorists compared to their victims, the perception that terrorism constituted a threat to international peace and security and the compulsory and institutional power available to the USA, meant that illegitimacy was translated into a collective international commitment to physically destroy the organization. But to what extent did Al Qaeda succeed in legitimizing its behaviour within its 'in-group'? Ideologies of selective extermination can sustain themselves in the face of outsider opposition through legitimation within an in-group.

It is difficult to precisely measure the degree of legitimacy enjoyed by Al Qaeda in the Muslim world and there is much conflicting evidence. One 2006 study points to a 'recent survey' showing that 'as much as 60 per cent of the population in some Arab countries' declared support for Osama Bin Laden—though without indicating which countries, when the survey was taken, or what questions were asked.[66] In November 2003 more than half of Saudis polled indicated support for Bin Laden's message.[67] It is also reported that in Nigeria, 70 per cent of boys born in the months after 9/11 were named 'Osama'—though this finding is contradicted by other polls showing that over 70 per cent of Nigerians support American counter-terrorism policies.[68] There is also circumstantial evidence for the view that Al Qaeda has secured significant support from parts of the Muslim world. Judging by the persistence of terrorist attacks since 9/11, the radical Islamist message has evidently garnered support among some Muslims, especially in the Middle East, Pakistan, and Afghanistan and among some disaffected Muslims in the West.[69] Support was reported to be particularly strong in Yemen, where it became common practice to hang Bin Laden's portrait in homes.[70] Al Qaeda's message seemed to resonate among some parts of the Muslim world because it spoke to social and political grievances, tapped into pervasive anti-Semitic and anti-

65 Boulden, 'Council and Terrorism', p. 621.

66 Abdel Bari Atwan, *The Secret History of al Qaeda* (Berkeley, CA: University of California Press, 2006), p. 40.

67 Atwan, *Secret History*, p. 40.

68 Atwan, *Secret History*, p. 59. The other polls were taken by the Pew International Attitudes Survey and are available on their website.

69 Leonard Weinberg, 'Democracy and Terrorism', in Louise Richardson (ed.), *The Roots of Terrorism* (New York: Routledge, 2006), p. 52.

70 Atwan, *Secret History*, p. 59.

American attitudes, and because in some parts of the Muslim world it was the only version of Islam taught in *madrassahs*.[71]

Another source of evidence for the depth of support for Al Qaeda is the number of members and affiliates it has attracted. One estimate in 2004 calculated that Al Qaeda had 'thousands' of members and over sixty active cells, although this is impossible to verify.[72] In addition to 'cells' and 'members' there were numerous Al Qaeda 'affiliates'. After its defeat in Afghanistan in 2001, Al Qaeda became more of a network than an organization, comprising various home grown 'affiliates'. Affiliates share Al Qaeda's basic ideology and sometimes include radicals trained in Al Qaeda's camps in Afghanistan or veterans of the war in Afghanistan.[73] At the time of writing, there were Al Qaeda affiliates operating in Lebanon, Algeria, Yemen, Egypt, Iraq, Pakistan, the Philippines, Indonesia, Somalia, and Mali. One estimate suggests that there are between 30 and 40 affiliates overall and that each comprises an average of 500 fighters, suggesting that the movement has directly recruited around 20,000 people to the cause.[74] Muslim sympathy for Al Qaeda and hostility towards the USA was only reinforced by the invasion of Iraq in 2003 and the mounting civilian casualties caused by the war in Afghanistan.[75] But the total number of recruits is comparatively small and sympathy evident in the wider Muslim community has not been translated into generalized political, ideological, or military support.

It is sometimes argued that Islamic religious leaders and institutions were reluctant to condemn acts of Al Qaeda terrorism, boosting its legitimacy in the Muslim world.[76] But in fact, Al Qaeda has been widely criticized by religious authorities and several *fatwas* and statements of condemnation were issued against it. Of particular interest is the role of civilian immunity in shaping

[71] Sonbol, 'Norms of War', p. 301. In Lebanon, Palestine, Egypt, and Afghanistan, radical Islamism had already proven popular among the young, due largely to the fact that it seemed to explain the problems faced by Muslim youths and offer a route to empowerment. See Fouad Ajami, *The Arab Predicament: Arab Political Thought Since 1967* (New York: Cambridge University Press, 1989), pp. 177–81. The role of education is indicated in the relatively well-to-do origins of many terrorist leaders. See Fareed Zakaria, 'The Allies Who Made Our Foes', *Newsweek*, 1 October 2001, p. 34. Walter Laqueur argues that anti-Americanism is a product simply of American power and that 'more gentle' policies would do little to stem it. See Walter Laqueur, *No End to War: Terrorism in the Twenty-First Century* (New York: Continuum, 2007), p. 161.

[72] J. Fox and S. Sandler, *Bringing Religion into International Relations* (New York: Palgrave, 2004), p. 76.

[73] Jonathan Schanzer, *Al-Qaeda's Armies: Middle East Affiliate Groups and the Next Generation of Terror* (Washington, DC: Washington Institute of Near East Policy, 2005), pp. 16 and 23.

[74] Schanzer, *Al Qaeda's Armies*, p. 24.

[75] On the radicalizing role of Iraq especially, see Jeffrey Haynes, 'Al Qaeda: Ideology and Action', *Critical Review of International Social and Political Philosophy*, 8 (2) 2005, p. 178–9.

[76] A point discussed by Adam L. Silverman, 'Just War, Jihad, and Terrorism: A Comparison of Western and Islamic Norms for the Use of Political Violence', *Journal of Church and State*, 44 (1) 2002, pp. 73–92.

these assessments. Perhaps the most thorough, coherently argued, and politically significant religious response to Al Qaeda was the *fatwa* issued by the head of the Supreme Council of 'Ulama of Saudi Arabia, Sheikh Salih bin Muhammed al-Lahiddan on 14 September 2001. This *fatwa* insisted that the following acts were clearly prohibited by Islam: aggression against those who have committed no crime; killing innocent people, the weak, infants, women and the elderly; destroying property; laying waste to land. These acts could not be condoned by any Islamic scholar, and those who committed such acts were declared to be 'the worst of people'.[77] The mufti of Saudi Arabia issued a *fatwa* that described the 9/11 attack as 'actions that shari'ah does not sanction' and 'not from this religion'. Two years later, the Saudi Council of 'Ulama issued a further *fatwa* expressly forbidding attacks on non-Muslims anywhere in the world on the grounds that the shedding of innocent blood is forbidden by Islamic law. Likewise, Sheikh Yousuf Qaradawi issued a *fatwa* on 12 September stating that 9/11 was illegitimate because Islam does not permit the deliberate killing of civilians. If a Muslim commits such an act, the *fatwa* read, 'we condemn and incriminate him in the name of our religion and our law'.[78] The Islamic Commission of Spain issued a *fatwa* specifically targeting Al Qaeda in the wake of the Madrid bombings. Defined as 'a *fatwa* against Osama bin Laden, al-Qa'ida, and those who claim to justify terrorism based on the Holy Qu'ran', the *fatwa* pointed to Qu'ranic verses on corruption, the permission that Allah grants to non-Muslims to live in peace, and the duty to respect those not waging war, to accuse Bin Laden of falsifying and manipulating the sacred texts to justify that which was expressly forbidden.[79]

Another significant *fatwa* was issued by King Abdallah II of Jordan in November 2004. Citing relevant verses from the Qur'an, King Abdallah's *fatwa* insisted that the principles of Islam forbade acts of terrorism and demanded respect for human life.[80] The King then brought together a conference of religious leaders from all the main Islamic traditions to reach a consensus on the matter in 2005. After much wrangling, the conference failed to find agreement and instead issued a declaration that indirectly challenged the authority of Bin Laden's *fatwa* (by clarifying the question of who may issue a *fatwa* in such a way as to exclude Bin Laden) and insisted that no Muslim may declare another Muslim to be a heretic.[81] The Islamic Supreme Council of America and its equivalent in South Africa issued a joint ruling which insisted

[77] Shmuel Bar, *Warrant for Terror: Fatwas of Radical Islam and the Duty of Jihad* (Lanham: Rowman and Littlefield, 2006), p. 107.

[78] Bar, *Warrant for Terror*, pp. 108–9.

[79] Bar, *Warrant for Terror*, p. 99.

[80] Bar, *Warrant for Terror*, p. 101.

[81] Bar, *Warrant for Terror*, p. 101, n. 8.

that the only legitimate *jihad* was a defensive one in response to armed attack. Similarly, Pakistani Islamic scholar, Mo'iz Ahmed rejected Bin Laden's reasoning on the grounds that the Qur'anic verses he used in the 1998 *fatwa* must be read in their historic context, invalidating Bin Laden's usage.[82]

Al Qaeda has also been criticized by other arms of Islam, including moderates, conservatives, and even other radicals. Some moderate Islamic clerics focused their criticism on the radical ideologies that underpin Al Qaeda's thinking. For example, Sheikh Abd al-Hadi Palazzi of Rome denounced two of its key claims: the definition of the *Dar al-Harb* and the idea that in the path of God, necessity permits what is otherwise forbidden. In relation to the former, he argued that so long as Muslims are permitted to practise their faith the Western world cannot be considered *Dar al-Harb*. On necessity permitting forbidden acts, he maintained that this holds only when the very survival of the Muslim community is at stake.[83] The ultra conservative Salafi sheikhs criticized Al Qaeda for spreading discord and enjoining Muslims to commit prohibited acts (such as suicide).[84] The imprisoned head of the radical Egyptian group, Gama'ah Islamiyah, Sheikh Karam Zuhdi, described 9/11 as unlawful because of the Islamic law prohibiting the killing of merchants.[85]

Many Western-based scholars have also argued that Bin Laden's *fatwa* was inconsistent with the Qur'an and Islamic law. Abdullah Saeed argues that Al Qaeda's position is 'illegitimate' because *jihad* may only be used defensively, may never be used against countries that enjoy peaceful relations with the Muslim world, and gives permission only for limited and discriminate war.[86] Among non-Muslim experts, John Kelsay argues that the injunction to kill civilians violates Islamic tradition on the rules of war, especially Qur'anic teachings relating to proportionality and the killing of innocent people; Natana DeLong Bas maintains that Bin Laden is hard pressed to find support for his views even in the work of Sayyid Qutb, and Rohan Gunaratna maintains that the Qu'ran prohibits the deliberate killing of civilians and that even Ibn Taymiyah, a religious scholar often quoted by Bin Laden, forbade indiscriminate killing.[87]

The claims advanced by Bin Laden and al-Zawahiri were not validated by many Muslim governments either—although of course governments may

[82] Bar, *Warrant for Terror*, pp. 102–3.

[83] Bar, *Warrant for Terror*, p. 104.

[84] Bar, *Warrant for Terror*, pp. 105–6.

[85] Bar, *Warrant for Terror*, p. 108.

[86] Abdullah Saeed, 'Jihad and Violence: Changing Understandings of Jihad Among Muslims', in Tony Coady and Michael O'Keefe (eds), *Terrorism and Justice: Moral Argument in a Threatened World* (Melbourne: Melbourne University Press, 2002), pp. 72–86.

[87] John Kelsay, 'The New *Jihad* and Islamic Tradition', Foreign Policy Research Institute' DeLong Bas, *Wahhabi Islam*, p. 266; Gunaratna, *Inside Al Qaeda*, p. 85; Silverman, 'Just War, Jihad and Terrorism', p. 91; and Saul Smilansky, 'Terrorism, Justification and Illusion', *Ethics*, 114 (4), 2004, pp. 796–7.

have been guided to this by material self-interest in a context of extreme international hostility to such ideas. With the notable exceptions of the Taliban which ruled Afghanistan for five years (1996–2001) and the Islamic Courts which ruled parts of Somalia for an even shorter time, Muslim governments have tended to reject Bin Laden's case. By and large, they condemned Al Qaeda and many have participated in some aspects of the War on Terror. Nor have the Muslim masses been enjoined to rise up against their un-Islamic governments as demanded by Al Qaeda. Indeed, when there were mass uprisings in the Muslim world, in 2011, the masses demanded democracy not Islamism. Although affiliates have proliferated, these have mainly failed to recruit significant numbers. Only Afghanistan, Pakistan, and Yemen have been seriously challenged by groups following Al Qaeda's ideology and local and historical factors were critically important to each of these. Indeed, the general failure of Muslim societies and governments to respond to Al Qaeda's call to arms was repeatedly criticized by Bin Laden and al-Zawahiri.[88] The main explanation for this apparent disjuncture between evidence of sympathy for Al Qaeda and the reluctance of governments and societies to take up its fight is that although many Muslims see Bin Laden as a 'brave champion' of rebellion who has restored Muslim dignity after decades of defeat, they do not support his political agenda (the caliphate) or his brand of Shari'a law, and many are persuaded that killing the innocent is prohibited by the Qur'an.[89]

In summary, developing ideas presented by three earlier radical writers, Al Qaeda launched a global *jihad* against the West, secular Muslim leaders, and others it considered to be apostate, with the ultimate aim of establishing a global Islamic state. This *jihad* targeted civilians principally. To justify this, Al Qaeda issued a *fatwa* making it a religious duty for Muslims to kill Americans and their allies, including civilians. This was justified by reference to God's will expressed through Qu'ranic teachings, the intractable conflict between the *Dar al-Islam* and *Dar al-Harb*, the impossibility of coexistence between Muslims and non-Mulims, collective Western guilt for the oppression of Muslims and occupation of Muslim lands, and the unrestrained nature of *jihad*. As with all doctrines of selective extermination, Al Qaeda's arguments had little appeal outside its 'in group'. It is not surprising, therefore, that it has been repeatedly and comprehensively denounced. This illegitimacy, combined with contextual factors resulted in the establishment of a widely supported international coalition aimed at its physical destruction.

Within the Muslim world, Al Qaeda proved divisive. Whilst governments and some religious leaders tended to either condemn the organization or fault its religious reasoning, Al Qaeda enjoyed a degree of popular support,

[88] Blanchard, 'Al Qaeda', p. 6.
[89] Atwan, *Secret History*, p. 40.

particularly among some disaffected youths in the Middle East, Pakistan, Iraq, Afghanistan, and the West. This level of support was sufficient to enable periodic terrorist attacks, as well as the insurgency in Afghanistan, and less successful violent uprisings in Iraq and Pakistan, but insufficient to propel insurrections against established governments in the Muslim world considered un-Islamic by Al Qaeda. Significantly, Muslim variations on the norm of civilian immunity featured prominently in criticisms of Al Qaeda.

Al Qaeda and its ideology of selective extermination are only part of the challenge to civilian immunity to emerge from the September 11 massacre. Radical Islamism posed a threat to Western security, forcing political and military leaders there to confront once more the tension between civilian immunity and necessity that was so much in evidence during the Cold War. The following section examines how this tension played out focusing especially on how the Bush Administration articulated the case for revising principles around civilian immunity and US conduct in Fallujah in 2004.

## THE WAR ON TERROR

Like other insurgent or terrorist groups, Al Qaeda operated in clandestine cells making its terrorists often indistinguishable from civilians. In Afghanistan, Pakistan, Iraq, and elsewhere, Al Qaeda operatives, their allies, and supporters concealed themselves within the civilian population.[90] In these circumstances the tension between civilian immunity and necessity, evident in Western debates about the conduct of armed conflict during the Cold War, returned to the fore. As in some of the Cold War conflicts, there was a strong temptation in such conditions to prioritize tactical gains and force protection above civilian immunity.[91]

Facing these dilemmas, whilst outwardly attempting to comply with civilian immunity, the Bush Administration contemplated the prioritization of necessity over the protection of civilians. It repeatedly claimed to be complying with the norm civil immunity but just as often invoked necessity by pointing to the gravity and uniqueness of the threat posed by radical Islamism to excuse civilian casualties. This section focuses only on a small number of these issues,

[90] Michael Skerker, 'Just War Criteria and the New Face of War: Human Shields, Manufactured Martyrs, and Little Boys with Stones', *Journal of Military Ethics*, 3 (1) 2004, pp. 27–31. It is endorsed by Michael Ignatieff, 'Ethics and the New War', *Canadian Military Journal*, Winter 2001–02, p. 7.

[91] That this should be so was a view expressed by US military personnel during a workshop on collateral damage. See John F. Kennedy School of Government, Harvard University, Project on the Means of Intervention, 'Understanding Collateral Damage Workshop', 4–5 June 2002, workshop report, p. 12.

examining the use of necessity arguments to justify the treatment of prisoners in a manner inconsistent with civilian immunity and the tactics employed to retake the city of Fallujah in Iraq. It examines the extent to which behaviour was inhibited by civilian immunity, the way in which civilian casualties were justified and how those arguments were judged by others. I argue that civilian immunity played a greater role in US decision-making than in any of the other cases involving the USA discussed in this book and that the USA tried to act in a manner consistent with the norm—suggesting that it has begun to be internalized there—but that sometimes its actions skirted the edge of compliance and its arguments tacitly resurrected the principle of necessity. I also argue that these claims failed to secure sufficient legitimacy, that civilian casualties were widely seen as illegitimate, and that this illegitimacy had negative material and political consequences for the USA, demonstrating the embeddeness of civilian immunity.[92]

Although torture is not specifically forbidden by civilian immunity, the killing of captives is prohibited by the norm and the general use of torture certainly violates the spirit of the principle. For our purposes, though, the key points here relate not to the treatment of prisoners per se but rather to the general attempt to rehabilitate necessity as a plausible reason for sometimes transgressing shared norms. In the early days of the War on Terror, political and public discourse in the USA especially became suffused with the idea that although it was legally and morally prohibited, torturing terrorist suspects was sometimes necessary in order to extract vital information. These ideas were expressed by figures from both sides of American politics.

Commenting on the arrest of a senior Al-Qaeda figure in late 2002, Senator Jay Rockefeller (Democrat, West Virginia), Chair of the Senate Select Committee on Intelligence, told CNN that 'I wouldn't take anything off the table where he is concerned because this is a man who has killed hundreds and hundreds of Americans over the last ten years'.[93] One anonymous Defence official told the *Washington Post* 'if you don't violate someone's human rights some of the time, you probably aren't doing your job'.[94] Another unnamed official told *Newsday* that in the case of one suspect rendered from Guantanamo to Egypt 'they promptly tore his fingernails out and he started telling things'.[95] A circuit judge went as far as to insist that 'if the stakes are high enough, torture is permissible. No one who doubts that this is the case should be in a position of responsibility'.[96] Prominent American lawyer, Alan

[92] See Pape, *Dying to Win*, pp. 243–5.

[93] Cited by Harry Rosenberg, 'Terror and Immigration Law', *The Nation*, 1 December 2003, p. 7.

[94] Staff Writers, 'US Decries Abuse but Defends Interrogators', *Washington Post*, 26 December 2002, p. A12.

[95] Eyal Press, 'In Torture we Trust?', *The Nation*, 13 March 2003, p. 2.

[96] Richard Posner, 'The Best Offense', *The New Republic*, 2 September 2002, p. 28.

Dershowitz, even presented a detailed case for legalizing the torture of suspected terrorists.[97]

Torture became a fairly routine form of interrogation in the War on Terror. Sometimes euphemistically called 'enhanced interrogation', torture was commonly used in three settings. First, on suspects captured in or transferred to prisons and bases in Iraq and Afghanistan—with Abu Ghraib prison and Bagram air base being only the most notorious. In October 2003, coalition forces in Iraq captured the head of Iraqi air defence, General Abed Hamed Mowhoush. He died in custody on 26 November at an unnamed detention centre. The Pentagon released a death certificate declaring that Mowhoush had died of 'natural causes'. The *Denver Post* pursued the case and forced the Pentagon to admit that an autopsy report had found that Mowhoush died of 'asphyxia due to smothering and chest compression' compounded by 'evidence of blunt force trauma to the chest and legs'.[98] Second, psychological mistreatment, though generally not overt physical abuse, was also practised at the Guantanamo Bay detention centre.[99] Third, other captives were secretly 'rendered' from the country of their capture to third countries where the torture of prisoners is routine.[100] The use of torture was therefore widespread and systematic. Indeed, when the US military police investigated claims of abuse at Baghdad's now notorious Abu Ghraib prison, it found that the '*systematic* and illegal abuse of detainees was intentionally perpetrated by several members of the military police guard force'.[101] There is no reason to think that the same was not true of other installations which housed prisoners.[102]

The US Aministration denied that it had authorized unlawful behaviour, typically arguing that undisputable cases of 'abuse' were caused by individual 'rogue elements' and that its policies were consistent with international norms. Defence Secretary, Donald Rumsfeld, for example, condemned the Abu Ghraib abuses as 'terrible' and 'inconsistent with the values of our nation', though he also made a point of distinguishing them from 'torture'.[103] But

[97] See Alan M. Dershowitz, *Why Terrorism Works* (New Haven, CT: Yale University Press, 2002).

[98] Anthony Lewis, 'Making Torture Legal', *The New York Review*, 15 (12), 15 July 2004, p. 4.

[99] E.g. David Rose, 'How I Entered the Hellish World of Guantanamo Bay', *Observer*, 6 February 2005.

[100] Jane Mayer, 'Outsourcing Torture: The Secret History of America's "Extraordinary Rendition" Program', *New Yorker*, 14 February 2005.

[101] Investigation of the 800th Military Police Brigade at http://news.findlaw.com/hdocs/docs/iraq/tagubarpt.htm accessed 14 July 2006. This quote is from part 1, para. 5.

[102] As was clearly documented by Human Rights Watch in its landmark report, *Getting Away with Torture*, April 2005. Also see in K. J. Greenberg and J. L Dratel (eds), *The Torture Papers: The Road to Abu Ghraib* (New York: Cambridge University Press, 2005).

[103] Donald Rumsfeld, Testimony Before the Senate and House Armed Services Committees, 7 May 2004.

there is ample evidence to suggest that senior leaders encouraged operatives to skirt the edges of compliance with norms regulating the treatment of captives and that those directly responsible for abuses often believed that they were acting in a manner consistent with the expectations set down by their commanders.[104]

A normative context that enabled non-compliance was established by successive US Attorney's-General who pointed to necessity as excusing at least a liberal interpretation of what was permitted by law. John Ashcroft (2001–05) condemned those who demanded that the treatment of captives be improved, warning: 'to those who scare peace-loving people with phantoms of lost liberty; my message is this: Your tactics only aid terrorists'.[105] His successor, Alberto Gonzales (2005–07) had earlier drafted a now infamous memorandum to the President on 25 January 2002, in which he argued that aspects of the 1949 Geneva Conventions were 'quaint' and 'obsolete': 'the nature of the new war [on terrorism] places a high premium on other factors, such as the ability to quickly obtain information from captured terrorists and their sponsors in order to avoid further atrocities against American civilians.... This new paradigm renders obsolete Geneva's [the 1949 Geneva Protocol on the Treatment of Prisoners of War] strict limitations on questioning of enemy prisoners'.[106] Necessity also underpinned arguments which held that because the USA was acting in self-defence in the wake of an unprovoked attack, the President's constitutional authority to take whatever action thought necessary to protect Americans was uninhibited by international law or other foreign constraints.[107]

These claims won some support from American conservatives and the US secured the (albeit clandestine) cooperation of a number of countries (including Syria, Egypt, the UK, Uzbekistan, and others), but also received widespread criticism both at home and abroad. In 2008, the incoming Obama Administration promised an end to torture and distanced itself from the necessity based claims of its predecessor. Obama's Republican opponent in

[104] This is set out in detail in Philip Zimbardo, *The Lucifer Effect: How Good People Turn Evil* (London: Rider Books, 2007), pp. 324–79.

[105] Attorney-General John Ashcroft before the Senate Judiciary Committee, 'Preserving our Freedoms while Defending Against Terrorism: Hearing Before the Senate Committee on the Judiciary, 107th Congress, 2001. Available at www.senate.gov/judiciary/print_testimony.cfm?id=12&wit_id=42

[106] Cited by Lewis, 'Making Torture Legal', p. 2; and David Cole, 'Human Rights and the Challenge of Terror', in Leonard Weinberg (ed.), *Democratic Responses to Terrorism* (New York: Routledge, 2008), p. 159.

[107] Anon, 'Ashcroft Hold Torture Memo', *AFP*, 9 June 2004. Accessed at www.news24.com/News24/World/Iraq/0,6119,2-10-1460_1539584,00.html on 28 March 2005. A small group of Justice Department lawyers, all appointed by the Bush administration, arguing vociferously against the abrogation of unlimited powers by the administration, many of them paying with their jobs. See Anthony Lewis, 'Introduction' in Greenberg and Dratel (eds), *Torture Papers*, p. viii.

the 2008 election, Senator John McCain, was also a staunch critic of the Bush Administration's stance on this issue. In 2005, McCain sponsored an amendment to the Defence Budget Bill which demanded the humane treatment of prisoners. Despite the Administration's best efforts to block it, the bill passed by 90 votes to 9.[108] In *Newsweek*, McCain argued that skirting the edges of law and morality eroded the normative distinction between the terrorists and their opponents:

> This is a war of ideas, a struggle to advance freedom in the face of terror in places where oppressive rule has bred the malevolence that creates terrorists. Prisoner abuse exacts a terrible toll on us all in this war of ideas. They inevitably become public, and when they do they threaten our moral standing. . . . The mistreatment of prisoners harms us more than our enemies.[109]

Reactions outside the USA were also generally critical. In 2006, for example, the UN's High Commissioner for Human Rights, Louise Arbour, commented that the practices were having an 'acutely corrosive effect' on global human rights norms.[110]

It is the effect of these arguments on the norm of civilian immunity, though, that is of particular interest to us. Across the different theatres of the War on Terror there is evidence that US commanders and soldiers occasionally allowed necessity to override civilian immunity—a problem starkly exposed by the 2010 publication of documents by *Wikileaks* showing countless cases of the wilful killing of civilians by US forces.

The US-led invasion of Iraq in 2003 and the subsequent insurgency and civil war there seriously damaged the legitimacy of the War on Terror. Although the coalition attempted to comply with civilian immunity, when faced with problems of necessity its actual conduct sometimes 'skirted the edges' of the rule. From the beginning, the number of civilian deaths in Iraq was higher than in Afghanistan. One account suggests that between 5,500 and 7,500 civilians were killed by coalition forces during the 'major combat operations' phase, the majority by aerial bombardment. Another report put that figure at approximately 3,750.[111] This generated a widely held perception that the USA 'didn't try very hard' to avoid Iraqi civilian casualties. A Pew Global Attitudes survey taken in June 2003, showed that more than 90 per cent of Jordanian, Moroccan, Palestinian, and Turkish respondents held this view,

[108] Cole, 'Human Rights', p. 161.

[109] John McCain, 'The Truth About Torture', *Newsweek*, 21 November 2005, p. 35.

[110] Laurenti, 'The United Nations and Terrorism', p. 80.

[111] See Martin Shaw, *The New Western Way of War* (Cambridge: Polity, 2005), pp. 115–23. And it is also worth noting that the war in Afghanistan exacted more civilian casualties with fewer bombs than the war in Kosovo. See Richard Falk, *The Great Terror War* (New York: Olive Branch Press, 2003), p. 68.

as did more than 70 per cent of Brazilian, French, Russian, and South Korean respondents.[112] In the counter-insurgency that followed, US forces perpetrated several massacres, such as the killing of over twenty civilians in Haditha on 19 November 2005. Although those responsible have been investigated and sometimes prosecuted, only a few were actually punished. By 2007, some six hundred investigations into alleged war crimes had resulted in only twelve soldiers serving prison time.[113] The most serious questions about systematic non-compliance with civilian immunity in Iraq, however, relate to the two assaults on Fallujah in 2004.

The city of Fallujah was relatively quiet immediately after the US invasion, and the city's mayor welcomed US troops. Lying to the west of Baghdad, Fallujah had escaped violence during the 'major combat operations' phase of the war. The situation soon deteriorated, however. After a series of incidents at checkpoints, on 28 April US soldiers fired on civilian protestors, killing between thirteen and eighteen and injuring up to ninety-one. The US claimed that its troops were fired on first, but eyewitnesses report that the civilians were unarmed and Human Rights Watch concluded that 'physical evidence does not support claims of an effective attack on the building as described by US troops'.[114] Relations between locals and US soldiers deteriorated sharply and the city became a major base for both local and foreign resistance, including Abu Musab al-Zarqawi's 'Al Qaeda in Iraq' and former Baathists.[115] As al-Zarqawi's campaign and the former-Baathist's insurgency spread, the USA stepped up its attacks on Fallujah, increasing the number of civilian casualties. In late March 2004, an airstrike purportedly targeting al-Zarqawi destroyed several homes, killing eighteen civilians. A few days later, four American private security contractors were ambushed and killed by a mob which then mutilated and paraded their bodies. The US Administration promised that this crime would 'not go unpunished' and US forces besieged the city.[116] Military commanders argued against an all-out assault, preferring to allow the situation to settle before launching a limited and precisely targeted campaign. But military concerns were overruled by the White House which insisted on a show of strength as retribution for the killing of Americans.[117] General James Conway later criticized the decision. He told the *Washington*

[112] Reported in Krahl, 'In the Crossfire or the Crosshairs?', p. 7.

[113] Krahl, 'In the Crossfire or the Crosshairs?', pp. 34–5.

[114] Human Rights Watch, *Violent Response: The US Army in al-Fallujah*, Human Rights Watch Report, 15 (7) June 2003. See Matt Carr, 'The Barbarians of Fallujah', *Race & Class*, 50 (1) 2008, p. 26.

[115] By most accounts though, foreign fighters constituted a small part of the Fallajuh resistance. E.g. Jonathan Steele, 'Driven by National Pride', *The Guardian*, 2 April 2004; and Carter Malkasian, 'Signaling Resolve: Democratization and the First Battle of Fallujah', *Journal of Strategic Studies*, 29 (3) 2006, p. 428.

[116] Alice Hills, 'Fear and Loathing in Falluja', *Armed Forces and Society*, 32 (4) 2006, p. 626.

[117] Hills, 'Fear and Loathing', p. 628.

*Post* that he had 'resisted calls for revenge and instead advocated targeted operations and continued engagement with municipal leaders. . . . We felt like we had a method that we wanted to apply to Fallujah: that we ought to probably let the situation settle before we appeared to be attacking out of revenge'.[118]

On 5 April, the USA launched *Operation Vigilant Resolve* to punish the insurgents and retake the city. The strategy involved cutting off escape routes and then taking the city street by street. Any resistance would be met with overwhelming firepower.[119] As one army commander indicated, 'if we take fire from it, we destroy the whole building'.[120] *New York Times* reporters embedded with the Marines in Fallujah compiled a description of the rules of engagement that applied immediately after the ceasefire but before the lifting of the siege. They give us good reason to think that discrimination was not a priority during the combat phase. The six principles they identified were: (1) snipers should shoot anyone approaching any US position; (2) any male of military age on the streets after dark should be shot whether they are armed or not; (3) soldiers should shoot anyone with a gun, irrespective of hostile intent; (4) hostile fire should be returned and helicopters should be called in to annihilate the position. If that failed, air strikes should be called in to destroy the structure; (5) no men should be allowed to leave the town; (6) civilians driving on closed sections of highway may be engaged with deadly force.[121]

Once they entered the city, US Marines encountered heavy resistance and four were killed. They responded by calling in close air support, making steady gains though slower than anticipated. Few reporters were in the city to record the devastation but soon accounts of civilian casualties began to emerge. *Al Jazeera* broadcast footage of civilian casualties and was accused by the USA of acting as a propaganda vehicle for the insurgents. The few Westerners present inside the city confirmed *Al Jazeera*'s account. Jo Wilding, a British human rights worker observed that 'US snipers in Fallujah shoot unarmed men in the back, old woman with white flag, children fleeing their homes and the ambulance that we were going in to fetch a woman in premature labour'.[122] Most estimates agree that between 600 and 650 civilians were killed in the

[118] 'Key General Criticizes April Attack in Fallujah: Abrupt Withdrawal Called Vacillation', *Washington Post*, 13 September 2004. For a discussion of this view, see Malkasian, 'Signaling Resolve, p. 434.

[119] Krahl, 'In the Crossfire or the Crosshairs?', p. 30.

[120] Cited by Michael Schwartz, 'Why the United States is Losing the War in Iraq', *Contexts*, winter 2005, p. 16.

[121] Schwartz, 'Why the United States is Losing the War in Iraq', p. 17.

[122] Cited in Jonathan Holmes, *Fallujah: Eyewitness Testimony from Iraq's Besieged City* (London: Constable and Robinson, 2007), p. 30.

space of five days, though some reports go up to 700 and the Iraqi Minister of Health estimated a much lower civilian toll of 220.[123]

Reports of civilian casualties sparked sharp criticism both within and outside Iraq (see below). Most notably, criticism came from the Iraq Governing Council which had not been consulted about the assault, undercutting any hope the Americans had of legitimizing these actions inside Iraq.[124] This prompted the USA to call off the attack and declare a conditional ceasefire. The siege lasted for another three weeks, during which time US aircraft and Marines launched sporadic attacks against insurgent positions. Then, the USA announced that responsibility for security in the city would be handed over to the hastily constituted 'Fallujah brigade', comprising former soldiers from Saddam's army, and withdrew.

The Fallujah brigade soon proved itself corrupt and incompetent. Fallujah rapidly became a centre of insurgent activity once again, although this time the ranks of local insurgents were swelled with new volunteers. On 8 November 2004, with British and Iraqi support, the US launched a second attempt to retake the city. The second operation, *Al Fajr* (new dawn) was more carefully planned than the first. The Iraqi Governing Council was brought on board in advance and a cordon thrown around the city. Residents were urged to leave, but men of military age were prevented from doing so in order to thwart expected insurgent attempts to melt away from battle.[125] Many women and children opted to stay as well, meaning that between 30,000 and 50,000 civilians remained in the city when the assault began. In line with the general theory of 'free-fire zone' counter-insurgency, once combat operations began US forces tended to assume that everyone left in the city was a combatant. This is made clear even by accounts of the battle that are gushing in their praise for the USA. Writing in the *Marines Gazette*, 'Bing' West claimed that 'the absence of civilians meant that Marines could employ blast weapons prior to entering houses that had become pillboxes not homes'.[126] Of course, civilians were not 'absent' and the treatment of houses as 'pillboxes' sometimes resulted in the killing of civilians. One such incident was recounted in detail by Hudda Fawzi Salam Issawi. During Operation *Al Fajr*, US troops arrived at a home where a family and neighbour were hiding. They shot Issawi's father and

[123] E.g. Carr, 'Barbarians', p. 28; Malkasian, 'Signaling Resolve', p. 437; Stephen Graham, 'Remembering Fallujah: Demonising Place, Constructing Atrocity', *Environment and Planning D: Society and Space*, 23 (1) 2005, p. 4 (puts the estimate at 600–880); Robert M. Entman, 'Punctuating the Homogeneity of Institutionalized News: Abusing Prisoners at Abu Ghraib Versus Killing Civilians at Fallujah', *Political Communication*, 23, 2006, p. 216. The Minister of Health's low estimate is especially interesting given the Ministry's very high estimate of casualties in the Operation Al Fajr—the second assault on Fallujah.

[124] It also generated a 'popular backlash against the coalition'. Malkasian, 'Signaling Resolve, p. 424.

[125] Mike Marqusee, 'A Name that Lives in Infamy', *The Guardian*, 10 November 2005.

[126] F. J. 'Bing' West, 'The Fall of Fallujah', *Marine Corps Gazette*, July 2005.

neighbour as they opened the front door.[127] One of the few journalists to remain in Fallujah, Lebanese television's Burhan Fasa'a, reported that 'Americans did not have interpreters with them, so they entered houses and killed people because they didn't speak English. They entered the house where I was with 26 people and shot people because they didn't obey the soldiers' orders, even just because the people couldn't understand a word of English'.[128]

The false assumption that everyone inside Fallujah was a combatant also permitted the use of 'fuel-air' weapons explosives, similar to those used by Russia against Grozny. 'Bing' West recounts that the Marines used warheads containing 'about 35 per cent thermobaric novel explosive and 65 per cent standard high explosive' in order to 'cause the roof to collapse and crush the insurgents fortified inside interior rooms'. The weapon was used repeatedly: 'the expenditure of explosives clearing houses was enormous', West tells us.[129] As the *Marine Corps Gazette* noted in 2000, 'fuel-air weapons' form a cloud of volatile gases or explosive particles and then ignite the cloud, creating a fireball and consuming all the oxygen in the area. People underneath the bomb are crushed to death by the pressure created, those caught in the fireball die from burns, and those on the perimeter suffer major burns, broken bones, and blindness. This weapon, the *Gazette* observed, 'can have the effect of a tactical nuclear weapon'.[130] Employed in an area containing civilians, it is an inherently indiscriminate weapon. Among the other weapons used in the second assault was white phosphorous, a chemical weapon whose use in civilian areas is prohibited by the Chemical Weapons Convention.[131] There were also unconfirmed reports of the use of napalm and of civilians being shot by snipers. An American cameraman took footage of a US Marine killing an injured man. Media outlets also published a photo of hospital workers and patients being forced by Marines to lie face down on the floor with their hands bound.[132] On 14 November, *Reuters* reported a 'sea of rubble and death' in Fallujah.[133]

It is difficult to know how many civilians were killed in the second attack on Fallujah. The US claimed only that 1,200 'insurgents' were killed in the fighting. Iraqi NGOs estimated a total of 6,000 deaths, including insurgents. Australia's ABC claimed that between 1,200 and 1,600 insurgents and up to

[127] Naomi Klein in Richard Falk, Irene Gendzier, and Robert Jay Lifton (eds), *Crimes of War: Iraq* (New York: Nation Books, 2006), p. 99.

[128] Falk, Gendzier, and Lifton, *Crimes of War*, p. 418.

[129] West, 'Fall of Fallujah'.

[130] Lester W. Grau and Timothy Smith, 'A "Crushing Victory": Fuel-Air Explosives and Grozny', *Marines Corps Gazette*, 2000.

[131] For a discussion of the use of white phosphorous and its legality, see Roman Reyhani, 'The Legality of the Use of White Phosphorus by the United States Military During the 2004 Fallujah Assaults', *Journal of Law and Social Change*, 10, 2007, pp. 1–45.

[132] Falk, Gendzier, and Lifton, *Crimes of War*, p. 184.

[133] Carr, 'Barbarians of Fallujah', p. 34; and Graham, 'Remembering Fallujah', p. 6.

2,000 civilians were killed.[134] In January 2005, the director of Fallujah's hospital told the UN that a hospital emergency team had recovered more than 700 bodies from the rubble, of which 550 were women and children. In March 2005, a deputation from the Iraqi ministry of health found that between 75 and 85 per cent of the city's buildings had been destroyed or heavily damaged.[135] Hafid al-Dulaimi, the US appointed head of the compensation commission, reported than 36,000 houses, 8,400 shops, 60 schools, and 65 mosques were destroyed.[136]

It seems clear that at the very least, US forces in Fallujah employed an exceptionally narrow definition of what civilian immunity prohibited and, in line with the general trend towards rehabilitating necessity, privileged tactical advantage over the protection of civilians. There are plausible grounds for going further and arguing that the USA revived the 'free-fire' strategy employed in Vietnam and collapsed the distinction between combatants and civilians in order to justify indiscriminate targeting.

In its attempt to justify US behaviour, political leaders, soldiers, officials, and commentators presented three lines of argument. First and foremost, they argued that US behaviour was consistent with the norm of civilian immunity and that the use of force was discriminate and precisely targeted. Military leaders invariably described US tactics as 'humane' and 'deliberate, precise and robust'.[137] The first response to reports of civilian casualties was to deny that they had been caused by US forces and where that was not possible casualties were portrayed as unintended but 'nearly unavoidable'.[138] Journalists embedded with US forces repeated this logic. Robert Kaplan, for example, argued that civilian casualties were minimal and caused by crossfire from fire fights 'usually perpetrated by the enemy'.[139] With the second assault, this line of argument was supported by a clear collapsing of the distinction between soldiers and civilians permitted by the prior issuing of a warning and the evacuation of some civilians prior to the assault. Repeating rhetorical and military practices developed during the Cold War, US forces operated on the false assumption that everyone who remained inside the city was a combatant.

Second, the US created and leveraged uncertainty by controlling information and downplaying and disregarding evidence of civilian casualties

[134] 'US Death Toll in Fallujah Reaches 71', *ABC News*, 2 December 2004.

[135] Cited in Carr, 'Barbarians of Fallujah', p. 33.

[136] Falk, Gendzier, and Lifton, *Crimes of War*, p. 417.

[137] Hills, 'Fear and Loathing', p. 634.

[138] Entman, 'Punctuating the Homogeneity', p. 221. Col. John R. Ballard, 'Lessons Learned from Operation Al Fajr: The Liberation of Fallujah', paper presented to the 10th Annual Command and Control Research and Technology Symposium, 2005, p. 6.

[139] Robert D. Kaplan, 'The Real Story of Fallujah', *Wall Street Journal*, 27 May 2004. Kaplan also claimed that the use of the term 'hadji' as a label for Iraqis (very reminiscent of the use of 'gooks' as a label for Koreans) was not racist but a term of endearment 'to wit . . . let's drink tea and hang out with the haji's'.

(especially those that appeared to be intentionally caused). Generally, the USA emphasized that reports of civilian casualties were grossly exaggerated. This was no doubt true in some cases but this was used to provide blanket justification in the face of evidence of civilian casualties.[140] Nowhere was this more in evidence than on the question of the use of white phosphorous. The USA initially denied using the weapon, and then when confronted with video imagery of artillery units firing white phosphorous shells admitted using the weapons but only as tracer fire. That too was proven incorrect when US soldiers published an article in a military journal saying that the weapons were used against targets in order to flush out insurgents.[141] Finally, the Pentagon admitted that white phosphorous 'was used as an incendiary weapon against enemy combatants' whilst claiming that such usage was not legally prohibited.[142]

Third, and more worryingly from the perspective of civilian immunity, commentators intimated that concern for unintended civilian casualties should be balanced against recognition of necessity. This helped create a context that supported the previous two lines of argument. In the wake of the killing of the security contractors, US politicians, military leaders, and commentators denounced Fallujah in apocalyptic terms. Head of the transitional authority, Paul Bremer pointed to the attacks as 'a dramatic example of the struggle between human dignity and barbarism' and vowed that the 'ghouls and cowards' responsible would be punished.[143] Using biblical language, Marine Colonel Gareth Brandl told the BBC shortly before the second assault: 'The enemy has got a face. He's called Satan. He lives in Fallujah'.[144] This line of reasoning was readily endorsed by the US media. Indeed, some media commentators were more vociferous. Fox's Bill O'Reilly demanded the destruction of Fallujah as a whole: 'you're not going to win their hearts and minds. They're going to kill you at the very end. They've proven that. So let's knock this place down'.[145] Writing in the *New York Post*, soldier-turned-'analyst' Ralph Peters argued (apparently without recognizing the irony) that 'the most humane thing we can do in that tormented city is just

[140] Malkasian, 'Signaling Resolve', p. 438.

[141] Reyhani, 'Legality of the Use of White Phosphorus', pp. 6–7.

[142] In fact, the US military acknowledges that White Phosphorus is prohibited. Openly available training manuals from Fort Leavenworth state bluntly that 'it is against the law of warfare to employ WP against personnel targets', *US Command and General Staff College Battle Book*, ch. 5, section III. Available at www.fas.org/man/dod-101/army/docs/st100-3/c5/5sect3.htm See George Monbiot, 'A War Crime Within a War Crime Within a War Crime', *The Guardian*, 22 November 2005.

[143] Cited by Carr, 'Barbarians of Fallujah', p. 22.

[144] Quoted in Naomi Klein, 'Die, then Vote: This is Falluja', *The Guardian*, 13 November 2004.

[145] Cited by Jeremy Scahill, *Blackwater: The Rise of the World's Most Powerful Mercenary Army* (New York: Nation Books, 2007), p. 107.

to win, to burn out the plague of fanaticism and prove to Iraq's people that the forces of terror will not be allowed to enslave them. . . . If that means widespread destruction, we must accept the price. . . . Even if Fallujah has to go the way of Carthage, reduced to shards, the price will be worth it'.[146] Former Reagan advisor, Jack Wheeler, insisted that 'Fallujah must be destroyed. I don't mean metaphorically, I mean for the entire population of the city, every man, woman and child, given 24 hours to leave and be dispersed in resettlement camps . . . and the town turned into a ghost town. . . . Fallujah must be physically obliterated from the face of the earth'.[147] Although officials and serving soldiers steered clear of this line of argument for obvious reasons, this rhetoric helped create the impression that the destruction of Fallujah was necessary for the defeat of Islamist extremism and that this necessity gave a licence to temporarily set civilian immunity aside.

US tactics in the two Fallujah campaigns were widely criticized in Iraq, the region, and globally, and were also seen by many US allies in Europe and Australia as 'inappropriate and counterproductive'.[148] Even the British government, America's staunchest ally in Iraq, expressed misgivings.[149] Under intense domestic pressure, Tony Blair urged restraint, privately informing President Bush that civilian casualties were hurting the coalition's legitimacy and that a renewed offensive threatened to break the coalition.[150] Just as notable was the criticism levelled by the liberal Israeli newspaper, *Haaretz*, which accused the USA of having 'committed war crimes in Fallujah on a scale unprecedented for this war'.[151] The head of the UN's Mission in Iraq, Lakhdar Brahimi, indicated his strong disapproval and threatened to resign.[152]

As might be expected, Iraqi opinion was uniformly hostile—leading one analyst to conclude in 2005 that the battle for hearts and minds had already been lost.[153] 'The overwhelming majority of Iraqis', Samer Shehata noted, 'perceived US military conduct in Fallujah in March 2004 as an unjustified and disproportionate use of force against a civilian population'.[154] We noted earlier that it was opposition from the Iraqi Governing Council that prompted the USA to prematurely terminate *Vigilant Resolve*. Indeed, Iraq's human

[146] Ralph Peters, 'Finishing Fallujah', *New York Post*, 9 November 2004.

[147] Jack Wheeler, 'Fallujah delenda est', *Newsmax.com*, 2 April 2004.

[148] Hills, 'Fear and Loathing', p. 623.

[149] Hills, 'Fear and Loathing', p. 626.

[150] Bing West, *No True Glory: A Frontline Account of the Battle for Fallujah* (New York: Bantam, 2005), pp. 159–60.

[151] Orit Shohat, 'Remember Fallujah', *Haaretz*, 28 April 2004.

[152] L. Paul Bremer, *My Year in Iraq: The Struggle to Build a Future of Hope* (New York: Simon and Schuster, 2006), pp. 326–7.

[153] Samer Shehata, 'Losing Hearts and Minds: Understanding America's Failure in Iraq', *Georgetown Journal of International Affairs*, 6, Winter/Spring 2005, p. 71.

[154] Shehata, 'Losing Hearts and Minds', p. 76.

rights minister and interior minister resigned in protest.[155] Adnan Pachachi, a member of Iraq's Governing Council described the first Fallujah operation as 'unacceptable and illegal'.[156] Subsequent polling showed that a large majority of Iraqis believed that both US operations in Fallujah were illegitimate. Shi'ites and Sunnis protested together in Baghdad and US action apparently encouraged a surge in volunteers for the resistance.[157] Polls taken immediately after the first assault found that 89 per cent of Iraqis considered the coalition to be an occupying force and 76 per cent believed that the USA should move its forces outside of the cities.[158] The moderate major of Fallujah, handpicked by the USA, resigned in protest, arguing that 'American behaviour is increasing the size of the resistance... [making] everyone seek revenge.... Falluja has become a symbol for those who reject the occupation'.[159]

In summary, sometimes confronted with the tension between necessity and civilian immunity, some aspects of the War on Terror skirted the edges of the norm. In some of its comments and legal work in relation to the treatment of captives, Bush Administration officials maintained that necessity and the imperatives of self-defence might sometimes override legal and other moral concerns. Within this context, it is not surprising that US forces in the field occassionally privileged tactical advantage and force protection over civilian immunity. In Fallujah, the USA employed a strategy very similar to that employed in Korea and Indochina—warning residents to leave and then collapsing the distinction between soldiers and civilians by assuming that all those who chose not to evacuate were combatants and could be treated accordingly. Among other things, this permitted the use of weapons that are prohibited for use in proximity to civilians, allowed US forces to destroy whole buildings with artillery and aerial bombardment without regard for the presence of civilians, and facilitated a general lack of discrimination in close-quarter targeting. Against a background context emphasizing the necessity of destroying Fallujah, the USA argued that its actions were consistent with civilian immunity and created and leveraged uncertainty to support its case.

Although US claims won some domestic support, they were sharply criticized elsewhere for three key reasons. First, extensive media coverage sometimes graphically documented abuses and civilian casualties. Although this was truer of Afghanistan and the prisoner abuse scandal than of Fallujah, the destruction of the Iraqi city was documented in real-time, as was evidence of civilian casualties. Publics and governments outside the USA had difficulty reconciling these images with the claim that the USA was conducting precise

155 Shehata, 'Losing Hearts and Minds', p. 77.

156 Cited by Entman, 'Punctuating the Homogeneity', p. 220.

157 Malkasian, 'Signaling Resolve', p. 439.

158 Malkasian, 'Signaling Resolve', p. 441.

159 Cited by Hills, 'Fear and Loathing', p. 626.

and discriminate military activities, creating a widely shared belief that the USA was violating civilian immunity. In this context, attempts to portray the Geneva Conventions as 'obsolete' only helped distance the USA further from world opinion and confirmed in the minds of some that the USA was not conducting itself with due respect for shared rules. Second, whilst the USA certainly enjoyed more international legitimacy than Al Qaeda, this did not translate into relative legitimacy vis-à-vis Afghan or Iraqi civilians. What is more, the widely perceived illegitimacy of the US invasion of Iraq established a degree of international sympathy for Iraqi civilians which heightened sensitivity to civilian casualties. Third, partly because civilian immunity played such a major role in the critique of Al Qaeda, governments and publics outside the USA tended to prioritize the minimization of civilian harm above potential tactical or strategic gains. The minimization of civilian casualties was widely seen as a key priority, generating intense criticism of careless, indiscriminate, or abusive behaviour.

## CONCLUSION

Civilian immunity may have won its battle of ideas against the twentieth-century's anti-civilian ideologies, but this is not a permanent victory. As this chapter demonstrates, new ideologies of selective extermination will arise from time to time and governments will continue to be forced to choose between necessity and civilian immunity. Significantly, though, neither Al Qaeda nor the USA secured sufficient legitimacy and both paid a price for killing civilians: Al Qaeda was confronted militarily by a coalition of over forty states supported by most of the rest of international society; the USA faced sharp criticism and armed insurrection, and a distinct lack of friends willing to share its burdens in Iraq. Whilst the structural limits of selective extermination played an important role in the case of Al Qaeda, contextual factors were also important in both cases.

Al Qaeda advocated an ideology of selective extermination which purported to justify the killing of Americans and their allies, including civilians. Predictably, these claims were resoundingly rejected outside the Muslim world and intervening variables, especially relative legitimacy, policy prioritization, and the balance of compulsory and institutional power, coalesced to ensure that this illegitimacy was translated into decisive punishment. However, as during Cold War insurgencies, Islamist terrorism and insurgency presented particular problems in relation to distinguishing soldiers and civilians. Responding to the threat posed by Al Qaeda, the USA and its allies tentatively moved towards resurrecting necessity to justify skirting the edges of civilian immunity in certain circumstances. Against this backdrop, the USA attempted to create and leverage uncertainty to secure sufficient legitimacy for behaviour that probably violated civilian immunity. Although these claims enjoyed different degrees of support within the USA, they were generally dismissed outside the USA and civilian casualties were criticized as illegitimate. Once again, contextual factors that had once stymied civilian immunity worked in the norm's favour: extensive reporting of civilian casualties challenged the claim of norm compliance and a combination of the absence of countervailing interests and belief that successful counter-insurgency requires legitimacy elevated concerns about civilian casualties.

Left unchecked, both the articulation of a new ideology of selective extermination and the creeping return of necessity might have threatened progress towards embedding and internalizing civilian immunity charted in the previous chapters. However, both lines of argument were met with sharp condemnation and resistance. Al Qaeda received little other than condemnation and punishment from outside the Muslim world and its ideas remain deeply divisive within. Whether deliberately caused or not, civilian casualties at the hands of the USA and its allies were widely criticized, undermined the legitimacy of the War on Terror itself, and caused divisions within the US-led coalition. In clear contrast to the Cold War, countervailing strategic interests have generally not trumped concerns about civilian immunity in the War on Terror, suggesting that the norm has become well embedded in international society if not equally well internalized within its members.

# Conclusion

I opened this book by observing a troubling paradox: whilst the deliberate killing of civilians is prohibited by the norm of civilian immunity, not only do mass atrocities persist but perpetrators of these grave wrongs sometimes escape punishment and criticism. Mass atrocities persist and new episodes erupt at least partly because perpetrators persuade themselves that the advantages of killing civilians outweigh the anticipated costs. Would-be perpetrators have reasonably good grounds for optimism on this score. The past two centuries are replete with examples of governments and others literally getting away with mass murder. And whilst, with the end of the Cold War and changes to the global context, it has certainly become more difficult to get away with mass murder, it is still not impossible to do so as the examples of Russian atrocities in Chechnya and Rwandan Patriotic Front (RPF) atrocities in Zaire demonstrated only too well.

The key to understanding this paradox lies in the politics of legitimacy. I suggested in Chapter 1 that behaviour is commonly regarded to be legitimate if it is seen to correspond with agreed standards of behaviour (norms). Legitimacy judgements guide how actors respond to what others do. Simply put, things judged legitimate tend to enjoy the support or voluntary acquiescence of others, reducing anticipated transaction costs. Things thought to be illegitimate are likely to be criticised, resisted, and punished, increasing anticipated transaction costs. Governments try to justify their behaviour to others by reference to agreed standards of behaviour because they want to legitimize their action and therefore reduce the likely costs. Justifications, of course, also help with the internal validation of a course of action by closing what psychologists call 'cognitive dissonance' created when one's outward behaviour fails to correspond with inner moral beliefs. In line with these logics, Quentin Skinner argued that actors are inhibited from acting in ways that they cannot plausibly justify to others.

But things are more complicated than this because there are multiple norms and because norms, arguments, and actors do not exist within a vacuum—they operate within contexts that exert a significant degree of influence. To justify behaviour that violates a particular norm such as civilian immunity, governments might point to other norms that are considered either more important or more appropriate to the circumstances at hand. The relationship between the norm of civilian immunity and mass atrocities was therefore at least in part a story about competition between different types of norms: a norm prohibiting mass atrocities (civilian immunity) and other norms that provided plausible grounds for legitimizing atrocities in certain circumstances. Part of the story of this book, therefore, was about the transformation of civilian immunity from a shared moral principle to a norm embedded in, and legislated by, international society—though not internalized by many of its members. I labelled the ideational competitors to civilian immunity 'anti-civilian ideologies' and pointed to two types that were evident over the past two centuries or so—necessity and selective extermination. Necessity held that in certain circumstances—most notably in the face of domestic revolts or insurgencies—legitimate authorities might use violence against civilians to achieve their purposes. Ideologies of selective extermination held that civilian immunity did not apply to particular groups and that the killing of civilian members of those groups could be both blameless and praiseworthy. During the long nineteenth century, governments almost always employed arguments drawing on one of these two sets of norms in order to justify the commission of mass atrocities.

The rise of liberal humanitarianism and the strengthening of civilian immunity helps to explain why, as the nineteenth century progressed, the principle of necessity became less effective as a source of legitimacy for mass atrocities. The tireless advocacy of Henri Dunant and others in the Red Cross movement and the creeping codification of the laws of war which made much of the Just War tradition's distinction between combatants and non-combatants, gradually transformed necessity from an enabler of mass atrocities into more of a restraint. Thus, whilst at the beginning of the nineteenth century Napoleonic France's claim that necessity permitted the killing of Spanish civilians as reprisal for guerrilla attacks on French troops was accepted as legitimate by the British, the almost identical German claim in relation to Belgian civilians at the beginning of the twentieth century was rejected by Britain and condemned by other members of international society. The rise of liberal humanitarianism gradually reduced the level of deliberate civilian devastation that could be justified by reference to necessity to the point where—in the twentieth century—it offered little prospect of legitimacy.

There were important differences, however, between similar nineteenth century cases in which perpetrators invoked necessity as a justification that could not be explained by reference to the effect of liberal humanitarianism on the relative weight given to civilian immunity and necessity alone. This is why the strengthening of civilian immunity as an international norm could only be part of the story told in this book. Why, in 1848, was Austria criticized by international society more sharply than France even though it subjected fewer civilians to summary execution? Why was the Ottoman Empire subjected to intervention in 1827 when it responded to an insurrection by killing civilians whilst France escaped with relatively mild criticism when it massacred civilians in Paris in 1872, even though civilian immunity should have been more influential in 1872 than in 1827? Why was Spain punished for its misrule of Cuba in 1901 by losing the right to govern whilst Turkey was permitted to continue governing Turkish Armenia despite committing genocide in 1915? I argued that these apparent anomalies could not be explained by either the relative weight given to the norms involved or the persuasive skills of the perpetrators alone. Instead, they pointed to the role of contextual factors in shaping how external actors evaluate legitimacy claims and the consequences that flow from those judgements. The context also determined just *how much* legitimacy a particular perpetrator required. Flowing from this insight, two of the central claims of this book were: *(1) that the context in which justificatory arguments are aired is as important as what is argued in influencing legitimacy judgements and the consequences that flow* and *(2) actors need only secure sufficient legitimacy for their actions, thereby preventing the illegitimacy of their actions from being converted into perceptions that they are illegitimate actors.* These two points help explain why perpetrators sometimes continued to avoid major criticism for mass atrocities even after necessity and selective extermination ceased to function as sources of potential legitimacy for mass atrocities.

Arguments are not aired and received in a vacuum. In almost all the cases that I examined in this book, the social context played a critically important role in influencing how external actors judged and responded to grave violations of civilian immunity. Identified in Chapter 1, among the most important contextual factors were the availability and clarity of information, the prior relationship between the perpetrators and outside actors, the interests and priorities of external actors, the material and institutional power of external actors, and the material and institutional power of the perpetrators. These factors also determined the extent to which international society was challenged to respond to mass atrocities and influenced the extent to which justifications presented by perpetrators were accepted. Where atrocities were reported, governments tended to validate, tolerate, or excuse mass atrocities committed by their allies irrespective of the plausibility of the justificatory arguments they offered. Seldom did such relationships break down as a result of the commission of mass atrocities, though in some protracted cases—notably that of El Salvador and—although not considered here—Guatemala—allies applied different forms of pressure on perpetrators in order to encourage them to change their course of action. At other times, governments were prepared to excuse or tolerate mass atrocities simply because it suited their immediate interests to do so. During the Cold War, the strategic interests of the superpowers commonly overrode everything else, including fidelity to civilian immunity. This was most obvious and egregious, perhaps, in the diplomatic and material support that the genocidal Khmer Rouge received from the West. But it was a common practice on both sides of the Iron Curtain. More mundane interests also sometimes overrode concern about civilian immunity: US isolationism played an important role in limiting the punishment of Turkey after the Armenian genocide; Western preferences for democratic reform in Russia overrode concerns about Russian atrocities in Chechnya; global guilt about international society's failure to halt the Rwandan genocide created a climate of impunity for the RPF.

By shaping the politics of legitimation, contextual factors also influenced the behaviour of perpetrators to an extent. For instance, where limited reporting created a climate of impunity, perpetrators sometimes did very little to explain or justify their behaviour to outsiders. Most obviously, Mao's China killed millions of Chinese civilians without coming close to offering a plausible justification to international society. Instead, it relied on a combination of international isolation and communist solidarity to protect it from censure. Likewise, the Khmer Rouge barely paid lip service to civilian immunity and the arguments it offered to outsiders were patently absurd. During its wars in Indochina, the USA complied with civilian immunity only when it believed that violations would be widely reported. Where it believed that violations would not be reported, as in Laos and Cambodia, US strategy paid much less respect to the norm.

This brings us to the question of how much legitimacy is required. There is a tendency to view legitimacy in zero-sum terms whereby governments or their actions are portrayed as either legitimate or illegitimate. This, of course, is misleading. Because legitimacy is inherently social, it is almost always relative. It is rare that a government or action is judged to be legitimate or illegitimate by everyone, or even by every government. Certainly, none of the episodes of mass killing examined in this book were so judged. There were always some governments willing to validate, excuse, or tolerate mass killing, just as there were others prepared to condemn and punish it. We need to talk, therefore, in terms of degrees of legitimacy. Accepting this point brings us to the question of *how much* legitimacy perpetrators require in order for them to be persuaded that mass atrocities are a viable and cost-effective option. In the timeframe covered by this book, perpetrators were never likely to persuade everyone (or even all other governments) that their mass atrocities were legitimate. Indeed, given the importance of prior social relations in shaping legitimacy judgements, it is likely that in each case some governments may have accepted almost any justificatory argument presented by their friends regardless of its merits, whilst others would have condemned almost any argument, no matter how plausible, uttered by their enemies. If, as I suggested earlier, governments are interested in securing legitimacy in order to reduce the anticipated costs associated with violating civilian immunity, there is likely to be no need for them to persuade everyone of their case. We might therefore talk in terms of perpetrators wanting *sufficient legitimacy*. This might be measured in two ways. Most obviously, we might ask how widespread is the international support or condemnation of perpetrators. Of course, it is not just the number of supporters or critics that matters, but their relative power—the support of the USA or Soviet Union during the Cold War might have been worth more to some perpetrators than the opinions of the rest of international society combined. The degree of legitimacy also matters. There is a big gap between a government validating an argument and thereby legitimizing a practice and condemning or punishing that practice because it judges that it violates a cherished norm and there are many possible types of response in between these two poles. Governments could acknowledge that a behaviour might violate the norm but choose to excuse or tolerate the behaviour. It excuses the behaviour when it acknowledges that the norm has been violated but points to extenuating circumstances to mitigate criticism or punishment. Both the Carter and Reagan administrations did this to some extent in relation to Latin America. Governments tolerate a behaviour when they acknowledge that the norm has been violated but fail to criticize it, though without trying to excuse the perpetrators. The West's response to the 'Katyn massacre' of Polish officers and the post-war killing of Cossacks and other returnees by the Soviet Union are good examples. Measuring legitimacy overall therefore requires complex judgements about the width and depth of legitimation. What perpetrators require, and tend to make judgements about prior to committing mass atrocities, is sufficient legitimacy—a sufficiently wide and deep degree of legitimacy to avoid the imposition of transaction costs they judge to be excessively high. Just how much legitimacy is sufficient is, of course, context-dependent. At one extreme, I argued that during the Cold War, client states that perpetrated mass atrocities effectively had a constituency of one. Latin American states needed only to persuade the USA of their cause and communist states only the Soviet Union in order to win the support of a sufficiently large bloc of international society.

Acknowledging the role that context plays in shaping the politics of legitimacy helps to explain how some perpetrators continued to secure sufficient legitimacy for mass atrocities even after civilian immunity became embedded as a norm in international society. We can see this perhaps most clearly in the persistence of selective extermination as a viable anti-civilian ideology well into the twentieth century. With their roots in European colonialism, ideologies of selective extermination rejected the universality of civilian immunity and insisted that certain groups were beyond protection, whether because of their race, class, political views, or some other marker. Because they rejected universalism, these ideologies were effectively closed moral systems, appealing only to their 'in-group' for legitimacy—white Europeans in the case of colonialism, Aryans and other preferred races in the case of Nazism, the working class in the case of Stalinism, poor peasants in the case of Maoism, Khmer peasants in the Khmer Rouge's case, and Muslim fundamentalists in the case of Al Qaeda. The capacity of these actors to secure sufficient legitimacy by reference to selective extermination was therefore heavily influenced by the material power of the 'in-group'. European colonialism sustained its ideology of selective extermination for a century and the ideology helped legitimize countless mass atrocities largely because of the preponderance of power held by Europeans and the strength of consensus within that community about European racial superiority. Despite the incorporation of civilian immunity into international law in the immediate aftermath of the Second World War, Stalinism continued to articulate an ideology of selective extermination and secure sufficient legitimacy for its mass atrocities. Only Stalin's death and the new Soviet leadership's change of course—itself a product of domestic considerations not themselves related to civilian immunity—brought an end to selective extermination in the Soviet Union. Until then, contextual factors including the West's preference for Stalin over Hitler, uncertainty about the facts surrounding reports about mass killing, the Second World War alliance, and the Soviet Union's emergence from the war as a superpower had helped sustain sufficient legitimacy for Soviet mass killing. To the extent that the Khmer Rouge succeeded in securing sufficient legitimacy—and it is worth remembering that without Vietnam's widely condemned intervention it would in all likelihood have remained in power well after 1979—the Khmer Rouge's ideology of selective extermination played no role whatsoever. No government or outside actor validated the Khmer Rouge's arguments yet many Western and Southeast Asian governments were prepared to forge diplomatic ties with it and supply it with diplomatic and material support after their ousting by Vietnam. The key factor here was that these same actors saw the Khmer Rouge as a balance to Vietnamese hegemony in Indochina. Domestic politics and the decline of the material power of its principal adherents did most to rid the world of its three bloodiest forms of selective extermination—colonialism, Nazism/fascism, and communism.

The first few historical chapters charted the gradual demise of necessity and selective extermination as viable counterweights to civilian immunity, but this relationship formed only part of the story. This was because perpetrators were sometimes still able to secure sufficient legitimacy for mass atrocities without appealing to anti-civilian ideologies. Indeed, barely any non-communist perpetrators did appeal to anti-civilian ideologies after 1945. Instead, they tried to manipulate the context in order to avoid responsibility for violating civilian immunity. As I noted earlier, actors do not judge legitimacy claims in a vacuum. How they perceive a situation influences how they respond. All other things being equal, absent plausible anti-civilian ideologies, external actors are much more likely to criticize or punish obvious violations of civilian immunity committed by identifiable perpetrators than they are when uncertainty remains about the nature of the situation. Perceptions are most immediately shaped by the explanations proffered by the perpetrators and their relation to the *reported facts* of the case at the time. Outsiders are unlikely to adopt strong positions when faced with incomplete, inconsistent, or uncertain information unless such a position corresponds closely with existing preferences, interests, and future expectations. As such, incomplete information and unclear interpretations of the situation, aided by factors such as geographical remoteness, contexts of war, or generalized chaos, and tight government restrictions and censorship of the media, sometimes granted perpetrators sufficient latitude to create uncertainty. Uncertainty about the facts was evident in many of the cases where mass killing was not widely criticized or punished. For example, the land reform, Great Leap, and Cultural Revolution massacres in China, and the massacres of suspected communists in Indonesia. Conversely, extensive reporting and the dissemination and proper analysis of accurate information reduced the range of plausible justifications that are available to the perpetrators and increases the likelihood of third-party criticism and punishment.[1] Extensive, almost real-time, reporting of the 1989 Beijing massacre and 1999 ethnic cleansing of Kosovar Albanians quickly dispelled the veracity of the perpetrators' arguments.

Perpetrators can play an important part in shaping perceptions to their advantage and, beginning with the UK and the USA during the Second World War, they have tended to prefer to create and leverage uncertainty in order to claim that their behaviour was consistent with the norm of civilian immunity rather than try to justify such violations. During the Second World War, the British and American governments justified the intentional bombing of German and Japanese civilians by arguing that civilians were not the actual targets of attack, a position that both governments knew to be inaccurate. Rather than justify mass atrocities, perpetrators argued—among other things—that massacre reports were false, that the victims were not civilians, that civilians were not killed deliberately, and that undeniable massacres were committed by 'rogue elements' or uncontrollable militia. Sometimes, of course, perpetrators used more than one of these arguments, hoping that a combination of arguments would prove more effective, and augmented them with arguments designed to denigrate the legitimacy of the victims or that of those who presented evidence of massacres. The very fact that these arguments so often succeeded in securing sufficient legitimacy for mass atrocities is testament to the capacity of the context to shape the politics of legitimacy.

[1] See Gary J. Bass, *Freedom's Battle: The Origins of Humanitarian Intervention* (New York: Alfred A. Knopf, 2008), pp. 25–38.

The context sometimes worked against putative perpetrators. The US Administration endured stinging criticism for its *Linebacker* operations over Vietnam even though these operations were almost certainly compliant with civilian immunity. International responses to communist China's various massacres are also instructive in this regard. Although the death toll from the 1989 Beijing massacre was tiny by Chinese standards up to that point, the regime was much more sharply criticized for this massacre than it had been for much larger episodes of mass killing in earlier decades. It was also punished with economic sanctions. The principal reasons for the stark differences between international society's responses to Chinese massacres were contextual. Whereas earlier massacres were poorly reported, often portrayed as communist in-fighting, and were outweighed as a policy priority by strategic considerations, the 1989 massacre was graphically reported in real-time, involved the killing of unarmed student protestors by soldiers, and occurred in a geopolitical context characterized by Western ascendancy and much reduced Cold War tension.

Combined with the steady strengthening of civilian immunity evidenced by the proliferation of institutions, laws, and practices intended to give effect to the norm, these changes to the international context made it more difficult—but not impossible—for perpetrators to secure sufficient legitimacy for mass atrocities in the post-Cold War era. There remained opportunities for perpetrators to create and leverage uncertainty and concerns about the violation of civilian immunity continued to co-habit with other interests and policy priorities. Moreover, as I argued in the previous chapter, the demise of anti-civilian ideologies was far from permanent. The rise of Al Qaeda showed the potential for new ideologies of selective extermination to arise. A smarter terrorist leadership might have proven more effective in securing legitimacy for Islamist mass atrocities, and may do so yet. Aspects of the US response to the Islamist threat showed that even governments that have made some strides towards internalizing civilian immunity might—in the right circumstances—be encouraged to revert to necessity arguments. Had Al Qaeda killed 30,000 or 300,000 Americans, how much more purchase would those necessity based arguments for sidelining civilian immunity have secured? Whilst the world's rhetorical commitment to civilian immunity is strong, the norm is both relatively recent and relatively fragile. It is also, evidently, subject to repeated challenges.

There are some important lessons here for those interested in strengthening civilian immunity and preventing future mass killing. Two stand out. First, *the dissemination, analysis, and interpretation of information is vitally important.* The first step to criticizing, punishing and deterring perpetrators is the early and proper identification of mass killing and the global dissemination of this analysis. I argued that one of the principal reasons why it became more difficult for perpetrators to get away with violating the norm of civilian immunity was the strengthening of global communications. Especially once anti-civilian ideologies proved insufficient as grounds for justifying mass atrocities, this played an important role in reducing the capacity of perpetrators to create and leverage uncertainty in order to portray their behaviour as being consistent with the norm. But although the reporting of atrocities improved significantly during the period covered by this book, the degree and quality of reporting remained geographically patchy and analytical capacity weak. As a result, for all the talk about the 24/7 global news cycle, uncertainty about the facts (i.e. were civilians being massacred?) and how to interpret them remained an important factor in many post-Cold War cases, including the Rwandan genocide and post-genocide massacres, Chechnya, and US conduct in Fallujah. There are a number of measures that might be taken to address these problems. In the short term, individual states and international institutions such as the UN could strengthen their analytical capacity to ensure that decision-makers are presented with timely and accurate assessments of situations that involve the violation of civilian immunity.

In relation to the UN, one of the most promising developments was the General Assembly's decision in late 2010 to strengthen the Office of the Special Adviser for the Prevention of Genocide (OSAPG) by granting it a role in early warning and assessment and expanding its mandate to include mass atrocities. An atrocity-specific office such as the OSAPG could be well placed to provide timely analysis of on-going situations and recommend strategies for mitigating the risks. The OSAPG participates in the UN's decision-making about conflict prevention, could engage in dialogue with relevant member states and regional arrangements, and provide advice directly to both the Secretary-General and, through him, to the Security Council. Where atrocities are judged to have occurred, the OSAPG might be charged with providing information and coordinating an integrated system-wide UN response. This could go a long way towards closing some of the information gaps that occasionally give leeway to the perpetrators of mass atrocities.

There are also steps that national governments might take to strengthen their own analytical capacity. National governments could give effect to their international commitments to prevent and punish genocide and uphold the Responsibility to Protect (RtoP) principle discussed in Chapter 1 by mainstreaming atrocity prevention and response into national policy. A useful starting point is a 2010 proposal by the Global Centre for RtoP, for governments to appoint national focal points for mass atrocity prevention and response. Among other things, national focal points could:

- provide early analysis of emerging situations;
- provide advice directly to the executive about matters relating to the prevention of genocide and mass atrocities;
- coordinate national responses to mass atrocities—thereby providing an atrocity lens to national decision-making;

- spearhead cooperation with the OSAPG and other relevant agencies and offices;
- help foster international consensus on the results of early analysis;
- make it possible for governments to respond to mass atrocities in a timely and decisive fashion;
- collaborate with other national focal points.[2]

Responding to findings by the Genocide Prevention Task Force, the Obama Administration in the USA appointed David Pressman as Director for War Crimes Atrocities and Civilian Protection within the Office of the National Security Advisor.[3] Denmark and Australia followed suit. Although a modest first step, the appointment of national focal points creates the potential for governments to strengthen their own analytical capacity, helping to further reduce the information gap and ensure that the imperative to uphold civilian immunity gets a serious airing in national policy debates.

Of course, whilst increments to global communications and analytical capacity will make it more difficult for perpetrators to create and leverage uncertainty, it will only indirectly affect their capacity to secure sufficient legitimacy from great and powerful friends, escape punishment on the grounds of their relative legitimacy, or attempt to revive an anti-civilian ideology. The key to overcoming these potential sources of legitimacy lies in *persuading international society to act to protect its shared norms from grave violations*. In relation to the norm of civilian immunity, the most promising avenue lies with the implementation of the Responsibility to Protect (RtoP).

Few would disagree with the proposition that RtoP has become a prominent feature in international debates about preventing genocide and mass atrocities and protecting the intended victims. Adopted unanimously by Heads of State and Government at the 2005 UN World Summit, it has been reaffirmed twice since by the UN Security Council and the General Assembly has agreed to give the principle its continuing consideration (see Chapter 1). Indeed, the aforementioned strengthening of the OSAPG came as part of this on-going consideration. In 2011, the UN Security Council specifically referred to the concept when authorizing the use of force to protect civilians in Libya (Resolution 1973). RtoP's capacity to inhibit the protection of perpetrators of mass killing by their powerful friends is intimately connected to the question of whether it is a norm and, if it is, what sort of norm it is? If RtoP is a norm, it stands to reason that this will make it more difficult for states to protect their allies when

[2] Global Centre for the Responsibility to Protect, 'Fulfilling the Responsibility to Protect: Strengthening Our Capacities to Prevent and Halt Mass Atrocities', meeting summary, 24 September 2010.

[3] Genocide Prevention Task Force, *Preventing Genocide: A Blueprint for US Policymakers* (Washington, DC: American Academy of Diplomacy, US Holocaust Memorial Museum, and USIP, 2008).

they commit mass atrocities. Whilst there is a wide consensus that RtoP is a norm, there is much less agreement about what sort of norm it is.[4] There are two elements to this particular problem. First, RtoP is not a single norm but a collection of shared expectations which have different qualities. On the one hand, RtoP involves expectations about how states relate to populations under their care. These expectations derive from civilian immunity and as such predate RtoP and are embedded in international humanitarian and human rights law.[5] Although there are arguments at the margins about their scope (especially concerning crimes against humanity) and the extent to which they are embedded or internalized (this book suggests that, at the time of writing, civilian immunity is more embedded than internalized), the basic proposition that states are legally and morally required to not intentionally kill civilians is well established.[6] RtoP's first pillar, the notion that states have a responsibility to protect their own populations, is therefore best understood as a reaffirmation and codification of already existing norms, including civilian immunity.

RtoP also places demands on states as members of international society. Not least, it requires them to assist and encourage their peers in the fulfilment of their responsibilities (pillar two) and to take timely and decisive action in cases where a state has manifestly failed in its duty to protect populations from genocide, war crimes, ethnic cleansing, and crimes against humanity (pillar three). Obviously, this should rule out protecting one's friends, allies, or acquaintances from international censure and punishment when they commit mass atrocities. But it is much less certain that this aspect of RtoP constitutes a norm and, if it can be so-called, there remains a serious question as to whether it is sufficiently determinate to exert compliance-pull that would alter state behaviour in this regard.[7] After all, as with the norm of civilian immunity, the manner in which RtoP influences state behaviour is heavily influenced by contextual factors.

The test of whether this second element of RtoP has become a norm is the extent to which there is a *shared expectation* that governments will exercise

[4] E.g. on RtoP as a norm, see Evans, *Responsibility to Protect*, p. 55; Ramesh Thakur, 'Goals and Action', *Ottawa Citizen*, 15 February 2008 (at http://www.canada.com/ottawacitizen/news/opinion/story.html?id=83ab727c-430b-4507-b2b0-ffcf96d93a19); and Teresa Chataway, 'Towards Normative Consensus on Responsibility to Protect', *Griffith Law Review*, 16 (1) 2007.

[5] As the Secretary-General noted. Ban Ki-Moon, *Implementing the Responsibility to Protect: Report of the Secretary-General*, A/63/677, 12 January, para. 13. See William Schabas, *Genocide in International Law: The Crimes of Crimes* (Cambridge: Cambridge University Press, 2000); and Yoram Dinstein, *The Conduct of Hostilities under the Law of International Armed Conflict*. Cambridge: Cambridge University Press, 2004).

[6] See Ward Thomas, *Ethics of Destruction: Norms and Force in International Relations* (Ithaca: Cornell University Press, 2001); Hugo Slim, *Killing Civilians: Method, Madness and Morality in War* (New York: Columbia University Press, 2008).

[7] See Thomas Franck, *The Power of Legitimacy Among Nations* (New York: Oxford University Press, 1990), p. 49.

their responsibility to criticize and sometimes punish perpetrators of mass atrocities even when it is not convenient for them to do so. There is some evidence to support the view that a duty to prevent mass killing is gradually emerging. In the case of *Bosnia vs. Serbia*, which concerned Serbia's alleged responsibility for genocide in Bosnia, the International Court of Justice found that states have a legal obligation to take all measures reasonably available to them to prevent genocide. Moreover, as well as prohibiting the intentional killing of civilians, International Humanitarian Law requires that states 'ensure respect' for the law. Moreover, the International Law Commission's Draft Articles on the Responsibility of States for Internationally Wrongful Acts give states a duty to cooperate to bring an end to breaches of the law. Finally, the UN recognized its failure to prevent the Rwandan genocide as a failure of the whole UN system—implicitly recognizing a collective responsibility to prevent genocide, intervene to protect the victims, and/or punish the perpetrators.[8] But translating these isolated findings into a general duty to criticize and punish perpetrators of mass killing requires a very liberal interpretation of the law.[9] Also, the case history documented in the previous chapters suggests that mutual recognition of such a duty is inconsistent at best.

Even if we can say that RtoP gives states a theoretical duty to criticize and punish perpetrators irrespective of their allegiances or preferences, the norm's capacity to impel this behaviour is fundamentally weakened by the problem of indeterminacy which leaves it as exposed to the vagaries of context as civilian immunity itself. Whilst norms shape shared understandings and can in some circumstances limit the behaviours that can be justified by reference to them, what a norm prescribes in a certain situation is never fixed or absolute. The more precisely a norm indicates the behaviour it expects in a given situation, the stronger its compliance pull.[10] Civilian immunity, for example, is a highly determinate norm: it demands that states refrain from deliberately killing civilians. Despite this clarity, actors still argue about whether civilians were being killed at a particular time and place, whether their deaths were

[8] See Edward C. Luck, 'The United Nations and the Responsibility to Protect', Policy Analysis Brief for the Stanley Foundation, August, p. 5; International Law Commission (ILC), Draft Articles on the Responsibility of States for Internationally Wrongful Acts, 2001 (available at http://untreaty.un.org/ilc/texts/instruments/english/commentaries/9_6_2001.pdf); Louise Arbour, 'The Responsibility to Protect as a Duty of Care in International Law and Practice', *Review of International Studies* 34(3), 2008, pp. 445–58; and A/CN.4/553, para. 10.

[9] Jose E. Alvarez, 'The Schizophrenias of RtoP', Panel Presentation at the 2007 Hague Joint Conference on Contemporary Issues of International Law: Criminal Jurisdiction 100 Years After the 1907 Hague Peace Conference, The Hague, The Netherlands, 30 June 2007, p. 12 (http://www.asil.org/pdfs/RtoPPanel.pdf); and Jerry Fowler, 'A New Chapter of Irony: The Legal Definition of Genocide and the Implications of Powell's Determination', in Samuel Totten and Eric Markusen (eds), *Genocide in Darfur: Investigating the Atrocities in the Sudan* (London: Routledge, 2006), p. 131.

[10] Franck, *Power of Legitimacy*, p. 52.

deliberate, and who was responsible. By comparison to civilian immunity, the demands imposed on international society by RtoP are highly indeterminate. In this context, it is rarely clear precisely what the RtoP requires in a given situation. This is partly because of the indeterminacy of the norm itself and partly due to the inevitable effects of contextual factors in shaping the way that different actors interpret cases and arrive at judgements about the most prudential courses of action. The indeterminacy of what RtoP requires in specific cases weakens its compliance-pull because it is difficult to know with any certainty what is required and therefore the extent to which actors are satisfying shared expectations of appropriate behaviour. Of course, as Quentin Skinner argued, actors 'cannot hope to stretch the application of the existing principles indefinitely; correspondingly, [the actor] can only hope to legitimate a restricted range of actions'.[11] It is fair to say, therefore, that active support for perpetrators or complete and disinterested inaction in the face of clear and undisputed evidence of mass atrocities would be obviously inconsistent with RtoP, partly explaining why it has become more difficult to get away with mass murder. But usually the facts of the case are open to dispute and indeed are disputed. The advent of global communications has not remedied this problem. Among the more recent cases examined in this book, the US government and *al Jazeera* gave very different accounts of what happened in Fallujah; until recently, the UN's account of post-genocide killings in Rwanda was very different to that offered by Médecins sans Frontières; the Russian government provided a different assessment of events in Chechnya to that given by sections of the Russian media and the Russian NGO, Memorial. Even when there is complete agreement about what is happening it is one thing for states to agree that civilians ought not be deliberately killed and something else entirely for them to agree to not excuse or tolerate violations of civilian immunity or agree on what should be done to criticize or punish perpetrators and protect the victims.

Thus, whilst RtoP certainly represents the most promising avenue for addressing the problem of states placing their interests, preferences, and sympathies ahead of their commitment to civilian immunity in the way they respond to grave violations of the norm, the principle remains vulnerable to the same challenges that bedevil civilian immunity. We can hope that, over time, RtoP will create shared expectations that make it more difficult—but probably not impossible—for states to protect others from censure when they violate civilian immunity. To achieve this, it will be necessary to maintain forward momentum in giving institutional meaning to the norm whilst protecting its greatest asset—the global consensus that underpins it.

[11] Quentin Skinner, 'Some Problems in the Analysis of Political Thought and Action, *Political Theory*, 2 (3) 1974, p. 117.

In the final analysis, mass atrocities persist and their perpetrators sometimes go unpunished, despite a deep consensus that such atrocities are gravely wrong, because a politically significant part of international society privileges other concerns above the defence of civilian immunity. This constituency is not evident in every case and its identity changes from case to case. States that lead international demands to punish some perpetrators are sometimes the very states that protect others from punishment. The privileging of other concerns over the defence of civilian immunity became more difficult to sustain in the first part of the twentieth century when anti-civilian ideologies became markedly less plausible as sources of legitimacy for mass killing. It became more difficult still towards the end of the century due to the strengthening of global communications that lifted some of the veil of uncertainty which often protected perpetrators from opprobrium, the lessening of Cold War rivalries shifted global priorities and reoriented patterns of amity and enmity, and the embedding and, in some places, internalizing of civilian immunity. But the capacity of context to determine how actors interpret and respond to mass atrocities means that it is still not impossible to get away with mass atrocities. This is at least partly why some governments and non-government actors continue see mass atrocities as a viable strategic path. What is more, although it is deeply embedded as a norm of international society, civilian immunity is not yet widely internalized by governments. Governments and others will, periodically, try to revive the anti-civilian ideologies or create entirely new ideologies to compete with civilian immunity. What is needed, therefore, is a persistent and determined politics that demands compliance with civilian immunity and denies honour to those who fail to act to defend humanity's cherished shared norms.

# *Bibliography*


Adams, Nina S. and Alfred W. McCoy (eds) (1970), *Laos: War and Revolution* (New York: Harper & Row).

Adams, William C. (ed.) (1982), *Television Coverage of International Affairs* (Norwood, NJ: Ablex).

Adas, Michael (1979), *Prophets of Rebellion: Millenarian Protest Movements against the European Colonial Order* (Chapel Hill: University of North Carolina Press).

Africa Watch (1992), *Rwanda: Talking Peace and Waging War. Human Rights Since the October 1990 Invasion*, 27 February.

Ahmed, Ishtiaq (1987), *The Concept of an Islamic State: An Analysis of the Ideological Controversy in Pakistan* (London: Pinter).

Ajami, Fouad (1989), *The Arab Predicament: Arab Political Thought Since 1967* (New York: Cambridge University Press).

Akçam, Taner (2004), *From Empire to Republic: Turkish Nationalism and the Armenian Genocide* (London: Zed Books).

——(2006), *A Shameful Act: The Armenian Genocide and the Question of Turkish Responsibility* (New York: Metropolitan Books).

Al-Zayyat, Montasser (2004), *The Road to Al-Qaeda: The Story of Bin Laden's Right Hand Man* (London: Pluto Press).

Aldrich, George H. (2000), 'The Laws of War on Land', *American Journal of International Law*, 94 (1).

Aldrich, Robert and Martyn Lyons (eds) (1999), *The Sphinx in the Tuileries and other Essays in Modern French History* (Sydney: University of Sydney).

Alexander, Don W. (1985), *Rod of Iron: French Counterinsurgency Policy in Aragon During the Peninsular War* (Washington, Delaware: Scholarly Resources Inc.).

Alexander, Yonah and Kenneth A. Myers (eds) (1982), *Terrorism in Europe* (London: Croom Helm).

——and Dennis A. Pluchinsky (eds) (1992), *Europe's Red Terrorists: The Fighting Communist Organizations* (London: Frank Cass).

——and Michael S. Swetnam (2001), *Usama Bin Laden's Al-Qaida: Profile of a Terrorist Network* (New York: Transnational Publishers).

Alexandrowicz-Alexander and Charles Henry (1954), 'The Legal Position of Tibet', *American Journal of International Law*, 48 (2).

Alexseev, Mikhail A. (ed.) (1999), *Center–Periphery Conflict in Post-Soviet Russia* (New York: St. Martin's Press).

Allen, Garland E. (1983), 'The Misuse of Biological Hierarchies: The American Eugenics Movement, 1900–1940', *History and Philosophy of the Life Sciences*, 5 (2).

Allen, Thomas B. and Norman Polmar (1995), *Code-Name Downfall: The Secret Plan to Invade Japan—and Why Truman Dropped the Bomb* (New York: Simon & Schuster).

Allman, T. D. (1970), 'Laos: The Labyrinthine War', *Far Eastern Economic Review*, 12 March.

Alperovitz, Ger (1965), *Atomic Diplomacy: Hiroshima and Potsdam* (New York: Simon and Schuster).

Alvarez, Jose E. (2007), 'The Schizophrenias of RtoP', Panel Presentation at the 2007 Hague Joint Conference on Contemporary Issues of International Law: Criminal Jurisdiction 100 Years After the 1907 Hague Peace Conference, The Hague, The Netherlands, 30 June.

Americas Watch and American Civil Liberties Union (1982), *Report on Human Rights in El Salvador* (New York: Vintage Books).

Amnesty International (1983), *Annual Report 1983* (London: Amnesty).

——(1984), *Annual Report 1984* (London: Amnesty).

——(2001), *Democratic Republic of Congo: Rwandese-controlled East: Devastating Human Toll*, London: Amnesty, 19 June.

Anderson, David L. (ed.) (1998), *Facing My Lai: Moving Beyond the Massacre* (Lawrence: University Press of Kansas).

Anderson, M. S. (1966), *The Eastern Question 1774–1923* (London: Macmillan).

Anderson, Rachel (2005), 'Redressing Colonial Genocide Under International Law: The Hereros' Cause of Action Against Germany', *California Law Review*, 93 (4).

Andreopoulos, George J. (ed.) (1997), *Genocide: Conceptual and Historical Dimensions* (Philadelphia: University of Pennsylvania Press).

Anstey, Roger (1966), *King Leopold's Legacy: The Congo Under Belgian Rule 1908–1960* (Oxford: Oxford University Press).

Arbour, Louise (2008), 'The Responsibility to Protect as a Duty of Care in International Law and Practice', *Review of International Studies*, 34 (3).

Arendt, Hannah (1951), *The Origins of Totalitarianism* (New York: Schocken).

——(1994), *Eichmann in Jerusalem: A Report on the Banality of Evil* (London: Penguin).

Armstrong, Karen (2000), *The Battle for God* (New York: Alfred A. Knopf).

Armstrong, Robert and Janet Shenk (1982), *El Salvador: The Face of Revolution* (Boston: South End Press).

Arnold, Henry H. and Ira C. Eaker (1941), *Winged Warfare* (New York: Harper and Brothers).

Arnson, Cynthia (1982), *El Salvador: A Revolution Confronts the United States* (Washington, DC: Institute for Policy Studies).

Ashe, Robert Pickering (1971), *Chronicles of Uganda*, 2nd edn (London: Frank Cass).

Ashley, Evelyn (1876), *The Life of Henry John Temple, Viscount Palmerston*, Vol. 1 (London: R. Bentley and Son).

Atwan, Abdel Bari (2006), *The Secret History of al Qaeda* (Berkeley, CA: University of California Press).

Autusserre, Severine (2010), *The Trouble with the Congo: Local Violence and the Failure of International Peacebuilding* (Cambridge: Cambridge University Press).

Avni, Haim (1982), *Spain, the Jews and Franco* (Philadelphia: Jewish Publication Society of America).

Baeur, Yahuda (1982), *History of the Holocaust* (New York: Franklin Watts).

Bailey, Paul J. (2001), *China in the Twentieth Century* (Oxford: Wiley-Blackwell).

Bain, Will (2003), *Between Anarchy and Society: Trusteeship and the Obligations of Power* (Oxford: Oxford University Press).

Baker, Keith Michael (ed.) (1994), *The French Revolution and the Creation of Modern Political Culture*, Vol. IV: *The Terror* (Oxford: Pergamon Press).
Balakian, Krikoris (1977), *Hai Koghkotan* (Beirut: Plenetta Printing).
Balakian, Peter (2004), *The Burning Tigris: The Armenian Genocide and America's Response* (New York: Perennial).
Ban Ki-moon (2009), *Implementing the Responsibility: Report of the Secretary-General*, A/63/677, 12 January.
Bar, Shmuel (2006), *Warrant for Terror: Fatwas of Radical Islam and the Duty of Jihad* (Lanham: Rowman and Littlefield).
Baranowski, Shelley (2011), *Nazi Empire: German Colonialism and Imperialism from Bismarck to Hitler* (Cambridge: Cambridge University Press).
Barker, J. Ellis (1920), 'Germany, Turkey and the Armenian Massacres', *Quarterly Review*, 233.
Barkin, J. Samuel (2010), *Realist Constructivism* (Cambridge: Cambridge University Press).
Barnett, A. Doak (1964), *Communist China: The Early Years, 1949–1955* (London: Pall Mall).
Barnett, Michael (2002), *Eyewitness to a Genocide: The United Nations and Rwanda* (Ithaca: Cornell University Press).
——and Raymond Duvall (eds) (2005), *Power in Global Governance* (Cambridge: Cambridge University Press).
Barnett, Robert (ed.) (1994), *Resistance and Reform in Tibet* (London: Hurst and Co.).
Barrett, Nicole (2001), 'Holding Individual Leaders Responsible for Violations of Customary International Law: The US Bombardment of Cambodia and Laos', *Columbia Human Rights Law Review*, 32.
Barry, Michael (1982–83), 'Statement to the Bar Association, 28 January 1983', *World Affairs*, 145 (3).
Bartov, Omer (1998), 'Defining Enemies, Making Victims: Germans, Jews and the Holocaust', *The American Historical Review*, 103 (3).
Bas, Natana DeLong (2004), *Wahhabi Islam: From Revival and Reform to Global Jihad* (New York: Oxford University Press).
Bass, Gary J. (2008), *Freedom's Battle: The Origins of Humanitarian Intervention* (New York: Alfred A. Knopf).
Baum, Richard (1994), *Burying Mao: Chinese Politics in the Age of Deng Xiaoping* (Princeton: Princeton University Press).
Bauman, Zygmunt (1989), *Modernity and the Holocaust* (Ithaca: Cornell University Press).
Beattie, John (1960), *Bunyoro: An African Kingdom* (New York: Holt, Rinehart and Winston).
Becker, Elizabeth (1998) *When the War was Over: Cambodia and the Khmer Rouge Revolution*, rev. edn (New York: Public Affairs).
Becker, J. (1996), *Hungry Ghosts* (New York: Free Press).
Beckett, Ian F. W. (2001), *Modern Insurgencies and Counter-Insurgencies: Guerrillas and their Opponents since 1750* (London: Routledge).
Beitz, C., M. Cohen, T. Scanlon, and A. J. Simmons (eds) (1990), *International Ethics: A Philosophy and Public Affairs Reader* (Princeton: Princeton University Press).

Bell, David A. (2001), 'Violence, Terror and War: A Comment on Arno Mayer's *The Furies*', *French Historical Studies*, 24 (4).

Bellamy, Alex J. (2002), *Kosovo and International Society* (London: Palgrave).

——(2009), 'Military Intervention' in Donald Bloxham and Dirk Moses (eds), *The Oxford Handbook of Genocide Studies* (Oxford: Oxford University Press).

——(2009), *Responsibility to Protect: The Global Effort to End Mass Atrocities* (Cambridge: Polity).

——(2011), 'Mass Atrocities and Armed Conflict: Links, Distinctions and Implications for the Responsibility to Protect', *Stanley Foundation Policy Analysis Brief*, January.

——and Paul D. Williams (2010), *Understanding Peacekeeping*, 2nd edn (Cambridge: Polity).

————(2012), 'On the Limits of Moral Hazard: Rebellion, Intervention and the Responsibility to Protect', *European Journal of International Relations*, 18 (3).

Benn, David Wedgwood (2006), 'On Comparing Nazism and Stalinism', *International Affairs*, 82 (1).

Berdal, Mats and Spyros Economides (eds) (2007), *United Nations Interventionism, 1991–2004* (Cambridge: Cambridge University Press).

Berenbaum, Michael and Abraham J. Peck (eds) (2002), *Holocaust and History: The Known, the Unknown, the Disputed, the Re-examined* (Bloomington: Indiana University Press with the US Holocaust Memorial Museum).

Bergerud, Eric M. (1991), *The Dynamics of Defeat: The Vietnam War in Hau Nghia Province* (Boulder: Westview).

Bernstein, Barton J. (ed.) (1970), *Politics and Policies of the Truman Administration* (Chicago: Quadrangle Books).

——(1976), *The Atomic Bomb: The Critical Issues* (Boston: Little, Brown).

——(1998), 'Truman and the A-Bomb: Targeting Noncombatants, Using the Bomb, and His Defending the "Decision"', *Journal of Military History*, 62 (3).

Best, Geoffrey (1980), *Humanity in Warfare: The Modern History of the International Law of Armed Conflict* (London: Weidenfeld and Nicolson).

——(1983), 'The Bishop and the Bomber', *History Today*, 33.

——(1994), *War and Law since 1945* (Oxford: Clarendon Press).

Bethell, Nicholas (1974), *The Last Secret: Forcible Repatriation to Russia 1944–47* (London: Andre Deutsch).

Biddle, Tami Davis (1999), 'Bombing by the Square Yard: Sir Arthur Harris at War: 1942–1945', *The International History Review*, 21 (3).

——(2002), *Rhetoric and Reality in Air Warfare: The Evolution of British and American Ideas about Strategic Bombing, 1914–1945* (Princeton: Princeton University Press).

——(2005), 'Sifting Dresden's Ashes', *The Wilson Quarterly*, 29 (2).

Binder, Martin (2009), 'Humanitarian Crises and the International Politics of Selectivity', *Human Rights Review*, 10.

Bird, Kai and Lawrence Lifschultz (eds) (1998), *Hiroshima's Shadow* (Stony Creek, Conn: Pamphleteer's Press).

Black, Jeremy (2005), *Introduction to Global Military History: 1775 to the Present* (London: Routledge).

Blair, Clay (1987), *The Forgotten War: America in Korea, 1950–1953* (New York: Times Books).

Blanchard, Christopher M. (2007), 'Al Qaeda: Statements and Evolving Ideology', Congressional Research Service report, 9 July.

Bland, Larry and Sharon Ritenour Stevens (eds) (1981), *The Papers of George Catlett Marshall*, Vol. II (Baltimore: Johns Hopkins University Press, 1981).

Blix, Hans (1979), 'Area Bombardment: Rules and Reasons', in *British Yearbook of International Law* (Oxford: Clarendon Press).

Bloxham, Donald (2005), *The Great Game of Genocide: Imperialism, Nationalism and the Destruction of the Ottoman Armenians* (Oxford: Oxford University Press).

——(2009), *The Final Solution: A Genocide* (Oxford: Oxford University Press).

Blum, William (2003), *Killing Hope: US Military and CIA Interventions since World War II* (London: Zed Books).

Bodansky, Yossef (2001), *Bin Laden: The Man Who Declared War on America* (New York: Random House).

Bond, Brian (1979), *Liddell Hart* (London: Cassell).

Bonney, Richard (2004), *Jihad: From Qur'an to bin Laden* (Basingstoke: Palgrave).

Boog, Horst (ed.) (1992), *The Conduct of the Air War in the Second World War* (Oxford: Berg).

Boulden, Jane and Thomas G. Weiss (eds) (2004), *Terrorism and the UN: Before and After September 11* (Bloomington: Indiana University Press).

Bouloiseau, Marc (1987), *The Jacobin Republic 1792–1794*, trans. Jonathan Mandelbaum (Cambridge: Cambridge University Press).

Bourgois, Philippe (2001), 'The Power of Violence in War and Peace: Post Cold War Lessons from El Salvador', *Ethnography*, 2 (1).

Bourke, Joanna (1999), *An Intimate History of Killing: Face-to-Face Killing in Twentieth Century Warfare* (London: Granta Books).

Boutros-Ghali, Boutros (1994), *Special Report of the UN Secretary-General on UNAMIR*, S/1994/470, 20 April.

——(1999), *Unvanquished: A US–UN Saga* (New York: Random House).

Brackman, Arnold C. (1969) *The Communist Collapse in Indonesia* (New York: W. W. Norton).

Bradsher, Harry S. (1999), *Afghan Communism and Soviet Intervention* (Oxford: Oxford University Press).

Brady, Christopher (1999), *United States Foreign Policy Towards Cambodia, 1977–1992: A Question of Realities* (London: Macmillan).

Braham, Randolph L. (1981), *The Politics of Genocide: The Holocaust in Hungary*, Vol. 1 (New York: Columbia University Press).

——(1994), *Tragedy of Romanian Jewry* (New York: Columbia University Press).

Brands, H. W. (1989), 'The Limits of Manipulation: How the United States Didn't Topple Sukarno', *The Journal of American History*, 76 (3).

Branfman, Fred (1972), *Voices from the Plain of Jars: Life Under an Air War* (New York: Harper & Row).

Bredvold, Louis and Ralph G. Ross (eds) (1960), *The Philosophy of Edmund Burke* (Ann Arbor: The University of Michigan Press).

Brekke, Torkel (ed.) (2006), *The Ethics of War in Asian Civilizations: A Comparative Perspective* (London: Routledge).

Bremer, L. Paul (2006), *My Year in Iraq: The Struggle to Build a Future of Hope* (New York: Simon and Schuster).

Brenet, A. (1902), *La France et l'Allemagne devant le droit international pendant les operations militaries de la guerre de 1870–1871* (Paris: A. Rousseau).

Brett-James, Antony (ed.) (1961), *Wellington at War 1794–1815: A Selection of His Wartime Letters* (London: Macmillan and Co.).

British War Office (1914), *Manual of Military Law* (London: War Office).

Brittain, James J. (2010), *Revolutionary Social Change in Colombia: The Origin and Direction of the FARC-EP* (London: Pluto).

Brittain, Vera et al. (1944), 'Massacre by Bombing', *Fellowship*, 10: 50–64.

Brittain, Victoria (1999), 'Colonialism and the Predatory State in the Congo', *New Left Review*, 236, July/August.

Browning, Christopher (1992), *The Path to Genocide: Essays on Launching the Final Solution* (Cambridge: Cambridge University Press).

Brugger, Bill (1981) *China: Liberation and Transformation 1942–1962* (London: Croom Helm).

Bruun, Geoffrey (1958), *Revolution and Reaction: 1848–1852* (New York: Van Nostrand).

Brym, Robert J. (1994), *The Jews of Moscow, Kiev and Minsk: Identity, Antisemitism, Emigration* (New York: New York University Press).

Brzezinski, Zbigniew (1956), *The Permanent Purge* (Cambridge, MA: Harvard University Press).

——(1983), *Power and Principle: Memoirs of the National Security Adviser 1977–1981* (London: Weidenfeld and Nicolson).

Buckley, John (1999), *Air Power in the Age of Total War* (Bloomington: Indiana University Press).

Bukovansky, Mlada (2002), *Legitimacy and Power Politics: The American and French Revolutions in International Political Culture* (Princeton, NJ: Princeton University Press).

Bullock, Alan (1962), *Hitler: A Study in Tyranny* (Harmondsworth: Penguin).

Bundy, McGeorge (1988), *Danger and Survival: Choices About the Bomb in the First Fifty Years* (New York: Random House).

Bunnell, Frederick (1990), 'Low Posture Policy Towards Indonesia in the Months Leading up to the 1965 Coup', *Indonesia*, 50.

Burke, Edmund (1987 [1790]). *Reflections on the Revolution in France*, ed. Conor Cruise O'Brien (London: Penguin).

Burke, Jason (2003), *Al-Qaeda: Casting a Shadow of Terror* (London: I. B. Tauris).

Burleigh, Michael and Wolfgang Wippermann (1991), *The Racial State: Germany 1933–1945* (Cambridge: Cambridge University Press).

Byers, Michael (2005), *War Law: International Law and Armed Conflict* (London: Atlantic Books).

Byrne, Hugh (1996), *El Salvador's Civil War: A Study of Revolution* (Boulder: Lynne Rienner).

Byung-joon Ahn (1976), *Chinese Politics and the Cultural Revolution: Dynamics of Policy Processes* (Seattle: University of Washington Press).

Calhoun, Craig (1994), *Neither Gods nor Emperors: Students and the Struggle for Democracy in China* (Berkeley: University of California Press).

Campbell, S. (1998), 'What Kabila is Hiding: Civilian Killings and Impunity in Congo', *Human Rights Watch*, 9 (October), 5a.

Cantor, Norman (1995), *The Sacred Chain: A History of the Jews* (London: Fontana).

Caridi, J. (1968), *The Korean War and American Politics: The Republican Party as a Case Study* (Philadelphia: University of Pennsylvania Press).

Carothers, Thomas (1991), *In the Name of Democracy: US Policy towards Latin America in the Reagan Years* (Berkeley: University of California Press).

Carpenter, Humphrey (ed.) (1995), *The Letters of J. R. R. Tolkien* (London: Harper Collins).

Carr, E. H. (1946), *The Twenty Years' Crisis 1919–1939* (London: Macmillan).

Carr, Matt (2008), 'The Barbarians of Fallujah', *Race & Class*, 50 (1).

Cattier, Felicien (2009, [1906]), *Etude sur la situation de l'etat indépendent du Congo* (Brussels: Kessinger Publications).

Central Intelligence Agency (1980), *Kampuchea: A Demographic Catastrophe*, National Foreign Assessment Centre, May.

Ceserani, David (1977), *Genocide and Rescue: The Holocaust in Hungary 1944* (Oxford: Berg).

——and Paul A. Levine (2002), *Bystanders to the Holocaust: A Re-Evaluation* (London: Frank Cass).

Chalk, Frank and Kurt Johanssohn (1990), *The History and Sociology of Genocide: Analyses and Case Studies* (New Haven: Yale University Press).

Chanda, Nayan (1986), *Brother Enemy: The War after the War* (New York: Harcourt Brace Jovanovich).

Chandler, David P. (1999), *Voices from S-21: Terror and History in Pol Pot's Secret Prison* (St. Leonards, UNSW: Allen and Unwin).

——, Ben Kiernan, and Anthony Barnett (eds) (1983), *Revolution and its Aftermath in Kampuchea: Eight Essays* (New Haven: Yale University Southeast Asian Studies).

————and Chanthou Boua (eds) (1988), *Pol Pot Plans the Future: Confidential Leadership Documents from Democratic Kampuchea, 1976–1977* (New Haven: Yale University Southeast Asia Studies).

Chang, Joseph (1973), *The North Korean Economy: Structure and Development* (Stanford, CA: Hoover Institution Press).

Chang, Jung (1992), *Wild Swans: Three Daughters of China* (London: Flamingo).

Charny, Israel (ed.) (1994), *The Widening Circle of Genocide: A Critical Bibliographic Review* (New Brunswick: Transaction).

Chary, Frederick B. (1972), *The Bulgarian Jews and the Final Solution, 1940–1944* (Pittsburgh: University of Pittsburgh Press).

Chataway, Teresa (2007), 'Towards Normative Consensus on Responsibility to Protect', *Griffith Law Review*, 16 (1).

Chayes, Abram and Antonia Handler Chayes (1995), *The New Sovereignty: Compliance with International Regulatory Agreements* (Cambridge, MA: Harvard University Press).

Checkel, Jeffrey (2001), 'Why Comply? Social Learning and European Identity Change', *International Organization*, 55 (3).

Chen Jian (2006), 'The Tibetan Rebellion of 1959 and China's Changing Relations with India and the Soviet Union', *Journal of Cold War Studies*, 8 (3).

Chen, Theodore H. E. (1967), *The Chinese Communist Regime: Documents and Commentary* (New York: Frederick A. Praeger).

Chesterman, Simon (2001), *Just War or Just Peace? Humanitarian Intervention and International Law* (Oxford: Oxford University Press).

Chickering, Roger and Stig Förster (eds) (2000), *Great War, Total War: Combat and Mobilization on the Western Front, 1914–1918* (Cambridge: Cambridge University Press).

——, Stig Förster, and Bernd Greiner (eds) (2005), *A World at Total War: Global Conflict and the Politics of Destruction, 1937–1945* (Cambridge: Cambridge University Press).

Chigas, George (2000), 'The Politics of Defining Justice After the Cambodian Genocide', *Journal of Genocide Research*, 2 (2).

Ching-wen Chow (1960), *Ten Years of Storm: The True Story of the Communist Regime in China* (New York: Holt, Rinehart and Winston).

Chirot, Daniel and Clark McCauley (2006), *Why Not Kill Them All? The Logic and Prevention of Political Mass Murder* (Princeton, NJ: Princeton University Press).

Chomsky, Noam and Edward Herman (1979), *After the Cataclysm: Postwar Indochina and the Reconstruction of Imperial Ideology* (Cambridge, MA: South End Press).

Christopher, Paul (1994), *The Ethics of War and Peace: An Introduction to Legal and Moral Issues* (Englewood Cliffs, NJ: Prentice Hall).

Churchill, Ward (1997), *A Little Matter of Genocide: Holocaust and Denial in the Americas from 1492 to the Present* (San Francisco, CA: City Light Books).

Churchill, Winston (1929), *The World Crisis*, Vol. 5: *The Aftermath* (London: Butterworth).

——(1948), *The Second World War*, Vols I–II (London: Cassell and Co.).

——(1953), *The Second World War*, Vol. VI: *Triumph and Tragedy* (Boston: Houghton Mifflin).

——(1966), *My Early Life 1874–1904* (London: Scribner).

Cienciala, Anna M., Natalia S. Lebedeva, and Wojciech Materski (eds) (2007), *Katyn: A Crime Without Punishment* (New Haven: Yale University Press).

Clark, Ian (2003), 'Legitimacy in a Global Order', *Review of International Studies*, 29: S1.

——(2005), *Legitimacy in International Society* (Oxford: Oxford University Press).

Clendenen, Clarence D. (1969), *Blood on the Border: The United States Army and the Mexican Irregulars* (New York: Macmillan).

Clodfelter, Mark (1989), *The Limits of Airpower: The American Bombing of North Vietnam* (New York: Free Press).

Clubb, O. Edmund (1978), *20th Century China*, 3rd edn (New York: Columbia University Press).

Coady, Tony and Michael O'Keefe (eds) (2002), *Terrorism and Justice: Moral Argument in a Threatened World* (Melbourne: Melbourne University Press).

Coates, W. P. and Zelda K. Coates (1944), *A History of Anglo-Soviet Relations* (London: Lawrence and Wishart).
Cobban, Alfred (1951), 'An Age of Revolutionary Wars: An Historical Parallel', *The Review of Politics*, 13 (2).
Cohen, Michael J. (1986), 'Churchill and the Jews: the Holocaust', *Modern Judaism*, 6 (1).
Coicaud, Jean Marc and Nicholas J. Wheeler (eds) (2008), *National Interest and International Solidarity: Particular and Universal Ethics in International Life* (Tokyo: UN University Press).
Coker, Christopher (2001), *Humane Warfare* (London: Routledge).
Colby, Elbridge (1927), 'How to Fight Savage Tribes', *American Journal of International Law*, 21 (2).
Cole, Wayne S. (1971), *America First: The Battle against Intervention 1940–1941* (New York: Octagon Books).
——(1971), *Charles A. Lindbergh and the Battle against American Intervention in World War II* (New York: Harcourt Brace Jovanovich).
Coleman, Katharina P. (2007), *International Organisations and Peace Enforcement* (Cambridge: Cambridge University Press).
Colville, Sir Henry (1895), *The Land of Nile Springs: Being Chiefly an Account of How we Fought Kabarega* (London: Edward Arnold).
Commission on Central America (led by Henry Kissinger) (1984), *The Report of the President's National Bipartisan Commission on Central America* (New York: Macmillan).
Commission of the Churches on International Affairs (1981), *El Salvador: One Year of Repression* (Geneva: World Council of Churches).
Connelly, Mark (2002), 'The British People, the Press and the Strategic Air Campaign Against Germany, 1939–1945', *Contemporary British History*, 16 (2).
Conquest, Robert (1970), *The Nation Killers: The Soviet Deportation of Nationalities* (London: Macmillan).
——(1978), *Kolyma: The Arctic Death Camps* (London: Macmillan).
——(1986), *The Harvest of Sorrow: Soviet Collectivization and the Terror-Famine* (New York: Oxford University Press).
——(1992), *The Great Terror: A Reassessment* (London: Pimlico).
Conrad, Joseph (1998), *The Heart of Darkness and Other Tales* (Oxford: Oxford University Press).
Conway-Lanz, Sahr (2005), 'Beyond No Gun Ri: Refugees and the United States Military in the Korean War', *Diplomatic History*, 29 (1).
——(2006), *Collateral Damage: Americans, Noncombatant Immunity and Atrocity after World War II* (New York: Routledge, 2006).
Cookey, S. J. S. (1964), 'Great Britain and the Congo Question, 1892–1913' (unpublished PhD thesis, University of London).
Cornwell, John (1999), *Hitler's Pope: The Secret History of Pius XII* (London: Viking).
Courtois, Stephane, Nicolas Werth, Jean-Louis Panne, Andrzej Paczkowski, Karel Bartosek, and Jean-Louis Margolin (1999), *The Black Book of Communism: Crimes, Terror, Repression* (Cambridge, MA: Harvard University Press).

Crane, Conrad C. (1999), 'Raiding the Beggar's Pantry: The Search for Airpower Strategy in the Korean War', *Journal of Military History*, 63 (4).

——(2000), *American Airpower Strategy in Korea, 1950–1953* (Lawrence: University Press of Kansas).

Crankshaw, Edward (ed.) (1971), *Khrushchev Remembers* (London: Sphere Books).

Crawford, James (2006), *The Creation of States in International Law*, 2nd edn (Oxford: Oxford University Press).

Crawford, Neta C. (2002), *Argument and Change in World Politics: Ethics, Decolonization and Humanitarian Intervention* (Cambridge: Cambridge University Press).

Crawley, C. W. (1930), *The Question of Greek Independence: A Study of British Policy in the Near East, 1821–1833* (Cambridge: Cambridge University Press).

Cribb, Robert (ed.) (1990), *The Indonesian Killings 1965–1966: Studies From Java and Bali* (Melbourne: Centre of Southeast Asian Studies, Monash).

——(2001), 'Genocide in Indonesia, 1965–1966', *Journal of Genocide Research*, 3 (2).

——and Colin Brown (1995), *Modern Indonesia: A History since 1945* (London: Longman).

Criddle, Joan D. and Teeda Butt Mam (1987), *To Destroy You is No Loss* (New York: Anchor).

Cronin, Isaac (ed.) (2002), *Confronting Fear: A History of Terrorism* (New York: Thunder's Mouth Press).

Crouch, Harold (1978), *The Army and Politics in Indonesia* (Ithaca: Cornell University Press).

Crummey, Donald (ed.) (1986), *Banditry, Rebellion and Social Protest in Africa* (London: James Currey).

Cumings, Bruce (1990), *The Origins of the Korean War*, Vol. II: *The Roaring of the Cataract, 1947–1950* (Princeton, NJ: Princeton University Press).

——(1997), *Korea's Place in the Sun: A Modern History* (New York: W. W. Norton and Co.).

Cuny, Frederick (1995), 'Killing Chechnya', *New York Review of Books*, 6 April.

Cutforth, Rene (1969), 'A Generation Ago', *The Listener*, 11 September.

d'Encausse, Hélène Carrère (1981), *Stalin: Order Through Terror* (London: Longman).

Dadrian, Vahakn H. (1994), 'A Review of the Main Features of the Genocide', *Journal of Political and Military Sociology*, 22 (1).

——(2003), 'The Signal Facts Surrounding the Armenian Genocide and the Turkish Denial Syndrome', *Journal of Genocide Research*, 5 (2).

——(2004), *Warrant for Genocide: Key Elements of the Turko-Armenian Conflict* (New Brunswick: Transaction Publishers).

Dakin, Douglas (1973), *The Struggle for Greek Independence 1821–1833* (London: B. T. Batsford).

Dalin, David G. (2005), *The Myth of Hitler's Pope: Pope Pius XII and His Secret War against Nazi Germany* (New York: Regnery Publishing).

Dallaire, Lt. Gen. Romeo (2004), *Shake Hands with the Devil: The Failure of Humanity in Rwanda* (London: Arrow Books).

Damrosch, Lori Fisler (1993), *Enforcing Restraint: Collective Intervention in Internal Conflicts* (New York: Council on Foreign Relations Press).

Danchev, Alex and Thomas Halverson (eds) (1996), *International Perspectives on the Yugoslav Conflict* (London: Macmillan).
Danner, Mark (1994), *The Massacre at El Mozote: A Parable of the Cold War* (New York: Vintage).
Davies, Joseph E. (1942), *Mission to Moscow: A Record of Confidential Dispatches to the State Department, Official and Personal Correspondence, Current Diary and Journal Entries, Including Notes and Comment up to October, 1941* (Sydney: Angus and Robertson).
Davies, Sara E. (2010), *Global Politics of Health* (Cambridge: Polity).
De Crespigny, Rafe (1992), *China this Century* (Melbourne: Oxford University Press).
De Cuellar, Javier Perez (1991), *Report of the Secretary-General on the Work of the Organization.*
De Jaegher, Raymond and Irene Corbally Kuhn (1952), *The Enemy Within: An Eyewitness Account of the Communist Conquest of China* (New York: Doubleday).
De Tocqueville, Alexis (1949), *The Recollections of Alexis de Tocqueville*, ed. J. P. Mayer and trans. A. D. de Mattos (New York: Harvill).
De Vattel, Emmerich (1916 [1758]), *The Law of Nations or the Principles of Natural Law Applied to the Conduct and to the Affairs of Nations and of Sovereigns*, trans. C. G. Fenwick (Washington, DC: Carnegie Institution).
De Waal, Alex and Bridget Conley-Zilkic (2006), 'Reflections on How Genocidal Killings are Brought to an End', *Social Science Research Council*, 22 December.
De Zeeuw, Jerden (ed.) (2008), *From Soldiers to Politicians: Transforming Rebel Movements after Civil War* (Boulder: Lynne Rienner).
Deitelhoff, Nicole (2009), The Discursive Process of Legalization: Charting Islands of Persuasion in the ICC Case', *International Organization*, 63 (2).
Del Boca, Angelo (1965), *The Ethiopian War 1935–1941* (Chicago: University of Chicago Press).
Dershowitz, Alan M. (2002), *Why Terrorism Works* (New Haven, CN: Yale University Press).
Des Forges, Alison (1999), *Leave None to Tell the Story: Genocide in Rwanda* (New York: Human Rights Watch).
Destexhe, Alain (1999), *Rwanda and Genocide in the Twentieth Century* (New York: New York University Press).
Detter De Lupis, Ingrid (1987), *The Law of War* (Cambridge: Cambridge University Press).
Didian, Joan (1983), *Salvador* (New York: Simon and Schuster).
Dietrich, Craig (1994), *People's China: A Brief History*, 2nd edn (New York: Oxford University Press).
Dikotter, Frank (2010), *Mao's Great Famine: The History of China's Most Devastating Catastrophe, 1958–1962* (London: Bloomsbury).
Diner, Dan (2008), *Cataclysms: A History of the Twentieth Century from Europe's Edge*, trans. William Templer with Joel Golb (Madison: University of Wisconsin Press).
Dinstein, Yoram (2004), *The Conduct of Hostilities under the Law of International Armed Conflict*. Cambridge: Cambridge University Press).
Doswald-Beck, Louise (1987), 'The Civilian in the Crossfire', *Journal of Peace Research*, 24 (3).

Douhet, Giulio (1942), *The Command of the Air*, trans. Dino Ferrari (New York: Coward McCann).

Downes, Alexander B. (2010), 'Review of Hugo Slim, *Innocent Civilians . . .*', *Journal of Strategic Studies*, 33 (1).

——(2008), *Targeting Civilians in War* (Ithaca: Cornell University Press).

Doyle, Michael W., Ian Johnstone, and Robert C. Orr (eds) (1997), *Keeping the Peace: Multidimensional UN Operations in Cambodia and El Salvador* (Cambridge: Cambridge University Press).

Drechsler, Horst (1980), *'Let Us Die Fighting': The Struggle of the Herero and Nama Against German Imperialism (1884–1915)* (London: Zed Books).

Dreyer, Edward L. (1995) *China at War, 1901–1949* (London: Longman).

Duffet, John (ed.) (1970), *Against the Crime of Silence: Proceedings of the International War Crimes Tribunal* (New York: Simon and Schuster).

Dunkerley, James (1982), *The Long War: Dictatorship and Revolution in El Salvador* (London: Junction Books).

——(1994), *The Pacification of Central America: Political Change in the Isthmus, 1987–1993* (London: Verso).

Dunn, Dennis J. (1998), *Caught Between Roosevelt and Stalin: America's Ambassadors to Moscow* (Lexington: University Press of Kentucky).

Dunne, Tim and Nicholas J. Wheeler (eds) (1999), *Human Rights in Global Politics* (Cambridge: Cambridge University Press).

Duong, Liai (2006), 'Racial Discrimination in the Cambodian Genocide', Genocide Studies Program, Yale University, Working Paper No. 34.

Dutt, R. Palme (1964), *The Internationale* (London: Lawrence and Wishart).

Dyadkin, Iosif G. (ed.) (1983), *Unnatural Deaths in the USSR, 1928–1954*, trans. Tania Deruguine (New Brunswick, NJ: Transaction).

Eade, Charles (ed.) (1951), *The War Speeches of the Rt. Hon. Winston Churchill*, Vol. 1 (London: Cassell and Co.).

Easherwick, Joseph W., Paul G. Pickowicz, and Andrew G. Walder (eds) (2006), *The Chinese Cultural Revolution as History* (Stanford: Stanford University Press).

Economy, Elizabeth and Michel Oksenberg (eds) (1999), *China Joins the World: Progress and Prospects* (New York: Council on Foreign Relations).

Editor's Note (1982–3), 'Atrocities and Violations of Human Rights and International Law in Afghanistan', *World Affairs*, 145 (3).

Edwards, R. Randle, Louis Henkin, and Andrew J. Nathan (1986), *Human Rights in Contemporary China* (New York: Columbia University Press).

El Salvador Truth Commission (1993), *From Madness to Hope: The 12-Year War in El Salvador* (San Salvador: Commission on the Truth for El Salvador).

Elliott, George Fielding and R. Ernest Dupuy (1937), *If War Comes* (New York: Macmillan).

Elterman, Howard R. (1978), 'The State, the Mass Media, and Ideological Hegemony: United States Policy Decisions in Indochina, 1974–75: Historical Record, Governmental Pronouncements and Press Coverage', Dissertation, New York University.

Emizet, Kisangani N. F. (2000), 'The Massacre of Refugees in Congo: A Case of UN Peacekeeping Failure and International Law', *Journal of Modern African Studies*, 38 (2).

Emmerson, Donald K. (ed.) (1999), *Indonesia beyond Suharto: Polity, Economy, Society, Transition* (Armonk, NY: M. E. Sharpe).

English, Allan D. (1993), 'The RAF Staff College and the Evolution of British Strategic Bombing Policy', *Journal of Strategic Studies* 16 (3): 408–31.

Entman, Robert M. (2006), 'Punctuating the Homogeneity of Institutionalized News: Abusing Prisoners at Abu Ghraib versus Killing Civilians at Fallujah', *Political Communication*, 23.

Ermacora, Felix (1985), *Report on the Situation of Human Rights in Afghanistan*, E/CN.4/1985/21, 19 February.

——(1986), *Report on the Situation of Human Rights in Afghanistan*, E/CN.4/1986/24, 17 February.

Esdaile, Charles (1988), 'War and Politics in Spain, 1808–14', *The Historical Journal*, 31 (2).

Esmein, Jean (1973), *The Chinese Cultural Revolution*, trans. W. J. F. Jenner (New York: Anchor Press, Doubleday).

Esposito, John L. (2002), *Unholy War: Terror in the Name of Islam* (Oxford: Oxford University Press).

Etcheson, Craig (1999), 'The Number—Quantifying Crimes Against Humanity in Cambodia', Documentation Centre of Cambodia.

Evangelista, Matthew (2002), *The Chechen Wars: Will Russia Go the Way of the Soviet Union?* (Washington, DC: The Brookings Institution).

Evans, Gareth (2008), *The Responsibility to Protect: Ending Mass Atrocity Crimes Once and for All* (Washington, DC: The Brookings Institution).

Evans, Grant and Kelvin Rowley (1984), *Red Brotherhood at War: Vietnam, Cambodia and Laos Since 1975* (London: Verso).

Evans, R. J. W. and Helmut Pogge von Strandmann (eds) (2000), *The Revolutions in Europe, 1848–1849* (Oxford: Oxford University Press).

Ewans, Martin (2002), *European Atrocity, African Catastrophe: Leopold II, the Congo Free State and its Aftermath* (London: Routledge Curzon).

Fainsod, Merle (1953), *How Russia is Ruled* (Cambridge, MA: Harvard University Press).

Falk, Richard (ed.) (1976), *Vietnam War and International Law: Volume 4 The Concluding Phase* (Princeton, NJ: Princeton University Press).

——(2003), *The Great Terror War* (New York: Olive Branch Press).

——, Irene Gendzier, and Robert Jay Lifton (eds) (2006), *Crimes of War: Iraq* (New York: Nation Books).

Fanon, Frantz (1965), *The Wretched of the Earth* (London: Grove Press).

Farer, Tom J. (1971), 'The Laws of War 25 Years After Nuremberg', *International Conciliation*, 583.

Farid, Hilmar (2005), 'Indonesia's Original Sin: Mass Killings and Capitalist Expansion, 1965–1966', *Inter-Asia Cultural Studies*, 6 (1).

Farwell, Byron (1976), *The Great Anglo-Boer War* (New York: Harper and Row).

Favez, Jean-Claude (1999), *The Red Cross and the Holocaust*, trans. John and Beryl Fletcher (Cambridge: Cambridge University Press).

Fein, Helen (1979), *Accounting for Genocide* (New York: Free Press).

——(1993–4), 'Discriminating Genocide from War Crimes: Vietnam and Afghanistan Reconsidered', *Denver Journal of International Law and Policy*, 29.

——(1993), *Genocide: A Sociological Perspective* (London: Sage).

——(1993), 'Revolutionary and Anti-Revolutionary Genocides: A Comparison of States Murders in Democratic Kampuchea, 1975 to 1979, and in Indonesia, 1965 to 1966', *Comparative Studies in Society and History*, 35 (4).

Fenby, Jonathan (2008), *The Penguin History of Modern China: The Fall and Rise of a Great Power 1850–2009* (London: Penguin).

Fest, Joachim (1970), *The Face of the Third Reich: Portraits of the Nazi Leadership* (New York: Weidenfeld and Nicolson).

——(1974), *Hitler* (Orlando, FL: Harcourt Brace).

Fewsmith, Joseph (2008), *China Since Tiananmen: From Deng Xiaoping to Hu Jintao* (Cambridge: Cambridge University Press).

Findlay, Trevor (2002), *The Use of Force in UN Peace Operations* (Oxford: Oxford University Press for SIPRI).

Finnemore, Martha (1996), *National Interests in International Society* (Ithaca: Cornell University Press).

——(2003), *The Purpose of Intervention: Changing Beliefs About the Use of Force* (Ithaca: Cornell University Press).

——and Kathryn Sikkink (1998), 'International Norm Dynamics and Political Change', *International Organization*, 52 (4).

Fitzgerald, Frances (1972), *Fire in the Lake: The Vietnamese and Americans in Vietnam* (Boston: Little, Brown and Co.).

Fitzpatrick, Matthew P. (2008), 'The Pre-History of the Holocaust? The *Sonderweg* and *Historikerstreit* Debates and the Abject Colonial Past', *Central European History*, 41: 477–503.

Fitzpatrick, Sheila (1994), *Stalin's Peasants: Resistance and Survival in the Russian Village after Collectivization* (Oxford: Oxford University Press).

——(ed.) (2000), *Stalinism: New Directions* (London: Routledge).

Foner, Phillip S. (1972), *The Spanish–Cuban–American War and the Birth of American Imperialism, 1895–1902*, Vol. 1 (New York: Monthly Review Press).

Foot, Rosemary (2000), *Rights Beyond Borders: The Global Community and the Struggle Over Human Rights in China* (Oxford: Oxford University Press).

*Foreign Relations of the United States* (1928), 1915 Supp, 981, US National Archives, Record Group 59, 867.4016/67 (28 May).

Förster, Stig and Jorg Nagler (eds) (1997), *On the Road to Total War: The American Civil War and the German Wars of Unification 1861–1871* (Cambridge: Cambridge University Press).

Forsyth, Susan (2003), *Representing the Massacre of American Indians at Wounded Knee, 1890–2000* (Lewiston, NY: Edwin Mellen).

Fournet, Caroline (2007), *The Crime of Destruction and the Law of Genocide: Their Impact on Collective Memory* (Aldershot: Ashgate).

Fox, J. and S. Sandler (2004), *Bringing Religion into International Relations* (New York: Palgrave).

Franck, Thomas (1990), *The Power of Legitimacy Among Nations* (New York, Oxford University Press).

Franck, Thomas (2002), *Recourse to Force: State Action Against Threats and Armed Attacks* (Cambridge: Cambridge University Press).

Frank, Richard B. (1999), *Downfall: The End of the Imperial Japanese Empire* (New York: Random House).

Friedlander, Henry (1995), *The Origins of Nazi Genocide: From Euthanasia to the Final Solution* (Chapel Hill: University of North Carolina Press).

Fuller, John F. C. (1923) *The Reformation of War* (London: Hutchinson and Co.).

Furber, David (2004), 'The Near as Far in the Colonies: The Nazi Occupation in Poland', *International History Review* 26 (3).

Furet, François (1981), *Interpreting the French Revolution* (Cambridge: Cambridge University Press).

——(1990), 'A Commentary', *French Historical Studies*, 16 (4).

——, F. Michael, and Keith Michael (eds) (1994), *The Terror*, Vol. 4 (London: Pergamon).

Futrell, Robert F. (1983), *The United States Air Force in Korea, 1950–1953*, rev. edn (Washington, DC: Government Printing Office).

Gaddis, John Lewis (1990), *Russia, the Soviet Union and the United States: An Interpretive History* (New York: McGraw-Hill).

Gall, Carlotta and Thomas de Waal (1999), *Chechnya: Calamity in the Caucuses* (New York: New York University Press).

Gardam, Judith Gail (1993), 'Proportionality and Force in International Law', *American Journal of International Law*, 87 (3): 391–413.

——(2004), *Necessity, Proportionality and the Use of Force by States* (Cambridge: Cambridge University Press).

Garrett, Stephen (1997), *Ethics and Airpower in World War II: The British Bombing of German Cities* (New York: St. Martin's Press).

Gati, Charles (2006), *Failed Illusions: Moscow, Washington, Budapest and the 1956 Hungarian Revolt* (Stanford: Stanford University Press).

Gavin, James Lt.-Gen (1958), *War and Peace in the Space Age* (New York: Harper).

Gay, Peter (1961), 'Rhetoric and Politics in the French Revolution', *American Historical Review*, 66 (3).

Gaytisolo, Juan (2000), *Landscapes of War: From Sarajevo to Chechnya* (San Francisco: City Lights).

Geertz, Clifford (1995), *After the Fact: Two Countries, Four Decades, One Anthropologist* (Cambridge, MA: Harvard University Press).

Gellately, Robert and Ben Kiernan (eds) (2003), *The Specter of Genocide: Mass Murder in Historical Perspective* (Cambridge: Cambridge University Press).

Genocide Prevention Task Force (2008), *Preventing Genocide: A Blueprint for US Policymakers* (Washington, DC: American Academy of Diplomacy, US Holocaust Memorial Museum, and USIP).

George, David Lloyd (1939), *Memoirs of the Peace Conference* (New Haven: Yale University Press).

Gerlach, Christian (2010), *Extremely Violent Societies: Mass Violence in the Twentieth-Century World* (Cambridge: Cambridge University Press).

Gerwath, Robert and Stephan Malinowski (2009), 'Hannah Arendt's Ghosts: Reflections on the Disputable Path from Windhoek to Auschwitz', *Central European History*, 42.

Getty, J. Arch (1985), *The Origins of the Great Purges: The Soviet Communist Party Reconsidered, 1933–1938* (Cambridge: Cambridge University Press).

——and Roberta T. Manning (eds) (1993), *Stalinist Terror: New Perspectives* (Cambridge: Cambridge University Press).

——and Oleg V. Naumov (1999), *The Road to Terror: Stalin and the Self-Destruction of the Bolsheviks, 1932–1939* (New Haven: Yale University Press).

Geyer, Michael and Sheila Fitzpatrick (eds) (2009), *Beyond Totalitarianism: Stalinism and Nazism Compared* (Cambridge: Cambridge University Press).

Gibney, Mark (2007), 'Genocide and State Responsibility', *Human Rights Law Review* 7(4).

Gibson, James William (1988), *The Perfect War: The War we Couldn't Lose and How We Did* (New York: Random House).

Gifford, Prosser and W. M. Roger Louis (eds) (1971), *France and Britain in Africa: Imperial Rivalry and Colonial Rule* (New Haven: Yale University Press).

Gilligan, Emma (2010), *Terror in Chechnya: Russia and the Tragedy of Civilians in War* (Princeton, NJ: Princeton University Press).

Ginsburgs, George and Michael Mathos (1964), *Communist China and Tibet: The First Dozen Years* (The Hague: Martinus Nijhoff).

Giovannitti, L. and F. Freed (1967), *The Decision to Drop the Bomb* (London: Methuen).

Global Centre for the Responsibility to Protect (2010), 'Fulfilling the Responsibility to Protect: Strengthening Our Capacities to Prevent and Halt Mass Atrocities', meeting summary, 24 September.

Glover, Jonathan (2001), *Humanity: A Moral History of the Twentieth Century* (London: Pimlico).

Goertz, Gary (2003), *International Norms and Decision-Making: A Punctuated Equilibrium Model* (Lanham: Rowman & Littlefield).

Goldblatt, Israel (1971), *History of Southwest Africa* (Cape Town: JUTA).

Goldhagen, Daniel J. (1996), *Hitler's Willing Executioners: Ordinary Germans and the Holocaust* (New York: Knopf).

Gong, Geret (1984), *The Standard of 'Civilization' in International Society* (Oxford: Clarendon Press).

Gooch, John (2005), 'Re-Conquest and Suppression: Fascist Italy's Pacification of Libya and Ethiopia, 1922–39', *Journal of Strategic Studies*, 28 (6).

Goodin, Robert E. (1995), *Utilitarianism as Public Philosophy* (Cambridge: Cambridge University Press).

Goodman, David S. G. and Gerald Segal (ed.) (1991), *China in the Nineties: Crisis Management and Beyond* (Oxford: Clarendon Press).

Goodson, Larry P. (2001), *Afghanistan's Endless War: State Failure, Regional Politics, and the Rise of the Taliban* (Seattle: University of Washington Press).

Gott, Richard (2004), *Cuba: A New History* (New Haven, NY: Yale University Press).

Gould, Stephen Jay (1981), *The Mismeasure of Man* (New York: W. W. Norton).

Gourevitch, Philip (2000), *We Wish to Inform You that Tomorrow we will be Killed with our Families: Stories from Rwanda* (London: Picador).
Graham, Robert J. (1984), 'Vietnam: An Infantryman's View of Our Failure', *Military Affairs*, 48 (3).
Graham, Stephen (2005), 'Remembering Fallujah: Demonising Place, Constructing Atrocity', *Environment and Planning D: Society and Space*, 23 (1).
Granville, J. A. S. (1976), *Europe Reshaped 1848–1878* (London: Harvester Press).
Grau, Lester W. and Timothy Smith (2000), 'A "Crushing Victory": Fuel-Air Explosives and Grozny', *Marines Corps Gazette*.
Grayling, A. C. (2006), *Among the Dead Cities: Was the Allied Bombing of Civilians in WWII a Necessity or a Crime?* (London: Bloomsbury).
Greenberg, K. J. and J. L. Dratel (eds) (2005), *The Torture Papers: The Road to Abu Ghraib* (New York: Cambridge University Press).
Greer, Donald (1966), *The Incidence of the Terror During the French Revolution: A Statistical Interpretation* (Gloucester, MA: Peter Smith).
Gregory, Paul R. (2009), *Terror by Quota: State Security from Lenin to Stalin (An Archival Study)* (New Haven: Yale University Press).
Grieco, Joseph M. (1988), 'Anarchy and the Limits of Cooperation: A Realist Critique of the Newest Liberal Internationalism', *International Organization*, 42 (3).
Groves, Brigadier General P. R. C. (1922), *Our Future in the Air: A Survey of the Vital Question of British Air Power* (London: Hutchinson).
Grunfeld, A. Tom (1996), *The Making of Modern Tibet*, rev. edn (Armonk, NY: M. E. Sharpe).
Gullace, Nicolleta F. (1997), 'Sexual Violence and Family Honor: British Propaganda and International Law during the First World War', *American Historical Review*, 102 (3).
Gunaratna, Rohan (2003), *Inside al-Qaida* (London: Hurst).
Gutman, Roy and David Rieff (eds) (1999), *Crimes of War: What the Public Should Know* (New York: W. W. Norton).
Gutman, Yisrael and Efraim Zuroff (eds) (1977), *Rescue Attempts During the Holocaust* (Jerusalem: Yad Vashem).
Guttman, Joseph (1965) 'The Beginnings of Genocide', *Turkish Armenocide*, Documentary Series No. 2 (Philadelphia: Armenian Historical Research Association).
Haas, Michael (1991), *Cambodia, Pol Pot, and the United States: The Faustian Pact* (New York: Praeger).
Haas, Peter J. (1988), *Morality After Auschwitz: The Radical Challenge of the Nazi Ethic* (Philadelphia: Fortress Press).
Halpern, Sandra (2004), *War and Social Change in Modern Europe: The Great Transformation Revisited* (Cambridge: Cambridge University Press).
Hamilton-Merritt, Jane (1993), *Tragic Mountains: The Hmong, The Americans, and the Secret Wars for Laos, 1942–1992* (Bloomington: Indiana University Press).
Hammond, William M. (1988), *Military and the Media 1962–1968* (Washington, DC: US Army Centre of Military History).
——(1998), *Reporting Vietnam: Media and Military at War* (Lawrence: University Press of Kansas).

Hampson, Norman (1988), *Prelude to Terror: The Constituent Assembly and the Failure of Consensus, 1789–1791* (Oxford: Basil Blackwell).

Hannum, Hurst (1989), 'International Law and Cambodian Genocide: The Sounds of Silence', *Human Rights Quarterly*, 11 (1).

Hansell Jr., Heywood S. (1972) *The Air Plan that Defeated Hitler* (Atlanta: Higgins-McArthur).

Hansen, Greg and Robert Seely (1996), 'War and Humanitarian Action in Chechnya', War and Humanitarian Action Project Occasional Paper No. 26.

Harper, Stephen (1985), *Miracle of Deliverance: The Case for the Bombing of Hiroshima and Nagasaki* (London: Sidgwick and Jackson).

Harriman, W. A. and E. Abel (1976), *Special Envoy to Churchill and Stalin* (London: Hutchinson).

Harrison, Royden (1971), *The English Defence of the Commune 1871* (London: Merlin Press).

Harrison, Tom (1962), *Living Through the Blitz* (London: Collins).

Hartigan, Richard Shelly (1982), *The Forgotten Victim: A History of the Civilian in War* (Chicago: Precedent Publishing).

——(1983), *Lieber's Code and the Law of War* (Chicago: Precedent).

Haslam, Jonathan (1986), 'Political Opposition to Stalin and the Origins of the Terror in Russia', *The Historical Journal*, 29 (2).

Hastings, Max (1979), *Bomber Command* (New York: The Dial Press).

——(1987), *The Korean War* (London: Michael Joseph).

Haynes, Jeffrey (2005), 'Al Qaeda: Ideology and Action', *Critical Review of International Social and Political Philosophy*, 8 (2).

Hays Parks, W. (1982), 'Rolling Thunder and the Law of War', *Air University Review*, 33 (1).

——(1983), 'Linebacker and the Laws of War', *Air University Review*, 34 (2).

Headley, Phineas Camp (1852), *Life of Louis Kossuth: Governor of Hungary* (London: Darby and Miller).

Hefner, Robert W. (1990), *The Political Economy of Mountain Java: An Interpretive History* (Berkeley: University of California Press).

Hegghammer, Thomas (2006), 'Global Jihadism After the Iraq War', *Middle East Journal*, 60 (1).

Heinamaa, Anna, Maija Leppanen, and Yuri Yurchenko (1994), *The Soldiers' Story: Soviet Veterans Remember the Afghan War* (Berkeley: University of California, International and Area Studies).

Heller, Mikhail and Alexsandr Nekrich (1986), *Utopia in Power: The History of the Soviet Union from 1917 to the Present*, trans. Phyllis Carlos (New York: Summit).

Herman, Edward S. and Noam Chomsky (1988), *Manufacturing Consent: The Political Economy of the Mass Media* (New York: Pantheon).

Hermann, Richard K. and Vaughn P. Shannon (1999), 'Enacting International Norms: American Elite Thinking About Interests and Obligation'. Paper presented at the Annual APSA Conference, Atlanta, GA.

————(2001), 'Defending International Norms: The Role of Obligation, Material Interest and Perception in Decision-Making', *International Organization*, 55 (3).

Hersh, Seymour M. (1983), *The Price of Power: Kissinger in the Nixon White House* (New York: Summit Books).

Hesse, C. (1993), 'Silences and the History of Representations of War', *The Journal of Military History*, 57 (5).

Hewitt, J. Joseph, Jonathan Wilkenfeld, and Ted Robert Gurr (eds) (2008), *Peace and Conflict 2008* (Boulder: Paradigm).

Hicks, George (ed.) (1990), *The Broken Mirror: China after Tiananmen* (London: Longman).

Higgins, A. Pearce (1909), *The Hague Peace Conferences and Other International Conferences Concerning the Laws and Usages of War: Texts of Conventions with Commentaries* (Cambridge: Cambridge University Press).

Hilali, A. Z. (2001), 'China's Response to the Soviet Invasion of Afghanistan', *Central Asian Survey*, 20 (3).

Hilberg, Raul (1985), *The Destruction of the European Jews*, rev. edn (New York: Holmes and Meir).

Hildebrand, G. C. and G. Porter (1976), *Cambodia: Starvation and Revolution* (New York: Monthly Review Press).

Hills, Alice (2006), 'Fear and Loathing in Falluja', *Armed Forces and Society*, 32 (4).

Hiltermann, Joost R. (2000), 'Elusive Justice: Trying to Try Saddam', *Middle East Report*, 215 (2).

——(2007), *A Poisonous Affair: America, Iraq and the Gassing of Halabja* (Cambridge: Cambridge University Press).

Hinton, Alexander Laban (1996), 'Agents of Death: Explaining the Cambodian Genocide in Terms of Psychosocial Dissonance', *American Anthropologist*, 98 (4).

——(1998), 'A Head for an Eye: Revenge in the Cambodian Genocide', *American Ethnologist*, 25 (3).

——(1998), 'Why Did the Nazis Kill? Genocide and the Goldhagen Controversy', *Anthropology Today*, 14 (5).

——(ed.) (2002), *Annihilating Difference: The Anthropology of Genocide* (Berkeley: University of California Press).

——(2005), *Why Did They Kill?* (Berkeley: University of California Press).

Hirsch, John L. and Robert B. Oakley (1995), *Somalia and Operation Restore Hope: Reflections on Peacemaking and Peacekeeping* (Washington, DC: United States Institute of Peace).

Hitler, Adolf (1971), *Mein Kampf*, trans. Ralph Mannheim (Boston: Houghton Mifflin).

Hoannisian, Richard G. (ed.) (1997), *The Armenian People From Ancient to Modern Times*, Vol. II: *From Dominion to Statehood: The Fifteenth to the Twentieth Century* (New York: St. Martin's Press).

Hochschild, Adam (1998), *King Leopold's Ghost* (Boston: Houghton Mifflin).

Hoffmann, Bruce (2006), *Inside Terrorism*, rev. edn (New York: Columbia University Press).

Hollis, Martin and Steve Smith (1990), *Explaining and Understanding International Relations* (Oxford: Clarendon Press).

Holmes, Jonathan (2007), *Fallujah: Eyewitness Testimony from Iraq's Besieged City* (London: Constable and Robinson).

Holt, Victoria K. and Tobias C. Berkman (2006), *The Impossible Mandate? Military Preparedness, The Responsibility to Protect and Modern Peace Operations* (Washington, DC: The Henry L. Stimson Center).
Horis, Ole and Sefa Martin Yurukel (eds) (2011), *Contrasts and Solutions in the Middle East* (Aarhus: Aarhus University Press).
Horne, Alistair (1965), *The Fall of Paris: The Siege and the Commune 1870–1871* (London: Macmillan).
Horne, John and Alan Kramer (1994), 'German "Atrocities" and Franco-German Opinion, 1914: The Evidence of German Soldiers' Diaries', *Journal of Modern Military History*, 66 (1).
——(2001), *German Atrocities, 1914: A History of Denial* (New Haven: Yale University Press).
Howard, Lise Morje (2008), *UN Peacekeeping in Civil Wars* (Cambridge: Cambridge University Press).
Howard, Michael (1961), *The Franco-Prussian War: The German Invasion of France, 1870–1871* (London: Rupert Hart-Davis).
——George J. Andreopoulos, and Mark R. Shulman (eds) (1994), *The Laws of War: Constraints on Warfare in the Western World* (New Haven: Yale University Press).
Hovannisian, Richard G. (ed.) (1998), *The Armenian Genocide in Perspective* (New Brunswick: Transaction Publishers).
——(ed.) (1999), *Remembrance and Denial: The Case of the Armenian Genocide* (Detroit: Wayne State University Press).
Hoxie, Frederick E. (1984), *A Final Promise: The Campaign to Assimilate the Indians, 1880–1920* (Cambridge: Cambridge University Press).
Huang, Phillip C. C. (1995), 'Rural Class Struggle in the Chinese Revolution: Representational and Objective Realities from the Land Reform to the Cultural Revolution', *Modern China*, 21 (1): 105–43.
Hughes, John (1967) *Indonesian Upheaval* (New York: D. McKay Co.).
Hull, Isabel V. (2005), *Absolute Destruction: Military Culture and the Practices of War in Imperial Germany* (Ithaca, NY: Cornell University Press).
Human Rights Watch (1993), *Iraq's Crime of Genocide: The Anfal Campaign Against the Kurds* (New York: Human Rights Watch).
——(1999), *Casualties of War: Civilians, Rule of Law, and Democratic Freedoms*, report no. 11, February.
——(2003), *Violent Response: The US Army in al-Fallujah*, report, 15 (7) June.
——(2005), *Getting Away with Torture* (New York: Human Rights Watch), April.
Human Security Research Group (2011), *Human Security Report 2009/2010: The Causes of Peace and the Shrinking Costs of War* (Oxford: Oxford University Press).
Huntington, Samuel P. (1968), 'The Bases of Accommodation', *Foreign Affairs*, 46 (4).
Hurd, Ian (1999), 'Legitimacy and Authority in International Politics', *International Organization*, 53 (2).
Hutchings, Graham (2001), *Modern China: A Guide to a Century of Change* (Cambridge, MA: Harvard University Press).
Hutton, Paul Andrews (1985), *Phil Sheridan and His Army* (Lincoln: University of Nebraska Press).

Hyslop, Beatrice F. (1948), 'Historical Publications since 1939 on the French Revolution', *Journal of Military History* 20 (3).

Ignatieff, Michael (2001–02), 'Ethics and the New War', *Canadian Military Journal*, Winter.

International Commission of Jurists (1959), *The Question of Tibet and International Law* (Geneva: International Commission of Jurists).

International Committee of the Red Cross (ICRC) (2008), *Enhancing Protection for Civilians in Armed Conflict and Other Situations of Violence* (Geneva: ICRC), September.

International Law Commission (2001), *Draft Articles on the Responsibility of States for Internationally Wrongful Acts* (New York: International Law Commission).

Ionid, Radu (2000), *The Holocaust in Romania: The Destruction of Jews and Gypsies Under the Antonescu Regime, 1940–1944* (Chicago: Ivan Dee).

Isaacs, Arnold R. (1983), *Without Honor: Defeat in Vietnam and Cambodia* (Baltimore: Johns Hopkins University Press).

Jackson, Karl D. (1992), *Cambodia 1975–1979: Rendezvous with Death* (Princeton, NJ: Princeton University Press).

Jackson, Robert J. (1993), 'Armed Humanitarianism', *International Journal*, 48.

——(2000), *The Global Covenant: Human Conduct in a World of States* (Oxford: Oxford University Press).

Jacob Blaustein Institute for the Advancement of Human Rights (2011), *Compilation of Risk Factors and Legal Norms for the Prevention of Genocide* (New York: Jacob Blaustein Institute).

Jacquard, Roland (2002), *In the Name of Osama Bin Laden: Global Terrorism and the Bin Laden Brotherhood* (Durham: Duke University Press).

Jakobsen, Peter Viggo (2002), 'The Transformation of United Nations Peace Operation in the 1990s', *Cooperation and Conflict*, 37 (3).

James, David (1954), *Lord Roberts* (London: Hollis and Carter).

Janda, Lance (1995), 'Shutting the Gates of Mercy: The American Origins of Total War, 1860–1880', *The Journal of Military History*, 59 (1).

Jervis, Robert (1976), *Perception and Misperception in International Politics* (Princeton, NJ: Princeton University Press).

Johnson, James Turner (1975), *Ideology, Reason and the Limitation of War: Religious and Secular Concepts 1200–1740* (Princeton, NJ: Princeton University Press).

——(1981), *Just War Tradition and the Restraint of War: A Moral and Historical Enquiry* (Princeton, NJ: Princeton University Press).

——(1999), *Morality and Contemporary Warfare* (New Haven, CT: Yale University Press).

——(2000), 'Maintaining the Protection of Non-Combatants', *Journal of Peace Research*, 37 (4).

——(2005), *The War to Oust Saddam Hussein: Just War and the New Face of Conflict* (Lanham: Rowman and Littlefield).

Johnson, Lyndon B. (1971), *The Vantage Point* (New York: Holt, Rinehart and Winston).

Johnson, Paul (1984), 'Marxism vs. the Jews', *Commentary*, 77, April.

Johnston, Alistair Iain (2007), *Social States: China in International Institutions,* (Princeton, NJ: Princeton University Press).

Jonassohn, Kurt with Karin Solveig Bjornson (1999), *Genocide and Gross Human Rights Violations in Comparative Perspective* (New Brunswick: Transaction).

Jones, Adam (2006), *Genocide: A Comprehensive Introduction* (London: Routledge).

Jones, H. A. (1937) *The War in the Air* (London: Oxford University Press).

Joseph, William A. (1986), 'A Tragedy of Good Intentions: Post-Mao Views of the Great Leap Forward', *Modern China,* 12 (4).

——Christine P. W. Wong, and David Zweig (eds) (1991), *New Perspectives on the Cultural Revolution* (Cambridge, MA: Harvard University Press).

Judah, Tim (2000), *Kosovo: War and Revenge* (London: Yale University Press).

Judd, Denis and Keith Sturridge (2003), *The Boer War* (London: John Murray).

Kahin, George McT. (1979), *Intervention: How American Became Involved in Vietnam* (New York: Alfred Knopf).

Kalyvas, Stathis N. (2006), *The Logic of Violence in Civil War* (Cambridge: Cambridge University Press).

Kam-yee Law (ed.) (2003), *The Chinese Cultural Revolution Reconsidered: Beyond Purge and Holocaust* (London: Palgrave).

Kamenka, Eugene (ed.) (1983), *The Portable Karl Marx* (Hardmondsworth: Penguin).

Karnow, Stanley (1991), *Vietnam: A History,* rev. edn (New York: Viking Penguin).

Katzenstein, Peter J. (ed.) (1996), *The Culture of National Security: Norms, Identities and World Politics* (New York: Columbia University Press).

Kaye, David and Steven A. Solomon (2002), 'The Second Conference of the 1980 Convention on Certain Conventional Weapons', *American Journal of International Law,* 96 (4).

Kaye, James and Bo Strath (eds) (2000), *Enlightenment and Genocide, Contradictions of Modernity* (New York: Peter Lang).

Keane, Fergal (1995), *Seasons of Blood: A Rwandan Journey* (London: Penguin).

Keene, Edward (2002), *Beyond the Anarchical Society: Grotius, Colonialism and Order in World Politics* (Cambridge: Cambridge University Press).

Keith, Arthur Berriedale (1919), *The Belgian Congo and the Berlin Act* (Oxford: Clarendon Press).

Kelly, George Armstrong (1980), 'Conceptual Sources of Terror', *Eighteenth Century Studies,* 14 (1).

Kelly, Michael J. (2005), 'The Tricky Nature of Proving Genocide Against Saddam Hussein Before the Iraqi Special Tribunal', *Cornell International Law Journal,* 38.

——(2007), 'The Anfal Trial Against Saddam Hussein', *Journal of Genocide Research,* 9 (2).

Kelman, Herbert C. and V. Lee Hamilton (1989), *Crimes of Obedience: Toward a Social Psychology of Authority and Responsibility* (New Haven: Yale University Press).

Kelsay, John (2003), 'The New *Jihad* and Islamic Tradition', *Foreign Policy Research Institute Wire,* 11 (3).

——(2007), *Arguing the Just War in Islam* (Cambridge, MA: Harvard University Press).

Kelsen, Hans (1949), *General Theory of Law and State* (Cambridge, MA: Harvard University Press).

Kennan, George F. (1961), *Russia and the West under Lenin and Stalin* (London: Hutchinson).

——(1967), *Memoirs: 1925–1950*, Vol. I (Boston: Atlantic-Little Brown).

Kennedy, Michael L. (1989), 'The "Last Stand" of the Jacobins Clubs', *French Historical Studies*, 16 (2).

——(1994), *The Jacobin Club of Marseille* (Ithaca: Cornell University Press).

Kent, Ann (1993), *Between Freedom and Subsistence: China and Human Rights* (Hong Kong: Oxford University Press).

Kiernan, Ben (1986), 'Kampuchea's Ethnic Chinese Under Pol Pot: A Case of Systematic Social Discrimination', *Journal of Contemporary Asia*, 16.

——(1988), 'Orphans of Genocide: The Cham Muslims of Kampuchea under Pol Pot', *Bulletin of Concerned Asian Scholars*, 20.

——(ed.) (1993), *Genocide and Democracy in Cambodia: The Khmer Rouge, the United Nations and the International Community* (New Haven: Yale University Southeast Asian Studies Monograph, No. 41).

——(1996), *The Pol Pot Regime: Race, Power, and Genocide in Cambodia under the Khmer Rouge, 1975–79* (New Haven: Yale University Press).

——(2003), 'The Demography of Genocide in Southeast Asia: The Death Tolls in Cambodia, 1975–79, and East Timor, 1975–80', *Critical Asian Studies*, 35 (4).

——(2004), 'Coming to Terms with the Past: Cambodia', *History Today*, September.

——(2004), *How Pol Pot Came to Power: Colonialism, Nationalism, and Communism in Cambodia, 1930–1975* (New Haven: Yale University Press).

——(2007), *Blood and Soil: A World History of Genocide and Extermination from Sparta to Darfur* (New Haven: Yale University Press).

——(2010), 'External and Indigenous Sources of Khmer Rouge Ideology', Yale Cambodian Genocide Project, www.yale.edu/cgp accessed 15 March.

——and Chanthou Boua (eds) (1982), *Peasants and Politics in Kampuchea, 1942–1981* (London: Zed Books).

Kiljunen, Kimmo (ed.) (1984), *Kampuchea: Decade of the Genocide: A Finnish Inquiry* (London: Zed).

——(1985), 'Power Politics and the Tragedy of Kampuchea During the Seventies', *Bulletin of Concerned Asian Scholars*, 17.

Kim, Samuel S. (ed.) (1998), *China and the World: Chinese Foreign Policy Faces the New Millennium* (Boulder: Westview Press).

Kimball, Jeffrey (1998), *Nixon's Vietnam War* (Lawrence: University Press of Kansas).

Kissinger, Henry (1979), *White House Years* (Boston: Little, Brown & Co.).

——(1982), *The White House Years*, Vol. II: *Years of Upheaval* (New York: Little Brown and Co.).

——(2003), *Ending the Vietnam War: A History of America's Involvement in and Extrication from the Vietnam War* (New York: Simon & Schuster).

Klass, Roseanne (ed.) (1990), *Afghanistan: The Great Game Revisited* (New York: Freedom House).

Klinghoffer, Arthur J. (1998), *The International Dimensions of Genocide in Rwanda* (New York: New York University Press).

Knightly, Philip (1975), *The First Casualty: The War Correspondent as Hero, Propagandist, and Myth Maker from the Crimea to Vietnam* (London: Andre Deutsch).

Koch, H. W. (ed.) (1985), *Aspects of the Third Reich* (New York: St. Martin's Press).
——(1991), 'The Strategic Air Offensive Against Germany', *The Historical Journal*, 34 (1).
Kolko, Gabriel (1988), *Confronting the Third World: United States Foreign Policy, 1945–1980* (New York: Pantheon Books).
Kornberg, Judith F. and John R. Faust (2005), *China in World Politics: Policies, Processes, Prospects* (Vancouver: University of British Columbia Press).
Körner, Axel (ed.) (2000), *1848: A European Revolution? International Ideas and National Memories* (London: Palgrave).
Krahl, Colin H. (2007), 'In the Crossfire or the Crosshairs? Norms, Civilian Casualties, and US Conduct in Iraq', *International Security*, 32 (1).
Kratochwil, Friedreich V. and John Gerard Ruggie (1986), 'International Organization: The State of the Art of the Art of the State', *International Organization*, 40.
Krepon, Michael (1974), 'Weapons Potentially Inhumane: The Case of Cluster Bombs', *Foreign Affairs*, 52 (3).
Kroslak, Daniela (2007), *The Role of France in the Rwandan Genocide* (London: Hurst and Co.).
Kumar, Mahendra (1963), 'Sino-Indian Relations 1950–1959', *International Studies*, 5 (1–2).
Kuper, Leo (1981), *Genocide: Its Political Uses in the Twentieth Century* (New Haven: Yale University Press).
Laber, Jeri and Barnett R. Rubin (1988), *A Nation is Dying: Afghanistan under the Soviets 1979–87* (Evanston, IL: Northwestern University Press).
Labin, Suzanne (1960), *The Anthill: The Human Condition in Communist China* (New York: Praeger).
Lal, Vinay (1998), 'Genocide, Barbaric Others and the Violence of Categories: A Response to Omer Bartov', *American Historical Review*, 103 (4).
Landers, James (2004), *The Weekly War: Newsmagazines and Vietnam* (Columbia: University of Missouri Press).
Lapide, Pinchas (1967), *The Last Three Popes and the Jews* (London: Souvenir Press).
Laqueur, Walter (1977), *Guerrilla: A Historical and Critical Study* (London: Weidenfeld and Nicolson).
——(1998), *The Terrible Secret: Suppression of the Truth about Hitler's 'Final Solution'*, new edn (New York: Henry Holt and Co.).
——(2007), *No End to War: Terrorism in the Twenty-First Century* (New York: Continuum).
Law, Kam-Yee (ed.) (2003), *Chinese Cultural Revolution: Beyond Purge and Holocaust* (London: Palgrave).
Lee, Chae-Jin (ed.) (1991), *The Korean War: 40-Year Perspectives* (Claremont, CA: Keck Center for International and Strategic Studies).
Lee, Steven Hugh (2001), *The Korean War* (New York: Longman).
Legro, Jeffrey W. (1992), *Cooperation under Fire: The Conduct of the Air War in the Second World War* (New York: St. Martin's Press).
——(1997), 'Which Norms Matter? Revisiting the "Failure" of Internationalism', *International Organization*, 51 (1).

Lehmann, Hartmann and Hermann Wellenreuther (eds) (1999), *German and American Nationalism: A Comparative Perspective* (Oxford: Berg).
Leifer, Michael (1983), *Indonesia's Foreign Policy* (London: George Allen and Unwin for the Royal Institute of International Affairs).
Leiser, Burton M. (ed.) (1981), *Values in Conflict* (New York: Macmillan).
Lemarchand, Rene (1998), 'Genocide in the Great Lakes: Which Genocide? Whose Genocide?', *African Studies Review*, 41 (1).
Lendvai, Paul (2006), *One Day that Shook the Communist World: The 1956 Hungarian Uprising and its Legacy* (Princeton, NJ: Princeton University Press).
LeoGrande, William M. (1981), 'A Splendid Little War: Drawing the Line in El Salvador', *International Security*, 6 (1).
Lev, Daniel S. and Ruth McVey (eds) (1996), *Making Indonesia: Essays on Modern Indonesia* (Ithaca: Cornell University Press).
Levene, Mark (2000), 'Why is the Twentieth Century the Century of Genocide?', *Journal of World History*, 11 (2).
——(2005), *Genocide in the Age of the Nation-State*, Vol. I: *The Meaning of Genocide* (London: I. B. Tauris).
——(2005), *Genocide in the Age of the Nation-State*, Vol. II: *The Rise of the West and the Coming of Genocide* (London: I. B. Tauris).
——and Penny Roberts (eds) (1999), *The Massacre in History* (New York: Berghahn Books).
Levi, Werner (1954), 'Tibet under Chinese Communist Rule', *Far Eastern Survey*, 23 (1).
Levin, Nora (1990), *The Jews of the Soviet Union since 1917: Paradox of Survival* (New York: New York University Press).
Lewin, Moshe (1995), *Russia/USSR/Russia* (New York: The New Press).
Lewis, Lloyd (1958), *Sherman: Fighting Prophet* (New York: Harcourt, Brace and Co.).
Lewy, Guenter (1978), *America in Vietnam* (Oxford: Oxford University Press).
Leys, Simon (1977), *The Chairman's New Clothes: Mao and the Cultural Revolution* (London: Allison and Bushby).
Liang-Fenton, Debra (ed.) (2004), *Implementing US Human Rights Policy: Agendas, Policies and Practices* (Washington, DC: United States Institute of Peace Press).
Liddell Hart, Basil (1972 [1925]) *Paris or the Future of War* (London: Garland).
Lieven, Anatol (1999), *Chechnya: Tombstone of Russian Power* (New Haven: Yale University Press).
Lipman, Jonathan N. and Stevan Harrell (eds) (1990), *Violence in China: Essays in Culture and Counterculture* (New York: State University of New York Press).
Lipsman, Samuel and Edward Doyle (1983), *Fighting for Time* (Boston: Boston Publishing Co.).
Lipstadt, Deborah E. (1986), *Beyond Belief: The American Press and the Coming of the Holocaust 1933–1945* (New York: Free Press).
——(1990), 'America and the Holocaust', *Modern Judaism*, 10 (3).
Littauer, Raphael and Norman Uphoff (1972), *The Air War Indochina*, rev. edn (Boston: Beacon Press).
Locke, John (1952 [1690]), *Second Treatise of Government* (New York: Pearson Education).

Lorimer, James (2005 [1876]), *The Institutes of the Law of Nations: A Treatise on the Jural Relations of Separate Political Communities*, Vol. 2 (Clark, NJ: Lawbooks Exchange).

Lowe, Norman (2002), *Mastering Twentieth-Century Russian History* (London: Palgrave).

Lowe, Vaughn, Adam Roberts, Jennifer Welsh, and Dominic Zaum (eds) (2008), *The United Nations Security Council and War: The Evolution of Thought and Practice since 1945* (Oxford: Oxford University Press).

Lu Xiuyuan (1994–95), 'A Step Towards Understanding Popular Violence in China's Cultural Revolution', *Pacific Affairs*, 67 (4).

Luck, Edward C. (2008), 'The United Nations and the Responsibility to Protect', Policy Analysis Brief for the Stanley Foundation, August.

Lyons, Martyn (1994), *Napoleon Bonaparte and the Legacy of the French Revolution* (New York: St. Martin's Press).

McCormack, Gavan (1983), *Cold War, Hot War: An Australian Perspective on the Korean War* (Sydney: Hale and Iremonger).

McCoubrey, Hilaire (1998), *International Humanitarian Law: Modern Developments in the Limitation of Warfare* (Dartmouth: Ashgate).

McDonald, Callum (1986), *Korea: The War Before Vietnam* (London: Macmillan).

MacFarquhar, Roderick (1966–7), 'Mao's Last Revolution', *Foreign Affairs*, 45.

McIlwaine, Cathy (1998), 'Contesting Civil Society: Reflections from El Salvador', *Third World Quarterly*, 19 (4).

McKeogh, Colm (2002), *Innocent Civilians: The Morality of Killing in War* (Basingstoke: Palgrave).

Mackerras, Colin, Kevin Bucknall, and Russell Trood (1989), 'The Beijing Tragedy: Implications for China and Australia', Centre for the Study of Australia-Asia Relations, Griffith University, research paper no. 51.

——Pradeep Taneja, and Graham Young (1993), *China Since 1978: Reform, Modernisation and 'Socialism with Chinese Characteristics'* (New York: St. Martin's Press).

Mackie, J. A. C. (ed.) (1976), *The Chinese in Indonesia* (Melbourne: Australian Institute of International Affairs).

Maclean, Fitzroy (1949), *Eastern Approaches* (London: Jonathan Cape).

McMahan, Jeff (2003), 'The Ethics of Killing in War', *Ethics*, 114.

McMichael, Scott Ray (1991) *Stumbling Bear: Soviet Military Performance in Afghanistan* (London: Brassey's).

McQuaid, Kim (1989), *The Anxious Years: America in the Vietnam–Watergate Era* (New York: Basic Books).

Madden Congressional Committee (1952), *The Katyn Forest Massacre: Final Report of the Select Committee to Conduct an Investigation and Study of the Facts, Evidence and Circumstances on the Katyn Forest Massacre*, 22 December.

Maddux, Thomas R. (1980), *Years of Estrangement: American Relations with the Soviet Union 1933–1941* (Tallahassee: University Presses of Florida).

Madley, Benjamin (2005), 'From Africa to Auschwitz: How German South West Africa Incubated Ideas and Methods Adopted and Developed by the Nazis in Eastern Europe', *European History Quarterly*, 35 (3).

Magnus, Ralph H. (ed.) (1988), *Afghan Alternatives: Issues, Options and Policies* (New Brunswick: Transaction Books).

Makiya, Kanan (1992), 'The Anfal: Uncovering an Iraqi Campaign to Exterminate the Kurds', *Harper's Magazine*, May, pp. 57–61.

Maley, William (2002), *The Afghanistan Wars* (London: Palgrave).

Malhuret, Claude (1983–4), 'Report from Afghanistan', *Foreign Affairs*, 62.

Malkasian Carter (2006), 'Signaling Resolve: Democratization and the First Battle of Fallujah', *Journal of Strategic Studies*, 29 (3).

Malone, David M. (2006), *The International Struggle over Iraq: Politics in the UN Security Council 1980–2005* (Oxford: Oxford University Press).

Mamdani, Mahmood (2001), 'A Brief History of Genocide', *Transition*, 10 (3).

——(2002), *When Victims Become Killers: Colonialism, Nativism and Genocide in Rwanda* (Princeton, NJ: Princeton University Press).

Mandelstam, Andre N. (1917), *Le sort de l'Empire ottoman* (Lausanne: Payot).

Mann, Michael (2005), *The Dark Side of Democracy: Explaining Ethnic Cleansing* (Cambridge: Cambridge University Press).

Mao Tse-tung (1967), *Selected Works of Mao Tse-tung*, Vol. 4 (Beijing: Foreign Languages Press).

Margalit, Avishai and Gabriel Motzkin (1996), 'The Uniqueness of the Holocaust', *Philosophy and Public Affairs*, 25 (1).

Marlin IV, Robert O. (ed.) (2004), *What Does Al-Qaeda Want? Unedited Communiques* (Berkeley, CA: North Atlantic Books).

Marriott, J. A. R. (1940), *The Eastern Question: A Study in European Diplomacy* (Oxford: Blackwell).

Marrus, Michael R. and Robert O. Paxton (1982), 'The Nazis and the Jews in Occupied Western Europe, 1940–1944', *Journal of Modern History*, 54 (4).

Martel, Gordon (ed.) (2004), *The World War Two Reader* (New York: Routledge).

Martin, A. C. (1957), *The Concentration Camps 1900–1902: Facts, Figures and Fables* (Cape Town: Howard Timmins).

Marx, Karl and Fredreich Engels (1953), *The Russian Menace to Europe: A Collection of Articles, Speeches, Letters and New Dispatches*, ed. Paul Blackstock and Bert Hoselitz (London: G. Allen).

Materer, Timothy (ed.) (1991), *The Selected Letters of Ezra Pound to John Quinn, 1915–1924* (Durham, NC: Duke University Press).

Mathiez, Albert (1985), *Révolution Française*, Vol. III (Paris: Biblioteque Mediations).

Mattern, Janice Bially (2005), *Ordering International Politics: Identity, Crisis and Representational Force* (New York: Taylor and Francis).

Mawdudi, Sayyid Abul A'la (1995), *Jihad fi Sabillah: Jihad in Islam*, trans. Khurshid Ahmad and ed. Huda Khattab (Birmingham: UK Islamic Mission Dawah Centre).

May, Arthur J. (1927), 'Contemporary American Opinion of the Mid-Century Revolutions in Central Europe', doctoral dissertation, University of Pennsylvania, Philadelphia.

May, Ernest R. (1961), *Imperial Democracy: The Emergence of America as a Great Power* (New York: Harcourt, Brace and World).

Mayall, James (1991), 'Non-Intervention, Self-Determination and the "New World Order"', *International Affairs*, 67 (3).

Mayer, Arno J. (2002), *The Furies: Violence and Terror in the French and Russian Revolutions* (Princeton: Princeton University Press).

Mazower, Mark (2002), 'Violence and the State in the Twentieth Century', *The American Historical Review*, 107 (4).

Meade Jr., Robert C. (1990), *Red Brigades: The Story of Italian Terrorism* (London: Macmillan).

Medvedev, Roy A. (1972), *Let History Judge: The Origins and Consequences of Stalinism* (London: Macmillan).

Meilinger, Philip S. (2000), 'The Historiography of Airpower: Theory and Decline', *The Journal of Military History*, 64 (2).

Meiselas, Susan (1997), *Kurdistan: In the Shadow of History* (New York: Random House).

Meisner, H. O. (ed.) (1926), *Kaiser Friedreich III: Das Kriegstagbuch von 1870/1871* (Berlin: Mittler).

Melander, Erik, Magnus Oberg, and Jonathan Hall (2009), 'Are "New Wars" More Atrocious? Battle Severity, Civilians Killed and Forced Migration Before and After the End of the Cold War', *European Journal of International Relations*, 15 (3).

Melson, Robert (1992), *Revolution and Genocide: On the Origins of the Armenian Genocide and the Holocaust* (Chicago: University of Chicago Press).

Melvern, Linda (2000), *A People Betrayed: The Role of the West in Rwanda's Genocide* (London: Zed).

——(2004), *Conspiracy to Murder: The Rwandan Genocide* (London: Verso).

Meron, Theodor (1987), 'The Geneva Conventions as Customary Law', *American Journal of International Law*, 81 (2).

——(2000), 'The Martens Clause, Principles of Humanity, and Dictates of Public Conscience', *American Journal of International Law*, 94 (1).

Metzl, Jamie Frederic (1996), *Western Responses to Human Rights Abuses in Cambodia, 1975–1980* (New York: St. Martin's Press).

Meyer, Hershel D. (1956), *The Khrushchev Report and the Crisis of the American Left* (New York: Independence Publishers).

Michealis, Meir (1978), *Mussolini and the Jews: German-Italian Relations and the Jewish Question 1922–1945* (Oxford: Oxford University Press).

Middle East Watch (1992), *Endless Torment: The 1991 Uprising in Iraq and Its Aftermath* (New York: Middle East Watch).

——(n.d.), *Genocide in Iraq: The Anfal Campaign Against the Kurds* (New York: Middle East Watch).

——and Physicians for Human Rights (1992), *Unquiet Graves: The Search for the Disappeared in Iraqi Kurdistan* (New York: Middle East Watch).

Middlebrook, Martin (1980), *The Battle of Hamburg: Allied Bomber Forces Against a German City in 1943* (London: Allen Lane).

Midlarsky, Manus (2005), *The Killing Trap: Genocide in the Twentieth Century* (Cambridge: Cambridge University Press).

Milanovic, Marko (2007), 'State Responsibility for Genocide: A Follow-Up'. *European Journal of International Law*, 18 (4).

Miles, General Nelson A. (1911), *Serving the Republic* (New York: Harper and Brothers).

Miles Jr., Rufus E. (1985), 'Hiroshima: The Strange Myth of Half a Million American Lives Saved', *International Security*, 10 (2).

Mill, John Stuart (1977), *Collected Works*, Vol. 18: *Essays on Politics and Society* (London: Routledge).

Miller, Stuart Creighton (1982), *'Benevolent Assimilation': The American Conquest of the Philippines, 1899–1903* (New Haven: Yale University Press).

Millett, Stephen M. (1976), 'The Air Force, the Courts and the Controversial Bombing of Cambodia', *Air University Review*, July–August.

Ming Wan (2001), *Human Rights in China's Foreign Relations: Defining and Defending National Interests* (Philadelphia: University of Pennsylvania Press).

Misdaq, Nabi (2006), *Afghanistan: Political Frailty and External Interference* (London: Routledge).

Mitchell, Allan (1971), *Bismarck and the French Nation 1848–1890* (New York: Pegasus).

Montefiore, Simon Sebag (2003), *Stalin: The Court of the Red Tsar* (London: Weidenfeld and Nicolson).

Montesquieu, Baron de (1989 [1748]), *Spirit of the Laws*, ed. Ann M. Cohler, Basia Collier Miller, and Harold Samuel Stone (Cambridge: Cambridge University Press).

Montgomery, Tommie Sue (1995), *Revolution in El Salvador: From Civil Strife to Civil Peace*, 2nd edn (Boulder: Westview Press).

Moorhead, Caroline (1998), *Dunant's Dream: War, Switzerland and the History of the Red Cross* (New York: Carroll and Graf Publishers).

Morgan, J. H. (1916), *A Dishonoured Army: German Atrocities in France* (London: Spottiswoode).

Morgenthau, Henry (1918), *Ambassador Morgenthau's Story* (New York: Doubleday).

——(1918) *Secrets of the Bosphorus* (London: Hutchinson).

Mori, Jennifer (1997), 'The British Government and the Bourbon Restoration: The Occupation of Toulon, 1793', *The Historical Journal*, 40 (3).

Morris, W. Wayne (1994), *Stalin's Famine and Roosevelt's Recognition of Russia* (Lanham: University Press of America).

Mortimer, Rex (1974), *Indonesian Communism under Sukarno: Ideology and Politics, 1959–1965* (Ithaca: Cornell University Press).

Moses, A. Dirk (1998), 'Structure and Agency in the Holocaust: Daniel J. Goldhagen and His Critics', *History and Theory*, 37 (2).

——(ed.) (2004), *Genocide and Settler Society: Frontier Violence and Stolen Indigenous Children in Australian History* (New York: Berghahn Books).

——and Dan Stone (eds) (2008), *Colonialism and Genocide* (London: Routledge).

Mosher, Michael A. (1991), 'The Skeptic's Burke: Reflections on the Revolution in France, 1790–1990', *Political Theory*, 19 (3).

Moussalli, A. S. (1992), *Radical Islamic Fundamentalism: The Ideological and Political Discourse of Sayyid Qutb* (Beirut: American University of Beirut).

——(1999), *Moderate and Radical Islamic Fundamentalism: The Quest for Modernity, Legitimacy and the Islamic State* (Gainesville, FL: University of Florida Press).

Mumford, Lewis (1948), 'Atom Bomb', *Air Affairs*, 2 (3).

Muste, A. J. (1947), *Not by Might: Christianity, the Way to Human Decency* (New York: Harper).

Nabulsi, Karma (1999), *Traditions of War: Occupation, Resistance and the Law* (Oxford: Oxford University Press).

Naimark, Norman M. (2010), *Stalin's Genocides* (Princeton, NJ: Princeton University Press).

Nash, David (1999), 'The Boer War and its Humanitarian Critics', *History Today*, 49 (6).

Nasson, Bill (1999), *The South African War, 1899–1902* (London: Arnold).

Nathan, Andrew J. (1990), *China's Crisis: Dilemmas of Reform and Prospects for Democracy* (New York: Columbia University Press).

National Committee for Human Rights in Afghanistan (1986), *Russia's Barbarism in Afghanistan*, Vols I–III. Kabul: National Committee for Human Rights in Afghanistan.

Neff, Stephen C. (2005), *War and the Law of Nations: A General History* (Cambridge: Cambridge University Press).

Neillands, Robin (2001), 'Facts and Myths about Bomber Harris', *RUSI Journal*, 146 (2).

Nekrich, Aleksandr M. (1978), *The Punished Peoples: The Deportation, and Fate of Soviet Minorities at the end of the Second World War* (New York: W. W. Norton and Co.).

Nelson, Samuel H. (1994), *Colonialism in the Congo Basin 1880–1940* (Athens, OH: Ohio University Press).

Newman, Robert P. (1998), 'Hiroshima and the Trashing of Henry Stimson', *The New England Quarterly*, 71 (1).

Nicolson, Harold (1967), *The War Years 1939–1945* (New York: Atheneum).

Nixon, Richard (1978), *The Memoirs of Richard Nixon*, Vol. 1 (New York: Warner Books).

Noakes, J. and G. Pridham (eds) (1988), *Nazism 1919–1945*, Vol. 3: *Foreign Policy, War and Racial Extermination. A Documentary Reader* (Exeter: Exeter Studies in History, No. 13).

Nolan, Cathal J. (ed.) (2004), *Ethics and Statecraft: The Moral Dimension of International Affairs*, 2nd edn (Westport, CN: Praeger).

Noorani, A. G. (2002), *Islam & Jihad: Prejudice versus Reality* (London: Zed).

Norbu, Dawa (2001), *China's Tibet Policy* (London: Curzon).

Nys, Ernest (1911), 'Francis Lieber—His Life and Work: Part II', *American Journal of International Law*, 5 (2).

O'Brien, William V. (1981), *The Conduct of Just and Limited War* (New York: Praeger).

O'Kane, Rosemary H. T. (1996), *Terror, Force and States: The Path from Modernity* (Cheltenham: Edward Elgar).

O'Keefe, Kevin J. (1972), *A Thousand Deadlines: The New York City Press and American Neutrality, 1914–17* (The Hague: Martinus Nijhoff).

Oppenheim, Lassa (1912), *International Law* (London: Longman).

Orbinski, James (2008), *An Imperfect Offering: Dispatches from the Medical Frontline* (Melbourne: Text Publishing).

Osiander, Andreas (1994), *The States System of Europe, 1640–1990* (Oxford: Clarendon Press).
Overy, Richard (1997), *Why the Allies Won* (New York: W. W. Norton and Co.).
——(1998), *Russia's War: A History of the Soviet War Effort 1941–1945* (Harmondsworth: Penguin).
——(2004), *The Dictators: Hitler's Germany and Stalin's Russia* (London: Allen Lane).
Owen, Taylor and Ben Kiernan (2006), 'Bombs over Cambodia', *The Walrus*, October.
Oxfam International (2003), *Beyond the Headlines: An Agenda for Action to Protect Civilians in Neglected Conflicts* (Oxford: Oxfam GB for Oxfam International).
Ozouf, Mona (1984), *L'école de la France: Essais sur la Révolution, l'utopia et l'enseignment* (Paris: Editions Sociale).
Pakenham, Thomas (1997), *The Scramble for Africa, 1876–1912* (London: Weidenfeld and Nicolson).
Pal, Radhabinod (1953), *International Military Tribunal for the Far East, Dissentient Judgment* (Calcutta: Sanyal and Co.).
Pankhurst, Richard (1999), 'Italian Fascist War Crimes in Ethiopia: A History of Their Discussion, from the League of Nations to the United Nations', *Northeast African Studies*, 6 (1–2).
Pape, Robert A. (1996), *Bombing to Win: Air Power and Coercion in War* (Ithaca: Cornell University Press).
——(2005) *Dying to Win: The Strategic Logic of Suicide Terrorism* (New York: Random House).
Parker, R. A. C. (1990), *Struggle for Survival: The History of the Second World War* (Oxford: Oxford University Press).
Paskins, Barrie and Michael Dockrill (1979), *The Ethics of War* (London: Duckworth).
Paul, Allen (1996), *Katyn: Stalin's Massacre and the Seeds of Polish Resurrection* (Annapolis, MD: Naval Institute Press).
Pavlowitch, Stevan K. (2008), *Hitler's New Disorder: The Second World War in Yugoslavia* (London: Hurst and Co.).
Peers, Lt. Gen. W. R. (1979), *The My Lai Inquiry* (New York: W. W. Norton and Co.).
Pelletiere, Stephen (1992), *The Iran–Iraq War: Chaos in a Vacuum* (New York: Praeger).
——(2001), *Iraq and the International Oil System—Why America Went to War in the Gulf* (London: Greenwood).
Percy, Sarah (2007), *Mercenaries: The History of a Norm in International Relations* (Oxford: Oxford University Press).
Perl, William (1989), *The Holocaust Conspiracy: An International Policy of Genocide* (New York: Shapolsky).
Petersen, Jennifer L. (2010), 'Rwanda's Leveraging of Moral Authority in the International Realm', unpublished paper, available at www.users.polisci.wisc.edu/irc/Petersen.doc accessed 27 March 2012.
Pflanze, Otto (1990), *Bismarck and the Development of Germany*, Vol. 11: *The Period of Consolidation, 1871–1880* (Princeton, NJ: Princeton University Press).
Phares, Walid (2007), *The War of Ideas: Jihadism Against Democracy* (London: Palgrave).

Phillipson, Coleman (1915), *International Law and the Great War* (London: T. Fisher Unwin).

Pictet, Jean (ed.) (1960), *The Geneva Conventions of 12 August 1949—Commentary: III Geneva Convention Relative to the Treatment of Prisoners of War* (Geneva: ICRC).

Pierpaoli, Paolo G. (1999), *Truman and Korea: The Political Culture of the Early Cold War* (Columbia, MO: University of Missouri Press).

Plamenatz, John (1952), *The Revolutionary Movement in France 1815–1871* (London: Longmans).

Pohl, J. Otto (1999), *Ethnic Cleansing in the USSR, 1937–1949* (Westport: Greenwood Press).

Polish Cultural Foundation (1965), *The Crime of Katyn: Facts & Documents* (London: Polish Cultural Foundation).

Polvinen, Tuomo (1986), *Between East and West: Finland in International Politics, 1944–1947*, ed. and trans. D. G. Kirby and Peter Herring (Minneapolis: University of Minnesota Press).

Ponchaud, Francois (1978), *Cambodia Year Zero*, trans. Nancy Amphoux (Harmondsworth: Penguin).

Popovski, Vesselin, Gregory M. Reichberg, and Nicholas Turner (eds) (2009), *World Religions and Norms of War* (Tokyo: United Nations University Press).

Potter, Lawrence G. and Gary G. Sick (eds) (2004), *Iran, Iraq and the Legacies of War* (New York: Palgrave).

Pottier, Johan (2002), *Re-Imagining Rwanda: Conflict, Survival and Disinformation in the Late Twentieth Century* (Cambridge: Cambridge University Press).

Power, Samantha (2002), *A Problem from Hell: America and the Age of Genocide* (New York: Basic Books).

Prauser, Steffen and Arfon Rees (eds) (2004), 'The Expulsion of the "German" Communities from Eastern Europe at the End of the Second World War', European Union Institute, Working paper 2004/1.

Press, Eyal (2003), 'In Torture we Trust?', *The Nation*, 13 March.

Price, Richard (1998) 'Reversing the Gunsights: Transnational Civil Society Targets Land Mines', *International Organization*, 52: 613–44.

——(ed.) (2008), *Moral Limit and Possibility in World Politics* (Cambridge: Cambridge University Press).

Price, Roger (1971), 'Conservative Reactions to Social Disorder: The Paris Commune of 1871', *Journal of European Studies*, 1.

Primoratz, Igor (ed.) (2007), *Civilian Immunity in War* (Oxford: Oxford University Press).

——(ed.) (2010), *Terror from the Sky: The Bombing of German Cities in World War II* (New York: Berghahn Books).

Prunier, Gerard (1997), *The Rwanda Crisis: History of a Genocide* (London: Hurst and Co.).

——(2009), *Africa's World War: Congo, the Rwandan Genocide, and the Making of a Continental Catastrophe* (Oxford: Oxford University Press).

Puangthong Rungswasdisab (2010), 'Thailand's Response to the Cambodian Genocide', Yale University Cambodia Genocide Project, www.yale.edu/cgp accessed 28 March 2012.

Quigley, Harold S. (1962), *China's Politics in Perspective* (Minneapolis: University of Minnesota Press).

Quindry, Frank E. (1931), 'Aerial Bombardment of Civilian and Military Objectives', *Journal of Air Law*, 2 (4).

Qutb, Sayyid (1978), *Milestones* (Stuttgart: Ernst Klett Printers).

——(2004), *In the Shade of the Qur'an*, trans. and ed. Adil Salahi (Leicester: Islamic Foundation).

Radvanyi, Janos (1972), *Hungary and the Superpowers: The 1956 Revolution and Realpolitik* (Stanford: Stanford University Press).

Rais, Rasul B. (1994), *War Without Winners: Afghanistan's Uncertain Transition after the Cold War* (Oxford: Oxford University Press).

Ramcharan, Bertrand G. (ed.) (1985), *The Right to Life in International Law* (The Hague: Martinus Nijhoff).

Ramsey, Paul (2002), *The Just War: Force and Political Responsibility* (Lanham: Rowman and Littlefield).

Rasanayagam, Angelo (2005), *Afghanistan: A Modern History* (New York: I. B. Tauris).

Rauschning, Hermann (1939), *Hitler Speaks* (London: Thornton Butterworth).

Rees, David (1964), *Korea: The Limited War* (Oxford: St. Martin's Press).

Rees, E. A. (ed.) (2004), *The Nature of Stalin's Dictatorship: The Politburo, 1924–1953* (London: Palgrave).

Reisman, W. Michael and C. H. Norchi (1988), 'Genocide and the Soviet Occupation of Afghanistan', Institute for the Study of Genocide News.

——and James Silk (1988), 'Which Law Applies to the Afghan Conflict?', *American Journal of International Law*, 82 (3)

Remnick, David (1997), *Resurrection: The Struggle for a New Russia* (New York: Random House).

Reus-Smit, Christian (1999), *The Moral Purpose of the State* (Princeton, NJ: Princeton University Press).

Reyhani, Roman (2007), 'The Legality of the Use of White Phosphorus by the United States Military During the 2004 Fallujah Assaults', *Journal of Law and Social Change*, 10.

Reyntjens, Filip (2004), 'Rwanda, Ten Years On: From Genocide to Dictatorship', *African Affairs*, 103.

——(2006), 'Post-1994 Politics in Rwanda: Problematising "Liberation" and "Democratisation"', *Third World Quarterly*, 27 (6).

Rhodes, Richard (1986) *The Making of the Atomic Bomb* (London: Simon & Schuster).

Richardson, Hugh E. (1984), *Tibet and its History*, revised and updated (Boulder: Shambhala).

Richardson, Louise (ed.) (2006), *The Roots of Terrorism* (New York: Routledge).

Riggs, Henry H. (1997), *Days of Tragedy in Armenia: Personal Experiences in Harpoot 1915–1917* (Ann Arbor: Gomidas Institute).

Rittberger, Volker (ed.) (1993), *Regime Theory and International Relations* (Oxford: Clarendon Press).

Roberts, Adam (1993), 'Humanitarian War: Military Intervention and Human Rights', *International Affairs*, 69 (3).

Roberts, Jeffrey J. (1998), 'Peering Through Different Bombsights: Military Historians, Diplomatic Historians and the Decision to Drop the Atomic Bomb', *Airpower Journal*, 12 (1).

Robertson, Esmonde (1988), 'Race as a Factor in Mussolini's Policy in Africa and Europe', *Journal of Contemporary History*, 23 (1).

Robinson, Piers (2002), *The CNN Effect: The Myth of News, Foreign Policy and Intervention* (London: Routledge).

Rodley, Nigel S. (1987), *The Treatment of Prisoners Under International Law* (Oxford: Clarendon Press).

——(ed.) (1992), *To Loose the Bands of Wickedness* (London: Brassey's).

Rogers, Tom (1992), *The Soviet Withdrawal from Afghanistan: Analysis and Chronology* (Westport: Greenwood Press).

Ro'I, Yaacov (ed.) (1995), *Jews and Jewish Life in Russia and the Soviet Union* (London: Frank Cass).

Roosa, John (2006) *Pretext for Mass Murder: The September 30th Movement and Suharto's Coup d'Etat in Indonesia* (Madison, WI: University of Wisconsin Press).

Rosenblum, Mort (1979), *Coups and Earthquakes: Reporting the World for America* (New York: Joanna Cotler).

Rostow, Walt W. (1972), *Diffusion of Power* (New York: Macmillan).

Roth, Brad R. (2000), *Governmental Illegitimacy in International Law* (Oxford: Oxford University Press).

Rowland, Dunbar (1926), *Andrew Jackson's Campaign Against the British* (New York: Ayer Co.).

Rubinstein, William. D. (1997) *The Myth of Rescue: Why the Democracies Could Not Have Saved More Jews from the Nazis* (London: Routledge).

Rummel, R. J. (1991), *China's Bloody Century: Genocide and Mass Murder since 1900* (New Brunswick: Transaction).

——(1994), *Death by Government* (New Brunswick: Transaction Publishers).

Russell, Bertrand (1995), *Pacifism and Revolution 1916–1918*, ed. Richard Pempel (London: Routledge).

Russell, John (2006), 'Obstacles to Peace in Chechnya: What Scope for International Involvement?', *Europe-Asia Studies*, 58 (6).

Russell, Lord John (ed.) (1835), *Memorials and Correspondence of Charles James Fox*, Vol. III (London: Richard Bentley).

Sageman, Marc (2008), *Leaderless Jihad: Terror Networks in the Twenty-First Century* (Philadelphia: University of Pennsylvania Press).

Saich, Tony and Hans J. van de Ven (eds) (1995), *New Perspectives on the Chinese Communist Revolution* (London: M. E. Sharpe).

Scahill, Jeremy (2007), *Blackwater: The Rise of the World's Most Powerful Mercenary Army* (New York: Nation Books).

Schabas, William A. (2000), *Genocide in International Law: The Crimes of Crimes* (Cambridge: Cambridge University Press).

Schaffer, Ronald (1980), 'American Military Ethics in World War II: The Bombing of German Civilians', *Journal of American History*, 67 (2).

Schama, Simon (1989), *Citizens: A Chronicle of the French Revolution* (New York: Alfred A. Knopf).

Schanzer, Jonathan (2005), *Al-Qaeda's Armies: Middle East Affiliate Groups and the Next Generation of Terror* (Washington, DC: Washington Institute of Near East Policy).

Scharf, Andrew (1964), *The British Press and the Jews Under Nazi Rule* (Oxford: Oxford University Press).

Schechtman, Joseph B. (1953), 'Transnistria Reservation', *YIVO Annual of Jewish Social Sciences*, 8 (4).

Schell, Jonathan (1987), *The Real War: The Classic Reporting on the Vietnam War* (New York: Pantheon Books).

Schlesinger, Arthur (1978), *Robert Kennedy and his Times* (New York: Random House).

Schlesinger, Thomas O. (1972), 'The Army and the Guerrilla: The Strategy of the Expedient', *Polity*, 4 (3).

Schnabel, Albrecht and Ramesh Thakur (eds) (2000), *Kosovo and the Challenge of Humanitarian Intervention: Selective Indignation, Collective Action, and International Citizenship* (Tokyo: UN University Press).

Schroeder, Paul W. (1994), *The Transformation of European Politics, 1763–1848* (Oxford: Clarendon Press).

Schurmann, Franz (1966), *Ideology and Organization in Communist China* (Berkeley: University of California Press).

Schuuman, Susan J. (2007), 'An "Inconvenient Atrocity": The Chemical Weapons Attack on the Kurds of Halabja, Iraq', thesis, University of New Mexico.

Schwartz, Michael (2005), 'Why the United States is Losing the War in Iraq', *Contexts*, winter.

Scott, James Brown (1924), 'The Codification of International Law', *American Journal of International Law*, 18 (2).

Searle, Thomas R. (2002), '"It Made a Lot of Sense to Kill Skilled Workers": The Firebombing of Tokyo in March 1945', *The Journal of Military History*, 66 (1).

Security Council Report (2008), *Protection of Civilians* (Cross-Cutting Report No. 2, 14 October), available at http://www.securitycouncilreport.org/site/c.glKWLeMTIsG/b.4664099/k.1776/CrossCutting_Report_No_2brProtection_of_Civilians-br14_October_2008.htm accessed 27 March 2012.

Selden, Mark and Alvin Y. So (eds) (2004), *War and State Terrorism: The United States, Japan and the Asia-Pacific in the Long Twentieth Century* (Lanham: Rowman and Littlefield).

Semelin, Jacques (2007), *Purify and Destroy: The Political Uses of Massacre and Genocide* (New York: Columbia University Press).

Seton-Watson, R. W. (1976), *R. W. Seton-Watson and the Yugoslavs: Correspondence, 1906–1941*, (London: British Academy, 1976), vol. 1.

Setunga, Philip and Nick Cheeseman (eds) (2001), *Torture: A Crime against Humanity* (Hong Kong: Asian Human Rights Commission).

Seybolt, Taylor (2007), *Humanitarian Military Intervention: The Conditions for Success and Failure* (Oxford: Oxford University Press for SIPRI).

Shakya, Tsering (1999), *The Dragon in the Land of Snows: A History of Modern Tibet since 1947* (New York: Columbia University Press).

Shannon, Vaughn P. (2000), 'Norms Are What States Make of Them: The Political Psychology of Norm Violation', *International Studies Quarterly*, 44.

Shaplen, Robert (1970), 'Our Involvement in Laos', *Foreign Affairs*, April.

Shaw, Martin (2005), *The New Western Way of War: Transfer War and its Crisis in Iraq* (Cambridge: Polity).

——(2006), *What is Genocide?* (Cambridge: Polity).

Shawcross, William (1979), *Sideshow: Kissinger, Nixon and the Destruction of Cambodia* (New York: Simon and Schuster).

——(1984), *The Quality of Mercy: Cambodia, Holocaust and Modern Conscience* (New York: Simon and Schuster).

Sheehan, Neil (1989) *Bright Shining Lie: John Paul Vann and America in Vietnam* (New York: Vintage).

Shehata, Samer (2005), 'Losing Hearts and Minds: Understanding America's Failure in Iraq', *Georgetown Journal of International Affairs*, 6, Winter/Spring.

Shepherd, Robert (1988), *A Class Divided: Appeasement and the Road to Munich, 1938* (London: Macmillan).

Sheridan, James E. (1975), *China in Disintegration: The Republican Era in Chinese History, 1912–1949* (New York: The Free Press).

Sherry, Michael S. (1987), *The Rise of American Air Power: The Creation of Armageddon* (New Haven: Yale University Press).

Shevtsova, Lila (1999), *Yeltsin's Russia: Myth and Reality* (Washington, DC: Carnegie Endowment for International Peace).

Short, Philip (2004), *Pol Pot: The History of a Nightmare* (London: John Murray).

Shoumikhin, Andrei (1996), 'The Chechen Crisis and the Future of Russia', *Contemporary Strategy*, 15.

Shrivastava, B. K. (1968), 'American Public Opinion on the Tibetan Question', *International Studies*, 10 (4).

Shue, Henry and David Wippman (2002), 'Limiting Attacks on Dual-Use Facilities Performing Indispensable Civilian Functions', *Cornell International Law Journal*, 3.

Shulman, Mark R. (eds) (1994), *The Laws of War: Constraints on Warfare in the Western World* (New Haven: Yale University Press).

Shultz, Richard (1978), 'Breaking the Will of the Enemy During the Vietnam War: The Operationalization of the Cost–Benefit Model of Counterinsurgency Warfare', *Journal of Peace Research*, 15 (2).

Sigaud, Louis A. (1941), *Douhet and Aerial Warfare* (New York: Putnam's).

Sigmann, Jean (1973), *1848—The Romantic and Democratic Revolutions in Europe* (London: Allen and Unwin).

Sihanouk, Norodom (1980), *War and Hope: The Case for Cambodia* (New York: Random House).

Silverman, Adam L. (2002), 'Just War, Jihad, and Terrorism: A Comparison of Western and Islamic Norms for the Use of Political Violence', *Journal of Church and State*, 44 (1).

Sinclair, Andrew (2004), *An Anatomy of Terror: A History of Terrorism* (London: Pan Books).

Skates, John Ray (1994), *The Invasion of Japan: Alternatives to the Bomb* (Columbia, SC: University of South Carolina Press).

Skerker, Michael (2004), 'Just War Criteria and the New Face of War: Human Shields, Manufactured Martyrs, and Little Boys with Stones', *Journal of Military Ethics*, 3 (1).

Skidelsky, Robert (1990), *Sir Oswald Mosley* (London: Papermac).

Skinner, Quentin (1974), 'Some Problems in the Analysis of Political Thought and Action, *Political Theory*, 2 (3).

Skocpol, Theda (1979), *States and Social Revolutions* (Cambridge: Cambridge University Press).

Slessor, Sir John (1956), *The Central Blue* (London: Cassell and Co.).

Slim, Hugo (2008), *Killing Civilians: Method, Madness and Morality in War* (New York: Columbia University Press).

Small, Vaclav (1999), 'China's Great Famine: Forty Years On', *British Medical Journal*, 18–25 December.

Smilansky, Saul (2004), 'Terrorism, Justification and Illusion', *Ethics*, 114 (4).

Smith, J. (ed.) (1994), *Mark Twain on the Damned Human Race* (New York: Hill and Wang).

Smith, Melden E. (1977), 'The Strategic Bombing Debate: The Second World War and Vietnam', *Journal of Contemporary History*, 12 (1).

Soderlund, Walter C., E. Donald Briggs, Kai Hilderbrandt, and Abdel Salam Sidahmed (2008), *Humanitarian Crises and Intervention: Reassessing the Impact of Mass Media* (Stirling, VA: Kumarian Press).

Sollis, Peter (1992), 'Displaced Persons and Human Rights: The Crisis in El Salvador', *Bulletin of Latin American Research*, 11 (1).

Solzhenitsyn, Aleksander I. (1974–8), *The Gulag Archipelago*, Vols I–III (New York: Harper and Row).

Sorabji, Richard and David Rodin (eds) (2006), *The Ethics of War: Shared Problems in Different Traditions* (Aldershot: Ashgate).

Soulemanov, Emil (2007), *An Endless War: The Russia–Chechnya War in Perspective* (Frankfurt: Peter Lang).

Southwood, Julie and Patrick Flanagan (1983), *Indonesia: Law, Propaganda and Terror* (London: Zed).

Spanier, John W. (1959), *The Truman–MacArthur Controversy and the Korean War* (Cambridge, MA: Harvard University Press).

Spector, Ronald H. (1985), *Eagle Against the Sun: The American War with Japan* (New York: The Free Press).

Sperber, Jonathan (1994), *The European Revolutions: 1848–1851* (Cambridge: Cambridge University Press).

Spies, S. B. (1977), *Methods of Barbarism? Roberts and Kitchener and Civilians in the Boer Republics January 1900–May 1902* (Cape Town: Human & Rousseau).

Spriano, Paolo (1985), *Stalin and the European Communists*, trans. Jon Rothschild (London: Verso).

Stanley, William (1996), *The Protection Racket State: Elite Politics, Military Extortion and Civil War in El Salvador* (Philadelphia: Temple University Press).

Stanton, Gregory (2004), 'Could the Rwandan Genocide have been Prevented?', *Journal of Genocide Research*, 6 (2).

Steans, Peter N. (1974), *1848: The Revolutionary Tide in Europe* (New York: W. W. Norton).

Stedman, Stephen John and Fred Tanner (eds) (2003), *Refugee Manipulation: War, Politics and the Abuse of Human Suffering* (Washington, DC: The Brookings Institution).

Stepanova, Ekaterina (2009), 'Trends in Armed Conflicts: One-Sided Violence Against Civilians', in *SIPRI Yearbook 2009: Armaments, Disarmament and International Security* (Oxford: Oxford University Press).

Sterba, James P. (ed.) (2003), *Terrorism and International Justice* (New York: Oxford University Press).

Stern, Steve (ed.) (1998), *Shining and Other Paths: War and Society in Peru 1980–1995* (Durham, NC: Duke University Press).

Stewart, John Hall (1951), *A Documentary Survey of the French Revolution* (New York: Macmillan).

Stimson, Henry L. (1947), 'The Decision to Use the Atomic Bomb', *Harper's Magazine*, February.

Stone, Dan (ed.) (2008), *The Historiography of Genocide* (London: Palgrave).

——(2010), *Histories of the Holocaust* (Oxford: Oxford University Press).

Stone, J. (1959), *Legal Controls of International Conflict: A Treatise on the Dynamics of Disputes and War-Law* (London: Stevens).

Stoneman, Mark R. (2001), 'The Bavarian Army and French Civilians in the War of 1870–1871: A Cultural Interpretation', *War in History*, 8 (3).

Stowell, Ellery C. (1921), *Intervention in International Law* (Washington, DC: John Byrne and Co.).

Strauss, Julia C. (2002), 'Paternalist Terror: The Campaign to Suppress Counterrevolutionaries and Regime Consolidation in the People's Republic of China, 1950–1953', *Comparative Studies in Society and History*, 44 (1).

Stueck, William (2002), *Rethinking the Korean War: A New Diplomatic and Strategic History* (Princeton, NJ: Princeton University Press).

Stuermer, Harry (1917), 'Germany and the Armenian Atrocities', *Current History*, November.

Sundaussen, Ulf (1982), *The Road to Power: Indonesian Military Politics 1945–1967* (Kuala Lumpur: Oxford University Press).

Sun Tzu (1963), *The Art of War*, trans. Samuel Griffith (Oxford: Oxford University Press).

Sutton, Donald S. (1995), 'Consuming Counterrevolution: The Ritual and Culture of Cannibalism in Wuxuan, Guangxi, China, May to July 1968', *Comparative Studies in Society and History*, 37 (1).

Swain, Jon (1997), *A River of Time: Memoir of Vietnam and Cambodia* (Oxford: St. Martin's Press).

Szasz, Paul C. (2005), 'The Security Council Starts Legislating', *American Journal of International Law*, 96 (4).

Szilard, Leo (1949), 'A Personal History of the Atomic Bomb', *Roundtable*, no. 601, 25 September.

Tackett, Timothy (2000), 'Conspiracy Obsession in a Time of Revolution: French Elites and the Origins of the Terror, 1789–1792', *American Historical Review*, 105 (3).

Tackett, Timothy (2003), 'The Flight to Varennes and the Coming of the Terror', *Historical Reflections/Reflexions Historiques*, 29 (3).

Talaat Pasha (1921), 'Posthumous Memoirs of Talaat Pasha', *Current History*, 15 (2).

Tanaka, Yuki and Marilyn B. Young (eds) (2009), *Bombing Civilians: A Twentieth Century History* (New York: The New Press).

Taylor, Telford (1970), *Nuremberg and Viet Nam, an American Tragedy* (Chicago: Quadrangle).

Teiwes, Frederick C. with Warren Sun (1999), *China's Road to Disaster: Mao, Central Politicians, and Provincial Leaders in the Unfolding of the Great Leap Forward 1955–1959* (Armonk, NY: M. E. Sharpe).

Ternon, Yves (1990), *The Armenians: History of a Genocide*, 2nd edn, trans. Rouben C. Cholakian (Ann Arbor: Caravan Books).

Terry, Fiona (2002), *Condemned to Repeat? The Paradox of Humanitarian Action* (Ithaca: Cornell University Press).

*The Cuban Crisis as Reflected in the New York Press (1895–1898)* (New York: Octagon Books, 1965).

Thion, Serge (1993), *Watching Cambodia: Ten Paths to Enter the Cambodian Tangle* (Bangkok: White Lotus).

Thomas, Ward (2001), *The Ethics of Destruction: Norms and Force in International Relations* (Ithaca: Cornell University Press).

——(2006), 'Victory by Duress: Civilian Infrastructure in Air Campaigns', *Security Studies*, 15 (1): 1–33.

Thompson, Janice A. (1993), 'Norms in International Relations: A Conceptual Analysis', *International Journal of Group Tensions*, 23 (1).

Thorne, Richard (1985), *The Issue of War: States, Societies and the Far Eastern Conflict of 1941–1945* (London: Hamish Hamilton).

Thornton, Russell (1987), *American Indian Holocaust and Survival: A Population History since 1492* (Norman, OK: University of Oklahoma Press).

Thurston, Robert W. (1996), *Life and Terror in Stalin's Russia: 1934–1941* (New Haven: Yale University Press).

Tilly, Charles (1990), *Coercion, Capital and European States AD 990–1990* (Oxford: Basil Blackwell).

Tiruneh, Andargachew (1993), *The Ethiopian Revolution 1974–1987: A Transformation from an Aristocratic to a Totalitarian Autocracy* (Cambridge: Cambridge University Press).

Tishkov, Valery (2004), *Chechnya: Life in a War-Torn Society* (Berkeley: University of California Press).

Todorov, Tzvetan (2001), *The Fragility of Goodness: Why Bulgaria's Jews Survived the Holocaust*, trans. Arthur Denner (Princeton: Princeton University Press).

Tolstoy, Nikolai (1977), *Victims of Yalta* (London: Hodder and Stoughton).

——(1981), *Stalin's Secret War* (London: Jonathan Cape).

Tombs, Robert (1981), *The War Against Paris 1871* (Cambridge: Cambridge University Press).

Tone, John Lawrence (1994), *The Fatal Knot: The Guerrilla War in Navarre and the Defeat of Napoleon in Spain* (Chapel Hill: University of North Carolina Press).

——(2006), *War and Genocide in Cuba, 1895–1898* (Chapel Hill: University of North Carolina Press).

Totten, Samuel and Paul R. Bartrop (eds) (2009), *The Genocide Studies Reader* (London: Routledge).

——and Eric Markusen (eds) (2006), *Genocide in Darfur: Investigating the Atrocities in the Sudan* (London: Routledge).

——and William S. Parsons (eds) (1997), *Century of Genocide: Critical Essays and Eyewitness Accounts* (London: Routledge).

Townshend, C. (2002), *Terrorism: A Very Short Introduction* (Oxford: Oxford University Press).

Toynbee, Arnold J. (ed.) (1916), *The Treatment of the Armenians in the Ottoman Empire* (London: Hodder and Stoughton).

——(1917), *The German Terror in Belgium* (London: Hodder and Stoughton).

Traverso, Enzo (1996), *Origins of Nazi Violence*, trans. Janet Lloyd (New York: New Press).

Trask, David F. (1981), *The War with Spain in 1898* (New York: Macmillan).

Traxel, David (1998), *1898: The Birth of the American Century* (New York: Alfred Knopf).

Trenin, Dmitri V. (2002), *The End of Eurasia: Russia on the Border Between Geopolitics and Globalization* (Washington, DC: Carnegie Endowment for International Peace).

——and Aleksei V. Malashenko (2004), *Russia's Restless Frontier: The Chechnya Factor in Post-Soviet Russia* (Washington, DC: Carnegie Endowment for International Peace).

Trooboff, Peter D. (ed.) (1975), *Law and Responsibility in Warfare: The Vietnam Experience* (Chapel Hill: University of North Carolina Press).

Trythall, Anthony (1977), *'Boney' Fuller* (London: Cassell).

Tuchman, Barbara W. (1962), *August 1914* (London: Constable).

Tucker, Robert C. (1973), *Stalin as Revolutionary, 1879–1929* (New York: W. W. Norton).

Tully, James (ed.) (1988), *Meaning and Context: Quentin Skinner and His Critics* (Cambridge: Polity).

Turner, G. B. (ed.) (1952), *A History of Military Affairs* (New York: Harcourt Brace).

Turner, Thomas (2007), *The Congo Wars: Conflict, Myth and Reality* (London: Zed Books).

Ucles, Mario Lungo (1996), *El Salvador in the Eighties: Counterinsurgency and Revolution* (Philadelphia: Temple University Press).

Ulam, Adam B. (1974), *Expansion and Coexistence: Soviet Foreign Policy, 1917–73* (New York: Praeger).

Ullman, Richard H. (1957), 'The Davies Mission and United States–Soviet Relations, 1937–1941', *World Politics*, 9 (1): 216–25.

Ung, Loung (2000), *First They Killed My Father: A Daughter of Cambodia Remembers* (New York: HarperCollins).

United Nations (1997), *Comprehensive Report on Lessons Learned from United Nations Assistance Mission for Rwanda (UNAMIR), October 1993–April 1996* (UN: New York).

——(1998), 'Report of the Investigative Team Charged with Investigating Serious Violations of Human Rights and International Humanitarian Law in the Democratic Republic of Congo', S/1998/581, 29 June.

United Nations Commission on Human Rights (1997), 'Report on the Situation of Human Rights in Zaire, Prepared by the Special Rapporteur, Mr. Roberto Garreton in accordance with commission resolution 1996/77'.

United Nations High Commissioner for Human Rights (2010), 'Report of the Mapping Exercise Documenting the Most Serious Violations of Human Rights and International Humanitarian Law Committed Within the Territory of the Democratic Republic of Congo between March 1993 and June 2003', August.

Urban, George (1981), 'Was Stalin (the Terrible) Really a "Great Man"? A Conversation with W. Averell Harriman', *Encounter*, 57 (5).

US Senate Committee on Foreign Relations (1988), 'Chemical Weapons Use in Kurdistan: Iraq's Final Offensive', staff report, October.

Valentino, Benjamin (2004), *Final Solutions: Mass Killing and Genocide in the 20th Century* (Ithaca: Cornell University Press).

——, Paul Huth, and Dylan Balch-Lindsay (2004), 'Draining the Sea: Mass Killing and Guerrilla Warfare', *International Organization*, 58 (2).

Van Arsdale, Peter W. (2006) *Forced to Flee: Human Rights and Human Wrongs in Refugee Homelands* (New York: Lexington Books).

Van Leeuwen, M. (2001), 'Rwanda's *Imidugudu* Programme and earlier Experiences with Villagisation and Resettlement in East Africa', *Journal of Modern African Studies*, 39.

Venturi, Franco (1989), *The End of the Old Regime in Europe, 1768–1789*, 2 Vols, trans. R. Burr Litchfield (Princeton, NJ: Princeton University Press).

Verwimp, Philip (2003), 'Testing the Double-Genocide Thesis for Central and Southern Rwanda', *Journal of Conflict Resolution*, 47 (4).

Vickery, Michael (1984), *Cambodia 1975–1982* (Sydney: Allen and Unwin).

Waciorski, Jerzy (1939), *Le terrorisme politique* (Paris: A. Pedone).

Wagener, Hans (1900), *Falsche Propheten: Gouverneur von Liebert und seine Presse* (Charlottenburg: Selbstverlag des Verfassers).

Walker, Richard L. (1955), *China under Communism: The First Five Years* (New Haven: Yale University Press).

Walston, James (1997), 'History and Memory of the Italian Concentration Camps', *The Historical Journal*, 40 (1).

Walzer, Michael (1977), *Just and Unjust Wars: A Moral Argument with Historical Illustrations* (New York: Basic Books).

Ward, Chris (1999), *Stalin's Russia*, 2nd edn (London: Arnold).

Ward, Tony (2005), 'State Crime in the Heart of Darkness', *British Journal of Criminology*, 45 (4).

Wasserstein, Bernard (1979), *Britain and the Jews of Europe* (Oxford: Oxford University Press).

Watson, George (1984), 'Was Hitler a Marxist? Reflections About Certain Affinities', *Encounter*, 63, December.

Wawro, Geoffrey (2003), *The Franco-Prussian War: The German Conquest of France in 1870–1871* (Cambridge: Cambridge University Press).

Webster, Sir Charles and Noble Frankland (1961), *The Strategic Air Offensive Against Germany 1939–1945*, Vols I–IV (London: HMSO).

Weidenbaum, Paul (1938), 'Necessity in International Law', *Transactions of the Grotius Society*, 24.

Weigley, Russell F. (1973), *The American Way of War: A History of United States Military Strategy and Policy* (New York: Macmillan).

Weinberg, Leonard (ed.) (2008), *Democratic Responses to Terrorism* (New York: Routledge).

Weinstein, Jeremy M. (2007), *Inside Rebellion: The Politics of Insurgent Violence* (Cambridge: Cambridge University Press).

Weisbord, Robert (2003), 'The King, the Cardinal and the Pope: Leopold II's Genocide in the Congo and the Vatican', *Journal of Genocide Research*, 5 (1).

Weiss, Thomas G. (1999), *Civil-Military Interactions* (Oxford: Rowman and Littlefield).

——(2004), 'The Sunset of Humanitarian Intervention? The Responsibility to Protect in a Unipolar Era,' *Security Dialogue* 35 (2).

——and Sam Daws (eds) (2007), *The Oxford Handbook on the United Nations* (Oxford: Oxford University Press).

Weissberg, Alexander (1951), *The Accused* (New York: Simon and Schuster).

Weitz, Eric D. (2003), *A Century of Genocide: Utopias of Race and Nation* (Princeton, NJ: Princeton University Press).

Welch Jr., Richard E. (1974), 'American Atrocities in the Philippines: The Indictment and the Response', *Pacific Historical Review*, XLIII (2).

Wendell, C. (ed.) (1978), *Five Tracts of Hasan al-Banna, 1906–1949* (Santa Barbara, CA: University of California Press).

Wendt, Alexander (1987), 'The Agent–Structure Problem in International Relations Theory', *International Organization*, 41 (3).

——(1992), 'Anarchy is What States Make of It: The Social Construction of Power Politics', *International Organization*, 46.

——(1999), *Social Theory of International Politics* (Cambridge: Cambridge University Press).

Werner, Jayne S. and Luu Doan Huynh (eds) (1993), *The Vietnam War: Vietnamese and American Perspectives* (New York: M. E. Sharpe).

Werth, Nicolas (2007), *Cannibal Island: Death in a Siberian Gulag* (Princeton, NJ: Princeton University Press).

West, F. J. 'Bing' (2005), 'The Fall of Fallujah', *Marine Corps Gazette*, July.

——(2005), *No True Glory: A Frontline Account of the Battle for Fallujah* (New York: Bantam).

Westad, Odd Arne (2007), *The Global Cold War: Third World Interventions and the Making of Our Times* (Cambridge: Cambridge University Press).

Westlake, John (1910), *International Law*, 2nd edn (Cambridge: Cambridge University Press).

Westmoreland, General William C. (1976), *A Soldier Reports* (New York: Dell).
Weyler y Nicolau, Valeriano (1906), *Mi mando en Cuba: historia militar politica de la última guerra separatista* (Madrid: Felipe).
Wheeler, Nicholas J. (2000), *Saving Strangers: Humanitarian Intervention in International Society* (Oxford: Oxford University Press).
White III, Lynn T. (1989), *Policies of Chaos: The Organizational Causes of Violence in China's Cultural Revolution* (Princeton, NJ: Princeton University Press).
Whittaker, David J. (2002), *Terrorism: Understanding the Global Threat* (London: Longman).
Wiarda, Howard J. and Harry F. Kline (eds) (2007), *Latin American Politics and Development*, 6th edn (Boulder, CO: Westview).
Wight, Martin (1972), 'International Legitimacy', *International Relations*, 4 (1).
Wilkins, Burleigh Taylor (1992), *Terrorism and Collective Responsibility* (London: Routledge).
Williams, Paul L. (2002), *Al-Qaeda: Brotherhood of Terror* (New York: Alpha Press).
Williams, Roger L. (1969), *The French Revolution of 1870–1871* (London: Weidenfeld and Nicolson).
Wills, Siobhan (2009), *Protecting Civilians: The Obligations of Peacekeepers* (Oxford: Oxford University Press).
Wilson, Trevor (1986), *The Myriad Faces of War: Britain and the Great War 1914–1918* (Oxford: Polity Press).
Wittgenstein, Ludwig (1953), *Philosophical Investigations*, trans. G. E. M. Anscombe (New York: Macmillan).
Woodhouse, C. M. (1965), *The Battle of Navarino* (London: Hodder and Stoughton).
Woodward, E. L. and Rohan Butler (eds) (1952), *Documents on British Foreign Policy, 1919–1939*, Vol. 4 (London: HMSO).
Wouters, Jan and Sten Verhoeven (2005), 'The Prohibition of Genocide as a Norm of *Ius Cogens* and Its Implications for the Enforcement of the Law of Genocide', *International Criminal Law Review* 5(3).
Wyman, David S. (1984), *The Abandonment of the Jews* (New York: The New Press).
Yahil, Leni (1987), *The Holocaust: The Fate of European Jewry* (Oxford: Oxford University Press).
Yang Su (2010), *Collective Killings in Rural China during the Cultural Revolution* (Cambridge: Cambridge University Press).
Young, Marilyn B. (1991), *The Vietnam Wars, 1945–1990* (New York: Harper Perennial).
Young, Oran (1989), *International Cooperation: Building Regimes for Natural Resources and the Environment* (Ithaca: Cornell University Press).
Youngs, Tim (1998), 'Kosovo: The Diplomatic and Military Options', *House of Commons Research Paper 98/93.*
Zawodny, J. K. (1972), *Death in the Forest: The Story of the Katyn Forest Massacre* (Notre Dame, IN: University of Notre Dame Press).
Zeidan, David (2001), 'The Islamic Fundamentalist View of Life as a Perennial Battle', *Middle East Review of International Affairs*, 5.
Zhang, L. and C. MacLeod (1999), *China Remembers* (Hong Kong: Oxford University Press).

Zhang Ling (2001), *The Tiananmen Papers*, ed. Andrew J. Nathan and Perry Link (New York: Public Affairs).

Zhang, Yongjin (1998), *China in International Society since 1949* (London: Macmillan).

Zheng, Y. (1996), *Scarlet Memorials: Tales of Cannibalism in Modern China* (Boulder, CO: Westview Press).

Zimbardo, Philip (2007), *The Lucifer Effect: How Good People Turn Evil* (London: Rider).

Zimmerer, Jurgen (2005), 'The Birth of the *Ostland* out of the Spirit of Colonialism: A Postcolonial Perspective on the Nazi Policy of Conquest and Extermination', *Patterns of Prejudice*, 39 (2).

Zimmerman, Joshua D. (ed.) (2005), *The Jews of Italy Under Fascist and Nazi Rule, 1922–1945* (Cambridge: Cambridge University Press).

Zorbas, Eugenta (2004), 'Reconciliation in Post-Genocide Rwanda', *African Journal of Legal Studies*, 1 (1).

# Index

Lightning Source UK Ltd.
Milton Keynes UK
UKOW04f0958230914

239016UK00001B/2/P